The Historical Construction of Southeast Asian Studies

The **Institute of Southeast Asian Studies (ISEAS)** was established as an autonomous organization in 1968. It is a regional centre dedicated to the study of socio-political, security and economic trends and developments in Southeast Asia and its wider geostrategic and economic environment. The Institute's research programmes are the Regional Economic Studies (RES, including ASEAN and APEC), Regional Strategic and Political Studies (RSPS), and Regional Social and Cultural Studies (RSCS).

ISEAS Publishing, an established academic press, has issued more than 2,000 books and journals. It is the largest scholarly publisher of research about Southeast Asia from within the region. ISEAS Publishing works with many other academic and trade publishers and distributors to disseminate important research and analyses from and about Southeast Asia to the rest of the world.

The Historical Construction of Southeast Asian Studies

Korea and Beyond

EDITED BY

PARK SEUNG WOO
VICTOR T. KING

LSEAS

INSTITUTE OF SOUTHEAST ASIAN STUDIES
Singapore

First published in Singapore in 2013 by
ISEAS Publishing
Institute of Southeast Asian Studies
30 Heng Mui Keng Terrace, Pasir Panjang
Singapore 119614

E-mail: publish@iseas.edu.sg   •   Website: bookshop.iseas.edu.sg

The responsibility for facts and opinions in this publication rests exclusively with the authors and their interpretations do not necessarily reflect the views or the policy of the publisher or its supporters.

ISEAS Library Cataloguing-in-Publication Data

The historical construction of Southeast Asian studies : Korea and beyond / edited by
  Park Seung Woo and Victor T. King.
  1. Southeast Asia—Study and teaching.
  2. South Asia—Research.
  I. Park, Seung Woo.
  II. King, Victor T.
DS524.7 H67   2013

ISBN   978-981-4414-58-6 (soft cover)
ISBN   978-981-4414-59-3 (E-book PDF)

Typeset by International Typesetters Pte Ltd
Printed in Singapore by Oxford Graphic Printers Pte Ltd

CONTENTS

LIST OF TABLES

LIST OF FIGURES

FOREWORD

It gives me great pleasure to write the Foreword for *The Historical Construction of Southeast Asian Studies: Korea and Beyond.* This book will indeed make its historical mark as the first edited volume for whose publication Korean scholars have taken the initiative and which addresses general issues in the development of Southeast Asian Studies. Within the past two decades the Institute of Southeast Asian Studies (ISEAS) has published three books whose contributors were mainly Korean, but the main subject of which was Korea, especially bilateral relations with Southeast Asia, ASEAN, or individual countries in the region. With this particular publication, I expect and hope that Southeast Asianists from Korea will assume a more active role in, and make greater contributions to, the global community of Southeast Asian Studies.

This edited volume is the result of an international conference organized by the Institute for East Asian Studies at Sogang University (SIEAS) on 19–20 March 2010. I have witnessed and appreciated the tremendous efforts and infinite time contributed by the co-editors Professors Park Seung Woo and Victor T. King, to negotiate with the publisher, edit and copy-edit the manuscripts, communicate with the authors, and write the introduction. I should also mention the patience and sacrifice of the ten authors who have waited a longer than usual time for publication and thus helped SIEAS and Southeast Asian Studies in Korea come of age and enter the international stage.

Since the mid-2000s, SIEAS has mobilized various resources and initiated various programmes to promote Southeast Asian Studies in Korea. Particularly with the ten-year grants from the National Research Foundation of Korea, in 2008 SIEAS embarked on a comprehensive research and educational project under the banner of *Southeast Asia as an Open Regional System: A New Paradigm for Communicating with the Globe and Reaching Out to the Public.* Among its specific programmes, SIEAS organizes international conferences every year, one for our research clusters and the other for our international journal *TRaNS: Trans-Regional and National Studies of Southeast Asia.* We offer these conferences as a new venue for academic discourse on a global level. I hope that this edited volume will serve as an important stepping stone towards our global initiatives.

Shin Yoon Hwan
Director of the Institute for East Asian Studies
Sogang University
Seoul, Korea

ACKNOWLEDGEMENTS

The current edited book is part of the long-term research project undertaken by the Institute for East Asian Studies at Sogang University (SIEAS) in the Republic of Korea. The essays in this volume were first delivered at a conference under the theme entitled "The Historical Construction of Southeast Asian Studies", which was organized by the SIEAS and held in Seoul in March 2010. The entire project is supported by the National Research Foundation of Korea Grant funded by the Korean Government (NRF-2008-362-B00018).

We would like to express our gratitude to Professor Shin Yoon Hwan, the Director of Sogang University's SIEAS, and his colleagues in the Institute for their enthusiastic support for this programme of work.

Victor King is sincerely grateful for the support and funding provided by The British Academy, the European Science Foundation and more recently the Research Committee of the Association of Southeast Asian Studies in the United Kingdom (ASEASUK) over a very long period of time for his work on the development of Southeast Asian Studies as a field of studies in the United Kingdom and continental Europe. In addition, the Association presented the opportunity for him to write a personal history of Southeast Asian Studies in the UK to mark the Association's fortieth anniversary in 2009, an exercise which contributed to his thinking for this present book. He is also mindful of the significance of the scholarly exchanges which he has enjoyed with colleagues in East Asian Studies at the University of Leeds and the Institute of Asian Studies at Universiti Brunei Darussalam.

Park Seung Woo would like to acknowledge the support from his colleagues in the Korean Association of Southeast Asian Studies (KASEAS) and the Korean Institute of Southeast Asian Studies (KISEAS).

Special thanks go to Triena Ong, Sheryl Sin and the editorial staff at the Institute of Southeast Asian Studies (ISEAS) in Singapore for their invaluable help and meticulous work in preparing the book for publication. The editors also wish to express their gratitude to the three anonymous reviewers of the manuscript who provided thoughtful critical commentary and, through their guidance, ensured that the final publication was a much improved contribution to the ongoing debates in Southeast Asian Studies.

Park Seung Woo and Victor T. King
Daegu, Korea and Brunei Darussalam
January 2013

ABOUT THE CONTRIBUTORS

CHOI Horim is HK Assistant Professor of the Institute for East Asian Studies, Sogang University in Korea. He received his Ph.D. in Anthropology from the Seoul National University in 2003. His main scope of research is Vietnamese ritual tradition, cultural policy, migration, and tourism. His recent works include *Museums in Southeast Asia: Cultural Politics of National Representation and Memory* (2011); *Southeast Asia and the World Beyond: From the Perspectives of Tradition, Colonialism, and Modernity* (2011); "Cultural Politics of Communal Festivals in Ha Noi" (2010); "Vietnamese Labor Migration to South Korea: Government Policies, Social Capital, Labor Exporting Agencies, and Chain Migration" (2010); "Ethnography of Korean Veterans' Battlefield Travel in Vietnam: 'Wol-nam War', Tourism, and Politics of Memory" (2010); "Vietnam War Memory and Tourism: Embodied History and Contested Authenticity" (2009); and "Ritual Revitalization and Nativist Ideology in Hanoi", in *Modernity and Re-Enchantment: Religion in Post-Revolutionary Vietnam*, edited by Philip Taylor (2007).

Freek COLOMBIJN graduated in cultural anthropology and history at Leiden University, the Netherlands, and obtained his Ph.D. degree also at Leiden University. He is currently Associate Professor at VU University Amsterdam. His research usually focuses on Indonesia. He has published *Under Construction: The Politics of Urban Space and Housing During the Decolonization of Indonesia, 1930–1960* (2010) and various articles on environmental history, communal violence, the social impact of new roads, pre-colonial state formation, football, and urban symbolism; he also co-edited *Urban Ethnic Encounters: The Spatial Consequences* (with Aygen Erdentug, 2002); *Roots of Violence in Indonesia: Contemporary Violence in Historical Perspective* (with J. Thomas Lindblad, 2002); and *The History of* *the Indonesian City Before and After Independence* (with Martine Barwegen et al., 2005). He is currently undertaking research on the perception of environmental problems, middle class consumption patterns and garbage collection by scavengers in Indonesian cities.

James J. FOX, who was previously Director of the Research School of Pacific and Asian Studies at the Australian National University, is now an Emeritus Professor based in the University's Resource Management in Asia Pacific Program. He has been doing research in Indonesia, particularly in the Timor area and on Java, since 1965. Over this period he has published widely on topics ranging from language and history to social organization and the environment. He has also been involved in a good deal of policy research and has served as the founding Director of the Korea Institute at the ANU.

Ariel HERYANTO is Associate Professor of Indonesian Studies and Head of Southeast Asia Centre, The School of Culture, History and Language, The Australian National University. He is the author of *State Terrorism And Political Identity In Indonesia: Fatally Belonging* (2007), editor of *Popular Culture in Indonesia: Fluid Identities in Post-Authoritarian Politics* (2008), and co-editor of *Pop Culture Formations Across East Asia* (2010). His areas of interest include everyday politics of identity and representation, media and cultural studies, as well as post-colonialism.

Victor T. KING is Emeritus Professor of Southeast Asian Studies at the University of Leeds, UK and former Executive Director of the White Rose East Asia Centre, which comprises a research partnership between the School of East Asian Studies at the University of Sheffield and East Asian Studies in the School of Modern Languages and Cultures at the University of Leeds. He is currently Eminent Visiting Professor at Universiti Brunei Darussalam. He is a former Chair of the Association of Southeast Asian Studies in the United Kingdom and the British Academy Committee for Southeast Asian Studies. He has published extensively on the sociology and anthropology of Southeast Asia, and most recently has published *The Sociology of Southeast Asia: Transformations in a Developing Region* (2011, reprint); *The Modern Anthropology of Southeast Asia: An Introduction* (with W.D. Wilder 2006, reprint); and with Michael Hitchcock and Michael Parnwell he has co-edited *Tourism in Southeast Asia: Challenges and New Directions* (2009) and *Heritage Tourism in Southeast Asia* (2010).

LEE Sang Kook is Assistant Professor at the Institute for East Asian Studies at Sogang University (SIEAS), Korea. He obtained his Ph.D. in Anthropology from the National University of Singapore. Before joining SIEAS in 2009, he had worked at the Ministry of Foreign Affairs and Trade of the Korean government as an area specialist in Southeast Asian affairs. He has done scholarly research on the issues of refugees, migration, and the border with a special focus on the Thailand-Myanmar borderland. He has coedited *Managing Transnational Flows in East Asia* (with Shirlena Huang and Mike Hayes, 2012) and a special issue of *Asian and Pacific Migration Journal* entitled "Transnational Migration in East Asia" (with Shirlena Huang and Mike Hayes, 2012). His journal articles include "Scattered but Connected: Karen Refugees' Networking in and beyond the Thailand-Burma Borderland" (2012) and "Borderland Dynamics in Mae Sot, Thailand and the Pursuit of Bangkok Dream and Resettlement" (2011).

PARK Sa-Myung is Professor of Political Science at Kangwon National University in Korea, Chairman of the Korean Institute of Southeast Asian Studies (KISEAS), and former President of the Korean Association of Southeast Asian Studies (KASEAS). After he received his Ph.D. in Political Science from State University of New York (SUNY) at Buffalo in 1988, he taught at Liaoning University, China in 1994–95 and studied at Columbia University, USA in 2001–02. He is particularly interested in socio-economic change, political development, and regional integration in East Asia encompassing Northeast and Southeast Asia. His recent publications include *A New Search for East Asia: Beyond Battlefields, Toward Marketplaces and Public Spaces* (2006) and other co-authored ones such as *Political Leadership for Crisis Management* (2007), *East Asian Community and Korea's Tomorrow* (2008), *In Search of East Asian Community* (2009), and *Southeast Asian Perceptions of Korea* (2010).

PARK Seung Woo is Professor of Sociology and Director of the Multicultural Education and Research Institute at Yeungnam University in Korea. He is currently serving as President of the Korean Association of Southeast Asian Studies (KASEAS) and is a member of the Board of Trustees at the Korean Institute of Southeast Asian Studies (KISEAS). Professor Park received his Ph.D. in Sociology from the University of Georgia in 1991. He has written extensively on Southeast Asia and on East Asian regionalism. His recent works include *East Asian Community and Korea's Tomorrow* (with Shin Yoon Hwan et al., 2008); *States of Democracy: Oligarchic Democracies* *and Asian Democratization* (with Cho Hee Yeon et al., 2008); *The Dynamic Transformation of Socio-Economic Inequality in the Asian Democratization* (2009); *Transnational Issues and Regional Governance in Southeast Asia* (with Yoon Jinpyo et al., 2010); and "Review of the Discourses on East Asian Community" (2011).

SONG Seung-Won is Assistant Professor at the Department of Malay-Indonesian Interpretation and Translation at Hankuk University of Foreign Studies, Korea. She acquired her Ph.D. from the Department of History at Ohio University, USA in 2008. She has written extensively on Indonesian contemporary political history and regionalism. Her recent works include *Museums in Southeast Asia* (with Choi Horim et al., 2011); *Southeast Asia and the World Beyond: From the Perspectives of Tradition, Colonialism, and Modernity* (with Kang Hee Jung et al., 2011); "An Analysis of the Nationalist History of Aceh: Based on the Writings of Yunus Djamil, Ali Hasjmy, and Hasan di Tiro" (2010); and "Indonesia's State Ideology and Its Interpretations across Orders: Based on the Analysis of Citizenship Education" (2010).

YU Insun is teaching Southeast Asian History at Sookmyung Women's University in Seoul. He is a former Professor of Southeast Asian History at Seoul National University. Prof. Yu earned his Ph.D. in Southeast Asian history at the University of Michigan in Ann Arbor, USA, in 1978. He has published extensively on Vietnamese history and most recently has published *Lê Văn Hưu and Ngô Sĩ Liên: A Comparison of Their Perception of Vietnamese History* (2006); *Vietnam-China Relations in the 19th Century: Myth and Reality of the Tributary System* (2009), and *The 1979 Sino-Vietnamese War from the Perspective of Historical Relations between the Two Countries* (2011). He is now working on the village regulations (hương ước), old and new, in Vietnam.

1

INTRODUCTION
The Historical Construction of Southeast Asian Studies and the Emergence of a Region

Park Seung Woo and Victor T. King

THE CONSTRUCTION OF REGIONS

It is a truism to state that regions are constructed. In our current globalizing world there appears to be an obsession and a need to establish regional organizations of various kinds as well as more disparate groupings of countries sharing certain interests, activities and objectives which in turn can be projected more successfully onto the global stage. It is also an obvious point, but worth making with reference to Southeast Asia, that some regions are much more easily defined and constructed than others, particularly if there is geographical or physical coalescence of some kind, shared histories and identifiable cultural characteristics. Regions also emerged in the context of economic, political and socio-cultural encounters between culturally different populations, especially following the expansion of Western trade, commerce and exploration some 400 years ago and the accompanying need by Western traders, administrators, missionaries and military personnel to map and locate territories and to classify and learn about those who resided there. However, with regard to the scatter of kingdoms, states and tribal groups and the geographical diversity and openness of those territories lying across the great sea routes between the Indian subcontinent and mainland China and Japan and which came to be called "Southeast Asia", there were special difficulties in identifying and demarcating a region. These difficulties persist.

SOUTHEAST ASIA AS A REGION: ORIENTATIONS

Those who have specialized in the study of Southeast Asia, and particularly those scholars located in Southeast Asian Studies centres, institutes and programmes, have frequently been engaged in debates and disagreements about what defines their region and what is distinctive about it; and this preoccupation has usually been much more intense when compared with the concerns of regionalist specialists in other parts of the world. In other words, Southeast Asianists have sought persistently for a rationale for what they do and, in order to serve their students and those they train, to provide an academic basis for considering the collection of countries and peoples which they are trying to understand as a viable and meaningful unit of analysis and scholarly speculation. Moreover, some academic disciplines have been exercised in these endeavours much more than others, and it is to historians, archaeologists and pre-historians, geographers, anthropologists and linguists that we turn when we wish to consider the main contributions to these debates and the reasons for the difficulties and disagreements. Historians in particular, and to some extent anthropologists, have played a major role in searching for the "essential" and "original" characteristics of Southeast Asia, the coherence of its history and the distinctive "genius" of Southeast Asian peoples. In our view the issue of regional demarcation seems to have been much less urgent and prominent for political scientists, economists, sociologists, international relations experts and development studies specialists who have tended to look in comparative terms for general trends, processes and characteristics across regions rather than focus on the details of origins, histories and cultures within defined and bounded spaces.

Aside from contributions to these matters in academic journals there have been at least two major volumes published in the last decade which have addressed issues of regional definition and which deserve to be mentioned in that they adopt rather different perspectives on the value of Southeast Asia as a unit for analysis: Paul Kratoska, Remco Raben and Henk Schulte Nordholt, eds., *Locating Southeast Asia: Geographies of Knowledge and Politics of Space* (2005*a*), and Cynthia Chou and Vincent Houben, eds., *Southeast Asian Studies: Debates and New Directions* (2006*a*). It so happens that both books were co-published in Singapore which is an appropriate location for them. Singapore is a country which, in some respects, can rightly be seen as occupying the geographical centre of Southeast Asia, and in scholarly terms, as being at the heart of Southeast Asian Studies in both teaching and research and, along with the area roughly within what is now Malaysia and some adjacent maritime territories, occupying the "low centre" of Anthony Reid's "saucer model of Southeast Asian identity" (1999*b*). Singapore was also one of the founding members of the Association of Southeast Asian Nations (ASEAN) which officially came into being on 8 August 1967. These two books, though by no means marking the culmination of the debate, brought together scholars across disciplines, research interests and nationalities to consider the significant moments, events, personages and issues in the development of the study of Southeast Asia, discuss the current "state-of-the-art", and look forward to some of the future prospects for this field of studies. Among other matters, Chou's and Houben's book explores the value of the area studies approach and its future viability in a relatively positive spirit, and, contrary to its critics, the editors argue that Southeast Asian Studies has been "an epicentre for theoretical knowledge production" (2006*b*, p. 1). More than this they point to the expansion of studies of Southeast Asia in the region itself, whilst noting the difficulties which this field of studies is experiencing elsewhere, especially in Europe (ibid., p. 2). Furthermore, Chou and Houben propose that, in a world in which there is the need to engage with other countries and regions from a position of strength, then a Southeast Asian regional identity through the ASEAN in particular is "becoming more and more self-evident" (ibid., p. 11). Overall the editors are optimistic and "although in some places [mainly Europe] there is reason for gloom, Southeast Asian studies as [a] whole is in the process of being reconfigured to become more of a central concern in our current world" (ibid., p. 20).

It is also our contention in this present volume that Southeast Asia as a region, concept and scholarly field of enquiry, though not a region that is necessarily fixed and unchanging, will continue to have resonance and relevance. This is in spite of the arguments frequently presented by globalization theorists and disciplinary specialists in particular that regions are rapidly losing their validity and viability in a world in which borders and boundaries are constantly traversed and transnational and cross-cultural encounters and hybridization have become increasingly apparent.

On the other hand, Kratoska's and his co-editors' book tends to be rather more sceptical about the utility of the concept of a Southeast Asian region and the appropriateness of attempting to understand it in terms of a multi-disciplinary area studies approach. They tend towards the very well-known view that Southeast Asia emerged as a regional concept because of external involvement and interest (from the U.S., Europe and Japan) so that these foreign powers could "deal collectively with a set of territories and peoples that felt no particular identification with one another" (2005*b*, p. 11). Their conclusion is that attempts to define and delimit Southeast Asia have been "inconclusive" and more than this that the term "Southeast Asia" continues to be used "as little more than a way to identify a certain portion of the earth's surface" (ibid., p. 14). The book focuses much more on regional constructs and concepts as, in Heather Sutherland's terms, "contingent devices" and not "fixed categories" (2005, pp. 20–59); the emphasis is much more on the contestation of space, the movement of populations, capital, cultures and ideas, and the importance of networks and brokerage (Kratoska, Raben, and Nordholt 2005*b*, pp. 12–15). This perspective is most consummately explored and evaluated in Howard Dick's contribution to the volume in his consideration of Southeast Asia as "an open system" (2005, pp. 250–74). Of course, we also recognize the value of conceptualizing Southeast Asia as "a contingent device" and one which will shift its boundaries and character depending on scholarly objects of enquiry and academic disciplinary interests and inclinations. In our opinion there is no contradiction between acknowledging the continuing importance of Southeast Asia as a region and the field of studies devoted to it on the one hand, and proposing that the region, as a concept and as a focus of scholarly investigation and analysis, can mean different things to different people.

Interestingly the significance of Southeast Asia as a region has recently been reinforced and strengthened with the publication in Singapore of yet another edited volume arguing the case for Southeast Asian Studies (Goh 2011*a*). Goh Beng Lan and her contributors present convincing arguments for the importance and vitality of scholarship within the region and of the contribution of local scholars to understanding the region within which they live. In the process of, in Goh's terms, "decentring" and "diversifying" Southeast Asia she proposes that we develop and deploy regional perspectives, "local dimensions", and provide the stage for "local", "native", or "indigenous voices" which are based, not on the interests and priorities of those outside the region, but "on local priorities" (2011*b*, p. 1). Moreover, she emphasizes the importance of contextualizing knowledge production on the future of Southeast Asian Studies, and, in arguing for the continued relevance of "area studies" and the need to explore its "afterlives", she and her contributors address the distinctions and mutually enriching interactions between locally generated ("insider") and Euro-American-derived ("outsider") perspectives on Southeast Asia and examine the opportunities provided by cross-disciplinary understanding. Therefore, for Goh, it is vital, in the continuing enterprise of Southeast Asian Studies, to consider the experiences, practices and views of local scholars. This also requires us to take account of "the alternative, albeit emergent, models of area studies in the region" (ibid., p. 15) and "alternative perceptions of Southeast Asia" (ibid., p. 44). The crucial need is "to create a platform to speak about Southeast Asian perspectives" so that those who come from and live in the region and share "the same convictions" can debate issues which "may not be of concern to those outside of the region", and in addition "explicate lived realities and understandings of normative social science concepts within the region, rather than taking wider social theories emanating from the West/outside as the formulae for defining the region" (ibid., p. 15). We agree very much with the spirit and intent of this volume, and we acknowledge that through the development of regional connections and institutions, there is vibrancy in academic studies on Southeast Asia from within the region.

Nevertheless, there is a danger and difficulties, as we shall see in our volume, in drawing too sharp a distinction between "insider" and "outsider" perspectives and interests, and a problem in determining what the alternative, emergent models of area studies from within the region comprise and whether or not they are sufficiently different from the kinds of models and concepts that have been developed from outside Southeast Asia. After providing a flavour of recent deliberations on Southeast Asia and how best to approach studying it as a region, we do not intend to dwell for too long on the intricacies of these debates about the value or otherwise of studying a region in its own right (which of course does not preclude considering its relations with other regions and the borderlands between regions) and the use of a multi-disciplinary approach in that endeavour. There have been some important publications and landmarks in these debates and their findings and arguments do not require repeating. Among the most significant contributions, in our view, have been those by Ananda Rajah (1999), Barbara Watson Andaya (1997), Benedict Anderson (1978, 1992), John Bowen (1995, 2000), Donald Emmerson (1984), Russell Fifield (1976, 1983), Ariel Heryanto (2002), Charles Hirschman (1992), Charles Keyes (1992), Victor Lieberman (1993, 1995, 2003, 2009), Denys Lombard (1995), Ruth McVey (1995, 1998), Anthony Reid (1988, 1993, 1994, 1999*a*, 1999*b*), Craig Reynolds (1995, 1998), Shamsul Amri Baharuddin (1994), Wilhelm G. Solheim (1985), Mary Steedly (1999), Heather Sutherland (2003, 2005) and Willem van Schendel (2005). We are sure that readers would choose other publications too, but it is our view that these mark out much of the scholarly terrain and it can also be argued that most of the strands of the debate have been brought together in the subtle, detailed and carefully crafted classic study by Oliver Wolters, reproduced in a later revised and extended edition (1982/1999). What is more, and perhaps unsurprisingly, the debate has been dominated by American-based scholars and to lesser extent academics from other Western countries conducted in the medium of the English language, and their preoccupations have often been on the history, current state, and the future of the study of Southeast Asia in the United States and other Western countries (including Australia and New Zealand).

There was a notable flurry of concern and anguish among regional specialists when there was a decline in official and student interest in Southeast Asia and area studies more generally in the United States and Europe from the mid-1970s through to the 1990s. In this connection the interventions by local Southeast Asian researchers and their role in the debates have been relatively thin on the ground though increasingly important, and in a powerful counter to perceived Western dominance in Southeast Asian Studies, Ariel Heryanto has identified the obstacles to a local contribution and has argued the case, as has Goh Beng Lan subsequently, for an "indigenous Southeast Asian Studies" as a way forward (2002; and see King 2001, 2005, 2006). In support of Heryanto and Goh it is clear that much of the future for the development of both multi-disciplinary programmes in Southeast Asian Studies and the study of Southeast Asia from disciplinary perspectives must lie within the region itself, and we venture to suggest in adjacent regions and countries as well (East Asia in particular including The People's Republic of China, the Hong Kong SAR, Japan and the Republic of Korea). That future has been based on the strong foundations which have been built in Singapore through the Institute of Southeast Asian Studies, the Faculty of Arts and Social Sciences, the Asia Research Institute and the Southeast Asian Studies programme at the National University of Singapore, and in regional and disciplinary programmes in Malaysia at the University of Malaya in Kuala Lumpur, Universiti Kebangsaan Malaysia, Universiti Sains Malaysia, and Universiti Putra Malaysia, and at Silpakorn, Thammasat and Chulalongkorn Universities in Thailand. In much of Southeast Asia there has been a focus, for obvious reasons, on studies within national boundaries and on Southeast Asia as an element in the wider field of Asian Studies. But within such countries as Indonesia, Vietnam, Thailand, the Philippines and Brunei in the past couple of decades there has also been a noticeable increase in interest in, and the deployment of resources to support specific programmes of study on Southeast Asia and in acquiring much deeper knowledge of one's neighbours.

Nevertheless, Southeast Asian Studies still seems to be in a double-bind. First, as a region it has been difficult to define in any case. Its cultural diversity, its political and geographical fragmentation, its varied historical experiences under different kinds of Euro-American colonialism, and its status as a crossroads and as a place which was subject to powerful influences and forces from outside, particularly India, China and the Middle East, have tended to render it as a region by default (King 2005). In other words it is defined by what it is not rather than what it is. Secondly, multi-disciplinary or in some cases interdisciplinary, language-based regional or area studies as the approach which has been deployed to study and understand the region had started to come in for sustained criticism from the 1970s purportedly because of its weaknesses in disciplinary, theoretical and methodological terms, its Western-centred perspectives and its association with colonial Orientalism and the post-colonial Cold War. More seriously the critics of the area studies approach have pointed to the inadequacies of drawing boundaries, whether national or regional, around units of analysis in the era of globalization and the transnational flows of people, culture, information, knowledge, capital and goods. As we have noted in Europe in particular the study of Southeast Asia has been in decline since the 1970s interspersed with a few modest revivals. There have also been ups and downs in the United States with the heyday of area studies in the first two decades or so after the Second World War, and a relative decline since then, though with resurgence from the 1980s with the influx of refugees into the United States from Indochina and then Burma, the settlers' interest in sustaining and studying their own cultures and languages, and the interest that American students showed in knowing more about these recent immigrants.

THE RATIONALE OF THE BOOK

So what is the purpose of yet another set of narratives and reflections on Southeast Asia as a region and the historical construction of the field of Southeast Asian Studies both within and outside Southeast Asia? A principal focus of interest is that this volume emerged from exchanges and interaction between Korean researchers and a selection of specialists from outside East and Southeast Asia who have a wide experience of the region. There is very little by way of published material in English providing overviews on and an appreciation of Korean research and perspectives on Southeast Asia, and this current volume attempts to begin to fill this gap in our knowledge. There is a focus on institutional developments in Southeast Asian Studies and on knowledge production on Southeast Asia (both colonial and post-colonial) within the Republic of Korea (ROK) and in the wider East Asia, as well as in the Southeast Asian region itself, the United Kingdom and the wider Europe, Australia and the United States. The book is not so much concerned with engaging in the central debates, theories and methodologies in Southeast Asian Studies or in addressing such issues as disciplinary versus area studies. The three edited publications to which we have just referred provide ample illustration of the major issues and concerns.

The field of Southeast Asian Studies is relatively recent in the Republic of Korea. In the pre-Second World War period Korea had been subject to Japanese colonialism; it then went through a bitter civil war and partition in which the major international powers played an important role, and it was not until the 1960s and 1970s under American tutelage in the south that the Republic of Korea began to accumulate sufficient resources to support research and to consider other countries beyond East Asia as possible fields for Korean diplomatic and economic interest. In the emergence of foreign policy and in becoming a major economic force in the region Korea saw the need for the development of linguistic expertise and more detailed knowledge of its Southeast Asian neighbours. A small number of Korean scholars were active in the 1960s and 1970s in the disciplines of history, language and literature, but very little in depth research was published at this time. In establishing the infrastructure of the study of Southeast Asia a crucial need early on was to develop Southeast Asian language programmes and produce language textbooks for teaching purposes; the early focus was on Vietnamese and Thai in particular, as well as Malay-Indonesian.

The main research developments in a recognizably Southeast Asian field of studies did not really begin to emerge until the late 1980s and early 1990s, following the completion of the doctoral training of a handful of pioneering scholars in the 1970s. This body of work was located primarily in the disciplines of political science and international relations and significant numbers of Korean research students from the 1970s onwards went abroad for doctoral study, and, for obvious reasons given close South Korean-American ties, particularly to the United States. The Republic of Korea's emerging position in the international relations and security environment and in the economic development of East Asia and Southeast Asia, accompanied by increasing political liberalization following military dictatorship which enabled Koreans to travel, work and study abroad, generated a concern from Korean scholars to investigate the wider Asian region, including Southeast Asia, in their academic research. Korean research also focused on political and economic relations between Korea and Southeast Asia and on such matters as Korean capital investment in the regions to the south. There were also comparative studies of Korean and Southeast Asian political and economic development.

In spite of this exposure to Western scholarship Korean scholars have also shown a special interest in the work undertaken on the region by Chinese and Japanese observers, as their closest neighbours in East Asia, and as countries with which they have shared histories and educational and other experiences. Korean scholars also have linguistic advantages in working in Chinese and Japanese and in accessing archival and other materials in these languages. It is also important to note that the very noticeable expansion of the Korean economy and the resources that were made available from that expansion, particularly from the 1980s, ensured that Korean scholars could undertake field research in Southeast Asia, develop a more intense and detailed knowledge of the region, and become increasingly involved in international scholarship. Park Seung Woo's chapter 4 provides more detailed information on the character, development and contribution of Korean scholarship on Southeast Asia and the reasons for it.

An important contribution to the development of the infrastructure of Asian Studies in the Republic of Korea, and within that Southeast Asian Studies, was the establishment of the Institute for East Asian Studies (IEAS) at Sogang University in Seoul in 1981. It is one of the leading research institutes for Asian Studies in the country and since its foundation it has fostered a greater understanding of Asia, including Southeast Asia, through a wide variety of high profile programmes. IEAS also sponsored the programme of work from which this present edited book emerged. In 2008 IEAS commenced a ten-year project of the Humanities Korea (HK) Program with the financial support of the National Research Foundation, a government-affiliated institution under the ROK Ministry of Education, Science and Technology. The objectives of the project, "Southeast Asia as an Open Regional System: A New Paradigm for Communicating with the Globe and Reaching Out to the Public" have been to explore the historical construction of Southeast Asia as a regional unit and of Southeast Asian Studies as the vehicle to study this region, as well as the mosaic formation of Southeast Asian cultures and the phenomena of regional cooperation and integration across and beyond the Association of Southeast Asian Nations. To carry out the project effectively and cohesively, IEAS formed themed research clusters to which domestic and international academics have been invited for collaborative work. One of the clusters was formed in 2009 around the research themes entitled "The Historical Construction of Southeast Asian Studies" and "Perceiving Southeast Asia". It was these themes which provided the focus of a conference held in Seoul on 19–20 March 2010 to enable Korean and non-Korean scholars to debate the issues, and from which some of the papers delivered at that gathering were selected for this present edited volume.

The main objective of this research cluster has been to trace the historical development of Southeast Asian Studies as an academic subject in major parts of the world, and particularly to focus on countries and regions where Southeast Asian Studies have been largely fostered and developed into an independent academic field of studies during the past century. Among them are various countries in Europe, as well as Australia, the USA, China, Japan, Korea, and in Southeast Asia itself. A country-by-country examination procedure was adopted whereby each cluster member chose or was assigned one country for his or her research area. Through the country-by-country investigation, the cluster attempted to reassess the historical legacies of Southeast Asian Studies in each country or region. An associated theme has been the ways in which the world has perceived and imagined Southeast Asia, particularly in Korea, Japan, China, India, the Middle East and Europe. Other clusters have followed. These comprised in 2010 "Historical and Cultural Formation of Southeast Asia: External Influences and Indigenization"; in 2011 "Colonization, Decolonization and the Formation of Plural Societies in Southeast Asia"; and in 2012 "Social Formations of Southeast Asian Frontier Societies".

In the programme of work, the 2009 cluster was able, first, to trace how the imagination and perception of Southeast Asia was transformed into an academic subject in these countries or regions. Second, the researchers examined the major reasons within particular national or international circumstances for the development or the decline of Southeast Asian Studies over the years. Third, keeping a close eye on the trajectories of Southeast Asian Studies in each country, the cluster focused on an exploration of the dominant research issues in particular periods. Fourth, it also considered interactions between Southeast Asian Studies and other academic disciplines, especially those in the fields of the social sciences and the humanities. Finally, the researchers have also given detailed accounts of some individual scholars who pioneered the advancement of Southeast Asian Studies as a field of scholarly endeavour.

A significant contribution of this volume is that, for the first time, it presents the work and perspectives of leading Korean scholars on the development of Southeast Asian Studies both within and outside the region. Six of the eleven chapters have been written by Korean researchers, along with a jointly written editorial introduction. The remaining contributions are provided by scholars with long established interests in the cultures and histories of Southeast Asia and who have brought perspectives from Europe, Australia and from within Southeast Asia itself. One observation might be that there is insufficient involvement of local scholars in this programme of work, but the intention has been to provide a platform for the expression and development primarily of Korean perspectives and thoughts on Southeast Asia as a region and on the histories of the development of Southeast Asian Studies both within Southeast Asia itself and beyond, and particularly in East Asia, hence the three chapters which deal specifically with the development of scholarly work in Korea, China and Japan. For obvious reasons Korean scholars have shown a particular interest in and have been influenced by the work undertaken by Chinese and Japanese researchers on Southeast Asia, and have developed expertise in a literature which has continued to remain largely inaccessible to English speaking audiences.

THEMES, ISSUES AND PERSPECTIVES IN THE HISTORICAL CONSTRUCTION OF SOUTHEAST ASIAN STUDIES

Southeast Asia: The Emergence of a Regional Concept

We have noted the problems of defining Southeast Asia as a region. Several of the contributors to this volume pay some attention to this issue, including Ariel Heryanto, Yu Insun and Victor King. It is still uncertain when the concept of a region with a distinctive personality separate from India and China was first formulated. The Chinese and Japanese had the long established notion of the "the South" (Japanese: *nanpo*), "the Southern Ocean" (Chinese: *nanyang*; Japanese: *nanyo*), "South[ern] Sea[s]" (Chinese: *nanhai*) or Eastern and Western Oceans (Chinese: *Dongxiyang*) which for them usually included, at various times, some or all of what is now Southeast Asia, with the addition of parts of India and some of the Pacific Islands as well. The regional concept therefore referred to a rather ill-defined and shifting entity with equally vaguely drawn subdivisions: "eastern", "western", "inner", "outer", "rear" and "frontal". Early Indian traders used the terms Suvarnabhumi (Land of Gold) and Suvarnadvipa (Golden Island/Peninsula) for regions to the east which included parts of Burma and Thailand, the Malayan Peninsula, Sumatra and Java. Some British residents in early Singapore in the first half of the nineteenth century also had a regional vision, although this was somewhat indeterminate and extended outwards from the Straits of Malacca. These early notions of a region were ill-defined but they certainly drew attention to a spread of territories which

were located between the Indian subcontinent and mainland China and
Japan and which were different from them. The concept of a much more
clearly delineated and conceptualized region which came to be referred to
as "Southeast Asia" came much later.

Reid has argued for the first, what might be termed scientific use of
the term "Southeast Asia" (*Südostasien*) in German-speaking scholarship at
the turn of the twentieth century (though note the indeterminate use of the
term "South-eastern Asia" by the American pastor Howard Malcolm as
far back as 1839, see chapter by Yu Insun, and Emmerson 1984, p. 5)
and from then on it became a term which was used relatively frequently
among German and Austrian pre-historians and ethnologists like Robert
von Heine-Geldern (Reid 1999*b*, pp. 9–10). However, the concept of a
Southeast Asian region in pre-historical and cultural terms was obviously
rather different from the later nation-state-based concept, bequeathed by
the departing colonial powers and the Japanese, which emerged during
the 1940s. This is speculation, but it does seem that for English- and
French-speakers at least who were familiar with the literature in German
that the concept of a Southeast Asian region (which was still usually
referred to by other terms) was circulating in various European scholarly
circles in the 1920s and 1930s. For example, a Department of South East
Asia and the Islands was established at the School of Oriental and African
Studies (SOAS) in London in 1932, though it was discontinued four
years later. It is very likely that British scholars and scholar administrators
based in Rangoon and Singapore in the interwar years had already arrived
at the concept of a Southeast Asian region, although whether or not it
included the American dependency of the Philippines is debateable. It is
an interesting coincidence that there was also a strong presence of Burmese
specialists in SOAS during the 1930s, the region which was geographically
close to the Indian subcontinent, but in the eyes of expatriate scholars in
Burma like John Stewart, who was appointed to SOAS in 1933 and who
had worked with John Furnivall, was undoubtedly conceived as culturally
separate from it.

In similar fashion the Japanese had also formulated a more precise
concept of Southeast Asia which emerged from its increasing imperialist
interests in the "south seas" (or more specifically "the outer south seas")
and they used the term *Tōnan Ajiya*, which directly translates into the
English term "Southeast Asia" as early as 1919 (Shimizu Hajime 2005,
pp. 89–91). The Chinese too were developing what they referred to as
"Nanyang Studies" in the interwar years. Among the expressions of an
increasing crystallization of this regional concept were the founding and

development of research institutes in China and Japanese-occupied Taiwan in the 1920s and 1930s and a "South Seas" society among overseas Chinese in Singapore in 1940.

As we know the firm creation and consolidation of Southeast Asia as the region which we are familiar with today was a product of the Japanese occupation of their "southern resources area" during the Pacific War, post-war Western decolonization and the emergence of newly independent nation-states, and strategic considerations in relation to the encounter, competition and conflict between Western liberal democracy, capitalism and the market, on the one hand and Soviet and Chinese communism, one-party authoritarian governance and centralized socialist state planning on the other. Once specific programmes, centres, departments and institutes with named journals and academic posts were established to study the region under the term "Southeast Asian Studies" then the region duly came into being and was given scholarly legitimacy and authenticity.

Very important developments were the establishment of Southeast Asian Studies programmes at SOAS, Yale and Cornell in 1946, 1947 and 1950 respectively which was followed by the foundation of further programmes and centres in the 1960s, 1970s and 1980s, not only in the United States but also in Europe, Australia, Japan, Singapore and Malaysia (Chou and Houben 2006*b*, pp. 5–6). We tend to think that the post-war construction of Southeast Asia was something generated and owned by the West; but it was not simply the stream of publications which came out of the University of Malaya in the 1950s which began to argue for the scholarly viability and significance of a Southeast Asian region, but most importantly the launch of the *Journal of Southeast Asian History* in Singapore (1960–69), later to become the *Journal of Southeast Asian Studies* in 1970 and the founding of the Centre for South-East Asian Studies there in 1963 as a forerunner of the Institute of Southeast Asian Studies which was established by the Singapore government in 1968. However, this developing Southeast Asian identity was not without dispute and contention, as we have already noted, and the boundaries of the region, depending on whether one viewed them as a pre-historian or archaeologist, an anthropologist, a linguist, a geographer or a political scientist, were not coincident and provided a series of overlapping and interlocking physical, social, cultural, historical, economic and political spaces. As Kratoska, Raben and Nordholt pertinently observe, the political boundaries of the region are "[a]n arbitrary imposition arising from the territorial preoccupations of European colonialism ... [and] ... these borders do not demarcate distinct cultural or ecological zones, or historical polities" (2005*b*, p. 3).

However, it was to be expected that when the term "Southeast Asia", which had already been used officially to refer to Lord Louis Mountbatten's South East Asia Command (SEAC) created in 1943 and the Southeast Asia Treaty Organization (SEATO) which emerged from the Manila Pact in 1954, was used by a collection of neighbouring countries that came together to recognize their shared regional interests and identity in the Association of Southeast Asian Nations (ASEAN) then the region was truly institutionalized in the global imagination. Nevertheless, in the sense that the definition of Southeast Asia very much depends on one's disciplinary perspective and research focus then we also have to accept that in conceptual terms there are several possible "Southeast Asias" within academic debates and discussions.

Southeast Asian Studies: Area Studies and Disciplines

In addition to the issues of regional definition, identity and borders this present volume has also addressed the matter of what constitutes Southeast Asian Studies. Is it the multi- and inter-disciplinary study of a defined region which also ideally requires knowledge of a local language (or languages), cultural and historical sensitivity and the need to understand the region from within? Or does it also embrace scholars who are working primarily from a disciplinary basis and in a disciplinary department and who happen to apply their expertise to a particular case (or cases) within the Southeast Asian region? Does it include scholars who concentrate on only one country in the region and do not stray beyond its borders, and, as is often the case with local researchers, focus on their own country without taking a wider comparative view? We find all these elements included, for various purposes, within this book, so that in some chapters more than others the discussion of studies of Southeast Asia range over multi-disciplinary regional perspectives, single country research as well as work on Southeast Asia or a country or a specific location within Southeast Asia in a particular discipline.

When contributors are considering the institutional development of area studies they tend to examine multi-disciplinary centres and programmes of study on Southeast Asia as in the chapters by Choi Horim on Vietnam, Yu Insun on Japan, Victor King on the United Kingdom and the wider Europe, Lee Sang Kook on Singapore, Park Sa-Myung on China, Park Seung Woo on Korea, and Song Seung-Won on the United States. When authors take the wider view of the contributions to scholarship and our understanding of Southeast Asia they tend to include those researchers (or at least some of them) who are primarily disciplinary-based and/or working on one country in the region as in James Fox's survey of Australia. In examining local perspectives and contributions to Southeast Asian Studies then local researchers who work on their own country are also usually included; in any case there is a strong tendency within the region to work on one's own country primarily, or at the most to extend one's range to very immediate neighbours (see Choi on Vietnam and Lee on Singapore).

We shall also find that country specialisms within the wider Southeast Asia are also considered in Colombijn's discussion of the development of Indonesian Studies in the Netherlands and Fox's consideration of the importance of not only Asian Studies, Asia-Pacific Studies and Southeast Asian Studies in Australia but also more specifically Indonesian and Indonesian-Malayan Studies. The Australian contribution, for quite obvious reasons, has been located overwhelmingly in Indonesian Studies. What is more in some countries Southeast Asian Studies has been more commonly embedded in the wider field of Asian, East Asian or Asia-Pacific Studies. Fox, in particular, in making the point that Southeast Asian Studies as a whole has never constituted a unified field of studies in Australia, also ranges over Australian-based disciplinary contributions to our understanding of Southeast Asia or parts of it and examines such fields as anthropology, history, archaeology and prehistory, language and literature, economics and demography. Similarly, in his appreciation of Japanese scholarship on Southeast Asia, Yu Insun chooses to focus on the very important discipline of history in Japan rather than on area studies more generally. This raises the question of whether or not the positive and developmental contributions to our understanding of Southeast Asia have come from researchers working in a particular discipline, and those who have focused on a country or sub-region within Southeast Asia; or those who have worked in multi-disciplinary area studies programmes across the region. Although this is a subject for debate we probably have to come down on the side of those who work in a disciplinary context and have focused on a country or sub-region. Even those scholars who have worked in area studies centres and institutes have usually approached their research from the perspective and training of a particular discipline.

Country-based Scholarship: Problems of Definition

Yet another complication is the determination of what constitutes "American", or "Singaporean", or "British" or "Australian research" on Southeast Asia. The academic world is extraordinarily mobile and scholars move between countries for training and work; this is especially the case in the English-speaking world where there has been considerable movement between the U.S., the UK, Australia, Canada and New Zealand and various former colonial dependencies. Some academics move very frequently and they have made a contribution to scholarship in several countries. Where, for example, would we place such distinguished scholars as Anthony Reid? We are sure that several Southeast Asian Studies/Asian Studies centres and programmes would want to claim him as a contributor to their endeavours: a New Zealander who followed his early education in his home country, then his Ph.D. at Cambridge, and who has worked in Malaysia, Singapore, Australia and the United States. His longest sojourn has been at the Australian National University where he holds an Emeritus Professorship, and so it seems that Southeast Asian Studies in Australia has the greatest claim to him. Another is Paul Wheatley, a British geographer who spent his academic career between Britain, then Malaya, and the United States. The major part of his career was in the U.S. where he held an Emeritus Professorship in Chicago, but, having been educated in the UK, he was also an important force in the British colonial institution of the University of Malaya when the study of Southeast Asia was in its infancy.

This brings us to the issue of colonial outliers. King, for example, has examined the University of Malaya within the context of the development of Southeast Asian Studies in the United Kingdom, but this, from the perspective of local scholars might be seen to be an unwarranted claim. Nevertheless, it does seem that as a colonial institution which was initially staffed primarily by expatriate academics (though not just from the UK but importantly from other Commonwealth countries and elsewhere), then its inclusion within an imperial rather than a local enterprise might be justified. The same case might be argued for the Ecole Française d'Extrême-Orient in Hanoi and the role that it played in the development of Southeast Asian Studies in France through the work of such distinguished scholars as Georges Coedès.

There is no easy answer to these issues raised by country-based reviews; the general rule of thumb seems to be that citizenship and place of birth might not be the main criterion for including an individual within the scholarly activities of a particular country and that, as Lee Sang Kook suggests, it is "the location of knowledge production itself". A case in point is Benedict Anderson, born in Kunming, China to an Anglo-Irish father and an English mother. He spent some time in Ireland and was educated at Eton College and Cambridge, but was brought up in California and spent almost his whole career at Cornell where he undertook his postgraduate studies and where he is now an Emeritus Professor. Here the United States can rightly claim him as a major contributor to Southeast Asian Studies in America. Then there is Oliver W. Wolters, the late Goldwin Smith Emeritus Professor of Southeast Asian History, who had been a major force in the early development of the Southeast Asian programme at Cornell University from 1964. Born in Britain, much of his early career from 1937 had been spent in Malaya and Singapore as a colonial official after graduating from Oxford with a degree in History. He then left Malaya for the UK in 1957 to a lectureship in History at the School of Oriental and African Studies in London and worked there with D.G.E. Hall. Finally he became the first Professor of Southeast Asian History at Cornell in 1964. His main contribution has been to the development of American scholarship on Southeast Asia.

However, even "the site of knowledge production" itself presents particular difficulties and it finds expression in debates about academic colonization and the dominance of expatriate scholarship in certain countries like Singapore, as we shall see in the next section.

Local and Foreign Scholarship: Does It Matter?

There is an obvious anxiety about the dominance of Western scholarship in the study of Southeast Asia (though we must beware of the assumption that this scholarship has been in some way homogeneous), and the subordinate position of local contributions to the development of our understanding of the region. The anxiety is at its most acute among researchers in Southeast Asia itself and the arguments against Western dominance are rehearsed in Choi Horim's examination of Vietnamese critical views on Western scholarship. But it has also been expressed by Western observers themselves, often because of a level of unease about accusations of ideological and academic hegemony, which harks back to earlier criticisms of Western perspectives as "Orientalist" and ethnocentric. There is also the matter of the commitment of countries outside Southeast Asia to the continuation of support and funding for these studies and the conviction that if the study of the region is to have a future then this must rely on the Southeast Asian countries themselves.

In his chapter in this volume Ariel Heryanto suggests that, in the examination of the historical construction and development of Southeast Asian Studies, the greater contribution to the field of studies from outside the region (in terms of key texts, ideas, individual scholars and institutions) as against that of local scholars raises several political, ethical and intellectual issues. He notes the "rather limited range of locally published and accessible ideas". In one respect this unequal contribution should not be unduly problematic; scholarship and knowledge are international and should be shared and open to all. Some local scholars have been trained abroad; some work abroad; local researchers contribute to international research programmes and to publications which involve participants from countries outside Southeast Asia; foreign researchers work, study and are trained in higher education and other research-based institutions in Southeast Asia. Lee Sang Kook's chapter argues, for example, that the study of Southeast Asia in Singapore was, as a British dependency, historically dominated by expatriate scholars, and the development of Southeast Asian Studies there has continued to rely heavily on foreign scholars in the post-war and post-independence period. Part of the explanation for this is that for much of its history after 1962 the [National] University of Singapore was primarily a teaching and training institution and not one which was devoted to the renewal of the senior generation of university scholars with locally trained postgraduates; Singaporean graduates usually moved into the public and corporate sectors and not into higher education. Moreover, when Singaporean scholars did take up posts in the local universities and research institutes they tended to focus on Singapore rather than extend their reach to other countries within the region. Local Singapore-based Chinese-language-medium regional research on Southeast Asia was also increasingly marginalized by English-language-medium studies which served to open Singapore to expatriate academics. What should also be emphasized is that, as a global city, Singapore has also sought out (and continues to do so) research and educational expertise from outside its borders, and offers attractive salaries, grants, fellowships and academic facilities to ensure that it does secure internationally recognized scholars, that it competes globally, and that it continues to play a significant role in supporting regional scholarship by bringing scholars from neighbouring Southeast Asian and other Asian countries to Singapore. In this regard the first four Directors of the Institute of Southeast Asian Studies were expatriates: Harry Benda, John Legge, Josef Silverstein and Kernial Singh Sandhu (though a Malaysian and a graduate of the University of Malaya); and the first Director of the Asia Research Institute at the National University of Singapore was Anthony Reid.

We should also acknowledge the fact that within the region it is not only in Singapore that expertise on Southeast Asia resides. ASEAN pronounced its policy for the promotion of Southeast Asian Studies programmes in the region itself in 1976 (Chou and Houben 2006*b*, p. 7). A multi-disciplinary programme of Southeast Asian Studies was established at the University of Malaya in the 1970s but prior to that and from the foundation of the university, research and teaching on Southeast Asia was conducted in a range of disciplinary departments (history, geography, sociology and anthropology, economics, politics). Along with Singapore, between 1959 and 1962 the Kuala Lumpur campus of the University of Malaya was an important site for the early development of research and teaching on Southeast Asia as a region in its own right. Choi Horim also draws attention to the fact that Vietnam established a research institute for Southeast Asian Studies within the Vietnam Academy of Social Sciences in Hanoi as early as 1973. At that time the Vietnamese divided a broader East Asia into two sub-regions: North Asia which included China, Japan and Korea, and South Asia which brought together Southeast Asia with the Pacific islands. The analytical frameworks were primarily derived from anti-imperialist, anti-neocolonialist and anti-feudal "socialist doctrines and concepts" within a nationalist context, and the programmes of research were located in government-supported and funded institutions. The emphasis was on localizing and indigenizing Southeast Asian Studies, on directing scholarship to address domestic and overseas development strategies, and on locating Vietnam within a Southeast Asian historical and cultural context. After 1986 and the introduction of the renovation policy (*doi moi*) the number of research and training organizations in Hanoi and Ho Chi Minh City increased significantly. A crucial development was the formation of the Southeast Asian Research Association of Vietnam in 1996 which now has a membership of over 2,500. Other Southeast Asian programmes and centres in other universities within the region have followed: for example, in Thailand at Mahidol, Silpakorn and Chiang Mai Universities, in Indonesia at Gadjah Mada University, and at Universiti Brunei Darussalam.

Nevertheless, and in spite of the difficulty of delimiting local and foreign scholarship, a major concern is that a dependence on foreign or external research may lead to agendas, priorities and interests which are different from those which are designed to serve local needs and concerns. The American preoccupation with modernization and nation-state building in post-war Southeast Asia and the problems engendered by notions of modernity and the cultural, political and economic institutions which accompanied it, all set within a Western frame of reference, are cases in point. There is also an obvious partisan or nationalistic impulse which wants the study of one's own country, society, culture and region to be generated primarily by and in the hands of one's own academic community.

Yet Ariel Heryanto points to a number of important regionally-based scholarly initiatives to develop region-wide networks, though with sponsorship from funding bodies in the United States and Japan and with mixed results. However, in Heryanto's view, what seems to hold out real promise is not so much regional knowledge emerging from the academy, but from non-academic constituencies particularly in the entertainment and media industries which have considerable economic and political clout (producers, retailers, advertisers, journalists, artists, activists, cultural critics and consumers of popular culture). In particular Heryanto refers to the influence of the new media and information technologies and popular culture (in music, film, theatre, art, radio, television, magazines, books, newspapers, the internet, public events, parades, festivals) and the importance of engaging with these cultural expressions in our examination and understanding of changing secular and religious values and identities in Southeast Asia. He argues that out of the study of the creative industries and the new media is likely to come a shift in our perspectives on the region, no longer so much focused on the nation-state and associated political elites as units of analysis, but on transnational, sub-national, cross-regional, hybrid social groups and on such principles of organization as gender, age, occupation, social class, religion and ethnicity. In his focus on networks, Heryanto's approach is similar to some of the contributions to the volume edited by Kratoska, Raben and Nordholt in honour of Heather Sutherland (2005) which focuses on Southeast Asia as an open system, on networks, corridors, communication and transnational flows rather than on national units, or on the delineation of boundaries and fixed territorial categories. The Korean research programme also emphasizes the need to view Southeast Asia as "an open system", and one which reaches out to East Asia, including Korea, and beyond. The developing connections between Southeast and East Asia are of special concern to Korea, Japan, the People's Republic of China and Taiwan, and, in our opinion, this will be a major focus in local and wider Asian scholarship. In this regard, it is likely that the West will be increasingly marginalized in these exchanges.

Interestingly, the anxiety about the subordinate position of local scholarship on Southeast Asia is paralleled in Western concerns about the colonial origin of most of the major pioneering studies of the region. Freek Colombijn ably demonstrates these concerns with regard to the Dutch relationship with its former East Indies Empire, and more particularly how those Dutch scholars currently working on Indonesia have come to terms with the colonial relationship and attempted to "decolonize" this field of studies. In our view nowhere in the history of colonialism has the relationship between the metropolitan power and the dependent territory been so long-established and intense, and the engagement, memories and images of the past and the continuing moral issues which Dutch colonialism raises are nowhere matched in French Indochina, British Burma and Malaya or Portuguese Timor. The quantity and quality of Dutch scholarship on the territories and populations which eventually came to be known as the post-war Republic of Indonesia is considerable. The knowledge amassed by the Dutch in history, geography, geology, ethnology and the social and natural sciences is immense. Colombijn refers to the colonial relationship as "a burden", particularly for Dutch historians and historically inclined social scientists in three senses: (1) with regard to access in the Netherlands to the most comprehensive collections of material on Indonesia anywhere in the world and the consequences of this for the ways in which Dutch scholars have studied and understood its former colony; the importance of a strong empirical, factual, archival emphasis in Dutch scholarship which has tended not to relate case studies to theoretical considerations, but rather assume that issues and topics should emerge from the empirical material; (2) the problem for the Dutch and particularly Dutch scholars following Indonesian independence, in positioning themselves in relation to the policies, practices and consequences of Dutch rule in the East Indies; and (3) a parochial, inward-looking orientation to things Indonesian which eschewed comparisons with places and peoples beyond Indonesia and which has emerged from the necessary engagement of academics with the Dutch public and the need to debate the value or otherwise of Dutch involvement in Indonesia.

Overall Dutch studies on Indonesia, many of them written in Dutch, did not attract the attention they deserved after the Second World War and Indonesian independence. The preoccupations of American-dominated social science on Indonesia and the wider Southeast Asian region, exemplified most obviously in the work of Clifford Geertz and his fellow researchers, meant that pre-war Dutch studies, although they were of obvious empirical and historical importance and were used by American, other European and Australian social scientists, were seen as largely irrelevant and old-fashioned in theoretical terms and in understanding the processes of post-war modernization and nation-building (though we should not forget the influential work of Julius H. Boeke [1953], Jacob Cornelis van Leur [1955] and Bertram J.O. Schrieke [1955–57] when they appeared in English translation). The trauma of the Indonesian revolution and the expulsion of the Dutch from their former colony also led to an increasing neglect of Indonesia in Dutch academic life in the 1950s and 1960s, though there has been some fitful resurgence of interest since the 1970s, with a further apparent decline in interest in the past decade.

Genealogies of Scholarship

Several of the chapters draw attention to the importance of the contribution of individual scholars in founding and/or developing programmes of study — whether multi-disciplinary, region-wide area studies programmes, or those within disciplines and on specific countries. Fox especially, in anthropological mode, constructs a genealogy of some of the main founding figures of this field of studies in Australia, and other chapters in our volume also select specific scholars for attention in tracing founders, lines of succession and scholarly networks. This exercise also requires the location of these scholars in particular institutions where programmes of study were first developed and, in most cases, sustained and, in Robert Cribb's terms where "circles of esteem" were established (2006, pp. 50–52). Fox, for example, considers the pioneering role of the Australian National University (ANU) in Canberra, and the Universities of Sydney, Melbourne, Monash (also in Melbourne), and Queensland, in the development of Southeast Asian, Asian and Pacific Studies from the mid-1950s.

Again the international character of scholarship is amply demonstrated in the Australian case and perhaps nowhere are the cross-national networks of academic training and career development more obvious than in Australia because of the major role that academics there played in Commonwealth-sponsored research on and in British dependencies in Southeast Asia and of the close relationships which existed between higher education institutions in Australia, New Zealand and the UK (at Oxford, Cambridge, SOAS and the London School of Economics [LSE]). In the development of Indonesian Studies in Australia, as in SOAS and Oxford, close links were also developed with Dutch institutions, particularly Leiden University, and with leading universities in the United States, especially Cornell. Overwhelmingly the Australian contribution to the study of Southeast Asia focused on the Indonesian-Malay world and rather than Southeast Asian Studies programmes, which were pursued prominently at Monash, the major interest was on Indonesian-Malayan Studies at the ANU, Sydney, Melbourne and Queensland, or in the location of Southeast Asia within wider Asian Studies programmes.

Important figures in this early work in Australia were, for example, Anthony H. Johns, who had been trained at SOAS and who developed Indonesian language and cultural studies, particularly the study of Islam and philology at the ANU in the formative period of the programme. In those early years Johns relied heavily on Indonesian language teachers to deliver his programme. Another prominent figure, this time in the development

of the study of Indonesian economics at the ANU, was Heinz Wolfgang
Arndt, who was born in Germany in 1915, trained at Oxford, and who
taught at the LSE and Manchester University before settling in Australia
in 1946 and taking Australian citizenship. Both Johns and Arndt were
instrumental in training a whole generation of Australian-based scholars
in the study of the Indonesian-Malay world. In addition, and although he
was not usually thought of in Southeast Asian terms, J. Derek Freeman
was another ANU-based scholar who made a major contribution to the
development of the anthropological study of the region; he too had an
international background — a New Zealander who was employed by
the Colonial Social Science Research Council in London to work in the
then Crown Colony of Sarawak, and who then pursued doctoral studies
at Cambridge. The density of scholarly networks in the development of
Southeast Asian Studies is also illustrated by the arrival of Wang Gungwu
at the ANU in the late 1960s. Born in Indonesia, he had been at the
University of Malaya during the crucial period when the post-war concept
of Southeast Asia as a region was formulated and was being fleshed out.
From his post as Head of East Asian History at the ANU he was then
appointed as Director of the Research School of Pacific Studies in 1975
where, among other things, he promoted the study of Southeast Asia. We
have already indicated the international connections which Anthony Reid
enjoyed; he arrived at the ANU in 1970.

   In the development of Indonesian and Malayan Studies in Sydney
again the international character of the Australian enterprise comes to the
fore: early appointments were F.H. van Naerssen who was trained in Leiden
and Russell Jones at SOAS; two of their most prominent students — Peter
Worsley and Stuart Robson — also went on to do doctoral research in
Leiden, with Robson remaining in Leiden for a considerable part of his
career, and Worsley returning to build the programme in Sydney. The
anthropologist, William R. Geddes, also developed programmes of research
on Southeast Asia at Sydney; like Freeman, Geddes was a New Zealander,
who had worked for the Colonial Social Science Research Council in
Sarawak, and then took his Ph.D. in London. At Melbourne the pioneer,
in this case in the combined fields of political and economic development,
was Jamie (J.A.C.) Mackie, who was educated at Melbourne and Oxford
and who also spent time in Cornell. At Monash it was the historian John
Legge, who had spent time in Cornell, and Herbert Feith, who did his
Ph.D. there, who established a truly multi-disciplinary Southeast Asian
Studies programme which gained international recognition. Southeast
Asian history at Queensland tells a similar story. The historian John Bastin

arrived from Britain to inaugurate the teaching of Southeast Asian history before returning to the UK, followed by Nicholas Tarling, British-born and educated at Cambridge, and who, after his sojourn in Cambridge and then Australia, spent most of his career at the University of Auckland in New Zealand.

The next generation of scholars were equally international and mobile. Three cases at the ANU serve to make our point. Heather Sutherland, who gained her undergraduate degree at the ANU and then went on to pursue her doctoral studies at Yale University, is currently Professor of History at the Vrije Universiteit in Amsterdam. Barbara Watson Andaya was educated at Sydney University; she then undertook her postgraduate studies in Hawai'i and her Ph.D. at Cornell before being appointed to the ANU in 1977. James Fox, an American, who undertook doctoral studies at Oxford, then spent time at Harvard before he arrived at the ANU in 1975.

In King's chapter on the United Kingdom similar genealogical connections can be discerned based on descent from a few senior scholars. The outstanding figure in the development of the study of Southeast Asia in the UK was undoubtedly D.G.E. Hall who occupied a key position at SOAS in the formative post-war years when government funding was made available. He gathered around him an outstanding group of historians (Charles Boxer, C.D. [Jeremy] Cowan, Hugh Tinker, Oliver Wolters and Merle Ricklefs among others) and oversaw the growth of the study of Southeast Asian languages in London. J.S. Furnivall, another leading British scholar in the realization of Southeast Asia as a region of study in its own right, was not particularly involved in building departments and programmes, but was extremely influential in developing the field of studies through his publications. Of the second generation of scholars in the UK it was Charles Fisher and Cowan at SOAS and a group of social anthropologists based at the LSE (Raymond Firth, Maurice Freedman and Edmund Leach [who then moved to Cambridge], all of them involved in the work of the Colonial Social Science Research Council in British dependencies in Southeast Asia) who did much, from a disciplinary perspective at least, to promote scholarly interest in the region. The anthropologist, Rodney Needham at Oxford, who had undertaken field research in British Borneo in the 1950s, also trained a considerable number of anthropologists, many of whom worked in Malaysia and Indonesia.

The attempt to identify the development of the study of Southeast Asia in the UK is also complicated by the fact that we have to examine educational developments, colonial administration and military service in the former British dependencies in the region. The careers of Hall, Furnivall and Fisher have to be seen in this wider imperialist light. The important training ground for British scholars, some of whom then went on to lay the foundations for Southeast Asian Studies in the home country, was in Burma (particularly in the University of Rangoon and the colonial administration in Burma) during the interwar years, and the Malay States and Singapore (especially following the foundation of the University of Malaya in Singapore in 1949 and its extension to the Kuala Lumpur campus in 1959). In the 1950s E.H.G. Dobby, in geography, and Cyril Northcote Parkinson, in history, were important senior figures in the recruitment and, in many cases, the training of both local and expatriate scholars at the University of Malaya, many of whom went on to play leading roles in Southeast Asian scholarship both within the region and beyond: Paul Wheatley, Kernial Singh Sandhu, David Bassett, Wang Gungwu, Wong Lin Ken, Khoo Kay Kim, Ken Tregonning and Mary Turnbull among many others. The role of Ken Tregonning in promoting Southeast Asian Studies and Southeast Asian history in Singapore in the early 1960s was especially significant.

In the United States too genealogical connections can be traced from the founding scholars of the 1940s and 1950s who established programmes of study in particular institutions. As Song Seung-Won indicates American scholarly interest was primarily driven by the need to understand and engage with Southeast Asia (in political, economic, geographical, historical and cultural terms) during the Japanese Occupation and in its aftermath with the emergence of new nation-states and the onset of the Cold War. However, the American colonial presence in the Philippines provided an early pre-war training ground for scholarly interest in the region, though, for obvious reasons, this focused almost exclusively on the colony and not on the region as a whole. Important senior scholars in this Philippine endeavour were Henry Otley Beyer in his contribution to the development of anthropology at the University of the Philippines in Manila. He also established the Institute and Museum of Ethnology and Archaeology there (see King and Wilder 2006/2003, p. 41). Another early figure in the promotion of the study of Philippine sociology and anthropology was Fred Eggan at the University of Chicago. A student of both Beyer and Eggan was Frank Lynch, who played a crucial role in the development of sociological studies in the Philippines itself in establishing a Department of Sociology and Anthropology and the Institute of Philippine Culture at the Ateneo de Manila (ibid., p. 71).

One of the outstanding and enduring programmes for the study of Southeast Asia in the U.S. during the post-war boom in this field of studies was that at Cornell University in New York State initially under the direction of Lauriston Sharp. In 1947 he founded the Cornell-Thailand Project and then became founding Director of the Cornell Southeast Asia Program in 1950 with the support of a grant from the Rockefeller Foundation. For a time Sharp had also studied under Robert von Heine-Geldern in Vienna, receiving a qualification in anthropology there in 1931. His colleague, George McTurnan Kahin, who succeeded him as Director in 1961, founded the Cornell Modern Indonesia Project in 1954. There were many other researchers who worked at Cornell in the early days and were part of these formative developments, among them Lucien and Jane Hanks, Robert Textor, Herbert Phillips and George William Skinner. Other crucial personages in the American contribution to the study of Southeast Asia were Clifford and Hildred Geertz along with Robert Jay who worked in Java and Bali in the 1950s under the auspices of the Center for International Studies at the Massachusetts Institute of Technology. Yale University established its Southeast Asia Program before that of Cornell in 1947 and key figures in its founding and development were Raymond Kennedy, Karl J. Pelzer and Harry J. Benda.

There are two important points to make about the American contribution which connects with themes which we have already raised. First, although major regional programmes of study were established early on at Yale, Cornell and the University of California at Berkeley (and later at the Universities of Michigan, Wisconsin-Madison, Hawaii-Manoa, Northern Illinois, Ohio, University of California-Los Angeles and California State Fresno, Washington, Johns Hopkins [School of Advanced International Studies], Arizona State, Harvard, Stanford, and Ohio State), it is noticeable just how strongly American scholars held to the importance of disciplinary training and perspectives and to the focus on one country in the region with the command of the necessary local language(s). Early on there was intensive and detailed attention paid to America's former colony, the Philippines, as well as to Indonesia and Thailand, and, although these countries came under the umbrella of the wider region, they were nevertheless treated as discrete national units for certain scholarly purposes (the separate Cornell projects on Thailand and Indonesia are cases in point). Secondly, the early development of Southeast Asian Studies in the United States depended significantly on contributions from outside the country, as one might expect given the international and immigrant character of the American academy. Von Heine-Geldern who left Vienna in 1938 for New York, returning to his homeland in 1950, played an important part in raising the profile of Southeast Asia in Cornell and New York and had been a mentor of Lauriston Sharp. Another German-speaker, Karl Pelzer moved from Germany to the

United States and played a leading role in building Southeast Asian Studies at Yale. Harry J. Benda, or Heinz Jindrich Benda, was a Prague Jewish refugee who had lived in the Dutch East Indies, spoke Dutch fluently, and attended university in New Zealand before moving to the United States; in the 1960s, like Pelzer, he did much to build Yale's reputation in the study of Southeast Asia, and especially Indonesia. The Yale-German-speaking connection had another interesting development when Bernhard Dahm spent time there in the early 1970s and eventually became founding Professor and Director of one of the few multi-disciplinary Southeast Asia programmes in Germany at the University of Passau in 1984; he continued in that role until his retirement in 1997. Hans-Dieter Evers also spent time at Yale as Professor of Sociology and Director of the Graduate Program in Southeast Asian Studies in the late 1960s and then went on to play a formative role in the development of research on Southeast Asia in Singapore, Bielefeld and Bonn, among many other places.

Southeast Asia and Its East Asian Neighbours

It goes without saying that political and economic interests very often drive the interests of external powers in a particular region. As we have seen post-war Western, particularly American scholarly engagement with Southeast Asia was intimately intertwined with international and strategic concerns in the context of super power conflict, the Cold War and global ideological confrontation. In the case of the perspectives of the Chinese, Japanese and Koreans, these were coloured by their close proximity to the regions to the south. What were and should be the attitudes to their close neighbours? What were the similarities and differences (historical and cultural) between them and us? Were there common political and economic interests? Were the territories to the south to be considered as part of a wider East Asia? What of the migrant populations from East Asia who had settled in Southeast Asia? What of the issues arising from transborder populations, particularly minority upland communities which resided within and beyond Southeast Asia? These considerations certainly influenced research agendas and the ways in which scholars in East Asia thought about and wrote about their neighbours to the south. In addition, their preoccupations and analyses had to be understood within particular national political, economic and educational contexts. China, Japan and Korea have also produced a very substantial literature on Southeast Asia, though because it has been written primarily in the vernacular has remained largely outside what might be termed the mainstream Anglo-American scholarship on the region. In this connection Yu Insun suggests, for example, that Japan can boast the largest number of historians of Southeast Asia in the world with generous financial support from such bodies as the Nippon Foundation and the Toyota Foundation as well as Japan's Ministry of Education and Science. Yet their contributions, primarily published in Japanese, are seldom considered in the major debates on Southeast Asian history.

In the case of China Park Sa-Myung argues that since the reforms of the late 1970s, and especially from the 1990s, the development of Southeast Asian Studies there has to be understood in relation to Chinese national strategies towards neighbouring countries. A China Association of Southeast Asian Studies was founded in 1979 and five institutions in southern China carried the responsibility to promote the study of Southeast Asia: Jinan and Xiamen Universities, which had been established very early on in the Chinese efforts to understand their southern neighbours and the Chinese communities in Southeast Asia; and then Zhongshan University in Guangzhou, Guangxi University in Nanning and Yunnan University in Kunming. The opening up of China to the outside world and especially the movement of people in and out of the country have changed the nature and direction of the Chinese academy's interests in and motivations for the study of Southeast Asia. An added dimension of these interests is the presence in Southeast Asia and the strategic importance of ethnic Chinese populations. Furthermore, China shares a long border with three mainland Southeast Asian countries: Vietnam, Laos and Myanmar, with upland minority communities spread across political boundaries, and long-established historical and cultural connections with Vietnam, which was once incorporated into the Han Chinese Empire, and subject to intense processes of Sinicization. Given its long historical involvement with the region, Chinese immigration and settlement to the region as well as the movement of a range of ethno-linguistic groups into mainland Southeast Asia from territories which are located within what is now the People's Republic of China, and its position (territorially, demographically, culturally, politically and economically) as a major power in Asia, it is to be expected that Chinese scholarly perspectives on Southeast Asia have been coloured by a strong Sino-centrism.

Park Sa-Myung indicates that Chinese work from the nineteenth century translated into a thesis of "Chinese colonization of Southeast Asia", and just like Western colonial perspectives did not allow for an autonomous history of its southern neighbours and its definition as a region in its own right. Nevertheless, China never projected colonial rule in Southeast Asia and therefore did not require the kind of systematic knowledge of the region which the European powers and the United States required, or even

Japan during its brief interregnum. There was a strong focus in Chinese scholarship on the overseas Chinese in Southeast Asia, their nationalistic and then subsequently communist aspirations, and their contribution to the development of the home country (see Saw and Wong 2007). One might refer to Chinese perspectives, though different in content and motivation from Western ones, as "Oriental Orientalism"; Southeast Asians were constructed and then viewed through a Chinese politico-cultural and historical lens.

Moreover, just as Europeans in Southeast Asia played a very significant role in the development of scholarship on the region in the home country, so overseas *nanyang* Chinese performed a similar function in mainland China. Some overseas Chinese were also trained in Japan in the pre-war period. The origin of modern Southeast Asian Studies in China owed much to the initiatives of overseas Chinese nationalists who established "South Seas [*Nanyang*] Studies" at Jinan School [later University] (1906) and Xiamen University (1921) and focused on the history of Chinese communities in Southeast Asia and China's relations with them. In 1928 the Nanyang (Cultural Services) Division was also established at Jinan University in Shanghai to promote the study of Southeast Asia, and a journal *Nanyang Yanjiu* (*Nanyang Research*) was also produced (Wang 2005, p. 65). These developments "had been stimulated by the intensive Japanese interest in the Nanyo or Nanyang" in the interwar years (ibid.) (see below).

In a parallel development these studies were continued in the region itself when Chinese who were born in mainland China in the 1910s and 1920s fled to Southeast Asia to escape Japanese aggression. Both Park Sa-Myung and Lee Sang Kook draw attention to the importance of *Nanyang* Chinese in Singapore who founded the China South Seas Society there in 1940 with its own *Journal of the South Seas Society*; in its formative years it was closely associated with Jinan University, and its members looked to China, and not Singapore as their homeland. But the allegiance of the membership shifted progressively to Singapore after the Second World War and the Society became linked to Nanyang University which was founded in Singapore in 1956 as a Chinese-language-medium institution. However, these Chinese scholars used the Chinese language in the Society's publications and research activities which was progressively marginalized by the increasingly mainstream English language scholars at the University of Malaya and then the [National] University of Singapore. Eventually Chinese language scholarship was eclipsed with the merger between Nanyang University and the University of Singapore in 1980 to form the English-language-medium, National University of Singapore.

With regard to subsequent developments in China it was overseas Chinese involved in the Singapore-based Society, many of whom returned to China in the post-war period, who were instrumental in the promotion of Southeast Asian Studies and the training of the next generation of specialists in Chinese universities. This younger generation were born in China in the 1930s and 1940s and trained in universities during the post-1949 Maoist regime; familiar subjects were on the agenda — the history of Southeast Asia, the overseas Chinese, China's relations with the region and the economy of Southeast Asia. It was clear that China had to deal with Southeast Asia as a regional entity after the founding of ASEAN in the late 1960s. Yet China's scholarship on Southeast Asia during the first three decades of Communist rule was driven by ideological concerns which favoured local anti-Western and communist movements in the region and was critical of continuing neo-colonialism.

Park Sa-Myung indicates that it was only after the opening up of China from the 1980s onwards and the emergence of a generation of more Westernized scholars, some of whom had studied abroad, that modern Southeast Asian Studies in China began to move into such fields as religion, gender, the environment, the media and cultural studies, and to draw on modern social science methods of investigation. Nevertheless, Park argues that this welcome modernization of Southeast Asian Studies in China is still tempered by a prevailing Sino-centrism and a preoccupation with the overseas Chinese, the continuing strength of traditional library- and archive-based academic approaches rather than field studies, and the focus on applied, policy-oriented and empirical work rather than more analytical theory-based approaches. For much of the post-war period studies of Southeast Asia in China have been hampered by inadequate funding, the difficulties of scholars undertaking fieldwork in and gaining first-hand contact with the region, and the problem of accessing primary source materials and research findings published in English (see Wang 2005, pp. 68–69).

The Japanese relationship with Southeast Asia was rather different from that of the Chinese in that during the period of modernization from the second half of the nineteenth century, and particularly after the Russo-Japanese war of 1904–05 when Japan emerged victorious and as a major power in the East, the Japanese began to extend their imperial ambitions to other parts of Asia. Southeast Asia came to be seen as an essential element in an economically and politically expanding Japanese Empire. Interestingly the Japanese promotion of the study of Southeast Asia in the interwar years was located not in higher education institutions in Japan, but in Japanese-occupied Taiwan at the Taipei Imperial University. A Japanese pioneer in Southeast Asian history, Fujita Toyohachi, was invited to take up the position of Dean of the College of Letters and Politics at Taipei in 1928. He was instrumental in establishing a Department of *Nanyo* History there. He was succeeded by Iwao Seiichi, who occupied the post from 1929 to 1946; Iwao Seiichi was proficient in the Dutch language and, using Dutch archival material, developed a research interest in Japanese residents in the expanding spheres of Dutch influence in the East Indies in the seventeenth century.

Therefore the regions to the south of Japan, dominated by Western imperial powers, began to crystallize in the Japanese mind into a distinguishable geographical entity prior to the Second World War. Indeed Yoko Hayami suggests that the term and concept of Southeast Asia "had already been in use by World War I in the context of Japan's southward imperialist expansion" (2006, p. 66). Similarly Shimizu Hajime maintains that the Japanese term *Tōnan Ajiya* which translates as "Southeast Asia" was "the expression of an original, autonomous Japanese concept, and not the translation of an English term" (2005, pp. 83–93). It was Japanese ambitions and their subsequent invasion and occupation of Southeast Asia which more than anything else served to delimit and define the region as separate from East Asia. One could argue that the Japanese invaded and occupied what they had previously conceived. In that Japan was not a Southeast Asian colonial power in the interwar years, cluttered with the problems of delimiting and administering separate territories within the Southeast Asian region, then the concept of Southeast Asia as a general area of economic and political opportunity would seem to have been a much more immediate and straightforward idea for them to develop and embrace. As we have seen, in somewhat similar fashion Austrians and Germans, free of colonial preoccupations, were able to think across the artificial territorial boundaries imposed and operated by the British, French, Dutch, Spanish, Portuguese and Americans. Yet the Japanese had a certain advantage over Europeans; despite the diversity of Asia, they could claim that they were Asians like their neighbours to the south, and they also had access to the Chinese literature on the region which they could then develop for their own purposes.

Therefore, it would seem that Japan, rather than adopting this regional concept from the West, already had a developed sense of what it constituted and what role it would play in an increasingly dominant Japanese presence across the western Asia Pacific. Moreover unlike China, Japan did not have the complication of a highly visible, economically vibrant expatriate population in Southeast Asia to command their attention (and the cultural and historical connections which went with the presence of the overseas Chinese there), although there was certainly some Japanese labour migration and investment in the region. Nor did they have shared land borders with their southern neighbours. In this sense Japanese perspectives were less partisan and nationalistic, and were therefore probably more regional in scope. But the interesting twist was, in contrast to China, Japan became an occupying power, and the Japanese engagement with Southeast Asia, however brief, was nevertheless qualitatively different from their Chinese neighbours; a considerable amount of Japanese scholarly attention in the post-war period was devoted to the Japanese occupation and to Japanese-Southeast Asian relations. Nevertheless, early Japanese historical research, which goes back to the Tokugawa period and the early eighteenth century, was particularly dependent on the re-examination of Chinese materials written in classical Chinese.

As Yu Insun indicates much of the major and lasting Japanese scholarship on the region only really began to be conducted after the Second World War, and especially after 1949 and the emergence of the People's Republic of China when the United States began to promote Japan and its economic advancement in Southeast Asia as a counter to the Chinese-dominated communist advance. In this regard Japanese scholars during the 1950s and 1960s were increasingly influenced by post-war Western conceptions of Southeast Asia and by the ways in which Western observers analysed and defined the region, including work by Harry Benda, John Smail and Georges Coedès. After an earlier more Japanese-centred interpretation of Southeast Asia, there was an increasing interest, as in the West, with Southeast Asian history as an autonomous field of study. Among the senior pioneering scholars in Japan in the early post-war years who were focusing on *Nanpo* history were Yamamoto Tatsuro, Ishii Yoneo, Hirasawa Ko, Nagazumi Akira, Ikehada Setsuho and Sakurai Yumio.

In spite of a long-standing interest in Southeast Asia it was not until 1963 that a multi-disciplinary Centre for Southeast Asian Studies, including natural scientists, was founded at Kyoto University, and The Study Group of *Nanpo* History, which was founded in 1942 and subsequently based itself at Tokyo University, became the Japan Society for Southeast Asian History in 1966. Unlike Chinese scholars who, by force of circumstance, have usually had, until recently at least, to examine Southeast Asia from a distance, well-funded Japanese researchers have had the opportunities to undertake field research in the region from the 1960s. They have engaged with the on-the-ground realities of the region using the vernacular, especially, and among other activities, with their involvement in the preservation of

Angkor Wat and the amount of first-hand research conducted in Cambodia. But Japanese researchers have been undertaking work across much of Southeast Asia, early on in Thailand and Laos, and then extending to Malaysia, Indonesia and the Philippines. We would suggest that, in contrast to China, Japan conforms, with some qualifications, to the Western view of Southeast Asia in that in historical terms it was a region to be occupied, exploited, dominated, and constructed to accommodate the needs and interests of the occupying power. For this reason prior to the Second World War Japanese historians were especially interested in the Western colonial experience in Southeast Asia and then, following the Japanese defeat, the post-colonial processes of economic development, international relations and security issues, nation-building and state formation. In the post-war period Japanese researchers have also made contributions to the history of port-cities and trade in maritime Southeast Asia, and, for obvious reasons, have paid special attention to the Japanese occupation of the region and the Pacific War. But Japanese reflections and findings on Southeast Asia are still largely inaccessible to an English-speaking audience, and Yu Insun argues pertinently that this renders international scholarship on Southeast Asia "incomplete". One could say the same for the lack of attention in English-language-medium scholarship to the important contributions of the Chinese.

In contrast to the rather different imperial viewpoints of the Chinese and the Japanese in Southeast Asia and therefore the more established status of their scholarship on the region, the development of Southeast Asian Studies in the Republic of Korea is a much more recent phenomenon. It is still in its experimental stage. As Park Seung Woo indicates the genealogy of Southeast Asian researchers in Korea commences from the early 1960s and began to take off in earnest from the late 1980s. Interest in Southeast Asia began to emerge with the increasing economic involvement of Korea in the regions to the south as an arena for capital accumulation and investment, and with the "opening and liberalization" of Korea in the 1980s. It began, as Park states, at Hankuk University of Foreign Studies in the 1960s and its development of teaching programmes in Malay-Indonesian, Thai and Vietnamese. But up until the 1980s Korean research interests were confined to history, language and literature; the widening of Korean research on Southeast Asia awaited the training of young Korean scholars in the 1970s.

According to Park Seung Woo the first generation of scholars who were considered as acknowledged Southeast Asian specialists did not begin to appear in Korea until the late 1980s and the early 1990s; many of them went abroad for their doctoral studies, overwhelmingly to the United States, and they were mainly in the disciplines of political science, comparative politics and international relations. As one would expect, some of this work examined Korean-Southeast Asian relations. Park suggests this first generation was "to a large extent self-motivated and self-recruited". This early growth of interest was accompanied by the institutionalization of Southeast Asian Studies, with the formation of the Korean Association of Southeast Asian Studies in 1991 with its journal *The Southeast Asian Review*, which began publication in 1992. A small Study Group on Southeast Asian Politics was established in 1990; it became the Study Group on Southeast Asian Studies in 1992, and was then reorganized into the government-registered Korean Institute of Southeast Asian Studies in 2003.

The second generation was the product of funded and systematic training in area studies. These scholars had the benefit of supervision and mentoring from the first generation and they emerged from the mid-1990s. They also went through training in the appropriate Southeast Asian language and had the opportunity to spend time, some of it extended, undertaking field research in the region. Although some continued to go overseas for their doctoral studies, most young Korean scholars were able to pursue their studies at local universities. Even those who studied abroad went to a range of destinations; no longer was the U.S. the preferred location: Australian, French, British and Southeast Asian universities were chosen, and there was movement into other disciplines, particularly anthropology, and cross-regional issues such as regionalism, international migration, migrant labour, cross-cultural marriage, and the influence of Korean popular culture on Southeast Asia.

Yet as with the overall appreciation of the Chinese contribution to the study of Southeast Asia, Park Seung Woo suggests that Korean studies too have tended to adopt descriptive, empirical, policy and applied approaches. Korean scholars have also preferred to work on an individual basis and there has not been much in the way of collaborative team research bringing together research from different disciplines and different methodological and theoretical training backgrounds.

CONCLUSIONS

The research agenda which the Korean Southeast Asianists have adopted for themselves is an ambitious one and this current edited volume provides only a taste of some of the work which has been undertaken to date. As we have seen the development of expertise in the Republic of Korea has been a quite recent phenomenon, but the signs are that the interest in Southeast Asia will continue to grow and diversify, and that the research environment in Korean universities and the funds available to undertake field research in Southeast Asia are in a relatively healthy state.

Although there have been frequent calls for the further development of Southeast Asian Studies in Southeast Asia itself, and Ariel Heryanto has continued to press the importance of the case (though the case for indigenization has been made often before [see, for example, Mohammed Halib and Huxley 1996, pp. 8–9), we should also welcome the continuing scholarly interest in the region from China (including Hong Kong), Japan and more recently the Republic of Korea, and, of course, from the non-Asian traditions of Australia, and to a lesser extent New Zealand (which we have not addressed in this volume). We should also not forget an emerging interest in the region from India — again a country which we have not examined here. Indian scholars have tended to study Southeast Asia in relation to South Asia, and, for obvious reasons, to focus on the Indian cultural heritage in Southeast Asia as well as more topical issues such as international relations and the strategic importance of the Indian Ocean area. There are active programmes of research on the region at Kolkata University and the Institute of Asian Studies there, as well as the School of International Studies at Jawaharlal Nehru University, Sri Venkateswara University (Tirupati), and Madras University among others. An exploration of the Indian contribution would certainly be a very worthwhile exercise as their interest in Southeast Asia is likely to continue to increase.

It is our view that the need to continue the Southeast Asian Studies project which began primarily in the West in the late 1940s will depend on a wide range of support for the necessary research and teaching to be undertaken. The core of that support will have to be from the region itself, but it will require collaboration across the Asian region. In addition to examining Southeast Asian Studies in Singapore and Vietnam we have referred to other programmes of work, whether specifically in Southeast Asian Studies or in the wider field of Asian Studies, in Malaysia, Thailand, Indonesia, Brunei and the Philippines. Overall then the study of Southeast Asia in the Asia-Pacific region including India appears to be in a relatively vibrant condition, and Singapore, as the scholarly hub in this field of studies, will continue undoubtedly to play a significant coordinating and sponsoring role.

However, there are still mixed views about the actual and potential role of local scholars and institutions to carry forward Southeast Asian Studies as our main agents of research. Chou and Houben, on a rather apologetic note, say that they had hoped that there would have been more contributions in their volume from scholars of Southeast Asian origin to debate new directions in this field of studies, but for various reasons this was not to be (in the event only two of the eight contributors are Asian, and one of those is Japanese); they also draw attention to the dominance of English language scholarship in Southeast Asian Studies, and the fact that "English language literature on the region by indigenous scholars remains limited" (2006*b*, pp. 17–18). They suggest that a translation programme is needed to bring publications in the vernacular into the global domain. Another issue is that, for many local scholars, a concern with their own country, based on national and nationalistic preoccupations conducted and published in the national language, has tended to preclude the adoption of a wider regional vision and the dissemination of research findings to a global audience. In this connection, Wang Gungwu, in his evaluation of the different trajectories of Southeast Asian Studies in Singapore and the People's Republic of China, remarks that "in Singapore as elsewhere, the desultory efforts by local scholars to nail down a Southeast Asian regional identity still depends on encouragement from outside the region" (2005, p. 74). In addition, Thongchai Winichakul, in assessing Thailand's contribution to Southeast Asian Studies and referring to the views of Charnvit Kasetsiri, the champion of Southeast Asian Studies in Thailand, characterizes the country's contributions to regional scholarship as "Thai-centric" in that "they mostly focus on subjects related to Thailand, consider Thai interests and adopt Thai perspectives. It is rare to find serious studies on Thailand's neighbours in their own right, rather than in relation to Thailand" (2005, p. 115). Aside from national preoccupations, there is usually the need to learn another language (other than English), if one wishes to move beyond the study of one's own country and culture. This has been of particular concern in the Philippines with its heavily Americanized linguistic and cultural traditions, and Serena Diokno notes that "[t]he language requirement obviously adds years of study to doctoral learning, which explains why many Filipinos who take Southeast Asian studies abroad choose to write about the Philippines". And she adds, perhaps rather defensively, "[o]ther Southeast Asian students abroad also tend to write about their own countries" (2005, pp. 133–34).

As with Chou's and Houben's volume, with reference to the edited book by Kratoska, Raben and Nordholt, of the fifteen contributors to that book only five are Asian; the main debate has yet again been set by outsiders. Interestingly the two volumes are dominated by contributions from European- and Australian-based scholars. Perhaps the crisis in area studies in Europe, or at least outside Southeast Asia, is continuing to prompt a concern to debate the value and rationale of Southeast Asian Studies whilst American and Asian researchers are now rather more relaxed about the project. In addition, Duncan McCargo, in a very blunt assessment of the field of Southeast Asian political studies, states that "it seems unlikely that the full-blown "indigenization" of Southeast Asian political studies will take place any time soon"; and he continues, "There is little evidence that large numbers of scholars from Southeast Asia are actually able or willing to engage in systematic, critical research on potentially sensitive political issues within their own societies without some external impetus or support" (2006, pp. 119–20). He goes into some detail on the reasons for this, but he holds to the importance of the continuing involvement of "international scholars" along with and in collaboration with, of course, the contributions of "local scholars" (ibid.).

Our volume has drawn attention to processes of decline in some area studies and Southeast Asian Studies programmes, notably in Europe (as has Chou and Houben 2006*b*, p. 20), but it is clear that not only in the Asia-Pacific region, but also in North America, especially the United States, there are signs of revitalization. It is also difficult to see how any serious scholarship on Southeast Asia can develop further without the involvement of American-based scholars (again we have not considered the contribution of Canada in Southeast Asian Studies in such universities as Victoria and Toronto). At least fourteen universities in the United States, including the premier institutions of Cornell, California at Berkeley and Los Angeles, Harvard, Johns Hopkins, Stanford and Yale, have active programmes of Southeast Asian and Asian Studies research. Many of the theoretical developments and paradigm shifts in the study of the region also continue to be generated in the West and especially in the United States.

It goes without saying that we, along with many before us, argue for the importance of collaboration among researchers not only across the Southeast Asian region and the Asia Pacific but also across the globe. We do not argue for indigenization at the expense of promoting the understanding of Southeast Asia in whichever country scholars (who are equipped with the necessary disciplinary, linguistic and area studies skills) choose to pursue knowledge. Inevitably in a globalizing world researchers from different countries must and, of course do come together to debate, discuss and discover, and to develop research projects and programmes. They also increasingly collaborate across disciplinary boundaries; it is an approach which Yoko Hayami argues vigorously for in a review of Japanese perspectives on Southeast Asia and the need for multi-laterality in scholarship (2006, pp. 78, 82). Globalization processes and increasing interaction across national boundaries and regions also require not only cross-disciplinary perspectives but also the adoption of comparative analyses. But we should not be overawed by globalization; it cannot tell us anything unless it is located in "the local". Our research has to be rooted in local realities and Southeast Asia as a region and its constituent sub-regions and populations have to be understood both in their own terms and as part of the global system before globalization can have any real meaning at all.

References

Acharya, Amitav and Ananda Rajah, eds. "Reconceptualizing Southeast Asia". Special focus. *Southeast Asian Journal of Social Science* 27, no. 1 (1999).

Ananda Rajah. "Southeast Asia: Comparatist Errors and the Construction of a Region". In *Reconceptualizing Southeast Asia*, edited by Amitav Acharya and Ananda Rajah. Special focus. *Southeast Asian Journal of Social Science* 27, no. 1 (1999): 41–53.

Andaya, Barbara Watson. "The Unity of Southeast Asia: Historical Approaches and Questions". *Journal of Southeast Asian Studies* 28 (1997): 161–71.

Anderson, Benedict. "Studies of the Thai State: The State of Thai Studies". In *The State of Thai Studies: Analyses of Knowledge, Approaches, and Prospects in Anthropology, Art History, Economics, History, and Political Science*, edited by E. Ayal. Athens, OH: Ohio University Centre for International Studies, Southeast Asia Program, 1978.

———. "The Changing Ecology of Southeast Asian Studies in the United States". In *Southeast Asian Studies in the Balance: Reflections from America*, edited by Charles Hirschman, Charles F. Keyes, and Karl Hutterer. Ann Arbor, MI: The Association for Asian Studies, 1992.

Boeke, Julius H. *Economics and Economic Policy of Dual Societies*. New York: Institute of Pacific Relations, 1953.

Bowen, John R. "The Forms Culture Takes: A State-of the-field Essay on the Anthropology of Southeast Asia". *The Journal of Asian Studies* 54 (1995): 1047–78.

———. "The Inseparability of Area and Discipline in Southeast Asian Studies: A View from the United States". *Moussons. Recherche en sciences humaines sur l'Asie du Sud-Est* 1 (2000): 3–19.

Chou, Cynthia and Vincent Houben, eds. *Southeast Asian Studies: Debates and New Directions*. The Netherlands: International Institute for Asian Studies and Singapore: Institute of Southeast Asian Studies, 2006*a*.

———. "Introduction". In *Southeast Asian Studies: Debates and New Directions*, edited by Cynthia Chou and Vincent Houben. The Netherlands: International Institute for Asian Studies and Singapore: Institute of Southeast Asian Studies, 2006*b*.

Cribb, Robert. "Region, Academic Dynamics, and Promise of Comparitivism: Beyond Studying 'Southeast Asia'?". In *Southeast Asian Studies: Debates and New Directions*, edited by Cynthia Chou and Vincent Houben. The Netherlands: International Institute for Asian Studies and Singapore: Institute of Southeast Asian Studies, 2006.

Dick, Howard. "Southeast Asia as an Open System: Geo-politics and Economic Geography". In *Locating Southeast Asia: Geographies of Knowledge and Politics of Space*, edited by Paul Kratoska, Remco Raben, and Henk Schulte Nordholt. Singapore: Singapore University Press and Athens, OH: Ohio University Press, 2005.

Diokno, Ma. Serena I. "Southeast Asia and Identity Studies in the Philippines". In *Locating Southeast Asia: Geographies of Knowledge and Politics of Space*, edited by Paul Kratoska, Remco Raben, and Henk Schulte Nordholt. Singapore: Singapore University Press and Athens, OH: Ohio University Press, 2005.

Emmerson, Donald K. "'Southeast Asia': What's in a Name?". *Journal of Southeast Asian Studies* 15, no. 1 (1984): 1–21.

Fifield, Russell H. "Southeast Asian Studies: Origins, Development, Future". *Journal of Southeast Asian Studies* 7 (1976): 154–61.

———. "Southeast Asia as a Regional Concept". *Southeast Asian Journal of Social Science* 11 (1983): 1–14.

Goh Beng Lan, ed. *Decentring and Diversifying Southeast Asian Studies: Perspectives from the Region*. Singapore: Institute of Southeast Asian Studies, 2011a.

———. "Disciplines and Area Studies in the Global Age: Southeast Asian Reflections". In *Decentring and Diversifying Southeast Asian Studies: Perspectives from the Region*, edited by Goh Beng Lan. Singapore: Institute of Southeast Asian Studies, 2011b.

Hayami Yoko. "Towards Multi-Laterality in Southeast Asian Studies: Perspectives from Japan". In *Southeast Asian Studies: Debates and New Directions,* edited by Cynthia Chou and Vincent Houben. The Netherlands: International Institute for Asian Studies and Singapore: Institute of Southeast Asian Studies, 2006.

Heryanto, Ariel. "Can There Be Southeast Asians in Southeast Asian Studies?". *Moussons. Recherche en sciences humaines sur l'Asie du Sud-Est* 5 (2002): 3–30.

Hirschman, Charles. "The State of Southeast Asian Studies in American Universities". In *Southeast Asian Studies in the Balance: Reflections from America*, edited by Charles Hirschman, Charles F. Keyes, and Karl Hutterer. Ann Arbor, MI: The Association for Asian Studies, 1992.

Keyes, Charles F. "A Conference at Wingspread and Rethinking Southeast Asian Studies". In *Southeast Asian Studies in the Balance: Reflections from America*, edited by Charles Hirschman, Charles F. Keyes, and Karl Hutterer. Ann Arbor, MI: The Association for Asian Studies, 1992.

King, Victor T. "Southeast Asia: An Anthropological Field of Study". *Moussons. Social Science Research on Southeast Asia* 3 (2001): 1–31.

————. *Defining Southeast Asia and the Crisis in Area Studies: Personal Reflections on a Region*. Working Papers in Contemporary Asian Studies, no. 13. Lund University Centre for East and South-East Asian Studies, 2005.

————. "Southeast Asia: Personal Reflections on a Region". In *Southeast Asian Studies: Debates and New Directions*, edited by Cynthia Chou and Vincent Houben. The Netherlands: International Institute for Asian Studies and Singapore: Institute of Southeast Asian Studies, 2006.

King, Victor T. and D. William Wilder. *The Modern Anthropology of South-East Asia: An Introduction*. London: RoutledgeCurzon and New York: Routledge, reprint, 2006. Originally published in 2003.

Kratoska, Paul, Remco Raben, and Henk Schulte Nordholt, eds. *Locating Southeast Asia: Geographies of Knowledge and Politics of Space*. Singapore: Singapore University Press and Athens, OH: Ohio University Press, 2005*a*.

————. "Locating Southeast Asia". In *Locating Southeast Asia: Geographies of Knowledge and Politics of Space*, edited by Paul Kratoska, Remco Raben, and Henk Schulte Nordholt. Singapore: Singapore University Press and Athens, OH: Ohio University Press, 2005*b*.

Lieberman, Victor. "Local Integration and Eurasian Analogies: Structuring Southeast Asian History, c.1350–c.1830". *Modern Asian Studies* 27 (1993): 475–572.

————. "An Age of Commerce in Southeast Asia? Problems of Regional Coherence — A Review Article". *The Journal of Asian Studies* 54 (1995): 796–807.

————. *Strange Parallels: Southeast Asia in Global Context, c800–1830*. Vol. 1, *Integration on the Mainland*, and Vol. 2, *Mainland Mirrors: Japan, China, South Asia, and the Islands*. Cambridge: Cambridge University Press, 2003/2009.

Lombard, Denys. "Southeast Asian Studies in France". In *A Colloquium on Southeast Asian Studies*, edited by Tunku Shamsul Bahrin, Chadran Jeshurun, and A. Terry Rambo. Singapore: Institute of Southeast Asian Studies, 1981.

————. "Networks and Synchronisms in Southeast Asian History". *Journal of Southeast Asian Studies* 26 (1995): 10–16.

McCargo, Duncan. "Rethinking Southeast Asian Politics". In *Southeast Asian Studies: Debates and New Directions*, edited by Cynthia Chou and Vincent Houben. The Netherlands: International Institute for Asian Studies and Singapore: Institute of Southeast Asian Studies, 2006.

McVey, Ruth. "Change and Continuity in Southeast Asian Studies". *Journal of Southeast Asian Studies* 26 (1995): 1–9.

————. "Globalization, Marginalization, and the Study of Southeast Asia". In *Southeast Asian Studies: Reorientations*, edited by Craig J. Reynolds and Ruth McVey. Ithaca, NY: Cornell University, Southeast Asia Program Publications, 1998.

Mohammed Halib and Tim Huxley. "Introduction". In *An Introduction to Southeast Asian Studies*, edited by Mohammed Halib and Tim Huxley. London and New York: Tauris Academic Studies, I.B. Tauris Publishers, 1996.

Reid, Anthony. *Southeast Asia in the Age of Commerce: 1400–1600*. Vol. 1, *The Land Below the Winds*, and Vol. 2, *Expansion and Crisis*. New Haven, CT: Yale University Press, 1988/1993.

———. "Recent Trends and Future Directions in Southeast Asian Studies (Outside Southeast Asia)". In *Towards the Promotion of Southeast Asian Studies in Southeast Asia*, edited by T. Abdullah and Y. Manuati. Jakarta: Indonesian Institute of Sciences, 1994.

———. "Studying 'Asia' in Asia". *Asian Studies Review* 23 (1999*a*): 141–51.

———. "A Saucer Model of Southeast Asian Identity". In *Reconceptualizing Southeast Asia*, edited by Amitav Acharya and Ananda Rajah. Special focus. *Southeast Asian Journal of Social Science* 27, no. 1 (1999*b*): 7–23.

Reynolds, Craig J. "A New Look at Old Southeast Asia". *The Journal of Asian Studies* 54 (1995): 419–46.

———. "Self-cultivation and Self-determination in Postcolonial Southeast Asia". In *Southeast Asian Studies: Reorientations*, edited by Craig J. Reynolds and Ruth McVey. Ithaca, NY: Cornell University, Southeast Asia Program Publications, 1998.

Saw Swee-Hock and John Wong, eds. *Southeast Asian Studies in China*. Singapore: Institute of Southeast Asian Studies, 2007.

Schrieke, Bertram J.O. *Indonesian Sociological Studies: Selected Writings of B. Schrieke*. Two vols. The Hague: W. van Hoeve, 1955–57.

Shamsul Amri Baharuddin. "A Comment on Recent Trends and the Future Direction of Southeast Asian Studies". In *Towards the Promotion of Southeast Asian Studies in Southeast Asia*, edited by T. Abdullah and Y. Manuati. Jakarta: Indonesian Institute of Sciences, 1994.

Shimizu Hajime. "Southeast Asia as a Regional Concept in Modern Japan". In *Locating Southeast Asia: Geographies of Knowledge and Politics of Space*, edited by Paul Kratoska, Remco Raben, and Henk Schulte Nordholt. Singapore: Singapore University Press and Athens, OH: Ohio University Press, 2005.

Solheim II, Wilhelm G. "'Southeast Asia': What's in a Name: Another Point of View". *Journal of Southeast Asian Studies* 16 (1985): 141–47.

Steedly, Mary. "The State of Culture Theory in the Anthropology of Southeast Asia". *Annual Review of Anthropology* 28 (1999): 431–54.

Sutherland, Heather. "Southeast Asian History and the Mediterranean Analogy". *Journal of Southeast Asian Studies* 34 (2003): 1–20.

———. "Contingent Devices". In *Locating Southeast Asia: Geographies of Knowledge and Politics of Space*, edited by Paul Kratoska, Remco Raben, and Henk Schulte Nordholt. Singapore: Singapore University Press and Athens, OH: Ohio University Press, 2005.

Thongchai Winichakul. "Trying to Locate Southeast Asia from Its Navel: Where is Southeast Asian Studies in Thailand?". In *Locating Southeast Asia: Geographies of Knowledge and Politics of Space*, edited by Paul Kratoska, Remco Raben, and

Henk Schulte Nordholt. Singapore: Singapore University Press and Athens, OH: Ohio University Press, 2005.

van Leur, Jacob Cornelis. *Indonesian Trade and Society: Essays in Asian Social and Economic History*. The Hague and Bandung: W. van Hoeve, 1955.

van Schendel, Willem. "Geographies of Knowing, Geographies of Ignorance: Jumping Scale in Southeast Asia". In *Locating Southeast Asia: Geographies of Knowledge and Politics of Space*, edited by Paul Kratoska, Remco Raben, and Henk Schulte Nordholt. Singapore: Singapore University Press and Athens, OH: Ohio University Press, 2005.

Wang Gungwu. "Two Perspectives of Southeast Asian Studies: Singapore and China". In *Locating Southeast Asia: Geographies of Knowledge and Politics of Space*, edited by Paul Kratoska, Remco Raben, and Henk Schulte Nordholt. Singapore: Singapore University Press and Athens, OH: Ohio University Press, 2005.

Wolters, O.W. *History, Culture and Region in Southeast Asian Perspectives*. Southeast Asia Program Publications, Studies on Southeast Asia, No. 26. Ithaca, NY: Cornell University, 1999. Revised edition in cooperation with the Institute of Southeast Asian Studies. Originally published by the Institute of Southeast Asian Studies, Singapore, 1982.

PART I
NORTHEAST ASIA

2

SOUTHEAST ASIAN STUDIES IN CHINA
Progress and Problems

Park Sa-Myung

INTRODUCTION

The progress of Southeast Asian Studies in China, a country with about twenty countries as its close neighbours, reflects its strategic needs which are common to all adjacent regions. In the three decades after the Communist revolution of 1949, area studies could not develop into an autonomous academic field beyond fragmented research on individual countries, owing to institutional dislocation and the lack of interest and demand of the government. In the three decades after the Reform and Opening of 1978, however, area studies recorded a marked growth, as government demand increased in step with the acceleration of China's globalization and the institutionalization of foreign policy-making. Thus, the development of Southeast Asian Studies in China should be understood in the context of its national strategies toward all neighbouring regions (Tang and Zhang 2004; Tang, Zhang, and Cao 2005).

In the meantime the progress of Southeast Asian Studies in China reflects the particular importance of the region. For China, Southeast Asia is a region not just with rich economic resources but with spatial, temporal, and human conditions most ideal for area studies (He 2003, p. 107; Yu 2005; Liang Z. 2007, p. 16). There exist very close geographic connections between China and Southeast Asia. Historically, they formed intimate "lips-to-teeth" relations. As a result, they share special "blood connections" through overseas Chinese communities and cross-border ethnic groups (Liang Z. 2007, p. 16). In this context, and given the very close relations between East Asia and Southeast Asia, Southeast Asian Studies in China has been especially preoccupied with the importance of Southeast Asia in understanding the past, present, and future of China within East Asia. As Wang Hui (2009) has indicated,

> There exist cultural differences between all countries. China is a Southeast Asian country as well as a Northeast Asian country. China serves as a link between many regions in Asia. China is close to many civilisations in the Asia-Pacific region and serves as a link between them. The world order excessively dominated by the United States should be changed. The future international order will be a relatively more pluralized order based on several regional associations.

Since the end of the Cold War objective conditions for Southeast Asian Studies have been improved in East Asia (Reid 2003; Chou and Houben 2006; Saw and Wong 2007). In China such historical junctures as the Reform and Opening in the late 1970s, the end of the Cold War in the late 1980s, and the East Asian economic crisis in the late 1990s gave crucial impetus to the progress of Southeast Asian Studies there. The relevance of a holistic perspective on East Asia encompassing both Northeast and Southeast Asia also increased (Yang and Zhang 2006; Li 2007).[1] Even a call for "Sino-Southeast Asian Studies" has been presented, based on cross-border linkages of individuals, groups, communities and networks (Liu 2000, 2001; Zheng 2002; Zeng 2003; Yu 2005).

Like other countries in East Asia, however, Southeast Asian Studies in China suffers from the "import-substituting" syndrome due to its "language [English] handicap" in contrast with the "export-oriented" tendency of the West owing to its "language [English] hegemony" (Hayami 2006). In East Asia, indeed, barriers to inter-regional and intra-regional communications on Southeast Asian Studies are still formidable. Nevertheless, the belated emergence of an East Asian perspective in China indicates that Southeast Asian Studies is faced with a critical juncture in its progress. Such a fresh perspective reflects the special status of China in the history of Southeast Asia, on the one hand, and represents the dynamic reality of geopolitical, geo-economic, and geo-cultural changes in East Asia, on the other.

This study examines the past changes, present conditions, and future prospects of Southeast Asian Studies in China in a holistic perspective on

East Asia. In the following section the historical development of Southeast Asian Studies in China will be reviewed in four stages, comprising "traditional Southeast Asian Studies" in the dynastic period, "formative Southeast Asian Studies" after 1911, "closed Southeast Asian Studies" after 1949, and "opened Southeast Asian Studies" after 1978. The third section will illuminate the recent achievements of "opened Southeast Asian Studies", focusing on the rapid growth in academic institutions and activities. In the fourth section, the future prospects of Southeast Asian Studies in China will be discussed, focusing on some salient problems such as biased perspectives, traditional methods and national subjects.

POLITICS AND SOUTHEAST ASIAN STUDIES

The gradual collapse of the "Chinese world order" in the nineteenth century was followed by drastic political change in the twentieth century, such as the Nationalist Revolution of 1911, the Communist Revolution of 1949, and the Reform and Opening of 1978. These events exerted a profound influence on Southeast Asian Studies, resulting in four stages of development comprising "traditional", "formative", "closed", and "opened" Southeast Asian Studies. The "formative Southeast Asia Studies" of the Nationalist period (1912–48) was replaced by the "closed Southeast Asian Studies" under the Communist regime (1949–78) dominated by the revolutionary politics of Mao Zedong. Finally, the "opened Southeast Asian Studies" following the Reform and Opening of 1978 initiated by the pragmatic leadership of Deng Xiaoping made great strides.

Traditional Southeast Asian Studies

In Chinese historical documents Southeast Asia was recorded as *Nanhai* [Southern Sea], *Dongxiyang* [Eastern and Western Oceans], and *Nanyang* [Southern Ocean]. The concept of *Nanhai* appeared in the Han dynasty (206 BC–AD 220), and circulated in the dynasties of Tang (618–907) and Song (960–1279). Both *Nanhai* and *Dongxiyang* were used in the Yuan (1271–1368) and integrated into *Xiyang* [Western Ocean] in the Ming dynasty (1368–1644). In Qing China (1644–1911) *Nanyang* was the most common term used (Wang 1984; Wang et al. 1994, pp. 3–4).[2] From *Shiji* [Historical Record] (91 BC) by Sima Qian to *Zhongguo Bada Zhimin Weirenquan* [China's Eight Greatest Colonisers] (1905) by Liang Qichao, thus, "traditional Southeast Asian Studies" accumulated the richest historical sources for Southeast Asian Studies in the world (Wang 1991, pp. 27–28; Yu 2005: Yuan 2006; Liang Z. 2007, p. 16).

China's interests in Southeast Asia increased rapidly in the nineteenth century, due to the growing human connections of Chinese emigrants including merchants and workers as well as the existing geographical and economic connections. In the Ming dynasty various travel accounts, such as Gong Zhen's *A Record of Vassal States in the Western Ocean* (1434), Ma Huan's *An Account of the Ocean Circuit* (1451), and Zhang Xie's *A Study of the Eastern and Western Oceans* (1617), recorded the geography, politics, economy, and culture of Southeast Asia as well as the life of Chinese emigrants. In the Qing dynasty various reports, such as Wang Dahai's *An Account of Exotic Islands* (1791), Wei Yuan's *A Treatise on Maritime Kingdoms* (1852), and Li Zhongjue's *An Account of the Singapore Climate* (1887), covered the Southeast Asian region and the overseas Chinese (Li 2002, pp. 998–99; Leonard 2009, pp. 22–67).

In general, "traditional Southeast Asian Studies" suffered from serious weaknesses in Sino-centric perspectives and descriptive methods. Modelled after Western imperialism, Sino-centrism was translated into a thesis of "Chinese colonisation" in Southeast Asia. Notwithstanding significant differences between the traditional Sino-centric concept of *Tianxia* [all under heaven] and the modern Western concept of imperialism, the hierarchy of the Sino-centric order precluded the possibility of an autonomous Southeast Asia (Li 2002, pp. 1000–1002; Yu 2005; Liang Y. 2008, p. 86). For Liang Qichao, Chinese communities in Southeast Asia represented colonialism which was led by the people in contrast with Western colonialism led by the government: "As the people of more than 100 countries in the South Sea are mostly descendants of the Chinese nation, they are naturally Chinese colonies" (Li 2002, p. 1000).

Formative Southeast Asian Studies

As "traditional Southeast Asian Studies" lost their political bases after 1911, the seeds of modern Southeast Asian Studies grew under the conservative Nationalist regime (1912–48). The institutional bases of "formative Southeast Asian Studies" were Jinan University (1906) and Xiamen University (1921), which had been established by overseas Chinese nationalists. The former launched a journal *Zhongguo yu Nanyang* [China and the South Seas] in 1918 and organized the Bureau of Nanyang Cultural Affairs in 1927. The Bureau published a periodical *Nanyang Yanjiu* [South Seas Studies] and the forty volumes of South Seas series, founding the institutional infrastructure of Southeast Asian Studies (Cao 2007, p. 62). The first official Nanyang Institute was established in 1942 to promote studies on the history of the overseas Chinese in Southeast Asia (Li 2002, pp. 1005–9).

However, "formative Southeast Asian Studies" was focused on the translation of foreign publications, and independent research was limited to the superficial description of the history, geography, culture, and environment of Southeast Asia. Achievements at an acceptable academic level were secured in the history of relations between China and Southeast Asia and the history of Chinese communities in Southeast Asia. In fact, the senior generation of "formative Southeast Asian Studies" consisted of overseas Chinese, who were born in mainland China in the 1910s and 1920s and who emigrated to Southeast Asia to escape the turmoil of Japanese aggression in the 1930s. In spite of their direct and long encounters with local societies in Southeast Asia, however, in-depth studies on the real conditions of local societies were very rare.

In 1940 the senior generation organized the China South Seas Society in Singapore. Many of them returned to China after World War II or the Communist Revolution, and trained a new generation of Southeast Asian specialists in various Chinese universities (Liao 2007, pp. 10–11; Suryadinata 2007, pp. 33–34). In general, however, their contributions were limited to the replacement of traditional Sino-centrism with modern nationalism. Following the tradition of Liang Qichao, they interpreted Chinese emigration to Southeast Asia as "colonization" or "transplantation" (Wang 1991, pp. 25–30; Li 2002, pp. 1003–4). The Sino-centric nationalistic bias was especially serious in studies on the overseas Chinese, as exemplified by such subjects as "the nationalism of the overseas Chinese", "the contribution of the overseas Chinese to the fatherland", and "the overseas Chinese as the mother of Chinese revolution".

The period of "formative Southeast Asian Studies" was represented by *The Chinese Overseas* (1927) and *A Chinese History of Colonisation* (1937) by Li Zhangfu and *A Revolutionary History of the Chinese Overseas* (1933) and *Contributions of the Chinese Overseas to the Fatherland* (1940) by Huang Jingwan (Li 2002, p. 1004). Meanwhile, modern Southeast Asian Studies influenced by Western social sciences emerged for the first time. The pioneering works were *The Chinese Emigration* (1923) and *Southeast Asia's Chinese Overseas and Fujian-Guangdong Societies* (1938) by Chen Da. Chen Da analysed the internal structure and economic function of Chinese communities in Southeast Asia as well as their international and domestic causes and effects (Li 2002, pp. 1007–8; Liang Y. 2008, pp. 86–88).

Closed Southeast Asian Studies

The revolution of 1949 occasioned the rise of radical "closed Southeast Asian Studies", which culminated in the turbulence of the Vietnam War and the Cultural Revolution from the 1960s to the 1970s. They were opposed to both traditional Sino-centrism and conservative nationalism which had been mobilized as ideological instruments for a new international order in East Asia. Because of strategic considerations, various institutes for Southeast Asian Studies were established in major universities and the Academies of Social Sciences in the capital and southern provinces. This phase was led by an intermediate generation between the senior and junior ones, consisting of a large proportion of returned overseas Chinese. Nevertheless, their earlier activities were still centred on the history of the overseas Chinese (Yuan 2007, p. 29). With the advent of the Cultural Revolution, even those studies were to meet with serious constraints (Liang Z. 2007, p. 17; Cao 2007, p. 64; Liao 2007, pp. 11–15; Suryadinata 2007, pp. 34–37).

The closed tendency of Southeast Asian Studies was conditioned by the revolutionary foreign policy of China toward Southeast Asia. At an earlier stage, China accepted national sovereignty as the fundamental principle of a new international order against imperialist domination and exploitation. At a later stage China underwent a strategic shift toward a united front against the "revisionism" of the Soviet Union. In the process of the transformation, China's propagation of the so-called "five principles of peaceful coexistence" and its prohibition of double nationalities were closely associated with its policies toward Southeast Asia. Despite the principle of sovereign equality invalidating traditional Sino-centrism, however, China made a distinction between "state diplomacy" and "people's diplomacy" to justify its radical foreign policy to "export revolution" to Southeast Asia. It supported various communist movements in Thailand, Malaysia, Indonesia, Burma, and the Philippines as well as those in Indochina (Park 2006, pp. 249–56).

In these radicalized circumstances, Southeast Asian Studies was closed to the development of the outside world in their perspectives, methods, and subjects. Their perspectives were dominated by the economic and structural paradigms of Marxism, Leninism, and Maoism; their methods were characterized by macro and superficial descriptions instead of micro and in-depth analyses; and their subjects were overwhelmed by political and ideological themes such as national liberation, peasant revolution, and class struggle (Wang 1991, pp. 32–33; Yu 2005). Such a closed character was most typically witnessed by historical studies. Their sources and contents depended heavily on those of the Communist bloc led by the Soviet Union. As a necessary consequence, the historical dynamism and contemporary diversity of Southeast Asia were either concealed or overlooked (Yuan 2007, p. 30).

Except for some historical studies, therefore, the first three decades of the radical Communist period produced almost little academic work of serious quality. Even the studies of the history of the overseas Chinese in Southeast Asia were uninspiring (1950–66) and entirely closed (1967–78), as attested by the dearth of publications (Li 2002, p. 1011). However, some traditional bibliographical studies based on the rich historical sources of China were still commendable. Moreover, the collection of primary sources through field work on the hometowns, farms, and enterprises of the overseas Chinese in southern coastal areas, the exploration and compilation of historical materials, and the introduction and translation of foreign publications must be their invaluable contributions to the restoration and development of Southeast Asian Studies in the wake of the Reform and Opening of 1978 (Yuan 2007, p. 31).

Opened Southeast Asian Studies

After 1978 Southeast Asian Studies was opened to diverse channels for international communication and, thus, to diverse perspectives, methods, and subjects (Chen 1992, pp. 16–18; Dai and Wang 1992, pp. 8–9; Yu 2005). The progress in Southeast Asian Studies was facilitated by growing government demands, deepening interdependence with Southeast Asia, and spreading mass media on foreign affairs (see Table 2.1) (Tang and Zhang 2007, pp. 60–61). It was furthered by diplomatic normalization with Indonesia, Singapore, Brunei, Laos, Vietnam and Cambodia after the end of the Cold War in 1989; economic transformation into a "socialist market economy" after the collapse of the Soviet Union in 1991; regional cooperation after the financial crisis of East Asia in 1997; and free trade agreements with the Association of Southeast Asian Nations (ASEAN) after admission to the World Trade Organisation (WTO) in 2001.

The progress of "opened Southeast Asian Studies" was evident in their institutions, methods, and subjects. The institutions have been restructured from hierarchical to competitive ones. The methods have been transformed

Table 2.1
Mass Media on International Affairs, 2006

Type	Title	Circulation
Newspaper	*Cankao Xiaoxi* [News for Reference]	Over 2.00 mil.
	Huanqiu Shibao [Global Times]	Over 1.00 mil.
	Guoji Xianqu Daobao [International Herald Tribune]	Over 0.20 mil.
Magazine	*Huanqiu* [Globe Biweekly]	Some 0.25 mil.
	Shijie Zhishi [World Affairs]	Some 0.14 mil.
TV Programme	*Guoji Guancha* [International Observer]	
	Jinri Huati [Today Topics] (English)	

Sources: Tang and Zhang (2007), pp. 61, 72 note 13.

from monistic to pluralistic ones. The subjects have been moved from history to reality and, thus, from the superficial description of national liberation and class struggle to the concrete analysis of historical realities and current dynamics. As a result "opened Southeast Asian Studies" has marked rapid progress in both quantitative and qualitative terms (Yuan 2007, p. 31). The process can be divided into two stages: "restoration" since the Reform and Opening in 1978 up to the collapse of the Soviet Union in 1991 and "development" in step with the accelerated transformation of the planned economy into the "socialist market economy" since 1992.

At the stage of "restoration", the old institutions for Southeast Asian Studies were fully restored. While they conducted research and translation to provide the government with background information on policy-making, they focused on the publication of previous research findings, including bibliographic studies, field work, and research articles (Yuan 2007, p. 32). The revitalization of research activities was closely associated with the restoration and diversification of research institutions. Diverse research institutes were reopened or newly organized by universities and the Academies of Social Sciences, and diverse academic journals were republished or newly launched. Central and local governments established affiliated institutes to study the politics, economy, and security of Southeast Asia (Yuan 2007, p. 32).

The "restoration" of Southeast Asian Studies was led by the intermediate generation, still consisting of a considerable proportion of returned overseas Chinese. In general, they were born in China in the 1930s and 1940s, trained through regular university education after the Revolution of 1949, and subjected to the academic destruction occasioned by the Cultural Revolution. They initiated the foundation of the China Association of Southeast Asian Studies in 1979. The five central bases for Southeast Asian Studies in the southern region included Xiamen University, Jinan University, Zhongshan University, Guangxi Academy of Social Sciences, and Yunnan Academy of Social Sciences (Liao 2007, pp. 11–15; Suryadinata 2007, pp. 34–37). They played the role of an effective bridge between the more localized generation and the more Westernized one. In the meantime, the China Association of Overseas Chinese History was founded in 1981, and the China Institute of Overseas Chinese History was opened in 1991 (Li 2002, pp. 1012–13).

The main subjects of research at the stage of "restoration" were the history of Southeast Asia, the history of the overseas Chinese, China's relations with Southeast Asia, and the economy of Southeast Asia. The widespread interest in overseas Chinese capital and the potential for its investment in China stimulated the rapid growth in studies of the history of overseas Chinese communities in Southeast Asia. As new studies repeated the practice of old studies, however, they could not break through the deadlock of "traditional Southeast Asian Studies", such as outdated sources, conventional theories, biased perspectives, and the narrow scope of political history. Despite the strategic importance of Southeast Asia, for instance, no serious political analysis has been attempted beyond the general description of government policies (Yuan 2007, p. 33). Indeed, it attests to certain constraints underlying "Southeast Asian Studies with Chinese characteristics" which still fall short of wholehearted opening (Dai and Wang 1992, pp. 14–15).

In this regard the generational transition from the more localized seniors to the more Westernized juniors seems to be the most significant factor in the future prospects of Southeast Asian Studies in China (Zhang 2007, p. 57). The junior generation, leading the stage of "development" of "opened Southeast Asian Studies," was trained through regular Chinese and foreign university education after the Reform and Opening (Liao 2007; Suryadinata 2007). They have diversified their research interests into religion, gender, disease, and environment, and their research methods into sociology, anthropology, international relations, and political economy (Cao 2007, pp. 64–69). Except for those in southern areas benefiting from rapid economic growth, nonetheless, their achievements were less than satisfactory largely because of their lack of opportunities for field work in Southeast Asia.

PROGRESS IN SOUTHEAST ASIAN STUDIES

The "opened Southeast Asian Studies" with the two stages of "restoration" and "development" has achieved impressive results in expanded institutions, increased publications, and diversified research subjects. The national spread of Southeast Asia specialists beyond their institutional bases in the southern provinces has also involved a rapid growth in research activities. For example, the subjects of research have diversified from the traditional subjects of history and the overseas Chinese into a variety of new subjects, such as politics, economy, law, geography, nationality, culture, education, religion, military affairs, international relations, and the natural sciences. However, in spite of marked growth in their quantity and certain improvements in their methods, various limitations in the quality of their research are considered as continuing and serious problems (Liang Z. 2007, pp. 16–18).

Expanded Institutions

The central locomotive of "opened Southeast Asian Studies" are various research institutes, which were restored or founded after the Reform and Opening. The inauguration of the China Association of Southeast Asian Studies in 1979 was an important milestone in the restoration and development of Southeast Asian Studies (Liang Z. 2007, p. 17). Headquartered at the Nanyang Institute of Xiamen University, its membership exceeds 600. The division of labour between general universities and special institutes, including those affiliated with central and local Academies of Social Sciences, resulted in the division of labour in Southeast Asian Studies. Whereas the primary function of special institutes lies in responding to the practical demands of the central and local governments, it is just a secondary function for research institutes affiliated with general universities (Tang and Zhang 2007, 55–57).

As one of the most important institutes in China, the Nanyang Institute of Xiamen University was established in 1956, and reorganized into the Research School of Southeast Asian Studies in 1996. It launched *Nanyang Ziliao Yicong* [*Southeast Asian Studies: A Quarterly Journal of Translations*] in 1957 and *Nanyang Wenti Yanjiu* [*Southeast Asian Affairs*] in 1974. It opened the Center for Southeast Asian Studies in 2000 to play a "pivotal role" in Southeast Asian Studies in China. The Center comprises four divisions: politics and economy, international relations, the overseas Chinese, Chinese literature (Liang Z. 2007, p. 17).[3] The junior generation leading the School represents the rapid internationalization of Southeast Asian Studies in China. As of 2008 the School boasted 176 graduate students, including 67 in the doctoral programme and 109 in the master's programme.

In addition to the southern "big five", many other universities and research institutes in northern and eastern regions have conducted various interdisciplinary projects on history, politics, economy, society, and culture (Huang and Cao 2007).[4] The quantity and quality of academic journals on Southeast Asian Studies have also been significantly improved. Three major journals, including *Dongnanya Yanjiu* [*Southeast Asian Studies*] of Jinan University, *Nanyang Wenti Yanjiu* [*Southeast Asian Affairs*] of Xiamen University, and *Yatai Pinglun* [*Asia Pacific Review*] of Zhongshan University, represent the recent achievements of "opened Southeast Asian Studies". In addition, *Dongnanya Zongheng* [*Around Southeast Asia*] of Guangxi Academy of Social Sciences and *Dongnanya Nanya Yanjiu* [*Studies on Southeast and South Asia*] of the Yunnan Academy of Social Sciences developed a good reputation (see Table 2.2).

In particular, *Southeast Asian Studies* played a leading role in the restoration and development of Chinese research on the region. Its trajectory of rise and fall represents the turbulent history of Southeast Asian Studies in China. After the Jinan University of Shanghai under the Nationalist regime was restored in Guangzhou in 1958, its Institute of Southeast Asian Studies launched a quarterly journal *Sources for Southeast Asian Studies* in 1959. It was suspended during the Cultural Revolution in 1966, and revived in 1979 after the Reform and Opening. It was reorganized

Table 2.2
Major Institutes and Journals on Southeast Asian Studies

Agency	Institute	Journal	Frequency
Xiamen U	Center for SEA Studies	*Southeast Asian Affairs*	Quarterly
Jinan U	Institute of SEA Studies	*Southeast Asian Studies*	Bimonthly
Zhongshan U	Institute of SEA Studies	*Asia Pacific Review*	Biannual
Guangxi A	Institute of SEA Studies	*Around Southeast Asia*	Monthly
Yunnan A	Institute of SEA Studies	*SEA and SA Studies*	Quarterly
Chinese A	Institute of A-P Studies	*Contemporary A-P Studies*	Monthly

Notes: U (University); A (Academy of Social Sciences); SEA (Southeast Asian); A-P (Asia-Pacific).
Sources: Tang and Zhang (2007); Zhang (2007); Huang and Cao (2007).

into the quarterly *Southeast Asian Studies* in 1987, and then developed to
the current bimonthly in 1995. It boasts the longest history and highest
frequency of publication and the widest distribution of authors in China
(Zhang 2007; Cao 2007).

Increased Publications

The progress of "opened Southeast Asian Studies" is also attested to by the
rapid growth in the publication of books on Southeast Asia. According
to an analysis of the catalogues of the National Library of China, the
books published in the 22 years from 1958 to 1979, largely corresponding to the period of "closed Southeast Asian Studies", were no more than
11 volumes. However, they increased to 24 volumes in the 10 years from
1980 to 1989, largely corresponding to the stage of "restoration", and
increased further to 158 volumes in the 15 years from 1990 to 2004,
largely corresponding to the stage of "development" (see Table 2.3). The
publication of books reflects the impressive quantitative achievement, and
implies considerable optimism for the qualitative development of Southeast
Asian Studies.

Likewise, the publication of articles has increased rapidly, with the
first decade of "opened Southeast Asian Studies" overwhelming the three
decades of "closed Southeast Asian Studies". In comparison with 1979,
the number of articles increased by 174 per cent in 1980, 370 per cent in
1981, 393 per cent in 1982, 390 per cent in 1983, 445 per cent in 1984,
and 516 per cent in 1985. In the first ten years, the subjects of research
were diversified to politics (30 per cent), economy (30 per cent), history
(28 per cent), culture (11 per cent), and military matters (1 per cent) (Dai
and Wang 1992, pp. 9–10). The objects of study were also diversified to

Table 2.3
Publication of Books on Southeast Asia

Period	1958–79	1980–89	1990–99	2000–04
Total Volumes	11.0	24.0	115.0	43.0
Annual Average	0.5	2.4	11.5	8.6

Sources: Tang and Zhang (2007), p. 61.

Table 2.4
Objects of Southeast Asian Studies
(%)

Object	1992	1994	1996	1998	2000	2002	2004	*
SEA Region	23.7	15.6	18.8	28.0	21.5	16.9	29.9	–
Countries	61.4	61.0	54.2	57.0	40.5	44.2	34.0	–
Indonesia	13.2	10.4	4.2	6.0	10.8	7.8	7.2	7.5
Malaysia	2.6	10.4	7.3	13.3	7.0	11.7	6.7	8.5
Singapore	8.8	11.7	7.3	10.0	7.6	3.9	6.2	31.9
Thailand	9.2	5.2	5.2	7.0	5.1	3.9	2.1	9.1
Vietnam	8.8	13.0	14.6	9.3	2.5	2.6	2.1	24.2
Philippines	8.8	2.6	8.3	9.3	6.3	5.2	4.6	6.6
Myanmar	5.7	6.5	2.1	1.0	1.3	9.1	4.1	6.0
Cambodia	0.9	1.3	3.1	0.0	0.0	0.0	0.0	3.3
Laos	2.6	0.0	2.1	1.0	0.0	0.0	0.0	1.9
Brunei	0.9	0.0	1.0	0.0	0.0	2.6	1.0	1.0
Chinese	12.3	18.2	21.9	15.0	24.1	18.2	19.6	–
Chinese-SEA	7.9	18.2	14.6	9.0	27.8	27.3	21.6	–
SEA Studies	0.9	1.3	5.2	3.0	0.0	3.9	6.2	–
Total**	106.2	114.3	114.7	112.0	113.9	110.5	111.3	100.0

Notes: * Data on most academic journals of China (1994–2004).
      ** Annual totals exceed 100 per cent because of articles on two and more countries.
Sources: Wong and Lai (2007), p. 18; Tang and Zhang (2007), p. 62.

all countries in Southeast Asia. An analysis of articles in *Southeast Asian Studies* and *Southeast Asian Affairs* from 1992 to 2004 indicates that most of the countries of the region were included every year, though case studies on individual countries decreased from 61.4 per cent to 34.0 per cent (see Table 2.4).[5]

Diversified Research Subjects

The development of Southeast Asian Studies is also attested to by the broader diversification of research subjects. Southeast Asian Studies in China in the last three decades has been opened to the methodological pluralism of the West. Consequently, the diverse perspectives, approaches, theories, and concepts of various academic disciplines in the West influenced the "opened Southeast Asian Studies" of China in diverse ways, away from the previously dogmatic studies on history, politics, economy, society, and culture. In the "development" of Southeast Asian Studies beyond their "restoration", a crucial juncture was the bold initiative of Deng Xiaoping for the "socialist market economy" in response to the end of the Cold War in 1989 and the collapse of the Soviet Union in 1991 (Yuan 2007, p. 36; Cao 2007, pp. 70–71).

The methodological changes in Southeast Asian Studies resulted from dynamic interactions between the transition of specialists and the diversification of subjects. With the rapid spread of the market economy and the gradual opening of the political system, a junior generation interested in diverse subjects emerged to lead Southeast Asian Studies. As Southeast Asian Studies was opened to non-specialists, moreover, many institutions and researchers previously with no or little interest in Southeast Asia were attracted to the field of studies. They produced many significant outcomes, offering new research subjects such as the Chinese media, theatrical literature, religious culture, cultural exchange, legal systems, educational systems, agricultural geography, maritime emigration, cross-border minorities, and economic regionalism (Yuan 2007, pp. 33–35; Zhuang 2008).

The opening of Southeast Asian Studies to diverse disciplines, including political science, sociology, economics, anthropology, religious studies, law, literature, and linguistics, contributed further impetus to the development of Southeast Asian Studies (Chen 1992, pp. 16–17; He 2003; Yu 2005; Yuan 2007, pp. 35–36). The focus of Chinese research was switched from past history to present reality. In the late 1990s, the frequency of the subjects in new books appeared in economics, politics, culture, and history. Such a trend of diversification is also evident in the articles in academic journals. In place of the enduring dominance of historical studies, studies in diverse modern social sciences saw a remarkable growth (He 2003). Thus, the prolonged reign of history throughout the "traditional", "formative", and "closed" stages of Southeast Asian Studies was eclipsed by the robust rise of economic studies (Zhao 2000).

However, an analysis of articles in *Southeast Asian Studies* and *Southeast Asian Affairs* indicates that economic studies exceeded 60 per cent in 1992, and declined sharply to 16 per cent in 2004. By contrast, political studies increased rapidly from 11 per cent in 1992 to 45 per cent in 2004, while other multi-disciplinary studies increased slowly (Wong and Lai 2007, pp. 20–22). Another analysis of articles in three major journals from 2000 to

Table 2.5
Subjects of Southeast Asian Studies, 2000–05
(%)

Subject	SEA Studies	SEA Affairs	AP Review
External Relations	25	15	35
Chinese	19	17	0
Politics	18	5	17
Society	11	4	3
Economy	7	40	5
Regional Cooperation	6	3	5
History	5	12	22
Security	5	2	11
Religion	4	2	7
Total	100	100	105*
Number	359	227	81

Notes: * It exceeds 100 per cent due to some articles covering both economy and politics.
Sources: Zhang (2007), pp. 49–50.

2004 suggests a different order of frequency: external relations in *Southeast Asian Studies* and *Asia Pacific Review* and economics in *Southeast Asian Affairs*. Nevertheless, they share a basic similarity in the diversity of research subjects (see Table 2.5). In particular, multi-disciplinary approaches increased in the studies of globalization and regionalization (Wong and Lai 2007, pp. 17–19; Cao 2007, p. 70).

PROBLEMS IN SOUTHEAST ASIAN STUDIES

Despite the rapid growth of Southeast Asian Studies after the Reform and Opening, there are still some conspicuous constraints. First, the most serious problem lies in Sino-centrism, either explicit or implicit, in their fundamental perspectives on Southeast Asian Studies, as their research questions tend to be raised in terms of the national interests of China. Second, despite the significant opening to the diverse methods of modern social sciences, traditional bibliographic studies and descriptive methods still occupy the mainstream. Third, applied policy-oriented studies tend to prevail over basic theory-oriented studies. In particular, however, studies on national subjects are extremely prone to Sino-centric biases due to China's extraordinary position in the history and reality of Southeast Asia. The most obvious example of this involvement is the question of the overseas Chinese.

Biased Perspectives

The recent debate in China on the conceptual implications of Tianxia [all under heaven], which represents the traditional Sino-centric worldview, has revealed the confrontation between two diametrically opposed perspectives: one, the vertical, monistic, and hegemonic order and the other, the horizontal, pluralistic, and harmonious order (Zhao 2005; Zhang S. 2006; Ke and Xu 2008; Zhao 2008). Nevertheless, both agree on the historical, though not on the theoretical dimension that the concept effectively served the hierarchical Sino-centric order of East Asia. The Sino-centric worldview, most deeply projected into "traditional Southeast Asian Studies", is yet to be overcome even in "opened Southeast Asian Studies". The atavistic Sino-centric worldview continues to stimulate ethnocentric biases in the basic perspectives of Southeast Asian Studies in China.

Indeed, it is quite evident that Sino-centric biases are reflected in "opened Southeast Asian Studies" in various ways (Liang Y. 2002; Tang, Zhang, and Cao 2005; Liang Y. 2008; Zhang Z. 2007; Tang and Qi 2008; Zhang 2008). In view of the "Sino-centricity" embedded in the basic perspectives of China on Southeast Asia (Ho 2007), there still looms the risk of increasing disjuncture between the objective realities of de-Sinicization in Southeast Asia and the subjective perceptions of Sinicization in China. The most typical example may be the "tributary illusion" of the traditional dynasties, in which even tribute for trade purposes was conceived as evidence of political subordination (Zhuang 2005). The question is so important that serious reflections are required of contemporary China, as it stands for the "revival of the great Chinese nation".

A Sino-centric perspective may be either the result of a passive response or the result of an active choice (Chen 1992, pp. 18–19). Although political control of academic activity has been relaxed in the liberal atmosphere of "seeking truth from facts", the ideological parameters of "socialism with Chinese characteristics" still constrain research. In Southeast Asian Studies, thus, the prevalence of pragmatic studies on economic development and nationalistic studies on the overseas Chinese seems quite natural (Liang Y. 2002; Liang Y. 2008, p. 89). In this regard the most reasonable alternative suggested by Southeast Asian specialists in China may be Southeast

Asia-centric perspectives based on global consciousness. For instance, a representative of the intermediate generation has emphasized:

> Chinese scholars studying Southeast Asia should make efforts to overcome Euro-centrism and, at the same time, avoid Sino-centric tendencies. At present, what is necessary for the development of Southeast Asian Studies is to nurture global consciousness and observe and study the history and reality of Southeast Asia in global and Southeast Asian perspectives (Liang Z. 2007, p. 18).

How much consensus is possible in China on such an alternative is questionable, nonetheless. It is a stark reality that the ideological constraints of "socialism with Chinese characteristics" contribute to conservative biases in Southeast Asian Studies. For example, the political problems of Myanmar seem to belong to "forbidden zones" because of the practical necessity of China's national interests, let alone the normative principle of Myanmar's national sovereignty. It is, in fact, difficult to collect primary sources and publish research products on the historical conflicts with China as well as the domestic politics and foreign policies of Southeast Asian countries. As a result, political studies are lagging far behind economic studies, further widening the gaps between objective realities and subjective perceptions (Liang Z. et al. 2002, p. 91).

Traditional Methods

In the three decades of "closed Southeast Asian Studies", many Southeast Asian countries, afraid of the political consequences, did not admit scholars from China, and China, short of financial resources, did not send scholars to Southeast Asia. As a result, field work was completely excluded from the methods of Southeast Asian Studies in China (Wang 2004, p. 8). Even the senior generation with the capacity for fieldwork was satisfied with the traditional methods of historical and descriptive studies. By contrast, the junior generation of "opened Southeast Asian Studies" tends to depend largely on the secondary sources of the West because of their weakness in local languages (Liang Z. et al. 2002; Liu 2003; Zhang 2007, p. 57; Zhang 2008, p. 48; Wong and Lai 2007, p. 15; Tang and Zhang 2007, pp. 68–69).

Therefore, the mainstream work of "opened Southeast Asian Studies" still indulges in traditional methods which are macro, superficial, descriptive, and historical, in contrast with the micro, empirical, analytical, and systematic methods of the modern social sciences (Zhu 1992; Liang Z. et al. 2002;

Tang, Zhang, and Cao 2005, p. 12). In the circumstances, policy-oriented studies, rather than basic theory-oriented studies are prevalent (Zhu 1992; Yuan 2007). Such applied studies are conducted by special institutes affiliated with government agencies or state enterprises. They tend to concentrate on superficial reports on the economy, politics, diplomacy, and security of Southeast Asian countries, which rarely contribute to the quality of Southeast Asian Studies in China (Zhongguo Xiandai 2002; Tang and Zhang 2007, pp. 64–66).

A leader of Southeast Asian Studies in China, Zhu Jieqin, has stressed the important point that "From the olden times, Southeast Asian Studies were the pragmatic studies of statecraft [Jingshi Zhiyong]. They should serve China's national interests and contribute to its 'four modernisations'" (Dai and Wang 1992, p. 12). Government demands and market incentives have served to promote policy-oriented studies and simplistic literature reviews and assessments of current affairs (Tang and Zhang 2007, pp. 64–67). Nevertheless, if it is the case that China's regional strategies are derived from the prevailing realist paradigm of power politics, policy-oriented studies are likely to engender serious difficulties. From Chinese perspectives, Southeast Asia, conceived of as an "abridged world" with geographical, economic, religious, and national diversities, will be expected to serve as China's springboard towards becoming a global power (Zeng 2003).

National Subjects

The development of "opened Southeast Asian Studies" is also constrained by the national subjects of research, which can be divided into the question of the overseas Chinese and the question of cross-border nationalities. While the former was the most popular subject in Southeast Asian Studies for a very long time, the latter is one of the most recent subjects reconsidered in a new perspective in response to processes and issues of globalization and regionalization (Ren 2002; Liu 2007). The significance of national subjects lies in their strategic location as "contact zones" or "intersections" between China and Southeast Asia (Liu 2000, pp. 3–6; Liu 2001). If the questions of Sino-centric perspectives and policy-oriented studies are not adequately addressed, the national subjects of research are likely to pose serious obstacles to really opened, informed and evidentially-based Southeast Asian Studies.

The subject of the overseas Chinese is the most sensitive focus of research in Southeast Asian Studies in China, in that it represents the "blood connections" of China with Southeast Asia. In 1978 Deng Xiaoping visited Thailand, Malaysia, and Singapore to gain an understanding of their current economic activities and their prospects for future economic development (Lee 2000, pp. 595–603). After the Reform and Opening, he established four special economic zones — Shenzhen, Zhuhai, Shantou, Xiamen — in the southern coastal areas of mainland China to induce the overseas Chinese capital of Hong Kong, Macao, Taiwan, and Southeast Asia to invest in the homeland (Ren and Zhao 1999, pp. 292–96). In practice, overseas Chinese capital is estimated to have exceeded two-thirds of the total inflow of foreign capital (Ren and Zhao 1999, pp. 287–309). The question is likely to amplify Sino-centric biases, as a representative of the junior generation suggests:

> As compared with studies in other countries on the emigrants and their descendants, China's studies on the overseas Chinese have particular significance beyond their general academic values. As the most important overseas resources, the huge size of the overseas Chinese [population] will offer important locomotive power for the resurgence of the Chinese nation, let alone their special role for the social development of China in the past (Zhuang 2008, p. 93).

The question of the overseas Chinese has been approached in terms of a "China-dominant paradigm" (Ho 2007, p. 89), but not by adopting an inter-subjective perspective of the Chinese community in the context of the local society within which they currently reside. However, more than 90 per cent of the overseas Chinese [Huaqiao] oriented toward Sinicization [Luoye Guigen] have been transformed into the ethnic Chinese [Huaren] oriented toward localization [Luodi Shenggen]. Sino-centric perspectives on the overseas Chinese are too anachronistic to understand the dynamic realities of Southeast Asia. While certain shifts in discourse to localization are discerned, the recent waves of Chinese citizens [Xin Huaqiao] all over the world stimulate academic interests in re-Sinicization. Nevertheless, the relationships between China and the ethnic Chinese are not the latter's unilateral contribution to their "fatherland" but reciprocal exchange through complex mutual interaction (Liang Y. 2002; Liang Y. 2008, pp. 86–92; Zhang 2008, p. 47). A scholar of the intermediate generation has pointed to the crux of the matter in a sensitive and informed assessment of the problem. He says:

> In Southeast Asia the history of the ethnic Chinese is the history of their immigration to a country and their gradual integration as a part of the nation. The ethnic Chinese economy constitutes a part of the

national economy, and Chinese capital is a part of the national capital. Therefore, China's policy toward the overseas Chinese should encourage their naturalisation into the local society and their contribution to the development of the national economy, rather than the economic construction and educational projects of China ... and promote the internationalism of the ethnic Chinese instead of their [Sino-centric] patriotism.

(Wang 1992, pp. 25–26)

However, Chinese historians tend to stress the passive aspects of Southeast Asian history, and neglect its positive aspects. Most studies on the overseas Chinese in Southeast Asia define them as an independent variable influencing local societies, but not as a dependent variable influenced by the latter (Ho 2007). The membership of the China Association of Overseas Chinese History which stands at over 300, as compared with the approximately 600 members of the China Association of Southeast Asian Studies, illustrates the importance of scholarly interest in and research on the overseas Chinese for "opened Southeast Asian Studies" (Liang Z. 2002, p. 2). In this context, any studies undertaken on the national identity, international relations, economic structure, and foreign investment strategies of the overseas Chinese can potentially raise all kinds of very sensitive questions (Liang Y. 2002; Ren 2002; Li 2002, pp. 1032–34).

Unlike the question of the overseas Chinese, the question of cross-border nationalities has emerged afresh in response to issues of globalization and regionalization (Liu 2000; Liu 2001; Liu 2007; Zhongguo yu Dongnanya 2007; Zhou 2008). Like the overseas Chinese, however, it is another empirical subject closely associated with the "blood connections" across national borders between China and Southeast Asia. In effect, the various nationalities scattered across southern China and northern Southeast Asia may offer an important clue, in theory as well as in practice, to the development of regionalism in East Asia encompassing Northeast and Southeast Asia. In this regard two pioneering works which counter the nature of the artificial borders and boundaries between China and Southeast Asia, *Sino-Southeast Asian Studies* (Liu 2000) and *East Asian History* (Yang and Zhang 2006), are highly commendable (Zheng 2002; Zeng 2003; Wang 2004; Wu 2005).

The question of cross-border nationalities is characterized by a fundamental ambivalence, nonetheless. Like the overseas Chinese, studies of cross-border minorities emphasize the organic linkages between China and

Southeast Asia overshadowing the artificial political and territorial boundaries which divide them. On the one hand, they extend further the spatial
and temporal scope of "opened Southeast Asian Studies" to East Asia. The
theoretical and practical relevance of such an East Asian perspective may
be deemed quite reasonable in this regard. On the other hand, Sino-centric
biases on Southeast Asia may be reproduced much more extensively if various
research subjects on the region are contextualized within an East Asian
rather than a Southeast Asian regional perspective. One of the most urgent
tasks of "opened Southeast Asian Studies" is, therefore, to break through the
historical predicament of Sino-centric perspectives. Indeed, other countries
in East Asia will never be receptive to such excessive and continuing Chinese
ethnocentrism in Southeast Asian Studies.

CONCLUSIONS

China and Southeast Asia share intimate relationships based on close spatial,
temporal, and human conditions. Accordingly, Southeast Asian Studies
in China boast a long lineage of "traditional", "formative", "closed", and
"opened" Southeast Asian Studies. In the modern period the "formative
Southeast Asian Studies", professing conservative nationalism in line with
traditional Sino-centric perspectives, accumulated elementary knowledge
of the history of Sino-Southeast Asian relations and overseas Chinese
communities in Southeast Asia. However, "closed Southeast Asian Studies",
in the period of radical communism, suffered from chronic stagnation.
After the Reform and Opening, "opened Southeast Asian Studies" has undoubtedly recorded impressive progress in the restoration and development
of Southeast Asian Studies.

Nevertheless, "opened Southeast Asian Studies" is faced with some serious
problems such as biased perspectives, the continuation of traditional methods,
and the focus on research which addresses Chinese national interests. Above
all else, it is most urgent to address and overcome Sino-centric perspectives
on Southeast Asia. What is more despite the opening of Southeast Asian
Studies to the diverse methods of the modern social sciences, descriptive
studies prevail over analytical ones. Finally, regardless of the diversification
of research subjects, national questions such as the overseas Chinese and
cross-border nationalities are prone to the adoption of the perspective of
excessive nationalism. In the meantime, the emergence of an East Asian
perspective, focused on organic linkages between China — thus, Northeast
Asia — and Southeast Asia beyond their artificial territorial boundaries, may,

if used with care and sensitivity, provide a positive element in the future prospects of the "opened Southeast Asian Studies" of China.

To conclude, a profound problem lies in the continuing importance of Sino-centric perspectives. "Opened Southeast Asian Studies" is indeed, "Southeast Asian Studies with Chinese characteristics" constrained by "socialism with Chinese characteristics". In the worst case, "opened Southeast Asian Studies" could follow the precedent of "closed Southeast Asian Studies" as an ideological instrument for regional hegemony. In the best case, "opened Southeast Asian Studies" could contribute to an equitable regional order in East Asia. All historical orders of East Asia were hierarchical ones of domination and dependence. The only sustainable regional order in the future will be a liberal and pluralistic one of multilateral and multilayered interdependence (Adler 1997; Zhang X. 2006; Zhang S. 2006). Thus, it is to be hoped fervently that the welcome advent of "opened Southeast Asian Studies" in Chinese scholarship will be able to overcome its excessive Sino-centric biases.

Notes

[1]   In the perspective of *East Asian History* it is too artificial to separate southern China and northern Southeast Asia, since the two regions share a similar natural environment, economic structure, national composition, and traditional culture. In fact such a historical perspective has already been presented in such concepts as "the Sino-centric order", "the tributary system", and "the East Asian order" (Yang and Zhang 2006, p. 141).

[2]   "Southern Sea" and "Southern Ocean" largely overlap with present "Dongnanya [Southeast Asia]". While "Eastern Ocean" included Borneo, Java, and the Philippines, "Western Ocean" included all maritime areas west of "Eastern Ocean" (Wang 1984). As "Southern Ocean" was generally used until the 1970s, "Southeast Asia" began to be socialized from the 1980s (Wang 2004, p. 9).

[3]   It was selected by the Ministry of Education as one of the 100 central research bases for the humanities and social sciences in 2000, and it was recognized by the central government as one of the most innovative institutes in philosophy and the social sciences in 2004.

[4]   Eastern and northern universities and institutes are more interested in comparative studies on the broader Southeast Asian region, and those in southern China are more interested in case studies on individual countries. In the case of the latter, however, universities and institutes in the eastern provinces of Guangdong and Fujian tend to focus on maritime Southeast Asia, and those in the western provinces Guangxi and Yunnan on mainland Southeast Asia (Wong and Lai 2007, pp. 14–16).

5   An analysis of a total 2,320 articles on Southeast Asia from 1994 to 2004 shows the dominance of Singapore (about 1/3) and Vietnam (about 1/4) in case studies on individual countries, indicating their special significance to China. Meanwhile, studies on relations between Greater China — China, Hong Kong, Macao, Taiwan — and Southeast Asia increased from 7.9 per cent in 1992 to 21.6 per cent in 2004, suggesting rapidly growing interest in the economic integration of East Asia (see Table 2.4).

References

Adler, Emanuel. "Seizing the Middle Ground: Constructivism in World Politics". *European Journal of International Relations* 3, no. 3 (1997): 319–63.

Cao Yunhua. "Guangdong de Dongnanya Yanjiu" [Southeast Asian studies in Guangdong]. In *Zhongguo de Dongnanya Yanjiu* [Southeast Asian Studies in China], edited by Huang Chaohan and Cao Yunhua. Beijing: Shijiezhishichubabshe, 2007.

Chen Qiaozhi. "Dui Woguo de Dongnanya Renshi" [On our country's perceptions of Southeast Asia]. In *Zhongguo de Dongnanya Yanjiu* [Southeast Asian Studies in China], edited by Chen Qiaozhi, Huang Zisheng, and Chen Senhai. Guangzhou: Jinandaxuechubanshe, 1992.

Chen Qiaozhi, Huang Zisheng, and Chen Senhai, eds. *Zhongguo de Dongnanya Yanjiu* [Southeast Asian Studies in China]. Guangzhou: Jinandaxuechubanshe, 1992.

Chou, Cynthia and Vincent Houben, eds. *Southeast Asian Studies*. Singapore: Institute of Southeast Asian Studies, 2006.

Dai Kelai and Wang Jienan. "Zhongguo Shinianlai dui Dongnanya de Yanjiu" [China's Southeast Asian Studies in recent 10 years]. In *Zhongguo de Dongnanya Yanjiu* [Southeast Asian Studies in China], edited by Chen Qiaozhi, Huang Zisheng, and Chen Senhai. Guangzhou: Jinandaxuechubanshe, 1992.

Hayami Yoko. "Towards Multi-Laterality in Southeast Asian Studies: Perspectives from Japan". In *Southeast Asian Studies*, edited by Cynthia Chou and Vincent Houben. Singapore: Institute of Southeast Asian Studies, 2006.

He Shengda. *Dongnanya Wenhua Fazhanshi* [A history of cultural development in Southeast Asia]. Kunming: Yunnandaxuechubanshe, 1996.

———. "Zhongguo Dongnanyashi Yanjiu de Chengjiu yu Zhanwang" [The achievements and prospects of Chinese studies on the history of Southeast Asia]. *Shijie Lishi* [World History], no. 2 (2003): 102–12.

Ho Khai Leong. "From 'Sino-Centricity' to 'Autonomous Narrative' in Southeast Asian Chinese Studies in China". In *Southeast Asian Studies in China*, edited by Saw Swee-Hock and John Wong. Singapore: Institute of Southeast Asian Studies, 2007.

Huang Chaohan and Cao Yunhua, eds. *Zhongguo de Dongnanya Yanjiu* [Southeast Asian Studies in China]. Beijing: Shijiezhishichubanshe, 2007.

Ke Lanan and Xu Jin. "Zhongguo Shiyexia de Shijie Zhixu" [World order in Chinese perspectives]. *Shijie Jingji yu Zhengzhi* [World economics and politics], no. 10 (2008): 49–56.

King, Victor T. "Southeast Asia: Personal Reflections on a Region". In *Southeast Asian Studies*, edited by Cynthia Chou and Vincent Houben. Singapore: Institute of Southeast Asian Studies, 2006.

Lee Kuan Yew. *From Third World to First*. New York: HarperCollins, 2000.

Leonard, Jane Kate. "Extracts from Wei Yuan and China's Rediscovery of the Maritime World". In *China and Southeast Asia*, vol. 4, edited by Geoff Wade. London: Routledge, 2009.

Li Anshan. "Zhongguo Huaqiao Huaren Yanjiu de Lishi yu Xianzhuang Gaishu" [An introduction to the past and present of Chinese studies on the overseas Chinese]. In *Huaqiao Huaren Baike Quanshu: Zonglunjuan* [Encyclopedia of the overseas Chinese: Overview volume], edited by Zhou Nanjing. Beijing: Huaqiaochubanshe, 2002.

Li Wen. "Goujian Dongya Rentong" [Constructing an East Asian identity]. *Dangdai Yatai* [Contemporary Asia-Pacific studies], no. 6 (2007): 3–10.

Liang Yingming. "Haiwai Huaren Jingji Huodong Yanjiu Ruogan Wenti" [Some problems of studies on the economic activities of the overseas Chinese]. In *Huaqiao Huaren Baike Quanshu: Zonglunjuan* [Encyclopedia of the overseas and ethnic Chinese: Overview volume], edited by Zhou Nanjing. Beijing: Huaqiaochubanshe, 2002.

————. "Huaqiao Huaren Xueke Jianshe yu Xueshu Dingwei" [Constructing the disciplinary status of the overseas Chinese studies]. In *Zhongguo Huaqiao Huaren Yanjiu* [Chinese studies on the overseas Chinese], edited by Wu Xiaoan and Wu Jiewei. Hong Kong: Wenhuichubanshe, 2008.

Liang Zhiming. "Shijizhijiao Zhongguo Dalu Xueshujie Guanyu Huaqiao Huaren Yanjiu" [The overseas Chinese studies in China's academic community at the turn of the century]. *Huaqiao Huaren Lishi Yanjiu* [Studies on the history of the overseas Chinese], no. 1 (2002): 1–8.

————. "Guanyu Zhongguo Dongnanyaxue Yanjiu de Jige Wenti" [On some problems of Southeast Asian Studies in China]. *Dongnanya Yanjiu* [Southeast Asian studies], no. 2 (2007): 14–19, 49.

Liang Zhiming, Li Mou, Yang Baoyun, and Fu Zengyou. *Gudai Dongnanya Lishi yu Wenhua Yanjiu* [Studies on the history and culture of ancient Southeast Asia]. Beijing: Kunlunchubanshe, 2006.

Liang Zhiming, Zhang Xizhen, and Yang Baojun. "Mianxiang Xinshiji de Zhongguo Dongnanyaxue Yanjiu" [Toward a new century of Southeast Asian Studies in China]. In *Mianxiang Xinshiji de Zhongguo Dongnanyaxue Yanjiu* [Toward a new century of Southeast Asian studies in China], edited by Liang Zhiming. Hong Kong: Shehuikexuechubanshe, 2002.

Liao Jianyu. "Zhongguo de Dongnanya Xuezhe" [Chinese scholars in Southeast Asian studies]. In *Zhongguo de Dongnanya Yanjiu* [Southeast Asian Studies in China], edited by Huang Chaohan and Cao Yunhua. Beijing: Shijiezhishichubanshe, 2007.

Liu Hong. *Zhongguo–Dongnanya Xue* [Sino-Southeast Asian Studies]. Beijing: Shehuikexuechubanshe, 2000.

———. "Sino-Southeast Asian Studies: Towards an Alternative Paradigm". *Asian Studies Review* 25, no. 3 (2001): 259–83.

———. "Jiu Lianxi, Jiu Wangluo" [Old linkages, old networks]. In *Huaqiao Huaren Baike Quanshu: Zonglunjuan* [Encyclopedia of the overseas Chinese: Overview volume], edited by Zhou Nanjing. Beijing: Huaqiaochubanshe, 2002.

———. "Southeast Asian Studies in Greater China". *Kyoto Review of Southeast Asia*, no. 3 (2003). <http://kyotoreview.cseas.kyoto-u.ac.jp/issue/issue2/index.html> (accessed 5 January 2011).

Liu Zhi. *Zhongguo-Dongnanya Kuajie Minzu Fazhan Yanjiu* [A Study on the development of Sino-Southeast Asian cross-border nationalities]. Beijing: Minzuchubanshe, 2007.

Park Sa-Myung. *Dongasiaeo Saeroun Mosaeg* [A new search for East Asia] (in Korean). Seoul: Imagine, 2006.

Reid, Anthony, ed. *Southeast Asian Studies*. Tempe, AZ: Program for Southeast Asian Studies, Arizona State University, 2003.

Ren Guixiang. "Huaqiao Huaren yu Zujiguo Guanxi Gailun" [An introduction to the relationships between the overseas Chinese and their nationality]. In *Huaqiao Huaren Baike Quanshu: Zonglunjuan* [Encyclopedia of the overseas Chinese: Overview volume], edited by Zhou Nanjing. Beijing: Huaqiaochubanshe, 2002.

Ren Guixiang and Zhao Hongying. *Huaqiao Huaren yu Guogong Guanxi* [The overseas Chinese and GMD-CPC relations]. Wuhan: Wuhanchubanshe, 1999.

Saw Swee-Hock and John Wong, eds. *Southeast Asian Studies in China*. Singapore: Institute of Southeast Asian Studies, 2007.

Suryadinata, Leo. "Southeast Asianists in China in the Last Three Decades". In *Southeast Asian Studies in China*, edited by Saw Swee-Hock and John Wong. Singapore: Institute of Southeast Asian Studies, 2007.

Tang Shiping, Luo Zhihan, and Sun Deng, eds. *Dongnanya Shigang* [A concise history of Southeast Asia]. Kunming: Yunnandaxuechubanshe, 1994.

Tang Shiping and Qi Dapeng. "Zhongguo Waijiao Taolun Zhongde 'Zhongguo Zhongxin Zhuyi' yu 'Meiguo Zhongxin Zhuyi'" [China-centrism and America-centrism in debates on Chinese diplomacy]. *Shijie Jingji yu Zhengzhi* [World economics and politics], no. 12 (2008): 62–70, 5.

Tang Shiping and Zhang Jie. "The State of Southeast Asian Studies in China". In *Southeast Asian Studies in China*, edited by Saw Swee-Hock and John Wong. Singapore: Institute of Southeast Asian Studies, 2007.

Tang Shiping, Zhang Jie, and Cao Xiaoyang. "Zhongguo de Diyu Yanjiu" [Area studies in China]. *Shijie Jingji yu Zhengzhi* [World economics and politics], no. 11 (2005): 9–17, 6.

Tang Shiping and Zhang Yunling. "Zhongguo Diqu Zhanlue" [The regional strategy of China]. *Shijie Jingji yu Zhengzhi* [World economics and politics], no. 6 (2004): 8–13, 4.

Wang Gungwu. "Southeast Asian Huaqiao in Chinese History-Writing". In *China and the Chinese Overseas*, edited by Wang Gungwu. Singapore: Times Academic Press, 1991.

———. "Xinjiapo he Zhongguo Guanyu Dongnanya Yanjiu de Liangzhong Butong Guandian" [Two different perspectives on Southeast Asian Studies in Singapore and China]. *Nanyang Wenti Yanjiu* [Southeast Asian affairs], no. 2 (2004): 1–15.

Wang Hui. "Minjuhua neon 1980 Niandae eo Munjae" [Democratisation was an issue of the 1980s] (in Korean). *Joongang Sunday*, 4 October 2009.

Wang Mintong. "Dongnanya Mingcheng Yange" [The terminological history of Southeast Asia]. *Dongnanya* [Southeast Asia], no. 2 (1984): 2–4.

Wang Mintong, Luo Zhihan, and Sun Cheng, eds. *Dongnanya Shigang* [A concise history of Southeast Asia]. Kunming: Yunnandaxuechubanshe, 1994.

Wang Muheng. "Youguan Dongnanya Wenti Yanjiu de Jidian Tihui" [Some understandings about studies on Southeast Asian problems]. In *Zhongguo de Dongnanya Yanjiu* [Southeast Asian Studies in China], edited by Chen Qiaozhi, Huang Zisheng, and Chen Senhai. Guangzhou: Jinandaxuechubanshe, 1992.

Wong, John and Lai Hongyi. "Changing Academic Challenges of the Southeast Asian Studies Field in China". In *Southeast Asian Studies in China*, edited by Saw Swee-Hock and John Wong. Singapore: Institute of Southeast Asian Studies, 2007.

Wu Qianjin. "Kuaguo de Shiye, Tixi de Jianguo" [A cross-border perspective, systematic construction]. *Guoji Guancha* [International review], no. 3 (2005): 73–77.

Wu Xiaoan and Wu Jiewei, eds. *Zhongguo Huaqiao Huaren Yanjiu* [Chinese studies on the overseas Chinese]. Hong Kong: Wenhuichubanshe, 2008.

Yang Jun and Zhang Naihe, eds. *Dongyashi* [East Asian History]. Changchun: Changchunchubanshe, 2006.

Yu Xiangdong. "Zhongguo de Yuenanxue Yanjiu Zhuangkuang ji Sikao" [Some thoughts on the current conditions of Vietnamese studies in China]. *Zhengzhou Daxue Xuebao* [Zhengzhou University journal of philosophy and social science], no. 6 (2005): 156–59.

Yuan Ding. "Ping Zhongguo Youguan Dongnanya Yanjiu" [A critique of Southeast Asian Studies in China]. *Dongnanya Zhongheng* [Around Southeast Asia], no. 3 (2006): 41–47.

――――. "Zhongguo de Dongnanya Yanjiu zhi Yanbian" [Changing Southeast Asian Studies in China]. In *Zhongguo de Dongnanya Yanjiu* [Southeast Asian studies in China], edited by Huang Chaohan and Cao Yunhua. Beijing: Shijiezhishichubanshe, 2007.

Zeng Ling. "Yanjiu he Jianguo Zhongguo yu Dongnanya Zhijian de 'Jiechuqu'" [Studying and constructing "contact zones" between China and Southeast Asia]. *Beijing Daxue Xuebao* [Beijing University journal of philosophy and social science] 40, no. 2 (2003): 152–55.

Zeng Pinyuan. "Zhongguo Dongnanya Zhanluelun" [On Chinese strategies toward Southeast Asia]. *Shiji Zhongguo* [Centurial China], October 2003. <http://bbs.cqzg.cn/thread-86127-1-1.html> (accessed 15 December 2010).

Zhang Shuguang. "Tianxia Lilun he Shijie Zhidu" [Tianxia theories and world institutions]. *Zhongguo Shuping* [China book review], no. 5 (2006): 5–49.

Zhang Xiaoming. "The Rise of China and Community Building in East Asia". *Asian Perspective* 30, no. 3 (2006): 129–48.

Zhang Xiuming. "Jinnian Guonei Huaqiao Huaren Yanjiu de Qushi yu Zhanwang" [Trends and prospects of Chinese studies on the overseas Chinese]. In *Zhongguo Huaqiao Huaren Yanjiu* [Chinese studies on the overseas Chinese], edited by Wu Xiaoan and Wu Jiewei. Hong Kong: Wenhuichubanshe, 2008.

Zhang Zhenjiang. "Zhongguo de Dongnanya Yanjiu: Chengjiu, Shijiao yu Wenti" [Southeast Asian studies in China: achievements, perspectives, and problems]. In *Zhongguo de Dongnanya Yanjiu* [Southeast Asian Studies in China], edited by Huang Chaohan and Cao Yunhua. Beijing: Shijiezhishichubanshe, 2007.

Zhao Heman. "Mainxiang 21 Shiji de Zhongguo Dongnanya Yanjiu" [Toward the twenty-first century's Southeast Asian studies in China]. In his *Mianxiang 21 Shiji de Dongnanya* [Southeast Asia meets the twenty-first century]. Guangzhou: Jinandaxuechubanshe, 2000.

Zhao Tingyang. *Tianxia Tixi* [The tianxia system]. Nanjing: Jiangsujiaoyuchubanshe, 2005.

――――. "Tianxia Tixi de Yige Jianyao Biaoshu" [A concise presentation of the tianxia system]. *Shijie Jingji yu Zhengzhi* [World economics and politics], no. 10 (2008): 57–65, 5.

Zheng Yisheng. "Yibu Yanjiu Zhongguo yu Dongnanya Wenti de You Changjianxing Lizuo" [A creative masterpiece in studies on the problems of China and Southeast Asia]. *Shijie Lishi* [World history], no. 2 (2002): 112–15.

Zhongguo Xiandai Guoji Guanxi Yanjiusuo [China Institute of Contemporary International relations]. "Zhongguo dui Dongmeng Zhengce Yanjiu Baogao" [A report on Chinese policies toward Southeast Asia]. *Xiandai Guoji Guanxi* [Contemporary international relations], no. 10 (2002): 1–10.

Zhonguo yu Dongnanya Minzu Luntan Bianweihui [Editorial Committee of the China and Southeast Asia Forum on Nationalities], ed. *Dierjie Zhongguo-Dongnanya Minzu Luntan Lunwenji* [The second China-Southeast Asia forum on nationalities]. Beijing: Minzuchubanshe, 2007.

Zhou Jianxin. *Heping Kuaju Lun* [On peaceful cross-border coexistence]. Beijing: Minzuchubanshe, 2008.

Zhu Zhenming. "Zhongguo Dongnanya Yanjiu de Xianzhuang yu Fazhan" [Trends and prospects of Southeast Asian Studies in China]. In *Zhongguo de Dongnanya Yanjiu* [Southeast Asian studies in China], edited by Chen Qiaozhi, Huang Zisheng, and Chen Senhai. Guangzhou: Jinandaxuechubanshe, 1992.

Zhuang Guotu. "Luelun Chaogong Zhidu de Xuhuan" [A short discussion on the illusions of the tributary system]. *Nanyang Wenti Yanjiu* [Southeast Asian affairs], no. 3 (2005): 1–8, 96.

————. "Duoxueke, Jiangou Lishi yu Xianzhuang, Jiaoxue Xiangzhang" [A multidisciplinary approach, considering both history and reality as well as promoting both teaching and learning]. In *Zhongguo Huaqiao Huaren Yanjiu* [Chinese studies on the overseas Chinese], edited by Wu Xiaoan and Wu Jiewei. Hong Kong: Wenhuichubanshe, 2008.

3

STUDIES OF SOUTHEAST ASIAN HISTORY IN CONTEMPORARY JAPAN
The 1990s and 2000s

Yu Insun

There are several complications in discussing the contribution of Japanese historians to the understanding of Southeast Asian history. The fact that Southeast Asia includes eleven countries, usually divided into mainland and maritime sub-regions, with different environments and histories makes it difficult to discuss an overarching research theme that can cover the entire region. Whilst countries in mainland Southeast Asia have existed as identifiable states from a relatively early stage in history, those constituting the maritime sub-region were created as states through Euro-American colonial occupation. A further complicating element has been the ethnic diversity within each country, which has generated significant tensions and in some cases open conflict. Finally, the difficulty in writing an essay on the contribution of Japanese scholars to Southeast Asian history is that Japan has the largest number of Southeast Asian history scholars in the world. The academic organization called *Tonan ajia shigakkai* [Japan Society for Southeast Asian History] represents the nation's fertile academic interest in this area.[1] Japanese research has dealt with very detailed questions in each Southeast Asian country. Therefore, in many cases, it is difficult to determine the period of history and the country discussed in the literature just through a cursory look at the titles of the published works produced by Japanese historians.

The reason why so many Japanese scholars can actively engage in Southeast Asian historical research is because organizations such as the Nippon Foundation (which surpasses the United States' Ford Foundation in terms of research grants and the funds available), the Ministry of Education and Science, and the Toyota Foundation provided generous financial support to promote humanities studies. Researchers can spend a year or two in any country or region he or she wishes and collect the most recent data and information (Shiraishi 2003, pp. 141–47).

Due to the massive number of researchers, tracking down each of the numerous research papers and periodicals generated from all the university research institutions and publishers is an extremely daunting task. Fortunately, it was possible to solve this problem by using the *Tonan aija — rekishi to bunka* [Southeast Asia: History and Culture], the academic journal of *Tonan aija shigakkai,* which provides the *"Tonan aija kankei bunken mokuroku"* [A list of publications on Southeast Asia] published in the previous year. Furthermore, the most important books and papers of the previous year are introduced in every May issue of *Shigaku Zasshi* [Journal of Historical Studies], which includes *"Rekishi gakkai — kaiko to tenbo"* [Historical Study in Japan: Retrospect and Prospect]. By referring to the Southeast Asia category in this issue, I was able to grasp the general trends in studies of Southeast Asian history in Japan. I would like to highlight the fact that I relied heavily on the above two publications in writing this chapter. What should also be emphasized is the substantial amount of scholarly work which has been produced and which is largely beyond the reach of Western and indeed Southeast Asian academics because it is written in the Japanese language. It represents in many respects a separate discourse on Southeast Asia which has never been considered by what we might term the dominant English-medium discourse.

After contemplating the time-frame for analysis, I decided to focus on the trends in Japanese studies of Southeast Asian history between 1990 and 2007.[2] One reason for this is that, despite prominent academic accomplishments prior to the 1990s, there is a need for a more up-to-date point of reference. Another more important reason is that previous works have already discussed research trends in Japan through the late 1980s. For example, in June 1987, the Japan Society for Southeast Asian History held a symposium regarding research in five Southeast Asian countries — the Philippines, Indonesia, Vietnam, Thailand, and Burma — under the theme of "Past Accomplishments and Future Tasks for Studies of Southeast Asian History in Japan". The papers were initially presented in Japanese but, after a review process, were published in English in 1991 (*Asian Research*

Trends, vol. 1, 1991, pp. 30–133). While works on Malaysia, Cambodia and Singapore were not presented, the five papers included in this publication are critical for the understanding of the nature and scope of Japanese research on Southeast Asian history up until the late 1980s.

The final point I would like to make is that this chapter intends to assist the reader by first discussing the process through which the regional concept of Southeast Asia emerged and then by exploring the history of Japanese research on Southeast Asian history. I then move on to analyse the quantity and content of the historical research that has been undertaken from the 1990s to 2007. However, even the time span of 1990 to 2007 is too broad and comprises such a large literature for discussion as a whole and it cannot be dealt with satisfactorily in a single section. Therefore, I have chosen to divide the discussion into two sub-sections: research trends from 1990 to 1999 and then those from 2000 to 2007.

CONCEPTUALIZATION PROCESS OF SOUTHEAST ASIA AS AN AREA

It is a widely known fact that the Japanese word *Tonan ajia* is a translation of the English words "South East Asia". The English term first emerged in official circles in August 1943, at the height of the Second World War, when the then U.S. President Franklin D. Roosevelt and then British Prime Minister Winston Churchill met at a conference held in Quebec. The two leaders agreed to install the "South East Asia Command"[3] in order to combat the Japanese forces that controlled most of Southeast Asia at the time. Since the term "South East Asia" did not exist in official terms prior to the conference, the new headquarters was initially called the "East Asia Command" but was renamed after the conference (Shimizu 1987*a*, p. 6).

While the term Southeast Asia was utilized a year before the Quebec conference in Rupert Emerson's *Government and Nationalism in Southeast Asia*, it did not gain widespread currency at the time (Emerson et al. 1942; Shimizu 1987*a*, p. 5). The term Southeast Asia was first used by an American pastor called Howard Malcolm in his book entitled *Travels in South-Eastern Asia,* which was published in Boston in 1839 (Malcom 1839; Emmerson 1984, p. 5). The regional scope discussed in Malcolm's book only includes the mainland section of what is now Southeast Asia and does not discuss the region's maritime territories. As the Western powers divided and colonized Southeast Asia soon afterwards, a new term which encompassed the entire region was difficult to come by. The exceptions to this problem were those countries which did not have any colonial possessions in the region such as Austria and Germany. They perceived the region as a whole and utilized the term *Südostasien* (the German word for Southeast Asia). An important figure in this regard in the first half of the twentieth century was a Viennese scholar, Robert von Heine-Geldern, who is widely acknowledged as a pioneer of the early study of Southeast Asia as a region (Emmerson 1984, p. 5).

In Japan, prior to the Second World War, Southeast Asia was generally referred to as *nanyo* (literally "the Southern Ocean") or *nampo* (the South). The term *nanyo* was adopted from Chinese. In ancient times, the Chinese referred to Southeast Asia and India collectively as "*nanhai*" (South Seas). This practice gradually changed during the Song dynasty when the words "*nanhai*" and "*nanyang*" (Southern Ocean) were used interchangeably. Moreover, since the area was vast, the Chinese drew a straight line southward from Guangzhou and divided the area in two. The area east of the line was dubbed "East *nanhai*" or "East *nanyang*" and the area west of the line was dubbed "West *nanhai*" or "West *nanyang*". Afterwards, from the end of the Yuan dynasty (1206–1368) to the Ming dynasty (1368–1644), the *nan* was omitted and the areas were simply referred to as *dongyang* (East Seas) and *xiyang* (West Seas). Luzon, the Sulu Islands, the Moluccas and other eastern Indonesian islands were included in the East Seas while Vietnam, Siam, and Bantam were incorporated into the West Seas. Through the above division, the Chinese formulated their views on "Southeast Asia". By the Qing period (1644–1912), Chen Lun Jiong's *Hai guo jian wen lu* [Observation on the Overseas Countries] referred to Europe as "Big *xiyang*" and India as "Small *xiyang*". In a separate development, the Chinese began to distinguish between East *nanyang* and *nanyang*. The former referred to the regions of Taiwan, the Philippines and Borneo while the latter referred to those of Indochina, Java and Sumatra. Through such divisions, the conceptualization of *nanyang* became even more concrete (Miyazaki 1942, p. 1–22; Hamashita 1991, pp. 123–27).[4]

The term *nanyo* was first utilized in Japan towards the end of the Tokugawa period (1603–1868). In 1798, Honda Toshiaki, in his *Saiiki monogatari* [Tales of the Western Regions], wrote the following: "In the past, the Japanese vessels also crossed the seas from China's Zhejiang and Guangdong to Annam, Cochinchina, Champa and *nanyang* to procure necessary goods for the country through commerce." In the same book, the East Indies are referred to as *higashi tenjiku nanyo* (East Indies South Seas). In *Chokiron*, written in 1801, places such as Borneo and Java are referred to as *nanyo*. Based on the above facts, one can deduce that his conceptualization of *nanyo* included what is currently known as Southeast Asia's maritime regions (Shimizu 1987*a*, p. 8; Shimizu 2005, pp. 85–86).[5]

However, the meaning of the term *nanyo* differed depending on the time period and the person. Despite such variance, the term generally referred to the islands of the Southwest Pacific and what is today understood as the maritime regions of Southeast Asia. The term, therefore, did not include the mainland section. In other words, *nanyo* was understood as an area separate from the Asian mainland (Shimizu 1987*a*, pp. 8–9).

Such a conceptualization of *nanyo* started to change after the Russo-Japanese War of 1904–05. The mainland section and the maritime section were referred to as Indochina and Malaya respectively, and the Japanese started to categorize the region as part of a greater Asia. Notably, the concept of *nanyo* became much clearer during the First World War. The main reason behind this change was the rapid penetration of Japanese products and commerce into the region which had been left in a power vacuum. Japan became de-facto controller of Micronesia, a former German colony, in the form of a trusteeship. Micronesia was referred to as *"inner nanyo"* or *"rear nanyo"* while the rest of Southeast Asia was dubbed *"outer nanyo"* or *"frontal nanyo"*. The conceptualization of today's Southeast Asia materialized through this process.

The distinction between inner *nanyo* and outer *nanyo* appears to be related to Japanese advancement in *nanyo*. There were two directions for Japan's southward advancement: the first was towards Okinawa, Taiwan, and today's Malayan Peninsula; the second was towards the Bonin Islands, the Philippines, and Oceania (Yano 1979, pp. 12–13). It is reasonable to assume that the Japanese distinguished these two and named the more proximate route as *inner* and the more distant one as *outer*.

Meanwhile, the term *tonan ajiya* appeared in an elementary school geography textbook, published in February 1919, while a middle school textbook also used the term *tonan ajia* (Shimizu 1987*a*, pp. 9–13; Shimizu 2005, pp. 89, 91). Of course, these terms were used for convenience unlike other terms such as Central Asia which had already gained wide international currency at the time. In general, today's Southeast Asia was still referred to as two separate areas: Indochina and the Malay Archipelago (Shimizu 1987*b*, pp. 22, 27; Shimizu 2005, p. 92). The Japanese were more devoted to utilizing the Western geographical concepts than adopting their own creative terms.

One point that needs to be raised here is that even if the Japanese perceived Southeast Asia as a single region, they did so in order to serve their imperialist policies. Therefore, important issues including the differences and similarities in social developmental stages, environmental aspects such as Southeast Asia's terrain and climate and anthropocentric elements such as demographics, language, religion, and culture were not seriously pursued in their research (Shimizu 1987*b*, pp. 34–35; Shimizu 2005, p. 101).

With the end of the Second World War, the Civil Information and Education Section (established by MacArthur's General Headquarters for the purpose of setting directives regarding Japan's general education) attempted to exclude all militaristic elements in Japan by forbidding education in various subjects such as ethics, Japanese history, and geography. Consequently, the use of the pre-war terminology of Southeast Asia became rather rare (Shimizu 1987*b*, p. 35). However, this silence only lasted for a short while as the Japanese proceeded to use the term *tonan ajia,* a direct translation of the word "South East Asia". Such change refuelled the country's deep interest in the region. The Japanese government, which had already expressed a continuing interest in Southeast Asia in August 1949 through its *White Paper on Education*, began to implement its policies in a full-fledged manner after Ikeda Hayato, then Minister of Finance, made a statement during a plenary session of the Diet held in May 1952. Hayato's statement was significant as it included the phrase "joint U.S.-Japan development of Southeast Asia" (Shimizu 1987*b*, p. 36; Shimizu 2005, p. 104). Following his statement, the use of the term "Southeast Asia" rapidly spread amongst the Japanese people. Of course, the concept of Southeast Asia had become something completely different from what was used prior to the war. Regardless, two factors played an important role in the rapid dissemination of the term: first, the Cold War altered the international environment and, secondly, American policy toward Japan shifted. Especially after China became a communist state in October 1949, the U.S. implemented an open door policy and promoted Japan's advancement in the Southeast Asian market in order to obstruct China's expansion in the region. In other words, the U.S. intended to transform Japan into a bastion of anti-communism (Hagiwara 1978, p. 117). The Japanese government, which became highly interested in Southeast Asia after it lost the Chinese market, moved quickly to seize the opportunity. In June 1953, then Prime Minister Yoshida Shigeru made the following statement in his parliamentary speech (Yano 1985, pp. 179–80):

As the current situation is such that we cannot expect much from our trade with China, I do not have to explain in detail the critical importance of Southeast Asia. For the prosperity of all countries of Southeast Asia, the Japanese government will not hold back in cooperating in various aspects including capital, technology, service etc. and further deepen mutually prosperous relationships.

Following such a development, in April 1954 Japan became a member of the Economic Commission for Asia and the Far East (ECAFE) and the Colombo Plan in October of the same year. These measures brought legitimacy to Japan's plan to expand economically into Southeast Asia.

It goes without saying that such generalization and dissemination of the term Southeast Asia influenced historical studies. The *Toyo shiryo shusei* [A Collection of Historical Materials on Asia], edited by Shimonaka Kunihiko in 1956, includes a separate section for Southeast Asia and introduces history, research and historical materials on Burma, Siam, Indochina, Vietnam and Malaysia. Also, in every May issue of the *Shigaku Zasshi*, the previous year's "Historical Study in Japan: Retrospect and Prospect" contains a separate section exclusively devoted to Southeast Asia. Up until 1956, the *Shigaku Zasshi* (vol. 65) treated Southeast Asia and India in the same category but after 1957 the journal treated Southeast Asia as an independent category (*Shigaku Zasshi* 66, no. 5).

The Japanese perception of Southeast Asia at the time was still problematical with regard to today's perspective. As can be seen from the aforementioned *Toyo shiryo shusei*, Thailand was referred to as Siam, whilst Vietnam and Indochina were regarded as separate entities, and Indonesia and the Philippines were not included at all. It is not unreasonable to assert that the modern conceptualization of Southeast Asia came about in 1963 when Kyoto University founded its Center for Southeast Asian Studies and the *Nampo shi kenkyu kai* [Study Group of *nanpo* History] was reorganized the following year to form the Preparatory Committee for the Japan Society for Southeast Asian History. These developments will be discussed in more detail later.

PROCESS OF RESEARCH ON SOUTHEAST ASIAN HISTORY

In addition to Heine-Geldern's research, the emergence of the term Southeast Asia during the Second World War helped people understand Southeast Asia as a unified concept and region. Consequently, for the first time in the world, the University of London opened a course on "Southeast Asian History" in 1949. The lecturer in charge was Professor D.G.E. Hall, a former Professor of Burmese History at Rangoon University. He concurrently served as the Chairman of the Department of Southeast Asian Languages and Cultural Studies at the School of Oriental and African Studies (SOAS), and worked relentlessly to improve educational programmes related to Southeast Asia and he trained the future generation of Southeast Asian history scholars.

At the same time, Professor Hall wrote *A History of South-East Asia* in 1955. This book can be seen as the world's first standard text for Southeast Asian history and opened a whole new dimension for researchers in this field of study. A qualifying point that must be made is that the Philippines was excluded in the first edition of the book but was later incorporated in the revised version published in 1964.

Japanese research on Southeast Asia first started with *tozai koshoshi* (*History of East-West interactions*), which was initially part of the Japanese studies of East Asian History. It would not be an overstatement to say that Japanese scholars developed their interests in Southeast Asia mostly through their Chinese history research since they were used to dealing with the historical materials written in classical Chinese.[6] Of course, this was not always the case. Hikida Toshiaki, an instructor at the Japanese Military Academy, had already written the *History of Annam* and *Gazetteers of Cambodia* in 1881. Furthermore, in 1884, he reprinted the *Dai Viet su ky toan thu* [Complete History of Dai Viet] which became the basic historical material for studying pre-modern Vietnamese history. These works were generated by a Japanese pioneer who was alarmed by the French invasion of Vietnam. Similarly, in 1884, Kishida Ginko reprinted the *An Nam chi luoc* [An Nam Gazetteer] which described Vietnam's history, civilization, and institutions up until the Mongol invasion of 1285. The book was written by Le Tac who had surrendered to the Mongols. This book is also an important historical resource for those interested in pre-modern Vietnamese history (Katakura 1977, pp. 12–13).

In 1896, several years after the above publications, Takaku Junjiro, who studied at Oxford University, annotated and translated *Nan hai ji gui nei fa chuan* [南海寄歸內法傳]. The original text was written by a seventh-century Tang dynasty monk, Yi Jing, who visited India and maritime Southeast Asia. The English title of the book is *A Record of the Buddhist Religion as Practiced in India and the Malay Archipelago (A.D. 671–695)* (1896). Takakusu's work deservedly received critical acclaim from academia. While there are certain parts of the book which require revision, there is not much disagreement that this seminal work helped later scholars understand Yi Jing's original text (Ishida 1945, pp. 125–26). From this aspect, Takakusu's translated and annotated text can be seen as the first global contribution by a Japanese scholar to the study of Southeast Asian history.

It was only at the start of the twentieth century that Japanese scholars started to show serious interest in Southeast Asia and this was mainly due to historical materials written in classical Chinese. Even Fujita Toyohachi (1869–1929), an eminent scholar who made a distinguished contribution to early research on East-West interactions, was initially interested in Chinese history, philosophy, and literature, but later switched his focus to East-West interactions during the Taisho period (1912–1925). He is recognized as the pioneer in what was referred to in pre-Second Word War Japan as *nankaishi · nanyoshi · namposhi* or what is now referred to as Southeast Asian history. His posthumously published *Tozai koshoshi no kenkyu · nankai hen* [A Study on the History of East-West Interactions: South Seas] is considered to be his *magnum opus*.[7] Kuwabara Jitsuzo (1870–1931) also wrote a book titled *Hoiyuko no jiseki* [Traces of Pu Shou Geng] which is considered to be a masterpiece in the history of East-West interactions.

Recognizing his significant contribution to academia, the Taipei Imperial University invited Fujita Toyohachi to leave his former position at Tokyo Imperial University and take up a new position as the Dean of the College of Letters and Politics at Taipei Imperial University in 1928. Taipei Imperial University became the first Japanese university to establish a Department of *Nanyo* History. According to the Taiwan Governor at the time, Taipei Imperial University established the College of Letters and Politics in order to disseminate Imperial Japan's culture into the South Seas regions (Oyanagi 1933, pp. 13–14) and the Department of *Nanyo* History was a crucial link in implementing this plan. Iwao Seichi and Yanai Kenji were appointed full-time lecturers in the Department of *Nanyo* History; Kuwata Rokuro of the Department of East Asian History and Obata Jun of the Department of National History also took part in research on Southeast Asian relations. Such developments made Taipei the early nexus of Japanese research on Southeast Asian history (Yamamoto 1991, p. 133).

Fujita Toyohachi passed away a year after he assumed the post but his successor, Iwao Seiichi, kept the post for eighteen years from 1929 to 1946. After his tenure, Iwao returned to his home country and taught Japan-Europe relations in the pre-modern era for fifteen years (until 1961). One of his academic advantages was his proficiency in Dutch. His language proficiency enabled him simultaneously to teach the language to his students and utilize seventeenth-century historical data retrieved from the Dutch East India Company [VOC] records. However, as his major work, *Nanyo nihon machi no kenkyu* [A Study on a Japanese Town in Nanyo] demonstrates, Seiichi was more interested in seventeenth-century Japanese residents in Indonesia rather than in Indonesian history itself (Nagazumi 1988, p. 217).

In a separate development, scholars such as Yamamoto Tatsuro at Tokyo Imperial University, Sugimoto Naojiro at Hiroshima University of Education and Matsumoto Nobuhiro at Keio Gijuku University actively engaged in *nanyo* research in Japan. Notably, among the students who enrolled in Yamamoto Tasturo's History of Indochina class in 1940–1941, there were those with shared interests in Southeast Asian and Indian history and culture and they started to hold meetings which were eventually organized into a study group in 1942. After several name changes, the group settled on calling itself *Nanposhi kenkyukai* [The Study Group of *Nanpo* History] and started to hold regular meetings (Shiratori 1991, p. 136).

Even before the above developments, societal and governmental interest in Asia gained momentum in Japan with the Sino-Japanese War and the Pacific War. As a result, organizations such as *Toa kenkyujo* [Centre for East Asian Studies], *Mantetsu toa keizai chosa kyoku* [Research Department of East Asian Economy in Manchurian Railroad Co.] and *Taiheiyo mondai chosa kai* [Research Center for Pacific Affairs] started to execute systematic activities. Other groups such as *toa minzoku chosa shitsu* [Research Section of East Asian People] of *Teikoku gakushiin* [Imperial Academy of Japan] (today's Japanese Academy of Arts and Sciences), *minami ajia kenkyujo* [Centre for Southern Asian Studies] and *indoshina kenkyu kai* [Study Group of Indochina] established close relations with research on Southeast Asian history. While these groups engaged in active research, they conducted much flawed research since their work was undertaken during the war and suffered from ideological and other distortions. This flawed research was discontinued after Japan's defeat (Yamamoto 1991, pp. 133–34).

In the ensuing post-war chaos, The Study Group of *Nampo* History discontinued its activities for a brief while but quickly resumed during 1949 to 1954 at Yamamoto's office for Asian history research at Tokyo University where the members held academic discussions. As a preparatory step towards resuming full scale research activities, the group applied for a research grant from the *Monbu-kagakushō* [Ministry of Education, Culture, Sports, Science and Technology] and eventually published the *Nihon kokunai shuyo toshokan shozo, obun tounan ajia bunken sogo mokuroku — shakai kagaku • jinbun kagaku hen* [A List of Publications on Southeast Asia in Western Languages at Major Japanese Libraries: Social Sciences and Humanities] in 1955 and *Nihon kokunai shuyo toshokan shozo, obun indo kankei bunken sogo mokuroku* [A List of Publications on India in Western languages at Major Japanese Libraries] in 1956. Furthermore, the group, after selecting materials related to Southeast Asian history from "the biography of Southwest barbarians" and "the biography of Southern barbarians" in the *Twenty-Five Histories*, edited them in chronological order and published the *nampo shokoku kankei kanbun shiryoshu hen dai ikki dai ikkan* [A Collection of Historical Materials in Classical Chinese on Southern Countries, vol. 1, no. 1] with Yamamoto Tasturo as the chief editor in 1957. The following year, the group also published the *Nampo shokoku kankei kanbun shiryoshu hen dai niki dai nikan* [A Collection of Historical Materials in Classical Chinese on Southern Countries, vol. 2, no. 2] (Shiratori 1991, pp. 137–39).

In the meantime the lectures on *nampo* history, which were discontinued after the end of the Second World War, were reoffered at Tokyo University's Faculty of Literature in 1957. Around the same time, The Study Group of *Nampo* History developed into a nationwide organization. It became something akin to an academic society and felt the need for its own academic journal. Thus, the organization published the first volume of *Namposhi kenkyu* [Journal of nampo History] in June 1959, followed by the second volume in 1960 and the third volume in 1963 (Yamamoto 1971, p. 5; Shiratori 1991, p. 139).

Another notable development occurred in *Shigaku Zasshi*, a journal which includes a "Retrospect" and "Prospect volume" of historical research in every May issue of its monthly publication. Specifically, starting from its May issue of 1957 [vol. 66, no. 5], the journal separated the "Southeast Asia" category from what was previously lumped into the "Southeast Asia · India' category".[8] Despite such developments, it seems that research on Southeast Asian history did not gain full momentum at this point. As Nagazumi Akira points out in the "Retrospect" and "Prospect" included in the May volume of 1959, incommensurate to the high level of public interest in Southeast Asia, research on the region did not yield much fruit and the relative lack of full scale research was regretful (Nagazumi 1959, pp. 149–50).

It seems safe to say that Japanese studies of Southeast Asian history gained momentum in the mid-1960s when *Tonan ajia kenkyu senta* [Kyoto University's Center for Southeast Asian Studies] was established and when The Study Group of *Nampo* History was transformed into the Japan Society for Southeast Asian History. President Hirasawa Ko's efforts played a crucial role in establishing Kyoto University's Center for Southeast Asian Studies. Hirasawa first started to draw the blueprints of a general research centre on Southeast Asia in 1958 and, in June 1959 he founded the *tonan ajia kenkyukai* [A Study Group of Southeast Asia] through which he held monthly meetings and presentations. In the following year, with promise of support from the Ford Foundation, the plan to establish a research centre progressed rapidly. Finally, in January 1963, these efforts bore fruit and the Center for Southeast Asian Studies came into being.[9] However, as economics professors from the Marxist school of thought refused to participate in the new research institute, the researchers became more focused on fieldwork in such subjects as botany, public sanitation, soil science and rice cultivation, despite having set the main research agenda of the first five years as "The Modernization of Southeast Asia" (Suehiro 1997, p. 59).[10]

By this time, membership in The Study Group of *Nampo* History increased even further to the point where weekly meetings were separated into a Southeast Asia Group and an India Group. In 1964, the group reached a consensus on the need for an organization by the name of the "Society for Southeast Asian History". A preparatory committee was formed and the first volume of *Tonan ajiashi kenkyu kai kaiho* (*Newsletter of The Study Group of Southeast Asian History*) was published. The *Tonan ajiashi kenkyu kai kaiho* continued to be published until volume 5 of 1966 and was renamed as *Tonan ajiashi gakkai kaiho* [*Newsletter of the Japan Society for Southeast Asian History*] following the founding of *Tonan ajia shigakkai* [Japan Society for Southeast Asian History] in November 1966 (Shiratori 1991, p. 140). It is reasonable to conclude that the underlying concept of Southeast Asian history became firmly established at this point. The Japan Society for Southeast Asian History[11] started publishing the *Tonan ajia — rekishi to bunka* [Southeast Asia: History and Culture], the official academic journal of the group, in October 1971 which continues to this day.

The ten volumes of *Iwanami koza tonan ajiashi* [Iwanami Lectures on Southeast Asian History, 2001–2003], which Yamamoto Tatsuro compiled and to which 140 members of the Japan Society for Southeast Asian History contributed, are both the grand summation and a demonstration of world class quality evident in studies of Southeast Asian History in Japan. As an end note, one very important aspect to note at this juncture in regard to Japan's Southeast Asian History research is that it generally demonstrates a special interest in the issues related to the Japanese occupation of Southeast Asia during the Pacific War. This topic will be thoroughly analysed in the latter part of this chapter.

QUANTITATIVE ANALYSIS OF RECENT JAPANESE RESEARCH ON SOUTHEAST ASIAN HISTORY

In order to analyse the trends in research on Southeast Asian History in Japan, one must first look at the quantity of books and academic papers published. As mentioned in the introduction, I relied on the "A List of Publications on Southeast Asia", included in *Tonan ajia — rekishi to bunka*, as the primary resource. Among the many publications listed, I selected the literatures that I assess to be related to research on Southeast Asian history. The recent research trend in Japan is such that the traditional academic boundaries have been eroded and various researches are simply being categorized under "Southeast Asian Studies" (Shiraishi 2003, p. 144). Consequently, the assessment of whether or not a particular piece of research can be classified under the discipline of history is strictly based on my subjective judgment. Naturally, the numbers may vary depending on the viewpoint but I still believe that my analysis will help readers grasp the general trend in Japan's research in Southeast Asian history. Please note that I have not included works by non-Japanese scholars including the Japanese translated versions of their research and their book reviews.

As illustrated in Tables 3.1, 3.2, 3.3 and 3.4, I have treated books and academic papers separately as these have different characteristics. I have further classified the books and academic papers according to their respective national focus and historical time period. Works that do not focus on any particular country (those that deal with the entire region or more than two countries) have been included in the Southeast Asia category. Also, I have divided the historical time period into four categories: pre-1800, 1800–1945, post-1945 and "general". The "general" category includes works that do not deal with a specific time period or historical era. I would also like to add that I have included works on international politics, diplomacy and economics in the post-1945 era when I thought that they have relevance to the discussion.

Table 3.1 shows the number of books on Southeast Asia published in Japan between 1990 and 1999 by category. Figure 3.1 illustrates the proportion of books according to the historical time period and Figure 3.2 illustrates the proportion by national focus.

As we can see from the table and two figures, books that deal with either Southeast Asia as a whole or with more than two countries in Southeast Asia, make up the largest share followed by books related specifically to Indonesia. Unexpectedly, the third largest number of published books focuses on Cambodia. While this phenomenon will be analysed later, it is mainly because of the high level of Japanese interest in the temple complex at Angkor.

By time period, post-Second World War books take up the largest share. This is because, as mentioned before, I have included a certain number of works that deal with the politics, diplomacy and economics of this era. Next in line comes the "general" category which includes books that do not deal with any particular time period. The proportion of books dealing with 1800–1945 contains a similar share. The reason why works on 1800–1945 account for a sizeable share is deeply related to Japanese interest in colonial history and the Japanese occupation of the region during the Second World War. In fact, one of the distinctive characteristics of research on Southeast Asian history in Japan is its deep involvement with issues related to the Japanese occupation.

Table 3.1
Books 1990–99

	General	pre-1800	1800–1945	post-1945	Total
Southeast Asia	38	5	16	24	83
East Timor	0	0	0	5	5
Laos	1	0	0	0	1
Malaysia	0	0	3	6	9
Myanmar	1	0	3	2	6
Vietnam	4	4	7	12	27
Brunei	0	1	0	0	1
Singapore	1	0	0	1	2
Indonesia	6	4	16	12	38
Cambodia	6	11	0	14	31
Thailand	2	0	5	5	12
Philippines	2	0	7	6	15
Total	61	25	57	87	230

Figure 3.1
Portion of Books by Historical Time Period, 1990–99

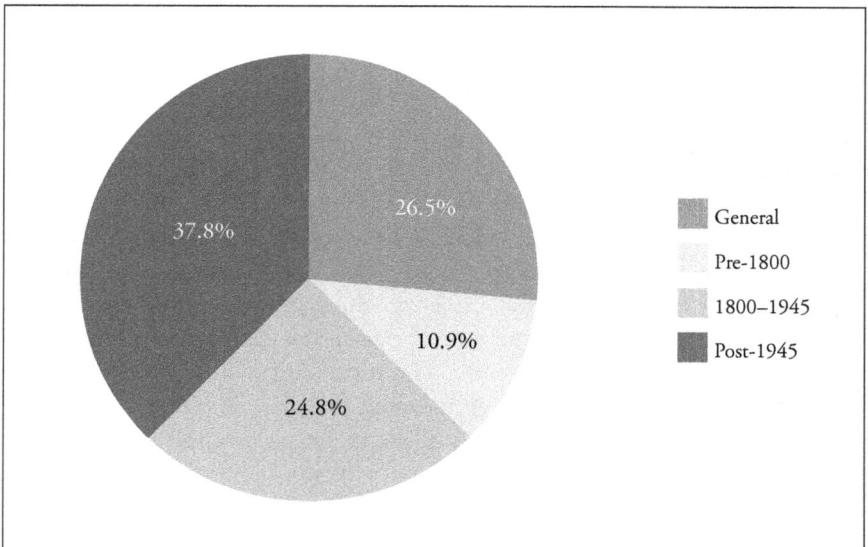

Table 3.2
Academic Papers 1990–99

	General	pre-1800	1800–1945	post-1945	Total
Southeast Asia	34	48	65	67	214
East Timor	0	0	0	5	5
Laos	1	1	3	3	8
Malaysia	0	3	23	44	70
Myanmar	2	28	22	18	70
Vietnam	7	41	43	53	144
Brunei	0	0	0	1	1
Singapore	1	0	6	20	27
Indonesia	11	82	99	63	255
Cambodia	3	20	3	15	41
Thailand	10	23	39	33	105
Philippines	2	10	51	44	107
Total	71	256	354	366	1047

Figure 3.2
Portion of Books by National Focus, 1990–99

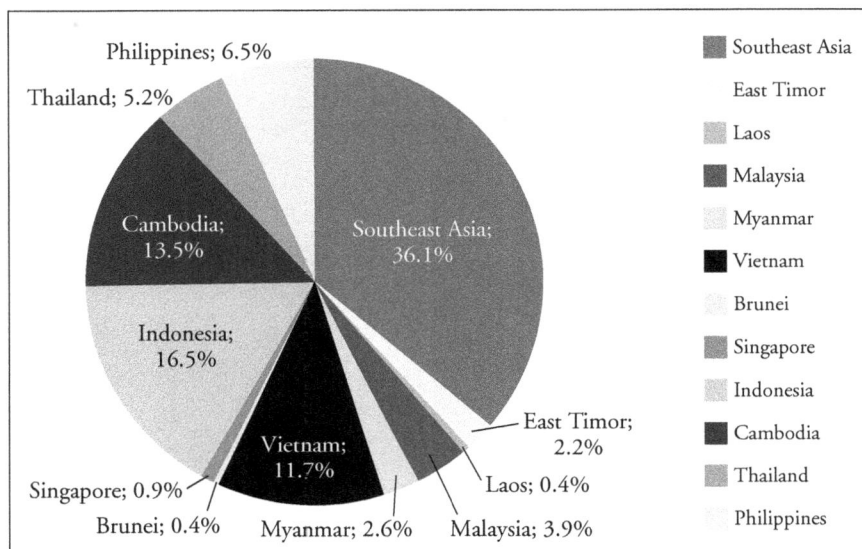

Philippines; 6.5%
Thailand; 5.2%
Cambodia; 13.5%
Indonesia; 16.5%
Singapore; 0.9%
Brunei; 0.4%
Myanmar; 2.6%
Malaysia; 3.9%
Laos; 0.4%
East Timor; 2.2%
Vietnam; 11.7%
Southeast Asia; 36.1%

Southeast Asia
East Timor
Laos
Malaysia
Myanmar
Vietnam
Brunei
Singapore
Indonesia
Cambodia
Thailand
Philippines

As in Table 3.1, Table 3.2 classifies academic papers written from 1990 to 1999 according to their respective categories. Academic papers related to Indonesia take up the largest share as Indonesian-history scholars are most numerous.[12] Next come papers in the Southeast Asia "general" category, which include those that deal with the inter-regional relationships between or among two or three countries. The reason why Vietnam-related papers account for the third largest group is because access to Vietnam-related information has become easier after Hanoi instituted the *doi moi* (renovation) policy which opened the country to the world in 1986. Lastly, the abundance of academic papers related to 1800–1945 is due to the 50th anniversary of the end of the war which heightened Japanese interest in this time period.

Table 3.3 classifies the books published from 2000 to 2007 according to their national and time-period focus. Figure 3.3 categorizes the books according to their historical time period and Figure 3.4 illustrates the percentage of books by respective country.

As indicated in Figure 3.4, books dealing with the entire region or more than two countries take up the largest share. Next, in descending order, are books on Indonesia, Cambodia and Vietnam. In terms of historical period,

Table 3.3

Books 2000–07

	General	pre-1800	1800–1945	post-1945	Total
Southeast Asia	14	11	41	11	77
East Timor	0	0	1	6	7
Laos	0	0	0	0	0
Malaysia	1	1	4	7	13
Myanmar	0	3	2	0	5
Vietnam	2	4	3	7	16
Brunei	0	0	0	0	0
Singapore	0	0	1	2	3
Indonesia	2	2	8	14	26
Cambodia	1	11	1	10	23
Thailand	1	1	5	3	10
Philippines	2	1	5	3	11
Total	23	34	71	63	191

Figure 3.3
Portion of Books by Historical Time Period, 2000–07

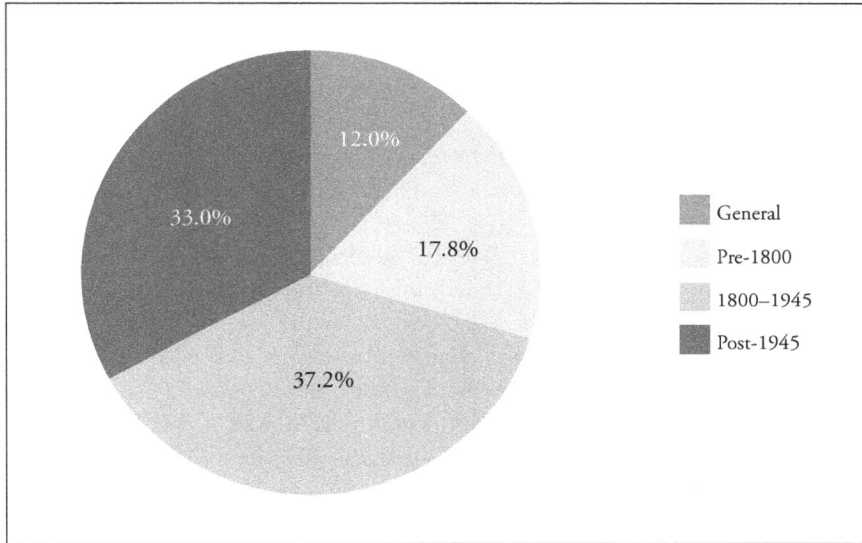

- 12.0% General
- 17.8% Pre-1800
- 37.2% 1800–1945
- 33.0% Post-1945

Figure 3.4
Portion of Books by National Focus, 2000–07

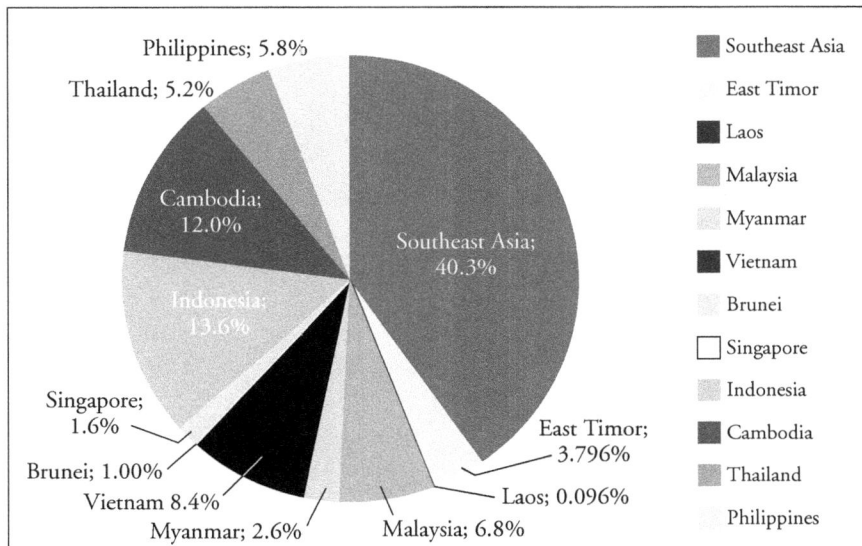

- Philippines; 5.8%
- Thailand; 5.2%
- Cambodia; 12.0%
- Indonesia; 13.6%
- Singapore; 1.6%
- Brunei; 1.00%
- Vietnam 8.4%
- Myanmar; 2.6%
- Malaysia; 6.8%
- Laos; 0.096%
- East Timor; 3.796%
- Southeast Asia; 40.3%

Legend:
- Southeast Asia
- East Timor
- Laos
- Malaysia
- Myanmar
- Vietnam
- Brunei
- Singapore
- Indonesia
- Cambodia
- Thailand
- Philippines

Figure 3.3 shows that the period 1800–1945 contains the bulk of the
books, followed by post-1945.

Comparing the absolute number of books published in the 1990s
(1990–99) to those published in the 2000s (2000–07), one can observe
that the former number is slightly higher. This is because of the simple
arithmetic fact that the former time period incorporates two more years
than the latter. In terms of national focus, the proportion remains the
same (in descending order: Indonesia, Cambodia, Vietnam), but the
number of books on Indonesia and Vietnam have slightly declined
in the 2000s.

Comparing 1990–99 and 2000–07 in terms of historical time periods,
the former time period shows that books dealing with the post-1945 era
take up the largest share, followed by books in the "general" category. The
latter time period shows a slight change in ranking as books dealing with
the 1800–1945 period take up the highest share, followed by books on
the post-1945 era. The reason why books related to 1800–1945 account
for the largest share in the 2000s is because of the publication of the
twenty-two volume, *Nampogun gunsei sokanbu chosabu marai gunsei kanbu
chosabu hokokusho* [Reports by the Research Department of the Malay

Table 3.4
Academic Papers 2000–07

	General	pre-1800	1800–1945	post-1945	Total
Southeast Asia	8	38	30	27	103
East Timor	0	0	0	10	10
Laos	0	3	1	5	9
Malaysia	3	5	20	38	66
Myanmar	3	19	25	24	71
Vietnam	4	49	38	39	130
Brunei	0	0	0	1	1
Singapore	0	0	8	10	18
Indonesia	6	36	56	71	169
Cambodia	3	33	8	17	61
Thailand	9	17	34	34	94
Philippines	4	10	41	30	85
Total	40	210	261	306	817

Military Government], written during the Second World War (Akashi 2007), and the ten volume *Daitoa ho chitsujyo · nihon teikoku hosei kankei shiryo* (nampo gunsei kankei shiryo) [Materials on the Legal Order of Great East Asia and the Legal System of Imperial Japan] (Asano 2007). Another notable point is the relative increase in books that deal with pre-1800 history.

As with Table 3.2, Table 3.4 classifies academic papers published from 2000 to 2007 according to their respective national and historical time period focus. By national focus, Indonesia represents the largest number of papers, followed by Vietnam, and then the "general" category. Unlike the 1990s, the results from the 2000s show that Vietnam-related academic papers come in second place. This is probably because all the Vietnam-related historical materials that have been collected after the *doi moi* of 1986 started to bear fruit during this time period in the form of academic papers. In terms of historical time period, the post-1945 period takes up a large share. This is quite different from 1990–99 and this seems to be intrinsically related to the significant Japanese interest in Southeast Asia's present.

Table 3.5
Books 1990–99
(1800–1945 related)

	General	Japanese Relations	Total
Southeast Asia	1	15	16
East Timor	0	0	0
Laos	0	0	0
Malaysia	0	3	3
Myanmar	3	0	3
Vietnam	6	1	7
Brunei	0	0	0
Singapore	0	0	0
Indonesia	2	14	16
Cambodia	0	0	0
Thailand	4	1	5
Philippines	1	6	7
Total	17	40	57

Table 3.6
Academic Papers 1990–99
(1800–1945 related)

	General	Japanese Relations	Total
Southeast Asia	22	43	65
East Timor	0	0	0
Laos	3	0	3
Malaysia	12	11	23
Myanmar	16	6	22
Vietnam	40	3	43
Brunei	0	0	0
Singapore	5	1	6
Indonesia	74	25	99
Cambodia	3	0	3
Thailand	33	6	39
Philippines	30	21	51
Total	238	116	354

Table 3.7
Books 2000–07
(1800–1945 related)

	General	Japanese Relations	Total
Southeast Asia	5	36	41
East Timor	0	1	1
Laos	0	0	0
Malaysia	3	1	4
Myanmar	0	2	2
Vietnam	3	0	3
Brunei	0	0	0
Singapore	0	1	1
Indonesia	2	6	8
Cambodia	1	0	1
Thailand	4	1	5
Philippines	2	3	5
Total	20	51	71

Table 3.8

Academic Papers 2000–07

(1800–1945 related)

	General	Japanese Relations	Total
Southeast Asia	22	8	30
East Timor	0	0	0
Laos	1	0	1
Malaysia	11	9	20
Myanmar	15	10	25
Vietnam	37	1	38
Brunei	0	0	0
Singapore	7	1	8
Indonesia	40	16	56
Cambodia	8	0	8
Thailand	26	8	34
Philippines	28	13	41
Total	195	66	261

CONTENT ANALYSIS OF RECENT RESEARCH ON SOUTHEAST ASIAN HISTORY

As mentioned in the introduction, research on the Japanese contribution to Southeast Asian history is not an easy task due to the diversity and complexity of the natural environment, ethnic groups, and culture. Just looking at the cultural aspect, various distinct cultures existed during prehistoric times (Coedès 1968, pp. 8–9).[13] From proto-historic times the region was influenced by Chinese, Indian, and Islamic cultures. Furthermore, one cannot disregard the influence of Western powers which colonized the region in modern times.

Yamamoto Tatsuro asserts that research on Southeast Asian history requires an understanding of all the diverse cultures that have influenced the area. Additionally, historical materials utilized in studies of Southeast Asian history are written in various languages including Chinese, Sanskrit, and various local and Western languages. Yamamoto states that a broad understanding of English, French, Dutch, Japanese, and local languages is a prerequisite for digesting recent research accomplishments. Another factor which makes research in this field even more difficult is the dearth of historical materials. This makes fieldwork an essential component of most research in Southeast Asian history, especially when it comes to uncovering pre-historic cultures, because researchers must rely on materials and findings from other disciplines such as linguistics, historical anthropology, and archaeology. Therefore, Yamamoto proposes that future research on Southeast Asian history requires a broad and global perspective, intimate knowledge in various languages within the relevant specialized fields, and willingness to delve deeply into the historical facts (Yamamoto 1992, pp. 304–6). Yamamoto assesses Nagazumi Akira (1929–87) to be an exemplary scholar who possessed all of the above qualities. Nagazumi Akira received his Ph.D. from Cornell University in 1967 through his research on Indonesian nationalism. Afterwards, he returned to his homeland to take up a professorship at Tokyo University where he made great contributions to Japan's research on Indonesian history and Southeast Asian historical research as a whole.[14]

As Yamamoto Tatsuro played a leading role in Japan's post-war research on Southeast Asian history, his words are very important in terms of understanding the trends in research. The *Tonan ajia sekai no rekishiteki iso* [The Historical Phase of the Southeast Asian World], in which Yamamoto Tatsuro's piece was included, was actually written to commemorate Nagazumi Akira's accomplishments, and the articles in it were in line with the assertion of Yamamoto Tatsuro. The book comprises fourteen academic papers that deal with Southeast Asian history from the ancient to the nineteenth-century colonial period and finally recent history when modern nation-states emerged in the region. A notable characteristic of the book is that it re-examines Southeast Asian history primarily based on literature written in classical Chinese or Western languages, utilizing fieldwork and empirical analysis of local (Southeast Asian) historical materials. Another distinct aspect is that, instead of seeing Southeast Asia as a unique and separate entity, the book incorporates and establishes Southeast Asia within the larger framework of world history.

In fact, even without relying on Yamamoto Tatsuro's assessment, one can see that Japanese scholars of Southeast Asian history relentlessly sought ways to move further ahead. For example, in June 1987 the aforementioned Japan Society for Southeast Asian History held an academic symposium under the title "Past Accomplishments and the Way Forward for Research on Southeast Asian History in Japan". This symposium is the product of determined efforts by researchers to advance their knowledge and understanding and their discipline. Another example is the twentieth anniversary of the foundation of the "Japan Society for Southeast Asian History" in

1986. From 31 May to 1 June, under the common theme of *"tonan ajia kenkyu no kadai to tenbo"* [Task and Prospect of Southeast Asian Studies], discussions and presentations related to archaeology, cultural anthropology, economics, and area studies, were held for two days. This event also showed the intention to promote interdisciplinary cooperation to further advance research on Southeast Asian History (Tsuchiya 1987, pp. 146–54).

The synthesis of all these interdisciplinary research efforts are included in *Koza tonan ajia gaku* [Lectures in Southeast Asian Studies] (11 vols.), planned and edited by Yano Toru. From its first edition in 1990 to the special edition in 1992,[15] these lectures have dealt with various disciplines and produced independent publications on various subject matter including methodology, nature, society, history, culture, ideology, politics, economics, international relations, and Japanese relations. These eleven volumes are regarded as a landmark achievement in Japan's Southeast Asian history research with 85 scholars authoring 144 academic papers (Tominaga 1993, p. 280).

Of the eleven volumes, the fourth one is entitled *Tonan ajia no rekishi* [A History of Southeast Asia], which was edited by Ishii Yoneo. This book does not assume the format of an introductory text to each time period or area. Rather it takes the form of each author presenting a scholarly inquiry based on his or her respective research interest. Furthermore, the authors include not only historians but also ecologists, archaeologists, economists, and anthropologists. The other volumes of the lectures also deal with historical issues. For example, *Tonan ajia no shiso* [Thought of Southeast Asia] deals with the history of ideas, *Tonan ajia no shakai* [Southeast Asian Society] discusses the formation of urban space or immigrant societies and *Tonan ajia no kokusai kankei* [International Relations of Southeast Asia] focuses on modern history. One advantage of this book is that it connects Southeast Asian history to the larger framework of world history through comparative studies with other areas. At the same time, the book conveys solid research foundations such as meticulous literature research and field investigation (Shimao 1992, pp. 93–100).

Other notable achievements of the 1990s are the publication of Ishii Yoneo and Sakurai Yumio, *Tonan ajiashi* I, *tairikubu* [Southeast Asian History, vol. 1, Mainland] (1999), and Ikehata Setsuho's edited volume *Tonan ajiashi* II, *toshobu* [Southeast Asian History, vol. 2, Islands] (1999). Prior to the publication of the above works, Nagazumi Akira's *Ajia no tatokai* [Asian Archipelago] (1977) and Ishii Yoneo's *Indoshina bunmei no sekai* [The World of Indochinese Civilisation] (1977) were two works that provided a general overview of Southeast Asian history. Both were published in 1977 and the former dealt with the maritime section of Southeast Asia while the latter discussed the mainland section of Southeast Asia. Therefore, the two publications of the 1990s update the two general history texts written in 1977.

Even without considering Yamamoto Tatsuro's comments, it is common knowledge that the process of acquiring a comprehensive understanding of Southeast Asian history is a very difficult one. Japanese academics have felt the need for a general text on Southeast Asian history but were hesitant to undertake this difficult task. The fact that a general text was finally published in the late 1990s is evidence of how Japanese academics managed to accumulate sufficient research materials and findings by then. Indeed, volume one (mainland) is authored by twenty-four scholars (although it must be noted that half of the content was authored by the two editors, Ishii Yoneo and Sakurai Yumio). Furthermore, volume one deals with formerly omitted topics such as "post-Angkor" history, the history of "Northern Thailand" and the history of the Shan people of Myanmar. These accomplishments illustrate the great strides made by Japanese academics over the years. Volume two lists eleven works (although the actual writers were five). The text first illustrates the process through which the pre-modern network of maritime trade, based on the Malacca Straits and Java, led to the establishment of burgeoning port-city states. The text continues to show how, starting from the end of the nineteenth century, the region became increasingly shaped by the progression of land-based rule which led to the early form of the nation-states we see today.

By the early 2000s, however, a vastly superior text entitled *Iwanami koza tonan ajiashi* [Iwanami Lectures on Southeast Asian History] (10 vols.) was published. *Tonan ajia: rekishi to bunka* (vol. 22, 2003, pp. 64–132) assessed the new text to be a seminal achievement in the development of research on Southeast Asian history in Japan and published a special edition comprising various reviews. The ten volumes are composed of 146 works by 86 scholars and this further affirms the assessment that the text is a momentous achievement for research on Southeast Asian history in Japan.

Quoting the editorial board, Japanese academia initially adopted the American "area studies" format, the French Annals School tradition, and research methodologies from social science and ecology, and fused them with traditional literature research in order to understand the dramatic changes taking place in Southeast Asia. This was initially a difficult process of trial and error, however, and these efforts led to an accumulation of research findings and a new generation of researchers armed with new analytical methods. Hence, the editorial board noted that the up-and-coming researchers might well produce texts that may deviate significantly from the established works and theories (Iwanami koza tonan ajiashi Editorial Board 2001, pp. vi–vii).

Indeed, the format of the first four out of the nine volumes is based on the historical time division by Sakurai Yumio who wrote the introduction in volume one. His classification of periods is very different from what past Western scholars had suggested. For example, Harry Benda designates history until the thirteenth century as the classical period,[16] the fourteenth to sixteenth century as the post-classical period and the seventeenth to nineteenth century as the early colonial period (or the period of Western imperialism) (Benda 1962, pp. 106–38). Another example is Anthony Reid who regards the fifteenth to seventeenth century as the early modern period, because it was during this time in history that developments in Southeast Asia's international trade led to the establishment of a new type of nation-state (Reid 1988).

Sakurai Yumio divides Southeast Asian history into the following four periods: (1) formation of pre-historic period: 1000 BCE–tenth century CE, (2) formation of Southeast Asian World historic period: eleventh century–fourteenth century, (3) formation of commercial historic period: fifteenth century–seventeenth century, and (4) eighteenth century–early nineteenth century (Sakurai 2001, pp. 10–12).[17] The titles of volume one to four are: (1) *Genshi tonan ajia sekai* [Proto-history of the Southeast Asian World], (2) *Tonan ajia kodai kokka no seiritsu to tenkai* [Formation of Ancient Southeast Asian States and their Development], (3) *Tonan ajia kinsei no seiritsu* [Formation of Modern Southeast Asia], and (4) *Tonan ajia kinsei kokkagun no tenkai* [Development of Modern Southeast Asian States].

Volume five, *Tonan ajia sekai no saihen* [Reorganization of the Southeast Asian World], and volume six, *Shokuminchi keizai no hanei to choraku* [Prosperity and Decline of the Colonial Economy] deal with the beginning of colonial rule and the issues of colonial governance. Volume seven, *Shokuminchi teiko undo to nashonarisumu* [Resistance to Colonialism and Nationalism], volume eight, *Kokumin kokka no keisei* [Formation of Nation-states] and volume nine, *Kaihatsu no jidai to mosaku no jidai* [Period of New Development and Attempts], deal with the efforts which were directed toward colonial liberation, the subsequent formation of nation-states and the collective sense of community that was formed through post-colonial economic development policy.

A separate volume titled *Tonan ajiashi kenkyu annai* [Guidebook to the Study of Southeast Asian History] contains an introduction to the recent research texts and an academic paper entitled *Tonan ajiashi kenkyu no kako · genzai · mirai* [A Study of Southeast Asian History: Past, Present and Future]. Additionally, under the category of original sources and archives, the separate volume includes an explanatory note on the characteristics of, and instructions for utilizing the main historical materials.

Aside from these general history texts, notable books in the "general" category from the 1990s include those such as *Historical Phase of the Southeast Asian World,* which compiles various academic papers according to their respective focus period between ancient and modern history. Ikehata Setsuho's edited book *Kawaru tonan ajiashi zo* [The Changing Image of Southeast Asian History] (1994), comprising fifteen academic papers, is also another part of a larger effort to promote a new historical image of Southeast Asia by bringing together a wide range of areas and eras. Conversely, it could be said that the *Iwanami Lectures on Southeast Asian History* materialized through the accumulation of these previous efforts. In the modern history category, books related to themes such as Southeast Asian issues in the post-Vietnam War era (e.g., Mio 1993) and international relations (e.g., Miwa 1994) comprise the mainstream.

A notable feature, as previously mentioned, is that there is a surprising number of Cambodia related books. This reflects the Japanese government's enthusiasm towards the preservation of Angkor Wat (e.g., Nakagawa and Japanese Government's Angkor Remains Relief Team 1995) and the reports (e.g., Ishizawa 1998) by Sophia University's Angkor Wat Research Group. Another reason is closely related to Cambodia's political tragedy after 1975 (e.g., Miyoshi 1994).

Of the post-1945 related academic papers published in the 1990s, many deal with the issue of national integration. As is widely known, Southeast Asian countries are composed of diverse ethnic groups and, furthermore, Indonesia and Malaysia became modern nation-states only after the Second World War. As these countries have a very short history of modern statehood, their efforts to integrate people into the modern nation are a topic of significant interest. These efforts have been made mostly through religion and education (e.g., Takahashi 1995; Nezu 1995). However, countries such as Myanmar, Thailand and the Philippines showed similar interest in national integration. Another theme is military dictatorship and the dangers it poses for democratization in Myanmar and other countries (e.g., Shibata 1996; Kurasawa 1998; Suehiro 1993; Ito 1998). A notable element in the academic papers related to the colonial period is the large number of those that deal with Japanese colonial rule. These will be treated together in the later part of this chapter. While there is a relative dearth of academic papers that deal with pre-1800 history, Japanese scholars demonstrate much interest in the issue of port-city states. In the sixteenth century, prior to the European advance, Southeast Asia's port-cities became major strategic and trade hubs that connected East Asia, India, and Southwest Asia. Based on these port-cities, states such as Srivijaya, Ayuthaya and Palembang emerged. Notable papers on these topics include Fukami Sumio (1994), Ishii Yoneo (1992) and Suzuki Tsuneyuki (1992, 1994).

Next, we should consider the contents of the books and academic papers published between 2000 and 2007. It goes without saying that the most important achievement of the 2000s is the aforementioned *Iwanami Lectures of Southeast Asian History* (10 vols.). Other notable publications include *Tonan ajia no koshi sekai: chiiki shakai no keisei to sekai chitsujo* [Port-city States of Southeast Asia: Formation of Regional Society and the World Order] by Hirosue Masashi (2004) and *Koshi kokka banten to toji boeki* [A Port-city State of Bantam and the Ceramics Trade] by Sakai Takashi (2002). In a review of Masashi's book, Ikuta Shigeru assessed the work to be a ground-breaking accomplishment which attempted to provide a general understanding of maritime Southeast Asia (Ikuta 2004, pp. 136–37). The latter work is an accomplishment based on the rigorous investigations of the Bantam Port remains and is part of an effort to reconstruct a complete picture of Southeast Asia's maritime ceramic trade.

Another point is that, compared to the 1990s, the 2000s are marked by a relative increase in the number of books on pre-1800 history. The reason behind this difference seems to be the publication of the first four volumes of the *Iwanami Lectures on Southeast Asian History* and *Tonan ajia no kenkoku shinwa* [Birth-myths in Southeast Asia] by Hirosue Masashi (2003).

Reviewing the academic papers published between 2000 and 2007, one can observe that, as in the 1990s, those that dealt with post-1945 history take up the largest share. The major part of the content discusses the issue of national integration through religion or education. A notable paper on the issue of nation and religion is Torii Takashi's edited book *Mahatiru seikenka no mareshia* [Malaysia under the Mahathir Regime] (2007) which deals with the issues of development policies and the influence of Islam during the Mahathir administration (1981–2003). As Islam is of considerable national and societal importance in Malaysia and Indonesia, the issue is being treated from multiple perspectives. For example, Miichi Ken (2003) delves into the relationship between Indonesia's Islamism and modernization. Democratization is also another significant focus and Kurasawa Aiko's work on post-Suharto Indonesia (2006a) and Nemoto Kei's paper on Aung San Suu Kyi's ideology (2001) demonstrates this interest. On the relationship between national integration and education, Murata Yokuo (2007) provides a detailed discussion of Thailand's education system and how Buddhism and language played a role in assimilating ethnic minorities.

Analysis on ethnic relations and the overseas Chinese is also one of the important research agendas in Japan. This is only natural since the Chinese have played a dominant role in the region's economy since the nineteenth century. On this topic, one notable research accomplishment of the 2000s is Tanaka Kyoko's *Kokka to imin: tonan ajia kajin sekai no henyo* [State and Immigration: Changing Ethnic Chinese Groups in Southeast Asia] (2002). This book examines the acculturation process of ethnic Chinese groups in British Malaya and Singapore from their initial mass immigration in the nineteenth century to the present. At the same time, with the new interest in overseas and ethnic Chinese groups in both Southeast Asia and China (mostly due to the recent emergence of China-related issues and elements in Southeast Asia), the Center for Southeast Asian Studies at Kyoto University hosted a seminar in September 2005 and published the results as a special edition in *Tonan ajia kenkyu* (vol. 43, no. 4). The intention was to look back at the previous research accomplishments and establish a new research direction. The seminar materialized because of the increasingly blurred conceptual boundaries of Southeast Asia as a region (Koizumi 2006, pp. 327–28). Sugaya Nariko noted that it is important to deploy multiple perspectives on overseas and ethnic Chinese related research, depending on the locations in which different overseas and ethnic Chinese groups are rooted (Sugaya 2006, pp. 374–96).

As was the case in the 1990s, the main research interest regarding the pre-modern era has concentrated on issues related to trade and port-cities. The importance of Hirose Masashi's and Sakai Takashi's works has already been mentioned. In terms of academic papers, Fukami Sumio's *Gendai no marakka kaikyo* [Malacca Straits during the Yuan Dynasty] (2004) is a notable work. Based on historical materials from the thirteenth to fourteenth century, this chapter shows that port-cities of the Malacca Straits went through a transition period during which they transformed from a piratical, entrepôt-trading city state to a convenience-providing port-city state.

Lastly, the research area in which Japanese academia shows the greatest interest is Japan-Southeast Asia relations, especially relations during the Second World War. As is widely known, during the Pacific War the Japanese occupied a major part of the region with the exception of Thailand, and thus a high level of enthusiasm on this topic can be seen as a natural outcome. The "Japanese Relations" category of Tables 3.5, 3.6, 3.7, and 3.8 mostly refer to works related to Japanese colonial rule in the region. The numbers clearly demonstrate the intensity of interest which Japanese scholars have on this topic. The reason why I included these tables is succinctly to demonstrate the high level of importance Japanese scholars place on the topic of Japan-Southeast Asia relations. Around 70 per cent of the books are related to Japanese relations while 30 per cent of academic papers are related to Japan.

After the Second World War, North American scholars were the first to initiate research on Japanese colonial rule while Japanese scholars started actively participating in the 1980s (Kurasawa 1996, pp. 191–92).[18] Because 1995 marked the 50th anniversary of the end of the Pacific War, the 1990s saw relatively more academic papers on the topic than even during the 2000s. The reason why many books on the topic were published in the 2000s was because of the source book authored by Akashi Yoji (2007) and Asano Toyomi (2007).

In the meantime, in order to commemorate the 50th anniversary of the end of the Pacific War by comprehensively synthesizing the research on Japan's colonial rule in Southeast Asia, a symposium under the theme of *tonan ajiashi no nakano nihon senryo* [Japanese Occupation in the History of Southeast Asia] was held. This event was divided into five parts and a total of twenty-one papers were presented. The outcome of this symposium was published two years later in Kurasawa Aiko's edited volume, *Tonan ajiashi no nakano nihon senryo*, in which eighteen of the twenty-one papers were included. According to the editor, the five parts were divided not according to country classification but according to themes. The intention was to compare and review the history of each Southeast Asian country (Kurasawa 1997*a*, p. x). Other notable works, published around the same time, are Goto Kenichi's book *Kindai nihon to tonan ajia — nanshin no shogeki to isan* [Modern Japan and Southeast Asia: Impact and Legacy of Southward Expansionism] (1995) and Ikehata Setsuho's book *Nihon senryoka no firipin* [The Philippines during the Japanese Occupation] (1996). The most notable research publication of the 2000s is Takeshima Yoshinari's *Nihon senryo to biruma no minzoku undo: takin seiryoku no seijiteki jyosho* [Japanese Occupation and the Burmese Nationalist Movement: Political Advance of the thakin] (2003).

Of the academic papers presented during the 1990s, Kozano Yako's *Nihon senryoka no jyawa sonraku shucho* [Village Chiefs of Java during the Japanese Occupation] (1997) takes issue with the influence of the Japanese occupation on local political leadership while Matsunaga Noriko's [Teaching of Japanese during the Japanese Occupation of Malaya] (1998) deals with the issue of loyalty toward Japan through education.

A notable publication from the 2000s is *Jochi ajia gaku* [Sophia Asian Studies] vol. 19 (2001), special edition titled *Nihon senryoki no indoneshia to firipin* [Indonesia and the Philippines during the Japanese Occupation], which presented the results of several years of fieldwork conducted by the respective authors. These works deserve acclaim not only because they provide comparative analyses of various records and data but also because they delve into areas and issues that previous research on Japanese colonial occupation did not examine. Next, Kurasawa Aiko (2006*b*) pays attention to the logistics and distribution during the Japanese occupation of the region. She claims that the military railroads built during those times actually harmed civilian supply transportation and eventually led to the mal-distribution of rice. Lastly, Hara Makoto's findings (2001) indicate that the occupying Japanese forces investigated the local churches in order to utilize the religious establishments for advancing the Japanese war effort.

CONCLUSIONS

Current Japanese research on Southeast Asian history is clearly world-class. This achievement is the product of sustained efforts by numerous scholars in the last century. The discipline, which started as a part of Asian history research, soon firmly established itself as an independent field of study in the 1960s. Today, it is attempting to advance one step further by incorporating Southeast Asian history into the larger framework of world history rather than leaving the discipline in the field of area studies.

Of course, this evolution was not without pains, especially when it came to the issue of language and data. As mentioned before, initial Japanese research utilized primarily historical materials written in classical Chinese. Even in the 1960s, researchers relied heavily on previous research findings by Western scholars. The importance of Western academics foris undeniable as scholars such as Benda (1962), who asserts the need to adopt social scientific methodologies in historical research, and Smail (1963), who criticizes the colonial view of history and instead proposes an "autonomous history" approach (making Southeast Asia the subject rather than the object of history), have been very influential. The list of required readings for Southeast Asian history also includes Coedès' *The Indianized States of Southeast Asia* (Ishii 1984, p. 256; 1991, p. 10).

The first Japanese scholar to synthesize primary historical materials and original sources was Nagazumi Akira. His work succeeded in bringing Japanese Southeast Asian history research to another level and led to original research accomplishments from the late 1970s and throughout the 1980s.

In the 1980s, it became the norm for Japanese researchers of pre-modern history to learn the local languages by residing in the region for prolonged periods of time. This was a notable change from previous scholars who relied heavily on literature in classical Chinese and Western languages. Instead of viewing Southeast Asia as an "object" moulded by foreign civilizations, the newer generation of scholars established the region as a "subject" with unique characteristics and autonomy (Momoki 2003, p. 8). Meanwhile, the main research themes of pre-modern Southeast Asia in the 1990s and 2000s have been the region's maritime trade network, port-cities, and port-city states. This research is a continuation of the earlier research conducted in the 1980s and has partially influenced Chinese and Japanese historical research (Momoki 2003, p. 8).

However, the accumulation of these research accomplishments further fuelled the need for a methodological direction in Southeast Asian historical research. The aforementioned *Koza tonan ajia gaku* [Lectures of Southeast Asian Studies] (11 vols.) seems to have come about as a response to such a need. Undoubtedly it is works such as *Tonan ajia sekai no rekishiteki iso* [The Historical Phase of the Southeast Asian World] (Ishii, Karashima, and Wada 1992) and *Kawaru tonan ajiashi zo* [The Changing Image of Southeast Asian History] (Ikehata 1994) which were attempts to synthesize the research results that had accumulated up until the end of the 1980s. These achievements led to two important general history texts, Ishii Yoneo's and Sakurai Yumio's edited book *Tonan ajiashi* I, *tairikubu* [Southeast Asian History, vol. I, Mainland] (1999) and Ikehata Setsuho's edited book *Tonan ajiashi* II, *toshobu* [Southeast Asian History, vol. 2, Islands] (1999) in the late 1990s and, by the early 2000s, the grand summation in the *Iwanami Lectures of Southeast Asian History* (10 vols) (2001). In sum, the overall trend in Japanese research up until the end of the 1990s was to synthesize previous accomplishments. At the turn of the century, the advent of the *Iwanami Lectures on Southeast Asian History* effectively concluded the prolonged effort towards a comprehensive synthesis and the general trend seems to be directed back towards pursuing detailed research themes. Some recent Japanese research has been based on previously undiscovered historical materials but a sizeable proportion of the work focuses on tracing the process of establishing past analytical frameworks through a critically retrospective examination of previous research and then attempting to correct the flaws in this research. Researchers pursuing the detailed research path must be aware that becoming excessively obsessed with a single micro-research agenda could lead to forgetting the importance of the larger effort to incorporate "Southeast Asia" into the wider framework of world history (Yamada 2006,

p. 280). In the latter case, it seems that maintaining a mutual channel of communication between researchers will become an important task (Osada 2007, p. 276).

Another point is that research on Southeast Asian history in Japan shows considerable interest in the region's history during the Japanese occupation. This period is an important issue not only for Southeast Asia but also for Japanese history. Furthermore, as Japan maintains a significant interest in the region, it is safe to assume that a high level of research will continue to be conducted.

As a final point, I would like to express my regret at the lack of Japanese research that is translated into other languages. In the future I hope that many Japanese research accomplishments become available in Western languages so that this world-class research can make significant contributions not only to Japan but also to the wider scholarship on the Southeast Asian region. In an important sense, without taking into account the Japanese contribution then scholarly work on Southeast Asia is incomplete.

Notes

[1]   *Tonan ajia shigakkai* will be discussed in more detail in the latter part of this chapter.

[2]   The reason for limiting the time-frame to 2007 is because the 2009 edition of *Tonan ajia — rekishi to bunka* was unavailable at the time of writing, and, therefore, it is impossible to know the research accomplishments of 2008.

[3]   The commonly used expression "Southeast Asia" emerged after the "Division of Southeast Asian Affairs" became established within the U.S. State Department. However, the British still use either "South East Asia" or "South-East Asia".

[4]   The modern Korean terms of "Dongyang" (East) and "Seoyang" (West) were first adopted by the Japanese during the nineteenth century based on this conceptualization.

[5]   Shimizu (2005) is a revised and translated (in English) version of his past papers (Shimizu 1987*a* and 1987*b*). The original English version was first presented in *The Japanese in Colonial Southeast Asia* (SEAP Series, Translation of Contemporary Japanese Scholarship on Southeast Asia, Cornell University, 1993), pp. 21–61.

[6]   This was also true of early twentieth-century French scholars such as Henri Maspéro.

[7]   The *Tozai koshoshi no kenkyu* is composed of two volumes, the former titled *Nankai hen* (South Seas) and the latter *Saiiki hen* (Silkroads). Vol. 1, *South Seas*, contains twenty-three papers which he published during his lifetime, while vol. 2, *Silkroads*, is composed of thirteen papers.

[8] *Shigaku Zasshi* previously used the term *nanyo* but started to adopt the term "Southeast Asia" in 1956.

[9] In 2004 the *tonan ajia kenkyu senta* renamed itself as *tonan ajia kenkyujo*. The English name remains the same.

[10] The early symposium special editions of the research centre's official publication, *Tonan ajia kenkyu* [Southeast Asian Studies], were composed of topics such as "rice farming in Malaya" (January 1965), and "utilization of water resources" (March 1966). The official publication did not have special editions on humanities and social sciences until the 1970s.

[11] The society renamed itself "Japan Society for Southeast Asian Studies" in 2007. While the exact number of members is unclear due to the unavailability of a member registry, it is estimated to be around 670 of which 200 are historians. Information regarding each scholar's focus country or focus era etc. is unavailable.

[12] As a point of reference, albeit slightly outdated, the total number of members in the Japan Society for Southeast Asian History was 276, of which 51 were Indonesia specialists (Nagazumi 1988, p. 212).

[13] The original title is *Les états hindouisés d'Indochine et d'Indonésie* (Paris, 1964).

[14] His major works include *Indoneshia minzoku ishiki no keisei* [Formation of national consciousness in Indonesia] (Tokyo: Tokyo Daigaku shuppan kai, 1980) and *Ajia no tatokai* [Asian Archipelago] (Tokyo: Kodansha, 1977).

[15] The special edition is Yano Toru's edited work, *Tonan ajia nyumon* [Introduction to Southeast Asia] (1992).

[16] This is because Benda adopted G. Coedès' theory (Coedès 1966, pp. 119–34).

[17] In this classification, the first period is the most problematic. Treating 1000 BCE, when even the early form of nation-states did not exist in the region, to tenth century CE, when numerous nation-states started to emerge in various parts of the region, as a single time period is clearly a stretch (Nishimura Watanabe 2003, pp. 65–66).

[18] Notable researches by early North American scholars are: W.H. Elsbree, *Japan's Role in Southeast Asian Nationalist Movements 1940–1945* (New York: Russell & Russell, 1953); Harry Benda, *The Crescent and the Rising Sun: Indonesian Islam under the Japanese Occupation 1942–1945* (The Hague: Van Hoeve Ltd., 1958).

References

1. Publications in Japanese

Akashi, Yoji, ed. *Nampogun gunsei sokanbu chosabu marai gunsei kanbu chosabu hokokusho* [Reports by the research department of Malay military government]. 22 vols. Tokyo: Ryukei Shosha, 2007.

Asano, Toyomi, ed. *Daitoa ho chitsujyo · nihon teikoku hosei kankei shiryo: nampo gunsei kankei shiryo* [Materials on the legal order of Great East Asia and the legal system of Imperial Japan]. Tokyo: Ryukei Shosha, 2007.

Asian Research Trends, vol. 1 (1991).

Fujita, Toyohachi. *Tozai koshoshi no kenkyu: nankai hen* [A study on the history of East-West interactions: south seas]. Tokyo: Hagiwara Seibunkan, 1933.

Fukami, Sumio. "Shurivijyaya teikoku" [The empire of Srivijaya]. In *Kawaru tonan ajiashi zo* [The changing image of Southeast Asian history], edited by Setsuho Ikehata. Tokyo: Yamakawa Shuppansha, 1994.

————. "Gendai no marakka kaikyo" [Malacca Strait during the Yuan Dynasty]. *Tonan Ajia — rekishi to bunka* 33 (2004).

Goto, Kenichi, ed. *Kindai nihon to tonan ajia — nanshin no shogeki to isan* [Modern Japan and Southeast Asia: the impact and the legacy of southward expansion]. Tokyo: Iwanami Shoten, 1995.

Hagiwara, Yoshiyuki. "Sengo nihon to tonan ajia no ichi zuke — haisen kara 10 nen no kiseki" [The mutual relations between Japan and Southeast Asia after World War II: ten-year traces since the defeat]. In *Kindai nihon no tonan ajia kan* [The modern Japanese view of Southeast Asia], edited by Kenichiro Shoda. Tokyo: Ajia Kenkyujo, 1978.

Hamashita, Takeshi. "Chugoku to tonan ajia" [China and Southeast Asia]. In *Koza tonan ajia gaku 4 — tonan ajia no rekishi* [Lecturers on Southeast Asian studies, vol. 4, A history of Southeast Asia], edited by Yoneo Ishii. Tokyo: Kobundo, 1991.

Hara, Makoto. "Nihon senryoka indoneshia ni okeru shukyo seisaku" [Policy on religion in Indonesia during the Japanese occupation]. *Jyochi ajia gaku* 19 (2001).

Hirosue, Masashi. *Tonan ajia no kenkoku shinwa* [Birth-myths in Southeast Asia]. Tokyo: Yamakawa Shuppansha, 2003.

————. *Tonan ajia no koshi sekai: chiiki shakai no keisei to sekai chitsujyo* [Port-city states in Southeast Asia: the formation of regional society and world order]. Tokyo: Iwanami Shoten, 2004.

Ikehata, Setsuho, ed. *Kawaru tonan ajiashi zo* [The changing image of Southeast Asian history]. Tokyo: Yamakawa Shuppansha, 1994.

————, ed. Nihon senryoka no firipin [The Philippines during the Japanese occupation]. Tokyo: Iwanami Shoten, 1996.

————, ed. *Tonan ajiashi*, II *toshobu* [A history of Southeast Asia, vol. II, islands]. Tokyo: Yamakawa Shuppansha, 1999.

Ikuta, Shigeru. "Kaiiki tonan ajiashi kenkyu no kaiko to tembo" [Retrospect and prospect on the study of maritime Southeast Asian history]. *Toyoshi kenkyu* 63, no. 3 (2004).

Ishii, Yoneo. *Indoshina bunmei no sekai* [The world of Indochinese civilisation]. Tokyo: Kodansha, 1977.

————. "Tonan ajia soron" [An introduction to Southeast Asia]. In *Ajia rekishi kenkyu nyumon* [An introduction to the study on Asian history], vol. 5, by Shimada Kenji et al. Kyoto: Dohosha, 1984.

————. "Koshi kokka to shiteno ayutaya" [Ayuthaya as a port-city state]. In *Tonan ajia sekai no rekishiteki iso* [The historical Phase of the Southeast Asian World], edited by Yoneo Ishii, Karashima Noboru, and Wada Hisanori. Tokyo: Tokyo Daigaku Shuppankai, 1992.

Ishii, Yoneo et al. *Tonan ajia no rekishi* [A history of Southeast Asia]. Tokyo: Kobundo, 1991.

Ishii Yoneo, Karashima Noboru, and Wada Hisanori, eds. *Tonan ajia sekai no rekishiteki iso* [The historical phase of the Southeast Asian world]. Tokyo: Tokyo Daigaku Shuppankai, 1992.

Ishii Yoneo and Sakurai Yumio, eds. *Tonan ajiashi* I *tairikubu* [A history of Southeast Asia: vol. 1, mainland]. Tokyo: Yamakawa Shuppansha, 1999.

Ishida, Mikinosuke. *Nankai ni kansuru shina shiryo* [Chinese historical sources on the South Seas]. Tokyo: Seikatsusha, 1945.

Ishizawa, Yoshiaki, ed. *Kambojia no bunka fukko* [Cultural revival of Cambodia]. Tokyo: Jochi Daigaku Ajia Bunka Kenkyujo, 1998.

Ito, Nobufumi. "Minshuka katei ni okeru gunbu no tettai to bunmin tosei — firipin no baai" [Military withdrawal and civilian control in the process of democracy: a case of the Philippines]. *Seiji keizaishi gakkai* 381 (1998).

Iwanami Koza Tonan Ajiashi Henshu Iinkai. "Kanko no kotoba" [Preface]. In *Iwanami koza tonan ajiashi* [Iwanami lectures on Southeast Asian history], vol. 1. Tokyo: Iwanami Shoten, 2001.

Iwao, Seiichi. *Nanyo nihon machi no kenkyu* [A study on Japanese town in nanyo]. Tokyo: Nan A Bunka Kenkyujyo, 1940.

Jochi ajia gaku, vol. 19 (2001).

Katakura, Minoru. *Betonamu no rekishi to higashi ajia — zen kindai hen* [Vietnamese history and East Asia: pre-modern period]. Tokyo: Sugiyama Shoten, 1977.

Koizumi, Jyunko. "Tokushu ni yosete" [For the special edition]. *Tonan ajia kenkyu* 43, no. 4 (2006).

Kozano, Yako. "Nihon senryoka no jyawa sonraku shucho" [Village chiefs in Java during Japanese occupation]. *Tonan ajia — rekishi to bunka* 26 (1997).

Kurasawa, Aiko. "Shimpojiumu tonan ajiashi no nakano nihon senryo — hyoka to ichi zuke" [Symposium: Japanese occupation in Southeast Asian history: evaluation and positioning]. *Ajia keizai* 37, nos. 7–8 (1996).

————, ed. *Tonan ajiashi no nakano nihon senryo* [Japanese occupation in Southeast Asian history]. Tokyo: Waseda Daigaku Shuppanbu, 1997*a*.

————. "Hajimeni" [Introduction]. In *Tonan ajiashi no naka no nihon senryo* [Japanese occupation in Southeast Asian history], edited by Aiko Kurasawa. Tokyo: Waseda Daigaku Shuppanbu, 1997*b*.

————. "Suharuto seiken hokai no rekishiteki igi" [Historical meaning of Suharto regime's collapse]. *Rekishigaku kenkyu* 718 (1998).

————. "Posuto kaihatsu to kokumin togo · minshuka" [Post-development, and national unity and democracy]. In *Gurobaruka to ajia shakai — posuto koroniaru no chihei* [Globalism and Asian society: the prospect for post-colonialism], edited by Niitsu Koichi and Yoshihara Naoki. Tokyo: Toshindo, 2006*a*.

————. "Teikoku nai no butsuryu" [Circulation of materials in the empire]. In *Shihai to Boryoku* [Rule and violence], edited by Aiko Kurasawa et al. Tokyo: Iwanami Shoten, 2006*b*.

Kuwabara, Jitsuzo. *Hojyuko no jiseki* [Traces of Pu Shou Geng]. Reprinted. Tokyo: Iwanami Shoten, 1935.

Matsunaga, Noriko. "Gunseika maraya ni okeru nihongo kyoiku" [Teaching of Japanese during Japanese occupation of Malaya]. *Tonan ajia — rekishi to bunka* 27 (1998).

Miichi, Ken. "Indonesia ni okeru isuramu shugi to modaniti no kosaku" [A mixture of Islam and modernity in Indonesia]. *Chiiki kenkyu ronshu* 5, no. 2 (2003).

Mio, Tadashi, ed. *Posuto reisen no indoshina* [Indochina in the post-cold war]. Tokyo: Nihon Kokusai Mondai Kenkyujyo, 1993.

Miyazaki, Ichisada. "Nanyo wo tozaiyo ni wakatsu konkyo ni tsuite" [On the ground of the division of *nanyo* between the East Seas and the West Seas]. *Toyoshi kenkyu* 4, no. 7 (1942).

Miyoshi, Norihide. *Kambojia PKO — chiiki funso kaiketsu to kokuren* [PKO in Cambodia: the settlement of the regional conflict and the UN]. Tokyo: Aki Shobo, 1994.

Miwa, Yoshihiko. *Beikoku no indoshina gaiko* [American foreign policy toward Indochina]. Tokyo: Nihon Boeki Shinkokai, 1994.

Momoki, Shiro. "Tonan ajiashi kenkyu no kako · genzai · mirai" [A study on Southeast Asian history: past, present, and future]. In *Iwanami koza tonan ajiashi* [Iwanami lectures of Southeast Asian history], edited by Hayase Shinzo and Momoki Shiro. Appendix: *Tonan ajiashi kenkyu annai* [A guidebook to the study of Southeast history]. Tokyo: Iwanami Shoten, 2003.

Murata, Yokuo. *Tai ni okeru kyoiku hatten: kokumin togo · bunka · kyoiku kyoryoku* [The development of education in Thailand: national integration, culture and educational cooperation]. Tokyo: Toshindo, 2007.

Nagazumi, Akira. "Tonan ajia" [Southeast Asia]. *Shigaku Zasshi* 68, no. 5 (1959).

————. *Ajia no tatokai* [Asian archipelago]. Tokyo: Kodansha, 1977.

————. *Indonesia minzoku ishiki no keisei* [Formation of national consciousness in Indonesia]. Tokyo: Tokyo Daigaku Shuppankai, 1980.

Nakagawa, Takeshi and Japanese Government's Relief Team of Angkor Remains, ed. *Ankoru iseki chosa hokokusho 1995* [A report of examination of Angkor remains, 1995]. Tokyo: Zaidan Hojin Nihon Kokusai Kyoryoku Senta, 1995.

Nemoto, Kei. "Aunsansuchi shiso to kodo" [Aung San Suu Kyi's thought and her action]. *Ajia bunka kenkyu bessatsu* 10 (2001).

Nezu, Atsushi. 1995. "Gengo to minzoku aidentiti mondai no seijika — shu genjyumin" [Politicisation of the issue of language and national identity: regional natives]. *SFC Journal of Language and Communication* (Keio Gijyuku Daigaku) 4 (1995).

Nishimura Masanari and Watanabe Yoshinari. "Tonan ajia kodai · chusei no rekishizo wo motomete" [In search of the historical image of ancient and medieval Southeast Asia]. *Tonan ajia — rekishi to bunka* 32 (2003).

Osada, Noriyuki. "Tonan ajia" [Southeast Asia]. *Shigaku Zasshi* 16, no. 5 (2007).

Oyanagi, Shigeta. "Bungaku hakase fujita toyohachi gimi ryakuden" [Fujita Toyohachi's short biography]. In *Tozai koshoshi no kenkyu · nankai hen* [A study on the history of East-West interactions: South Seas], by Fujita Toyohachi. Fujita, Tokyo: Hagiwara Seibunkan, 1933.

Sakai, Takashi. *Koshi kokka banten to toji boeki* [A port-city of Bantam and ceramic trade]. Tokyo: Doseisha, 2002.

Sakurai, Yumio. *Iwanami koza tonan ajiashi* [Iwanami lectures of Southeast Asian history], vol. 1. Tokyo: Iwanami Shoten, 2001.

Shibata, Kazuharu. "Myanma hatten no kagiwa minshuka" [Democratisation: a key for the development of Myanmar]. *Kaigai jijyo* 44, no. 6 (1996).

Shigaku Zasshi 66, no. 5 (1957).

Shimao, Minoru. "Shohyo, ishii yoneo hen, tonan ajia no rekishi" [Book review: Ishii Yoneo, ed. A history of Southeast Asia]. *Shigaku Zasshi* 101, no. 4 (1992).

———. "Tokushu iwanami koza tonan ajiashi" [Special Issue: Iwanami lectures of Southeast Asian history]. *Tonan ajia — rekishi to bunka* 22 (2003).

Shimizu, Hajime. "Kindai nihon ni okeru tonan ajiya chiiki gainen no seiritsu" [Southeast Asia as a regional concept in modern Japan]. *Ajia keizai* 28, no. 6 (1987*a*).

———. "Kindai nihon ni okeru tonan ajiya chiiki gainen no seiritsu" [Southeast Asia as a regional concept in modern Japan]. *Ajia keizai* 28, no. 7 (1987*b*).

Shiratori, Yoshiro. "'Tonan ajia shigakkai' seiritsu no enkaku" [A History of "Japan Society for Southeast Asian History"]. *Tonan ajia — rekishi to bunka* 20 (1991).

Suehiro, Akira. "Tai no gunbu to minshuka undo — 73 nen 10 gatsu seihen kara 92 nen 5 gatsu ryuketsu jiken e" [The Thai military regime and democratising movement]. *Shakai kagaku kenkyu* [Tokyo Daigaku] 44, no. 5 (1993).

———. "Sengo nihon no ajia kenkyu — ajia mondai chosakai, ajia keizai kenkyujyo, tonan ajia kenkyu senta" [Asian studies in Japan after World War II: ajia mondai chosakai, ajia keizai kenkyujyo, tonan ajia kenkyu senta]. *Shakai kagaku kenkyu* 48, no. 4 (1997).

Sugaya, Nariko. "Supeinryo firipin ni okeru chugokujin" [The Chinese in Spanish Philippines]. *Tonan ajia kenkyu* 43, no. 4 (2006).

Suzuki, Tsuneyuki. "Parenban oken no kakuritsu" [The establishment of Palembang kingship]. In *Tonan ajia sekai no rekishiteki iso* [The historical phase of the Southeast Asian world], edited by Ishii Yoneo, Karashima Noboru, and Wada Hisanori. Tokyo: Tokyo Daigaku Shuppankai, 1992.

———. "Koshi kokka parenban" [The port-city of Palembang]. In *Kawaru tonan ajiashi zo* [The changing image of Southeast Asian history], edited by Setsuho Ikehata. Tokyo: Yamakawa Shuppansha, 1994.

Takahashi, Muneo. "Kokumin togo to Pancharashira" [National integration and *Pantjasila*]. In *Gendai indoneshia no seiji to keizai* [Politics and economy in contemporary Indonesia], edited by Yasunaka Akio and Mihira Norio. Tokyo: Ajia Keizai Kenkyujyo, 1995.

Takeshima, Yoshinari. *Nihon senryo to biruma no minzoku undo: takin seiryoku no seijiteki jyosho* [Japanese occupation and Burmese nationalist movement: the political uprising of the *Thakin*]. Tokyo: Ryukei Shosha, 2003.

Tanaka, Kyoko. *Kokka to imin: tonan ajia kajin sekai no henyo* [State and immigration: the change of ethnic Chinese groups in Southeast Asia]. Nagoya: Nagoya Daigaku Shuppankai, 2002.

Tominaga, Yasuyo. "Tonan ajia" [Southeast Asia]. *Shigaku Zasshi* 102, no. 5 (1993).

Tonan ajia: rekishi to bunka 22 (2003).

Torii, Takashi, ed. *Mahatiru seikenka no mareshia* [Malaysia under the Mahathir regime]. Tokyo: Ajia Keizai Kenkyujyo, 2007.

Tsuchiya, Kenji. "Tonan ajia kenkyu no kadai to tenbo" [The task and the prospect of Southeast Asian studies]. *Tonan ajia — rekishi to bunka* 16 (1987).

Yamada, Naoko. "Tonan ajia" [Southeast Asia]. *Shigaku Zasshi* 115, no. 5 (2006).

Yamamoto, Tatsuro. "Tonan ajiashi no kadai" [The task of Southeast Asian history]. *Tonan ajia — rekishi to bunka* 1 (1971).

———. "Tonan ajia shigakkai souritsu 25 shunen" [The 25th anniversary of Japan Society for Southeast Asian History]. *Tonan ajia — rekishi to bunka* 20 (1991).

———. "Owarini — nihon no tonan ajiashi kenkyu to nagazumi akira kyojyu" [An apologue: studies of Southeast Asian history in Japan and prof. Nagazumi Akira]. In *Tonan ajia sekai no rekishiteki iso* [The historical phase of the Southeast Asian world], edited by Ishii Yoneo, Karashima Noboru, and Wada Hisanori. Tokyo: Tokyo Daigaku Shuppankai, 1992.

Yamamoto, Tatsuro et al., eds. *Iwanami koza tonan ajiashi* [Iwanami lectures of Southeast Asian history]. 10 vols. Tokyo: Iwanami Shoten, 2001–03.

Yano, Toru. *Nihon no nanyoshi kan* [The Japanese view of *nanyo* history]. Tokyo: Chuo Koronsha, 1979.

———. *Nanshin no keifu* [Genealogy of southward expansionism]. Tokyo: Chuo Koronsha, 1985.

———, ed. *Koza tonan ajia gaku* [Lectures in Southeast Asian studies]. 11 vols. Tokyo: Kobundo, 1990–92.

———. *Tonan ajia gaku nyumon* [An introduction to Southeast Asian studies]. Tokyo: Kobundo, 1992.

2. Publications in Western Languages

Asian Research Trends: A Humanities and Social Science Review (Tokyo), vol. 1 (1991).

Benda, Harry. *The Crescent and the Rising Sun: Indonesian Islam under the Japanese Occupation, 1942–1945*. The Hague: Van Hoeve Ltd., 1958

————. "The Structure of Southeast Asian History". *Journal of Southeast Asian History* 3, no. 1 (1962).

Coedès, Georges. *Les états hindouisés d'Indochine et d'Indonésie*. Paris: Editions E. de Boccard, 1964.

————. *The Making of South East Asia*. London: Routledge & Kegan Paul, 1966.

————. *The Indianized States of Southeast Asia*. Honolulu: East-West Center Press, 1968.

Elsbree, W.H. *Japan's Role in Southeast Asian Nationalist Movements, 1940–1945*. New York: Russell & Russel, 1953.

Emerson, R., L.A. Mills, and V. Thompson. *Government and Nationalism in Southeast Asia*. New York: Institute of Pacific Relations, 1942.

Emmerson, Donald K. "'Southeast Asia': What's in a Name?" *Journal of Southeast Asian Studies* 15, no. 1 (1984).

Malcom, Howard. *Travels in South-Eastern Asia Embracing Hindustan, Malaya, Siam, and China, with Notices of Numerous Missionary Stations and a Full Account of Burman Empire*, 2 vols. Boston: Could, Kendall, and Lincoln, 1839.

Nagazumi Akira. "Japanese Studies on Indonesia". *Bijdragen tot de taal-, Land- en Volkenkunde* 144, nos. 2–3 (1988).

Reid, Anthony. *Southeast Asia in the Age of Commerce, 1450–1680*. New Haven: Yale University Press, 1988.

Shimizu Hajime. "Southeast Asia as a Regional Concept in Modern Japan". In *Locating Southeast Asia: Geographies of Knowledge and Politics of Space*, edited by Paul Kratoska et al. Athens: Ohio University Press, 2005.

Shiraishi Takashi. "New Initiatives from Japan". In *Southeast Asian Studies: Pacific Perspectives*, edited by Anthony Reid. Tempe, AZ: The Program for Southeast Asian Studies, Arizona State University, 2003.

Smail, John. "On the Possibility of an Autonomous History of Modern Southeast Asia". *Journal of Southeast Asian History* 2 (1963).

4

THE HISTORICAL CONSTRUCTION OF SOUTHEAST ASIAN STUDIES IN KOREA

Park Seung Woo

INTRODUCTION

The origin of "Southeast Asian Studies" in the Republic of Korea can be traced back to the early 1960s.[1] But it was not until the late 1980s that any serious academic research on Southeast Asia began in earnest. Since then many Korean scholars who can be regarded as Southeast Asia area specialists, or "Southeast Asianists" have joined this academic discipline or field of study. The exact number of Korean Southeast Asianists is not known, however, it can be estimated roughly at 150 to 200; the number varies in accordance with what criteria we use in determining the membership of the academy of Southeast Asianists. If we apply a relatively strict standard, as I do in this study, the number may not exceed 150.[2] Among them, the number of Southeast Asianists who are in the disciplines of social sciences and history will be around 120 or so; others are in the fields of Southeast Asian languages and literature (Park S.W. 2009).

The small size of the membership should not be denigrated, however, if we take into consideration the relatively short history — a little over twenty years — of Southeast Asian Studies in Korea and its humble origins. For those approximately 120 social scientists and historians working in this field, there are several possible ways of categorizing them. One way is to divide them into two categories or generations and draw a demarcation line around the mid-1990s. In this way, the first generation of local academics on Southeast Asia comprises those who began their careers as Southeast Asian area specialists prior to the mid-1990s, while the second category/ generation started their academic research careers after that period.

This chapter examines how the research undertaken by Korean area specialists on Southeast Asia has evolved over time in accordance with changes that have taken place from inside and outside the academia during the last three decades. In particular it seeks to map various research agendas and themes as well as methodologies that have been pursued by Korean academics in different periods — in the 1980s, the 1990s and the 2000s. It also attempts to identify the institutional developments that have been taking place with regard to Southeast Asian Studies.

THE DAWN OF SOUTHEAST ASIAN STUDIES IN KOREA

In the Republic of Korea (ROK) the first academic interest in Southeast Asia began early in the 1960s, when some language programmes were offered in college education. It is also around this time that the ROK entered into diplomatic relations with major nations in Southeast Asia and that some Koreans began to look at this region with a more sustained interest. ROK established diplomatic relations with Thailand and Malaysia in 1958 and 1960 respectively, although diplomatic ties with the Philippines started much earlier in 1949.

Hankuk University of Foreign Studies (HUFS), founded in 1954 as Korea's first institution of higher education focusing on foreign language training, has undoubtedly played a pioneering role in Korea's education on Southeast Asia at the tertiary level. It began to teach the languages and literatures of Southeast Asian countries in its undergraduate programmes during the early 1960s. It opened departments of Malay-Indonesian, Thai, and Vietnamese in 1964, 1966, 1967 respectively (Park S.W. 2010).[3]

Here some early trailblazers in the teaching of Southeast Asian languages and societies made important contributions to the training of future Southeast Asianists. Choi Chang-Sung and Lee Gyo-chung played a leading role in the development of HUFS's Thai Department in the 1970s; they were joined by Cha Sang-Ho and Kim Youngaih in 1982.[4] Choi and Lee had taught in HUFS from the late 1960s and early 1970s until their retirement. Choi and Lee taught Thai language, while Kim taught Thai literature and Cha, Thai politics. They also played an important role in the institutional development of Southeast Asian Studies in Korea. For instance, Choi Chang-Sung played an important role in the establishment of the Korean Association of Thai Studies (KATS) and became its first President, serving in that post for eight years (1987–95). In the Department of Vietnamese at HUFS, such figures as Kim Ki-Tae and Cho Jae-Hyun played important roles in its early development. Kim taught Vietnamese language and literature and Cho, Vietnamese society and literature.

However, as most previous studies on "the history of Southeast Asian Studies in Korea" pointed out (Cho H. 2001; Cho, Oh, and Park 1998; Jeon 2006; Oh et al. 2008; Shin and Rhee 1996), very little research was done during the 1960s and 1970s, apart from a few elementary studies in the areas of history, language, and literature. The major publications during this period were basically college textbooks for the language and literature classes. Some examples are Choi Chang-Sung's *A Study on Thai Language* (1968), *Intermediate Readings on Thai Language* (1969), and *Introduction to Thai Grammar* (1975); Kim Ki-Tae's *Elementary Vietnamese* (1970) and *Intermediate Vietnamese* (1971); and Cho Jae-Hyun's *Theories on Modern Vietnamese Poetry* (1976) and *An Outline of Modern Vietnamese Literature* (1981).

What can be regarded as the first acknowledged Southeast Asia area specialists in Korea only appeared from the 1980s. Yu Insun was one among them. He received his Ph.D. degree at the University of Michigan in 1978 for his study of Vietnamese history during the seventeenth and eighteenth centuries (Yu 1978). He began his career as a Southeast Asia specialist in the History Department of Korea University in the same year and later moved to Seoul National University (SNU) and taught there until his retirement in 2007.[5] Lee Eun-Ho was awarded his Ph.D. degree in political science at Southern Illinois University in 1972 for his comparative study of the military role in Korea and South Vietnam (Lee E. 1972). After years of teaching in American universities, he returned to Korea in 1981 to teach in the Political Science Department of a local university. There are others who have occasionally contributed to this area of study such as Ahn Chung-Si, Kang Tae-Hoon, and Kim Sung-Chul. However, except in the case of Yu Insun, these senior scholars can hardly be regarded as serious Southeast Asianists. Only Yu spent his entire academic career in teaching and undertaking research on Vietnamese history. There are also some publications which were produced during the 1980s that can be considered as "research on Southeast Asia". Among them, *Southeast Asia and ASEAN* and *The Local Political System in Asia* (Ahn et al. 1981, 1987), to which Ahn Chung-Si contributed his chapters are worth mentioning here.

More serious Southeast Asia area specialists began to appear from the late 1980s. Many Korean researchers who received doctoral degrees from various schools both at home and abroad during the late 1980s and early 1990s started to enter the academe of Southeast Asian Studies. They constitute the mainstay of "the first generation of Southeast Asianists" in Korea.[6] The most distinctive feature of the first generation of Southeast Asianists, which distinguishes them from the second, is that they are to a large extent self-motivated and self-recruited. On the other hand the second generation of scholars was encouraged and motivated by their first generation mentors and they received the appropriate and necessary training from the early stage of their education as area specialists.

Before moving on to discuss the emergence of first generation scholars and examine their work — scrutinizing who they are and what they did — I will discuss briefly the social and demographic features of Korean Southeast Asianists and identify the differences between the first and the second generation of Southeast Asianists. First of all, the field of Southeast Asian studies is male-dominated as are other fields of activity in Korea. However, there is a slight between-generation difference in gender ratio. The first generation is more male-dominated as more than 90 per cent are male, while the proportion of males for the second generation is slightly lower with around 80 per cent. The age range of the scholars is as expected: the mainstay of the first generation is in their fifties, while most second generation scholars are in their thirties and forties. When looking at their occupational status and institutional affiliation, we discover that most of the first generation scholars (more than 90 per cent) are full-time university professors. For the second generation, the proportion of full-time professors is relatively low with 50–60 per cent and the remainder is made up of part-time lecturers, researchers in both public and private research institutions, and research professors affiliated with universities (Park S.W. 2009).

THE EARLY YEARS OF SOUTHEAST ASIAN STUDIES IN KOREA

In contemporary Korean history, the 1980s will be remembered as the period of "opening and liberalization", although not all will agree with this observation. In the longer perspective of Korea's social history, this era is almost equivalent to the Chinese "Reform and Opening" of the 1980s and the Vietnamese *Doi Moi* in the late 1980s. Strict military rule still permeated every facet of people's lives during the 1980s, but the liberalization in some areas of social life proceeded steadily culminating in the political democratization of 1987. The Seoul Olympics in 1988 then accelerated the pace of liberalization in Korea.

The Korean government had gradually lifted many bans on overseas visits during the 1980s. A strict ban on studying abroad was eased in 1981 and the general liberalization of travelling abroad was put into effect from 1989. It is around this time that many Korean people began to show their interest in other foreign countries and peoples living there, particularly in less well-known countries in the "Third World" including Southeast Asia. It is also from the early and mid-1980s that many young Korean students started to go abroad to pursue their graduate studies. Some of them took a keen interest in Southeast Asia for various reasons and through various channels. They began to return home with their doctoral degrees from the late 1980s. This is when Southeast Asian Studies as a serious academic discipline began.

The door of the nation opened much wider to the strong current of "globalization" and "regionalization" at the beginning of the 1990s. President Kim Young Sam made it public that globalization was his top priority on the national agenda during his presidency (1993–97). Not only commodities and money investments but also businesspeople, tourists, and migrant workers crossed national borders. Economic, socio-cultural and personal exchanges between Korea and other countries expanded on an unprecedented scale. The exchanges between Korea and Southeast Asian countries, both human and material, were also increased significantly.

The Advent of the First Generation of Southeast Asianists

It is under this circumstance that the first generation of Southeast Asianists emerged. And, it is also perhaps because of this circumstance that the proportion of those who obtained Ph.D.s from foreign universities is higher (around 80 per cent) among the first generation Southeast Asianists than for the second generation (50–60 per cent). And the majority of the first generation foreign-educated scholars gained their doctorates from universities in the United States (around 80 per cent of foreign Ph.D.s). The most popular major for the first generation Southeast Asianists is political science; six out of ten majored in this discipline. Those who majored in anthropology, economics, history, and sociology are few; just two or three for each discipline.

The majority of first generation Southeast Asianists received their undergraduate education during the 1970s with such majors as political science, anthropology, economics, history and law as well as Southeast Asian languages. They studied in graduate schools both at home and abroad from the late 1970s through to the 1980s. And they received their

Ph.D. degrees during the late 1980s and early 1990s. Below I select some of the first generation Southeast Asianists to examine their academic career trajectories and review some major research results that they have produced during the 1990s.

The majority of the first generation Southeast Asianists who started their academic careers during the late 1980s and early 1990s majored in political science and in comparative politics and international relations in particular. Park Sa-Myung is among the first stream of scholars who received their Ph.D.s in political science from universities in the U.S. He was awarded his doctorate from the State University of New York (SUNY) at Buffalo in 1988. His Ph.D. dissertation was the result of a comparative study between Indonesia and the Philippines on state transformation (Park S. 1988). He returned home and was appointed Professor in the Department of Political Science and Diplomacy at Kangwon National University (KNU) in 1989, where he has served until now. By inviting three more researchers on Southeast Asia into its faculty since then, KNU has positioned itself as one of the finest institutions for Southeast Asianists in Korea. Bae Geung-Chan, who was awarded his doctoral degree in political science at Claremont Graduate School, USA, also did a comparative study in his Ph.D. dissertation, dealing with the formation processes of authoritarian states in Korea, Indonesia and the Philippines (Bae 1988). He later became affiliated with the Institute of Foreign Affairs and National Security (IFANS), a state-run educational and research institution. Yoon Jinpyo's Ph.D. dissertation also undertook a comparison between Indonesia, Thailand and Vietnam in relation to their modern state formations (Yoon 1990). After receiving a doctorate from the University of South Carolina, he returned home and was appointed to the Korea Institute for Defense Analysis from 1990 to 1995 and later moved to Sungshin Women's University in 1995.

More scholars followed suit. Jeon Je-guk received his Ph.D. from Ohio State University in 1990; Ko Woo-Seong, from Northern Illinois University in the same year; Park Kie-Duck, from the University of Chicago in 1993; and Seo KyoungKyo, from Southern Illinois University in 1993. All of them carried out comparative studies in their doctoral dissertations (Jeon 1990; Ko 1990; Park K. 1993; Seo 1993), The comparison was either between or among Southeast Asian countries, or between a Southeast Asian country (countries) and a country (or countries) in another region(s). After acquiring their Ph.D.s, Park joined the Sejong Institute in 1994 and Seo was appointed Professor in the Political Science Department at HUFS in 1996.

Single case/country studies were very rare in the field of political science during this period. Shin Yoon Hwan's Ph.D. dissertation stands out among them. He studied at Yale University under the supervision of James Scott and his doctoral dissertation analysed the state of Indonesia under Soeharto's rule, focusing on political patronage, bureaucracy, and the business class (Shin 1989). He returned home to find a position in the Political Science Department at Sogang University in 1989 and has since taught and undertaken research there. Under his tutelage, Sogang soon became one of the fertile cradles for young researchers on Southeast Asia. Meanwhile, Kim Sung-Joo and Park Kwang Seop did doctoral research by looking at the Southeast Asian region in general as one unit of analysis. Kim received his doctorate from the SUNY-Buffalo in the U.S. in 1986, whereas Park earned his from the University of the Philippines in 1995 (Kim S. 1986; Park K. 1995).

Byun Chang-Koo, Kim Hong-Koo, and Yang Seungyoon, on the other hand, are among the important first generation political scientists in Southeast Asian Studies who received doctorates from local universities. Byun was awarded his Ph.D. from Kyungpook National University in 1987 and his dissertation was on ASEAN and its regional security issues (Byun 1987). Kim Hong-Koo obtained his Ph.D. from HUFS in 1990 and his dissertation dealt with the military intervention in politics in Thailand (Kim H.-K. 1990). Yang, on the other hand, received his first Ph.D. from Kyungnam University in 1992 with his study on Islam and politics in Indonesia (Yang 1991) and his second from Gadjah Mada University in Indonesia in 2006 with a study on Korean-Indonesian relations (Yang 2006). Doctoral degree holders from local universities at the time were likely to start their teaching careers much earlier before they obtained their Ph.D.s. Byun was appointed to Busan National University of Education in 1981 before he moved to the Catholic University of Daegu. Kim Hong-Koo joined the Faculty of Pusan University of Foreign Studies (PUFS) Department of Thai early in 1983 and Yang, the Department of Malay-Indonesian at HUFS in 1984.

In other disciplines other than political science, the production of Ph.D. holders majoring in Southeast Asian Studies was limited. In the field of anthropology, Oh Myung-seok studied the Malay peasantry and obtained his Ph.D. from Monash University, Australia in 1994 (Oh 1994). He returned to Korea and was appointed Professor in the Department of Anthropology at SNU in the same year. As an anthropologist and area specialist, he set an example to some of the SNU graduates, who later conducted field research in various Southeast Asian countries — Indonesia, Malaysia, Thailand, Vietnam, and the Philippines.

In the field of history, three historians returned home with doctorates from universities in three different foreign countries. Kwon Oh Shin was awarded his Ph.D. from the University of the Philippines in 1992 with his study of Philippine history during the Commonwealth Period (Kwon 1992). Cho Hung-guk received his doctorate from the University of Hamburg in Germany in 1993 with his study of the modern history of Thailand (Cho H. 1993). In the same year Soh Byungkuk obtained a Ph.D. degree from Ohio University, USA, majoring in Malaysian modern history (Soh 1993). Kwon joined the Faculty of History at KNU and Soh, the Department of Malay-Indonesian at HUFS, in 1996, while Cho became a full-time faculty member in the Graduate School of International Studies at Pusan National University later in 2003.

Lastly, in the field of sociology Park Seung Woo was awarded his Ph.D. from the University of Georgia, USA, in 1991 with a comparative study of agrarian transformation in Korea and the Philippines (Park S.W. 1991). After returning home, he joined the faculty at Yeungnam University in 1992. In the field of international economics, Park Innwon earned his Ph.D. from the University of Pennsylvania in 1993 with his study of regional economic integration in ASEAN (Park I. 1993). After sojourning in the National University of Singapore for five years (1993–98), he was appointed to Korea University's Graduate School of International Studies in 1998.

The Early Works of the First Generation Southeast Asianists in the 1990s

The major works in the field of social sciences on Southeast Asia which were produced during the 1990s and deserve mention are basically of the following three types: first, the Ph.D. theses written by the first generation scholars during the first half of the 1990s, most of which were mentioned above; second, the follow-up research done by them after their Ph.D. thesis writing; and third, the studies done by the subsequent generation for their Ph.D.s during the latter half of the 1990s. In this section we will briefly review the second category of work.

Most research done by the first generation scholars during the 1990s are some kind of follow-up work. The research subjects and themes were developed and data were gathered during their doctoral thesis writing. For instance, Park Sa-Myung wrote several articles on Indonesia and the Philippines during this time, whose themes parallel those in his dissertation (1991, 1993, 1996, 1999). Shin Yoon Hwan's papers on Indonesia are also part of a follow-up study (1991, 1993). In a similar vein, Yoon Jinpyo published one paper on Thailand's state and market and another to compare Thailand and Indonesia (1996, 1997); Kim Hong-Koo, on Thai Buddhism and politics (1996); Yang Seungyoon, on Islam in Southeast Asia (1992); Park Kie-Duck, on the Philippine military (1994); and Seo Kyoung-Kyo on Thailand and the Philippines (1993, 1994, 1997, 1999). All of them published in such journals as the *Korean Journal of International Relations* (published by the Korean Association of International Studies), *Korean Political Science Review* (by the Korean Political Science Association), *Journal of Korean Association of Thai Studies*, and the *Dongnam-asia yeon'gu* [*Southeast Asian Review*] (the official journal of the Korean Association of Southeast Asian Studies).

In anthropology, Oh Myung-seok's papers on the rural society of Malaysia were also closely related to his doctoral thesis (1993, 1999*a*). In history, Yu Insun published articles on the Vietnamese family system (1997) and Kwon Oh Shin published a book depicting Philippine history under American colonial rule (2000). In sociology, Park Seung Woo delivered some papers comparing Philippine agriculture and rural class relations with those of Korea (Park S.W. 1993, 1998*a*; Park and Green 1995).

On the other hand, some researchers sought new research themes which have little to do with the ones developed in their doctoral theses. For instance, Shin Yoon Hwan delved into several diverse issues such as Korea's investment in Southeast Asia, the behaviour of Korean business corporations in Southeast Asian countries, the relationship between Indonesia and Korea, and an analysis of foreign area studies in Korea (Shin 1995*a*, 1995*b*, 1998; Shin and Rhee 1996). Similarly Park Sa-Myung delivered a paper on globalization (2000); Yu Insun, on *Doi Moi* policy (1994); Oh Myung-seok, on Islam and Chinese society in Malaysia (1997, 1999*b*); and Park Seung Woo on the Philippine agricultural production system (1998*b*, 1998*c*).

Lew Seok Choon, another first generation scholar, published two articles on the social systems of the Philippines and Malaysia (1994, 1995). Although his doctoral study (1986) did not deal directly with Southeast Asia, he later turned his attention to the issues on Southeast Asia, and the Philippines in particular. Similarly, Park Jang Sik, an expert on Myanmar, wrote several articles on Myanmar society and people and Sino-Myanmar relations (1993, 1995, 1996*a*, 1999), although he earned his Ph.D. in the field of linguistics (1996*b*).

During the same period, two primers on Thailand came out: one is a collection of papers edited by the Korean Association of Thai Studies, entitled *An Understanding of Thailand* (KATS 1998), and the other, by Kim Hong-Koo (1999). Such experts on Thailand as Lee Gyo-chung (President of the KATS at the time), Cha Sang-Ho, Choi Chang-Sung,

Kim Hong-Koo, Kim Youngaih, Lee Byungdo, Song In-seo, and many others contributed to the former.

Institutional Development in Southeast Asian Studies during the 1990s

An important institutional development in Southeast Asian Studies in Korea witnessed during the early 1990s was the inauguration of the *Han'guk dongnama hakhoe* (Korean Association of Southeast Asian Studies or KASEAS) and the formation of *Dongnama jeongchi yeon'guhoe* (Study Group on Southeast Asian Politics or SGSEAP), the predecessor of the Korean Institute of Southeast Asian Studies (KISEAS).

KASEAS, the most important academic society in the field of Southeast Asian Studies in Korea, was established in June 1991. It is an academic association which is open to any scholars interested in the study of Southeast Asia. Its first President was Han Sung-Joo, a prominent political scientist in Korea University who later served as ROK's Foreign Minister and Ambassador to the United States. It started to publish its own official journal, *Dongnam-asia yeon'gu* [*The Southeast Asian Review*], a year after. This soon became the most important outlet for Southeast Asian Studies in Korea. It has been published biannually until 2009, when it started to be published triannually. The latest issue of the journal was volume number 22, issue number 3, which was published in October 2012. Today total membership of the KASEAS stands at 330.

SGSEAP was formed in December 1990 with eight political scientists including Bae Geung-Chan, Kim Sung-Joo, Ko Woo-Seong, Lee Eun-Ho, Park Sa-Myung, Shin Yoon Hwan, Yang Seungyoon, and Yoon Jinpyo, all of whom except Lee had just finished their doctoral studies. And, except Yang, all of them obtained their Ph.D.s in the U.S. Later recruiting more scholars in other disciplines such as anthropology, economics and sociology, it was expanded into the *Dongnama jiyeok yeon'guhoe* (Study Group on Southeast Asian Studies or SGSEAS) in 1992. (Later in 2003, it was further expanded and reorganized into the present form of KISEAS, a more formal academic organization registered with the government.) Scholars involved in the research activities of the KISEAS jointly produced many research results during the 1990s. It includes some translations (SGSEAP 1991, 1992; SGSEAS 1993) and compilations of research papers (SGSEAS 1994, 1995, 1996, 1997).

Another noteworthy development is the establishment of the Center for Southeast Asian Studies (CSEAS) at HUFS in November 1990. Comprised mostly of the faculty members and former students of HUFS College of Oriental Languages, CSEAS has continued to play an important role in the development of Southeast Asian Studies in Korea. It started to publish its journal, *Dongnama yeon'gu* [*Journal of Southeast Asia*], from 1991 and the latest issue (vol. 22, no. 1) came out in May 2012.

Academic societies for the scholarship on individual countries of Southeast Asia are not many. There are only two of them at present: one is the Korean Association of Thai Studies (KATS), and the other, the Korean Association of Vietnamese Studies (KAVS). The former was established early in 1987, several years before the emergence of the KASEAS, while the latter appeared later in 1999. The KATS started its official journal (*Journal of the Korean Association of Thai Studies*) in 1988. Being published irregularly during the early years, it came out annually during the years 2004–08 and became biannual from 2009. The latest issue of the journal was number 2 of volume 18, published in February 2012.

All the journals mentioned above are published in Korean, although articles written in other languages such as English and Southeast Asian languages have also been included. They are all accredited by the National Research Foundation of Korea and listed in the Korea Journal Citation Index (KCI). *Donanam-asia yeon'gu* has been listed in KCI since 2003, while both *Dongnama yeon'gu* and the *Journal of KATS* became KCI journals in 2010.

THE DEVELOPMENT OF SOUTHEAST ASIAN STUDIES IN THE 2000s

The Birth of the Second Generation Southeast Asianists

From around the mid-1990s a new generation of Southeast Asia area specialists began to join this academic field and Southeast Asian Studies in Korea developed from an early childhood stage and entered a kind of young adulthood. These second generation researchers had a keen interest in the area of Southeast Asia from the early stage of their academic careers and received more systematic training both in undergraduate and graduate schools. In contrast to the previous generation who were self-trained, they had mentors; they were encouraged, motivated and even inspired by their seniors, i.e. the first generation scholars. They were also stimulated by the enthusiastic academic atmosphere created by the proliferation of academic societies such as KASEAS, *Dongnama jiyeok yeon'guhoe* (today's KISEAS), and KATS. The first cohort of the second generation were very active in the academic societies even before they obtained their Ph.D. degrees, and published several papers (e.g., Hong 1993; Jeon 1998, 1999; Kim M. 1993, 1997; Park E. 1994).

Another significant feature of the second generation is that most of them did some kind of field research and spent some time — some for several years and others briefly — in the country of their interest. In contrast, except for a few scholars such as Shin Yoon Hwan, most of the first generation Southeast Asianists were not able to stay in the country (or countries) which they focused on in their study. Second generation scholars have also shown more expertise in local languages than the first generation; many of them have a good command of a local language.[7] Below we will look at the work by some selected second generation scholars produced during the late 1990s. The focus here is on their Ph.D. dissertations.

In the field of anthropology, Hong Seok-Joon received his Ph.D. from Seoul National University (SNU) in 1997 and Kim Hyung-Jun from the Australian National University (ANU) in 1996. Hong's dissertation dealt with Islamization in Malaysia (1997) and Kim's, with Muslims in Indonesia (1996). Afterwards they actively contributed important articles to major journals (e.g., Hong 1999; Kim H.-J. 1998a, 1998b). Both Hong and Kim are graduates of the SNU Department of Anthropology. After graduation, Hong pursued his doctorate at his *alma mater*, while Kim went abroad to Australia to do his Ph.D. Receiving their doctoral degrees, Kim worked in the Department of Anthropology at Kangwon National University (KNU) in 1997, and Hong became affiliated with Mokpo National University in 2000.

In the field of political science, Yang Gil Hyun (1996) obtained his Ph.D. from SNU with a comparative study of political democratization in Third World countries including Myanmar. He joined the faculty at Jeju National University a few years later. Jeong Yeonsik, a graduate of HUFS Department of Chinese Language, received his Ph.D. from the University of South Carolina with a comparative study of social market economies in China and Vietnam (Jeong 1997a). He found a full-time post at Changwon National University the following year and continued to work on the research topic that he developed (Jeong 1997b, 1999). Park Eunhong and Lee Hanwoo had their Ph.D.s from Sogang University; Park, with his study of the political economy of Thailand; and Lee, on the reform policy in contemporary Vietnam (Park E. 1998; Lee H. 1999). Both Park and Lee were guided into Southeast Asian Studies during their graduate years under the tutelage of Shin Yoon Hwan.

In the field of economics and international trade, Kwon Yul was awarded his Ph.D. from Sogang University and Park Bun Soon, from HUFS in

1999. Kwon's Ph.D. thesis was on economic reform in Vietnam and Park's on Korean investment in Southeast Asia (Kwon 1999; Park B. 1999). Both of them have been affiliated with research institutes since the early 1990s. Kwon has been working in the Korean Institute for International Economic Policy (KIEP), a government-funded economic research institute, and Park, in Samsung Economic Research Institute (SERI), an affiliated organization of Samsung Group.

In the field of history, Song Jungnam obtained his Ph.D. from Hanoi National University in Vietnam in 1996 and Choi Byungwook, from ANU in 1999. Both of them focused on Vietnamese history. Song's study was a comparison of social changes in rural villages in Vietnam and Korea, while Choi did research on mid-nineteenth century Vietnamese history (Choi B. 1999; Song 1996). Song joined the faculty of HUFS Department of Vietnamese right after he was awarded his Ph.D., while Choi was appointed to the Department of History at Inha University in 2006, after having had part-time teaching jobs for several years.

Thus the late 1990s became a more productive period for Korean Southeast Asian area studies, proliferated with both the works by the first generation scholars and the doctoral studies done by the young scholars in the second generation. However, a much more promising milieu unfolded after the year 2000.

Continuing Stream of the Second Generation Southeast Asianists in the 2000s

With the beginning of the 2000s, more and more young scholars with their Ph.D.s in various disciplines were entering the field of Southeast Asian Studies. They were more diverse in terms of academic majors and the universities from which they graduated. More Ph.D. holders were produced in such disciplines as anthropology. The United States was no longer the main ground where Korean Southeast Asianists were educated; they were trained in various countries: Australia, France, UK, as well as Southeast Asian countries. Local universities also emerged as the main outlet of Southeast Asianists.

More than any other fields, anthropology was the main field in which more area specialists were trained in the past decade. Chae Suhong obtained his Ph.D. from the City University of New York in 2003 with his study of political processes in the post-reform industrial factories in Vietnam (Chae 2003a). He was appointed to the Department of Archaeology and Cultural Anthropology at Chonbuk National University (CNU) in 2004.

Kang Yoonhee (2002) was awarded her doctorate from Yale University with a study of languages and rituals of Petelangan people in Indonesia, after which she continued to publish some important follow-up studies in major journals (2003, 2006). Kim Ye-kyoum (2003*a*) obtained his Ph.D. on women and gender in northern Sulawesi, Indonesia from the University of Hull in the UK. Universities in Southeast Asian countries also produced two young scholars in this field; Cho Youn-Mee (2005) graduated from Gadjah Mada University in Indonesia and Lee Sang Kook (2007) from the National University of Singapore (NUS). Cho's Ph.D. thesis dealt with vigilantism in Java and Lee's on the social system in "border society" in the Thailand-Burma borderland. Except Kim Ye-kyoum, all others did their undergraduate studies in the Department of Anthropology at SNU.

There were also three local university-trained anthropologists in the area of Southeast Asian Studies: Kim Minjung (2002), Choi Horim (2003) and Kim Yi Seon (2003), all of whom obtained their Ph.D.s from SNU. Kim Minjung's dissertation was on women and family in Philippine rural village; Kim Yi Seon's, on tourism and handicraft in Thailand; and Choi's, on the problem of ritual and the state's role in ritual revitalization in Vietnam. Both Choi Horim and Kim Yi Seon are graduates of SNU Department of Anthropology, while Kim Minjung did her undergraduate study in the Sociology Department of Sogang University. Kim Yi Seon has been working in the Korean Women's Development Institute from the early 1990s, while Kim Minjung has worked in the Department of Anthropology at KNU from 2005, where Park Sa-Myung (Political Science Department), Kwon Oh Shin (History Department), and Kim Hyung-Jun (Anthropology Department) had already settled.

In the field of political science, Hwang In-Won (2001) and Choi Nankyung (2004) received their Ph.D.s from ANU, Lee Jaehyon (2005) from Murdoch University in Australia, and Choi Jungug (2001*a*) from the University of Texas, USA. Hwang's Ph.D. thesis was on Malaysian politics and he later elaborated and updated it to publish a volume which became a best-seller in Kuala Lumpur's bookstores (Hwang 2003). Choi Jungug published some articles on the Philippines and Malaysia afterwards (Choi J. 2001*b*, 2003). Choi joined the faculty at Konkuk University in 2004, while Hwang was appointed to Gyeongsang National Univerisity in 2006. On the other hand, Kang Young Soon (2002) was awarded her Ph.D. from the University of Indonesia; and Kim Dong-Yeob (2003*a*) obtained his from the University of the Philippines, based on which he delivered further studies in major journals (Kim D. 2002, 2003*b*). Kim is now serving as a research professor in the Institute for Southeast Asian Studies (ISEAS) at PUFS, which is under the directorship of Park Jang Sik.

Over the last decade local universities have also played the role of main educator of Korean Southeast Asianists in the political science field. Jeon Je Seong (2002) obtained his Ph.D. from SNU with his study on the labour movement in Indonesia, Lee Dong-Yoon (2002) from Yonsei, Cho Young Hee (2006) from Inha, and Song Kyung-Ah (2011) from SNU. After teaching part-time at some local universities and doing research in private research institutes, Jeon and Lee found their niches in Chonbuk National University (CNU) in 2006 and Silla University in 2009 respectively. Not many universities in Korea are accommodating more than one Southeast Asianist with a full-time post. CNU is one of the rare cases, by employing two of them: Jeon in the Political Science Department and Chae Suhong in the Anthropology Department.

However, HUFS was the mainstay of educating Southeast Asianists, where Lee Byungdo (2000), Lee Yohan (2000), Choi Kyunghee (2004), Lee Kyung Chan (2006), and Jang Jun Young (2008) received their doctorates in political science. Lee Byungdo joined the faculty of the Thai Department at HUFS, his *alma mater*, in 2000; Lee Kyung Chan has been in the Department of Business in Asia at Youngsan University from 1997; Lee Yohan is now affiliated with Souphanouvong University in Laos; and Choi Kyunghee is currently affiliated with the KISEAS as a research fellow.

Formally launched in December 2003, one of the important roles played by the KISEAS is to provide a kind of incubator for the young scholars who have just started their academic career. Many people including Lee Hanwoo, Hwang In-Won, Jeon Je Seong, Cho Young-Hee, and Choi Kyunghee had once served or currently serve as research fellows there. Some of them have used the opportunity wisely as a stepping stone to find a full-time post in local universities. More will follow below on the KISEAS.

In the field of history, Nho Young Soon (2000) received her Ph.D. from the University of London, Youn Dae Yeong (2007) from the University of Paris, Song Seung-Won (2008) from Ohio University, USA, and Kim Jongouk (2009) from the National University of Vietnam at Hanoi. After receiving their Ph.D.s, both Youn and Song joined the Institute for East Asian Studies at Sogang University (SIEAS) as Humanities Korea (HK) research professors. The two anthropologists mentioned above, Lee Sang Kook and Choi Horim, both of whom are graduates of SNU, are also affiliated with the SIEAS as HK professors. There will also be more to follow on the SIEAS.

We also have new members of the Southeast Asian Studies community in other minor fields: Ra Hee-Ryang from the University of Hawaii in the field of international economics, Eom Eunhui from SNU in the field of environmental education, and Kim Yi-jae from SNU in the field of geography. Ra (2007) wrote his Ph.D. thesis on international reserves; Eom (2008), on the environmental movement in the Philippines; and Kim Yi-jae (2005), on reinterpreting the Southeast Asian region from a geographer's view. In the field of sociology we have Yoon Chung Ro (2005) from Dongguk University and Kim Jeehun (2009) from the University of Oxford. Kim's Ph.D. thesis dealt with transnational migration and he moved to Inha University recently, after staying in the SIEAS for one-and-a -half years.

The Major Works of Korean Southeast Asianists in the 2000s

It may be premature to judge the first decade of the twenty-first century to be the most fertile period in the history of Southeast Asian Studies in Korea. But it is nonetheless fair to say that it was an era of very productive, progressive, and promising, academic work both in quantity and in quality. Many area specialists in various disciplines, educated in very diverse universities in different countries around the world have flowed in to join the academia of Southeast Asianists. They have produced a large amount of scholarly work in various academic meetings and have published numerous important articles and books during the past decade. Since it is almost impossible to review all of them here in this small space, I will just give a cursory glance at some selected works produced during this period.

One of the noteworthy characteristics of the last decade is that many new research issues and themes have been developed and pursued in the study of Southeast Asia. Firstly, there have been a series of studies on regionalism in Southeast Asia and East Asia including such themes as regional cooperation and regionalization in either ASEAN or ASEAN+3 frameworks, economic integration and the formation of ASEAN or East Asian Free Trade Areas (AFTA/EAFTA), and East Asian community and identity building. These issues have so far been hotly debated by many Korean area specialists (Bae 2001, 2003; Hwang 2008; Jeon 2007; Kwon 2003, 2004, 2005; Lee H. 2007; Lee J. 2007*a*, 2007*b*; Lee Y. 2000, 2003; Park B. 2005, 2010; Park I. 2006; Park I. and Kwon 2007; Park S. 2006, 2007; Park S. et al. 2008; Park S. and Supachai 2003; Park S.W. 2008*a*, 2011; Ra 2009; Shin 2009; Shin et al. 2008; Yang G. 2005).

Secondly, many Korean researchers have more recently become interested in such trans-border human exchange issues as transnational migrations, international marriages, migrant labourers, and the resultant social problems (Chae 2007; Choi H. 2010; Kim D. 2009, 2010; Kim J. 2009, 2010, 2011; Kim M. 2007, 2009, 2011; Kim M. et al. 2006; Lee S. 2007, 2008, 2011). Among them, Kim Dong-Yeob (2010) and Kim Minjung (2009, 2011) have shown an interest in intermarriage migration and Southeast Asian migrants in Korea and Kim Jeehun (2009, 2010, 2011), in Korean sojourners in Singapore. Lee Sang Kook (2007, 2011), on the other hand, has been dealing with the "border society" issues, based on his field study in Mae Sot area in the Thai-Burma borderland.

Thirdly, "*Hallyu*", or the Korean Wave, in Southeast Asia is also an issue that has recently been in debate (Kim H.-K. 2005; Lee H. 2002; Shin 2002; Shin and Lee 2006). In particular, Shim Doobo, a specialist on popular culture and media studies who obtained his Ph.D. from the University of Wisconsin-Madison (2000), has been actively engaged in this issue and recently published important pieces of work in foreign refereed journals (Shim 2006, 2007). Also, some have recently turned their attention to the issue of "Southeast Asian Waves" in Korea (e.g., Kim H.-K. 2009, 2011).

Fourthly, the relations between Southeast Asia or Southeast Asian countries and other countries or regions (e.g., Korea, China, Northeast Asia, U.S., etc.) comprise another issue that has been frequently pursued by Korean Southeast Asianists (Cho H. 2000, 2008, 2009; Lee H. 2003; Lee K. 2006; Park S. 2005*a*; Shin and Chayachoke 2005; Soh 2010; Yang S. 2006). Some are interested in the historical relations and others, more contemporary ones. Cho Hung-guk, for instance, is interested in the historical relations between Northeast Asia (Korea, in particular) and Southeast Asia. He published a volume titled *History of Exchanges between Korea and Southeast Asia* in 2009. Shin Yoon Hwan's and Chayachoke's volume, *Relations between Korea and Southeast Asia in the Past* (2005) is also worth noting here.

Finally, very recently some scholars including Hong Seok-Joon (2007) and Kim Dong-Yeob (2011) have begun to show interest in East Asia's and South Asia's trade networks in the past and the place of Southeast Asia in these. This is a good sign; it shows that Korean Southeast Asianists are beginning to see in earnest the Southeast Asian region as an open system, whose boundaries are permeable, and its interactions with outer regions or civilizations as having always been ongoing in its history.

Another outstanding feature of Korean Southeast Asian Studies in the last decade is that collaborative research projects have been quite in fashion. Many researchers formed their own research teams and conducted research on common agendas and issues for a year or multiple years. The resultant outcomes include: studies on Chinese society (Park S. et al. 2000), political change (Park S. 2004), economic development (Yoon 2004), economic crisis and reform (Park S. 2005*b*; Yoon 2005), ethnic conflicts (Oh 2004*a*), civil movements and local society (Kim M. 2005), electoral politics (Shin 2008*a*, 2008*b*), and political leadership (Park S. et al. 2007) in Southeast Asia, as well as on regional cooperation and East Asian regionalism (Park S. et al. 2008; Shin et al. 2008).

And, on top of that, most Korean Southeast Asianists in this period were conducting business as usual, doing research on various issues and themes that they had developed for a long time since their doctoral thesis writing. Some of those research themes and results, especially by the political scientists, are quite classic: political changes and democratization (e.g., Choi J. 2001*b*, 2003; Choi N. 2004; Park E. 2007; Park K. 2002; Park S.W. 2008*b*; Seo 2005); political processes including electoral and party politics (e.g., Cho 2006; Choi J. 2010; Choi K. 2004; Hwang 2002; Jeong 2006, 2009; Lee B. 2000; Lee J. 2006; Lee J. and Hwang 2008; Shin 2008*a*, 2008*b*); civil society and social movements (e.g., Jeon 2002; Oh 2005; Park E. 2003; Park K. 2002); and state and state-society relations (e.g., Choi H. 2003; Jeon 2002, 2010; Kim D. 2005; Park S.W. 2006; Yoon C. 2005; Yoon J. 2007).

Anthropologists and historians have developed other research themes of their own. The favourite topics of Korean anthropologists on Southeast Asia are: religion (Islam in particular) and religion-politics or church-state relations (e.g., Hong 2001; Kim H.-J. 2003, 2007, 2011); national identity, ethnicity, ethno-linguistic groups, ethnic conflicts, and ethnic relations (e.g., Hong 2003; Oh 2004*a*, 2004*b*); and tourism (Choi H. 2009; Kim Y. 2003). Chae Suhong and Kim Ye-kyoum, however, have their own research interests: Chae's interest is in the political economy of factory regimes and production processes (2003*b*, 2009) and Kim's, in Indian language and culture in Southeast Asia (2004), NGOs and Indonesian development (2003*b*), and ethnographic studies of Indonesian women (Kim Y. and King 2004, 2005). Hwang In-Won (2009) and Kang Young Soon (2007, 2010), though political scientists, share the same interest with anthropologists, in ethnic politics in Malaysia and religion (Islam) and politics in Indonesia respectively.

Historians of Southeast Asia, however, do not seem to have any especially favourite or typical topics; theirs are very diverse. Both Choi Byungwook (2004, 2010) and Youn Dae Yeong (2007) have shown interest in the nineteenth and early twentieth century history of Vietnam; Cho Hung-guk

(2008, 2009), in the historical relations between Korea and Southeast Asia; Soh Byungkuk (2005), in Malaysian nationalism under Japanese rule; and Song Seung-Won (2009, 2010), in the Pancasila ideology in Indonesia. They have also published several important books during this period. Cho Hung-guk and Soh Byungkuk presented their reviews of Thai and Malaysian histories in a typically historian's perspective (Cho H. 2007; Soh and Cho 2004), while Choi Byungwook (2006) published a primer on the pre-modern history of Southeast Asia. Yu Insun also published a volume entitled *New History of Vietnam* in 2002.

Lastly, there are also other noteworthy works on a variety of research themes, either in the form of an independent volume or an article in a refereed journal, which need to be briefly considered below. Shin Yoon Hwan's (2001) and Park Sa-Myung's (2006) volumes are important collections of various research carried out during the previous years. Shin's volume contains his research results on Indonesian politics and economy that he had conducted during the 1990s, while Park's book comprises fifteen articles on Southeast Asia's political and economic changes, Chinese economy and Chinese relations with Southeast Asia, and East Asian regionalism that he had written during the years, 1994–2006. Shin's other volume on Southeast Asian cultures (2008c) is a collection of essays on various cultural issues including customs, cuisines, costumes, and other lifestyles, which is quite unique if we consider that he is a political scientist. His book seems to have gained huge popularity among general readers, though. His is a praiseworthy attempt to get closer to the ordinary citizens and to familiarize them with Southeast Asian cultures and peoples.

On the other hand, Yang Seung Yoon's articles on Indian society in Southeast Asia (Yang S. 2001, 2008) and Lew Seok Choon and his colleague's (2009) research on the dynamics of Philippine local politics based on their field study in Mindanao are also noteworthy. Comparative studies between Southeast Asian countries on any issues have been few during the last decade. This is in contrast to the proliferation of comparative studies in the 1990s. Among such rare cases are Kim Ye-kyoum's (2002), Park Seung Woo's (2006), Ra Hee-Ryang's (2008a, 2008b, 2011), Shim Doobo's (2010), and Yoon Jinpyo's (2007) works.

Most of the Korean researchers on Southeast Asia focus more on major countries in Southeast Asia such as Indonesia, Malaysia, the Philippines, Thailand, and Vietnam. However, some of them have shown an interest in other minor countries: Cambodia (Cho Y. 2006, 2009; Jeong 2006, 2009), Laos (Lee Y. 2009), Myanmar (Jang 2008; Lee S. 2010; Park J. 2009; Park J. and Kim 2008), and Timor Leste (Yang S. 2009).

Institutional and Other Important Developments in the 2000s

The first decade of the twenty-first century also witnessed notable progress in terms of the institutional development in Korean Southeast Asian Studies. All Korean academics with research interests in Southeast Asia were affiliated with either local universities or public/private research institutes or both. Southeast Asian area studies programmes in these institutions have grown rapidly. They are also connected with each other through academic societies. Based on this development, collaborative research projects among Korean Southeast Asianists proliferated during the period. Below I will note some major developments.

First of all, the role of local universities should be noted. As far as Southeast Asian Studies is concerned, the importance of HUFS, PUFS, SNU, and Sogang Universities cannot be overstated. The undergraduate programme of HUFS can be considered to be one of the best training grounds for local scholars in the study of Southeast Asia. Around twenty Korean Southeast Asianists in the fields of history and social sciences are graduates of HUFS, most of whom are from Southeast Asian languages departments in the College of Oriental Languages. Around half of them did their Ph.D.s in their *alma maters* and eight of them are now working there as full-time faculty members.

SNU should be proud of its Department of Anthropology. Most Korean anthropologists on Southeast Asia are SNU graduates. SNU's undergraduate programme has produced more than twenty Southeast Asianists and a dozen of them are Anthropology Department graduates. It has also produced seven Ph.D.s who have specialized in Southeast Asia.

PUFS and Sogang University, on the other hand, are among the best cradles of Southeast Asianists in Korea. PUFS is currently employing more than seven social scientists in Southeast Asian Studies and Sogang University and its Institute for East Asian Studies, around seven.

To the development of Southeast Asian Studies in Korea, the public and private research institutes have made a significant contribution. *Dongnama jiyeok yeon'guhoe* (SGSEAS), a network organization which had provided the most important medium of communication and forum of academic dialogues for Southeast Asianists in Korea during the 1990s, was dissolved in December 2003, and its forty full members (full membership requires a doctoral degree in Southeast Asian Studies and approval of full members at the Annual General Meeting) and twenty-five associate members (graduate students in this field who are admitted to the institute with the recommendation of three full members and the approval of majority of the full members) were reorganized into a new research institute called the Korean Institute of Southeast Asian Studies (KISEAS).

KISEAS is a more formalized academic organization and it was registered with the Ministry of Foreign Affairs and Trade (MOFAT) of the Korean government. It has continued to play its previous role by providing an academic arena where scholars and researchers in the field of Southeast Asia meet regularly and exchange their ideas and discuss each others' research results. It is part of the members' obligations to attend monthly seminars and to present research papers once every one or two years.

Since its reorganization the KISEAS has produced several important publications, most of which are collections of papers contributed by its members. They include *Political Leadership in Coping with the Crisis in Southeast Asia* (Park S. et al. 2007), *Beyond Crisis, Toward Cooperation: Widening and Deepening Regional Cooperation in Southeast Asia* (Park S. et al. 2008), *In Search of East Asian Community* (Park S. et al. 2009), and *Transnational Issues and Regional Governance in Southeast Asia* (Yoon et al. 2010). There has recently been a collaborative work published by the KISEAS (2011) that demands special mention. It is the results of a survey on the attitudes and perceptions of peoples of ten ASEAN countries toward Korea and Korean people. The survey was conducted by many able researchers affiliated with the KISEAS for two years 2008–10. It was funded by the ASEAN-Korea Special Cooperation Fund.[8]

The Institute for East Asian Studies at Sogang University (SIEAS) established in 1981 is one of the outstanding university-affiliated research institutes, which have played a leading role in East Asian and Southeast Asian Studies in Korea. Shin Yoon Hwan assumed the post of its Director in 2002 and under his leadership SIEAS has achieved a remarkable development. During the years 2002–04, it undertook a series of huge research projects, working as the hub institution in a research consortium consisting of several universities and research institutes. It collaborated with more than sixty scholars and forty research associates in the fields of East and Southeast Asian Studies. Among the research outcomes are Kim M. (2005); Oh (2004*a*); Park S. (2004, 2005*b*); and Yoon J. (2004, 2005).[9] In 2006–07 Shin Yoon Hwan led another research project dealing with elections and electoral system/process in Southeast Asian countries, the results of which were published in two volumes (Shin 2008*a*, 2008*b*).[10]

In 2008, SIEAS was selected as the first local research institute in Southeast Asian Studies to receive a ten-year research grant under the Humanities Korea (HK) programme sponsored by the National Research

Foundation and the Republic of Korea (ROK) Ministry of Education, Science and Technology. The total amount of the grant is expected to be around 9 million U.S. dollars. This funding enabled the institute to employ ten full-time faculty members, most of whom are specialists in Southeast Asian Studies whose names were mentioned above. The institute launched a ten-year research project, entitled "Southeast Asia as an Open Regional System", of which the present work is part.

Finally, the role played by the KASEAS should also be mentioned. KASEAS has long held regular academic conferences twice (or thrice) a year from its inception. A list of the themes of conferences that have been held for the last twelve years is shown in Table 4.1. Since the early 2000s, it has also held academic conferences regularly every two years in

Table 4.1

Themes of the Conferences Organized by the Korean Association of Southeast Asian Studies (KASEAS), 2001–12

Year	Season*	Main Theme
2001	Annual	The Changes in and the Identities of Southeast Asia
2001	Summer	The Revival of Islam and the Separatist Movements in Asia
2002	Annual	The Political Economy and Social Changes in Southeast Asia
2002	Summer	Women, Social Structure and Cultural Identities of Southeast Asia
2002	Fall	The Development, Crisis and Cultural Identities of Southeast Asia
2003	Annual	The Political Systems and the Economic Transformation of Southeast Asia
2003	Summer	The Culture of Southeast Asia and the Social Changes in the Philippines
2003	Fall	The Political Economy and Socio-Cultural Dynamics of Southeast Asia
2004	Spring	The Historical Formation and Structural Transformation of Southeast Asia
2004	Fall	The Structural Differentiation and Cultural Assimilation in Southeast Asia
2005	Spring	The Politics in Southeast Asia: Electoral Politics and Political Leadership

Table 4.1 *(Cont'd)*

Year	Season*	Main Theme
2005	Fall	APEC and Southeast Asia: Changes and Cooperation
2006	Spring	International Cooperation and Political Changes in Southeast Asia
2006	Fall	Human Rights and Democracy in Asia
2007	Spring	Borders, Migration and Globalisation: Southeast Asia in Transition in the 21st Century
2007	Fall	The Accomplishment of Southeast Asian Studies in Korea since the 1990s: Retrospection and Reflection
2008	Spring	New Horizons for the Southeast Asian Studies in Korea: The Mutual Relationship between Korea and Southeast Asia and the Regional Governance
2008	Fall	Democracy and the Challenge of Civil Society in Southeast Asia
2009	Spring	Korea, Japan and Southeast Asia: The Migration, Investment, and Cultural Flow (The 1st KASEAS-CSEAS Joint International Conference)**
2009	Fall	The Interconnection between Northeast Asia and Southeast Asia: Their Different Dreams and Intentions on East Asian Regionalism
2010	Spring	The Outside World and Southeast Asia: The Influences from East Asia, India, Europe and the Mid East
2010	Fall	The Religion and Politics of Southeast Asia: The State, Society, and Individuals
2011	Spring	The Boundaries and Outer Limits of Southeast Asian Studies in Korea
2011	October	Green and Life in ASEAN: Coexistence and Sustainability in East Asian Connections (The 2nd KASEAS-CSEAS Joint International Conference)**
2011	Fall	The Present and Future of Southeast Asian Studies in Korea
2012	Spring	Transnational Southeast Asia: Comparative and Transnational Approaches

Notes: * Annual conferences were held in March during the 2001–03 period. In recent years Spring conferences used to be held in April or May and Fall conferences, in October or November.
** CSEAS refers to the Center for Southeast Asian Studies at Kyoto University, Japan. The 1st KASEAS-CSEAS Joint International Conference was held in Jinju city in Korea, while the 2nd in Kyoto University in Japan.

Table 4.2
Korea-ASEAN Academic Conferences Jointly Organized by
KASEAS and AUN (ASEAN University Network),
2003–11

Date	Venue	Theme
Feb. 2003	Quezon City, Philippines	Regional Cooperation and Identity Building in East Asia in the Age of Post-Cold War Globalization
June 2004	Penang, Malaysia	Southeast Asian Studies in Korea and Korean Studies in Southeast Asia
Nov. 2005	Seoul, Korea	East Asian Cooperation and Integration: Implications of the 1st East Asia Summit
Jan. 2007	Ho Chi Minh City, Vietnam	Information Revolution and Cultural Integration in East Asia
Feb. 2009	Chon Buri, Thailand	Pop Culture Formations across East Asia in the 21st Century: Hybridization or Asianization
Feb. 2011	Bali, Indonesia	Revisiting Transnationalism in East Asia: Emerging Issues, Evolving Concepts

cooperation with the ASEAN University Network (AUN) (see Table 4.2). It has continued to publish the collections of papers delivered in those conferences. Among the collections published during the 2000s are *Regional Cooperation and Identity Building in East Asia* (Park S. and Supachai 2003), *The Promise of ICTs in Asia: Key Trends and Issues* (Lim, Sison, and Kim 2008),[11] and *Pop Culture Formations across East Asia* (Shim, Heryanto, and Siriyuvasak 2010).[12]

CONCLUSIONS:
PROBLEMS AND LIMITATIONS

Southeast Asian Studies in Korea has shown in recent years promising signs of development. Many new young scholars and researchers have joined this field of study. And, more and more young students are showing interest in this region. Unlike the earlier generation of Southeast Asianists, they are oriented, from the beginning, more seriously toward the study of the Southeast Asian region and trained more systematically. They, together with the first generation seniors, have developed and pursued many diverse research issues and themes during the past decade. A lot of collaborative research projects have also been conducted, producing many new research results that deserve high praise. This positive and promising situation is in contrast to that of Europe and the U.S., where area studies on Asia in general, and Southeast Asia in particular, has been in decline since the 1990s.[13]

However, this encouraging picture is not without defects; Southeast Asian Studies in Korea, of course, has its own problems and limitations. Three points stand out. First, Korean social scientists engaged in studies of Southeast Asia have so far produced basically "descriptive" works. It is not that descriptive works are inappropriate and unimportant. The problem rather lies in the fact that more serious attempts at a causal explanation, in-depth analysis, theoretical interpretation and generalization using more elaborate theoretical and methodological frameworks are scarce. We can consider some of the reasons for this generally unsatisfactory condition. One is that more recently studies of Southeast Asian countries take the form of a single case/country study rather than a comparative study, the latter of which had once been in vogue during the early 1990s. The other is that much of the research on Southeast Asia is more of applied and/or policy-oriented studies, which tend to be more descriptive and normative rather than theoretical. Although what has been accomplished by Korean academics should not be underestimated, more analytical and theoretical endeavours by Korean academics on Southeast Asia are still needed.

Secondly, a more serious effort to transcend the disciplinary boundaries and to ultimately integrate them into a unique and independent discipline of "Southeast Asian Studies" or "Southeast Asiology" is still lacking. There have been many attempts by local social scientists on Southeast Asia at interdisciplinary research on the region. However, they have been below expectation in the sense that most Korean Southeast Asianists have engaged in the study of Southeast Asia on a basically individual basis and/or "in parallel" with each other. Even though they share an academic interest in and a commitment to Southeast Asia, there has not been much serious attempt at collaborative and "integrative" research. What is needed is not just an inter- or multi-disciplinary approach to the region but a trans-disciplinary and integrative approach to the study of Southeast Asia, although that might not be an easy task to accomplish in the near future.

Lastly, although more and more research results are being published in English and other languages, publications in Korean language are still overwhelming. There have been many praiseworthy achievements by Korean academics in Southeast Asian Studies written in Korean, but the language barrier has prevented them from being widely known, and not delivered to foreign audiences. Nor are the academic exchanges and cooperation with Southeast Asianists abroad satisfactory; they still come short of many people's expectations. More and more research conducted by Korean Southeast Asianists should reach academics in other countries, and more academic exchanges and collaborative research with them should also be encouraged.

If younger generation Southeast Asianists devote more effort and energy and show more enthusiasm and passion to deal with these problems and to cope with these limitations, then Southeast Asian Studies in Korea will surely show much brighter prospects in the coming decade.

Notes

[1] Some argue that Korean academic interest in Southeast Asia began as early as the 1930s (e.g., Youn 2009).

[2] In this study, one is acknowledged to be a "Southeast Asianist" when and if he or she has received a doctoral degree or publishes three or more academic research papers in refereed journal with his/her dissertation or research papers dealing with the issues or themes directly related to Southeast Asia.

[3] Pusan University of Foreign Studies (PUFS), established in 1981, followed suit. It began to offer undergraduate programmes in Southeast Asian languages when it started departments in Thai and Malay-Indonesian languages in 1982 and then Vietnamese and Myanmar languages in 1991 and 1992 respectively (Park S.W. 2010).

[4] Note on the transliteration of Korean personal names: all Korean names are given in the order of surname going first followed by first name(s) throughout the text in this chapter. This is the everyday practice in Korea. References are also arranged in such an order. Most Koreans do not have their middle name(s).

There are so many Kims, Lees, and Parks in Korea and naturally, if you look at the entries in the reference list at the end of this chapter, you will find many works by different authors with the same last name. In these cases the text citation will include an (or two if necessary) initial and there are many such cases.

[5] SNU, a prestigious local state-run university, together with HUFS, turned out the majority of Southeast Asian area specialists in Korea. The graduates of SNU constitute around one-fifth of Korean Southeast Asianists, while those of HUFS around one-sixth.

[6] Some previous studies on the history of Southeast Asian Studies in Korea label those scholars who started their academic careers as Southeast Asianists during the late 1980s and the early 1990s as the "second generation" (Cho, Oh, and Park 1998; Jeon 2006; Jeon and Lee 2008; Park S.W. 2009). On the

other hand, less than a dozen senior scholars including such figures as Ahn Chung-Si, Choi Chang-Sung, Kim Ki-Tae, Lee Eun-Ho and Yu Insun, who had taught and done research on Southeast Asia from the 1960s or 1970s, were seen as constituting the "first generation". This study, however, proposes a more conservative view that a "serious" and full-fledged area study on Southeast Asia has not started before the late 1980s.

[7]   Shin Yoon Hwan is one of the rare cases. Being one of the first generation scholars, Shin stayed in Indonesia for a long while doing his field research and learning the local language.

[8]   The researchers who participated in this project are listed below. All of them are members of the KISEAS. In parentheses is the name of country that they served as the main investigator or the research theme they were responsible for: Choi Horim (Vietnam), Hong Seok-Joon (Malaysia), Jeong Yeonsik (Cambodia), Kim Dong-Yeob (Philippines), Kim Hong-Koo (Thailand), Kim Hyung-Jun (Indonesia), Kim Ye-kyoum (Brunei), Lee Yohan (Laos), Park Jang Sik (Myanmar), Shim Doobo (Singapore), Yoon Jinpyo (General), and Park Sa-Myung, Bae Geung-Chan, and Lee Jaehyon (Southeast Asian people's perceptions toward China, Japan and Australia).

[9]   The Southeast Asia specialists who participated in this research project and contributed their papers to these volumes are as follows: Bae Geung-Chan, Cho Hung-guk, Choi Byungwook, Hong Seok-Joon, Hwang In-Won, Jeon Je-Seong, Je Dae-Sik, Jeong Yeonsik, Kim Dong-Yeob, Kim Hong-Koo, Kim Hyung-Jun, Kim Jongouk, Kim Minjung, Kim Youngaih, Kwon Yul, Lee Dong-Yoon, Lee Hanwoo, Lee Yohan, Nho Young Soon, Oh Myung-seok, Park Bun Soon, Park Kie-Duck, Park Sa-Myung, Park Seung Woo, Shin Yoon Hwan, Soh Byungkuk, and Yoon Jinpyo. In addition to them, many area specialists in the studies of China and Japan also took part in the programme.

[10] Those who participated in this research project are as follows: Hong Seok-Joon, Jeon Je-Seong, Kim Dong-Yeob, Kim Hyung-Jun, and Lee Choong Lyol.

[11] Those who contributed their papers to this collection are: Hong Seok-Joon, Hwang In-Won, Jeon Je-Seong, Kim Dong-Yeob, Kim Hong-Koo, and Kim Hyung-Jun.

[12] The local Southeast Asianists who contributed their papers to this collection are Kim Hyung-Jun, Kim Minjung, and Shim Doobo. Participants from Southeast Asian countries are Ariel Heryanto (ANU), Zawawi Ibrahim (Universiti Teknologi MARA, Malaysia), Rachmah Ida (Airlangga University, Indonesia), Liew Kai Khiun (NTU, Singapore), Joseph Salazar (ADMU, Philippines) and Ubonrat Siriyuvasak (Chulalongkorn University, Thailand).

[13] This assessment is found in "Futures of Asian Studies", *Asian Studies Newsletter* (USA) (Summer 1997): 7–12, cited in Milner (1999) and Ruth McVey's article (1998, p. 37). In Australia and Japan, however, Asian Studies seems to be still in vigor (Milner 1999; Suehiro 1999).

References

1. Publications in Korean

Ahn Chung-Si et al. *Southeast Asia and ASEAN*. Seoul: Seoul National University Press, 1981.

————. *The Local Political System in Asia: A Comparative Perspective*. Seoul: Seoul National University Press, 1987.

Bae Geung-Chan. "ASEAN+3 Regional Cooperation". *Korean Observation on Foreign Relations* 3, no. 1 (2001).

————. "ASEAN+3 Cooperation and Regional Identity". *Dongnam-asia yeon'gu* [Southeast Asian Review] (Korean Association of Southeast Asian Studies) 13, no. 1 (2003).

Byun Chang-Ku. "A Study on ASEAN's Regional Security Cooperation". Ph.D. dissertation, Kyungpook National University, Korea, 1987.

Chae Suhong. "The Ho Chi Minh City and the Political Economy of the Reform". *Cross-Cultural Studies* (Institute of Cultural Studies, SNU) 9, no. 1 (2003*b*).

————. "Vietnamese Returnees from Immigrant Work in Korea: Their Life and Human Exchange in East Asia". *Cross-Cultural Studies* 13, no. 2 (2007).

Cho Hung-guk. "The Trade between China, Japan, Korea and Southeast Asia in the 14th through the 17th Century Period". *International Area Review* (Center for International Area Studies, HUFS) 3, no. 2 (2000).

————. "Problems and Perspectives of South East Asian Studies in Korea". *International Area Studies Review* (International Association of Area Studies in Korea) 5, no. 1 (2001): 47–67.

————. *Thailand: Land of Buddhism and King*. Seoul: Sonamu, 2007.

————. "Contacts between Korea and Majapahit Kingdom in Indonesia in the Beginning of the Joseon Dynasty". *Donga yeon'gu* [East Asian Studies] (Institute for East Asian Studies, Sogang University) 55 (2008): 45–69.

————. *History of Exchanges between Korea and Southeast Asia*. Seoul: Sonamu, 2009.

Cho Hung-guk, Oh Myung-seok, and Park Sa-Myung. "The Present Status and Future Tasks of Southeast Asian Studies in Korea". In *The Present Status and Future Tasks of Foreign Area Studies in Korea*, edited by Yi Sang-seob and Kwon Tae-hwan. Seoul: Seoul National University Press, 1998.

Cho Jae-Hyun. *Theories on Modern Vietnamese Poetry*. Seoul: Yeongdong Munhwasa, 1976.

————. *An Outline of Modern Vietnamese Literature*. Seoul: HUFS Press, 1981.

Cho Young Hee. "Cambodia's Party Politics and Elections since the Introduction of Party Pluralism". Ph.D. dissertation, Inha University, Korea, 2006.

————. "The Development Path of Cambodian NGOs". *Democracy and Human Rights* (5–18 Institute, Chonnam National University) 9, no. 3 (2009): 137–69.

Choi Byungwook. "A Study on the Cao Ba Quat Rebellion, 1854". *Dongnam-asia yeon'gu* 14, no. 2 (2004).

————. *History of Southeast Asia: Traditional Age*. Seoul: Daehan Textbook Publisher, 2006.

————. "Vietnamese Annexation of Cambodia (1835–1847) with the Handling of the Queen Mei". *Dongnam-asia yeon'gu* 20, no. 2 (2010).

Choi Chang-Sung. *A Study on Thai Language*. Seoul: HUFS Press, 1968.

————. *Intermediate Readings on Thai Language*. Seoul: Yeonhapsa, 1969.

————. *Introduction to Thai Grammar*. Seoul: Samgyeongsa, 1975.

Choi Horim. "Ritual Revitalization and State-Society Relations in Vietnam". Ph.D. dissertation, Seoul National University, 2003.

————. "Vietnam War Memory and Tourism". *Donga yeon'gu* 57 (2009): 269–313.

————. "Transnational Labor Migration in Southeast Asia and Regional Governance". *Dongnam-asia yeon'gu* 20, no. 2 (2010).

Choi Jungug. "Capital Flows, Political Cleavages, and Economic Policy Choice: Malaysia during the Asian Economic Crisis". *Dongnam-asia yeon'gu* 13, no. 1 (2003): 383–400.

Choi Kyunghee. "Determinants of Democratic Quality of Political Regimes: An Empirical-Comparative Analysis of the Five East Asian Nations". Ph.D. dissertation, Hankuk University of Foreign Studies, Korea, 2004.

————. "The Intermediate Evaluation on Achievement and Anti-corruption Strategy of Yudhoyono's Government in Indonesia". *Korean Journal of International Relations* (Korean Association of International Studies) 48, no. 1 (2008).

Eom Eunhui. "Neoliberalization of the Environment and the Change of the Third World Environment: Political Ecology of the RapuRapu Mining Project in the Philippines". Ph.D. dissertation, Seoul National University, 2008.

Hong Seok-Joon. "The Cultural Meaning of National Identity of Malays in Contemporary Malaysia". *International and Area Studies Review* 2 (1993).

————. "The Islamization and Social Change in Malaysian Rural Society". Ph.D. dissertation, Seoul National Unversity, 1997.

————. "The Islamization and the Traditional Rituals in Contemporary Malaysia". *Journal of Rural Society* (Korean Rural Sociological Society) 9 (1999): 37–66.

————. "The Cultural Meanings of Islamic Revivalism in Contemporary Malaysia". *Dongnam-asia yeon'gu* 11, no. 1 (2001): 1–27.

————. "The Dynamics of Malay-Muslims Ethnic Identities: The Comparative Study of Malay Societies in Malaysia and Thailand". *Dongnam-asia yeon'gu* 13, no. 1 (2003): 101–29.

————. "Sea World of East Asia and the History and Culture of East Asian Port Cities". *Doseo munhwa* [Journal of the Island Culture] (Institute of Island Culture, Mokpo National University) 29 (2007): 403–39.

Hwang In-Won. "Mahathir's Political Legacy and Abdullah Badawi's Political Leadership". *Dongnam-asia yeon'gu* 17, no. 2 (2007): 207–39.

————. "ASEAN's Response towards the Widening and Deepening of East Asian Regionalism". *Donga yeon'gu* 54 (2008): 51–82.

————. "Revisiting Multi-Ethnic Politics in Malaysia". *Donga yeon'gu* 57 (2009): 315–52.

Jang Jun Young. "The Neo-Military and Political Change in Myanmar: Political Power of the Military and Prospects for Democratization". Ph.D. dissertation, Hankuk University of Foreign Studies, Korea, 2008.

Je Dae-Sik. "The Background and Development of Aceh Separatist Movement in Indonesia". *Dongnam-asia yeon'gu* 13, no. 1 (2003): 65–99.

Jeon Je Seong. "Labor Disputes and Indonesian Government in the 1990s". *Dongnam-asia yeon'gu* 6 (1998): 167–92.

————. "Economic Crisis, Political Reform and Labor Problems in Korean Companies in Indonesia: Focusing on Clothing and Factories in Jabetabek". *Dongnam-asia yeon'gu* 8 (1999): 117–54.

————. "Labor Politics in Democratizing Indonesia: The Collapse of State-Corporatism and the Rise of Working-Class Leadership". Ph.D. dissertation, Seoul National University, 2002.

————. "Dynamics and the Future of Southeast Asian Studies in Korea: Waiting for a Manifesto of the 'Third-Generation'". *Donga yeon'gu* 50 (2006): 109–40.

————. "Participatory Regionalism in Southeast Asia and Its Implications for 'East Asian Community'". *Dongnam-asia yeon'gu* 17, no. 2 (2007): 101–30.

————. "The Changing Relations between Indonesian State and Foreign Capital". *Dongnam-asia yeon'gu* 20, no. 1 (2010): 259–98.

Jeon Je Seong and Lee Jaehyon. "Education Process and a Model for Reproducing Southeast Asia Area Specialists in Korea". *Dongnam-asia yeon'gu* 18, no. 2 (2008): 255–97.

Jeong Yeonsik. "Social Market Economies and Corporatism: A Comparative Study of Civil Society in China and Vietnam". *Korean Political Science Review* (Korean Political Science Association) 33, no. 2 (1999): 303–24.

————. "The Electoral Process in Cambodia: Political Functions and Meanings". *Dongnam-asia yeon'gu* 16, no. 1 (2006): 93–118.

————. "Cambodia's 2008 Election: Consolidation of Electoral Authoritarianism". *Donga yeon'gu* 56 (2009): 139–70.

Kang Young Soon. "The Competition and Cooperation of Islamic Organizations in the Present Indonesia's Election Politics: Nahdlatul Ulama and Muhammadiyah". *Dongnam-asia yeon'gu* 17, no. 1 (2007): 69–113.

————. "A Study of Traditional Islamic Educational Institution in Indonesia: Pondok Pesantren". *Asia yeon'gu* [Journal of Asian Studies] (Korean Association of Asian Studies) 13, no. 1 (2010): 29–68.

Kim Dong-Yeob. "The Political Economy of Malaysia: Beyond Economic Crisis and Mahathir, Towards Neo-liberal State". *Donga yeon'gu* 48 (2005): 100–38.

————. "The Practice and Prospects of Korean Retirement Migration to Southeast Asia: The Philippine Case". *Donga yeon'gu* 58 (2009): 233–67.

————. "Intermarriage Migration and Transnationalism Focused on Filipina Wives in South Korea". *Dongnam-asia yeon'gu* 20, no. 2 (2010): 31–72.

———. "Nature and Changes of Southeast Asian Maritime Trade in 15–16 Century: Focused on Portuguese Contact and Influences". *Dongnam-asia yeon'gu* 21, no. 2 (2011): 1–41.

Kim Hong-Koo. "A Study on the Causes of Military Intervention in Politics during the Period from 1932 to 1976 in Thailand". Ph.D. dissertation, Hankuk University of Foreign Studies, Korea, 1990.

———. "Thai Buddhism and Political Legitimacy". *Dongnam-asia yeon'gu* 4 (1996): 57–92.

———. *Introduction to Thai Studies*. Busan, Korea: Pusan University of Foreign Studies Press, 1999.

———. "Korean Wave in Thailand". *Journal of Korean Association of Thai Studies* 12 (2005): 109–43.

———. "Thai Wave in Korea". *Journal of Korean Association of Thai Studies* 15, no. 2 (2009): 149–82.

———. "The Origin and Diffusion of 'Southeast Asian Phenomena' in Korea". *Dongnam-asia yeon'gu* 21, no. 2 (2011): 77–123.

Kim Hyung-Jun. "Formation of Religious Authority and Its Characteristics in Indonesian Islam". *Dongnam-asia yeon'gu* 13, no. 2 (2003): 223–50.

———. "Political Jihad: Participation of Muhammadiyah in the Indonesian Presidential Election of 2004". *Dongnam-asia yeon'gu* 17, no. 1 (2007): 33–68.

———. "Responses of Javanese Muslims to Islam: Analysis of Three Religious Texts". *Dongnam-asia yeon'gu* 21, no. 2 (2011): 155–82.

Kim Ki-Tae. *Elementary Vietnamese*. Seoul: HUFS Press, 1970.

———. *Intermediate Vietnamese*. Seoul: HUFS Press, 1971.

Kim Minjung. "A Study of Philippine Women Labor". *Dongnam-asia yeon'gu* 2 (1993).

———. "Family and Women in Southeast Asia". In *The Society and Culture in Southeast Asia*, edited by Study Group on Southeast Asian Studies (SGSEAS). Seoul: Oruem, 1997.

———. "Power, Gender and Motherhood in Philippine Rural Village". Ph.D. dissertation, Seoul National University, 2002.

———, ed. *Middle Classes, Civil Movements and Local Society in Southeast Asia*. Seoul: Politeia, 2005.

———. "International Marriage and Human Rights: International Marriages in Korea and the Philippines and the Issue of Human Rights". *Human Rights Review* 2 (2007).

———. "Filipina Singers on the Live Bar Stage in South Korea: Positioning between 'Musician' and 'Entertainer'". *Dongnam-asia yeon'gu* 19, no. 2 (2009): 219–51.

———. "Philippine Female Labor Migrants in Korea". *Korean Cultural Anthropology* (Korean Society for Cultural Anthropology) 44, no. 2 (2011).

Kim Minjung, Yoo Myungki, Lee Hyu-kyung, and Chung Kiseon. "Being 'Korean' Wives: Dilemmas and Choices of Vietnamese and Filipino Migrants". *Korean Cultural Anthropology* 39, no. 1 (2006): 159–93.

Kim Yi-jae. "Resisting the Stereotyped Southeast Asia in World Regional Geography". Ph.D. dissertation, Department of Social Studies, Seoul National University, 2005.

Kim Yi Seon. "Development of Tourism and the Change of Production and Meaning System of Thai Handicraft: A Case Study of Baan Thawai, a Woodcarving Village in Chiangmai". Ph.D. dissertation, Seoul National University, 2003.

Korean Association of Thai Studies (KATS), ed. *An Understanding of Thailand*. Seoul: HUFS Press, 1998.

Korean Institute of Southeast Asian Studies (KISEAS). *Southeast Asian Perceptions of Korea*. Seoul: Myung In Publishers, 2011.

Kwon Oh Shin. *American Imperialism*. Seoul: Munhakkwa Jiseongsa, 2000.

Kwon Yul. "A Study of the Gradualist Approach to Reform in Vietnam". Ph.D. dissertation, Sogang University, Korea, 1999.

———. *The Expansion of ASEAN Economic Integration and the Countermeasures of Korea*. Seoul: Korean Institute for International Economic Policy (KIEP), 2003.

———. "Regionalism in East Asia". *Dongnam-asia yeon'gu* 14, no. 1 (2004).

———. "East Asian Economic Integration". *Dongnam-asia yeon'gu* 15, no. 2 (2005).

Lee Byungdo. "A Study on Change and Institutionalization of Political Parties in Thailand". Ph.D. dissertation, Hankuk University of Foreign Studies, Korea, 2000.

Lee Choong Lyol and Lee Sun Ho. "The Export Direction and Strategies of Electronic Banking and Finance Market of Southeast Asian Countries". *Dongnam-asia yeon'gu* 19, no. 1 (2009): 29–66.

Lee Dong-Yoon. "Party Politics and Democracy in Southeast Asia: A Comparative Study of the Philippines, Thailand, and Indonesia". Ph.D. dissertation, Yonsei University, Korea, 2002.

Lee Hanwoo. "Agricultural Reform Policy in Vietnam, 1975–1993". Ph.D. dissertation, Sogang University, Korea, 1999.

———. "'Wave of Korean Cultures' in Vietnam: Its Formation and Socio-economic Influence". *Donga yeon'gu* 42 (2002): 93–113.

———. "Vietnam-China Relation in Historical Perspective: Cooperation and Conflict". *Donga yeon'gu* 44 (2003): 131–63.

———. "Japanese and Chinese Views on the East Asian Community". *Dongnam-asia yeon'gu* 17, no. 2 (2007): 65–100.

Lee Jaehyon. "Changing Malaysian Society in the 1990s and UMNO's Factional Dispute in 1998". *Dongnam-asia yeon'gu* 16, no. 2 (2006): 115–44.

———. "A Comparative Study of Visions for East Asian Regional Cooperation of Mahathir and Kim Dae-Jung". *Dongnam-asia yeon'gu* 17, no. 2 (2007a): 33–64.

————. "Mahathir's Discourse of East Asian Regionalism: A Quest for an Anti-West Developmental Coalition of Asia". *Korean Journal of International Relations* 47, no. 1 (2007*b*): 121–44.

Lee Jaehyon and Hwang In-Won. "The Analysis of Political Implications of the 2008 Malaysian General Election". *Sinasea* [New Asia] 15, no. 4 (2008): 64–92.

Lee Kyung Chan. "Malaysia's US Policy and Malaysian-US Relations under Mahathir". Ph.D. dissertation, Hankuk University of Foreign Studies, Korea, 2006.

Lee Sang Kook. "Migrants, Illegality and a Border Social System: A Study of a Border Social System in the Thailand-Myanmar Borderland". *Dongnam-asia yeon'gu* 18, no. 1 (2008): 109–50.

————. "White Saviors and the Karen: A Karen Myth Becoming Reality". *Korean Cultural Anthropology* 43, no. 1 (2010): 217–62.

Lee Yohan. "A Study on the Schemes of Regional Cooperation Change of Politico-economy in East Asia: Based on the Neo-liberal Institutionalism". Ph.D. dissertation, Hankuk University of Foreign Studies, Korea, 2000.

————. "Reappraisal of East Asia Cooperation Theory: ASEAN+3 Case". *Dongnam-asia yeon'gu* 13, no. 1 (2003): 313–39.

————. "A Study on the Efficiency Strategy of Korean Official Development Assistance for Lao PDR". *Dongnam-asia yeon'gu* 19, no. 1 (2009): 185–213.

Lew Seok Choon. "Social Systems in the Philippines". *Dongnam-asia yeon'gu* 3 (1994): 91–128.

————. "Social Systems in Malaysia". *Dongnam-asia yeon'gu* 4 (1995): 93–112.

Lew Seok Choon and Wang Hye Suk. "The Dynamics of Local Politics in the Philippines: A Case Study on the PBMA in Surigao del Norte Province". *Dongnam-asia yeon'gu* 19, no. 2 (2009): 1–56.

Oh Myung-seok. "The Origin and Social Characteristics of Malay Rubber Small Holders". *Dongnam-asia yeon'gu* 2 (1993): 85–109.

————. "Changing Identities of Malay Women: Between Islam, Adat, and Modernization". *Korean Cultural Anthropology* 30, no. 1 (1997): 3–51.

————. "Family Farm and Inheritance in Malay Rural Society". *Journal of Rural Society* 9 (1999*a*): 122–61.

————. "Chinese Society in Malaysia, 1945–1969". *Dongnam-asia yeon'gu* 7 (1999*b*): 245–69.

————, ed. *Regionalism and Ethnic Conflicts in Southeast Asia*. Seoul: Oruem, 2004*a*.

————. "Pork Consumption and Ethnic Relations in Malaysia". *Dongnam-asia yeon'gu* 14, no. 2 (2004*b*): 1–38.

————. "Malay Middle Class and Reformist Movement in Malaysia". *Cross-Cultural Studies* 11, no. 1 (2005): 187–224.

Oh Myung-seok et al. "Southeast Asian Studies in Korea since the 1990s" [Round-table discussion records]. *Dongnam-asia yeon'gu* 18, no. 2 (2008): 331–99.

Park Bun Soon. "A Study on the Evolution of Korean Investment in ASEAN". Ph.D. dissertation, Hankuk University of Foreign Studies, Korea, 1999.

————. *Asian Economy, Searching for Coexistence*. Seoul: Samsung Economic Research Institute, 2005.

————. *One East Asia*. Seoul: Samsung Economic Research Institute, 2010.

Park Eunhong. "A Study on Thai Democratization". *Dongnam-asia yeon'gu* 3 (1994): 149–87.

————. "The Political Economy of the Public Economy in Developing Countries: A Study on the Transformation of the State Owned Enterprises in Thailand". Ph.D. dissertation, Sogang University, Korea, 1998.

————. "The Emergence and Evolution of Civil Society in Southeast Asia: Focusing on the Thai Case". *Dongnam-asia yeon'gu* 13, no. 2 (2003): 39–68.

————. "Transformation of Thai Democracy". *Democratic Society and Policy Studies* 12 (2007): 129–52.

Park Jang Sik. 1993. "Ethnic Groups and Ethnic Conflicts in Myanmar". *Jiyeok yeon'gu* [International Area Studies] (Institute of International Area Studies, SNU) 2, no. 4 (1993): 57–76.

————. "Secessionist Movement of Karen People in Myanmar". *Dongnama yeon'gu* [Journal of Southeast Asia] (CSEAS, HUFS) 4 (1995): 255–82.

————. "The Aspects of Ethnic Conflict and the Prospect of National Integration in Myanmar". *Dongnam-asia yeon'gu* 4 (1996*a*): 29–56.

————. "Aspects of the Vicissitudes in Sino-Myanmar Relations from the Classical Era to the Premodern Period". *International Area Studies Review* 3, no. 1 (1999): 59–82.

————. "The Political Economy of Natural Gas in Myanmar". *Dongnam-asia yeon'gu* 19, no. 2 (2009): 1–38.

Park Jang Sik and Kim In-A. "A Reassessment of the Colonial Period in Myanmar". *Dongnam-asia yeon'gu* 18, no. 1 (2008): 73–107.

Park Kie-Duck. "Civil-Military Relationship and Socio-Economic Reform in the Philippines". *Korean Journal of International Relations* 34, no. 1 (1994): 171–200.

————. "Political Change and the Role of Civil Society in the Philippines". *Korean Political Science Review* 36, no. 1 (2002): 263–86.

Park Sa-Myung. "The Crisis and Transformation of State: A Comparison of Indonesia and the Philippines". *Korean Journal of International Relations* 31 (1991): 225–55.

————. "A Social Revolution at Transition: The Crisis and Future Direction of the Revolutionary Social Movement in the Philippines". *Dongnam-asia yeon'gu* 2 (1993): 111–43.

————. "Class Formation in Colonial Societies: A Historical Comparison of Indonesia and the Philippines". *Dongnam-asia yeon'gu* 4 (1996): 3–28.

————. "The Impact and Transformation of the Social Movements in the Philippines". *Korean Journal of International Relations* 39, no. 3 (1999): 219–41.

————. "Globalization and Southeast Asia: Challenge and Response". *Korean Political Science Review* 34, no. 4 (2000): 301–19.

————, ed. *The Dynamics of Political Change in Southeast Asia*. Seoul: Oruem, 2004.

————. "From Battlefield to Marketplace: Change and Continuity in China-ASEAN Relations". *Dongnam-asia yeon'gu* 15, no. 2 (2005*a*): 1–40.

————, ed. *The Economic Crisis and Political Responses in Southeast Asia*. Seoul: Politeia, 2005*b*.

————. *A New Search for East Asia: From Battlefield to the Marketplace, From the Marketplace to the Public Space*. Seoul: Imagine, 2006.

————. "From the Marketplace to the Public Space: Beyond Developmental Competition in East Asia". *Dongnam-asia yeon'gu* 17, no. 2 (2007): 1–31.

Park Sa-Myung, Hwang In-Won, Kwon Yul, Chae Suhong, Lee Jaehyon, and Jeon Je Seong. *Beyond Crisis, Toward Cooperation: Widening and Deepening Regional Cooperation in Southeast Asia*. Seoul: Imagine, 2008.

Park Sa-Myung, Lee Hanwoo, Kwon Yul, Chae Suhong, Lee Jaehyon, Jeon Je Seong, and Cho Young Hee. *In Search of East Asian Community*. Seoul: Imagine, 2009.

Park Sa-Myung, Shin Yoon Hwan, Oh Myung-seok, Cho Hung-guk et al. *Chinese Society in Southeast Asia*. Seoul: Tradition and Modernity, 2000.

Park Sa-Myung and Supachai Yavaprabhas, eds. *Regional Cooperation and Identity Building in East Asia*. Seoul: Korean Association of Southeast Asian Studies, 2003.

Park Sa-Myung, Yoon Jinpyo, Jeon Je Seong, Hwang In-Won, and Kim Minjung. *Political Leadership in Coping with the Crisis in Southeast Asia*. Seoul: Imagine, 2007.

Park Seung Woo. "Socio-Economic Changes in Korea and the Philippines under Colonialism and Their Implications". *Journal of Culture and Society* 8 (1993): 109–34.

————. "A Comparative Study on Post-War Agricultural Restructuring and Capitalist Industrialization between Korea and the Philippines". *Journal of Rural Society* 4 (1994): 241–70.

————. "The Origins and Production Systems of Sugar and Coconut Industries in the Philippines". *Journal of Humanities* 19, no. 2 (1998*b*): 159–87.

————. "Agricultural Production Systems and Structural Changes in Rural Society in the Philippines, 1960s–1970s: Focusing on Rice and Sugar Sectors". *Journal of Rural Society* 8 (1998*c*): 186–217.

————. "The Formation of the Indigenous Ruling Class in the Philippines under Spanish Colonialism". *Dongnam-asia yeon'gu* 13, no. 1 (2003): 1–34.

————. "The Dynamic Interplay of State, Social Class, and the Nation in Southeast Asia: The Cases of Malaysia and the Philippines". *Donga yeon'gu* 50 (2006): 184–233.

————. "Discourses on East Asian Regionalism and the Problem of Orientalism". *Donga yeon'gu* 54 (2008*a*): 9–49.

———. "Southeast Asian Studies in Korea: Focusing on the Second-Generation Southeast Asianists in the Field of Social Sciences". *Dongnam-asia yeon'gu* 19, no. 1 (2009): 215–75.

———. "Review of the Discourses on East Asian Community". *Asia Review* (SNU Asia Center) 1, no. 1 (2011): 61–110.

Ra Hee-Ryang. "Economic Integration of China and ASEAN". *Review of International and Area Studies* (Institute of International Affairs, SNU) 18, no. 1 (2009): 67–95.

———. "Southeast Asian Economy after the Global Economic Crisis: The Case Study for Thailand, Malaysia, and Indonesia". *Dongnam-asia yeon'gu* 20, no. 1 (2010): 143–80.

Seo Kyoung Kyo. "A Research on the Process of Democratization in Thailand, 1880–1992". *Journal of Korean Association of Thai Studies* 5 (1993): 157–73.

———. "A Study on Causes of Thai Military Intervention in Politics". *Dongnam-asia yeon'gu* 3 (1994): 127–48.

———. "Comparative Study on Democratization in Thailand and the Philippines". *Korean Journal of International Relations* 36, no. 3 (1997): 355–84.

———. "Electoral and Political Party Systems in the Philippines". *Dongnam-asia yeon'gu* 7 (1999): 3–45.

———. "Analysis on Philippine Democracy". *Dongnam-asia yeon'gu* 15, no. 1 (2005): 1–39.

Shim Doobo. "Comparative Research on the Reportage of Social Conflict Issues in the Newspapers of Three ASEAN Countries". *Dongnam-asia yeon'gu* 20, no. 1 (2010): 1–40.

Shin Yoon Hwan. "Modern Forms of 'Capitalist Accumulation': A Study of Capitalist Class Formation in New Order Indonesia". *Korean Political Science Review* 27, no. 2 (1993): 3251–74.

———. "Comparative Politics and Foreign Area Studies in Korea". In *The Present Status and Future Tasks of Foreign Area Studies in Korea*, edited by Yi Sang-seob and Kwon Tae-hwan. Seoul: Seoul National University Press, 1998.

———. *The Political Economy of Indonesia: The State, Capital and Labor under Soeharto's Rule.* Seoul: Seoul National University Press, 2001.

———. "The 'Wave of Korean Cultures' in East Asia: A Comparative Analysis". *Donga yeon'gu* 42 (2002): 5–34.

———, ed. *Elections and Political Processes in Southeast Asia.* Seoul: Sogang University Press, 2008*a*.

———, ed. *Elections and Socio-Political Changes in Southeast Asia.* Seoul: Sogang University Press, 2008*b*.

———. *Walking through the Southeast Asian Culture.* Paju, Korea: Changbi Publishers, 2008*c*.

———. "Regionalism in Southeast Asia: Implications for East Asian Community Building". *Donga yeon'gu* 56 (2009): 107–37.

Shin Yoon Hwan and Lee Han Woo. *Korean Wave in East Asia*. Seoul: Jeonyewon, 2006.

Shin Yoon Hwan, Park Sa-Myung, Bae Geung-Chan, Lee Jaehyon, Kwon Yul, Park Bun Soon, Lee Choong-Lyul, Park Seung Woo, Chae Suhong et al. *East Asian Community and Korea's Tomorrow: Beyond Northeast Asia, Toward East Asia*. Seoul: Imagine, 2008.

Shin Yoon Hwan and Rhee Sung-Hyong. "The Present Status of and Future Challenges for the Foreign Area Studies in Korea". *National Strategy* 2, no. 1 (1996): 155–87.

Soh Byungkuk. "Literary Activities of Malay Nationalists in Malaysia under Japanese Rule, 1942–45". *International Area Review* (HUFS) 8, no. 2 (2005): 94–106.

———. "Some Aspects of US-Thai Relations from 1973 to 1976". *Dongnama yeon'gu* 19, no. 3 (2010): 97–128.

Soh Byungkuk and Cho Hung-guk. *Buddhist Kings and Sultans*. Seoul: Tradition and Modernity, 2004.

Song Kyung-Ah. "A Study on Public Health Care in Thailand with a Focus on the Establishment of Thaksin's Universal Health Coverage". Ph.D. dissertation, Seoul National University, 2011.

Study Group on Southeast Asian Politics (SGSEAP), trans. *How the Dominoes Fell*, by John H. and Mae H. Easterline. Seoul: Bakyeongsa, [1986] 1991.

———. *Southeast Asian Politics and Society*. Seoul: Hanul, 1992.

Study Group on Southeast Asian Studies (SGSEAS), trans. *Southeast Asia in the New International Era*, by C. D. Neher. Seoul: Seoul Press, 1993.

———, ed. *The Political Change in Southeast Asia*. Seoul: 21st Century Korean Research Foundation, 1994.

———, ed. *The Political Economy of Southeast Asia*. Seoul: 21st Century Korean Research Foundation, 1995.

———, ed. *The Political Leaderships in Southeast Asia*. Seoul: 21st Century Korean Research Foundation, 1996.

———, ed. *The Society and Culture in Southeast Asia*. Seoul: Oruem, 1997.

———, ed. *The Religion and Society in Southeast Asia*. Seoul: Oruem, 2001.

Yang Gil Hyun. "A Comparative Study in the Political Dynamics of Third World Democratization: Focusing on the Experiences of Korea, Nicaragua, and Myanmar". Ph.D. dissertation, Seoul National University, 1996.

———. "Exploring the Possibilities and Strategies to Construct East Asian Community". *Donga yeon'gu* 48 (2005): 202–32.

Yang Seungyoon. "A Political Historical Study of Islam in Indonesian Politics". Ph.D. dissertation, Kyungnam University, Korea, 1991.

———. "A Brief History of Islam in Southeast Asia". *Dongnam-asia yeon'gu* 1 (1992): 165–208.

———. "A Study on the Lifecycle of Indonesian Muslims". *Dongnama yeon'gu* 5 (1996): 187–210.

————. "Indian Society in Southeast Asia: The Case of Indonesia". *Dongnama yeon'gu* 9 (2001).

————. "A Historical Review on the Influence of Indian Culture in Indonesia". *Journal of Indian Studies* (Korean Society for Indian Studies) 13, no. 1 (2008): 67–93.

————. "A Study on Timor Leste's Politics and International Relationship". *Asia yeon'gu* 12, no. 2 (2010): 165–90.

Yang Seungyoon et al. *Islam in Southeast Asia*. Seoul: HUFS Press, 2000.

Yoon Chung Ro. "A Comparative Study on the Formation of Anti-Communist Dictatorial States and Their State Capacities: Focused on the Ngo Dinh Diem Regime of South Vietnam and Syngman Rhee Regime of South Korea". Ph.D. dissertation, Dongguk University, Korea, 2005.

Yoon Jinpyo. "A Comparative Study of the Military in Thailand and Indonesia with Special Emphasis on Military Strategy and Armed Forces Structure". *Korean Journal of International Relations* 36, no. 2 (1996): 273–99.

————. "Changing Relationship between the State and the Market: A Case Study on Thailand". *Dongnam-asia yeon'gu* 5 (1997): 67–90.

————, ed. *Economic Growth and Developmental Strategy in Southeast Asia: A Retrospective Reassessment*. Seoul: Oruem, 2004.

————, ed. *The Political Economy of Reform and Restructuring in Southeast Asia*. Seoul: Politeia, 2005.

————. "Institutional Comparison of the State Structure in Indonesia, Thailand and Vietnam". *Journal of Korean Association of Thai Studies* 14 (2007).

Yoon Jinpyo, Cho Youn-Mee, Cho Young Hee, Choi Horim, Huh Chang-dug, Kim Ye-kyoum, Lee Dong-Yoon, Park Bun Soon, and Park Seung Woo. *Transnational Issues and Regional Governance in Southeast Asia*. Seoul: Myung In Publishers, 2010.

Youn Dae Yeong. "Vietnamese Intellectuals in the Early Twentieth Century and Their View of East Asia". *Donga yeon'gu* 53 (2007): 293–326.

————. "Kim Yung-kun's Course of Life and Vietnamese Studies in the 1930s and the 1940s". *Dongnam-asia yeon'gu* 19, no. 3 (2009): 57–100.

————. "Nguyen Dynasty's Response to Nguyen Trung To's Arguments for Reform in the Late 19th Century". *Yoksa hakbo* (Korean Historical Association), no. 206 (2010): 211–43.

Yu Insun. "The *Doi Moi* Policy and the Reinterpretation of Vietnamese History". *Dongnam-asia yeon'gu* 3 (1994): 1–26.

————. "Vietnamese Adaptations of Chinese Family System in the Premodern Period". *Dongnam-asia yeon'gu* 5 (1997): 25–50.

————. *New History of Vietnam*. Seoul: Isan Publisher, 2002.

2. Publications in English and Other Languages

Bae Geung-Chan. "International Impacts on the Formation of Modern Authoritarian States in East Asia: A Comparative Analysis of South Korea, the Philippines and Indonesia". Ph.D. dissertation, Claremont Graduate University, USA, 1988.

Chae Suhong. "Spinning Work and Weaving Life: The Politics of Production in a Capitalistic Multinational Textile Factory in Vietnam". Ph.D. dissertation, City University of New York, 2003*a*.

——. "The Political Economy of Multinational Factory Regimes and Recent Strikes in Vietnam". *Dongnam-asia yeon'gu* [Southeast Asian Review] 19, no. 1 (2009).

Cho Hung-guk. "Die politische Geschichte Thailands unter der Herrschaft König Narais" [in German]. Ph.D. dissertation, Universität Hamburg, Germany, 1993.

——. "The Trade between China, Japan, Korea and Southeast Asia in the 14th through the 17th Century Period". *International Area Review* (Center for International Area Studies, HUFS) 3, no. 2 (2000).

Cho Youn-Mee. "Main hakim sendir: Studi kasus *vigilantism* di klanten, Jawa tengah pada awal era Reformasi" [Mob Justice Actions in Java: A Study of Vigilantism in the Era of Indonesian Reformation] [in Indonesian]. Ph.D. dissertation, Universitas Gadjah Mada, Indonesia, 2005.

Choi Byungwook. "Southern Vietnam under the Reign of Minh Mang, 1820–1841". Ph.D. dissertation, Australian National University, 1999.

Choi Jungug. "Economic Crisis, Elite Cooperation, and Democratic Stability: Asia in the Late 1990s". Ph.D. dissertation, University of Texas-Austin, 2001*a*.

——. "Philippine Democracies Old and New: Election, Term Limits and Party Systems". *Asian Survey* 41, no. 3 (2001*b*).

——. "District Magnitude, Social Diversity, and Indonesia's Parliamentary Party System from 1999 to 2009". *Asian Survey* 50, no. 4 (2010): 663–83.

Choi Nankyung. "Democratisation, Decentralization, and Local Party Politics in Post-Soeharto Indonesia". Ph.D. dissertation, Australian National University, 2004.

Hwang In-Won. "Changing Conflict Configuration and Regime Maintenance in Malaysian Politics: From Consociational Bargaining to Mahathir's Dominance". Ph.D. dissertation, Australian National University, 2001.

——. "Authoritarianism and UMNO's Factional Conflicts". *Journal of Contemporary Asia* 32, no. 2 (2002).

——. *Personalized Politics: The Malaysian State under Mahathir*. Singapore: Institute of Southeast Asian Studies, 2003.

Jeon Je-guk. "The Political Economy of Micro-Variation in East Asian Development Patterning: A Comparative Study of Korea, Taiwan, Singapore and Thailand". Ph.D. dissertation, Ohio State University, 1990.

Jeong Yeonsik. "Interest Representation in Socialist Market Economies: A Comparative Study of Civil Society in China and Vietnam". Ph.D. dissertation, University of South Carolina, 1997*a*.

——. "The Rise of Corporatism in Vietnam". *Contemporary Southeast Asia* 19, no. 2 (1997*b*).

Kang Yoonhee. "Words of the Ancestors, Words for Survival: Marginality, Emotion, and the Power of Magical Words among the Petalangan of Riau, Indonesia". Ph.D. dissertation, Yale University, 2002.

———. "The Desire to be Desired: Magic Spells, Agency and the Politics of Desire among the Petalangan People in Indonesia". *Language and Communication* 23, no. 2 (2003).

———. "'Staged' Rituals, 'Veiled' Spells: Multiple Language Ideologies and Transformations in Petalangan Verbal Magic". *Journal of Linguistic Anthropology* 16, no. 1 (2006).

Kang Young Soon. "Antara Tradisi dan Konflik: Kepolitikan Nahdlatul Ulama, 1984–" [in Indonesian]. Ph.D. dissertation, Universitas Indonesia, 2002.

Kim Dong-Yeob. "The Politics of Market Liberalization: A Comparative Study of the Korean and Philippine Telecommunications Service Industries". *Contemporary Southeast Asia* 24, no. 2 (2002).

———. "The Political Economy of Telecommunications Service Market Liberalization: A Comparative Study of Korea and the Philippines". Ph.D. dissertation, University of the Philippines, Diliman, Quezon City, 2003*a*.

———. "Economic Liberalism and the Philippine Telecom Industry". *Journal of Contemporary Asia* 33, no. 4 (2003*b*).

Kim Hyung-Jun. "Reformist Muslims in a Yogyakarta Village: The Islamic Transformation of Contemporary Socio-Religious Life". Ph.D. dissertation, Australian National University, 1996.

———. "Unto You Your Religion and Unto Me My Religion: Muslim-Christian Relations in a Javanese Village". *SOJOURN: Social Issues in Southeast Asia* 13, no. 1 (1998*a*).

———. "Changing Concept of Religious Freedom in Indonesia". *Journal of Southeast Asian Studies* 29, no. 2 (1998*b*).

Kim Jeehun. "Research Notes on the Making of a 'Gated Community': A Study of an Inner City Neighbourhood, Jakarta, Indonesia". *Asian Journal of Social Science* 30, no. 1 (2002): 97–108.

———. "Managing Intergenerational Family Obligations in Transnational Migration Contexts: Korean Professional and Educational Migrant Families in Singapore". Ph.D. dissertation, University of Oxford, UK, 2009.

———. "'Downed' and Stuck in Singapore: Lower/Middle Class South Korean Wild Geese (*Kirogi*) Children in Singapore". *Research in the Sociology of Education* 17 (2010): 271–311.

———. "Living as Expatriate Wives/Mothers: Balancing Work and Family Issues among Korean Working Women in Singapore". *Dongnam-asia yeon'gu* 21, no. 1 (2011): 217–48.

Kim Jongouk. "Mot so bien doi o lang xa chau tho Song Hong tu dau the ky XIX den giua the ky XX: Qua truong hop lang Me Tri" [The Changes in Rural Society in Song Hong Region in Vietnam: The Case of Me Tri Village] [in

Vietnamese]. Ph.D. dissertation, Department of History, National University of Vietnam, Hanoi, 2009.

Kim Sung-Joo. "The Great Power Triangle and Southeast Asian Security, 1975–1984". Ph.D. dissertation, State University of New York at Buffalo, 1986.

Kim Ye-kyoum. "A Debate on Differences between the Vision and Path towards Development in South-East Asia: With Particular Reference to Thailand, Indonesia and Malaysia". *Kritis: Jurnal Studi Pembangunan Interdisiplin* (UKSW, Indonesia) 14, no. 1 (2002): 1–22.

———. "Living from Hand to Mouth Provided There is Happiness: Life-Dynamics of Tomohonese Women, Minahasa, North Sulawesi, Indonesia". Ph.D. dissertation, University of Hull, UK, 2003*a*.

———. "The Effectiveness of Non-Governmental Organisations in Contributing to More Appropriate Forms of Development in Indonesia". *Ekoton* (Unsrat, Indonesia) 3, no. 1 (2003*b*): 53–70.

———. "The Structural Analysis of the Hindi and Southeast Asian Versions of Indian Epic, Ramayana". *Antropologi* (Universitas Indonesia) 28, no. 75 (2004).

Kim Ye-kyoum and Victor T. King. "Regional Development Programmes and the Life-Dynamics of Women on an Eastern Indonesian Island". *SOJOURN: Social Issues in Southeast Asia* 19, no. 2 (2004).

———. "Reflexive Reactions of Eastern Indonesian Women to the Economic Crisis: An Ethnographic Study of Tomohon, Minahasa, North Sulawesi, Indonesia". *Indonesia and the Malay World* (SOAS, University of London, UK) 97, no. 33 (2005): 307–25.

Ko Woo-Seong. "Government Policies, Foreign Capital, State Capacity: A Comparative Study of Korea, Indonesia and Malaysia". Ph.D. dissertation, Northern Illinois University, 1990.

Kwon Oh Shin. "Dwight D. Eisenhower and the Philippines, 1935–1960". Ph.D. dissertation, University of the Philippines, Diliman, Quezon City, 1992.

Lee Eun-Ho. "The Role of the Military in Nation-Building: South Vietnam and Korea". Ph.D. dissertation, Southern Illinois University, 1972.

Lee Jaehyon. "UMNO Factionalism and the Politics of Malaysian National Identity". Ph.D. dissertation, Murdoch University, Australia, 2005.

Lee Ji-Eun. "Monsters in Contemporary Thai Horror Film: Image, Representation and Meaning". Ph.D. dissertation, Chulalongkorn University, Thailand, 2010.

Lee Sang Kook. "Integrating Others: A Study of a Border Social System in the Thailand-Burma Borderland". Ph.D. dissertation, National University of Singapore, 2007.

———. "Borderland Dynamics in Mae Sot, Thailand and the Pursuit of the Bangkok Dream and Resettlement". *Asian and Pacific Migration Journal* 20, no. 1 (2011): 79–99.

Lew Seok Choon. "The Contextual Effect of Dependency on Economic Development and Sectoral Inequality: A Cross-National Study". Ph.D. dissertation, University of Illinois at Urbana-Champaign, 1986.

Lim, Sun Sun, Raymund C. Sison, and Dong-Yeob Kim, eds. *The Promise of ICTs in Asia: Key Trends and Issues.* Seoul: Jimoondang, 2008.

McVey, Ruth. "Globalization, Marginalization, and the Study of Southeast Asia". In *Southeast Asian Studies: Reorientations*, edited by Craig J. Reynolds and Ruth McVey. Ithaca, NY: Cornell University Southeast Asia Program Publications, 1998.

Milner, Anthony. "Approaching Asia, and Asian Studies, in Australia". *Asian Studies Review* 23, no. 2 (1999).

Nho Young Soon. "A History of the Indochinese Communist Party, 1930–1936". Ph.D. dissertation, University of London, 2000.

Oh Myung-seok. "Other Malay Peasants: Making of Rubber Smallholders in Johor, Malaysia". Ph.D. dissertation, Monash University, Australia, 1994.

Park Innwon. "Static, Dynamic, and Trade-linked Computable General Equilibrium Model Estimations of Regional Economic Integration: The ASEAN Illustration". Ph.D. dissertation, University of Pennsylvania, 1993.

———. "East Asian Regional Trade Agreements". *Pacific Economic Review* 11, no. 4 (2006).

Park Innwon and Kwon Yul. "Regional Trade Arrangement between ASEAN and Korea". In *ASEAN-Korea Relations: Security, Trade and Community Building.* Singapore: Institute of Southeast Asian Studies, 2007.

Park Jang Sik. "Burmese Phonology and Morphology". Ph.D. dissertation, Banaras Hindu University, India, 1996*b*.

Park Kie-Duck. "Fading Reformism in New Democracy: A Comparative Study of Regime Consolidation in Korea and the Philippines". Ph.D. dissertation, University of Chicago, 1993.

Park Kwang Seop. "The Response of ASEAN and Its Member Countries to the Challenge of Global and Regional Changes Created by the Post-Cold War Era". Ph.D. dissertation, University of Santo Tomas, Philippines, 1995.

Park Sa-Myung. "The State, Revolution and Development: A Comparative Study of Transformation of the State in Indonesia and the Philippines". Ph.D. dissertation, State University of New York at Buffalo, 1988.

Park Seung Woo. "Agrarian Transformation and Colonialism in the Context of Capitalist Development: An Historical-Comparative Study of Korea and the Philippines". Ph.D. Dissertation, University of Georgia, 1991.

———. "The State and Social Classes in Korea and the Philippines". *Thammasat Review* 3, no. 1 (1998*a*): 97–119.

———. "Oligarchic Democracy in the Philippines: Democratization Sans Disintegration of Political Monopoly." In *State of Democracy: Oligarchic Democracies and Asian Democratization*, edited by Cho Hee Yeon, Lawrence Surendra, and Eunhong Park. Mumbai: Earthworm Books, 2008*b*.

———. "Korea's Preparation for Southeast Asia: Research and Education on Southeast Asian Studies in Korea". In *Korea's Changing Roles in Southeast Asia:*

Expanding Influence and Relations, edited by David I. Steinberg. Singapore: Institute of Southeast Asian Studies, 2010.

Park Seung Woo and Gary P. Green. "Agricultural Restructuring and Capitalist Industrialization: The Cases of South Korea and the Philippines". *Kasarinlan: Philippine Quarterly of Third World Studies* 11, nos. 1 and 2 (1995): 123–48.

Ra Hee-Ryang. "Four Essays on International Reserves". Ph.D. dissertation, University of Hawaii at Manoa, 2007.

──────. "Modeling the Dollarization: A Case Study for Cambodia, Laos, and Vietnam". *Global Economic Review* 37 (2008*a*): 157–69.

──────. "Financial Market Volatility and International Reserve Holding Behaviour: A Case Study for Korea, Indonesia, the Philippines, and Thailand". *Global Economic Review* 37 (2008*b*): 311–32.

──────. "Two Economic Crisis and Dollarization for Cambodia, Laos, and Vietnam". *Dongnam-asia yeon'gu* [Southeast Asian Review] 21, no. 2 (2011): 125–53.

Seo Kyoung Kyo. "Military Involvement in Politics and the Prospects for Democracy: Thailand, the Philippines, and South Korea in Comparative Perspective". Ph.D. dissertation, Southern Illinois University, 1993.

Shim Doobo. "Media Globalization and Korean Big Business". Ph.D. dissertation, University of Wisconsin at Madison, 2000.

──────. "Hybridity and the Rise of Korean Popular Culture in Asia". *Media Culture Society* 28, no. 1 (2006).

──────. "Korean Wave and Korean Women Television Viewers in Singapore". *Asian Journal of Women's Studies* 13, no. 2 (2007).

Shim Doobo, Ariel Heryanto, and Ubonrat Siriyuvasak, eds. *Pop Culture Formations across East Asia*. Seoul: Jimoondang, 2010.

Shin Yoon Hwan. "Demystifying the Capitalist State: Political Patronage, Bureaucratic Interests, and Capitalists-in-Making in Soeharto's Indonesia". Ph.D. dissertation, Yale University, 1989.

──────. "The Role of Elites in Creating Capitalist Hegemony in Post-Oil Boom Indonesia". In *Indonesia*. Ithaca, NY: Southeast Asia Program, Cornell University, 1991.

──────. "Korean Investment in Southeast Asia". *Journal of Contemporary Asia* 25, no. 2 (1995*a*).

──────. "Rethinking Indonesia-South Korea Relations". In *ASEAN and South Korea: Emerging Issues in Trade and Investment Relations*, edited by Daljit Singh and Reza Y. Siregar. Singapore: Institute of Southeast Asian Studies, 1995*b*.

Shin Yoon Hwan and Chayachoke Chulasiriwongs, eds. *Relations between Korea and Southeast Asia in the Past*. Bangkok: ASEAN University Network (AUN) and Korean Association of Southeast Asian Studies (KASEAS), 2005.

Soh Byungkuk. "From Parochial to National Outlook: Malay Society in Transition, 1920–1948". Ph.D. dissertation, Ohio University, 1993.

Song Jungnam. "Lang Yen So tu truyen thong den do moi va so sanh voi nhung bien doi o nong thon Han Quoc" [in Vietnamese]. Ph.D. dissertation, Hanoi National University, 1996.

Song Seung-Won. "Back to Basics in Indonesia? Reassessing the Pancasila and Pancasila State and Society, 1945–2007". Ph.D. dissertation, Ohio University, 2008.

———. "The Pancasila Industrial Relations and the New Order Regime's Views on Society". *Dongnama yeon'gu* [Journal of Southeast Asia] (CSEAS, HUFS) 19, no. 2 (2009): 155–90.

———. "A Discourse on the Pancasila State and Its Contemporary Appeal in Indonesia". *Asia yeon'gu* [Journal of Asian Studies] (Korean Association of Asian Studies) 13, no. 3 (2010): 1–40.

Suehiro Akira. "A Japanese Perspective on the Perception of 'Ajia': From Eastern to Asian Studies". *Asian Studies Review* 23, no. 2 (1999).

Suh Jiwon. "The Politics of Transitional Justice in Post-New Order Indonesia". Ph.D. dissertation, Ohio State University, 2012.

Yang Seungyoon. "Dynamics of South Korean-Indonesian Relations 1966–2000: A Study of Inter-Dependence". Ph.D. dissertation, Universitas Gadjah Mada, Indonesia, 2006.

Yoon Jinpyo. "Formation and Transformation of the Modern State: A Comparative Study of the Nature and Role of the State in Indonesia, Thailand and Vietnam". Ph.D. dissertation, University of South Carolina, 1990.

Youn Dae Yeong. "Les idées et les mouvements réformistes en Corée et au Vietnam, 1897–1911" [The Reformist Ideas and Movements in Korea and Vietnam, 1897–1911] [in French]. Ph.D. dissertation, University of Paris VII, 2007.

Yu Insun. "Law and Family in the 17th and 18th Century Vietnam". Ph.D. dissertation, University of Michigan, 1978.

PART II
SOUTHEAST ASIA

5

CONTENTIOUS DEVELOPMENT
Southeast Asian Studies
in Singapore

Lee Sang Kook

INTRODUCTION

Singapore has been identified as an ideal place for those who study the Southeast Asian region, as they are able to benefit from the world-class library facilities of the Institute of Southeast Asian Studies (ISEAS) and the National University of Singapore (NUS). Various types of academic gatherings take place all year around, including international conferences, seminars and talks, and these provide valuable opportunities for researchers to disseminate their findings and to develop social relationships with their fellow scholars. The number of prestigious scholarly journals published in Singapore, such as *Journal of Southeast Asian Studies, SOJOURN: Journal of Social Issues in Southeast Asia* and *Contemporary Southeast Asia, Asian Journal of Social Science* and *Singapore Journal of Tropical Geography*, and the proliferation of books published on the diverse issues that face the region, provide further evidence of the depth and breadth of Southeast Asian Studies practised in Singapore. Once one is located in Singapore, even with a short period of stay, one becomes widely exposed to lively exchanges of ideas and discussions as well as the state of the art of Southeast Asian Studies. It is truly a hot spot for this area of study.

However, one easily realizes that the constitution of Southeast Asian scholarship in Singapore is to a great degree different from that in other countries. Expatriate components are the substantial and inherent parts of scholarship in the country in comparison to other countries. This leads us to the following questions: Does Southeast Asian Studies conducted in Singapore *really* reflect Singaporean scholarship? To what extent can we say that it is Singaporean Southeast Asian Studies? How can we differentiate between foreign scholarship and local scholarship in Singapore? All of these questions converge on how to define Southeast Asian Studies in Singapore. The difficulties in coming up with a precise definition reflect the reality of scholarship that has developed not specifically in the realm of Southeast Asian Studies but also in academia in general in Singapore. This problem reflects the historical and geographical conditions within which Singapore is located.

What are the conditions that make it difficult to define Southeast Asian Studies in Singapore? What factors have shaped the current state of Southeast Asian Studies there? Here we need to take a close look at the historical role played by Singapore. Modern Singapore was developed by the British to be a place that connected the East and the West. This role has never lost its relevance, even after independence. Various groups of people, including colonial administrators, traders, entrepreneurs and labourers, have come to Singapore and made use of the advantages provided by their location. Scholars are no exception in this perennial ebb and flow of people. Fluidity has blurred the boundaries between the local and the global. In this sense, then, Southeast Asian Studies in Singapore could be defined as being conducted not just by local Singaporeans but also by expatriate scholars residing in Singapore. The key point in this definition does not lie in people's nationalities but rather in the location of knowledge production itself.

As such, Singapore pursued the development of Southeast Asian Studies by providing outlets to scholars. The pursuit of meritocracy in academia led to the seeking of foreign expertise and promoted the English medium for its educational system as well as knowledge production. This greatly contributed to the establishment of Singapore as one of the most important locations for conducting research in and on the region. With strong institutional support, this small country has become a major player in area studies, setting research agendas and framing the direction of Southeast Asian Studies in general.

This chapter traces the development path of Singapore. It explores what particular historical and political junctures have shaped scholarship in the country. It requires us to examine the development of Southeast Asian Studies in connection with the changing historical, societal and political conditions. For this purpose, the chapter engages in a comparative approach between English and Chinese scholarship in order to demonstrate the different paths of development and the resulting academic landscape of current Singapore. This comparative perspective sheds light not only on the different historical constructions of scholarship, but also on the different conflations of language, scholarship, identity and politics in Singaporean history.

THE INCEPTION OF SOUTHEAST ASIAN STUDIES IN SINGAPORE

Modern scholarship on Southeast Asia in Singapore can be said to have begun in 1819 with British colonization. Colonial scholars, most of whom were colonial administrators and journalists, began embarking on the production of knowledge of the region, particularly of the Malay world. Among them was J.H. Moor, a journalist who published the first regional study in English in 1837, based largely on the accounts of various countries that were published in the newspaper which he had edited (Reid 2004, pp. 12–13). John Crawfurd was influenced by Moor's endeavour to produce *A Descriptive Dictionary of Indian Islands and Adjacent Countries* in 1856, which covered all parts of Southeast Asia except Burma and the landlocked far north. Above all, J.R. Logan's unmatched endeavours led to the publication of *Journal of the Indian Archipelago and Eastern Asia* between 1847 and 1867 in Singapore (Reid 2004, p. 13; 1999, p. 12).

However, it was not until the formation of the Straits Branch of the Royal Asiatic Society that collective and more organized research began to be established. On 4 November 1877, a group of colonial administrators convened to embark on collaborative research on the Straits Settlements and its neighbouring countries. Those present at the meeting included Archdeacon G.F. Hose (President), N.B. Dennys, A. Gray, D.F.A. Hervey, C.J. Irving, W.E. Maxwell, F. Maxwell, W.A. Pickering, A.M. Skinner and J.D. Vaughan. This organization was initially called the "Straits Asiatic Society" but later changed its name to the Straits Branch of the Royal Asiatic Society after a proposal for affiliation with the Royal Asiatic Society in London was approved in May 1878 (*Journal of the Straits Branch of the Royal Asiatic Society*, vol. 1 [1878], p. iii). Later, the name was again changed to the Malayan Branch of the Royal Asiatic Society in 1923 and the Malaysian Branch of the Royal Asiatic Society in 1964. These name changes reflected the changing political landscape of the region.

At the very first meeting of the organization, the attendees agreed upon the objectives of the Society, and these are reflected in its Rules. These state that "the objects of the Society shall be (a) the investigation of subjects connected with the Straits of Malacca and neighbouring countries, (b) the publication of papers in a Journal, (c) the formation of a Library of books bearing on the objects of the Society". This statement shows that the Society was fully oriented towards academic purposes, with a focus on research, publication and library development. Research areas mentioned in the Rules attract our particular attention. A clear geographical range of the Straits of Malacca is immediately formed here, yet the extension to neighbouring countries raises questions. Archdeacon Hose, the founding President, elaborated upon the identification of neighbouring countries in his inaugural address.

> The expression "neighbouring countries" was selected as being a wide and comprehensive term, in order that the Society might feel as little restricted as possible in accepting communications respecting any part of Southern and Eastern Asia. But no doubt the attention of the Society will be chiefly concentrated upon the Peninsula of Malacca, as far North as the Tenasserim Provinces, and the great Indian Archipelago, that wonderful chain of Equatorial Islands stretching from Sumatra on the West to New Guinea of [sic] the East (1878, p. 1).

Although Hose did not restrict the range of what was referred to as the neighbouring countries, it is implied that it comprised all those territories which we now think of as maritime Southeast Asia. He continually conceptualized these areas from linguistic and cultural perspectives, and suggested that "Malaya" was the most simple and intelligible categorization to utilize. With his suggestion, the term "Malaya" was not meant to be confined to the administrative sphere of British Malaya, but was meant to refer to the Malay-speaking world in general.

Hose's statement and the rest of his address do not provide information about any geographical forms of what we call "Southeast Asia" today. Although he roughly described "Southern and Eastern Asia", he did not seem to conceive of it as the modern concept of what we now call Southeast Asia. Thus, it can be confidently assumed that the term Southeast Asia was created in the twentieth century, as stated by scholars who have traced the genealogy of the term (e.g., Emmerson 1984).

Why did scholars, who were mostly colonial administrators, begin to initiate this collective movement to engage in serious research on the

Straits of Malacca and neighbouring countries, namely Malaya, at that particular moment in time? Finding an explanation for this requires us to consider the historical juncture at which Malaya was located at that time. With the Pangkor Engagement signed in January 1874, the British began by placing a British official in Perak as an advisor who was entitled progressively to intervene in state affairs by "advising" the Sultan. This marked the beginnings of British expansion of territorial control in the Malay Peninsula. The Society was formed as a result of increasing interest in the Malay States because of British political intervention in the years after 1874 (Chee 1995, p. 87).

However, it is unfair to describe these scholars solely as the forerunners of British colonizers with political purposes hidden behind the guise of academic ones. In his inaugural address, Hose (1878, p. 3) stressed that knowledge should be sought for its own sake, and not merely for the purpose of applying it for personal and material benefit, but in order to contribute to the common stock. Indeed, the members of the Society mainly demonstrated their academic seriousness in the flagship journal of the Society, *Journal of the Straits/Malayan/Malaysian Branch of the Royal Asiatic Society*, whose name changed according to the changes to the Society's own name. As stated in the Rules of the Society, the publication of the Journal was the chief preoccupation of the scholars. Indeed, the Journal has been published regularly over time, except during the period of the Japanese occupation of Singapore (1942–45). The Journal served as a platform for establishing scholarship. Undoubtedly the substantial amount of knowledge contained in the Journal and other types of publications such as reprints and monographs is testimony to the Society's contribution to Malayan/Singaporean scholarship in terms of quantity and diversity. Chee (1995, p. 91) has categorized the contents of the Journal into three main areas: natural history (fauna, flora, ethnology, anthropology, geology and meteorology); Malay studies (Malay language, classics, custom, folklore, artifacts, etc.); and Malayan history. However, as Chee (1995, p. 91) has revealed, this simplistic categorization does not do full justice to the great range of subjects covered in the Journal. One needs to refer to the *Index Malaysiana* (Lim and Wijasuriya 1970), which covers the issues which appeared from 1878 to 1963, in order to appreciate the entire range of scholarship.

In the early days, scholars were interested in the history of specific states, which reflected growing British engagement and intervention in particular territories. Although important academic contributions had been made from the very inception of the Society, it was during the 1930s–40s that most of the valuable work appeared.[1] W.E. Maxwell and R.J. Wilkinson were the leading figures in this regard. Indeed, almost all the articles published in the Journal in the early days were concerned with the Malay world. They did not cover any areas beyond that, for instance, any part of modern day mainland Southeast Asia. Although research on the neighbouring countries was one of the Society's objectives, their interests were heavily focused on the Malay world, particularly the Peninsular Malay States, and they also showed far less interest in the Dutch colonies in the region. For example, although a considerable area of what became British Burma had been incorporated as a directly governed dependency of British India from the 1880s, it never attracted the scholarly attention of members of the Society. This research scope and range reveals that their immediate concerns were the administrative states in which they were directly involved. In fact, it would not be untrue to state, even while acknowledging their esteem as scholars, that this concern led them to provide historical accounts from an imperialist or British stance at times. For example Winstedt (1935, p. 256, cited in Chee 1995, p. 99) states:

> Dutch influence depended entirely on a trading company's stock-in-trade, on Dutch orderliness and on the example of cleanliness of the traders' houses, which actually monopoly the system more effectively than any Eastern system and its Portuguese predecessors, caused a decline in Malay wealth and therefore in Malay civilisation and promoted that anarchy which obtained in the Malay States before British intervention.

As seen from the above, colonial scholars tended to justify British intervention as a means to address the decline of stability and order in the Malay world. This later prompted criticism from post-colonial scholars and others who called for a reinterpretation and reassessment of Malayan history from the Malayan point of view (Lim 1959; Khoo 1968). However, it would only be fair to review the work of colonial scholars and point out their limitations in relation to the ecology within which they were situated. It was fundamentally unthinkable for individual scholars to place themselves as "pure" scholars in an age of high imperialism, totally disregarding any burdens, influences and pressures, whether imperialist or nationalist. Individuals are strongly connected to the particular historical and political environments in which they are located.

Within the limits of their ecology, the colonial writers thrust themselves into establishing a foundation for scholarship. They opened up a path for future generations to build on and develop further. This tradition was most successfully passed down to the scholars of the next generation with the establishment of the University of Malaya in Singapore in 1949. Scholars, both expatriate and local, were now mostly based at the University, and they engaged in the further development of scholarship in more professional and institutional ways. As English continued to be a medium of research and publication and it was also promoted as a medium of education in general and official communication in the post-colonial environment, the legacy of earlier English scholarship has been passed down to future scholars without interruption. However, it is also this legacy that has rendered local voices less prominent under the continuing dominance of expatriate scholars.

ANOTHER HERITAGE:
THE BUILDING-UP OF CHINESE SCHOLARSHIP

China began to express serious concerns about the region when large numbers of Chinese migrant labourers started populating the British colonies in the region, including Singapore, Penang and the Malay States (Wang 2005, pp. 64–65). This led to serious scholarly research breaking new ground from the turn of the twentieth century. It further developed into the need for the education of Nanyang Chinese migrants and their offspring. Eventually Jinan (暨南)[2] School was established to meet the need in Nanjing in 1906 (later its name changed to Jinan University in 1927). This served as the cornerstone of government efforts to educate Nanyang migrants (Seah 2008, p. 26).[3]

Jinan University's connection with Nanyang was not limited to education. The connection was extended to research as well. It established the "Nanyang Cultural and Educational Affairs Bureau" (南洋文化教育事業部) in 1927, which was the first institutional foundation to embark on the study of Southeast Asia. It is important to note that the establishment of the research institution was spurred by Japanese "South Seas (Nanyo) Fever" and their research centres in the colony of Taiwan during the first two decades of the early twentieth century (Liu 2003; Seah 2007, pp. 137–38; Wang 2005, p. 65). The fever was directly transferred to China by those who pursued their education in Japan during this period of time.

These endeavours to promote scholarly research on Nanyang were now transferred to Singapore, the heart of Nanyang, by a group of Chinese intellectual migrants to Singapore, some of whom had conducted research at the Bureau of Jinan University. On 17 March 1940, "the South Seas Society" (中國南洋學會) was established by eight co-founders[4] to engage in research on the Nanyang areas in a collective way. The Society was closely linked to "Sin Chew Jit Poh" (星州日報), a local Chinese-language newspaper: five[5] of the co-founders were from the newspaper. There was also a strong connection with Jinan University as three[6] of the co-founders were from the Bureau of this university. In addition, the influence of the Japanese Fever can be seen from the fact that two co-founders had studied in Japan (Seah 2007, pp. 138–41). The establishment of the Society can perhaps be considered as the Chinese equivalent of the Straits Branch of the Royal Asiatic Society (Franke 1978, p. ii).

The full Chinese name of the China South Seas Society (中國南洋學會) demonstrates that its members retained a strong affiliation to China. Although they were physically located in Singapore, they considered China as the "homeland" (祖國) and identified themselves as "huaqiao" (華僑). They were sojourners, following Wang's identification (2003, p. 55), who were making only a brief visit and definitely planned to return home. This orientation of their identity towards China can also be seen from the fact that the Society's flagship journal, *Journal of the South Seas Society* (南洋學報), adopted the Chinese style of periodization. For instance, the publication year of the first volume of the Journal (1940) is marked as the 29th year of the Republic of China (民國二十九年), with the formal establishment year (1912) of the Republic after the Xinhai Revolution (辛亥革命) serving as the starting point. However, this identity changed as the members gradually transformed from sojourners into settlers, as will be shown later.

Like *Journal of the Straits Branch of the Royal Asiatic Society*, *Journal of the South Seas Society* stipulated certain Rules which included the Society's objectives. The Rules state that "the objects shall be (a) the publication of a Journal and or works and maps, (b) the establishment of a library and a research institute, (c) the promotion of the cultural affairs of the South Seas countries." This statement shows that the Society was fully dedicated to scholarly activities as well as to increasing cultural awareness in Nanyang. Although there is no clear indication of the geographical scope of the South Seas countries, it can be assumed that this covers the Southeast Asian countries of today since the articles in the Journal, even in the early days, also concerned mainland Southeast Asia. For instance, the first volume contains topics such as "History of China-Thailand Relations" and "Folklores of Northeastern Thailand". Thus, it can be posited that the geographical concept of Nanyang had expanded to include all countries of Southeast Asia by that time. However, the direct linguistic translation of Nanyang to Southeast Asia and the interchangeable usage of the two terms only took place in the late 1940s.

Journal of the South Seas Society served as a platform to demonstrate the academic endeavours on Nanyang. Articles appearing in the Journal were mainly concerned with historical research, reflecting the fact that the founding members of this Society were mostly historians. The major topics included Nanyang areas in Chinese historical records, the Chinese in Nanyang, archeological studies, local customs, local flora and fauna, and belief systems. Early volumes of the Journal were written entirely in Chinese but articles in English later began to be included, albeit in small numbers.

Among the Society's members, Hsu Yun-Ts'iao (Xu Yunqiao, 许云樵) was considered to be the most prominent figure. As a rigorous scholar with a charismatic personality, he dominated the Society in the early days, taking up the position of the editor of the Journal. Tan Yeok Seong (Chen Yusong, 陈育崧), although not a founding member, also began to influence the Society not just by his scholarly research but also through financial support. These two scholars played a major role in establishing the tradition of Chinese scholarship in Singapore (Wang 2005, p. 66; 2004*a*, p. 94). Wang Gungwu's scholarship in the early days was very much influenced by these two scholars: the search for the Nanhai trade between China and Southeast Asia brought him in touch with the two scholars' work (Wang 2004*b*, p. 148). He has recollected that Hsu was a serious scholar and that today's scholars would not even be comparable to him in terms of academic rigour.[7]

However, not long after the formation of the Society, a turbulent situation arose: the Japanese occupation of Singapore during the period 1942–45. It was impossible for them to continue their activities in Singapore during this time and many of the members thus moved to and formed a daughter organization in Chungking, the wartime capital of China. However, Hsu remained in Singapore during the Japanese occupation because he "could not bear to abandon the (Society's) countless books and numbers of drafts". He made every effort to avoid getting caught by the Japanese while holding onto the Society's materials. This story became enshrined as a significant early historical moment in the organization's narrative (Seah 2007, p. 143). It is quite likely that it served to strengthen Hsu's later position in the Society.

When the Second World War ended, the Society resumed its activities in Singapore. However, there was now a great difference in their orientation compared with the past. Their activities began to take place with a stronger connection to the locality itself rather than with China. In general, people in Nanyang went through identity reformulation as it became a permanent place of residence and they took part in constructing a new nation state as settlers. In a reflection of these local conditions, the members decided to base the Society permanently in Singapore although its wartime activities had been undertaken elsewhere. In addition, they began to be very active in building-up scholarly relations with Western expatriate scholars, particularly members of the Malayan Branch of the Royal Asiatic Society, and extending invitations to them. At the eighth Annual General Meeting held on 3 May 1947, the decision to invite seven prominent scholars as Honorary Members was made. Among them were Richard Winstedt, George Coedès and C.O. Blagden (*Journal of the South Seas Society*, vol. 10, no. 2 [1954]). In turn, some members of the South Seas Society began to participate in the activities of the Malayan Branch of the Royal Asiatic Society. For instance, Hsu Yun-Ts'iao became a life member of the organization and maintained office as a Councillor from 1946 to 1955 (and later as Vice President from 1956 to 1973) (Seah 2007, p. 147). Scholarly exchanges between local Chinese and Western scholars inevitably influenced the former to adopt the Western conception of Southeast Asia. It also resulted in the inclusion of English articles in *Journal of the South Seas Society*.

However, Chinese scholars went through a period of internal strife in 1958, which was a watershed moment in terms of the direction that the Society was taking. Hsu, who had strengthened his position for so long, had to step down, as he was accused of wielding too much influence in the Society and of taking personal possession of its property. This opened up a new phase in the direction of scholarship. The scholars of the next generation took over leadership, with the editorship of the Journal being taken over by Wang Gungwu from 1958 to 1961. The Constitution of the Society was amended in 1959 to reflect the new spirit (Gwee 1978, pp. 4–5). Yet this did not signal the end of Chinese scholarship. Led by Wang, the Journal became more bilingual and more globalized with the inclusion of more articles in English than was the case in the past. The orientation of their identity began to lean more towards Singapore, with the eventual replacement of "China" (中國) with "Singapore" (新加坡) in the Chinese name of the Society in 1958.

The most important thing is that this tradition was passed down to the next generation with a strong institutional base at Nanyang University (Nan Tah), which was established in 1956. The Chinese scholars who were members of the Society, including Hsu, played an active role in developing Southeast Asian Studies at Nanyang University. The University provided a strong institutional base for them to gear up local scholarship in parallel with scholarship at the University of Malaya in Singapore. However, their destiny was interrelated with the changing post-colonial environments in Singapore and furthermore was influenced by the government's language policies on education. In the same vein, the ups and downs of local Southeast Asian Studies scholarship were closely linked to these political, social and educational factors.

As we have noticed, during the 1940s–50s, local scholarship in Singapore was developed in parallel to Western scholarship. However, the question of defining "the local" itself cannot be avoided. Could the Chinese scholars in the early days be considered as local people given that they regarded themselves only as sojourners? How much was scholarship by Malays and Indians included in "local" scholarship? If local scholarship is reduced to Chinese scholarship due to the exclusive dominance of Chinese scholars in academia, then how much of this Chinese scholarship can be considered to be local? As discussed earlier, Chinese scholars in the early days were heavily influenced by the Japanese Fever and later by Western scholars. All of these questions suggest that "local" is itself a problematic, constructed and hybrid term in the context of Singapore.

THE RISE AND FALL OF CHINESE SCHOLARSHIP

As mentioned earlier, the establishment of Nanyang University provided an institutional base for Chinese intellectuals to conduct scholarship on Southeast Asia. Prior to the formation of the University, a large number of Chinese students were pursuing their tertiary education in China. In particular, Jinan University and Amoy University catered to the needs of overseas Chinese students. However, with a Communist victory in China, it became impractical for them to pursue education there since the colonial administration now banned it. Thus, there was a simultaneous high demand for tertiary education among the Chinese community in Malaya and Singapore. In the end, Nanyang University was formally opened on 15 March 1956 (Doraisamy 1969, p. 94; Seah 2005, p. 59).

Nanyang University provided a base not just for research but also for training future Southeast Asian scholars. The University became a focal point for Chinese scholars to engage in Southeast Asian Studies in Chinese. A key figure among them was Hsu Yun-Ts'iao. He joined the University and started a movement to set up a research institute on Nanyang areas, which was in fact an initiative of the South Seas Society. Lee Kong Chian's[8] expression of support that he would sponsor the centre accelerated the progress of this movement. Eventually, the Institute of Southeast Asia (南洋 研究所, Nanyang Yanjiusuo) was established in 1957 and Hsu became the founding Director (Seah 2005, p. 61). With this naming, it is interesting that the Chinese character of Nanyang (南洋) was translated into "Southeast Asia". This provides a clear indication that by this time, the English term "Southeast Asia" had become the agreed term of use among Chinese scholars in general, reflecting the Western influences in post-colonial Southeast Asian Studies in Singapore.

Scholars at Nanyang University had an idea of Southeast Asia as a community, even though this was only a rough idea at this time. There is evidence of this in Hsu's remarks (1959, p. vii) in the flagship journal of the Institute, *The Bulletin of the Institute of Southeast Asia* (南洋研究).

> We study not merely Malaya, but Southeast Asia as a whole, because, politically or economically, Malaya cannot stand apart from the rest of Southeast Asia. Even more does this apply to Singapore. We hope that all the countries of Southeast Asia will cooperate intellectually after the pattern of "the European Common Market"; this is the only way out for Singapore, Malaya and the other Southeast Asian countries.

Hsu made this statement even before the formation of the predecessors of ASEAN (Association of Southeast Asian Nations), including the ASA (Association of Southeast Asia) in 1961 and the MAPHILINDO (Malaya, the Philippines and Indonesia) in 1963. With this growing sense of a regional identity, Nanyang University was intended to "not only supply spiritual and intellectual food to the Chinese in Southeast Asia for the promotion of cultural intercourse, but also serve as the centre of Southeast Asian Studies" (Hsu 1959, p. vii). In order to fulfill this objective, scholars at the University actively engaged in the development of perspectives on Southeast Asia, and were based at the Institute in the early days. Above all, they reproduced a group of scholars for the next generation. The students who graduated from the University under their supervision continued their postgraduate studies in Western countries such as the United States, the United Kingdom and Australia. They included Cui Guiqiang; Yen Ching Hwang; Yong Chit Fatt; and Ng Chin Keong.[9] This, in turn, strengthened the scholarship at the University and the South Seas Society, as the graduates played a major role in the Society after completing their degrees (Seah 2005, pp. 61–63).

During the 1960s–70s, Chinese language track scholarship on Southeast Asia which was developed at Nanyang University and the South Seas

Society formed a major strand of Southeast Asian Studies in Singapore in parallel to another large strand of scholarship developed at the University of Singapore.[10] Their scholarship became well recognized by scholars in the other research track. For example, Harry Benda (1969, p. 6), the founding Director of ISEAS, stated that the Institute of Southeast Asia at Nanyang University was a sister institution. K.G. Tregonning, who founded *Journal of Southeast Asian History/Studies* at the University of Singapore, invited the South Seas Society to send delegates to the first International Conference of Southeast Asian historians held in 1961. I suggest that the period of the 1960s–70s was the heyday of Southeast Asian Studies in Singapore in terms of the variety of publications: the Chinese language track scholars published journals such as the already existing *Journal of the South Seas Society*, *Journal of Southeast Asian Researches* (1965–71) published at the Southeast Asian Research Centre established by Hsu after he had resigned from Nanyang University, and *Nanyang Quarterly: Review of Southeast Asian Studies* (1971–85) (an English language journal published by the South Seas Society). This period also saw the establishment of ISEAS in 1968 and *Journal of Southeast Asian History/Studies* (from 1960) in the English language track scholarship. Moreover, although not exclusively related to the study of Southeast Asia, the Island Society[11] published periodicals such as *Journal of the Island Society* (1967–73), *Island Society Quarterly* (1968–74), and *Island Literature* (1967–72), with an emphasis on Chinese literature, overseas Chinese problems and Southeast Asian Studies.

However, the Chinese-track scholarship had to confront the ever grow-ing marginalization of the Chinese language. The origins of this problem can be traced back to the colonial period, when English-educated people had more opportunities. English became more dominant as they secured political power and promoted English as a market language in the post-colonial environment. Although the founding of Nanyang University was a watershed moment for Chinese education, the University had to face various obstacles in the process of rooting itself within the changing political conditions. When Singapore was a part of Malaya (before August 1965), it was pressed to recruit not just Chinese students but also other ethnic groups to the University, in order to be relevant in the broader context of Malaya. Thus, it was pressed to introduce more modules in the English medium. This pressure was not entirely intended for graduates of the University who had been far less valued than those of the University of Singapore who were favoured in the job market. The pressure was interpreted as a government endeavour to address anti-government activities at Nanyang University, a problem that had been haunting the People's Action Party (PAP) (Hong and Huang 2008, p. 113). The proposals for restructuring, including the Wang Gungwu Report,[12] were met with strong objections and anti-government activities organized by the members of the University, and these became much more rampant as time went on.

The marginalization of the Chinese language was reflected by a sharp drop in enrolments. Between 1959 and 1978, the proportion of pupils enrolled in Chinese primary schools plummeted from 46 per cent to 11 per cent (Goh et al. 1979, cited in Kwok 2001, p. 499). In contrast, by the mid-1970s, initiated by the government, English was gaining much more importance in all social fields: it was becoming the medium of government, the armed forces, schools and homes. Politicians and education leaders placed emphasis on the fact that "English was merely the language which Singaporeans needed to cope with modern technology and commerce" (Turnbull 1982, p. 315). The restructuring of the Singapore economy towards high-technology industries was gaining pace and one reason for the entry of foreign capital was identified as English proficiency (Gopinathan 1996, pp. 282–83).

In tandem with this marginalization of the Chinese language, the activities of Chinese-track scholars were becoming weaker from the 1970s. For instance, the number of South Seas Society members was 215 in 1971, and this decreased to 159 in 1974, 149 in 1976, and 102 in 1986 (Seah 2005, p. 88). Nanyang University, a breeding ground for Chinese scholarship, increasingly began to use English as the medium of teaching from 1975 onwards in the face of falling enrolments and heightened government pressure. The Joint Campus Scheme was then introduced in 1979, to allow first-year students at Nanyang University to attend classes conducted in English together with students at the University of Singapore, which effectively turned Nanyang University into an English-medium institution. In the end, the government merged Nanyang University with the University of Singapore in 1980 to form the National University of Singapore (Gopinathan 1996, p. 282; Seah 2005, pp. 91–92).

The actual closing down of Nanyang University had a major impact on Chinese scholarship on Southeast Asia. The building-up of scholarship which had begun with the establishment of the South Seas Society in 1940 and was further developed at Nanyang University from 1956 onwards now lost its institutional base. As Wang Gungwu (2005, p. 74) has noted, this alternative heritage in Singapore that had offered a parallel track for Southeast Asian Studies for several decades now became marginalized with the merging of Nanyang University into NUS. With the closure of the

University, local scholarship lost its momentum to push forward their endeavours. After the loss of this important foundation, a group of Chinese scholars continued their academic activities with the South Seas Society and the Singapore Society of Asian Studies (新加坡亚洲研究学会), which was formed in 1982 and has been publishing a journal, *Asian Culture* (亞洲文化, *Yozhou Wenhua*) (Suryadinata 1998, p. 102). However, their interests became limited to ethnic Chinese issues to a large extent rather than Southeast Asian Studies.

STRONG INSTITUTIONS, CONTENTIOUS SCHOLARSHIP

While Chinese-track education, particularly at the university level, became increasingly marginalized, English-track education had never lost its dominance since the beginning of modern Singapore, first under the leadership of colonial administrators/scholars and then under the leadership of the PAP government dominated by English-educated Chinese. What created even more of a contrast in the development of Southeast Asian Studies in the two tracks is that while in the Chinese-track, early endeavours to develop scholarship almost completely ceased with the demise of Nanyang University, the heritage of the English-track scholarship which was developed during the colonial period was successfully passed down to future generations through a much stronger institutional base, fully supported by the Singapore government.

The history of the University of Malaya that accommodated the heritage of the Straits/Malaya Branch of the Royal Asiatic Society dates back to 1905 when the King Edward VII Medical School was established. In 1928 Raffles College was formed to promote the arts and social sciences at the tertiary level for Malayan students. These two institutions were merged to form the University of Malaya in 1949. The first generation of Southeast Asianists at the University of Malaya included E.H.G. Dobby who wrote *Southeast Asia* (1960), a pioneering geographical-historical publication that demonstrated the environmental personality of the region (Reid 2004, p. 18). His junior colleagues included Paul Wheatley and Kernial Singh Sandhu both of whom were prominent historical geographers. Scholars at the University began to exert effort into searching for a local perspective on the history of the region. This took place in tandem with the forces of decolonization and nationalism. In reflecting on this situation, scholars attempted to uncover indigenous agency, i.e., the Southeast Asian

perspective. Above all, Cyril Northcote Parkinson,[13] who was the head of
the History Department in the early 1950s, recognized the importance of
teaching not just the history of Europe or America but also that of Southeast
Asia. Parkinson[14] guided his students to conduct research on an original
topic concerning Singapore or Malaya. His early students included Wang
Gungwu, Wong Lin Ken, Khoo Kay Kim, Eunice Thio, R. Suntharalingam,
and Chiang Hai Ding (Ho 2008, pp. 21–24). Ken Tregonning and Mary
Turnbull joined the department to teach in 1953 and 1955, respectively,
to strengthen Parkinson's endeavours.

It is not an exaggeration to state that the launch of *Journal of Southeast
Asian History* in 1960 by the department was a milestone in the history
of Southeast Asian Studies. The establishment of this journal heralded the
rise of a full-fledged scholarly platform for this area of research. It was
Ken Tregonning who contributed greatly to the launch of the journal. In
the late 1950s before the Journal was launched, he had felt the need for
a journal with a different emphasis from *Journal of the Malayan Branch of
the Royal Asiatic Society*. Although the journal had established a reputable
scholarship with the contributions of well-known scholar-administrators such
as Richard Winstedt and R.J. Wilkinson, its concerns were mostly limited
to the British colonies and, against the backdrop of decolonization, the
journal was considered to be old-fashioned and conservative. Tregonning
pursued a journal that, unlike this, would cover the whole of Southeast Asia
and reflect a perspective that was grounded in the region and overcame a
colonial one (Ho 2008, p. 17). Besides the launch of this regional history
journal, he also established another milestone in 1961, playing a crucial
role in organizing the first international conference of Southeast Asian
historians in Singapore (the impetus later behind the establishment of the
International Association of Historians of Asia) (Reid 2004, p. 14). These
two milestones convincingly displayed that Singapore was becoming a centre
for Southeast Asian Studies beyond Southeast Asia. As mentioned earlier,
even in the 1960s, Singapore boasted that it held a central position in terms
of research on Southeast Asia, by publishing journals such as *Journal of the
South Seas Society, Journal of the Malayan Branch of the Royal Asiatic Society*,
and now *Journal of Southeast Asian History*. Observing this development at
the time, Harry Benda (1969, p. 4) stated that, "As a matter of fact, the
availability of such rich human and organisational resources in the Republic
(of Singapore) — and, albeit to varying degrees, elsewhere in the region,
too — constitutes one of the most significant junctures where foreign and
Southeast Asian research endeavours and interests do intersect."

The University of Malaya in Singapore became the University of Singapore in 1962 and the newly named University grew fast and formed more departments. In addition to the Departments of History and Geography set up during the period of Raffles College, the Political Science Department was established in 1961 and the Sociology Department in 1965.[15] The establishment of the Centre for South-East Asian Studies in 1963 served as an impetus at the University to engage research on the region. The Centre brought together the Departments of Economics, Geography, History, Law, Political Science and Social Studies, as well as the University's library section, to sponsor and encourage postgraduate interdisciplinary research on various subjects concerning the region. Again Tregonning played a key role in engendering this institute. After visiting the research centres for Southeast Asian Studies in Yale and Cornell, and that for Asia in Harvard and Stanford for three months, Tregonning became the Secretary for this newly established Centre. However, the Centre never really took off, although it had initially promised to bring in international scholars, enhance staff exchanges and support publications and bibliographical work. It ceased its activities well before Tregonning left Singapore in 1967. Although short lived, the Centre had laid an institutional foundation which later initiatives such as ISEAS were built upon (Ho 2008, p. 30).

In order to reflect the emergence of the social sciences and interdisciplinary research, *The Journal of Southeast Asian History* changed its name to *The Journal of Southeast Asian Studies* in 1970. As Ho (2008, p. 70) has stated, the change in title legitimized a broader scholarship that reflected the closer relationship between Southeast Asian history and the social sciences. One of the main reasons for the creation of the journal was to serve as a platform for local and regional scholars. However, the contributions and participation of local scholarship remained low; the major contribution came from the outside. Statistical research shows that almost 60 per cent of the contributors to the journal from 1960 to 1979 came from outside the region (Ho 2008, p. 153). Indeed, local scholarship had not developed sufficiently to match foreign scholarship, in particular at the University of Singapore, and overall development of scholarship relied on expatriate scholars. It was ascertained from Ooi Jin Bee's (1971, p. 35) observation in the early 1970s.

> The difficulty is compounded in the University of Singapore by two
> factors: (1) the relative youthfulness of most of our social sciences

departments and (2) the lack of continuity arising from the low proportion of local staff in some departments as well as the high turnover of expatriate staff....

While it is necessary to have a proportion of expatriates to provide stimulus and intellectual ferment, too high a proportion and too rapid a turnover of such staff are obviously undesirable.

The above statement shows that the low proportion of local staff and the rapid turnover of expatriate staff had an undesirable impact on the firm establishment of scholarship in Singapore. However, this was not a particular phenomenon at that time. As mentioned earlier, from the development of modern Singapore in 1819, Singapore was intended to be a place that connected the East and the West. This function was entrenched not just in the trade sector but in all parts of society. Foreign components continued to be essential parts of the young state to accelerate the speed of development given the limited resources it had. Academia was no exception.

In the 1970s, in the face of the imminent task of economic development, the government's basic idea of university education was not oriented towards research institutions but rather toward teaching and training institutions. Hence, local students were not encouraged to engage in graduate level study and top-class students were encouraged to be civil servants rather than scholars. This can be ascertained from Peter S.J. Chen's observation (1971, p. 48) of the situation of the Department of Sociology at the University of Singapore in 1971, which had only four full-time postgraduate students then, none of whom was a Ph.D. student. It was only when stepping into the twenty-first century that the University was repositioned as a research institution.

The government dual language policy that began to be implemented in the late 1970s might have been also singled out as a restriction to the entry into Southeast Asian Studies. Although the Singapore government understood the need for research on the region, its dual language policy propelling people to equip themselves with both English and a "mother tongue" (Chinese, Malay, and Tamil) discouraged the learning of the languages of neighbouring countries, which is an essential part of engaging in research on Southeast Asia.[16]

With this shortage of local resources, the Singaporean government deliberately sought foreign experts to promote Southeast Asian Studies through the establishment of ISEAS in 1968 in the face of the emergence of a regional identity that was manifested in the formation of ASEAN in

1967. The establishment of ISEAS opened a new chapter in the history of Southeast Asian research in Singapore. It was not, of course, the first institute related to Southeast Asian Studies in the country. As mentioned earlier, Nanyang University and the University of Singapore had already formed research institutes before this. However, these institutes often came into being from individual endeavours of scholars at the universities and thus often encountered problems caused by financial constraints and a lack of human resources. For these reasons, they either ended up ceasing to operate or ran inefficiently. However, the birth of ISEAS was different. The main initiative came from the government but this did not mean that ISEAS was not an academic institute. With financial stability and equipped with human resources, ISEAS began firmly to establish its reputation not just in Singapore but also in the world. It is not an exaggeration to state that the Southeast Asian Studies of ISEAS is the Southeast Asian Studies of Singapore, and in the same measure, that the history of Southeast Asian Studies in Singapore is the history of Southeast Asian Studies of ISEAS. As such, ISEAS has promoted a Singaporean brand of Southeast Asian Studies to the world.

As mentioned earlier, the establishment of ISEAS reflected the regional situation in the 1960s when Singapore became independent and felt a need to cooperate with its neighbouring countries for its survival in tandem with the emergence of the spirit of regional integration in the form of ASEAN. In this context, establishing an institution for the scholarly study of the region was meant to fulfill one of the objectives stated in the Bangkok Declaration of ASEAN: "To Promote South-East Asian Studies" (Lim et al. 1998, p. 2). Indeed, one of the missions that ISEAS intended to achieve was to encourage Southeast Asians to study neighbouring countries, not their own one. Above all Goh Keng Swee, who spearheaded the formation of ISEAS as the then Minister for Defence, placed emphasis on the need for a regional perspective beyond myopic national interests (Wang 2005, pp. 71–72). It was Goh who searched for the best scholars to run the new institute from the U.S., Australia, Canada and Malaysia. He invited non-Singaporean directors to uphold its autonomy, academic credibility and regional focus. Invited by him, Harry J. Benda, a historian from Yale University, became the first Director from 1968 to 1969, followed by J.D. Legge, a historian from Monash University as the second Director from 1969 to 1970. Josef Silverstein, a political scientist from Rutgers University, served as the third Director from 1970 to 1972. K.S. Sandhu, a Malaysian geographer from the University of British Columbia, succeeded him as the fourth Director in 1972. In his twenty years of leadership until his sudden death in December 1992, Sandhu built up ISEAS to become a full-fledged world-class institute (Lim et al. 1998, p. ix).

The Directors promoted Southeast Asian Studies not from a nationalist perspective but rather from a regional one. They often travelled to neighbouring countries to strengthen scholarly relations. For instance, Harry Benda attended a conference of historians in Asia held in Kuala Lumpur, participated in a regional meeting of Asian Studies centres in Southeast Asia, and went to Indonesia to strengthen academic cooperation soon after he had arrived in Singapore. Legge also made trips to Manila, Bangkok and other cities in order to forge relations. Josef Silverstein was no exception in extending his cooperation to neighbouring countries, visiting Burma, Thailand, Sumatra and Java (ISEAS Annual Report 1968, p. 4; 1968/70, p. 3; 1970/71, p. 9). However, it was during Sandhu's period that ISEAS truly became a central institute for both the region and the world. Regional scholars enjoyed opportunities for interaction and discussion with the support of ISEAS research fellowships during Sandhu's directorship. He was identified as "the founder of Southeast Asian studies for Southeast Asians" (Lim et al. 1998, p. 25).

Although much effort was poured into nurturing Singaporean Southeast Asian scholarship in ISEAS throughout the years, it was indeed rare to see Singaporean scholars engaging in cross-national research. Only a handful of Singaporean scholars were doing so: Russell Heng on the media in Vietnam; Hong Lysa on Thai history; Ananda Rajah[17] on the anthropological study of Thailand and Burma; Leonard Sebastian on Indonesian politics; and Yong Mun Cheong on Indonesian history (Lim et al. 1998, p. 25). This shows that although ISEAS had now matured enough to become a regional and world institute, its production of local Southeast Asianists was not commensurate with the reputation of the Institute. To a large extent, the operation of institute activities was conducted by regional and international scholars under non-Singaporean leadership..

During the period of 1968–92, ISEAS balanced research activities between those disciplines which were rather more policy-oriented such as economics, politics, security studies, and international relations and those which were not such as anthropology, sociology, and history. However, throughout the 1990s, ISEAS increasingly focused on the former set of disciplines. This change is evidenced by the proportion of ISEAS researchers indicated in annual reports. In 1992/93, 32.1 per cent of researchers were located in a programme of social (cultural, historical) issues of ISEAS; 31.4 per cent in economic issues; 22.6 per cent in strategic issues; 8.8 per cent in a programme on Indochina; and the rest in other programmes including public affairs. During this period of time, in terms of discipline, anthropology, sociology and history still made up a sizeable portion of disciplinary studies, making up about 40 per cent of researchers (ISEAS Annual Report 1992/93, pp. 27–31). However, the proportion of these disciplines decreased each year over the course of the 1990s. Eventually, by 1998/99, economics had become the dominant field, making up 56.9 per cent, followed by politics, security and international relations, which made up 23.9 per cent, while the proportion made up of social and cultural studies and history decreased to 18.3 per cent (ISEAS Annual Report 1998/99, pp. 19–20). These figures show that ISEAS had become a much more policy-oriented institute. This change invited divided reactions: scholars of the marginalized disciplines lamented this change, while policy implementers and scholars of dominant disciplines took advantage of it. Southeast Asian Studies in ISEAS had taken a different path from the conventional one, which posed the conundrum of the identity of Southeast Asian Studies in ISEAS and to some extent in Singapore while impacting on the general direction of Southeast Asian Studies in the world with its established reputation.

The early 1990s brought another watershed moment in the development of Southeast Asian Studies. This time change did not arrive from ISEAS but from NUS. The undergraduate Southeast Asian Studies Programme was launched in the 1991/92 academic year under the coordinator, Tong Chee Kiong. In fact, the initial proposal to set up the Programme came out at the Faculty's Heads of Departments meeting in 1986 by the then Dean Edwin Thumboo. Year after year, Faculty members such as Chan Heng Chee, John Wong, Victor R. Savage and Tong Chee Kiong had prepared the inauguration of the Programme. The establishment of the Programme reflected a compelling sense that "Singapore has been and still remains an inextricable part of the economic, cultural and political network of Southeast Asian societies". One of the cornerstones of the Programme was to ensure that the students be equipped with a Southeast Asian language. This was meant to enhance the students' cultural and social understanding of the region. The Programme endeavoured to adopt interdisciplinary approaches to both teaching and research in cooperation with the departments in the Faculty of Arts and Social Sciences. It also collaborated with ISEAS for the students to benefit from its material and human resources and fellowship programmes. Unlike the early directorship of ISEAS, Singaporean scholars took up the directorships in the early stage. Tong Chee Kiong was succeeded by Victor Savage from 1992 to 1997, Hong Lysa from 1997 to 1999, Victor Savage again from 1999 to 2001, and Chua Beng Huat from 2001 to 2003. Then the Filipino scholar Reynaldo C. Ileto, an internal staff member of the Programme and the author of *Pasyon and Revolution: Popular Movements in the Philippines, 1840–1910* (1979) headed the Programme from June 2003 to December 2005, Brenda Yeoh from January 2006 to December 2008, and Goh Beng Lan from January 2009 until the time of writing. The Programme was accorded the status of a full-fledged department from 1 July 2011 as it gained recognition of its maturation as a field of study.[18] The establishment of the Programme/Department marked the endeavours of NUS to promote Southeast Asian Studies in the face of the increasing marginalization of Southeast Asian Studies in the U.S. and Europe.[19]

Over the years, other departments of NUS also strengthened their teaching and research capacities. In particular, the Department of Sociology had a critical mass of scholars. Although the Department began with a handful of staff, headed by Murray Groves, an Australian social anthropologist, in 1965, its development was impressive. Hans-Dieter Evers, a German sociologist, succeeded Groves and laid a strong foundation; during his term from 1971 to 1974, *Working Papers Series* and *Southeast Asian Journal of Social Science* (now *Asian Journal of Social Science*) were launched in 1972 and 1973 respectively.[20] Geoffrey Benjamin had played a substantial part in the development of Southeast Asian studies in the Department since 1967 when he began his career to 1998 when he departed. He was actively involved in research on the region as well as developing Southeast Asianists such as the late Ananda Rajah. Above all, Chua Beng Huat's participation in the Department from 1985 greatly increased the international reputation of the Department as well as Singapore sociology in general. He has also been active in nurturing the future generation of scholars. His critical and liberal stance[21] has influenced the Department so that it has become a dynamic place where a diverse range of ideas and research findings have been exchanged and communicated. The Department has been a mainstay of anthropologists, not just sociologists. Anthropologists including Geoffrey Benjamin, Vivienne Wee, Roxana Waterson, Maribeth Erb, the late Ananda Rajah, Saroja Dorairajoo, Vineeta Sinha, Eric Thompson and Mika Toyota advanced the profile of anthropology in the Department. Indeed, anthropologists have contributed to the outward looking character of the Department, overcoming an inherent nature of sociology departments in general to focus on their own countries.[22]

Other departments like Geography and Political Science, and even the Department of Architecture in the Faculty of Design and Environment, merit mention in the developing scholarship on Southeast Asia. In particular, the Geography Department can boast a high level and quality of research produced by faculty members, notably Brenda Yeoh and Henry Yeung. The

Department has been so influential that it has played a key role in setting current research agendas of NUS such as migration and city networks which of course has affected the trajectory of Southeast Asian Studies in general. The Department of Political Science has strengthened its capacity and expanded research on the region though perhaps it has not made the same impact as other departments. The Department of Architecture has also engaged in Southeast Asian Studies in particular in the areas of heritage and the historical development of cities.

NUS's endeavour to develop Southeast Asian Studies continued beyond the level of the Faculty of Arts and Social Sciences. Subsequently at the university level, a grand initiative was undertaken to establish a world-class institute at NUS. The Asia Research Institute (ARI) was formed as a university-level institute in July 2001. The impact of the establishment of ARI would be comparable to that of ISEAS in 1968, as it clearly marked a Singaporean initiative to advance Southeast Asian Studies beyond Singapore through the establishment of a world-class institution. After an extensive international search, Anthony Reid, a prominent scholar in Southeast Asian history, was invited to become the founding director. He arrived in Singapore in July 2002 and the official opening ceremony took place in March 2003. This search recalls the earlier search for Harry Benda, also a prominent scholar in Southeast Asian history, as the founding director of ISEAS. Under Reid's directorship, ARI was truly becoming a focal point for scholarly activities in diverse areas of Asian studies, particularly in Southeast Asian Studies. It was rare to see a single day pass without any activity in ARI. The research clusters brought ARI's research staff and visiting fellows from various countries together to work on specific research agendas. The research clusters included "The Changing Family in Asia" led by Gavin Jones, "Asian Migration" by Brenda Yeoh, "Cultural Studies in Asia" by Chua Beng Huat, "Religion and Globalisation in Asian Context" by Bryan Turner, "Southeast Asia-China Interactions" by Anthony Reid, and "Southeast Asian Archaeology" by John Miksic. Under the leadership of these leading scholars, the clusters produced high quality research outcomes. ARI also became a breeding ground for future generations. It provided various forms of financial support including fellowships, research grants, fieldwork grants and dissertation write-up grants to graduate students. Besides, it offered an opportunity for NUS faculty members to spend a leave period in refreshing their research endeavours.[23]

Anthony Reid completed his term as Director in 2007, leaving a lasting legacy on the scholarship of Southeast Asian Studies in Singapore. Lily Kong, a prominent local geographer succeeded him. Under her leadership,

ARI reorganized the scheme of research clusters where some previous clusters such as "Southeast Asia-China Interactions" were discontinued and new ones including "Asian Urbanism" and "Science, Technology and Society" were opened, further building on earlier success. It was thought that ARI's future was now in the hands of local leadership. However, it was not long before we saw again the introduction of foreign expertise. In January 2011, Prasenjit Duara, an internationally renowned historian of China and the wider Asia became the new Director. Indeed, in 2008 NUS had brought him to Singapore from the University of Chicago to promote research excellence.

Research clusters have been key schemes in conducting research and therefore defining research directions at ARI and NUS. If we see those clusters in operation now — "Asian Migration", "Asian Urbanism", "Changing Family in Asia", "Cultural Studies in Asia", "Meta Cluster: Asian Connections", "Religion and Globalisation in Asian Contexts", "Science, Technology and Society" — we can grasp the point that the presence of Southeast Asia is not prominent but is ambiguously located in a broader Asia. It demonstrates that ARI's focus has shifted to Asia in general. We can also observe from the themes of the Research Clusters the changing regional context which Singapore and its government are experiencing. We are therefore seeing the emergence of a new, broader understanding of "Southeast Asian Studies" and a change in the identity of "Southeast Asian Studies" which is intimately connected to the resources and institutions in Singapore. Like it or not, these research directions and changes in identity which are taking place in Singapore have been making a great impact on Southeast Asian scholarship in general and can be expected to affect the future of the field.

Over the years, as we have seen from the establishment of the Southeast Asian Studies Programme/Department, the capacity building of the existing departments and the operation of ARI, NUS has consolidated its pre-eminent position in Southeast Asian Studies. The fact that over one hundred Southeast Asianists are affiliated with NUS is evidence of this strength. The Directory of Southeast Asianists has stated that the number of Southeast Asianists was 80 in 1993, 112 in 1996–97, 107 in 2001 and 107 as of 2009. No other university in the world can boast such a rich pool of human resources in this field. With human resources and institutional support, NUS has become a major player to the degree to which it can shape the trends and trajectories of Southeast Asian scholarship. This development path has been different from that in other countries. Its development is attributed to the nexus of the government and academia and local and expatriate scholars. This nexus has turned the directions and identity of Southeast Asian Studies in the country into different forms.

CONCLUSION

Southeast Asian Studies in Singapore has had a problem with locating local scholarship from the outset. The development of English-track scholarship in this field, starting in the nineteenth century, was initiated by British scholars, who were mostly colonial administrators when Singapore was identified as a part of the Malay world. Scholarship in this period raises the question of whether Singapore could exclusively claim ownership of the scholarship developed during the colonial period, if this ownership belongs to the United Kingdom or whether it must be shared with current Malaysia? The fact that indigenous or local participation in the development of scholarship was absent makes its identification as the property of Singapore more difficult.

Chinese scholarship which began in the 1940s cannot avoid the identity problem either. At the outset, Chinese scholars were not considered as local people but as sojourners who identified China as their home country. The scholarship they conducted was very much influenced by mainland Chinese scholarship before they migrated to Nanyang and by Japanese scholarship while they were in Japan, having been saturated with "Japanese Fever" for Nanyo (Nanyang). The Chinese scholars were not indigenous scholars when they initiated Chinese-track Nanyang Studies through the establishment of the South Seas Society. Rather, they were hybrid scholars (Seah 2007), who had been exposed to diverse forms of scholarship which had their roots in the colonial, mainland Chinese and Japanese context.

Indeed for some time in the 1960s–70s, there existed a relatively strong local scholarship that was based mainly at Nanyang University. The heritage of Chinese-language track scholarship was transferred to the University in parallel to the English-track scholarship. However, the former became marginalized as English became dominant not just in education but also in Singapore society. Chinese-track scholarship lost an institutional base with the coming to an end of Nanyang University in 1980. Although this scholarship still continues in the long-existing South Seas Society and Singapore Society of Asian Studies, it is unable to match the rigorous English-track scholarship. Its focus tends to be on overseas Chinese issues, and it does not fully cover the various issues of Southeast Asia.

Unlike the Chinese-track scholarship, the English-track scholarship in Singapore has developed greatly over the years as English has become the medium of the globalizing world to which the development of Singapore has been tied and the government has intensified the promotion of Singapore as a central place for regional studies. The establishment of ISEAS crystallized Singapore's endeavours to develop a Singapore brand of Southeast Asian Studies for the world. The contributions of foreign scholars, including directors and research staff have contributed tremendously over the years to establishing ISEAS as a world-class institute. Despite the controversy over the issue that ISEAS has become a policy-oriented institute over the years, it has clearly brought Singapore to the front line of Southeast Asian Studies. Alongside ISEAS, NUS has carried on research on the region and become a world-class university in this academic field. The formation of the Southeast Asian Studies Programme/Department signified a clear effort on the part of NUS to develop the academic field. The Departments of Sociology, History and Geography have raised the profile of NUS. Needless to say, the establishment of ARI in 2001 marked a cornerstone for NUS in advancing Southeast Asian Studies. It was a focal point not just for Singapore but also for the world. This series of developments have strengthened scholarship at NUS.

In the post-colonial condition that Singapore lacked "indigenous" resources in overall areas including education and research, the typical way in which Singapore has chosen to develop Southeast Asian Studies has been to establish world-class institutes and to bring in foreign expertise. This strategy has paid off since it has situated Singapore as the prime place where scholars gather, information is exchanged and quality research outcomes are published. In following this development path, Southeast Asian scholarship in Singapore has turned out differently from other countries. At the moment the Singaporean context is also significantly associated with the development of research agendas and the future direction of Southeast Asian Studies. And the country affects and influences Southeast Asian Studies in general with the level of its human resources and institutional support devoted to the field. We are now therefore observing the emergence of Singapore-driven Southeast Asian Studies.

Notes

A very early version of this chapter in Korean appeared in *The Southeast Asian Review* 30, no. 3 (2010): 101–45.

1   These include R.O. Winstedt's "A History of Johor 1365–1895" (1932), "A History of Perak" jointly with R.J. Wilkinson (1934), "A History of Selangor" (1934), "A History of Malaya" (1935); R.J. Wilkinson's "Early Indian Influence in Malaysia" (1935*a*), "The Malacca Sultanate" (1935*b*); Anker Rentse's "History of Kelantan, Part 1" (1934); W. Linehan's "A History of Pahang" (1936); Roland Braddell's "An Introduction to the Study of Ancient Times in the Malay Peninsula" (1937), "Notes on Ancient Times of Malaya" (1947); and M.C. ff. Sheppard's "A Short History of Trengganu" (1949).

2   The Chinese scripts in this chapter conform to original forms.

3   Among the early Nanyang students in the school was Lee Kong Chian, who migrated to Singapore in 1905 at the age of six from Fujian Province in China. He studied at the school from 1908–11 and later became a great businessman and philanthropist in Singapore who made countless contributions to various sectors of society including education (Seah 2008; Huang 2009).

4   They were Kwan Chu Poh; Yue Daff; Yao Tsu Liang; Hsu Yun-Ts'iao; Chang Lee Chien; LouShih Mo; Lee Chan Foo; and Han Wai Toon (Seah 2007, p. 139).

5   They included Kwan Chu Poh; Yue Daff; Yao Tsu Liang; Hsu Yun-Ts'iao; and Chang Lee Chien (Seah 2007, p. 139).

6   They were Lou Shih Mo; Lee Chan Foo; and Yao Tsu Liang (Seah 2007, p. 141).

7   Personal communication on 5 January 2010.

8   See note 3 for the information on him.

9   The major of many students was history, influenced by Hsu (Seah 2005, p. 63).

10   The University of Malaya in Singapore became the University of Singapore in 1962.

11   The Island Society was established in 1966 by local scholars, many of whom were also members of the South Seas Society, to contribute to the nation building efforts of Singapore as well as to the promotion of scholarly research in the face of Singapore's independence in 1965 (Ong 1978, pp. 43–48).

12   Led by Wang Gungwu, the Wang Gungwu Curriculum Review Committee was formed in 1965 while Singapore was a part of the Federation of Malaysia. In an interview, Wang mentioned that the main idea in the Report was for graduates of Nanyang University to be treated equally (Yuan et al. 2004, pp. 31–32).

13   It was D.G.E. Hall who broke new ground in searching for this viewpoint in his book, *History of South-East Asia* (1955). He taught at Rangoon University from 1921 to 1934.

14   His main work includes *British Intervention in Malaya, 1867–1877* (1960).

15   This information was obtained from the NUS website, <http://www.nus.edu.sg>.

16   Personal communications with Huang Jianli on 7 January 2010 and Wang
     Gungwu on 5 January 2010.
17   He was my Ph.D. supervisor and passed away in January 2007 when I was in
     the last stages of completing my study.
18   This information was obtained from various issues of the Southeast Asian
     Studies Programme Handbook and the website of the Programme/Department,
     <http://www.fas.nus.edu.sg/sea>.
19   For the state of Southeast Asian studies, see Chou and Houben (2006);
     Halib and Huxley (1996); Hirschman et al. (1992); Reid (2003); and Sears
     (2007).
20   The information was drawn from the website of the Department <http://www.
     fas.nus.edu.sg/soc> and Benjamin (1996).
21   *Communitarian Ideology and Democracy in Singapore* (1995) represents these
     stances.
22   This section was largely derived from my own experiences and association with
     the Department.
23   This was obtained from my observations during my days in NUS from 2003
     to 2007 and from various issues of ARI annual reports in the ARI's website,
     <http://www.ari.nus.edu.sg>.

References

Benda, Harry J. "Research in Southeast Asian Studies in Singapore". *Journal of the
     South Seas Society* 24 (1969): 1–10.
Benjamin, Geoffrey. "Sociologie Singapurská". In *Velký Sociologický Slovník*, edited
     by H. Maríková, M. Petrušek and A. Vodáková. Charles University, Prague:
     Karolinum, 1996. (The orginal English text of the article was downloaded from
     the website <http://nanyang.academia.edu/GeoffreyBenjamin/Papers/1196367/
     Singapore_sociology>).
Braddell, Roland. "An Introduction to the Study of Ancient Times in the Malay
     Peninsula". *Journal of the Malayan Branch of the Royal Asiatic Society* 15, no. 3
     (1937): 64–126.
————. "Notes on Ancient Times in Malaya, Part 1". *Journal of the Malayan Branch
     of the Royal Asiatic Society* 20, no. 1 (1947): 161–86.
Chee, Choy Meh nee Lum. "History of the Malaysian Branch of the Royal Asiatic
     Society". *Journal of the Malaysian Branch of the Royal Asiatic Society* 68,
     no. 2 (1995): 81–148.
Chen, Peter S.J. "Teaching and Research in the Social Sciences in Singapore". *Nanyang
     Quarterly: A Review of Southeast Asian Studies* 1, no. 1 (1971): 45–51.
Chou, Cynthia and Vincent Houben, eds. *Southeast Asian Studies: Debates and New
     Directions.* Singapore: Institute of Southeast Asian Studies, 2006.

Chua, Beng Huat. *Communitarian Ideology and Democracy in Singapore*. London and New York: Routledge, 1995.

Crawford, John. *A Descriptive Dictionary of the Indian Islands and Adjacent Countries*. London: Bradbury and Evans, 1856.

Dobby, E.H.G. *Southeast Asia*. London: University of London, 1950.

Doraisamy, T.R., ed. *150 Years of Education in Singapore*. Singapore: Teacher's Training College, 1969.

Emmerson, Donald K. "'Southeast Asia': What's in a Name?". *Journal of Southeast Asian Studies* 15, no. 1 (1984): 1–21.

Franke, Wolfgang. "Introduction". In *Proceedings of Seminar on Societies for Southeast Asian Studies, Past, Present and Future*. Singapore: Nanyang University, 1978.

Goh, Keng Swee et al. *The Report on the Ministry of Education 1978*. Singapore: Ministry of Education, 1979.

Gopinathan, S. "Education". In *A History of Singapore*, edited by Ernest C.T. Chew and Edwin Lee. Singapore: Oxford University Press, 1996.

Gwee, Yee Hean. "South Seas Society: Past, Present and Future". In *Proceedings of Seminar on Societies for Southeast Asian Studies, Past, Present and Future*. Singapore: Nanyang University, 1978.

Halib, Mohammed and Tim Huxley, eds. *An Introduction to Southeast Asian Studies*. Singapore: Institute of Southeast Asian Studies, 1996.

Hall, D.G.E. *A History of South-East Asia*. London: Macmillan, 1955.

Hirschman, Charles, Charles F. Keyes, and Karl Hutterer, eds. *Southeast Asian Studies in the Balance: Reflections from America*. Ann Arbor, MI: The Association for Asian Studies, 1992.

Ho, Chi Tim. "A Situated History of the Journal of Southeast Asian History/ Studies (1960–1979)". Master's thesis, Department of History, National University of Singapore, 2008.

Hong, Lysa and Huang Jianli. *The Scripting of a National History: Singapore and Its Pasts*. Hong Kong: Hong Kong University Press, 2008.

Hose, M.A. "Inaugural Address of the President". *Journal of the Straits Branch of the Royal Asiatic Society* 1 (1878): 1–12.

Hsu, Yun-Ts'iao. "Prologue". *The Bulletin of the Institute of Southeast Asia* 1 (1959): vi–vii.

Huang, Jianli. "Shifting Culture and Identity: Three Portraits of Singapore Entrepreneur Lee Kong Chian (1893–1967)". *Journal of the Malaysian Branch of the Royal Asiatic Society* 82, no. 1 (2009): 71–100.

Ileto, Reynaldo C. *Pasyon and Revolution: Popular Movements in the Phillipines, 1840–1910*. Manila: Ateneo de Manila University Press, 1979.

Khoo, Kay Kim. "Recent Advances in the Study and Writing of Malaysian History". *Peninjau Sejarah* 3, no. 1 (1968): 1–12.

Kwok, Kian-Woon. "Chinese-Educated Intellectuals in Singapore: Marginality, Memory and Modernity". *Asian Journal of Social Science* 29, no. 3 (2001): 495–519.

Lim, Huck Tee and D.E.K. Wijasuriya. *Index Malaysiana: An Index to the Journal of the Straits Branch Royal Asiatic Society and the Journal of the Malayan Branch Royal Asiatic Society 1878–1963*. Kuala Lumpur: Malaysian Branch Royal Asiatic Society, 1970.

Lim, Pui Huen P. et al. *Institute of Southeast Asian Studies: A Commemorative History 1968–1998*. Singapore: Institute of Southeast Asian Studies, 1998.

Lim, Say Hup. "The Need for a Reinterpretation of Malayan History". *Malaya in History* 5, no. 2 (1959): 41–43.

Linehan, W. "A History of Pahang". *Journal of the Malayan Branch of the Royal Asiatic Society* 14, no. 2 (1936): 1–256.

Liu, Hong. "Southeast Asian Studies in Greater China". *Kyoto Review of Southeast Asia* 3 (2003). <http://kyotoreview.cseas.kyoto-u.ac.jp/issue/issue2/article_232_p.html> (accessed 8 March 2010).

Moor, J.H. *Notices of the Indian Archipelago and Adjacent Countries: Being a Collection of Papers Relating to Borneo, Celebes, Bali, Java, Sumatra, Nias, the Philippine Islands, Sulus, Siam, Cochin China, Malayan Peninsula, etc*. Singapore: [s.n], 1837.

Ong, Tee Wah. "The Island Society, Singapore: Its Past, Present and Future". In *Proceedings of Seminar on Societies for Southeast Asian Studies, Past, Present and Future*. Singapore: Nanyang University, 1978.

Ooi, Jin Bee. "Relevance in Social Science Research in Singapore". *Nanyang Quarterly: A Review of Southeast Asian Studies* 1, no. 1 (1971): 34–36.

Parkinson, C. Northcote. *British Intervention in Malaya, 1867–1877*. Singapore: University of Malaya Press, 1960.

Reid, Anthony. "A Saucer Model of Southeast Asian Identity". *Southeast Asian Journal of Social Science* 27, no. 1 (1999): 7–23.

———, ed. *Southeast Asian Studies: Pacific Perspectives*. Tempe, AZ: The Program for Southeast Asian Studies, Arizona State University and the UCLA Asia Institute, 2003.

———. "Studying Southeast Asia in a Globalized World". *Taiwan Journal of Southeast Asian Studies* 1, no. 2 (2004): 3–18.

Rentse, A. "History of Kelantan, Part I". *Journal of the Malayan Branch of the Royal Asiatic Society* 12, no. 2 (1934): 44–62.

Seah, Leander Tze Ling. "Historicizing Hybridity and Globalization: The South Seas Society in Singapore, 1940–2000". Master's thesis, Department of History, National University of Singapore, 2005.

———. "Hybridity, Globalization, and the Creation of a Nanyang Identity: The South Seas Society in Singapore, 1940–1958". *Journal of the South Seas Society* 61 (2007): 134–51.

————. "Conceptualizing the Chinese World: Jinan University, Lee Kong Chian, and the Nanyang Connection, 1900–1942". *BiblioAsia* 4, no. 1 (2008): 26–44.

Sears, Laurie J., ed. *Knowing Southeast Asian Subjects.* Seattle: University of Washington Press, 2007.

Sheppard, M.C. ff. "A Short History of Trengganu". *Journal of the Malayan Branch of the Royal Asiatic Society* 22, no. 3 (1949): 1–74.

Suryadinata, Leo. "Southeast Asian Studies in Singapore: Past and Present". In *Toward the Promotion of Southeast Asian Studies in Southeast Asia,* edited by Taufik Abdullah and Yekti Maunati. Jakarta: Program of Southeast Asian Studies, Indonesian Institute of Sciences, 1998.

Turnbull, C.M. *A History of Singapore 1819–1975.* Kuala Lumpur: Oxford University Press, 1982.

Wang, Gungwu. *The Nanhai Trade: The Early History of Chinese Trade in the South China Sea.* Singapore: Times Academic Press, 1998.

————. *Don't Leave Home: Migration and the Chinese.* Singapore: Eastern Universities Press, 2003.

————. "Chinese Political Culture and Scholarship about the Malay World". In *Diasporic Chinese Ventures: The Life and Work of Wang Gungwu,* edited by Gregor Benton and Hong Liu. London and New York: RoutledgeCurzon, 2004*a.*

————. "Mixing Memory and Desire: Tracking the Migrant Cycles". In *Diasporic Chinese Ventures: The Life and Work of Wang Gungwu,* edited by Gregor Benton and Hong Liu. London and New York: RoutledgeCurzon, 2004*b.*

————. "Two Perspectives of Southeast Asian Studies: Singapore and China". In *Locating Southeast Asia: Geographies of Knowledge and Politics of Space,* edited by Paul H. Kratoska, Remco Raben, and Henk Schulte Nordholt. Singapore: Singapore University Press, 2005.

Wilkinson, R.J. "Early Indian Influence in Malaysia". *Journal of the Malayan Branch of the Royal Asiatic Society* 13, no. 2 (1935*a*): 1–16.

————. "The Malacca Sultanate". *Journal of the Malayan Branch of the Royal Asiatic Society* 13, no. 2 (1935*b*): 22–67.

Winstedt, R.O. "A History of Johor 1365–1895". *Journal of the Malayan Branch of the Royal Asiatic Society* 10, no. 3 (1932): 1–167.

————. "A History of Selangor". *Journal of the Malayan Branch of the Royal Asiatic Society* 12, no. 3 (1934): 1–34.

————. "A History of Malaya". *Journal of the Malayan Branch of the Royal Asiatic Society* 13, no. 1 (1935): 1–270.

Winstedt, R.O. and R.J. Wilkinson. "A History of Perak". *Journal of the Malayan Branch of the Royal Asiatic Society* 12, no. 1 (1934): 1–180.

Yuan, Yaoqing et al. "Wang Gungwu on the Nantah Incident: An Interview". In *Diasporic Chinese Ventures: The Life and Work of Wang Gungwu,* edited by Gregor Benton and Hong Liu. London and New York: RoutledgeCurzon, 2004.

Periodicals
Asian Culture
Island Literature
Island Society Quarterly
Journal of the Island Society
Journal of the South Seas Society
Journal of Southeast Asian History
Journal of Southeast Asian Studies
Journal of the Straits/Malayan/Malaysian Branch of the Royal Asiatic Society
Nanyang Quarterly: Review of Southeast Asian Studies
SOJOURN: Journal of Social Issues in Southeast Asia

Annual Reports, Newsletters, Handbooks, Directory
Annual Reports of Asia Research Institute, National University of Singapore
Annual Reports of Institute of Southeast Asian Studies
Newsletters of Asia Research Institute, National University of Singapore
Newsletters of Institute of Southeast Asian Studies
Directory of Southeast Asianists at National University of Singapore
Southeast Asian Programme Handbook, National University of Singapore

Personal Communications
Huang, Jianli, 7 January 2010
Wang, Gungwu, 5 January 2010

6

THE CONSTRUCTION AND INSTITUTIONALIZATION OF SOUTHEAST ASIAN STUDIES IN VIETNAM
Focusing on Insiders' Perceptions and Assessment[1]

Choi Horim

INTRODUCTION

In Hanoi, **notably, a Department of Southeast Asian Studies was established in 1973**, within the government research organization then known as the Vietnam Social Sciences Committee.

(Reid and Diokno 2003, p. 101; my emphasis)

This sentence in a long paragraph, which considered the history of institutions which are engaged in Southeast Asian Studies within Southeast Asia itself, seems to have two implications: first, it is notable that an organization for Southeast Asian Studies was established in Vietnam relatively earlier than in some other Southeast Asian countries. Second, it is not clear whether this Department played its role as an independent research institute. Western scholars count Singapore's Institute of Southeast Asian Studies (ISEAS) and Malaysia's Department of Southeast Asian Studies, University of Malaya, among the leading institutions of this region. Until the 1990s, outsiders might have perceived that "Vietnam is not something" which falls within the scope of Southeast Asian Studies (Halib and Huxley 1996, p. 4; Reid 2004, p. 15).[2]

However, Vietnamese scholars contend that they have developed Vietnam's Southeast Asian Studies programme viewing Southeast Asia as both a geographical entity with a long history and cultural tradition and a strategic region for modern development. Based mainly on the arguments of Vietnamese scholars, this study has traced the construction of Southeast Asian Studies as an academic subject in Vietnam. The study has also paid heed to the institutionalization of Southeast Asian research institutions and their activities focusing on the perceptions and evaluation of Vietnamese scholars.

Firstly this chapter provides a historical overview of the institutionalization of Southeast Asian Studies focusing on the relevant research institutions in Vietnam. Secondly, it describes the perceptions of Southeast Asian Studies inside Vietnam and the local evaluation of the effort to indigenize Southeast Asian Studies. In this regard this study has taken note of Vietnamese scholars' perceptions and assessment of Southeast Asian Studies performed by outsiders, primarily by Western scholars; in other words it concerns the perceptions and evaluation of Southeast Asian Studies conducted by Southeast Asian insiders and its origin in an indigenous Vietnamese point of view. And finally, this chapter examines the construction and limitations of Southeast Asian Studies in Vietnam, including the issue of this field as one which advocates interdisciplinary regional studies.

In this study I visited local research institutes, interviewed leading researchers, and collected various documents and major journals and pamphlets for a literature review. The field research enabled me to gather information on the history of the construction and development of Southeast Asian Studies in Vietnam; relevant research and training programmes at research institutes, academic associations, and college departments; major publications and journals on this field of studies; leading scholars and researchers, their background and activities and so on.[3] As shown in Table 6.1, the in-depth interviews were carried out with ten current and former professors in Hanoi and Ho Chi Minh City. Of these, Professors Phạm Đức Dương, Nguyễn Van Chính, Ngô Văn Doanh, and Phan Thị Hồng Xuân provided insightful opinions and rich information on the history and current status of Southeast Asian Studies in Vietnam.

Table 6.1
List of Interviewees (July 2009)

Date of Interview	Interviewee	Affiliation	Status/Area of Research
July 6	Trần Đình Lâm	Center for Vietnam and Southeast Asian Studies (CVSEAS), College of Social Sciences and Humanities, Ho Chi Minh City National University	Director, economics
July 6	Thành Phần	CVSEAS	Vice director, ethnology, Study of Champa
July 6	Hoàng Văn Việt	Khoa Đông Phương (the Faculty of Oriental Studies), Ho Chi Minh City National University	Dean, Comparative politics of Southeast Asia (the Philippines) & Korea
July 6	Nguyễn Văn Tiệp	Khoa Nhân học (Department of Anthropology), Ho Chi Minh City National University	Head, Director of the Research Institutes for Applied Anthropology
July 7	Phan Thị Hồng Xuân	Department of Southeast Asian Studies, Ho Chi Minh City Open University	Vice head, anthropology, Malaysian-India-Chinese migrants
July 10	Nguyễn Văn Chính	Asia-Pacific Research Institute, Hanoi National University	Vice director, anthropology
July 10	Ngô Văn Doanh	Viện Nghiên cứu Đông Nam Á (Institute for Southeast Asian Studies), Vietnam Academy of Social Sciences (VASS)	Editor-in-chief of *Southeast Asian studies (Nghiên cứu Đông Nam Á)*
July 10	Nguyễn Duy Dũng	Viện Nghiên cứu Đông Nam Á	Vice director, Head of ASEAN-Japanese Studies Office
July 11	Phạm Đức Dương	Founder of the Institute for Southeast Asian Studies	Founder and director
July 14	Phan Huy Lê	Professor emeritus Department of History, Hanoi National University	Chairperson of Hội Lịch sử Việt Nam (the Vietnam Society of History)

FOUNDATION OF THE DEPARTMENT OF SOUTHEAST ASIAN STUDIES AND THE INSTITUTIONALIZATION OF SOUTHEAST ASIAN STUDIES IN VIETNAM

In 1972, a proposal was submitted to the Central government to establish a Southeast Asian research institution. Led by Professor Nguyễn Khánh Tòan (then-president of the *Ủy ban Khoa học Xã hội Việt Nam*, or Vietnam Social Sciences Committee), historians Phan Gia Bền, Phạm Nguyên Long and Đặng Bích Hà, archaeologist Cao Xuân Phổ, literary scholars Cao Huy Đinh and Nguyễn Tấn Đắc, and linguist Phạm Đức Dương played a crucial role in founding the institution. Most of them were then-executives of major state-run institutes in the humanities and social sciences, such as the Social Sciences Committee of Vietnam, the Institute of Literature, and the Institute of Archeology.

At the time of the foundation of *Ban Đông Nam Á* (the Department of Southeast Asian Studies), Professor Nguyễn Khánh Tòan's keynote speech included important information on the basic directions and perspectives of Southeast Asian Studies in Vietnam. East Asia (*Đông Á*) was divided into North Asia (*Bắc Á*), including China, Japan, and Korea, and South Asia (*Nam Á*), including Vietnam, Southeast Asia and the Pacific region, and the latter was considered as the comprehensive scope of studies and perceptions of the Southeast Asian region. He states that Southeast Asian culture has long been formed historically with diverse ethnic groups and it belongs to a South Asian linguistic system. The regional scope of Southeast Asian Studies should comprise the Asian continent without restricting it to Southeast Asia and be connected to studies of the Pacific region. Southeast Asia needs to be understood as the centre of the "Orient (*Đông Dương*)" (Nguyễn Khánh Tòan 1973, pp. 3, 8–9).

Nguyễn Khánh Tòan's speech adopted many socialist doctrines and concepts.

> As it is a strategically important region located between the Asian and American continents, Southeast Asia with its civilization formed from the prehistoric times emerged as the focus of interest in European colonialism from the inception of capitalism. Southeast Asia has been riddled with the world's major contradictions, such as those between empires, between socialist-nationalist liberation movements and colonialism, and between revolutionary forces and feudalism, etc. Southeast Asian Studies should serve the political mission for revolution. Its overriding

goal is to overthrow imperialism and neo-colonialism. The long-term goal is to make Southeast Asia a land of peace and friendship in order to guarantee each nation's freedom and independence, prosperity and happiness. In other words, the development of Southeast Asian Studies is needed to build Southeast Asia as a stable peaceful region which greatly contributes to the peace and wellbeing of Asia, the Pacific, and the world (ibid., pp. 7–8).

This attitude of putting political rhetoric before the goal of the studies itself is mirrored in the policy of operating most state-run research institutions. In addition, his speech represents a philosophy that historically embellishes the Southeast Asian region and stresses the unity of the oppressed nations under occupation. He emphasized that based on the common roots of Southeast Asian culture including rice farming, pole houses, and bronze drums, many nations and ethnic groups led peaceful lives and had no major clashes unlike other regions of the world. And because of this, each nation in the region was more likely to have collaborated with each other and achieved emotional unity than in any other region.

Researchers of Southeast Asian Studies in each country should make a concerted effort for peace, independence and prosperity. Today, nothing can prevent Vietnam and each nation in Southeast Asia from fighting for independence, freedom, peace, and social progress! (ibid., pp. 13–14).

The initial efforts in the post-colonial era to indigenize Southeast Asian Studies in Vietnam were very much part of an ideological orientation based on the concepts of socialism and nationalism as we have seen above. These efforts have been gradually expanded and diversified, mainly under the agenda of the Party-state's academic organizations.[4]

In 1984 the Department of Southeast Asian Studies was expanded to found the "Institute for Southeast Asian Studies" (Viện Đông Nam Á). On 10 April 1984 after preparations of over a decade, the chairperson of the Vietnam Social Sciences Committee announced a decision No. 312 (*số 312-KHXH/QĐ*) for the establishment of the Institute. According to the decision, the main responsibility of the Institute was to serve the Party and the state in devising development strategies for the social sciences concerned with the region, with domestic and overseas development strategies and programmes through scientific research of the history, politics, economy, society and culture of Southeast Asian countries. The basic role of the Institute was described as "serving scientific research and education about Southeast Asia, supporting the Vietnam Social Sciences Committee, and managing research projects on the Southeast Asian region at the national and regional levels".

Professor Phạm Đức Dương, the founder and Director of the Institute for Southeast Asian Studies, said the Institute had undertaken studies of the following five issues from 1973 to 1990: first, the study of traditional and native Southeast Asian civilizations as different from Sino-centric and Indian civilizations, focusing on each nation's characteristics formed through the conquest of nature and the history of social strife according to the culture and ethnic construction of each country; second, the study of the historical formation of each country and nation underpinned by the trajectory of the emergence of traditional culture, that is, the historical study of how Southeast Asian culture had appeared and changed through interaction and exchange with Sino-centric and Indian cultures as well as other cultures on the Asian continent; third, the historical study of the intervention of Western colonialism and administration and the local response in national liberation movements, with a focus on changes in economy, society, and traditional culture in the process of colonization and liberation; fourth, the study of the many routes to modernity in Southeast Asian countries today and the relationships between Southeast Asian countries and the international community; and finally, the study of the relationships between Vietnam and other Southeast Asian countries in the historical process (Phạm Đức Dương 1990, p. 12).

He also emphasized that Southeast Asian Studies in Vietnam should be more faithful to its two major responsibilities as follows: first, the academic discipline should carry out studies with a deeper and comprehensive under-standing of diverse cultural values in Southeast Asia. Specifically, he asserted that it should undertake deeper studies of historical and cultural development from the past traditions to the modern period as well as of the relations between Vietnam and Southeast Asian countries. To build peace and promote stability, cooperation and development in the region, he argued, Southeast Asian Studies should expand research projects to contribute to each nation's pride, unity, and friendship. He added that through its achievements, the academic subject should contribute to Vietnam's strategies for development and to the Communist Party and the socialist government in establishing overseas policies on Southeast Asia as a strategic sub-region of the Asia-Pacific region. Secondly, Southeast Asian Studies in Vietnam should not only strengthen basic research in various areas of study but also expand and deepen studies of a broad range of issues and problems in the social sciences. He emphasized an ambitious goal for Southeast Asian Studies in that it should contribute to enriching theories in each area of study not just at the regional level but also at the global level. To this end, he stressed studies of correlations between the Southeast Asian region and Vietnam. In other words, he contended that studies of Vietnam should be undertaken in relation to the study of Southeast Asia and Southeast Asian Studies should be deepened in relationship to the study of Vietnam (ibid., pp. 6–7).

With the above as goals, the Institute for Southeast Asian Studies published a variety of books and dissertations in broader areas in the 1990s. The publications include research books on Southeast Asian countries and nations in archaeology, anthropology, ethnology, linguistics, literature, geography, and economics as well as the research results of work on some Southeast Asian languages. In addition, the Institute has continued to publish introductory books on the history, culture, economy, and society of Southeast Asian countries for a domestic readership. It has also published academic dissertations on Southeast Asian countries for the degree of Associate Doctor (*phó tiến sỹ*) and Ph.D., and collections of research annals and bibliographical catalogues while accumulating a wealth of information in Southeast Asian Studies (Interview with Professor Nguyễn Duy Dũng and Phạm Đức Dương).

One of the noteworthy achievements of the construction and institutionalization of Southeast Asian Studies as an independent discipline since the establishment of the Institute for Southeast Asian Studies is the publication of an academic journal *Nghiên cứu Đông Nam Á* (*Southeast Asian Studies*) according to the permit No. 974 of the Ministry of Culture, Information, Sports and Tourism (*số 974 BC-GPXB do Bộ Văn hóa-Thông tin-Thể thao và Du lịch*) on 25 September 1990. Since the publication of the first issue in February 1991 up to now, the journal has remained the single journal for Southeast Asian Studies in Vietnam. "Southeast Asian Studies" is also the name of a publisher under the umbrella of the Institute for Southeast Asian Studies at the Vietnamese Academy of Social Sciences. The responsibilities and duties of the publisher are to publicize the programmes and research results of scientific studies of Southeast Asia in each area, publish each issue of the journal, and help manifest the scientific values of research activity along with information and knowledge of Southeast Asia (ibid., pp. 13–14; Interview with Professor Ngô Văn Doanh).

Nguyễn Quang Ngọc, then-head of the Department of History at Hanoi National University, participated as a representative of Vietnam together with Phạm Đức Thanh, then-director of the Institute for Southeast Asian Studies, in the international conference on Southeast Asian Studies in Asia held in Quezon City in the Philippines in January 2002. He said there that the orientation of the Vietnamese academic community began to change under the influence of reform policies in the mid-1980s (UP Asian Center et al. eds. 2003). In this context, the Vietnamese academy started to accelerate and intensify collaboration and reciprocal exchange between scholars from the major countries involved in the study of Southeast Asia in order to respond to the demand of ideological and national reform in Vietnam. Since the mid-1980s, there had been an increase in the need for mutual support and collaboration, and subsequently the demand and support from scientific institutions under the umbrella of the Ministry of Science, Technology and Environment and the Central Council for Scientific Theories had increased (Nguyen Quang Ngoc 2003, p. 105).

In the 1990s, the Institute for Southeast Asian Studies also had a mandate to address ASEAN issues. The Institute concentrated on Vietnam's regional research capacity in this mandate while developing and implementing independent programmes to reinforce international collaboration projects. Then, executives and scholars at state-run research institutions related to the Institute began to organize academic conferences or take part in conferences at home and abroad, and initiated joint research projects with well-known international scholars. In the early 1990s, the Institute placed the foremost priority on such research tasks as the basic study of Indochina and ASEAN members, the comparative study of religion in Southeast Asia, and the study of Southeast Asian people's adaptation to the environment (Phạm Đức Dương 1990, pp. 12–13).

Vietnam's courtship of this body was consummated with its entry into ASEAN in 1995, providing the justification for the Institute's glossy English-language publication, *Southeast Asian Studies*. In the late 1990s, translated research papers from foreign countries and scholars started to appear in the journal of *Southeast Asian Studies*. The Vietnamese academic community has expanded exchange and collaboration with major overseas Southeast Asian research institutions in recent years. With the opening of many areas according to the renovation policy, *đổi mới*, the academic community had already built close collaborative relationships with numerous universities and research centres across the world and also facilitated academic exchange since the late 1980s (Interview with Professor Trần Đình Lâm). Also, with the globally revived Vietnamese Studies, the academy began to hold frequent international conferences on Vietnam. Vietnamese researchers emphasize that Vietnamese Studies are an integral part of Southeast Asian Studies at the international level and therefore the expansion of international exchange in this area features a growing process of the development of Southeast Asian Studies in Vietnam (Interview with Professor Hoàng Văn Việt). Vietnamese Studies has actually played a great role in revitalizing Southeast Asian Studies in Vietnam.

The most significant achievement that served as a critical milestone in the development of Vietnamese Studies was the first International Conference on Vietnamese Studies organized in Hanoi from 15 to 17 July 1998. Over 300 overseas scholars from 26 countries and 400 local professionals attended the conference. The conference addressed a broad range of issues, such as history, traditions and modern society; culture and cultural exchange; economy and society; villages and agriculture; gender, family and population; etc. Another conference held in September 2000 in Hanoi was attended by over 100 and 200 overseas and local scholars respectively (Nguyen Quang Ngoc 2003, pp. 107–8).

In the mid-1980s, academic societies and research institutions started to be established more actively and the number of educational and research institutions for Southeast Asian Studies began to grow steadily. As shown in Table 6.2, most organizations came into being after the implementation of the renovation policy in 1986. With the speedy change in the global environment and economic and political renovation, an increasing demand for international cooperation from both inside and outside the region has triggered the proliferation of institutions for Southeast Asian Studies in Vietnam.

However, most of the research institutions were established in haste without sufficient preparation for strong academic infrastructure and manpower. Led by the government, many research institutes were hurriedly founded even when there were not many Vietnamese scholars specializing in Southeast Asian Studies (Interview with Professor Nguyễn Văn Chính).

Table 6.2
Research and Training Organizations for Southeast Asian Studies in Vietnam

Organization	Founding Year	Remarks
Institute for Southeast Asian Studies (*Viện Nghiên cứu Đông Nam Á*), VASS	1973	Journal: Nghiên cứu Đông Nam Á (since 1990, in Vietnamese, monthly) Southeast Asian Studies (since 1995, in English, yearly)
The Southeast Asian Research Association of Vietnam (SEARAV, *Hội Nghiên cứu Đông Nam Á Việt Nam*)	1996	Affiliated with the Vietnam Union of Science and Technology Associations (VUSTA) Chair person: Prof. Phạm Đức Dương
Center for Vietnamese and Southeast Asian Studies (CVSEAS), College of Social Sciences and Humanities, Vietnam National University in Ho Chi Minh City	1993	Established by the Ministry of Education and Training Current Director: Dr Trần Đình Lâm
Research Center for Asia-Pacific Studies, affiliated with the College of Social Sciences and Humanities, Hanoi National University, Vietnam	1985	Established by the Ministry of Education and Training Director: Prof. Đinh Văn Đức, linguist Vice Director: Nguyễn Văn Chính
Center for Southeast Asian Research, the Institute of International Relation Institute	1995	Affiliated with the Ministry of Foreign Affairs
Center for Southeast Asian Prehistory (CESEAP, *Trung tâm Tiền sử Đông Nam Á*)	1999	Non-Governmental Organization working on the field of Palaeo-Anthropology Established by Dr Nguyễn Việt, archaeologist, based in Hanoi

Table 6.2 (*Cont'd*)

Organization	Founding Year	Remarks
Department of Southeast Asian & Australian Studies, the College of Social Sciences and Humanities, Hanoi National University	1997	Head: Prof. Mai Ngọc Chừ, linguist Vice Head: Dr. Nguyễn Tương Lai, Thai Studies
Department of Southeast Asian Studies, Hong Bang University, Ho Chi Minh City	2001	Head: Dr Nguyễn Quốc Lộc, ethnologist
Department of Southeast Asian Studies, Ho Chi Minh City Open University	1991	Acting Dean: Dr Phan Thị Hồng Xuân
Vietnam Institute for Northeast Asian Studies (VINAS), VASS	1998	Offers projects related to Southeast Asia Director: Dr Ngô Xuân Bình, Vice Director: Dr Trần Quang Minh

Professor Chính cynically said, "Leaders of the institutes for Southeast Asian Studies can do everything". It would be fair to say that more scholars and researchers in Vietnam have been mobilized for business through international collaboration projects than for research tasks since the late 1990s.

In this regard one of the most interesting and noteworthy organizations is the Southeast Asian Research Association of Vietnam (SEARAV). This Association was established in 1996, based on the decision of the Prime Minister-Central Government (*Quyết Định của Thủ Tướng Chính Phủ*, 563/ TTg, Hanoi 20/8/1996) in affiliation with the Vietnam Union of Science and Technology Associations (VUSTA). As of 2006, the Association had over 2,500 members and 57 member organizations including 20 research institutes, 36 centres, 2 science research unions, 2 clubs, and 3 one-member limited liability companies. SEARAV is a professional organization of Vietnamese citizens working in the field of scientific research and performing professional work related to Southeast Asia (Article 2 of the Charter of SEARAV). This is categorized as a "social professional organization" in the context of the Vietnamese concept of civic organization or NGOs (see, Norlund 2007; Choi 2008).

As defined in its charter, the Association's goal is to unite people who work not only in the field of Southeast Asian Studies and ASEAN cooperation, but also in the general field of science-technology, education, economy and society, and so on.

> SEARAV is operating nationwide and participating actively and effectively in all the fields of science research, science-technology services, education and training, culture, healthcare, natural resources and environment protection, relief, poverty reduction, and community development assistance. They have provided employment for thousands of workers and made convincing contributions to the socialization cause launched by the Vietnam Communist Party and the State. The people and the international friends have highly appreciated those achievements and contributions. It is likely to be said SEARAV has secured a firm foothold as a social professional organization through its meaningful and fruitful contributions to the society.[5]

(SEARAV 2006, pp. 4, 14–15)

Organized with the support of the Party-state, this Association aims at private research and exchange for Southeast Asian Studies but it also pursues various social and international activities and functions. Its registered members and activities show that it placed more emphasis on its general social role than academic research and exchange. It has defined its academic mission in ambiguous terms. Furthermore, its membership does not require any practical qualifications related to Southeast Asian Studies and education and even foreigners or ethnic Vietnamese can become members if they pay the dues. It seems that SEARAV reflects the features of Vietnamese organizational culture: it values the formation of the social organization itself rather more than research, and it serves to strengthen social networks with related people and maximize personal and collective interests through these networks.

In general, research and training in the field of Southeast Asian Studies have not been conducted simultaneously in Vietnam. One exception would be the Department of Southeast Asian Studies at Ho Chi Minh City Open University. The Department gave the impression of being solely dedicated to Southeast Asian Studies and education in Ho Chi Minh City (Interview with Professor Phan Thị Hồng Xuân). Even in terms of Vietnamese Studies, it is a rare institution where research and education are carried out at the same time. On the other hand, there are a growing number of research centres and institutes which offer programmes of Vietnamese language courses and Vietnamese Studies, mainly Vietnamese history and culture, for foreign students and scholars. Most of them are not listed in Table 6.2. Nevertheless, they also have many projects to cooperate with Southeast Asian Studies institutions. So far training has been offered only in classes and to faculties or centres teaching the Vietnamese language to foreigners. The Faculty of Vietnamese Language at Hanoi University, founded in the mid-1960s, was considered the first and largest institution of its kind. In 1995, the Faculty started to offer Vietnamese language and culture courses which were designed to contribute to undergraduate degrees for foreign students who wanted to specialize in Vietnamese Studies. Since the late 1990s, many universities throughout the country began to offer programmes for foreigners. They have successfully attracted a large number of students; for example, Hanoi Teacher Training University, Hanoi University of Foreign Studies, Danang University, and the Vietnam National University in Ho Chi Minh City. The Faculty of Vietnamese Studies and Vietnamese Language for Foreigners at the College of Social Sciences and the Humanities, Vietnam National University in Ho Chi Minh City was incorporated into the Center for Vietnam and Southeast Asian Studies (CVSEAS). Recently, in CVSEAS the students are mainly foreigners learning the Vietnamese language.

PERCEPTIONS OF SOUTHEAST ASIAN STUDIES IN VIETNAM AND INDIGENIZATION EFFORTS

Vietnam's Perceptions and Assessment of Southeast Asian Studies outside the Region

There has indeed been a long-term tendency for outsiders to be more loquacious about the Southeast Asian region than its own inhabitants. A historian complains that "[i]t is remarkable that a region that for so long occupied the position of cross-waterway of the world should have had so little to say for itself. Like all multi-ethnic regional systems, it seemed more coherent to outsiders than to stay-at-home locals" (Abu-Lughod 1989, pp. 296–97; cited in Reid and Diokno 2003, p. 93). Founders of Southeast Asian Studies in Vietnam have also recognized this background quite well. Therefore, they have had a critical assessment of the influence of Europe, the former Soviet Union, the United States, China and Japan on this field of studies. In this manner they have stressed the need for indigenization. It was a natural process that they should also pay attention the role and influence of the French colonial period, more than anything else, in the pre-history of the formation of Southeast Asian Studies in Vietnam. They positively assessed that, from its establishment in 1898 in Saigon to 1954, the Ecole Française d'Extrême-Orient (EFEO, *Viễn Đông bác cổ Pháp*) was instrumental in the birth of Southeast Asian Studies in the Indo-China region (Phạm Đức Dương 1998*a*, pp. 19–22).[6] At the time, EFEO frequently organized research teams to collect materials in Vietnam, Laos, Cambodia, Thailand, Burma, and Java. These research cohorts also studied in many other countries beyond the Southeast Asia region including China, India, Japan and Russia. The scholars of Hanoi recognized early on that the EFEO had made diverse and profound achievements in research and they emphasized that its examination of many epigraphic materials particularly explained the existence of civilization unique to this region.

It is a well-known fact to Western scholars as well that the EFEO in the colonial period expanded its research focusing on Vietnam. Vietnamese culture and history appeared always opaque and alien to them, and they were inclined to interpret it as little more than a lesser variant of the Chinese. The Khmer monuments of Angkor, and to a lesser degree the Cham monuments in Central Vietnam, by contrast, stirred profound French interest and attracted the best of France's oriental scholars. Established in Saigon but subsequently headquartered in Hanoi, the most ambitious project of the EFEO was the restoration and analysis of Angkor which was systematically commenced in 1907 (Reid and Diokno 2003, pp. 97–98).

Although Vietnam's culture and history were regarded as being at the periphery and not the centre of the region in the colonial period, the institutionalization of studies on this region started from Vietnam.[7] The most natural places from which to conceive the coherence of Southeast Asia and the need for its study as a region were the entrepôts clustered around the Straits of Malacca. But educational and scholarly institutions were relatively slow to develop in British Malaya, and it was not until the 1950s that Southeast Asian Studies began systematically there. Before World War II in the colonial era proper, the lead was taken by Rangoon and Hanoi (ibid., p. 97). This was related to the inception period of the modern states. That is to say, as mainland Southeast Asia, including Vietnam and Burma, had already had a framework for institutional scholarship since the feudal kingdom period, modern educational systems could be built more systematically based on the traditional system in this region than in maritime Southeast Asia.

Vietnamese scholars, however, make the criticism that the EFEO and Western scholars, including Dutch and British, had clear limitations in spite of their important contributions to Southeast Asian Studies and their exploration in various areas such as archaeology, linguistics, ethnology, and history. First, the studies focused on European sensibilities and perceptions in judging Southeast Asia. Instead, Vietnamese scholars stress cultural relativism in that each nation has its unique value and world-view, which in turn form each nation's unique culture and history. Second, Europe's Oriental Studies are biased towards the major civilizations outside Southeast Asia from whence they commence their investigations, only then gradually moving towards the little traditions within the region. In other words, they point out that European scholars only examined Southeast Asia's unilateral acceptance of Indian and Chinese cultures because they first studied India and China, then Southeast Asia. Third, it is argued that Western scholars committed the error of viewing colonized or occupied nations as barbarous or retarded (Phạm Đức Dương 1990, pp. 4–5; 1998a, pp. 27–28). However, we cannot ignore the fact that criticisms of Western-centrism, ethnocentrism and Orientalism were also widely presented in the Western academic community.[8]

Vietnam's Southeast Asian Studies were greatly influenced by regional studies in China and Russia in the 1940s and 1950s. Vietnamese scholars often had opportunities to meet researchers and experts on India, Indonesia,

Laos and Middle Eastern countries in the former Soviet Union and began to receive a great influence from its social sciences from 1954. Many pioneers of Southeast Asian Studies in the Communist countries of Southeast Asia had studied in the former Soviet Union.[9]

Oriental Studies in Vietnam have a strong tendency to divide them into country studies (*đất nước học*) and regional studies (*khu vực học*), an influence from the Soviet Union. In particular, country studies in the Soviet Union were developed quite early on. Along with the growth of socialism in Southeast Asian countries during the Cold War in the 1950s and 1960s, the study of Southeast Asia in the Soviet Union had the opportunity to develop further and Russian scholars usually viewed the history and culture of the colonized countries from the perspective of national liberation (Phạm Đức Dương 1998a, pp. 30–32). But it was pointed out that these studies in the Soviet Union had a weak point of making use of research materials from the West rather than using findings from their own field-research at the local level. It has also been argued that Russian scholars tended to focus their interests on modern politics, while Western scholars took much more interest in the culture and history of Southeast Asia (Interview with Phạm Đức Dương).

Vietnam's pioneering scholars have also assessed Southeast Asian Studies in the USA. Quoting Emmerson (1984), Scott (1992) and Hirschman (1992), for example, Phạm Đức Dương paid heed to American scholars' evaluation that like scholars of the Soviet Union, American scholars tended to focus their interest on political research in Southeast Asian Studies during the Cold War and many of them received funds from large businesses or contributed to government agencies. He explained that this was in contrast to European scholars who published a number of achievements in anthropology, geography, linguistics and worked mainly at universities and research institutions (ibid., pp. 33–37). Vietnamese scholars thought that, although a latecomer compared to Europe, the United States accumulated a tremendous wealth of materials on Southeast Asian Studies in a short period of time, and in the 1970s, the USA research institutes had more active relationships with Southeast Asian scholars. With the restoration of formal diplomatic ties ahead in the 1990s, Vietnam too took greater interest in collaboration with academic circles in the USA.

In the case of Southeast Asian Studies in China, Vietnamese scholars suggest that, although China has been very interested in Southeast Asia over a long period of time, its studies originated largely from the perspective of

Sino-centrism (Đới Khải Lai 1992). Chinese people have a strong tendency of perceiving that southern China had a strong cultural impact on Southeast Asia and southern China and Southeast Asia share the same cultural roots (Phạm Đức Dương 1993). Vietnam too had already adopted a Sino-centric cultural model (*Văn hóa Trung Hoa*) over several centuries. The country introduced Chinese characters in writing and a number of historical materials were derived from China. Vietnam's Institute for Southeast Asian Studies collected these materials at the start of its establishment and published *Vietnam's Ancient Book on Southeast Asia* (*Thư tịch cổ Việt Nam viết về Đông Nam Á*) (Nguyễn Thị Thi sưu tầm 1977). This book comprised four volumes: Chenla (*Chân Lạp*), Siam (*Xiêm*), Laos (*Lào*), and Champa-Burma-Java (*Chiêm Thành, Myanma, Chà Và*). In the 1970s, many scholars were preoccupied with the translation of Chinese materials (Interview with Professor Phan Huy Lê).

Japan too has taken great interest in the Asian region over a long period of time under the influence of their reading of Chinese materials on the region. Vietnamese scholars have evaluated that Japan's studies of the Asian region are of long-standing. For example, using China's ancient books as early as in the Tokugawa period of the early eighteenth century, Japan published five volumes of a research book on transportation and exchange between Japan, China and Asian countries (Nguyễn Văn Chính 1995).

What message, then, does the history of Southeast Asian Studies by those outside the region give to Vietnam's Southeast Asian Studies programmes? First the accumulation of research and experiences in many fields of study across the world have laid the scientific foundation for establishing Southeast Asian Studies as an identifiable field of regional studies. Second, the efforts made by Western scholars in the past century have contributed to enhancing the awareness of this region. Native scholars should make efforts to succeed to these achievements and yet present their own perspectives different from those of Western scholars, and compare the viewpoints of the outsiders and the insiders. Third, Western scholars are divided in their opinions on whether Southeast Asia is a regional entity with an identity of its own. However, Vietnamese scholars should recognize the importance of Southeast Asian Studies and expand the content of these studies consistently from two perspectives: that Southeast Asia is indeed a cultural and historical region, and although this identity does not coincide with the modern definition of Southeast Asia, it can be traced back a long way in time, and that currently it is an important strategic region. Fourth, they should adopt an interdisciplinary approach which uses various methods of approach derived from different disciplines and research results from these different fields. For instance, archaeologists may collect linguistic research findings to use in their studies of ancient culture. Although archaeology and linguistics have their own methodologies and subjects of study as independent disciplines, research achievements and approaches in each study can be used to enhance our understanding of the complex characteristics of regions (Phạm Đức Dương 1998a, pp. 49–55; Interview with the author). In this context, Vietnam's early Southeast Asian researchers undertook their studies on the basis of what had been introduced to them on Southeast Asia by Western countries, China and Japan (e.g., Đới Khải Lai 1992; Phạm Đức Dương 1978; 1996 etc.). And increasingly some of these studies have considered and developed the achievements in Southeast Asian Studies from the insiders' view of the region.

Vietnam's Perceptions and Assessment of Southeast Asian Studies from within the Region

In general, scholars outside Southeast Asia think that studies of the region by Southeast Asians began, at the earliest, in the late 1970s when institutes for Southeast Asian Studies were established in this region, and most locally-based studies began to be undertaken in the 1980s and 1990s (Bahrin 1981, pp. 100–101; Halib and Huxley 1996, pp. 1–4). However, it is a common notion of Vietnamese scholars that the perceptions and viewpoints of this region by Southeast Asians themselves had existed even before the institutional establishment of Southeast Asian Studies in many countries.

> We need to understand the tribal and cultural origins and linguistic diversity inside Southeast Asia which had existed before the influence of Western scholarship. Before the influence of the West, there had already been a wealth of studies on various factors from the aspect of "Oriental Studies".

> (Nguyên Khánh Tòan 1973, p. 11)

According to the assertion of Phạm Đức Dương, there were active independence movements of colonized nations in the mid-twentieth century after World War II and an increased interest in the prosperity of the independent countries. At the time, Southeast Asians began to have self-awareness, posing fundamental questions such as "Who are we? Where did we come from? Where are we headed for?" He contended that these questions were a driving force for powerful implementation of Southeast Asian Studies as a field of regional studies (*khu vực học*) inside Southeast Asia (1990, p. 5). Perceptions of a common ancient civilization unique to Southeast Asia and cultural exchange have often been reflected in historical and archaeological studies and an emphasis has been placed on the fact that there existed a civilization of ancient countries that never fell behind other civilizations.

In the post-war era, studies of the Southeast Asian region have become more active because of the strategic needs of each country. There has also been a sharp increase in studies of ASEAN, specifically with regard to economic cooperation and international relations for the last two decades. One thing Vietnamese scholars acknowledge as a clear fact is that the emergence of ASEAN was instrumental in enhancing Southeast Asians' awareness of the importance of a broader and deeper understanding of other neighbouring countries within the region (Interview with Ngô Văn Doanh and Nguyễn Duy Dũng).

Vietnamese scholars have constantly maintained their interest in research findings from other Southeast Asian countries and have increased their contacts and exchange with scholars from outside Vietnam. In 1991, some papers were published in *Nghiên cứu Đông Nam Á*, which introduced in detail Southeast Asian Studies in Southeast Asia (Nguyễn Tấn Đắc 1991; Trần Khánh 1991). The Vietnamese assessment is that Singapore has very actively promoted and supported Southeast Asian Studies (both mainland and maritime areas) in many fields based on a rich pool of researchers and scholars not just from Southeast Asia itself but from Europe, China, Japan, and the United States, who have stayed in Singapore for a long-term period of time to carry out their research and writing. The papers also emphasize that attention should be paid to benchmarking the elements which contribute to Singapore's success: that it hosts various international seminars every year, accepts a great number of students from abroad, and receives support for research funds from the world's prestigious foundations (Trần Khánh 1991; Phạm Đức Dương 1998*a*, pp. 68–72). Quoting *Bibliography of Southeast Asian Studies in Thailand* (Charnvit et al. 1991), Nguyễn Tấn Đắc (1991) conducted a statistical analysis of research outcomes by country, including Southeast Asian Studies in Thailand. The researchers have also paid attention to the provision of teaching, research training and other programmes on

Southeast Asia in Malaysia and the Philippines. Since the mid-1980s, the Vietnamese Academy of Social Sciences has expanded its collaborative relationships with Southeast Asian research institutions, including Singapore's Institute of Southeast Asian Studies (ISEAS). They have noted that ISEAS has a world-class reputation in this region and in recent years a growing number of Vietnamese scholars and students have gone to study in Singapore.

The Perceptions of the Origin of Indigenous Southeast Asian Studies in Vietnam

Founding scholars who contributed to the establishment of the Institute for Southeast Asian Studies in Vietnam have emphasized that Vietnamese capabilities in Southeast Asian Studies have been developed over a long period of time with the long-established engagement of Vietnamese researchers in the region. In this regard Vietnamese scholars claim that Southeast Asian Studies has an indigenous origin from earlier times, and the starting point is not from the Western colonial period. They stress that Southeast Asian Studies in Vietnam was overshadowed by colonialism and Chinese influence but at the same time it has indigenous roots. According to them, this is verified in the fact that Vietnamese ancient books contained information on historic events, geography, diaries, and essays dealing with the culture and history of Southeast Asia from a long time ago. Nguyễn Lệ Thi (1993) argued that the history of Southeast Asian Studies in Southeast Asia dates back to the thirteenth century.

Vietnamese scholars say that the oldest book containing the records of Southeast Asia is *Đại Việt sử ký* (大越史記) by Lê Băn Huu in 1272, but it is no longer extant. Currently *An Nam chí lước* (安南志略) by Lê Tắc (1333) is the oldest book available. *Dư địa chí* (輿地誌) by Nguyễn Trãi (1438) explains the geography of present-day Southeast Asia and speaks highly of *Đại Việt sử ký*. In particular, the book noted that the then-Vietnam and neighbouring countries kept close relations with each other (Nguyễn Lệ Thi 1993, pp. 60–61).

At the end of the Lê Dynasty (1428–1788), Lê Quý Đôn wrote a number of books ranging from history, culture, geography, and biology. Especially two of them, entitled *Phủ biên tạp lục* (撫邊雜錄) and *Vân đài loại ngữ* (雲臺類語), showed great interest in the history of relationships between Vietnam and other countries within the region according to specific historical periods. Emperor Minh Mạng established the Quốc sử quán Triều Nguyễn (Library of Nguyen Dynasty) in the nineteenth century and this institution compiled two substantial sets of material, *Khâm định Việt sử thong giám cương mục* (欽定越史通鑑綱目) and *Đại nam thực lục chính biên* (大南寔錄正編). In particular, the latter carried political, military and cultural information on Southeast Asian countries for the first time. *Đại nam liệt truyện chính biên* (大南烈傳正編) described Vạn Tượng (Luang Prabang, Laos), Nam Chưởng (Vientiane, Laos), Xiêm La (Thailand) and Cao Miên (Cambodia) by time period. Others too touched on Southeast Asian countries: *Quốc triều xử trí Vạn tượng sự nghi lục* (國朝處置萬象事誼錄) edited by Quốc Sử quán Triều Nguyễn and *Ngũ man phong thổ ký* (五蠻風土記) by Ngô Cao Lãng (Nguyễn Lệ Thi 1993, pp. 61–68).

Meanwhile, Phan Huy Chú (1833) wrote about his experience of an official trip from Danang to Singapore and Batavia (Java) between 1832 and 1833 in *Hải trình chí lược* (海程志略). Indonesian scholar Asvi Warman Adam introduced his writing as "Vietnamese records on Batavia" (*Xưa Nay số* 24, November 1996; cited in Phạm Đức Dương 1998*a*, p. 79).

> Vietnam's ancient books include very important materials regarding historical relations between Vietnam and other Southeast Asian countries. These, however, reveal their own limitations as their details are fragmentary, sporadic and unsystematic. Nevertheless, they offer crucial information in the following aspects: First, cross-border trade was frequent from the ancient times. Second, their relationships contributed to exchange in national cultures and to building common cultural traits. Third, such exchange between local people promoted national competition and patriotism, achieved political development and helped create new dynasties. Fourth, in this process, the people in the region could strengthen their friendship and establish a tradition of peaceful relationships.
>
> (Nguyễn Lệ Thi 1993, pp. 77–78)

We can see this explanation also contains socialist doctrines which stress the national unity of peoples in the region that had experienced colonial rule. Vietnamese scholars also assessed their voluntary efforts to construct modern Southeast Asian Studies in Vietnam. In Vietnam, wider studies of Vietnam or of each country in the region have been performed in specialized fields of study including archaeology, anthropology (*nhân chủng học*), linguistics, and ethnology (*dân tộc học*), history, and economics since the 1950s.

However, Southeast Asian Studies was not yet formed as an independent field of study. With the foundation of the "Ban Đông Nam Á" in 1973, Southeast Asian Studies became a practically independent academic field. Vietnamese scholars maintain that this process was never a coincidence but the result of the passionate efforts of domestic and overseas institutions and researchers for the independence and progress of Southeast Asian Studies. Nevertheless, many of them agree that Southeast Asian Studies in Vietnam is still underdeveloped. Celebrating the first publication of the journal *Nghiên cứu Đông Nam Á*, Phạm Đức Dương said that, although Vietnam came into existence and grew in Southeast Asia and kept in touch and had long lasting relationships with other countries in the region, the country was still very much lacking in knowledge of Southeast Asian Studies by his estimation (1990, pp. 5–6).

DEVELOPMENT AND LIMITATIONS OF SOUTHEAST ASIAN STUDIES AS INTERDISCIPLINARY REGIONAL STUDIES

Vietnamese pioneers of modern Southeast Asian Studies shared the following perceptions on the scope of these studies which were based on the following principles and were designed to focus and promote this field of scholarship: first, the identification of a unique Southeast Asian civilization, which is different from Chinese and Indian civilizations, based on the assumption that it did indeed exist; second, the study of the processes of formation of Southeast Asian countries, peoples and traditional cultures based on their understanding that such formation was possible through contact with Chinese and Indian cultures as well as other Asian cultures; third, the study of European influence in the process of Western colonial intervention in the region, national liberation movements and Southeast Asia's modernization; fourth, study of the transition to modern society, namely, the industrialization processes of each Southeast Asian country and the prospects for the future of the region in the twenty-first century in the context of globalization and regional integration; fifth, the study of the relations between Vietnam and each of the other Southeast Asian countries (Phạm Đức Dương 1998*a*, pp. 262–63).

In particular, Vietnamese scholars highlight the need for an interdisciplinary approach. "Southeast Asian Studies should be conducted with synthetic methods (*phương pháp tổng hợp*), encompassing various fields of study, such as history, culture, geography, linguistics and economics. For example, archaeological research findings should be combined with those of ethnology, history, folklore, and linguistics." (Nguyên Khánh Tòan 1973, p. 13) The first issue of *Southeast Asian Studies* in 1990 stressed interdisciplinary methods and diverse and generic approaches as shown in the following quote, "Southeast Asian Studies should choose the right methodology of its own, especially putting weight on the notion of its generic nature. It needs to attempt various approaches connected with diverse fields of study and conduct comprehensive research" (Phạm Đức Dương 1990, p. 7). The Journal is also defined as a journal for Area Studies based on multi- and interdisciplinary approaches (*phương pháp tiếp cận đa ngành và liên ngành*).[10]

Interdisciplinary research began to flourish when social scientists and scholars of the humanities strived to explore the civilizations of Southeast Asia which Western scholars had not found or perceived. For examples of interdisciplinary researchers, historical folklorist Từ Chi and linguist and ethnologist Phạm Đức Dương highly admired the achievements of some geographers at Hanoi National University of Education, including Lê Bá Thảo (President of the *Hội Địa lý Việt Nam,* or the Vietnam Association of Geography). He positively introduced their contribution to Southeast Asian geography as part of world geography. In particular, he highlighted that there was a significant accumulation of human geographical studies in Laos, Cambodia and Thai.

Advocates of area studies in many countries have maintained that this field of research requires a multi- or interdisciplinary approach. However, in Centres of Southeast Asian Studies, the academic staffs are usually disciplinary specialists with specific interests in the region. This may create a problem: "disciplined" academics teach "multi-disciplinary" undergraduates who tend to lack disciplinary "backbone" (Halib and Huxley 1996, pp. 4–5). The same issue has been identified in Vietnam as well. While placing emphasis on interdisciplinary study and turning existing researchers of Vietnam into researchers of Southeast Asian Studies, Vietnam increased the pool of researchers. A good example is Lê Bá Thảo, the author of *Thiên nhiện Việt Nam (Nature of Vietnam)*. He is not a geographer of Southeast Asia for sure, but he led the interdisciplinary involvement of geography at the Southeast Asia Centre. In particular he made a contribution to nurturing future researchers in economic and archaeological geography. This gives a clue to Vietnam's capabilities in the study of Southeast Asia.

The participation of ethnology and cultural studies in interdisciplinary work was seen as vital to the cultural history area. The interdisciplinary involvement of archaeology, linguistics, and ecology were also regarded as essential. By its own estimation, Vietnamese academia has been relatively strong in ethnology for a considerable period of time. An especially famous study is about the cultural universality of rice-growing villages in Southeast Asia (Nguyễn Từ Chi 1996). Nguyễn Từ Chi is a leading scholar who initiated the participation of ethnology. In particular, underscoring field surveys, he thought that such tradition is necessary for the study of Southeast Asian history and culture. He designed ethnological programmes at the Southeast Asia research centre and published *Các dân tộc Đông Nam Á* [*Ethnic Groups of Southeast Asia*] (1997).

In ethnology, comparative research on agriculture and rural culture thrived. Ethnologists such as Nguyễn Từ Chi, Nguyễn Duy Thiệu, Bùi Xuân Đính, Nguyễn Quốc Hùng, and Vũ Huy Quang released *Tìm hiểu cảnh quan đồng bằng* (*Understanding Landscapes of the Plains*) together in 1983. The book, using a comparative perspective, explained that rural lives in the region are considerably different according to geographic features like coasts, deltas, islands, basins, highlands, and alpine areas.

Unlike field-based Vietnamese examples, research on other countries usually presents only simple and basic details from the existing literature. Although many ethnologists call themselves Southeast East Asian Studies professionals, most achievements of their research are actually confined to Vietnam. Almost every issue of the journal of *Southeast Asian Studies* has posted research findings by ethnologists, but most of them are rooted in Vietnam studies. They cover folk studies on Vietnamese ethnic minorities which usually has a Southeast Asian dimension. For example, research on the H'mong people is claimed to be part of and very conducive to the development of Southeast Asian Studies, because it pays attention to the residence of similar ethnic minorities in China, Myanmar, Thailand and Vietnam (Phạm Đức Dương 1998*a*, pp. 268–70).

These arguments are not necessarily unconvincing for the reason that the study of Vietnamese ethnic minorities has expanded to embrace other Southeast Asian countries. It is noteworthy that researchers of ethnic minorities were transformed into Southeast Asian Studies professionals after the development of the Institute for Southeast Asian Studies. For example, studies on the Tây–Thái people diversified into the examination of a variety of tribes on the Southeast Asian mainland.

Another point highlighted by Vietnamese scholars is that their study of Southeast Asia has a strong foundation for research on Thailand, Laos, and Myanmar. This is because Vietnamese scholars studied each country for a long period from the year of the inception of the Institute for Southeast Asian Studies to the late 1990s. Researchers on Thailand are Dương Xuân Dương, Trịnh Diệu Thìn, Nguyễn Chí Thông, Mai Văn Bảo, and Lê Ngọc Phương. In the case of Myanmar research, there is Professor Phạm Kim Hảo, and in research on Laos Professors Đào Văn Tiến and Phạm Đức Dương who visited the country over a long period. These scholars are well-versed in each national language. Besides, scholars of ethnic minority descent are contributing to the study of Southeast Asia through their work on their own ethnic minorities. They work at college history departments, not at the Institute for Southeast Asian Studies, but have published their research findings in the journal of *Southeast Asian Studies*. Such examples are Cầm Trọng, Lê Sỹ Giáo, Hoàng Lương, Vi Trọng Liên, and Lương Bèn. They have played an important part in Southeast Asian Studies in Vietnam for quite a long time as researchers in cultural studies, ethnology, and linguistics.

Archaeologists like Hà Văn Tấn, Ngô Thế Phong, Vũ Công Quý, Trình Năng Chung also made a contribution to the study of Southeast Asia by working on maritime cultures and models of agricultural formation. Among others, the point made by the Vietnamese academia is that linguistics has made a significant contribution to the development of Southeast Asian Studies (e.g., Phan Ngọc and Phạm Đức Dương 1983; Phạm Đức Dương 2007). Linguists who specialize in specific languages have taken charge of language education in the country-specific programmes. For example, Professors Phan Ngọc and Nguyễn Sỹ Tuấn have taught the Khmer language and designed related materials, and Professors Nguyễn Chí Thông, Phạm Đức Dương and Trương Duy Hoà for the Laos and Thai languages, and Professors Lê Văn Thọ and Nguyễn Thị Lương for the Indonesian language. Under the leadership of Phan Ngọc and Ngô Văn Doanh, former and incumbent chief editors of *Nghiên cứu Đông Nam Á*, they contributed to the publication of the *Dictionary of Southeast Asian Cultures*.

Literature has been an important element in Southeast Asian Studies in Vietnam too. Professor Cao Huy Đỉnh spearheaded the involvement as Chairperson of *Ban Đông Nam Á* from June 1973 to April 1975. He studied Indian literature in India for two years. A particular contribution has been made in comparative literature and in the introduction to and analysis of Philippine, Malaysian and Indonesian literary works as well as those from mainland countries such as Thailand and Laos. Especially noticeable is the publication of papers on Indonesian literature including works from the Dutch colonial period. A prime example is Nguyễn Đức Ninh (1983) who studied Indonesian literary contact with Dutch colonial and western literature. In addition, there are numerous doctoral theses on the ancient literature of Cambodia and the folk literatures of the Laos. Books on Southeast Asian folk literature are continually published. Moreover, research on folk cultures is ongoing. In particular, there have been a large number of studies undertaken on folk cultures and art in Thailand and Laos as well as on the folk cultures of the indigenous populations of Myanmar and Malaysia.

Compared with mainland Southeast Asian countries, research in Vietnam on maritime Southeast Asia is rare. In country studies, Laos and Cambodia have obviously played a pioneering role in Vietnam (Reid and Diokno 2003, p. 100). For its governing Communist Party insisted from the 1970s that Vietnam's victory held the same strategic and historical meanings as Communist revolutions in its brethren nations, Laos and Cambodia; and therefore Vietnam's revolution should be understood in the context of those in related and neighbouring Southeast Asian countries. However, studies on maritime and coastal regions have also developed to a certain degree, particularly in subjects like maritime trade and exchange between Vietnam and island Southeast Asia in the fields of archaeology and history (e.g., Phạm Đức Dương et al. 1996). Indonesia specialists in Vietnam are valued since researchers on maritime countries such as Indonesia and Malaysia are very few. However maritime research in Vietnam is still negligible with just a few students on Master's degrees at several universities and research centres.

Although a steady emphasis has been placed on the importance of interdisciplinary study, most papers are still published in separate disciplines. Moreover, Vietnamese Studies still account for a majority of studies included under the umbrella of Southeast Asian Studies. Tables 6.3 and 6.4 explain the trends and distribution of papers recently published in the journal of *Southeast Asian Studies*.

Of twenty-seven papers published in the English Journal in the years 2005–08, seventeen can be categorized as Vietnamese Studies, including research on overseas Vietnamese. Six articles on international relations or ASEAN are also directly related to Vietnam's foreign policies. The remaining four articles may be considered as of more general Southeast Asian interest; one of them was written by foreign co-authors and the other three were based on library studies in the disciplines of history and folk culture studies.

Table 6.3
Classification of the Papers Published in Southeast Asian Studies

Category	2005	2006	2007	2008	Sum
Vietnam	– Sea-posture culture – Cultural heritage – Ceramics trade – Value of VN Equitization	– Rural household economy – VN history – Hindu-Champa goddess	– Y A Na worship – Vietnam in the 20th century – the Dutch East Indian Company in Tonkin	– National unification – Po Nagar Temple	13
Ethnic minorities in Vietnam	– Festival in Central Highlands	– Muong (compare with Thai)		– Ethnic Chinese in South Vietnam	3
Overseas Vietnamese	– VN community in Thailand				1
Southeast Asian countries	– Akha in Laos	– Myanmar (by Myanmar & Japan scholars)	– Siam reformers	– Makassar, Sulawesi	4
ASEAN, International Relations		– VN's Exchange Museum programme with Thailand & Laos	– ASEAN economic integration – Globalization	– ASEAN community – Vietnam & UN – Cochinchina-Japan relations	6
Total	8	6	6	7	27

Table 6.4
Classification of the Papers Published in *Nghiên cứu Đông Nam Á*, in the 1st half of 2009

Catetory	2009–1	2009–2	2009–3	2009–4	2009–5	2009–6	Sum
Vietnam	6	–	5	3	5	6	25
Vietnam Ethnic minorities			1				1
Overseas Vietnamese						1	1

Note: Southeast Asian couonal languages about their own countries, and is published "locally" (Halib and Huxley 1996, pp. 5–6).

By contrast, in the six issues of the *Nghiên cứu Đông Nam Á* published in the first half of 2009, the articles categorized as Southeast Asian Studies in effect fall within Vietnamese Studies.[11] The problem is that no matter how many articles are published in the field of Southeast Asian Studies and more particularly Vietnamese Studies, there remains a major language barrier to foreign Southeast Asianists as they cannot read or review them in Vietnamese.[12]

CONCLUSIONS

This chapter has traced the construction of Southeast Asian Studies as an academic discipline in Vietnam through the studies and explanations of Vietnamese scholars. Its primary focus has been on the institutionalization of Southeast Asian Studies, taking note of the assessment and perceptions of Vietnamese scholars. It has also examined the construction and limitations of Southeast Asian Studies in Vietnam, which advocates Southeast Asian Studies as interdisciplinary Area Studies, whilst stressing the importance of discovering the origins of local or indigenous studies within the general field of Southeast Asian Studies. Based on this study, the features of Southeast Asian Studies in Vietnam can be summarized as follows:

First, Vietnamese scholars contend that they have developed Southeast Asian Studies viewing Southeast Asia as both a geographical entity with a long history and cultural tradition and a strategic region for modern development. They also argue that since the establishment of *Ban Đông Nam Á* in 1973, Southeast Asian Studies in Vietnam have been conducted in five categories: (1) the origin of Southeast Asian civilization as different from Chinese and Indian civilizations; (2) the formation of Southeast Asian countries and nations and the emergence of traditional cultures; (3) the colonial invasion and the response to this in national liberation movements; (4) the modernization process of each Southeast Asian country and its relationship with the international communities; and (5) the history of the relationships between Vietnam and Southeast Asian countries.

Second, the birth and growth of Southeast Asian Studies in Vietnam have been closely related to Vietnam's national efforts to overcome colonialism. Vietnamese scholars, in general, assess the influence of colonialism as two-sided and take a negative stance against Western-centred viewpoints. In Vietnam particularly, socialist and nationalist ideologies are deeply ingrained in the philosophy of researchers. Scholars are largely engaged in studies that serve the national identity of their countries. Whilst acknowledging Western scholars' important contributions to the development and the expansion of Southeast Asian Studies worldwide, they have criticized ethnocentrism and other clear limitations of these studies and have attempted to uncover the origins of indigenous Southeast Asian Studies in Vietnam. Vietnamese scholars who institutionalized Southeast Asian studies have highlighted the fact that there is already a wealth of local accumulated capabilities in Southeast Asian Studies in Vietnam and these studies have a long history. Vietnamese scholars also argue that Southeast Asian Studies has an indigenous origin from earlier times, and it did not start from the colonial period.

Third, a majority of scholars working at Southeast Asian research institutions can be called scholars of Vietnamese studies. In other words, it is hard to discuss Southeast Asian Studies without addressing Vietnamese Studies. Most scholars who studied in Europe (including the former Soviet Union), the United States, and Australia can also be called scholars of Vietnamese Studies. Researchers of Vietnamology in various fields of study have expanded their scope of study whilst working as researchers in Southeast Asian Studies, and researchers of other Southeast Asian countries have also addressed issues mostly related to Vietnam. If studies of Vietnam are excluded, Southeast Asian Studies are still undifferentiated and underdeveloped in a strict sense.

Fourth, since the foundation of the Institute for Southeast Asian Studies in 1984 and the publication of *Nghiên cứu Đông Nam Á* in 1990, this area of study has begun to see a more vigorous institutional development and academic progress. An accumulation of research in Southeast Asian Studies began with scholars working in established disciplines, such as archaeology, history, linguistics, ethnology, and geography. A comparison at the institutional level shows that after their entry into ASEAN, Southeast Asian research organizations in Vietnam became stronger and their collaboration with overseas research institutions became more active. Recently, studies of international relations including Vietnam-ASEAN and globalization issues have been published in increasing numbers.

Fifth, compared to other Southeast Asian countries, Vietnam has very actively established a range of research organizations. However, most of them have placed more emphasis on the policy agenda of the state or social functions than research, and researchers unrelated to Southeast Asian Studies or even non-researchers have played a leading role in some of these organizations. These institutional characteristics of Southeast Asian Studies in Vietnam are believed to reflect the features of the country's organizational culture. Vietnam has a strong tendency to organize researchers, expand the size of organizations, and focusing on active publications, scholarly seminars and overseas collaboration. In other words, it emphasizes the overt activities and the infrastructure of research but not necessarily the content and quality of the research. There is also a clear tendency to prioritize the strategic programmes of work and the tasks of the organization before personal interest in a particular research project.

Notes

[1]   This work was supported by the National Research Foundation of Korea Grant funded by the Korean Government (NRF-2008-362-B00018). This chapter is partly revised and translated from my paper in Korean which was originally published in *Dongnam Asia Yon-gu* [The Southeast Asian Review], vol. 21, no. 1 (February 2011): 93–135.

[2]   In the same vein, this is also noteworthy: "The Institute of Southeast Asian Studies in Singapore, established in 1971, had become a major meeting point for Southeast Asianists, as well as the leading publishing house for SEAS, but its focus was on the research rather than on the teaching of the region. Hence in 1976, Malaysia kicked off the first interdisciplinary SEAS program in the region at the University of Malaya. Three years earlier, an Institute for SEAS within the Vietnam Academy of Social Sciences with a narrower focus on Laos and Cambodia had been set up in Hanoi" (Chou and Houben 2006, p. 7).

3   This study does not aim at an in-depth review of individual works prepared by
     Southeast Asian researchers. Although such a review is essential and necessary, it
     goes beyond the temporal limitations and thus will be left for further studies.
4   In the post-war era, generally speaking, the state's role in the development of
     Southeast Asian Studies in other countries in the region was similar to that of
     Vietnam. New programmes have been established, new positions created and a
     spirit of optimism prevailed with the leading role of the state sector. National
     policy-makers recognized the need for acquiring solid knowledge about the
     region itself. This awareness has been fuelled by urgent social, political, and
     economic demands. Things of great magnitude are happening in the region itself.
     International attention has been transfixed on the social, political, economic,
     and technological developments in the region. In the aftermath of the Cold
     War, technological advances and the easing of earlier political and economic
     barriers have enabled the region to increase its global economic and cultural
     networks. Simultaneous to such moves are tremendous parallel domestic social,
     political, and economic developments. Global and regional developments such
     as these have raised the profile of the region, bringing it to the attention of
     broad public and professional audiences around the world (see, Chou and
     Houben 2006, pp. 2–3).
5   On the occasion of the 10th anniversary (1996–2006) of SEARAV, summarizing
     and appraising the development process, as well as introducing popularly the
     association and member organizations, SEARAV has assigned its central office
     and member organizations to compile the book entitled *SEARAV and Member
     Organisations*. You can see many member organizations listed in the book,
     which have nothing to do with Southeast Asian research. However, the current
     president of SEARAV is Professor Phạm Đức Dương, one of the most well-
     known Southeast Asianists in Vietnam.
6   For the study of the Historical Construction of Southeast Asian Studies in Viet-
     nam, there are few works as good as the book *25 năm Tiếp Cận Đông Nam Á
     Học (25 years' Approach to Southeast Asian Studies)* (Phạm Đức Dương 1998a).
     Most of the scholars I met in Vietnam agree that the author of this book has
     been one of the most influential leading scholars in the field of Southeast Asian
     Studies in Vietnam for the last four decades. He took the lead in pioneering
     and expanding this field of studies in Vietnam during his directorship of *Viện
     nghiên cứu Đông Nam Á* for twenty-one years (1973–94), and accomplished
     major academic achievements in linguistic and cultural studies. His study with
     the theme of *"25 năm một chặng đường đến với Đông Nam Á học ở Việt Nam"
     (25 years on the Road to Southeast Asian Studies in Vietnam)* summarized the
     entire history of Southeast Asian Studies in Vietnam. Born in 1930, he is still
     very energetic and active in teaching and writing. He opens his personal library
     for visitors' use.
7   The pioneering nationalist who most clearly became a "Southeast Asia scholar"
     was Nguyễn Văn Huyền. He taught Vietnamese at the Ecole des Langues

Orientales in Paris in the 1920s and 1930s, extended his studies to Leiden and London, and learned enough Dutch and English to be able to reconceptualize the region as an ethnographic whole. His pathbreaking investigation of common patterns of house building in the region was probably the first by an ethnically Southeast Asian author to use the term "Southeast Asia" in its title (Reid and Diokno 2003, p. 96).

[8]   Western-derived concepts have dominated practically most writings in the humanities and social sciences related to Southeast Asia. Local scholars have primarily been trained in the West; those who have been trained locally have often been supervised by those trained in the West. Thus, Western concepts and theories on regional realities and on processes of modernization have been perpetuated. Both foreign and local scholars have called for an "indigenized" approach in the social sciences and for the writing of "autonomous" history. Indeed, most academic researchers (Western as well as local) now routinely attempt to avoid ethnocentrism and "Orientalism" in their scholarly work on Southeast Asia (Halib and Huxley 1996, p. 6).

[9]   For example, Nguyễn Khánh Tòan was a "big" leading communist, influenced by the Soviet Union. He was a member of the Central Committee of the Communist party, in charge of Social Sciences. Phạm Đức Dương and Ngô Văn Doanh got their Ph.D.s in the Soviet Union. Anyway, since the 1990s, the academia of Southeast Asian Studies in Vietnam has seen a new generation studying in the U.S., Canada, Australia, Singapore, Japan, and Western Europe. Most of them wrote doctoral dissertations in the field of Vietnamese Studies but are working in the field of Southeast Asian Studies. For example, Professor Nguyễn Văn Chính studied in the Netherlands, where he obtained his Ph.D., and in Japan. He criticized the political and ideological orientation of the "old generation".

[10] Nguyễn Quang Ngọc has said Vietnamese Studies or "Vietnamology" is "multi- and interdisciplinary" in nature and Vietnamese Studies in Vietnam is considered "a generic, interdisciplinary science included in Area Studies". He proposed that in practice researchers depend on the particular purposes and depth of their research, focusing on research in specific fields of study. He contended that the interdisciplinary and generic nature of Vietnamese Studies should not be regarded as something extreme or absolute; rather, attention should also be paid to a number of disciplines that are conventionally considered essential such as history, language, demography or ethnology (Nguyen Quang Ngoc 2003, pp. 101–3, 108).

[11] Every ten issues that I counted above contain papers by Professor Ngô Văn Doanh, current chief editor of the Journal. He is a very prolific author but I do not know how they assess the originality and quality of the papers, or if they have any process of peer review.

[12] The situation is similar in other Southeast Asian countries except for Singapore. It restricts reviewing or introducing native scholars who work in Southeast Asian

Studies in their own national languages into the academic circles in which English-speaking scholars are dominant. The contributions of Western writers dominate in every discipline in the English-language literature on Southeast Asia, to which Southeast Asians have only recently begun to contribute significantly. A related point is that Southeast Asians have tended to research and write on their own countries: the number of true "Southeast Asianists" in the region remains limited. Thus, a large part of local scholars' work on the region has involved Indonesians, Thais and to a lesser extent Malaysian scholars writing in their national languages about their own countries, and is published "locally" (Halib and Huxley 1996, pp. 5–6).

References

Abu-Lughod, Janet. *Before European Hegemony: The World System A.D. 1250–1350*. New York: Oxford University Press, 1989.

Bahrin, Tunku Shamsul. "Southeast Asian Studies in Malaysia". In *A Colloquium on Southeast Asian Studies*, edited by Tunku Shamsul Bahrin, Chandran Jeshurun, and A. Terry Rambo. Singapore: Institute of Southeast Asian Studies, 1981.

Center for Vietnam and Southeast Asian Studies (CVSEAS). "Nội Dung Đề Án" [Contents of Suggestions]. Unpublished document. Hochiminh City: CVSEAS, 2009.

Charnvit Kasetsiri et al. *Bibliography Southeast Asian Studies in Thailand*. Bangkok: The Center for Southeast Asian Studies, Thammasat University, 1991.

Choi Horim. "Vietnam-eui Siminsahoe-wa NGO: Hyeonhwang-gwa Pyeongga". [Inquiring into Civil Society and in Contemporary Vietnam] [in Korean]. *Minjujueui wa Inkwon* [Journal of Democracy and Human Rights] (5·18 Research Center, Chonnam Nat'l University) 8, no. 2 (2008): 267–307.

Chou, Cynthia and Vincent Houben. "Introduction". In *Southeast Asian Studies: Debates and New Directions*, edited by Cynthia Chou and Vincent Houben. Singapore: Institute of Southeast Asian Studies, 2006.

Department of Oriental Studies, College of Social Sciences and Humanities, Hochiminh City National University of Vietnam. *Catalogue*.

Đới Khải Lai. "Tình hình Nghiên cứu Đông Nam Á của Trung Quốc gần đây" [Contemporary Tendencies of Southeast Asian Studies in China]. *Tạp chí Nghiên cứu Đông Nam Á* (Hà Nội: Viên nghiên cứu Đông Nam Á) 10, no. 1 (1992): 63–70.

Emmerson, Donald K. "Southeast Asia: What's in a Name?". *Journal of Southeast Asian Studies* 15, no. 1 (1984): 1–12.

Halib, Mohammed and Tim Huxley, eds. *An Introduction to Southeast Asian Studies*. Singapore: Institute of Southeast Asian Studies and London and New York: I.B. Tauris Publishers, 1996.

Hirschman, Charles. "The State of Southeast Asian Studies in American Universities". In *Southeast Asian Studies in the Balance: Reflections from America*, edited by Charles Hirschman, Charles F. Keyes, and Karl Hutterer. Ann Arbor, MI: The Association for Asian Studies, 1992.

Institute for Southeast Asian Studies, Vietnam Academy of Social Sciences (VASS). *Catalogue.*

Nguyễn Đức Ninh. *Tiểu thuyết Indonesia nửa đầu thế kỷ XX* [Indonesian Novels of the first half of 20th Century]. Hà Nội: Viện Đông Nam Á, 1983.

Nguyên Khánh Tòan. "Thay Lời Nói Đâu: Về Phương Hướng va Nhiệm vụ Nghiên cứu Đông Nam Á của Chúng ta" [Preface: Orientation and Misssion of Our Southeast Asian Studies]. In *25 năm Tiếp Cận Đông Nam Á Học*, by Phạm Đức Dương. Hà Nội: NXB Khoa học Xã hội, 1973/1998.

Nguyễn Lệ Thi. *Thư tịch cổ Việt Nam viết về Đông Nam Á trong sách: Việt Nam—Đông Nam Á quan hệ lịch sử văn hóa* [The Vietnamese Ancient Books on Southeast Asia: Historical and Cultural Relations between Vietnam and Southeast Asia]. Hà Nội: Nxb Chính trị quốc gia, 1993.

Nguyen Quang Ngoc. "A Glimpse of Vietnamese Studies: Research and Teaching in Vietnam". In *Southeast Asian Studies in Asia: An Assessment*, edited by Asian Center, University of the Philippines. Manila: University of the Philippines, 2003.

Nguyễn Tấn Đắc. "Quá trình nhận thực về khu vực Đông Nam Á" [Construction of Perceptions on Southeast Asian Region]. *Tạp chí Nghiên cứu Đông Nam Á* số 1, no. 2 (1991): 3–7.

Nguyễn Thị Thi sưu tầm, ed. *Thư tịch cổ Việt Nam viết về Đông Nam Á* [The Vietnamese Ancient Books on Southeast Asia]. Hà Nội, 1977.

Nguyễn Từ Chi. *Góp phần nghiên cứu văn hóa và tộc người* [Contribution to the Study of Culture and People]. Hanoi: Nxb Văn hóa Thông tin, 1996.

———. *Các dân tộc Đông Nam Á* [Ethnic Groups of Southeast Asia]. Hanoi: Nxb Văn hóa dân tộc, 1997.

Nguyễn Từ Chi (chief editor), Nguyen Duy Thieu, Bui Xuan Dinh, Nguyen Quoc Hung, and Vu Huy Quang, eds. *Tìm hiểu cảnh quan đồng bằng* [Understanding Landscapes of the Plains]. Hà Nội, 1983.

Nguyễn Văn Chính. "Nhật Bản và các mối quan tâm về khu vực học" [Japan and the Interests of Regional Studies]. Unpublished paper, 1995.

———. "Southeast Asia Viewed through the Medium of Vietnamese Primary and Secondary Schoolbooks". Unpublished paper, 2007.

Norlund, Irene. *Filling the Gap: The Emerging Civil Society in Vietnam*. Hanoi: VUSTA, SNV, and UNDP, January 2007.

Phạm Đức Dương. "Một số vấn đề dân tộc—ngôn ngữ ở nước ta" [Some Problems of Ethnic Groups and Languages in Our Country]. *Tạp chí Dân tộc học* số 4 (1978): 28–33.

————. "Đông Nam Á Học va Tạp Chí 'Nghiên Cứu Đông Nam Á'". *Nghiên Cứu Đông Nam Á số* 1, no. 1 (1990): 3–14.

————. "Giao lưu văn hóa ở Đông Nam Á" [Cultural Exchange in Southeast Asia]. In *Việt Nam—Đông Nam Á, quan hệ lịch sử văn hóa*. Hà Nội: Nxb Chính trị quốc gia, 1993.

————. "Giới thiệu một số ý kiến của A. G. Haudricpurt về việc phân loại các ngôn ngữ theo hệ tộc ở Đông Nam Á". *Tạp chí Nghiên cứu Đông Nam Á*. số 1, no. 22 (1996): 102–12.

————. *25 năm Tiếp Cận Đông Nam Á Học* [25 years' Approach for the Southeast Asian Studies]. Hà Nội: NXB Khoa học Xã hội, 1998*a*.

————. *Ngôn ngữ của văn hóa Lào* [Language of Laos Culture]. Hanoi: Nxb Chính trị quốc gia, 1998*b*.

————. *Bức Tranh Ngôn ngữ—Văn hóa Tộc người ở Việt Nam và Đông Nam Á* [Picture of Languages and Cultures of the Peoples of Vietnam and Southeast Asia]. Hà Nội: NXB Đại học Quốc gia Hà Nội, 2007.

Phạm Đức Dương, Trần Quốc Vượng, and Cao Xuân Phổ, eds. *Biển với người Việt cổ* [Ancient Vietnamese People with the Sea]. Hanoi: Nxb van hoa thong tin, 1996.

Phạm Đức Thành. "Cùng Bạn Đọc" [With Readers]. In *25 năm Tiếp Cận Đông Nam Á Học*, by Phạm Đức Dương. Hà Nội: NXB Khoa học Xã hội, 1998.

Phan Ngọc and Phạm Đức Dương. *Tiếp xúc ngôn ngữ ở Đông Nam Á*. Hanoi, 1983.

Reid, Anthony. "Studying Southeast Asia in a Globalized World". *Taiwan Journal of Southeast Asian Studies* 1, no. 2 (2004): 1–18.

Reid, Anthony and Maria Serena Diokno. "Completing the Circle: Southeast Asian Studies in Southeast Asia". In *Southeast Asian Studies: Pacific Perspectives*, edited by Anthony Reid. Tempe, AZ: Arizona State University, 2003.

Scott, James C. "Foreword". In *Southeast Asian Studies in the Balance: Reflections from America*, edited by Charles Hirschman, Charles F. Keyes, and Karl Hutterer. Ann Arbor, MI: The Association for Asian Studies, 1992.

SEARAV. *SEARAV và Các Tổ Chức Thành Viên* [SEARAV and Member Organisations]. Hanoi: SEARAV (Southeast Asian Research Association of Vietnam), 2006.

Trần Khánh. "Giới thiệu về Viện Nghiên cứu Đông Nam Á của Singapore" [Introduction to the Institute of Southeast Asian Studies in Singapore]. *Tạp chí Nghiên cứu Đông Nam Á*. số 1, no. 2 (1991): 71–74.

University of the Philippines Asian Center et al., eds. *Southeast Asian Studies in Asia: an Assessment*. Manila: University of the Philippines Asian Center, 2003.

Nghiên cứu Đông Nam Á (Institute for Southeast Asian Studies, VASS). *2009–1(106); 2009–2(107); 2009–3(108), 2009–4(109), 2009–5(110), 2009–6(111)*.

Southeast Asian Studies (Institute for Southeast Asian Studies, VASS). 2005; 2006; 2007; 2008.

7

POPULAR CULTURE FOR A NEW SOUTHEAST ASIAN STUDIES?

Ariel Heryanto

INTRODUCTION

Focusing on the prospect of a locally based Southeast Asian Studies in the near future, this chapter necessarily takes a different approach and framework from most of the other chapters. For political and historical reasons, Southeast Asian Studies, as we know it today, has for the past several decades had its major centres of excellence half a globe away from Southeast Asia, no matter how one might define the region. With the exception of Singapore, formal training and research in Southeast Asian Studies in the region are fairly new and small in size and impact in comparison both to academic activities in other fields of enquiry, as well as in comparison to area studies in several countries outside the region. Understandably, most historical analysis of area studies has referred largely to key texts, ideas, persons and institutions from other regions. While such an exercise is highly valuable, it raises a number of intellectual, political and ethical issues as I have explored them elsewhere (Heryanto 2002). Building on that article, I wish to consider below the prospects for a home-grown Southeast Asian Studies in the twenty-first century, and speculate what such studies might look like. I must admit from the start, I do not have any ready answers to these important yet difficult questions. However, I hope this modest attempt is a worthy step. More specifically, this is a preliminary attempt to consider the initial and potential contribution of intra-Asian popular cultural flows to the future of a locally based area studies of the region, its people and its historical trajectory, as one possible form of successor to the old Southeast Asian Studies from the Cold War era.

Unlike most analyses of prominent Southeast Asian Studies in other regions, we are faced with a rather limited range of locally published and accessible ideas when examining the case within the otherwise rich intellectual traditions of the region itself. Instead of following the usual practice of looking back to milestones, key texts, authors, and debates of area studies in the past, local conditions have led me to focus on the present potentials and possible future. Instead of confining the selection of materials for analysis to published academic works on locally produced Southeast Asian Studies, I take the liberty to consider various non-academic materials, especially popular cultural products that bear witness to the fervour of contemporary cross-regional networks, offering one potential basis for a future region-based area studies. Needless to say, such an approach is far from adequate. It is my hope, nonetheless, that the discussion below shows persuasively that post-Cold War areas studies has no or little choice but to go beyond its "regnant paradigm" (McVey 1995, p. 6) of the past, especially if it is to survive this century and particularly in the region itself. It is neither possible nor desirable for a home-grown Southeast Asian Studies to produce a replica of the exemplary models from the colonial and Cold War eras. Southeast Asian Studies in the present and future cannot afford to overlook the vibrant development of new media and popular cultures. Substantial sections in the middle of this chapter will be devoted specifically to a close examination of samples of what such cross-regional cultural flows look like and how they may be helpful in the formation of a locally-based area studies.

I will look at some of the dominant streams in the recent intra-regional popular cultural products, of which the so-called "Korean Wave" is a salient part. To complement that discussion, I will examine selected alternative samples of intra-regional popular cultural circulation that are politically sensitive to majority groups in the region. I refer to ethnicity and religion in Singapore, Indonesia and Malaysia. Both the dominant and the alternative intra-regional popular cultural flows in this new millennium signal new desires and anxieties among millions of people in this politically and economically dynamic region as they attempt to redefine their self-identities, and also a common commitment to embrace a modernity that better fits their specific, if diverse and fluid, historical circumstances and aspirations for their future. All these new developments require reconsideration not only of the selected contents or external contexts of Southeast Asian Studies from the past century, but also its dominant presuppositions, and its overall structural and defining framework.

AREA STUDIES RECONSIDERED

Centuries old commercial, religious, artistic and political links among the various states and people of what is currently called Southeast Asia have been well documented. However, until various colonial powers established the territorial boundaries of what are now different independent nation-states in Southeast Asia, the formal and systematic studies of the region have not taken the shape as we know them today. The colonial experience left a wealth of strong social and political legacies that persist in the contemporary social dynamics of these independent nations. The Cold War in the second half of the twentieth century gave rise to new imaginary and sponsored activities that grouped together some of these nation-states called Southeast Asia as if they constituted one bounded "region". Seen from this perspective, Southeast Asian Studies was to an important extent a by-product of these external forces, predicated on the assumption that Southeast Asia was arguably a region with sufficient unity for a viable and distinct unit of analysis that warranted a special category in the academy. Scholars in Southeast Asian Studies often had difficulty defending their special cluster of academic activities when questioned by their colleagues from the more established academic disciplines. What at first looked like a fiction (that is Southeast Asia as a bounded regional unit) became a relatively successful reality partly through (in other words "Southeast Asia" as a bounded regional unit) the activities of the people and the states in this region.

The fact that the centres of excellence in institutionalized Southeast Asian Studies during the Cold War were located outside the region, and were Euro- or American-centric, has been well documented and needs no further review (Emmerson 1984; Rafael 1994; Reynolds 1995). Observers have also noted that since the late 1990s, and with the end of the Cold War, many things have changed rapidly, giving some hope for the rise of locally-based Southeast Asian Studies at a time when such studies elsewhere had suffered major cuts in governmental and societal support with dire consequences to the enterprise (Reid 1999; Heryanto 2002). Two of the most recent related forces that have transformed the region are new media technology and industrial capitalist expansion. These new forces have the capacity to help integrate the region much better than any conscious efforts made by the political elite of the region. However, one must quickly add that the forces of the market and the new media were not necessarily a good thing for everyone in the region, as they are never meant to be. It is also worth noting that the new media might not have been so effective in integrating the region until they were accompanied by the recent boom in the production, circulation and consumption of popular culture across the national borders of North, East and Southeast Asia. Ironically, this took place not long after the infamous 1997 economic crisis and in the early 2000s.[1]

As Southeast Asian Studies waned in many parts of the world following the end of the Cold War, there have been some enthusiastic attempts to build locally based area studies in Southeast Asia. Most prominent among these attempts are the networks run by academics, with generous sponsorship from external philanthropic foundations from the USA and Japan.[2] One such network is the Southeast Asian Studies Regional Exchange Program (SEASREP), based in Manila, with sponsorship from the Japan and Toyota Foundations in the initial years in the late 1990s. Soon after that the Bangkok-based Asian Studies in Asia Fellowship Program (AsiA FP) was founded, then transformed into the Asian Scholarship Foundation (ASF) from 2002. ASF and its predecessor enjoyed generous support from the Ford Foundation. The third important network in the region is the Kuala Lumpur-based Asian Public Intellectuals (API) Fellowships with sponsorship from the Nippon Foundation. The Rockefeller Foundation sponsored the establishment of another Bangkok-based network called the Asian Muslim Action Network (AMAN). Several more projects along these lines have been evolving, including the ASEAN University Network.

It is hard to see the simultaneity of these new and comparable initiatives as purely accidental. There seems to be a common sense of urgency to salvage area studies, which had been deemed to be in irremediable crisis in many parts of the world outside the region. It was also clear there was a common commitment to innovation in building a locally based area studies, as well as attachments to the Cold War era area studies. Cognizant of the structural limitations that seriously impede academic rigour in the region (see McVey 1995; Heryanto 2002), many of these networks have been keen to collaborate with mid-career non-academic professionals who have the potential to make a significant contribution to building a strong home-grown area studies. Reminiscent of the studies of the Orient in colonial times, such persons may include those loosely labelled as "public intellectuals", as well as artists, civil servants, and journalists. It is also a common policy among members of these networks to give priority support to those who are both citizens and residents in the participating countries. These networks commonly encourage participants to study the less familiar among the participating countries, instead of their own country or their closest neighbouring countries.

Unfortunately, even the best intents and efforts do not readily equate to successes. One decade after these visions and commitments were first put into practice, their interim achievements deserve noting, and problems acknowledged. The number of young academics in selected universities studying other parts of the region may have grown. Some of them may have published work that will be recognized as important contributions to area studies. There has been a growing interest in scholarly study of this area among local intellectuals. Notwithstanding these, the scale and intensity of economic dynamics, urban growth, and cultural vibrancy of the region in the past three decades dwarfed the achievements of these new projects. More fundamentally, heavily reliant on external funding and the persistent legacies of the old "regnant paradigms" of area studies from the Cold War period have made it difficult for these projects to self-sustain over a long period and achieve their intended goals any time soon. Despite the aspiration of the founding members of the network to encourage innovation and collaboration with non-academics, conservative and narrow-minded academicism characterized many of the sponsored activities, leading to a general tendency to reproduce some of the less innovative practices of area studies from the Cold War era.

Largely overlooked, or misunderstood, or underestimated by students of Southeast Asia past and present is the growth of new strength in non-academic and non-state-sponsored knowledge production with potential impact on scholarly activities in Southeast Asian Studies. If the trends continue well into the next several decades, one can postulate a scenario where different locally-based producers, retailers, advertisers, journalists, artists, activists, cultural critics, and consumers of popular cultures have a lot to instruct each other about their neighbouring countries and the globalized region as a whole, but not in classrooms and not directly towards attaining academic degree.

No doubt, one dominant feature of such knowledge is the industrial interests of the sponsors, including those with questionable ethical and ideological overtones. While such knowledge will never replace what is commonly expected of a respectable scholarly work, students of Southeast Asian Studies must not rush to dismiss these non-academic knowledges, because the latter are part of the strongest forces that shape Southeast Asia today. This is not necessarily a one-way relationship. Academics in the region have been active in the production, circulation, regulation, and consumption of popular culture. What is new, for better or worse, is a major shift of power relations in the production of knowledge around intra-regional networks, between academics and those in the media and entertainment industry. Not only will academics have to be more attentive to sources of information and resources available from the media and entertainment industries, but an increasing number of graduates from academic institutions have sought and found employment in this fast developing industry. Following the "corporatization" of academic institutions in the region (Heryanto 2003) in the 1980s and 1990s, what we have seen since the late 1990s (and more so in the 2000s) is a series of new initiatives by major local industries to take part in investment in the establishment of tertiary institutions. It has become increasingly impossible or unacceptable, for students of contemporary Southeast Asia to overlook the work of the new media and widespread consumption of popular culture.

NEW MEDIA AND POPULAR CULTURE

Both the terms "new media" and "popular culture" have been casually used by many people from a wide range of backgrounds, including journalists and academics. However, among specialists each of these phrases is highly contested. It is unnecessary to go into detail about the ongoing debates about the concepts. For our immediate purpose, suffice it to note what senses of the terms will be adopted in this discussion, and to acknowledge that this preference is neither taken for granted nor free from objection.

Scholars (for instance Chun and Keenan 2006; Lister, Dovey, Giddings, Grant and Kelly 2003; McQuail 1994) have discussed at length the benefits of the commonly used term "new media" as well as the reasons for its popularity and some of the thorny issues surrounding its use. It is important to heed their advice that the adjective "new" here should not be taken to imply "better" for all beings, or to imply total separation from or incompatibility with the "old(er)" media. Even if "new" is taken to imply "better", it can never mean the same for different people. The term "new media" does not refer to a fully developed state of technology, but also to the potentials for the future that they still have. In the discussion below, the term "new media" (plural for "new medium") refers loosely and collectively to the different information technologies of communication — particularly but not exclusively the electronic and digital — with the following marked characteristics or features that distinguish them from the old media: interactivity, high capacity, decentralization, and flexibility of form, content, and use.

Beyond the specialist media studies circles who do not always agree with each other, discussions on new media technologies often revolve around what they do for us in important areas, such as governance, education, industry, personal relations and conflicts. These studies are definitely valuable. What is frequently missing in these discussions, however, is a consideration of what the new media have done *to* us, as opposed to *for* us. There is an assumption that the new technology changes many things around us, but not our inner selves which are autonomous and as if free from history. Such arguments presume the universalist idea that human beings are essentially the same and that across the globe they are trying to achieve the same ideals. Thanks to the new media, so the common wisdom goes, we can now do things better, easier, at a higher speed, and at lower cost. The notion that "new" will necessarily bring something "superior" or "better" is an index of a particular modernist bias from the previous century about progress and the evolution of history. The media themselves have generally been perceived — by political and economic elites as much as by lay people — first and foremost as a set of tools. They are perceived to be neither good nor bad in themselves. Their value is considered to depend on who owns them, or who has access to their use, and how they are used.

A humanist perspective of this kind was dominant for most of the last two centuries in the social sciences and humanities, and it has shaped the dominant paradigm in Southeast Asian Studies. Surprisingly, this dominant view survived the two World Wars that shattered the illusion of human reason and the capacity of human beings to bring about a better life with the use of science and technology. In any case, this past history helps explain why, until very recently, scholars in Southeast Asian Studies were never trained to recognize, let alone seriously examine, media technology as a social force with a significant degree of autonomy in the process of social change. In fact, instead of simply facilitating better human agency in communicating the same old types of messages with greater speed or size or detail, the new technology has challenged and subverted (if not uniformly) all of the old familiar institutions, practices and agencies. It has also helped give birth to new kinds of messages and new kinds of agency, and has reinvented a new kind of social relations. Accordingly, if area studies will survive well in the new social environment, it can be expected to undergo some substantial transformation from its predecessors.

As elaborated elsewhere (Heryanto 2008*b*), I use the term "popular culture" to refer to a variety of genres of communicative practices widely and prominently circulated for a large number of the people, or by such people, or a combination of both. The first category (for the people) refers to mass-produced commodified messages (including music, films, and television) and related signifying practices. The second category (by the people) includes non-industrialized, relatively independent, communicative practices that circulate through various means (public events, parades, festivals), often, but not always, in opposition or as alternatives to the mass-produced commodities of entertainment and lifestyles. To bring the concept into sharper relief, let me contrast it to what popular culture *is not*. Most past studies of Asian culture devoted attention to the so-called "traditional" or "ethnic" cultures (often exoticised as authentic cultures of specific peoples by the tourist industry, museums and the art world) which can be easily distinguished from the modern, urban-based popular culture which lacks a specific association to or embeddedness within any particularly ethnic group and its traditions. Popular culture is also distinguished from the state-sanctioned "official" version of national cultures (as often propagated in schools and ceremonies) or the "avant-garde" or "high" cultures of the nation's intelligentsia (as found in the academy, theatres and prestigious galleries). This is not to say that there is no borrowing or mutation of particular elements between one category and another. The contrary is true; borrowing of elements from one category to another has been common throughout history.

If media technology has been relegated to the status of a mere tool, and is thus considered secondary to something of greater importance (such as the "content", or the people who own and manipulate it), popular culture was obviously regarded as even less important.[3] Actually, there were more reasons than has usually been admitted for the lack of interest in popular cultures among scholars in Southeast Asian Studies during its peak in the Cold War period. One of these reasons is gender bias. Led by American social sciences, Southeast Asian Studies during the Cold War was preoccupied with issues of the region's march towards modernization, state-nation building or those hurdles that impede such projects (as poverty, Communism, local traditions, corruption, or violence). They all appear as primarily activities about and for men from a predominantly male authorial perspective. In contrast, entertainment and popular culture as disseminated via the mass media (radio and television) was seen as occupying the secondary "private" or "domestic" domain, mainly belonging to the second-class gender.

Additionally, a significant reinvigoration of popular culture is a fairly recent reality in many parts of Southeast Asia.[4] Although the early emergence of popular culture in Southeast Asia dates back around a century ago, it underwent difficulties during the political turmoil of decolonization and the Cold War. Although many todays' Southeast Asian consumers of popular cultures have fond memories of products in the middle of the twentieth century, only the last two or three decades of the twentieth century began to witness a major expansion of the mass production and consumption of popular cultures in this region. The new development was made possible by the sustained industrialization from the 1980s, the rapid growth of the media and entertainment industries (especially television network), and the increased capacity, affordability, and higher level of user-friendliness of the digital media technology.

From the 1950s, if not earlier, popular culture from India had already spread across the region, if unevenly. In the 1970s and 1980s martial arts and historical films from Hong Kong, China, Taiwan and telenovellas from Latin America found a huge and avid audience in the region. Japanese comics, toys, animated films, popular music and television dramas were a big hit in the 1980s and early 1990s (for details see Iwabuchi 2002*a*; Otmazgin 2007, 2008).[5] From the early 2000s Korean music, soap operas and video games have made a major presence in the region (for details see Merdikaningtyas 2006; Setijadi 2005; Shim 2006; Shim, Heryanto, and Siriyuvasak 2010; Siriyuvasak and Shin 2007). Despite all these developments, these phenomena still remain a sorely understudied area. The majority of writings and discussions available are from journalistic reports and blogs among fans. Although such publications have some merit, they often lack the analytical depth and rigour that can be expected of serious academic research work.

By definition, popular culture is a product of an industrialized society, where cultural practices and artefacts are produced, displayed, or consumed in a great number with the assistance of technologies of mass duplication, making them highly accessible to a large number of consumers across different locations and social backgrounds. Many of these technologies were not designed in Southeast Asia and their circulation is not within the control of Southeast Asians, although Southeast Asian labour often went into the process of production.[6] Even in those countries of the region where industrialization began slightly earlier or progressed more robustly, popular culture is a fairly new phenomenon, and the study of this phenomenon has only recently developed. In this sense, the absence or dearth of work on popular culture in Southeast Asian Studies can be understood as something other than the result of an oversight or gender bias alone.

Increasingly, the pace of producing scholarly work appears too slow to catch up with the progressively faster moving world pushed by the new media. Many scholars across the major disciplines, including (though not especially) those active in Southeast Asian Studies, were simply unprepared to take on the task of analysing something so new and something that until recently scholars had regarded so unworthy of close scrutiny and analysis. In addition to intellectual inhibitions, there are also serious practical issues. There are increasingly abundant quantitative data on the subject matter to be collected for analysis, and these data quickly become obsolete soon after — or even before — they are collected.[7] For these reasons, this study does not aim to add or emphasize any particular empirical details of a phenomenon per se which is still very much alive, changing, and in-progress. Instead, this study aims to highlight a few long-standing issues. These issues were selected specifically on the basis of their significance to the discussion of the future of locally-based area studies in Southeast Asia. A brief account of Asian popular culture flows in the region will be presented as no more than a cursory introduction to the general phenomenon. A few empirical details and references will follow mainly for illustrative purposes.

The dawn of this millennium witnessed, for the first time, how the West ceased to be the one and only centre of orientation for the consumption of popular culture in Asia. Although American popular music and Hollywood films continue to hold an important influence, they no longer have the sole and dominant power that they enjoyed for almost the entirety of the previous century. At precisely the time when more and more Asians, particularly the young, were switching their fascination to media representations of fellow Asians, "East versus West" as a discursive frame of thought or convenient trope was also declining dramatically in public discussion.[8] This is a profound transformation if one considers how the "East versus West" dichotomy was a central point of reference for nearly all discussion of nation-building during much of the history of the decolonization of the region. It was revived most strongly in the last decades of the twentieth century when "Asian Values" propaganda was in vogue. The fall of the "Asian Values" discourse was not only or directly the result of the 1997 economic crisis as many have suggested.[9] Rather, it was superseded by an intra-Asian focus and fascination among millions of people in the region, particularly in terms of consumerism, entertainment, and popular culture. The shift of power from formal state elite discourses to mass consumption of popular culture is probably part of a larger set of changes in the region. This, in turn, requires major shifts and adjustments in the study of the region if such studies are to have relevance.

Two qualifications are now called for. First, the declining concern with the "East versus West" dichotomy should not be taken as a sign of an absolute decline of Western power or cultural influence.[10] Rather, it indicates a strong trend in Asia, where selected iconic elements of

Western popular culture have now been creatively blended with those conventionally understood as "Asian" within a new aesthetics, sensibility and identity among Asian youths. Rather than being entirely wiped out, rejected or avoided, these elements of Western popular culture are modified, localized and incorporated. From the late 1980s a trend was already noticeable whereby in micro-level practices, the new rich in Asia "objectif[ied] the West in the form of commodities at their disposal ... Instead of ... regard[ing] the West as a major threat, or ... an object of obsessive idolisation, more and more Asians regard. ... Western things as pliable resources" like any other exoticized objects of consumption from 'Asia'" (Heryanto 1999, p. 169). While markers of distinction pertaining to "Asian" and "non-Asian" continue to be reproduced, repackaged and marketed and occasionally mixed, the two are no longer portrayed as opposites that shall never meet.

Second, I mentioned earlier that the trend towards better regional integration in Southeast Asia has been galvanized not so much by efforts of the region's top political elites as by forces of the new media and the market in the new environment of expanded industrial capitalism and the creative work of popular culture. Having said this, I must acknowledge that governments in the exporting countries of these popular cultural products have played an important role. Governments in Japan and South Korea made substantial investments in the creative industries from the late 1990s for economic and political reasons rather than reasons of cultural advancement or enlightenment. However, these efforts should not be equated with the outcome. In neither case, do these governments have the capacity to turn, direct or convert the successful expansion of popular cultural production, distribution and consumption in the region into greater political clout or, as some have called it, "soft power" and "diplomatic influence". Shim Doobo (2006) shows the concerted and long-term efforts of the South Korean government in investing in and engineering what is now commonly referred to as the "Korean Wave". Otmazgin (2008) provides details of Japanese state investment in cultural production and distribution, and its limited capacity to reap political gains. His analysis also shows how other governments (in Taiwan, South Korea, the Philippines and Malaysia) attempted unsuccessfully to restrict the inflow of Japanese popular culture into their respective territories as they had previously done with American popular culture. Even when it was evident that their earlier attempts had been to no avail, many governments in the region continued to ride the latest popular cultural wave and to seek short-term political and diplomatic gains in the name of the nation they represented.

The results have been varied but limited (for the case of Japan see Iwabuchi 2002*b*).

THE DOMINANT WITHIN INTRA-REGIONAL CULTURAL FLOWS

In the opening section I mentioned the need to look at what exists in the public space across Southeast Asia as a potential resource for a locally based area studies, given the limited size and range of scholarly debates that have been conducted thus far under the rubric of Southeast Asian Studies in the region. This section and the next will be devoted to examining selected samples of contemporary popular cultural products that have caught the imagination of millions of youths in the region.

Most observers now emphatically agree that audience reception matters. Ultimately the success story of the Northeast Asian popular cultures cannot be adequately assessed without due recognition of the role of the audience in making it happen. But "audience" is an extremely complex and elusive concept; it is certainly more problematic than can be addressed in this brief study. I mention this only as a reminder that analysing state policies or obtaining the record-breaking sales figures can be useful but never adequate for understanding the Asianization of Southeast Asian popular culture. Although such information is important it does not tell us why millions of Southeast Asians in the early 2000s spent hours each week passionately consuming recent popular culture from other Asian countries. What was it about these cultural products that the audience found compelling and appealing, and which they could not find in other cultural products?

Many analysts have explored possible answers (Otmazgin 2007; Shim, Heryanto, and Siriyuvasak 2010; also for Thailand see Siriyuvasak and Shin 2007; for Indonesia see Ida 2008; Merdikaningtyas 2006; Pravitta 2004; and Setijadi 2005; for Singapore Chua 2004). Understandably, none has claimed to know the answers with any certainty. With the notion of "audience" still highly contested, it hardly needs to be said that we should not assume uniformity of audience reception even in the most abstract and general sense. Although various popular cultural products were consumed more or less in the same period across the region, these products acquired different values and significance as they travelled in different locations and social groups. Here I do not refer primarily to individual consumers' subjective preferences or backgrounds, although these are an important factor that deserves study in their own right. Instead, my concern is with the different social histories that have produced different collective memories and "imagined audiences" across the societies of Southeast Asia, each with different (dis)abilities, expectations, and sensitivities in their acts of consumption. The next section will elaborate this point.

Below is a brief observation about some common thematic features that prevail in many of the popular Asian drama series. By no means does this provide a direct, let alone an adequate, answer to the question of why these series appeal to such a wide audience. However, it is an important step towards answering the question. Given the wide range of forms and genres of Asian popular cultures that have swept across the region (comics, music, films, television drama series, toys, video games, clothing and hairstyles, and so on), and the size of each form and genre, the case presented below is a fragment of the total picture with no claims to representativeness. The selection of genres and materials is based on what appeared to be the most prominent and accessible samples. I have chosen to comment on drama series in this section, and films in the next, because of their prominence in the region as well as for methodological reasons. Televised drama series (as discussed below) have the capacity to reach a large and broad audience, perhaps no less than what comic books, music, or films do.[11] Televised drama series as a medium can be more powerful than comic books and music, not only because of their moving images and sound. By presenting a realist portrayal of life situations which the majority of its target audience aspire to or feel familiar with, televised drama series promise to convey meaningful messages to their audience in a most direct and consumer friendly way.

With effective use of realist images, sound and narratives, dubbed or subtitled Japanese or Korean drama series and films can also strike a chord with various audiences in Southeast Asia who do not speak the original language used in them. Under the specific circumstances that prevail in the region today, drama series can also outdo films in their ability to reach and compel a loyal audience. Of late, films have attracted a narrower audience than television in the region, because the former are more demanding: a trip to the movie house, through the heavy traffic, on a particular date and at a particular hour, a ticket fee, and solitary consumption in a dark room.[12] Although purchasing and playing a DVD version of a film can mitigate the difficulties, this would usually still require more effort than simply sitting in one's living room (or the neighbour's, as is commonly the case in most parts of Southeast Asia) with a television set at the right time. Although watching films and televised drama series is usually a collective act, the latter is definitely more communal and participatory (inviting immediate comments and other reactions collectively from the audience) than the former.

One of the first things that stand out across the various drama series in the region, and perhaps beyond, is the popularity of melodrama, comprising a love story between two or more heterosexual urban-based young people who have a good education and career and live in material comfort. This love story is complicated by a third and sometimes also a fourth person who also loves, or is loved by, one protagonist or the other. In addition to these main characters, there are usually minor characters whose function is to supply intermittent comic scenes. The drama series *Meteor Garden* (2001), the four series of *Endless Love* [*Autumn in My Heart* (2000), *Winter Sonata* (2002), *Summer Scent* (2003) and *Spring Waltz* (2006)] and *Full House* (2004) are often cited as the first drama series to be popular across the region, and in some countries are still the most popular to date. They all come from Northeast Asia, and they all conform to the formula above. Horror and comedy are also fairly popular. However, for various reasons they do not enjoy the level of popularity and respectability as romantic melodrama.[13]

Another theme of many of these Oriental dramas is the importance of hard work and persistence, demonstrated particularly by the young female protagonist. Not surprisingly, most studies by others (as those already cited throughout this chapter) suggest that females outnumber males as viewers. The same gender imbalance can be seen among the fans of the predominantly male popular music singers from Japan and Korea.[14] Paradoxically, the merits of industriousness, patience and humility in these Korean and Japanese drama series are invariably counter-posed with exuberant displays of comfort, elegance, and luxury in the lifestyles of some of the wealthy characters. Such lifestyles are often more extensively shown and foregrounded in these drama series than in Hollywood films. In the stories presented, there is no one-to-one direct and causal link between industriousness and a luxurious lifestyle. Not all the industrious characters end up living in abundance. Not all who work hard do so with the intention to become wealthy. Not all who are wealthy appear to work harder than the less advantaged ones. We will return to this matter in a moment.

Although the love story sets the overall storyline of these Northeast Asian drama series, what gets foregrounded throughout the episodes is not the protagonist's preoccupation with her affectionate feelings towards someone she loves. Rather, the series presents a dramatic display of the protagonist's uphill struggle and gradual ability to overcome various challenges of living as part of a second-class gender in a rapidly industrializing Asian society with a strong patriarchal culture. This is so much so that the romantic relationship between the protagonists is occasionally pushed to the side. Indeed, another message typically conveyed in these dramas is the virtue of patience and self-restraint. This self-restraint often appears in these series as a response to various challenges, which range from ambitious demands and heavy pressures from the older generation, tradition, peer groups, competitive workplaces and health issues to sincere but complicated love for some other person. Reminiscent of the cinematic style found in Japanese films, many scenes where the protagonist is in the grip of strong emotions of deep sorrow and grief or anger are depicted in Korean dramas with very little or no sound or action.[15] Predictably, most of these stories end happily. The protagonist's struggle, hard work, patience and persistence are ultimately rewarded, presumably to the pleasure of the audience at the end of the series. Some moderate level of gender egalitarianism becomes the moral of the story.

To be sure, hard work and self-restraint are also valued in many liberal and industrial countries in the West and their former colonies, and feature prominently in their fiction. It is important to note some subtle distinctions between the two narrative traditions.[16] In many Hollywood-style narratives, hard work and a deliberate delay of gratification often appear to be a temporary measure, an unpleasant but necessary requirement for some sort of material reward to be earned by the character in the near future. In contrast, in many of these Oriental drama series hard work and self-restraint appear to have more than simply instrumental value. These acts are presented as morally virtuous in their own right, instead of as a means for some reward to be gained more or less immediately afterwards.

One can thus construct two models. In one narrative convention, exemplified by Hollywood films screened in the region, even an industrious protagonist appears natural or rational when s/he attempts to minimize her or his hard work and self-restraint to whatever level is technically necessary to meet the demands of a given situation in order to attain relief or claim a reward. In the other narrative convention, from Northeast Asian air, a protagonist will happily submit to hard work and self-restraint, regardless of the immediate rewards (if any), and will be grateful for whatever rewards that these might entail. The contrast in action and work can be further extended to that of speech. Unlike the extrovert characters in many Hollywood films, who appear normal when they are essentially "freely thinking and speaking subjects" who speak their minds to their interlocutors, the characters in many of these recent Asian drama series and films are marked as "normal" when they are self-restrained. At least at the level of appearance, decorum is prioritized over individual expression. This resonates with off-screen speech conventions in many parts of Asia where royal court cultures still retain some degree of respect and moral authority (of course, as with all models, there are some exceptions).[17]

Such cross-regional similarities have led some observers to make an argument for the "cultural proximity" of Northeast Asian popular cultures over those from North America. While not wanting to discount this argument outright, I find it inadequate. Audience preferences and pleasure can develop from contacts with the familiar and with sameness as much as from contacts with the unfamiliar and foreign.[18] On the other hand, I do not agree with some of the strong criticism of the "cultural proximity" thesis either. Of the critics of the "cultural proximity" thesis, more have objected to the modifier "cultural" than to the noun "proximity". The concept "cultural proximity" has some validity when one takes "culture" to refer to a contested field and a set of signifying practices in the world marked by unequal relations of power in both material and non-material terms. Even if it is inadequate to explain the popularity of Northeast Asian popular culture, the "cultural proximity" thesis has some value when the term "culture" is not understood as something static and unchanging or inertly or naturally belonging to a clearly bounded social group.

Let us move from abstract generalization to some specific examples. The storyline in *Meteor Garden* revolves around the love between Shan Cai and Dao Ming Tze, with several complications and sub-plots of additional love stories involving other characters.[19] Shan Cai is a girl from an economically modest family background. Dao is the spoilt son of an extremely rich family. He takes the lead in a group of four boys called F4, who are both feared and idolized for their wealth, good looks, and bullying. Despite their extreme contrast in material terms, Shan Cai and Dao are equally stubborn. Shan Cai's name, as she tells the audience in one scene, means "weed not to be trampled on". In the early episodes of the drama series, Shan Cai finds herself the object of repeated bullying by her schoolmates acting as a proxy for F4. She would not have been targeted by F4 and their supporters in the first place had she not confronted Dao in defence of her girlfriend who had previously made some minor mistake *vis-à-vis* Dao, which provoked a scolding from him. Far from accepting her fate and submitting herself to assaults and humiliation by F4, Shan Cai revolts and single-handedly strikes back. In one of the earlier scenes, she punches Dao to the ground!

Later on we learn that Dao has a crush on Shan Cai. To his surprise, however, Shan Cai rejects his affections outright. This rejection further deepens Dao's desire to conquer and possess Shan Cai by any means, including a willingness to publicly abase himself and compromise his reputation as the toughest guy in the school. Slowly but surely, Dao wins Shan Cai's heart. But with few exceptions, in the lengthy series of *Meteor Garden* the love story between Shan Cai and Dao is fraught with endless disagreements between them. Their squabbles are entry points for some of the comic situations that entertain the audience. In any case, for the period of time when Shan Cai and Dao feel mutual interest, each stubbornly represses her or his affectionate feelings for the other and maintains their own pride.

As a person with only modest economic resources, Shan Cai appears throughout the story as a hard-working person with a strong determination to maintain honour and self-esteem, and to delay self-gratification. Although she accepts that Dao will obviously shower her with material benefits, for a long time she is hesitant to accept his love. A substantial portion of the story also portrays how Shan Cai confronts threats from other people, including humiliation from Dao's mother who objects to Dao's relationship with her. So, while there is some element of a Cinderella complex in this series (as in nearly all the top titles in the region), Shan Cai exemplifies a female protagonist with a strong, uncompromising and confrontational nature and integrity, thus defying any simple parallel to Cinderella. In another important contrast to the many Cinderella-style stories, whether from Hollywood or locally made, *Meteor Garden* and most of the top Korean drama series show very little sexually-motivated body contact between the protagonists who are in love. Usually, there is no more than one kissing scene for the entire story, with multiple episodes. This last mentioned feature has drawn repeated commendation from viewers, predominantly female, of different national and religious affiliations and social classes.

In contrast to *Meteor Garden*, gentle expressions of tender love dominate the tetralogy *Endless Love*. The prevalent mood in the series is a combination of mellowness and melancholy that distinguishes it from the more youthful *Meteor Garden*. What *Meteor Garden* and *Endless Love* share, however, is the self-restraint of the protagonists, along with presentations of luxurious lifestyles. The *Endless Love* tetralogy has been noted by avid viewers and analysts alike for its beautiful natural and urban scenery, good looking actors, and the trendy lifestyles that appear in the *mise-en-scene*. The other big hit, *Full House*, is closer to *Meteor Garden* in that squabbles dominate the romantic relationship between the two equally stubborn protagonists: Han Ji-Eun (an economically modest female novelist) and Lee Young Jae (a rich and famous male actor). Despite their differences, the two protagonists are strongly committed to hard work and self-restraint, denying their true feelings towards each other.

Apart from the propagation of the values of hard work, persistence and self-restraint (plus the highly fashionable clothing depicted in these television series), there are limited historical facts that viewers can learn about Korea or Japan from their popular culture.[20] This is not surprising. These cultural products were designed specifically for a wide range of international audiences with various backgrounds and no prior knowledge of the exporting country. What unifies the diverse audiences is a presumed aspiration towards some sort of cosmopolitanism and a strong appetite for upper middle-class consumerism.[21] This seems to contradict my earlier suggestion that the recent spread of intra-regional cultural flows promise to enhance the growth of locally based area studies. What we have not discussed is the fact that the success of these soap operas has actually propelled a long series of learning experiences and a hunger for more knowledge about the countries of origin of those televised dramas. That these are not the countries of Southeast Asia must be appreciated as part of a larger learning process to be outlined below.

The number of Southeast Asian tourists visiting Japan and Korea (and particularly the sites selected for the scenes in the popular series) jumped dramatically. On one occasion, groups of rich youths from Jakarta travelled to Bangkok to attend a concert by singer Jihoon Jung aka Rain (who starred in the drama series *Full House*) when his manager included Bangkok, but not Jakarta, in a concert tour. On occasions the movement has been in the other direction, or to other major metropolitan sites in Southeast Asia. Cross-regional travels and interactions both online and offline takes place among Southeast Asians and beyond via the consumption of Northeast Asian popular culture, with Tokyo, Seoul, Hong Kong or Taipei being the centres of reference. New waves of interest in the formal study of Japanese and Korean in the region have reportedly been directly related to the new obsession with Northeast Asian soap operas. This has been accompanied by the establishment not only of fan groups, but also of more serious social organizations that collaborate with the Japanese or Korean diplomatic offices in the region to hold training courses, exhibitions and festivals promoting products and services from those countries. Information about opportunities for formal study in those countries, and about the limited number of scholarships that are available, is regularly disseminated by these local organizations. The full range and scope of such activities cannot be listed here, as they were continuing to expand when this essay was being prepared.

One can recognize these Northeast Asian popular cultures as an alternative expression of modernity in popular cultures to those produced in the major centres of the entertainment industry in North America. However, from the perspective of many communities in Southeast Asia, something is missing in those cultural products from Northeast Asia and North America alike. As noted earlier, one outstanding difference between these Northeast Asian products and their North American counterparts is the emphasis on pious but resilient feminine beauty in the former, and the prowess of a hypersexualized masculinity in the latter. What sets both of these dominant products apart from both life and its fictional representation in Southeast Asia is the absence of any intense engagement with the ethnic and religious tensions so prevalent in Southeast Asian societies.[22] These issues will be further discussed in the next section.

ALTERNATIVE ASIANIZATION OF POPULAR CULTURE

In contrast to the dominant intra-regional popular culture outlined above, the few alternative samples to be discussed below are products of illiberal Southeast Asian societies with a long history of artistic and cultural didacticism. The imported modern notion of a separation between fact and fiction remains thin and fragile. Normally the contents of these local works are richly endowed with information about and allusions to local or national historical and political events, making it potentially difficult to appeal to international audiences without prior knowledge of the region.[23] To those unfamiliar with them, some of the narratives from this region might appear rather inward-looking and parochial. But as should be self-evident, for the purpose of intra-regional area study, this is not necessarily a bad thing.

As Chua (2004) admits, Singapore is much closer culturally and economically to Northeast Asia than to its neighbours in Southeast Asia. Given Singapore's combination of strong Confucianism, patriarchy, secularism and economic power, it should not be a surprise that some aspects of the formula found in the Northeast Asian drama series identified above resonate well with a recently produced Singapore drama series entitled *The Little Nyonya* (2008). The series narrates the lives of four generations of three Peranakan Chinese families in Malacca and Singapore in the last three quarters of the twentieth century. In this series, Peranakan Chinese are (as described by one of the characters) descendants of Chinese male migrants to the Malay archipelago who married local women and developed a distinct culture, mixing Chinese, Malay and European elements.

In an echo of the thematic features of the Northeast Asian drama series, the female protagonist Yue Niang is unfairly treated as a servant in the home of a rich family. She shows unreserved filial piety to her grandmother, her only living relative. Despite her strong desire to rebel against the injustices around her, more often than not she chooses to conceal her feelings. She also decides not to express or pursue her love for Chen Xi, a rich and liberal-minded gentleman who is already deeply in love with her. Despite Chen Xi's insistence on proposing marriage to her, Yue Niang renounces her true feelings because Chen Xi is already arranged to marry someone whom his grandmother has chosen for him. *The Little Nyonya* has not been as widely shown in the region as have the Korean and Taiwanese titles. However, it was a big hit domestically and has the potential to attract television viewers across Southeast Asia.[24]

More importantly, rather than simply presenting an engaging storyline of industriousness, piety and beauty, *The Little Nyonya* claims to be semi-historical, with a somewhat anthropological tinge. In more than a few scenes, the film displays lengthy and detailed shots of the presumably nearly extinct cultural heritage of the Peranakan Chinese on both sides of the Malayan Peninsula. At several points, scenes in the series seem to forget the main storyline and transform into a documentary film for visitors to a museum, an exhibition, or seminar room. Highly exoticized images of Peranakan cuisine dominate these lengthy scenes, with details of the recipes narrated by the characters. There are also extensive displays of Peranakan art work in porcelain, architecture, clothing, embroidery, certain rituals, and songs. Then an elder character is heard reminding a younger one (and the viewer) what a shame it would be if the younger generation were to disavow this wealth of tradition. Despite this intellectual pretention, some local viewers critically questioned the portrayals of the Peranakan characters speaking in Mandarin, instead of Malay.[25]

This series is one vivid example of a locally based medium that attempts to produce and disseminate purportedly important information about a social group in the region. One can strongly question the accuracy of the historical information presented in this series, but to do so is to miss the point. What concerns us here is the fact that requires further analysis: the circulation of the series has caught the imagination of a huge audience across the region. Marginally added to the main storyline is a sub-plot, superimposed on the main story, about a young couple who meet the protagonist Yue Niang in her old age and eagerly ask her to recollect her life story. The main story then unfolds as a flashback to seventy years before. One of the young couple is Angela, the step granddaughter of the protagonist. Like the other female protagonists discussed above, Angela has a markedly stubborn character, especially in her interactions with the males of her own age. The other party in the couple is Jonathan Li Xiuwen, Angela's schoolmate in Canada, who is interested in Angela. Jonathan is projected as a model for viewers of the series to emulate. Showing great interest in learning about Peranakan culture, Jonathan takes many pictures of Peranakan artefacts and decides to write his thesis on Peranakan culture for his university degree.

Self-orientalism is blatant and unashamed in *The Little Nyonya*.[26] It is a recent manifestation of the long series of enterprises that the Singaporean government and people have been preoccupied with for decades in the nationalist project of building a nation to be reckoned with in the region. What the drama series *The Little Nyonya* does not tell us is that there is more than one homogeneous group of "Peranakan" among the many dispersed Malay-speaking communities in the region. The term "Peranakan" means different things among these groups. This is only a reminder of the potential debates that may ensue if and when such a series is aired more widely across the region.

In many parts of the region, identity politics and in particular politics pertaining to ethnicity and religion, are "dead serious" (Kahn 1998, p. 21), perhaps even more so than the politics of nationality. Few performing artists in the region have been more committed, creatively bolder or more widely respected in challenging the officially sanctioned ethnic division than the late film director Yasmin Ahmad (1958–2009). In her home country Malaysia, ethnic and religious identities are constitutionally demarcated (see Goh, Gagrielpillai, Holden, and Khoo 2009). To trespass these boundaries is risky, and in some cases is against the law. Yasmin's cinematic works — *Sepet* (2004), *Gubra* (2006), *Muallaf* (2008), and *Talentime* (2009) — challenge and subvert any frozen segregations. In her films, the officially sanctioned social identities are made fluid, with inter-ethnic and inter-religious love and commitment appearing not only possible, but indeed highly desirable. All kinds of censures make it difficult for Yasmin's work to be shown publicly in her home country (Khoo 2009; Muhammad 2009). Fortunately, her films occasionally have found venue for limited public screening in Singapore and Jakarta, where ethnic and religious issues are no less sensitive and politically explosive. Despite such occasional showings in neighbouring capital cities, her works have not been accessible to wider audiences in the region for reasons that have more to do with the system of distribution and (related to this) the commercial value (or lack thereof) of such films than with political censorship. As a result, although her works might easily appeal to a wide audience in the region, they have been screened mainly in selected film festivals abroad, making it difficult for them to occupy a central position in the category of popular culture as conceptualized in this study.

The ethnic segregation in many parts of the region undoubtedly has serious bearings upon the extent to which *The Little Nyonya* can be distributed and also the manner in which the series can be appreciated in countries where "ethnic Chinese" does not only signify a minority with substantial economic power but is also stigmatized as second class citizens. For these reasons, one cannot take for granted the great success of *Meteor Garden* in Indonesia or Malaysia (as distinct from the situation in Singapore, Hong Kong, or to some degree Thailand and the Philippines).[27] Based on her fieldwork on audience reception in Indonesia, Pravitta reports that several of her respondents admitted that it took them by surprise that they could have so adored the series protagonist Dao Ming Tze (played by Jerry Yan). They confessed, "one does not usually find a good-looking man in a Mandarin film" (Pravitta 2004, p. 7). This changed rapidly, at least among the small circle of respondents studied by Pravitta:

> one does not usually see "indigenous" Indonesians dating an ethnic Chinese. ... You don't usually hear an "indigenous" girl referring to a Chinese guy in endearing terms. This has all changed. Female students started to look at men of Chinese ethnicity, and coined all sorts of terms such as *cica* (*cina cakep*) [good-looking Chinese], *cihuy* (*cina uhuy*) [cool Chinese].
>
> (Pravitta 2004, pp. 18–19)

Obviously, for various reasons, this finding above is not valid for the whole of Indonesia. In almost the same period Rachma Ida found no positive correlations between the new fandom for oriental-looking, Mandarin-speaking protagonists on television and markedly improved inter-ethnic relations in the city of Surabaya where she conducted similar research (Ida 2008, pp. 106–7).

Except for the spillover of broadcasts from one country captured on the peripheries of neighbouring countries by satellite disks, and a few exceptions within mainstream broadcasting,[28] technical, administrative and commercial structures mean that it is easier to distribute local popular music than it is for local films and television series across national boundaries, and ethnic and religious divisions. This has clearly been the case with recordings by some of the top popular singers travelling from Indonesia to Malaysia, Singapore and East Timor (Heryanto 2008*b*, pp. 1–3; Khalik 2007; Sloman 2009). Similarly, the Filipino crooner Christian Bautista has found a huge number of fans in Indonesia and Thailand. These intra-regional cultural flows in Southeast Asia may expand further in size or kind, and it is not impossible that their future development may have long lasting impact. But for now, two alternative popular cultures deserve more attention than they have currently received. The first are works with a strongly Islamic content. The other is the range of popular cultural forms (music, films, drama series, and dance) which are heavily indebted to Indian popular cultures, especially to so-called Bollywood. It is unfortunate that owing to some political circumstances, these two streams of culture have been pitted against each other.[29]

A decade before the spread of East Asian popular culture, Indonesia and Malaysia witnessed the dawn of a new cultural politics of Islam involving the "gentrification" and commodification of Islamic lifestyles (Heryanto 1999). However, unlike the popular cultures from Northeast Asia that rose rapidly to prominence, the growth of Islamic popular cultures has been taking place in a slower and more timid manner. Their popularity is more restricted to Muslim-majority countries. Conservative Muslim leaders have been divided about the merits of popular culture as a mode of mass communication to convey religious messages, or as a source of entertainment for the religion's followers. Things changed for the better when the pious Jakarta-based Muslim Rhoma Irama transformed dangdut music in the late 1970s, and made himself the first important popular star with an explicitly Islamic identity (Frederick 1982; Lockhard 1998, pp. 94–105). Since then he has enjoyed the title of "King of Dangdut". One of the more recent eventful moments in the history of Islamic popular culture in the region took place in 2008 with record-breaking ticket sales for the Indonesian film *Ayat-ayat Cinta* (Verses of Love), surpassing the box office figures for any title of any genre in the country, including Hollywood blockbusters.[30] This was one of the very first Indonesian films to feature a female protagonist who is nearly fully veiled.

What is surprising about *Ayat-ayat Cinta* is not so much its enormous commercial success as why it took so long for the world's largest Muslim nation to produce a film like this at all. Prior to the release of *Ayat-ayat Cinta*, veiled women were nearly totally absent from the cinema screen in Indonesia, and were rarely seen on film posters in Malaysia. In any case, the release of *Ayat-ayat Cinta* and multiple copycat films took place in the wider context of "Islamization" in state politics and middle-class lifestyles from the 1980s. Like the new rich elsewhere, many newly wealthy Muslims in Indonesia, Singapore and Malaysia discovered a new preoccupation with the aesthetics of their newly established power, the display of wealth, and exuberant consumerist practices. Another conspicuous expression of the persona of the new trendy Muslim is noticeable in the rapidly growing fashion industry for Muslim women.

In the first few weeks after its release *Ayat-ayat Cinta* is being widely referred to as one of the most Islamic films ever made in Indonesia. The story is set in Egypt and revolves around Indonesian Muslim postgraduate students studying Islam. It focuses on a love story framed within moral propagation of what is and is not proper according to Islam. As the years pass, the film remains in the popular memory as a milestone in the history of Islamic popular culture. However, not all Muslims agree with this evaluation. In some circles, Muslim intellectuals have denounced the film as too liberal and un-Islamic in its portrayal of the romantic relations between the young protagonists. The behaviour of the leading actors off-screen was also criticized (Yumiyanti 2008). The editors of one Islamist journal accused *Ayat-ayat Cinta* as propagating pluralism, something they condemned, and alleged that the novelist and film-makers were "agents of Zionism" (*Risalah Mujahidin* 2008).

In my own assessment, *Ayat-ayat Cinta*'s popularity is attributable to its being both more and less than Islamic. It is hybrid, and perhaps cosmopolitan, in substance and in style. Despite its generous display of Islamic markers, in significant sections the film is redolent of Hollywood and Bollywood movies as well as Indonesian television dramas (*sinetron*). In contrast to the female characters in veils, the male protagonist Fahri wears Western-style casual clothes and a trendy haircut. He does not grow a beard. At his wedding ceremony Fahri wears a Western suit and tie. The scenes of the wedding itself are highly reminiscent of those in Bollywood movies. This kind of hybridity is characteristic also of the film's Northeast Asian-style counterparts and also runs through the popular songs, films and drama series already discussed.

I have made several references here to Bollywood films and to the immensely popular musical genre of dangdut which owes its sounds and beat to Bollywood music. Despite the long history and widespread of the consumption of popular culture from South Asia, this subject has received very little attention from the small but growing number of scholars studying culture in the region, popular or otherwise (for more see David 2008). Dangdut is a generic term referring to a uniquely Malay/Indonesian music style that mixes elements from Arabic, Indian and Malay traditions. Mainly sung and enjoyed among the urban poor, dangdut was strongly associated with "bad taste" and the preferences of the lower classes until the 1970s when Rhoma Irama turned it into a respectable music genre. Even after Rhoma successfully elevated the status of dangdut (thanks in part to the

Western musical instruments he used and the rock music he blended into his compositions), dangdut and Bollywood popular cultures more generally have not enjoyed the same level of public prestige as their counterparts from North America and Northeast Asia.[31]

The reasons for this unequal status are complex. However, for our present purposes, suffice it to note one small but important factor. Dangdut has spawned multiple sub-genres among diverse groups of people, ranging from the Islamic proselytizing type of sentimental popular to genitally-focused (Pioquinto 1995) dance music performances. In many parts of Java, indigenous mysticism is happily married to Hinduism blended with Islam that came from India (and not the Middle East). On this most industrialized island in Indonesia, the more erotic type of dangdut performance has prevailed, especially among the lower classes. In 2003 the then little-known Inul Daratista stirred up a nationwide controversy with her dangdut sensual singing and dancing. Professing to be a Muslim herself, Inul represents a new cultural icon, a non-aristocratic Javanese practice that celebrates bodily pleasure and sexuality with a nominal Islamic slant. To her critics, Inul epitomizes the moral corruption and decadence of the global Western-styled modernity that Indonesia has wrongly adopted. In an ironic twist, however, no less a figure than Rhoma Irama, the King of Dangdut himself, made a public attack on Inul and her rise to fame with a call for a boycott and a moralistic condemnation of what she represented. With edicts from local Muslim leaders and local government endorsement, Inul was banned from performing in several provinces in Indonesia, as well as in Malaysia.

The saga of dangdut may at first seem unrelated to the discussion in the previous sections. What is common to all the cultural forms discussed here is the prevailing consolidation of the new middle classes as a national bourgeoisie. The emergence and popular reception of contemporary popular cultures from Northeast Asia signals a strengthening of the moral position or legitimacy of the tastes and aspirations of the new middle classes across the region. The nostalgic quest for re-examination of past history and injustices, along with the implicit appeal for new legitimacy for an ethnic minority with significant capital as illustrated by *The Little Nyonya*, is an expression of the same ideology.

Although it is the world's largest Muslim nation, Indonesia for too long assigned to Muslims a status akin to that of a minority, and the majority of Muslims appeared to have adopted this "minority mentality" (Wertheim, cited in Vatikiotis 1998, p. 120). Until the 1980s Islam was widely associated with poverty, backwardness, and the countryside (Mahasin 1990). The commercial success of *Ayat-ayat Cinta* is one of a number of more recent affirmations for a series of events that have reversed that long history of condescension, signified by the newly acquired political status, new wealth, and preoccupation with the aesthetics of everyday life in ways not very different from those that appear in the drama series from Northeast Asia. There is a region-wide desire to consume the best from both East and West, without being either an Asian or a Westerner as stereotyped on and off screen. Like dangdut, Bollywood movies and music, were not taken seriously or accorded any respect by the middle classes in Malaysia, Singapore or Indonesia until the late 1990s when Bollywood movies began to be "gentrified" and to focus on romantic dramas (instead of masculine action and suspense as in the previous decades) with beautiful scenery, songs, and good-looking actors and actresses (David 2008, p. 180). Although there seems to be a common pursuit of upward class mobility as outlined above, it is clear that not all are equal among these different strands of cultural flows and styles. How these new social, cultural, and technological changes offer prospects and pose challenges to a locally based area studies in the region will be the focus of the concluding section below.

TOWARDS A POSSIBLE FUTURE

Recent changes in new media technology that injected new strength into media and cultural studies have, to an unprecedented extent, opened up new space for home-grown agency in the production of knowledge. Potentially, this also opens a new space for intellectual innovation for a locally based area studies. Under the ideal circumstances these developments (the new networks, the new media, and the growing interests in cultural and media studies) could have converged and sparked serious investigations of subject positions: what does it mean to be a "Southeast Asian" in the 2000s, studying "Southeast Asia" and employing analytical tools largely invented and acquired from outside the region? Unfortunately, to date such exploration has not gone very far. Cultural studies, media studies, and the labels of some of the approaches in those studies (post-structuralism, semiotics, post-modernism) have been received with mixed reactions. More than a few in area studies as well as those in the traditional academic disciplines have resisted, dismissed or avoided these new approaches and perspectives, some apparently out of suspicion, prejudice or unfamiliarity.[32]

Meanwhile, outside the formal academic confines of area studies, the turn of the new millennium has witnessed the promising networks with more or less the same spirit or similar goals. I do not have the knowledge or the space to offer a complete list. Within the limited areas of media and cultural studies alone, mention must be made of the extremely successful endeavour of the *Inter-Asia Cultural Studies* project led by Chua Beng Huat (Singapore) and Chen Kuan Hsing (Taiwan). The project brings together scholars, artists and activists in Asia and the Pacific for a range of activities, of which publishing the well-respected journal under the same name and organizing periodic conferences have been the most notable. More specifically focused on Southeast Asia is the commendable work of a smaller but no less active group under the name of the Association of Southeast Asian Cinemas, initiated by Khoo Gaik Cheng and her friends. Related to this is the Southeast Asia-Pacific Audiovisual Archive Association (SEAPAVAA), established in 1996. Yogyakarta has been hosting the Jogja-Netpac Asian Film Festival each year. In late 2009 the Jakarta-based NGO Rumah Film launched the first Islam-themed Film Festival in the region.

Notwithstanding all this, as discussed in earlier sections, even when all these media and cultural innovations are added together, their presence and impact on the growth of a locally-based area studies remains insignificant. The commercially driven waves of Japanese, Korean, Bollywood, and Islamic popular cultures have had far more impact on the development of a stronger sense of regional identity and integration. True, the commercially driven diffusion of popular culture is unlikely to become a site or mechanism for a new, locally based area studies in the region. The entertainment industry has neither the interest nor capacity to sponsor a sustained production of academic knowledge and activities as widely expected by the scholarly communities.

The future of an institutionalized network of locally based area studies remains unclear. If such studies do grow further, one should not expect them to come with the same name, geographical reference, focus, approach and character as the Southeast Asian Studies of the Cold War years. If a viable, locally based area studies is to grow and flourish, I imagine that it will not be able to ignore, resist, or dismiss contemporary developments in the new media as well as the entertainment and popular culture industry and the various non- as well as trans-disciplinary approaches. As the sights and sounds of omnipresent militarism gradually fade from the public space in Southeast Asia, those of intra-regional popular culture move in. Serious study of these new ubiquitous sounds and sights is no longer simply rewarding, but has become mandatory for any viable area study in this millennium.

A series of shifts will likely take place in such studies, in response to the region's changing character and social relations within it. These changes will include a reduction in emphasis on the nation-state as a unit of analysis, and correspondingly more emphasis on transnational, sub-national, cross-regional, social groups based on gender, age, profession, class, religious or ethnic affiliations. An important shift can also be anticipated in focus, from the study of formal political and economic institutions as well as the elite to examining the fast-growing, confusingly fluid, and highly mobile networks of social groups with hybrid, multiple and fragmented identities.

A soft narrative with a more nuanced textual or ethnographic approach will probably gain more currency at the expense of statistics, diagrams, and models. Increased attention will also likely be paid to the dialectics between subject positions and practice, in preference to the old emphasis on values, belief systems, or social structures. More than ever before, a high level or sophisticated mastery of at least one of the languages in the region and an understanding of the intricacies of the information technology will be pre-requisites in area studies. Under such circumstances locally based intellectuals, as native speakers, will find themselves in a more advantaged position than ever before in a new area studies that will be strongly interested in listening to the voices of fellow Asians as speaking subjects, instead of regarding them as mere objects for analysis in the manner that charac-terized area studies in the previous century. If any of the above scenarios makes sense, the increased cross-regional production and consumption of popular cultural products can be expected to constitute a major area of interest that did not exist in the previous periods of area studies.

This chapter has examined the potential contribution of the recent growth of inter-regional popular cultural products to the development of a new generation and to the potential development of locally-based regional studies that will succeed Southeast Asian Studies from the Cold War. By no means does this study suggest that contemporary popular cultural products are necessarily "neutral" or "good" in themselves or for the broader educational projects within the region or outside it. Obviously commercial interests dictate most of the production and dissemination of these cultural products, occasionally at the expense of historical facts, and aesthetic and moral values that are highly respected in academic settings. As hinted in most of the foregoing sections, a great number of the major entertainment products — including those that purport to preach moral or religious values — deserve critical assessment. These products are aimed to entertain the widest possible consumers for the greatest possible profit, and not to educate the public or challenge those in power. To achieve their aims, those behind the production of popular cultures often rely on the already dominant but problematic assumptions and prejudices and values (including various forms of racism, essentialism, sexism), often with the unintended consequence of reproducing and aestheticizing the status quo or promoting a new set of values of the wealthy urban middle classes. Thus, we have witnessed the dominance of sentimental melodramas that appeal to the bourgeois class across Asia over the "superstitious" horror or "macho" action-oriented narratives much enjoyed by the lower classes. Likewise, we have noted the dominant position of cultural products from the stronger capitalist networks in Northeast Asia and Singapore over those from the economically and politically less stable nations in the region. All these political and ethical issues are very important, and should be taken more seriously outside this present study. Admittedly being somewhat one-sided, this preliminary study focuses on the potential contribution of these popular cultural products to the making of a greater sense of regionalism or Asianness in the global world among millions of Southeast Asians from a wide spectrum of backgrounds. In turn, a stronger sense of regional identity promises to be one necessary, if not sufficient, condition for the possible and resilient growth of a locally-based area studies.

Notes

The author gratefully acknowledges the benefits of various critical comments on an earlier version of this paper from those who do not necessarily agree with many points presented here. They are alphabetically Bart Barendregt, Rommel Curaming, Barbara Hatley, Virginia Hooker, Joel Kahn, Hong Lysa, Sumit Mandal, Nissim Otmazgin, Adrian Vickers and Thongchai Winichakul, plus three anonymous reviewers and participants of a seminar at the Center for Southeast Asian Studies, Kyoto University, where the author was a Visiting Research Fellow. Persistent shortcomings in this chapter remain solely the author's. The study is part of a larger project with the generous assistance from the Australian Research Council Discovery Project and Australian National University as the hosting institution.

[1]   Interestingly, in what appear to be separate events, in Japan (Otmazgin 2008), Korea (Shim 2006), and certain countries of Southeast Asia (Heryanto 2008b), economic crises immediately preceded a series of events that led to a new vibrancy in popular cultural production.

[2]   I enjoyed the privilege of being involved in some of the first of these networks during their initial years, and I gratefully acknowledge the many insights I gained from participating in their activities.

[3]   Lockhard (1998), one of the earliest published books on popular cultures in Southeast Asia, and reviewers of this book (Lent 2000; Moro 2000) lament the general lack of recognition of the merits of studying popular cultures among scholars with an interest in the region or in any single country therein. When the Hong Kong Institute of Education organized an International Conference

on Popular Culture and Education in Asia on 11–13 December 2008, the organizer claimed that the event was the first of its kind.

4   During the nationalist movement for independence in the first half of the past century, it was common for "high cultured" men of letters (journalists and literary writers) to take a leading political role, before taking a top official position within the government of their newly independent nations. This trend disappeared when militarism swept across the region during the Cold War. Of late we see film actors and television entertainers entering state politics in the region (see Heryanto 2008*b*, 2010*a*, 2010*b*) in competition with the business people.

5   In more or less the same period, telenovellas from Latin America were highly popular, especially in the Philippines but also the neighbouring countries in Southeast Asia. As we currently focus on the intra-Asian popular culture flows from the turn of the century, many of the equally popular cultural products from other geographical areas (including Latin America) will not be included in our discussion.

6   This is one area that reminds us of the limited and unstable boundary that defines what is or is not "Southeast Asian", thus the need to use the term with some flexibility and caution.

7   Even as late as 1998 the publication of Craig Lockhard's *Dance of Life; Popular Music and Politics in Southeast Asia* was promoted in the book blurb as "a singularly original piece of scholarship, unmatched in both breadth and detail". Barely a year later, it appeared to have become history because it missed the next, and bigger developments of popular culture in Southeast Asia and beyond. The later developments were bigger not only in the sense that each of the countries he studied has produced works with multiple scales of commercial success and popularity. More importantly, as highlighted in this study, there was a remarkable increase in the scope and intensity of exchange as well as collaborative production and consumption of popular culture across the region and beyond.

8   As discursive signifiers, "East", "Asia/ns" and "West/ern/ers" in this study do not refer to some materially or physically objective entities, locations, persons, or qualities. Rather they have acquired multiple and competing meanings in our collective imaginations and speech through identifiable and analysable social histories.

9   In Singapore (where I lived when the 1997 crisis hit) and to a lesser degree in neighbouring Malaysia, more than a few local observers argued that these two countries had survived the crisis precisely because they had been more vigorously faithful than their neighbours to "Asian Values". For more recent comments on the issue, see Chua (2010).

10 The West's supremacy in the production and circulation of global popular culture remained intact even after the ascendancy of the Northeast Asian counterparts. Iwabuchi (2002*b*, p. 459) argues that some of the best examples of Japan's newly acquired global power in popular culture were restricted in Asia and not

in the West. Even in the case of selected Japanese cultural products that appear to be strongly popular in the West, their success was heavily indebted to the assistance of the industrial networks of selected major American companies. Shin (2009) describes in detail the series of ambitious attempts by popular singer Rain and his manager Jinyoung Park to make inroads into the U.S. market, but to no avail.

11   One caution is due with regard to such crude comparison. Television programmes often help popularise films, comics or music, but usually not the other way round.

12   In countries like Indonesia, access to movie theatres has recently become rather rare and difficult for those living outside major cities. The total number of movie theatres has shrunk dramatically. The few new ones are concentrated as cinemaplexes in up market shopping malls in a small number of capital cities. The majority of old movie theatres in many parts of the country have been abandoned by their owners, due to the rising costs of maintaining the business in the face of the expansion of private television networks, political liberalization, and the wide accessibility of DVD players and computers as well as the uncontrollable pirated DVD market.

13   Korean films have plenty of graphic violence scenes, perhaps even more than Hollywood titles do. This has not been the case with the Korean televised drama series that have been aired in the region and gained high ratings. Bollywood films that have circulated in the region have also exhibited a notable gentrification, with more romantic melodramas and fewer violence-focused action films (for details, see David 2008). In Southeast Asian countries where religion is a part of high-level politics, local horror films and television series have been frowned upon and discouraged by religious authorities as inappropriate. For some middle-class literati, horror stories signify backwardness and an antithesis to modernity. In Indonesia, horror stories find more freedom in the form of film and television programmes called "reality shows" (see van Heeren 2007). Local comedies often rely on crude references to sex and slapstick comedy, neither of which appeals to the middle-class audience that constitute the majority of the movie-goers in shopping malls. Instead of appearing fully as a genre, comedy often finds space as sub-plots or selected scenes in some of the successful romance stories of the melodrama genre.

14   See Siriyuvasak and Shin (2007, p. 124) for their comments on the case of the Korean Wave that created "male idols for young female consumption". For Indonesia see Ida (2008); Merdikaningtyas (2006); Pravitta (2004); and Setijadi (2005). For Taiwan, see Yang (2008).

15   The opposite is true in the majority of hyper-sentimental and caricature-style soap operas in several other countries in the region.

16   Surely, Hollywood movies do not represent American cinema, let alone "Western" narrative traditions. By no means is the following comment intended to recuperate the "East versus West" dichotomy.

17   Without resorting to overgeneralizing the heterogeneous region, examples of such speech conventions can be easily found in Thailand and Java as well as Bali. In all these places, Sultans and Kings still command significant reverence among ordinary people. To a significant degree such speech conventions can also be seen in Japan. To cite one example from a famous text in Japan: "in a love-story animation, *Kimagure Orenjirōdo*, the hero and heroine never confess their love for each other" (Iwabuchi 2002*b*, p. 455).

18   Anecdotal evidence suggests that part of the attractiveness of these recent drama series from Korea and Japan is their depiction of a somewhat distant, but desirable, quality of life: the combination of the industriousness and resilience of the protagonists with the exuberant lifestyle depictions in many scenes (fashion clothing, fine dining, boutique home interiors, and so on) that tantalize the viewers' imagination. For examples of critical discussion of the cultural proximity debate see Setijadi (2005); Iwabuchi (2002*a*, pp. 130–34); Otmazgin (2007).

19   The genealogy of *Meteor Garden* (*Liúxīng Huāyuán*) is interesting, and it deserves a separate comparative discussion. This 2001 Taiwan series was based on award-winning Japanese manga stories *Hana Yori Dango* (1992) authored by Yoko Kamio. *Meteor Garden* has been the most commercially successful series in Indonesia to date, and probably in the neighbouring countries in Southeast Asia too. (In other countries the Korean drama *Winter Sonata* was reportedly more popular.) Only after it had become evident that *Meteor Garden* generated a great deal of revenue was a sequel (*Meteor Garden II*) made in 2003. A Japanese version of the television series was then produced in 2005. Though neither of the two was a flop, neither was able to repeat the popularity or commercial success of the first series of *Meteor Garden*. Despite this, and inspired by other success stories of Korean hits, a Korean version of the series was produced in 2009 under the title *Kkotboda namja*, better known in English as *Boys Over Flowers*.

20   Some of the more semi-historical television series and films are exceptions. But even in the latter cases, what one can learn from these popular cultures about history is never presented in any straightforward way as the case of *The Little Nyonya* illustrates below. Historical accuracy or education is not necessarily essential in the historical genre stories when they are designed, manufactured and sold primarily for mass entertainment with the aim of maximum profit-making.

21   For discussion on the "odourless" (*mukokuseki*) or "faceless" nature of widely popular Japanese popular culture products see Iwabuchi (2002*b*, pp. 455–56) and Otmazgin (2007).

22   Secularity is common in Hollywood stories as well as Korean and Japanese stories, regardless of how strongly religious a significant number of the population in Northeast Asia and the U.S. may be.

23   Elsewhere, Chua (2004, p. 209) mentions a similar feature which he believes to have impeded the possibility for Chinese popular culture to reach the

scale of popularity achieved by its Korean, Taiwanese or Japanese counter-parts. We should note that Anderson (2002, p. 24) identifies similar reasons for the limited circulation of European films in comparison with North American ones.

24 As I prepared this essay, the series had been aired in Malaysia, Cambodia, The Philippines, Myanmar and Thailand. One local journalist reported that when aired in Singapore at one point it "chalked up a viewership rating of 26.3 per cent … beating the 22.5 per cent rating for the closing ceremony of the Beijing Olympics. … The 34-episode show is the most-watched Chinese drama serial in the past eight years" (Lee 2008).

25 Such criticism can be found in the "official" Facebook group pages of the drama series [Shu Qi, 21 February 2010, <http://www.facebook.com/#!/pages/The-Little-Nyonya/22268538302> (accessed 12 October 2010)]. I received a similar remark from another colleague in Singapore via private communication.

26 A Singaporean friend confessed privately to me that what she dislikes most about the television series is its "Singaporean Airlines" qualities, instead of the Peranakan Singaporeans as she knows them. While fully agreeing with such an apt observation, I am tempted to add that for the purpose of cross-regional cultural flows and interaction, the series serves a function not very different from the famous airlines company.

27 For discussion on the problematic representations of the Chinese Indonesians on and off the screen, see Sen (2006) and Heryanto (2008a, 2010b).

28 In 2009 a televised cartoon from Malaysia (*Upin & Ipin*) was aired on the Televisi Pendidikan Indonesia network and was a big success, The same was true of the animation from Singapore *Sing To Dawn* (2008), localized in Indonesia as *Meraih Mimpi* (2009) and screened across the Cinema 21 network, the largest distributor in the country.

29 I have discussed this issue more extensively elsewhere (Heryanto 2008b, 2010b), and limitations of space force me to do injustice to the subject matter by presenting no more than a few brief paragraphs below.

30 The most commercially successful foreign blockbusters reach around one million ticket sales. Since 2001 three Indonesian films sold more than 2 million tickets: *Ada Apa Dengan Cinta?* (2.5 million), *Get Married* (2.2 million), *Naga Bonar Jadi 2* (2.4 million). In the first month after its release *Ayat-ayat Cinta* sold more than three million tickets (Sasono 2008), and in the third month, the figure rose to 3.65 million (*Jakarta Post* 2008).

31 Interestingly, those behind the production and global distribution of Bollywood-styled films seem to prefer to direct their promotional work in North America and Western Europe than Southeast Asia. I thank Sumit Mandal for bringing my attention to this point.

32 For contesting views on this subject, see Reynolds (1995, 1998); McVey (1998); Reid (1999); Clammer (2000); Heryanto (2002), Jackson (2003); Burgess (2004); Curaming (2006).

References

Anderson, Perry. "Force and Consent". *New Left Review* 17 (2002): 5–30.

"'Ayat-Ayat Cinta' Celebrates Success". *Jakarta Post*, 14 May 2008.

Burgess, C. "The Asian Studies 'Crisis': Putting Cultural Studies into Asian Studies and Asia into Cultural Studies". *International Journal of Asian Studies* 1, no. 1 (2004): 121–36.

Chua Beng Huat. "Conceptualizing an East Asian Popular Culture". *Inter-Asia Cultural Studies* 5, no. 2 (2004): 200–21.

———. "Disrupting Hegemonic Liberalism in East Asia". *Boundary* 37, no. 2 (2010): 199–216.

Chun, Wendy Hui Kyong and Thomas Keenan. *New Media, Old Media*. New York and London: Routledge, 2006 .

Clammer, J. "Cultural Studies/Asian Studies". *SEA Journal of Social Science* 28, no. 1 (2000): 47–65.

Curaming, Rommel. "Towards a Poststructuralist Southeast Asian Studies?". *Sojourn* 21, no. 1 (2006): 90–112.

David, Bettina. "Intimate Neighbors: Bollywood, Dangdut music, and Glolbalizing Modernities in Indonesia". In *Global Bollywood; Travels of Hindi Song and Dance*, edited by Sangita Gopal and Sujata Moorti. Minneapolis and London: University of Minneapolis Press, 2008.

Emmerson, Donald K. "'Southeast Asia': What's in a Name?". *Journal of Southeast Asian Studies* 15, no. 1 (1984): 1–21.

Frederick, William. "Rhoma Irama and the Dangdut Style". *Indonesia* 34 (1982): 103–30.

Goh, Daniel P.S., Matilda Gagrielpillai, Philip Holden, and Gaik Cheng Khoo. *Race and Multiculturalism in Malaysia in Singapore*. London: Routledge, 2009.

Heryanto, Ariel. "The Years of Living Luxuriously". In *Culture and Privilege in Capitalist Asia*, edited by M. Pinches. London and New York: Routledge, 1999.

———. "Can There be Southeast Asians in Southeast Asian Studies?". *Moussons* 5 (2002): 3–30.

———. "Public Intellectuals, Media and Democratization". In *Challenging Authoritarianism in Southeast Asia: Comparing Indonesia and Malaysia*, edited by A. Heryanto and S.K. Mandal. London: RoutledgeCurzon, 2003.

———. "Citizenship and Indonesian Ethnic Chinese in Post-1998 Films". In *Popular Culture in Indonesia: Fluid Identities in Post-Authoritarian Politics,* edited by A. Heryanto. London & New York: Routledge, 2008*a*.

———. "Pop Culture and Competing Identities". In *Popular Culture in Indonesia: Fluid Identities in Post-Authoritarian Politics*, edited by A. Heryanto. London & New York: Routledge, 2008*b*.

———. "Entertainment, Domestication, and Dispersal: Street Politics as Popular Culture". In *Problems of Democratisation in Indonesia: Elections, Institutions and Society*, edited by E. Aspinnal and M. Mietzner. Singapore: Institute of Southeast Asian Studies, 2010*a*.

————. "The Look of Love: New Engagements with the Oriental in Indonesian Popular Culture". In *Pop Culture Formations Across East Asia*, edited by D. Shim, A. Heryanto, and U. Siriyuvasak. Seoul: Jimoondang, 2010*b*.

————. "Upgraded Piety and Pleasure: The New Middle Class and Islam in Indonesian Popular Culture". In *Islam and Popular Culture in Indonesia and Malaysia*, edited by A. Weintraub. London & New York: Routledge, 2011.

Ida, Rachmah. "Consuming Taiwanese Boys Culture". In *Popular Culture in Indonesia: Fluid Identities in Post-Authoritarian Politics*, edited by A. Heryanto. London & New York: Routledge, 2008.

Iwabuchi, Koichi. *Recentering Globalization: Popular Culture and Japanese Transnationalism*. Durham and London: Duke University Press, 2002*a*.

————. "'Soft' Nationalism and Narcissism: Japanese Popular Culture Goes Global". *Asian Studies Review* 26, no. 4 (2002*b*): 447–69.

Jackson, P. "The Dual Crises of Asian Area Studies and Cultural Studies". *Sojourn* 18, no. 1 (2003): 1–41.

Kahn, Joel. "Southeast Asian Identities". In *Southeast Asian Identities; Culture and the Politics of Representation in Indonesia, Malaysia, Singapore, and Thailand*, edited by J. Kahn. Singapore: Institute of Southeast Asian Studies, 1998.

Khalik, Abdul. "Timor Leste: An Outpost of RI culture?". *Jakarta Post*, 10 May 2007.

Khoo Gaik Cheng. "Reading the Films of Independent Filmmaker Yasmin Ahmad". In *Race and Multiculturalism in Malaysia in Singapore*, edited by Goh, Gagrielpillai, Holden and Khoo. London: Routledge, 2009.

Lee, Jocelyn. "Little Nyonya, Big Ratings". *Straits Times*, 24 December 2008.

Lent, John. "Review of *Dance of Life: Popular Music and Politics in Southeast Asia*, by C. Lockhard". *Pacific Affairs* 73, no. 1 (2000): 140–41.

Lister, Martin, John Dovey, Seth Giddings, Iain Grant, and Kieran Kelly. *New Media: A Critical Introduction*. London: Routledge, 2003.

Lockhard, Craig. *Dance of Life: Popular Music and Politics in Southeast Asia*. Honolulu: University of Hawaii Press, 1998.

Mahasin, Aswab. "The Santri Middle Class: An Insider's View". In *The Politics of Middle Class Indonesia*, edited by R. Tanter and K. Young. Clayton: Centre of Southeast Asian Studies, Monash University, 1990.

McQuail, Denis. *Mass Communication Theory: An Introduction*. London: Sage, 1994.

McVey, Ruth. "Change and Continuity in Southeast Asian Studies". *Journal of Southeast Asian Studies* 26, no. 1 (1995): 1–9.

————. "Globalization, Marginalization, and the Study of Southeast Asia". In *Southeast Asian Studies: Reorientations*, edited by Craig J. Reynolds and Ruth McVey. Ithaca, NY: Cornell Southeast Asia Program, 1998.

Merdikaningtyas, Yuli Andari. "Demam K-Drama dan Cerita Fans di Yogyakarta". *Clea*, no. 9 (December 2006): 41–60.

Moro, Pamela. "Review of *Dance of Life; Popular Music and Politics in Southeast Asia*, by C. Lockhard". *Indonesia* 70 (October 2000): 165–66.

Muhammad, Amir. *Yasmin Ahmad's Films*. Petaling Jaya: Matahari Books, 2009.

Otmazgin, Nissim K. "Contesting Soft Power: Japanese Popular Culture in East and Southeast Asia". *International Relations of the Asia-Pacific* 8, no. 1 (2008): 73–101.

———. "Japanese Popular Culture in East and Southeast Asia: Time for a Regional Paradigm?". *Kyoto Review of Southeast Asia* 8/9 (March/October 2007).

Pioquinto, Ceres. "Dangdut at Sekaten: Female Representations in Live Performance". *RIMA* 29 (Winter and Summer 1995): 59–89.

Pravitta, Gabrielle Medda Maya. "Menonton Perempuan Penonton Meteor Garden". *Clea*, no. 6 (December–January 2004): 1–29.

Rafael, Vicente. "The Cultures of Area Studies in the United States". *Social Text* 41 (Winter 1994): 91–111.

Reid, Anthony. "Studying 'Asia' in Asia". *Asian Studies Review* 23, no. 2 (1999): 141–51.

Reynolds, Craig. "A New Look at Old Southeast Asia". *The Journal of Asian Studies* 54, no. 2 (1995): 419–46.

———. "Self-Cultivation and Self-Determination in Postcolonial Southeast Asia". *Southeast Asian Studies: Reorientations*, edited by Craig J. Reynolds and Ruth McVey. Ithaca, NY: Cornell Southeast Asia Program, 1998.

Risalah Mujahidin. "Misi Pluralisme Di Balik Novel Ayat-ayat Cinta". 17 February–March 2008.

Sasono, Eric. "Fenomena Ayat-ayat Cinta". *Koran Tempo*, 28 March 2008.

Sen. "'Chinese' Indonesians in National Cinema". *Inter-Asia Cultural Studies* 7, no. 1 (2006): 171–84.

Setijadi, Charlotte. "Questioning Proximity: East Asian TV Dramas in Indonesia". *Media Asia* 32, no. 4 (2005): 197–202.

Shim Doobo. "Hybridity and the Rise of Korean Popular Culture in Asia". *Media, Culture & Society* 28, no. 1 (2006): 25–44.

Shim Doobo, Ariel Heryanto, and Ubonrat Siriyuvasak, eds. *Pop Culture Formations across East Asia*. Seoul: Jimoondang, 2010.

Shin Hyunjoon. "Have You Ever Seen the Rain? And Who'll Stop the Rain? The Globalizing Project of Korean Pop (K-pop)". *Inter-Asia Cultural Studies* 10, no. 4 (2009): 507–23.

Siriyuvasak, Ubonrat and Shin Hyunjoon. "Asianizing K-pop: Production, Consumption and Identification Patterns among Thai Youth". *Inter-Asia Cultural Studies* 8, no. 1 (2007): 109–36.

Sloman, Annie. "A Hybrid Popular Culture". *Inside Indonesia* 96 (April–June 2009).

van Heeren, Katinka. "Return of the Kyai: Representations of Horror, Commerce, and Censorship in Post-Suharto Indonesian Film and Television". *Inter-Asia Cultural Studies* 8, no. 2 (2007): 211–26.

Vatikiotis, Michael R.J. *Indonesian Politics under Suharto: The Rise and Fall of the New Order*. London: Routledge, 1998.

Yang, Fang-chih Irene. "Engaging with Korean Dramas: Discourses of Gender, Media, and Class Formation in Taiwan". *Asian Journal of Communication* 18, no. 1 (2008): 64–79.

Yumiyanti, Iin. "Kontroversi Dongeng Cinta Fahri". *detikNews*, 18 March 2008.

PART III
EUROPE

8

BRITISH PERSPECTIVES ON SOUTHEAST ASIA AND CONTINENTAL EUROPEAN COMPARISONS
The Making of a Region

Victor T. King

Although the contexts and institutional formats of area studies are in the process of being reconfigured, area studies remains crucial. The study of Southeast Asia is part of a broader issue. Its very existence should neither be hampered by profit-making nor political considerations. Its motivation lies in the central tenet of the pursuit and propagation of knowledge.

(Chou and Houben 2006a, p. 19)

INTRODUCTION

In this chapter I shall identify the origins of the making of Southeast Asia and Southeast Asian Studies in the United Kingdom* (with some comparative references to continental European activities) and attempt to establish those factors which encouraged the development of this enterprise and those which stood in its way. In this regard it is important to indicate the main moments, events and persons in this process of construction and provide some evaluation of the contribution which British scholarship has made to this field of studies. A most significant and preliminary observation is that not only is it problematical to define Southeast Asia but it is equally problematical to define precisely what constitutes British scholarship on Southeast Asia in that it was not confined to the shores of the United Kingdom. Of course, scholarship is seldom restricted by national boundaries, but in the particular case of British academic engagement with Southeast Asia we have to take into account the contribution which was made by expatriate researchers and teachers in centres of higher education in the colonies and dependencies. Prior to the 1940s Britain was not entirely dependent on the development of expertise on the Southeast Asian region in the home country. An important training ground for British academics and scholar-administrators was the University of Rangoon and Raffles College in Singapore (Selth 2010; and see Cowan 1980). Following the Pacific War an interesting shift in the locus of scholarship also took place. The British no longer had a base in Burma and the University of Rangoon after 1948, but they continued to have a presence in Singapore and Malaya and also Hong Kong during the 1950s and 1960s when we witnessed the making and consolidation of Southeast Asia as an internationally defined region for scholarly enquiry. Expatriate academics were appointed to the University of Malaya, which was established in Singapore in October 1949 from the merger of Raffles College and the King Edward VII College of Medicine, and then expanded to its Kuala Lumpur campus in 1959. We should also note the important contribution which expatriate scholars at the University of Hong Kong, formally established in 1911, made to the study of Southeast Asia.

It would be foolish to claim a greater role for the United Kingdom in making Southeast Asia than it deserves, but I would venture to suggest that the British and the wider Commonwealth contribution was crucial (particularly from Australia and New Zealand). It was crucial (and even more crucial than London) because Singapore and Kuala Lumpur, and to a degree Hong Kong became training grounds for local scholars in the study of Southeast Asia. More importantly the two universities which emerged after the partition of the University of Malaya in 1962 (to become the University of Malaya in Kuala Lumpur and in Singapore, the National University of Singapore) subsequently established successful Southeast Asian Studies programmes. The Singapore government also went further in setting up the Institute of Southeast Asian Studies in 1968 which has become one of the most prominent global research centres on the region for both Asian and non-Asian scholars alike. From the University of Malaya in its early days came a stream of publications not only focused on Malaya and Singapore but also on the wider region which repeatedly set down the case for the integrity and coherence of Southeast Asia as a subject of study in its own right. In addition, Singapore and Kuala Lumpur, and again to some extent Hong Kong became part of international networks of scholarship on the region, and many prominent scholars in the United Kingdom in the heyday of Southeast Asian Studies up to the 1970s had had the great good fortune to spend a period of their career engaged in teaching and research there. It might be worth emphasizing at this point that, although the USA was the prime mover in establishing Southeast Asian Studies outside Southeast Asia, I suggest that the British were the pioneers of this project within the region, though I shall want to acknowledge shortly (see below) some key contributions from continental European scholars.

Unfortunately I have not had the time to construct an academic pedigree of the development of the study of the region from a British perspective, although I trust that readers will begin to see one emerging in what I have to say about the development of British scholarship. Anthony Reid has already provided us with a relatively comprehensive list of scholars who contributed to the making of Southeast Asia in Singapore and Kuala Lumpur in his "saucer model" of Southeast Asian identity (1999, pp. 9–10, 14–15). It is immediately obvious what a closely interconnected academic network it was and how the career paths of individuals constantly crossed. This is unsurprising when a subject or field of study is being created because the numbers of researchers are small and in the early years they were mainly supervised and trained by a few senior scholars. The field was also dominated by a small number of core academic subjects which examined the region not from a multi-disciplinary perspective but from a firm base in a particular discipline: language and literature, geography, history, political science, anthropology, economics and economic history (ibid., p. 9). In other words rather than adopting an area studies perspective scholars approached the study of the region, or particular sub-regions or countries within Southeast Asia, from a specific academic discipline.

I would suggest that there were three generations of scholars who had a formative influence on the development of the field of British-generated Southeast Asian Studies (though the division between the generations is somewhat rough and ready). Some of them contributed very directly to the making of the region and to the promotion of a regional perspective through their writings and the training of the next generation of specialists (Daniel G.E. Hall, C.D. [Jeremy] Cowan and Charles A. Fisher are outstanding examples of them), whilst others kept to their academic disciplines but through their research on the region and their knowledge of it were involved in developing the infrastructure of Southeast Asian Studies in the United Kingdom (among them the anthropologists Raymond Firth, Maurice Freedman, Edmund Leach and Rodney Needham).

The first generation emerged in the interwar years and the late colonial period among a handful of expatriates who were teaching in Rangoon or occupied official positions in Burma, or were involved in administration and research in Malaya and the Straits Settlements; it included some local scholars as well who were trained in British colonial institutions (ibid., p. 15). This was the generation of Charles Otto Blagden, Ernest H.G. Dobby, Firth, John S. Furnivall, Hall, Gordon H. Luce, Victor Purcell, John Alexander Stewart, and Sir Richard Winstedt. The second was forged during the Pacific War and during the first couple of decades thereafter. Some saw military service in the Far East and some of them had benefited from the growth of interest in area studies following the publication of the *Scarbrough Report* in 1947; this generation included such scholars as Cowan, Fisher, Freedman, John Gullick, Brian Harrison, Leach, Cyril Northcote Parkinson, Harry Leonard Shorto, E.H.S. (Stuart) Simmonds and Oliver W. Wolters. The third generation emerged during the 1950s and 1960s. Some also played important roles in the developments which followed the publication of the so-called *Hayter Report* in 1962. This generation included John Bastin, Ian Brown, Dennis Duncanson, Denis Dwyer, Ian Glover, M.B. (Barry) Hooker, James C. Jackson, Mervyn Jaspan, T. (Terry) G. McGee, David K. Bassett, Michael Leifer, Leslie Palmier, Kernial Singh Sandhu, Khoo Khay Kim, Ralph Smith, Anthony (Tony) Stockwell, Syed Hussein Alatas, Robert Taylor, Kenneth Tregonning, Mary Turnbull, Paul Wheatley and Wang Gungwu. I count myself among the fourth generation which emerged in the late 1960s and into the 1970s, and included, among many others, Peter Ayre, Peter Carey, Clive J. Christie, Mark Hobart, Jeremy Kemp, Roger Kershaw, Oey Hong Lee, Andrew Turton, Richard Vokes and C.W. (Bill) Watson.

What I shall also propose in this chapter, and the proposal takes its lead from Anthony Reid's "saucer model", is that British perspectives on the concept of a Southeast Asian region were privileged because of the strategic location of a British imperial presence in the Straits Settlements of Penang (Pulau Pinang), Malacca (Melaka) and most importantly Singapore, and the close connections of these "nodal points" with neighbouring territories in what was to become the region which we now know as "Southeast Asia". There was an obvious tension in this locational advantage to which I have just referred, given British interests in other Asian areas outside Southeast Asia, but the British, and particularly those based in Singapore from the first part of the nineteenth century, also enjoyed the advantage of seeing those territories around the Straits of Malacca as connected (historically, culturally, politically and economically) with those in the mainly Muslim world of island Southeast Asia and the predominantly Buddhist world of the mainland. It seems that an early emerging British vision of a Southeast Asian region in the first half of the nineteenth century, unhindered at that time by territorial imperatives, was then overtaken by colonial preoccupations and the need to focus on the administration of those British territories which were acquired progressively from the mid-nineteenth century. Instead it was those continental Europeans, principally the Germans and Austrians, who were not encumbered by the blinkers imposed by discrete and defined empires in the East, who began to discern a Southeast Asian region from the turn of the twentieth century. Two German-speaking scholars in particular, Robert von Heine-Geldern and Karl Pelzer, were to develop a strong scholarly presence in the United States and they were crucial in the promotion of the concept of a culturally and historically defined region separate from India and China in the post-war American academic world (Reid 1999, pp. 10–11).

However, interestingly these wider regional visions resurfaced and began to have resonance with some British scholars, who were working in Burma in the interwar years, and who had become disaffected with the notion that Burma was merely part of a "Greater India". Furnivall and Hall, both of whom had lived and worked in colonial Burma and who were also aware of the emerging scholarship on the region (both in English and other languages), were prime movers in the project to define Southeast Asia in the post-war development of British university research and teaching on the newly emerging nations of Asia. Hall played this role from his base in the School of Oriental and African Studies (SOAS) in London and Furnivall from Cambridge.

What must be emphasized as well is that of all the colonial powers Britain was the only one to have possessions in both mainland and island Southeast Asia (with the minor exception of Portugal) and it is my contention that the mainland-island divide, which the British to some extent bridged, has been one of the major obstacles in conceiving Southeast Asia as a region. The French were preoccupied with their Indochinese mainland; the Dutch with their maritime East Indies territories; and the Americans, and before them the Spanish, with their Philippines outlier, which until recently was seen only rather equivocally as part of Southeast Asia and in historical, cultural and economic terms connected more to a trans-Pacific rather than an Asian world.

Another preoccupation of this chapter is to plot the institutional development of the study of Southeast Asia in the United Kingdom from the early twentieth century to the present. What is abundantly clear is that having eventually identified Southeast Asia as a region which deserved at least some coordinated attention the British government and its agencies had neither a clear idea whether and how best to fund its study and at what level nor a consistent and sustained national policy of support. Yet in the first two decades after the Second World War British strategic and commercial interests in Southeast Asia were substantial, following the loss of its Indian possessions: in the port city of Singapore and its military facilities, in the vitally important rubber and tin production belt of the Malay States and in the oil reserves of Brunei. Not only were these matters of vital concern to Britain but the Straits of Malacca and the South China Sea, which at the high point of nineteenth-century European imperialism had been turned into "a British lake", also provided the British with their gateway to Hong Kong and East Asia.

It is therefore somewhat surprising that more was not done before the Second World War to support these interests and develop a strong base of scholarship and training in the languages, cultures, geographies, histories and economies of the region. As we shall see the British approach, in contrast to that of some of its European neighbours, particularly the French, Dutch and Germans, was fitful and indecisive. Nevertheless, although it is true that British government support for the study of Southeast Asia was not as ambitious as it might have been, there was modest development in the 1920s and 1930s and some funds were forthcoming in the early post-war period. In the event, a handful of outstanding scholars were appointed who contributed significantly to "the making of a region". This national effort was primarily located in London, at the School of Oriental and African Studies (Braginsky 2002, pp. 1–48). Nevertheless, we should not forget that there was the important presence of senior scholars at the London School of Economics (LSE) including Raymond Firth and Maurice Freedman; they were not in an area studies institution, though they had a scholarly interest in the region and played their part in developing a language-based area studies infrastructure. There was also a scatter of researchers in Oxford and Cambridge, in particular Rodney Needham who trained considerable numbers of Oxford anthropologists who conducted field research in Indonesia and Malaysia and Edmund Leach in Cambridge, though originally at the LSE (Scarbrough 1947, p. 114; King 1989, pp. 19–20).

In order to provide an institutional framework for this history I shall also refer selectively to the major national reports and initiatives which were to shape area studies more generally and Southeast Asian Studies in the United Kingdom in particular from the 1940s through to the 1980s (and see King 1990). Three key national reports, which were usually referred to using the names of those who led the enquiries, were commissioned: Scarbrough (1947), Hayter (1961) and Parker (1986). All three provided some funding support but this was never administered in a sustained way and each report bemoaned the low level of provision in comparison with national needs which had preceded it, and the absence of a national policy, even when there had been some previous investment.

Moreover, in terms of the national centres of Southeast Asian Studies, the situation today has deteriorated considerably from the position which had been attained in the 1970s. In his survey of Southeast Asian Studies in the United Kingdom in 1977, Bassett counted almost 50 staff in the then three universities where there were designated programmes (SOAS, Hull and Kent) and when staff in other London colleges and in other departments at Hull were included the total reached almost 60 out of about 80 members of the Association of South-East Asian Studies (1981, p. 58). Since then two of the Centres have disappeared — Hull and Kent — and the only designated Centre now is that at SOAS which counts just under 30 members, with a modest programme of activity at the University of Leeds (with seven staff), which resulted from the transfer of five posts from Hull between 2003 and 2005. Currently the Association of South-East Asian Studies in the United Kingdom (ASEASUK) continues to be active with up to 200 members but the character of the constituency is rather different from what it was during the heyday of British Southeast Asian Studies in the 1960s and 1970s (see below).

These institutional developments have been amply covered and considered in the paper from which this current expanded and heavily revised chapter has emerged (see King 2010). What I shall do here is extract some of the salient points to illustrate my main theme of what we might characterize as British "vacillation" with regard to the importance of Southeast Asia for British national and global interests, and the inability of the British government and its higher education funding agencies to develop and sustain a coherent and considered national policy and to provide the necessary funding to support research and teaching on the region.

SOUTHEAST ASIA AS REGION:
A CONSTANT HEADACHE

First I have to say something about the problem of regional definition and then take up the theme of the apparent advantages that a small number of British scholars enjoyed from the first half of the nineteenth century in beginning to realize Southeast Asia as an historically and geographically interconnected set of territories separate from India and China. A considerable amount of time and energy has been devoted to debating and deliberating on the problems and prospects of defining Southeast Asia (see, for example, Acharya and Rajah 1999; Braginsky 2002; Chou and Houben 2006a, 2006b; King, 2005, 2006; Kratoska, Nordholt, and Raben 2005). When we thought that we had exhausted ourselves in attempts to grasp what constitutes Southeast Asia (exemplified, amongst many others, in the detailed and nuanced study of Oliver Wolters [1999]), we have recently witnessed a resurgence of scholarly interest in addressing issues of regional definition and the rationale of area studies (see King 2001a, 2005, 2006; and see Braginsky 2002). This is not only in response to what has been identified as "the crisis" in area studies and specifically Asian Studies (Jackson 2003a, 2003b), a crisis which is mainly located in the Western academy (in terms of the decline in government priorities, funding, intellectual commitment and student interest) (see Anderson 1978, 1992; McVey 1995, 1998), but is also an attempt to counter charges that: (1) area studies lacks a disciplinary spine, theoretical sophistication and a robust methodology; (2) that in the era of globalization it continues to present a parochial, inward-looking, boundary-obsessed perspective; and (3) that there was an uneasy, indeed unhealthy relationship between Western governments (anxious about the spread of Asian Communism) and their promotion of area studies during the Cold War. Of course the defence of area studies also has to address its origins in Western imperialism in that the academic project of Asian Studies in particular still carries residues of "Orientalism" and Western ethnocentrism. In my account in this chapter of the development in the United Kingdom and other parts of Europe of the study of Southeast Asia as a region, the colonial-imperial origin of area studies in the West and its prejudices are plain to see, but even at its most Orientalist, I am prepared to argue that there was a genuine attempt by what are seen to be the scholarly agents of imperialism to do more than simply shore up Western cultural, political and economic hegemony and give it intellectual justification (and see King 1990, 2001b; Braginsky 2002, pp. 11–12).

There are several major problems in defining Southeast Asia and there is no point in covering these in detail other than to note that, in any attempt to devise a region, there will always be problems of drawing boundaries and reconciling or at least explaining the diversities within the boundaries so drawn, and the cultural, historical and other connections beyond the boundaries. But I want to place emphasis in this introduction on two issues, and relate these firstly to the comparative history of colonialism in the region and where the interests of the colonial powers were focused, and secondly to the recent Southeast Asian diasporas and especially the relocation of various Southeast Asian ethnic groups in the West. On the first point I accept that my argument has to be qualified but I think it helps explain why some observers in the distant past tended to view matters in regional terms and others did not. In my view (not a new one) much of the difficulty which we experience in defining the region turns on the divisions, broadly speaking, between island and mainland Southeast Asia. Secondly, the more recent dispersal of populations out of Southeast Asia has, in my view, led not to a reinforcement of the idea of Southeast Asia but to narrower nation-state-based perspectives.

Firstly the division between the island and mainland worlds is strong and continues to have resonance (King 2001a). This has not been so much the result of intellectual construction and artifice, but rather has emerged from processes of migration, ethno-linguistic dispersal, external influences and cultural differentiation. Therefore it is not surprising that linguists of the mainland and island ethno-linguistic groups have usually formed their own separate scholarly organizations: based either on the Austronesian language family (which connects with cultures in Madagascar, Taiwan and the majority of the Pacific Islands, though it extends to a few outliers in Vietnam, Thailand and Cambodia), or on the Austro-Asiatic, Tai-Kadai or Sino-Tibetan families (which spill over into southern China and the northeastern regions of the Indian subcontinent). More generally rather than coming together as Southeast Asianists, scholars have usually felt more comfortable in Malay-Indonesian gatherings or Thai Studies, or Vietnamese Studies meetings and so on (King 2001a).

It is interesting in this respect that just after an Association of Southeast Asian Studies was established in the United Kingdom in 1969 by senior academics at SOAS, which was designed to unite Southeast Asianists across the nation, some scholars at the same School founded Indonesia Circle Society in March 1973 with its own association newsletter (later to become the journal *Indonesia and the Malay World*). This development was also accompanied by the setting up of the Malay-Indonesia Etymological

Project with British, French and Italian collaboration in Paris in July 1973 (Carey 1986, pp. 12–13; Lombard 1981, p. 56). European scholars with interests in Austronesian languages and literatures also came together to found the European Colloquium on Indonesian-Malay Studies which has held conferences since 1978 in universities across Europe and has been very active in promoting an island or maritime perspective on the languages and cultures of Southeast Asia (King 2009, pp. 10–11). In France too scholars committed to the Austronesian world founded the journal *Archipel* in 1971 in part to complement the emphasis on mainland Southeast Asia in the journal *L'Asie du Sud-Est and le monde insulindien* launched in 1970 (Lombard 1981, p. 57). Not to be outdone the major academic multi-disciplinary constituency of mainland Southeast Asia which focuses on Thailand and culturally related populations beyond the Thai nation-state (that is, the Tai-speaking communities) and which includes British scholars came together to organize a regular biennial International Conference on Thai Studies which was inaugurated in 1981.

On my second point it is well established that the colonial powers and the learned societies which emerged within the colonies and dependencies organized their scholarly activities within defined territorial units. Journals were established which usually focused on a particular colonial dependency (sometimes with some attention to the neighbouring countries) and not on the region, and were managed by learned societies, either located in the mother country or in the colony or both, whose members frequently comprised scholars and those involved professionally in colonial administrative, educational and commercial affairs. For example, the Dutch established journals devoted exclusively to their colonial possessions in the East; the most well-known was *Bijdragen tot de Taal-, Land- en Volkenkunde van Nederlandsch Indie* which first appeared as long ago as 1853. In French Indochina, l'École Française d'Extrême-Orient (EFEO) was founded in 1898 in Saigon and moved to Hanoi in 1901; it launched its journal *Le Bulletin de l'École Française d'Extrême-Orient* in 1901. In the British territories the Burma Research Society was founded on 29 March 1910 at a meeting in the Bernard Free Library in Rangoon and the *Journal of the Burma Research Society* commenced publication in 1911. The *Journal of the Straits Branch of the Royal Asiatic Society* which was first published in 1878 in Singapore, under the auspices of the Royal Asiatic Society of Great Britain and Ireland (RAS) (est. 1823) focused primarily on the British port settlements of Penang, Malacca and Singapore which until 1867 were administered from India, and then widened its interests more firmly to the neighbouring Malay States, later becoming the Malayan Branch of the RAS in 1923 and the Malaysian Branch in 1964. With expatriate, particularly British involvement, The Siam Society with its *Journal of the Siam Society* was established under royal patronage in 1904. A flurry of activity in the Philippines in the early 1950s in which prominent American academics were involved led to the inauguration of the journal *Philippine Studies* at the Ateneo de Manila in 1953, and the Philippine Sociological Society was founded in 1952 with its own journal, *Philippine Sociological Review*. Numerous specialist journals published by colonial museums and other educational and research institutions, which usually focused on a particular colony or territory, were also founded.

This national orientation has continued and has been strengthened especially by the Southeast Asian diaspora following the Indochinese wars and the debacle of Burma. Given the prominent position which the USA has in the global media and educational agendas and its capacity to organize and support scholarly activities then it is worth noting that the settlement of refugees from Indochina in the USA, the intense Western interest in and criticism of the activities of the military junta in Burma, and the very substantial and continued interest of American academics in that region have led to the development of nationally-focused associations and study groups in the USA. Ironically the post-war American-promoted construction of Southeast Asia and its central role in globalization now seems to be working against regional definition. It is no longer Southeast Asian Studies that command centre stage but increasingly the nationally and ethnically based organizations. The national Center for Burma Studies was established at Northern Illinois University in 1986 associated with the Burma Foundation and the Burma Studies Group, as a Sub-committee of the Southeast Asia Council (SEAC) of the Association for Asian Studies (AAS); it publishes *The Journal of Burma Studies* and *Bulletin of the Burma Studies Group*. The Center for Lao Studies was established in San Francisco with its own *Journal of Lao Studies* launched in 2010 and edited at Cornell University; an International Conference on Lao Studies was also inaugurated at Northern Illinois University. A Thailand, Laos, Cambodia Studies Group has also been established as an affiliate of the SEAC within the American Association for Asian Studies. At Ohio University a Cambodian Studies Forum was set up with a *Journal of Cambodian Studies*. Finally in 2006 a *Journal of Vietnamese Studies* was launched by the University of California Press through the Vietnam Studies Group again within the Southeast Asia Council of the Association for Asian Studies.

Yet this merely returns to the principles of American scholarship on Southeast Asia which emerged in the 1940s. In the anti-imperialist stance which the Americans adopted in relation to Southeast Asia, it was the nationalist agenda which was of utmost importance, and, though the United States was vitally important in the creation of Southeast Asia as a region, there has always been a tension between the wider regional perspective and the view that expertise should be developed on particular countries. This in turn arose primarily from the nation-state based preoccupations of American political science. As Smith observes in relation to the early years of the development of Southeast Asian expertise in the United States:

> Language was combined with specialisation in one or other discipline, on the assumption that a group of scholars working on a single country would then be able to share one another's expertise. The countries which received most emphasis, at Cornell and in the United States as a whole, were Thailand, Indonesia and the Philippines (1986, p. 16).

Of course, American attempts to define the region tended to divide between those who were mainland specialists of Thailand especially, but also to some extent Vietnam and Burma, and those who focused on the island world, particularly Indonesia and the Philippines. In this connection we should now turn to a major scholarly attempt at regional definition, which again evokes the division between mainland Southeast Asia and the islands. One of the most significant and outstanding contributions to regional historical scholarship and to the work of bringing Southeast Asian history into an integrated and coherent regional framework is Anthony Reid's *Southeast Asia in the Age of Commerce: 1400–1680* (in two volumes, 1988/1993). As we shall see Reid, a New Zealander who pursued his doctoral studies at Cambridge, was especially drawn into the historical study of Southeast Asia in regional terms during his time at the University of Malaya. Yet interestingly his *magnum opus* resulted in a debate which served to demonstrate more sharply the different trajectories of mainland and island Southeast Asian history. Victor B. Lieberman, who undertook his doctoral studies at SOAS, in his critical appreciation of Reid's work, forcefully separated mainland Southeast Asian experiences and brought them into relationship with Indo-European history and especially the administrative histories of France and Russia (1993, 1995). Again not to be outdone by a regional rival from the island world Lieberman has produced his own two-volume *magnum opus* which shows us that it is problematical to seek a unity in Southeast Asian history on the basis of the open commercial and international character of island Southeast Asia (2003, 2009). I shall return to Reid's contribution to regional definition later.

As I have already indicated, the division between mainland and island Southeast Asia was to some extent cemented by the colonial experience. The Dutch, Spanish, Portuguese and American focus was on island Southeast Asia, the French on the Indochinese mainland. The only major European colonial power which bridged the mainland-island divide in territorial terms was the British, and this bridge provided, to some extent at least, a route along which some scholars travelled in their attempt to find regional coherence. However, it is also true that this potentially broader vision was compromised by the British preoccupation with the Indian subcontinent. For much of the late colonial period the British saw their Southeast Asian dependencies as an extension of the Indian empire in the concept of "Further" or "Farther India", in that Burma and for a time the Straits Settlements were merely eastward administrative and provincial extensions of India. The perception of Southeast Asia as a region was also rendered problematical because of British East Asian interests, and though subordinate to India, the Straits Settlements in particular, whilst also an extension of the Indian subcontinent, were part of a commercial maritime perspective which brought Britain into relationship with China (particularly the "Treaty Ports") and Hong Kong as well.

Nevertheless, the British presence and their wider experiences and encounters in the region resulted in the nineteenth century in a relatively expansive and growing knowledge not only of Burma, the Malay States, the Straits Settlements and the northern Borneo territories, but also Thailand (Siam) especially following the Bowring Treaty of 1855, Sumatra, Java and even parts of the Philippine islands. Very gradually the British presence led to some administrators and scholars who had lived and worked in the region looking beyond a given European-administered territorial unit and beginning to see wider parallels and similarities. Burma and the University of Rangoon in particular, despite the close relations with India, was a training ground for some of these ideas, and as far back as the early to mid-nineteenth century the outward-looking perspectives of some British residents of the Straits Settlements, especially Singapore, also contributed to changing ideas about regional geography, culture and history. I must also emphasize that these visions of a wider Southeast Asian region were not confined to the British sphere; we also witness them among some French, Dutch, German and Austrian scholars, though, in my view, these perspectives on region were not nearly as widespread and embedded into university research as those of the British, nor did they embrace decisively a "modern" definition of Southeast Asia rather than one based on prehistory and ethnology.

THE COLONIAL DIMENSION AND THE NEED TO TRAIN THOSE WHO GOVERN

It is impossible to separate the creation of Southeast Asia from Britain's colonial past and its expanding international interests (and indeed those of the French and Dutch) and for that reason the kinds of regional studies that developed during the interwar years and more importantly during the immediate post-war period have often been the subject of severe criticism. The task of assisting in the training of colonial officers in the cultures, languages, histories and geographies of distant Asian dependencies and the Western interests and perspectives which were developed to understand them came to be criticized as "Orientalism". The ideological construction and domination and the continued economic exploitation of other peoples in the context of imperialism, came in for harsh criticism, particularly among post-war European activists, Asian nationalist leaders and scholars and social scientists of radical Marxist and political economy persuasions.

Yet, if the need to support colonialism was one of the main reasons for the foundation of appropriate programmes of regional study and training in the languages of the dependent and other territories of strategic, commercial and administrative interest, it is surprising how long it took the British government to establish a coordinated programme of academic training. If British imperialism had depended on an academically supported and sustained rationale then it was doomed from the start. Professor Sir Cyril Phillips, a former Director of the School of Oriental and African Studies, lamented the fact that the period during which the British established a colonial empire, when they were engaged in the "political and administrative reconstruction of India", and had expanded their economic and political interests in Southeast Asia, Africa, East Asia and the Pacific Islands, passed by without "the formation in London of an Imperial training centre" (1967, p. 11; and see 2003). As with much else in the United Kingdom the provision of expertise and training in area studies and languages was generally *ad hoc* and lagged behind the development of the study of Asia in other European countries: at the École Spéciale des Langues Orientales founded in 1795 in Paris (eventually to become l'Institut National des Langues et Civilisations Orientales [l'INALCO] in 1971], the School of Oriental Studies in Berlin and the Asiatic Museum in St Petersburg which was founded in 1818 (with the subsequent founding of the Institute for Oriental Studies there in 1930). On the publication of the Reay Report in London in 1909 not only had France, Germany and Russia already established institutions for the study of "living" Oriental languages and cultures but so too had Austria-Hungary, Italy and Holland (Scarbrough 1947, p. 22). In 1922, and with no significant political and economic interests in Asia, an Oriental Institute was also established in Prague shortly after the founding of SOAS.

As one might anticipate the perceived need to establish institutions and programmes to impart knowledge of Asia and to ensure some facility in Asian languages was tied very closely to Britain's presence in the Indian subcontinent. The call for the creation of a centre for Asian (or in those days "Oriental") Studies goes back at least to 1798 just after the French foundation of an Oriental Institute in Paris, when the newly appointed Governor-General of India, Richard Wellesley emphasized the need to educate civil servants of the East India Company not only in the basic knowledge and skills to enable them to discharge their professional administrative duties but also to be acquainted with "the history, languages, customs and manners of the people of India" (Phillips 1967, p. 9). Prior to this Sir William Jones had founded the Asiatic Society of Bengal in 1784 for the study of Sanskrit and Indo-Aryan philology (Scarbrough 1947, pp. 8–9). There were also short-lived attempts to establish an Oriental Institution in London from 1818 (Hartog 1917, p. 5).

Given this early British interest in India it is therefore surprising that by the end of the nineteenth century there was still no such British Asia centre, although professorships in Sanskrit and Chinese had been established in Oxford and Cambridge in the second half of the nineteenth century and chairs in Arabic had been founded in the two universities as long ago as the 1630s (ibid., p. 8). The study of Asian literatures and languages, including Hindustani and Chinese, had also been established in University College London (UCL) from the 1820s and soon after at neighbouring King's College (Hartog 1917, p. 5). There was also some training provided in Oxford, Cambridge and UCL for probationers in the Indian Civil Service (Phillips 1967, p. 11). Yet this was not provided and coordinated in a single institution where expertise could be concentrated and sustained.

Above all it was the growth of German commercial and imperial ambitions in Asia and Africa in the early twentieth century which re-awakened British interest in founding a special institute for the study of Asia (ibid., p. 12). A Committee of Enquiry, chaired by Lord Reay, a former Governor of Bombay and President of the Royal Asiatic Society, was set up in 1907 by His Majesty's Treasury to examine the proposal for a School of Oriental Studies in the University of London (and see Carey 1986, p. 5; Hartog 1917, p. 11). The Committee was guided by political, strategic, administrative and economic needs and recommended strongly

the establishment of a specialist School to cover the major languages of
the Middle East, India, Malaya and Burma, China and Japan, as well
as East and West Africa (Reay 1909; Phillips 1967, p. 12). But there
were further delays occasioned by the need to find financial support
and suitable premises, and obviously by the severe disruption caused by
the First World War. Eventually the School of Oriental Studies (which
included the study of Africa) was granted its Royal Charter in 1916 and
was officially opened on 23 February 1917 (Hartog 1917, p. 21). Its name
was changed to the School of Oriental and African Studies (SOAS) in 1938
(Scarbrough 1947, p. 10).

With regard to Southeast Asia two posts were established in 1917, a
Readership in Malay and a Lectureship in Burmese, and briefly a Lecture-
ship in the Oceanic (Pacific) Languages. However, over two decades later
and on the eve of the Second World War SOAS could still only muster a
Reader in Malay (Sir Richard Winstedt) and a Reader in Burmese (John
Alexander Stewart), who had been appointed to a lectureship in 1933.
There were, however, several external lecturers, usually from the military
or Christian missions, who were brought in from 1936 to teach some of
the languages of the upland minorities of Assam-Burma (Khasi, Chin,
Shan, and Kachin). For the first time an additional lecturer in Siamese
was appointed in 1936 and provision in Polynesian languages was also
re-introduced with extra support for Malay and Burmese. Although the
British did not anticipate that their empire would disintegrate as rapidly
as it did, it is salutary to note that the major institution for the study of
Asia (and Africa) in the capital city was established less than thirty years
before one of its major reasons for coming into existence, which was "to
provide practical training for those about to proceed overseas" (Phillips
1967, p. 17), began to be removed.

What is noteworthy is that in the interwar years there was a lack of
student interest in degree programmes offered by the School, though there
was recruitment to short elementary courses and sub-degree instruction;
there was also a constant struggle to fund the School's activities (ibid.,
pp. 19–22, 24–25). In any case many students who went for training
and study were from overseas (ibid., p. 25; Scarbrough 1947, p. 13).
Nevertheless, it is important to note that in the restructuring of the School's
programmes in 1932 (and even before the term Southeast Asia came into
much more regular use) six departments devoted to the study of regional
languages and cultures were established. One of these was "South East
Asia and the Islands" which, given the long-standing British interest in
the Malay-Indonesian world, recognized the Austronesian diaspora into the

Pacific Ocean as well. But the emergence of a clearly defined Southeast Asia programme was short-lived; it was discontinued in 1936 and absorbed into other departments (Phillips 1967, p. 23).

Although the School had made considerable progress, on the eve of war Phillips noted "the scantiness of the School's resources, the fragility of its academic structure, and the lack of British national policy". More than this he concluded that "compared even with the Reay proposals of 1909 [the School's] teaching establishment was still deficient in every department" (ibid., p. 29). With the obvious deficiencies in language training during the War and the lack of preparation for the great changes which would take place after it in the colonies and dependencies, the British government was eventually spurred into action. In June 1944 the then Secretary of State for Foreign Affairs, Mr Anthony Eden announced the setting up of a Commission under the chairmanship of the Earl of Scarbrough to examine the facilities offered by universities and other educational institutions in Great Britain for the study of Oriental, Slavonic, East European and African languages and cultures (ibid., p. 38).

THE SCARBROUGH REPORT (1947): THE WAY FORWARD

The Earl of Scarbrough's Report was a vital watershed in the development of Asian and other area studies and language instruction in post-war Britain. The context for the establishment of an Inter-departmental Commission of Enquiry on 15 December 1944 can be gleaned from the representation on the Commission which comprised sixteen members, nearly all senior figures from the Ministry of Defence, the Air Ministry, Foreign Office, War Office, Colonial Office, India Office, Burma Office along with The British Council, Ministry of Education, Department of Overseas Trade and the University Grants Committee. The Earl of Scarbrough had been Governor of Bombay from 1937 to 1943 and served as Under-Secretary of State for India and Burma in 1945.

In spite of Britain's global interests at that time the Scarbrough Commission observed that the engagement in a World War had led to the realization that Britain's understanding and knowledge of the peoples (and economy) of Africa and "the East" were "under-developed" and the nation "ill-equipped" to provide the necessary expertise and training (1947, p. 7). Even more strongly the Commission concluded that in the mid-1940s the provision in these studies was "unworthy of our country and people" and that "it would be harmful to the national interest to allow the present state of affairs to continue or even to deteriorate" (ibid., p. 8). The argument of course, given the composition of the Commission, was designed to address British political, strategic and economic interests but it was also based on the rationale of cultural understanding and the importance of encouraging "mutual interest in our respective ways of life and thought and in our cultural achievements" (ibid., p. 25; Phillips 1967, p. 39).

Even at that time Scarbrough made reference to "a revolution in com-munications", the crucial importance of knowing and understanding other peoples and cultures in order to discharge imperial responsibilities in the colonies, to the task of carrying forward relationships in the Dominions, some of which were also near neighbours of various African and Asian colonies and protectorates, and perhaps even more importantly to "the need to prepare for new relationships with India, Burma and Ceylon" (1947, p. 6). It has already been remarked upon amply elsewhere but it is worth re-emphasizing the fact that the experience of the Japanese occupation of large parts of Southeast Asia played a major role in the development of British perceptions of the region and scholarship on it. As Cowan states the experience of war brought large numbers of young men who would not otherwise have known anything about Southeast Asia into contact with the peoples and cultures of the region and some of them returned to take up further studies (1963, pp. 8, 12). Key figures in the shaping of post-war Southeast Asian Studies in the United Kingdom had also served in the military in the Pacific War. Therefore, the war was a key turning point in British perspectives on the region, made more directly relevant with the independence of India, Pakistan, Ceylon (Sri Lanka) and Burma and then the emerging threat, from a Western viewpoint, of communist governments and movements in the Cold War era in Asia (Chou and Houben 2006a, p. 4; Stockwell 1986, pp. 79–83).

The Scarbrough Commission, in imperialist mode, divided Asia into the sub-regions which were destined to persist throughout the post-war period. Within the general term "Oriental" were (1) Near and Middle Eastern; (2) Indian and Sinhalese (later to become South Asian); (3) Far Eastern (or East Asian); and (4) South-East Asian and Oceanic (comprising Burma, the Malay Peninsula, Siam, French Indo-China, the Netherlands East Indies and the Islands of the South Pacific) (1947, p. 79). Scarbrough's enquiry found that, although there was some coverage of Southeast Asia at Oxford and Cambridge in the fields of colonial administration, anthropology and applied economics, the study of the region was confined largely to London (at SOAS and the LSE) and primarily to language and linguistics. There were insignificant numbers of degree students, though "a number took limited courses, mainly in Burmese and Malay" (Phillips 1967, p. 13). The main focus was on Indian and Chinese Studies, though overall non-linguistic subjects were poorly represented, and there was some training of service students in Chinese and Japanese language at SOAS.

In contrast with other European countries the number of teaching posts in Oriental Studies in the United Kingdom compared unfavourably and the government had not established any scholarly institution in Asia of the stature of L'École Française d'Extrême-Orient in Saigon and then Hanoi or the Batavian Society of Arts and Sciences in Jakarta (established in 1778) (Scarbrough 1947, pp. 22, 119; Stokhof 2003, p. 126). The reasons Scarbrough gave for this British neglect were damning: "traditional exclusiveness which tends to disregard and even to look down upon culture which has little in common with our own" (ibid., p. 23). It is quite astonishing to read that, in a country with a large empire, apart from those who served it overseas, "an insignificant proportion of our population has visited or interested itself in countries which form the subject of our survey" (ibid., p. 24). But the experience of a World War did begin to open up other parts of the world to a much larger proportion of the British population and this was an additional argument mustered by the Scarbrough Commission in favour of an expansion in area studies provision (ibid., p. 25).

All the recommendations on behalf of area studies which Scarbrough made in the 1940s have been repeated ever since: the need for the development of a base of scholarship and research with supporting resources, the importance of language training but with the parallel expansion of non-linguistic subjects, the increase in attention to "the living present", increasing interaction between the humanities and social sciences and across disciplines, regular contact with the peoples and countries under study and disseminating knowledge to and engaging the wider public (ibid., pp. 28–35, 69–77).

For the purposes of this chapter we should note that the Scarbrough Commission established six regional sub-committees to assist it in data gathering and in devising recommendations; one of these covered "South-East Asian Studies". It had a membership of four including two academic members who were Raymond Firth (an anthropologist at the LSE who had undertaken research in Malaya and the Polynesian island of Tikopia, and was an external lecturer in Polynesian languages at SOAS from 1942) and John Sydenham Furnivall (who had been a colonial official in Burma, one of the founding members of the Burma Research Society, and associated with the University of Rangoon where he was later to be awarded an Honorary

Degree in 1957, and from 1936–41 Lecturer in Burmese Language, History and Law at Cambridge University).

Nevertheless, even with the plan to re-establish a focus for Southeast Asian Studies at SOAS, the Scarbrough Commission noted that it "would still leave wide fields of research untouched", in some of the important language groups, the archaeology and history of Indo-China, Buddhist philosophy, and the pre-history of "Farther India" (1947, p. 118). One important recommendation of the Commission was that the study of Southeast Asian languages should be concentrated in London. However, Scarbrough also proposed that, whilst other subjects in Oriental and African Studies should be more dispersed, this should still not go beyond a few major universities which already had some provision, including London, Oxford and Cambridge (ibid., p. 70). It was this last recommendation from which the Hayter Sub-committee was to depart some years later.

Following Scarbrough there was expansion at SOAS on the basis of earmarked grants. The Department of South East Asia and the Islands was re-established under John Stewart in 1946. He had been appointed to the Indian Civil Service in 1904 and served in Burma from 1905; for a time he worked with Furnivall. Following his return from Burma he was appointed as Lecturer in Burmese at SOAS from 1933 to 1935, a Senior Lecturer 1936–37, and then Reader and Head of the Department of India, Burma and Ceylon from 1937 to 1946, before serving as Professor of Burmese and Head of the Department of South East Asia and the Islands from 1946 until his death in 1948 (Dunn and Firth 1949, p. 264). Stewart was succeeded by Daniel (DGE) Hall who was to serve as Acting Head of the Department from 1949 to 1959. Hall, following his academic career in Burma where he was Professor of History at the University of Rangoon in the 1920s and early 1930s, returned to his homeland to a teaching career in Surrey, and was subsequently appointed to the newly created Chair in South East Asian History at SOAS in 1949 (Cowan 1980, pp. 149–54).

Under Stewart and Hall the department increased its range and depth of language provision. Even before Scarbrough there had been some developments. The first established Lectureship in Siamese had been introduced in 1941. From 1942 an additional external lecturer had been appointed in Tibeto-Burman, Old Burmese, Mon and Pyu (in the shape of the distinguished scholar of Burma Gordon Luce), and in Malay. From 1946 to the early 1950s language provision was further strengthened in Burmese, Mon, Malay, Tai/Siamese and Oceanic/Austronesian languages. New posts were also created in Old Javanese, Vietnamese (Annamese),

Cambodian and Art and Archaeology. Outside the language and area studies programmes the new Departments of Law and (Cultural) Anthropology were established, and there was expansion in the Departments of Phonetics and Linguistics, and in History (Carey 1986, p. 6; Phillips 1967, p. 44).

THE STUDY OF SOUTHEAST ASIA IN SOUTHEAST ASIA

As I have indicated it is important not to confine our attention to the British contribution to Southeast Asian Studies in the home country. We have seen how important expatriate officialdom from Burma and the University of Rangoon were to the development of the study of Southeast Asia at SOAS and Cambridge (through Furnivall, Hall and Luce) (and see Selth 2010, pp. 404–8). Furnivall founded the Burma Research Society in 1910 in which scholars such as Blagden, Luce and Stewart, who were later to play significant roles at SOAS, held membership (Dunn and Firth 1949, p. 261). It is also worth remembering that Rangoon College, which was established as an affiliated college of the University of Calcutta as long ago as 1878, was founded, on the merger with Judson College (American Baptist College) as an independent university in 1920 (Cowan 1980, p. 149). In the 1940s and 1950s it was also one of the most prestigious universities in Asia. However, with the political developments in Burma after independence it was the University of Malaya rather than Rangoon which was to carry forward the Southeast Asian project in Singapore, Kuala Lumpur and by extension the United Kingdom. Very notably Cyril Northcote Parkinson as Raffles Professor of History in Singapore in the 1950s did much to promote the study of Southeast Asia at the University (see, for example, 1937) and to develop links with American academia as Visiting Professor at Berkeley, Harvard and Illinois. Ernest HG Dobby, as Professor in the Department of Geography in the 1950s, enjoyed a similar high profile bringing young lecturers like Donald Fryer, B.W. Hodder and Paul Wheatley into the department. Dobby had also taught in Raffles College before and immediately after the war (see, for example, 1950). Interestingly, it was the Scarbrough Report which recommended that SOAS and the LSE should develop partnerships with Rangoon University and Raffles College, Singapore, to bring Burmese and Malay(an) graduates to London and to send young British scholars to Burma and Singapore (1947, p. 43). A further suggestion was to establish a Department of Malay Studies in Singapore to help facilitate cooperation between British, Australian and Dutch scholars (ibid.).

The importance of the study of Southeast Asia in Southeast Asia is attested to by Anthony Reid in his re-evaluation of the respective American and non-American contributions "in defining what Southeast Asian Studies was about" (1999, p. 9). He points out that his introduction to the study of Southeast Asia did not emerge from any contact with the major programmes of study in such places as Cornell. Instead, he tells us, that, as a newly appointed Lecturer in History fresh from Cambridge, he turned up at the University of Malaya in Kuala Lumpur with little knowledge of the region, and "was asked to teach the early modern history of Southeast Asia". He continues "I hardly knew what it was, but the process of finding out was unquestionably the formative experience for me in my subsequent writing" (ibid.). He like many others who played a vital role in the creation and development of Southeast Asia as a subject of scholarly contemplation served "their apprenticeships in the universities of Malaysia and Singapore" (ibid.).

Yet just at the time that enormous energy was being devoted to the study of Southeast Asia in Singapore and from 1959 in Kuala Lumpur the efforts in the home country had almost come to a standstill. A flurry of post-Scarbrough activity in the late 1940s and early 1950s petered out in the late 1950s. Obviously the expansion at SOAS was beyond anything that had been seen before and in that sense could be seen as a "heyday". But the momentum was in the region not in the United Kingdom. The number of academic posts available were increased in Singapore and Kuala Lumpur and from the 1950s began to decline at home. This unsatisfactory national situation needed a remedy, and it was found in Hayter.

THE HAYTER REPORT (1961):
THE GOLDEN YEARS

In spite of Scarbrough's eloquent and detailed case for the enhancement of provision and improved coordination in area studies, the financial strictures of the immediate post-war period meant that any increase in staff and facilities was to be relatively modest. Nevertheless, with earmarked grants between 1947 and 1952 staff numbers did increase across Oriental Studies from 95 to 220 with modest gains in Southeast Asian Studies, though the number of students increased very little (Hayter 1961, p. 3).

However, after 1952 increase in staff slowed dramatically with the ending of earmarked grants, although SOAS managed to keep up some momentum in the decade from 1952 to 1962 (ibid., pp. 11–33; Phillips 1967, pp. 48–57). It was no surprise, therefore, that looking across the

Atlantic Ocean to the enormous expansion in area studies in the USA and their dynamic and modern character, the University Grants Committee (UGC) decided in 1959 to set up another Enquiry, which was charged with the review of developments in Oriental, Slavonic, East European and African Studies since Scarbrough. An important part of the review was the examination of the American area studies model during a visit to North America in April 1960; the Sub-committee visited ten American universities (including Cornell, California and Stanford) and two in Canada. It did not look to continental Europe for inspiration, though we shall see that the concept of an overseas institute, like that which had been developed in the colonial period in Hanoi and Batavia (Jakarta) was on the agenda of the British Academy in the 1950s and 1960s. It is an interesting element of the history of Southeast Asian Studies in the United Kingdom that it also reflects wider tensions between the British orientation to a trans-Atlantic agenda with the USA and an attempt to address its relations with continental Europe. This tension is expressed very directly in Ralph Smith's attempt to discover "a British tradition" in Southeast Asian Studies where he refers to the continental European contribution but gives most attention to the American development of area studies.

The UGC Sub-committee of seven members chaired by Sir William Hayter, a former British Ambassador to Moscow (1953–57) and Warden of New College, Oxford, was a more streamlined affair than the Scarbrough Commission with its 16 members and 7 special sub-committees, involving an additional 18 advisers. The Hayter Sub-committee began its work in January 1960 and presented its report in May 1961 (1961, p. v). The context of the Sub-committee's deliberations was the gathering pace of decolonization and Britain's withdrawal from its overseas possessions. Hayter indicated the need for Britain to meet these challenges by forging new kinds of relations with the new nations, in a considerably more fluid and unpredictable world (ibid., pp. 34ff).

The Sub-committee concluded that "the overall pattern of development" of Oriental Studies in the 1950s was "disappointing". With regard to Southeast Asia, as well as Eastern Europe, the Middle East and the Far East, "[t]he study of these regions barely enters into the work of the non-language departments". In language departments the amount of work "devoted to modern studies is small" and at undergraduate and postgraduate level there was "little attention to these countries 'as living societies'" (ibid., p. 3). Over a decade after Scarbrough's criticisms of British parochialism, Hayter remarked that "the total amount of knowledge" of these other parts of the world was "inadequate" (ibid., p. 4). Even a half century ago the Sub-committee had already emphasized that the global "political centre of gravity" had moved from Western Europe but British education had not responded to this change in world affairs (ibid., p. 3). A major shift in the Hayter Report's recommendations was the importance of expansion not in language departments but in modern studies and specifically in history, geography, law, economics, anthropology and other social sciences. According to the Report the provision lacked vitality and relevance to the modern world (see Carey 1986, pp. 8–9).

The Hayter Report recommended the establishment of 125 new university posts and 100 postgraduate awards over ten years, travel grants to visit the areas under study, intensive language training, and the creation of six to eight new multi-disciplinary area studies' centres "on lines similar to those in America" spread between several universities, some of them outside the traditional heartlands of London and Oxbridge (ibid., p. 4). It was from this initiative that a Centre for South-East Asian Studies was established in Hull in 1962–63 emphasizing politics, geography, economics, history, sociology and anthropology. The Southeast Asian programmes at SOAS were strengthened in modern studies, with the establishment of a Department of Economic and Political Studies and a Department of Geography and the study of Southeast Asia was given coordination at the research and postgraduate level with the founding of a Centre there in 1966. Language study also continued to be concentrated in London (Phillips 1967, pp. 58–59). Later in 1969 additional funds became available after the Hayter initiative, and staff in Southeast Asian Studies began to be appointed at the University of Kent and a Centre established there in 1978. Developments also took place in several other British universities which strengthened the study of Southeast Asia. The 1960s and 1970s were, as Peter Carey states, "a golden age" in British Southeast Asian Studies (1986, pp. 9–14, 16).

By the early 1980s there were some 50 staff across the three established Centres with a further 50 or so individuals with a professional interest in the region spread across other universities, museums and libraries. Nevertheless, from 1975 there was some retrenchment followed by severe cuts in the early 1980s. Many of the gains of the Hayter years were soon lost with about one-third of the staff in Southeast Asian Studies retiring or leaving for other posts from the three designated Centres (King 1990, p. 13; Carey 1986, pp. 17–20). For example, in the Department of South East Asia at SOAS the staff base of 16 in 1976–77 had halved to 8 by 1986–87 (Shackle 2003, p. 73).

CONFIDENCE BREEDS SUCCESS

The Association of South-East Asian Studies in the United Kingdom (ASEASUK)

Let us now look at other developments from the 1960s. The academic expansion following Hayter gave a new found confidence to the senior figures in Southeast Asian Studies and they felt that the time was ripe to begin to coordinate this developing scholarly enterprise and raise its national profile. A proposal was agreed to found an Association to represent those professionally involved in the study of Southeast Asia. Even so the Southeast Asian Studies constituency was still relatively small and residentially concentrated in the 1970s in the three main Centres of Southeast Asian Studies. The major role played by senior academics of the Centre of South East Asian Studies at SOAS in the early years of the Association was to be expected.

The Association of South-East Asian Studies (recently its title was modified from "South-East" to "Southeast") was initially promulgated and administered by a primarily London-based professoriate comprising three Professors from SOAS: Jeremy Cowan, Charles Fisher, Stuart Simmonds, and one from the LSE, Maurice Freedman, joined by Dr David Bassett from Hull (King 2009, pp. 3–11). The reason for the Association's formation was stated in the brief circular of May 1969 which was intended to obtain expressions of interest from potential members. It stated "In view of the growth of South-East Asian Studies in the United Kingdom, and the need for co-operation and co-ordination in the development of these studies and in the advancement of our mutual interests, the Association for [sic] South-East Asian Studies has been formed."

At this juncture it is interesting to note with regard to Southeast Asian Studies at the national level that parallel developments were taking place elsewhere since it was in 1969 that senior members of The British Academy began to discuss the possibility of founding a British Institute in Singapore and encouraging the formation of an associated Society of Friends to coordinate and facilitate the development of British-based research in the region. This was another expression of the momentum that had been generated by Hayter and the more general "feel-good factor" in area studies. These Academy discussions achieved a real momentum in 1970 and 1971 just at the time that the ASEASUK was taking its first tentative steps and they involved prominent academics who were to play a role both in the early years of the Association and in the planning for a British Institute, particularly

Maurice Freedman and Jeremy Cowan. The first Committee comprised all
the members of the *ad hoc* Committee (with the exception of David Bassett),
in addition to Professor Mervyn Aubrey Jaspan from Hull, (John) Dennis
Duncanson from Kent and Dr Leslie Hugh Palmier from Bath. With the
exception of Maurice Freedman, who served as the first elected Chair, and
Leslie Palmier, the officers of the Association were drawn from the three
Centres of Southeast Asian Studies. The first list of members compiled in
1971 totalled 64, almost half (31) of whom came from SOAS, 9 from Hull
and 4 from Kent. Therefore, just over two-thirds of the membership came
from the three recognized Centres.

THE BRITISH INSTITUTE IN SOUTH-EAST ASIA: THE ACADEMY IN THE REGION

As we have seen Britain had never established a scholarly institute in Southeast
Asia along the lines of the EFEO in Hanoi and the Dutch Institute in
Batavia. However, the British Academy began to take steps to establish a
British Institute in South-East Asia (BISEA) in Singapore in the 1960s (see
King 2009, pp. 12–20; and Carey 1986, p. 16). Discussions in the Academy
and with The British Council and the Foreign and Commonwealth Office
about the need to found an Institute in Asia go back to at least the mid-
1950s, prompted by the Scarbrough Report (1947). Initially coordinated
by a Committee of the Universities of Oxford, Cambridge and London
the discussions focused on the possibility of establishing an Institute in Far
Eastern or East Asian Studies, concentrating primarily on China and Japan.
The preferred location was Tokyo. Largely for financial reasons the plans
for an Institute which originally was to share premises with The British
Council in Tokyo eventually fell through, though other locations in Kobe,
Kyoto and Yokohama were considered.

Given the long drawn out negotiations over locations in Japan and the
eventual collapse of British plans, it was not until mid-1969 that the Academy
began to entertain the idea of either an Institute of East Asian or South-East
Asian Studies in Singapore. The Singapore government had established its
own Institute of Southeast Asian Studies in 1968; possible accommodation
for a British scholarly presence was identified with the planned departure
of British military forces and the availability of vacant premises; positive
support from the Singapore government was forthcoming, and facilities
and communications were excellent. It was also felt that prospects for local
donations and the cooperation of Australian and New Zealand academies
would be much more likely in Singapore. The Academy proceeded to organize

an exploratory meeting in March 1970 and a follow up meeting in December, both chaired by Professor Grahame Clark FBA to which prominent scholars in the fields in which the Institute was to operate (archaeology, art history, history, social and cultural anthropology, and languages and literatures) were invited. Grahame Clark was to go on to serve as the first Chair of the Institute's Management Committee in London from August 1975, to be succeeded by Professor William Watson.

There were wide-ranging debates in these exploratory meetings in 1970 but two major issues surfaced: the regional scope of the Institute and whether or not it should include East Asia, especially China, and whether Singapore was the most appropriate location to support the Academy's efforts to promote archaeological work in a diverse region. There was also some concern whether Singapore's own Institute might present difficulties for the development of a British Institute covering the same region. Following the first meeting the Chair, Grahame Clark, wrote a brief paper for the Academy which began:

> As a meeting-ground of Indian and Chinese culture, the home of a number of indigenous peoples of outstanding interest and the source of great wealth, South-East Asia, comprising Burmah (sic), Thailand, Laos, Cambodia, Vietnam, Indonesia and the Phillipines (sic) [the former British dependencies were omitted from this statement and presumably taken for granted], has strong claims to the serious attention of scholars from a broad range of disciplines. The exploratory meeting held on 19th March 1970 in the Academy's rooms showed that British universities are becoming increasingly aware of the potentialities of this region both for teaching and research. Indeed studies in the geography, archaeology, art, history, economics, sociology and politics of South-East Asia promise to be one of the more significant areas of growth in a number of British universities. If this growing interest — and investment — is to be as productive as it might be, there is an obvious need for some coordination both in this country and in the field. The time is ripe while the situation is still fluid for the Academy to take a lead in this promising field (cited in King 2009, pp. 14–15).

Clarke's paper proposed that a "Society for South-East Asian Studies" be formed and an Institute or School "at some central point in the area" be established. Finally, it was suggested that there seemed to be "a strong case for seeking to coordinate United Kingdom and Australian and New Zealand endeavours in South-East Asia".

It was Edmund Leach who pressed for Maurice Freedman, his former colleague at the LSE and a fellow senior anthropologist, to be fully involved in the deliberations. Freedman was both a Southeast Asianist who had undertaken field research among the Chinese in Singapore and a Sinologist who had published extensively on Chinese society in mainland China, and was at that time involved in the setting up of the Association of South-East Asian Studies which he was then to chair. The possibility of combining Southeast and East Asian interests was therefore left open. Freedman was appointed to undertake a visit to the region on behalf of the Academy between 6 September and 9 October 1971 taking in Singapore, Jakarta, Kuala Lumpur, Bangkok, Manila, Hong Kong, Taipei and Canberra. He submitted his report soon after his return entitled *Proposed British Institute for and in South-East Asia* (November 1971). Given the diversity of the region, Freedman recommended that serious attention be turned to establishing a multi-site Institute with an administrative centre in Singapore and two bases with library resources to support field research in Bangkok (to cover mainland Southeast Asia) and Jakarta (for the island world); the mainland-island divide surfaced yet again. He also suggested that Manila might have its attractions if a single site Institute was established and he pointed to strong links between the Philippines and Hong Kong scholarship on Southeast Asia. Above all Freedman argued for the vigorous pursuit of a joint Australian-British Institute.

A third meeting, again chaired by Grahame Clark, was organized in February 1972 to consider the Freedman report. The decision was taken to recommend to the Council of the Academy that a British Institute be established. Proposals went to the Council at its meeting on 26 October 1972 and approval was given to proceed to found an Institute to be located in Singapore, for an initial period of three years. Its purpose was to promote joint endeavours with local scholars on research objectives of mutual interest in Southeast Asia (particularly in the fields of archaeology, history, art history and anthropology); to keep British scholars informed of needs and priorities in regard to research work in the region; and to arrange for collaboration and secure the necessary permits for British scholars to work there (see Carey 1986, p. 16; and Villiers 1980, p. 1).

The Institute Directorship was advertised in 1974. Dr Milton Osborne, an Australian citizen who was then in the Department of History at Yale, with experience in the Australian Foreign Service and good relations with French academe, and a distinguished historian of Indochina, was appointed to the post in October of that year. The link to Australia was confirmed. A Management Committee chaired by Grahame Clark was also established. Although Milton Osborne commenced his duties from August 1975 it was not until February 1976 that the Institute was finally registered in

Singapore under the Societies Act; it took up a small office suite in the International Building in Orchard Road. For Southeast Asianists in the UK who were undertaking research in the region the Institute provided valuable support, connections and facilities. It served to demonstrate forcefully that Britain was firm in its commitment to the development of scholarly activities in and on the area. The Institute also introduced Travelling Fellowships for British researchers from 1976, a welcome support for field research in the region.

To round off this brief excursion into the history of the Institute, Milton Osborne resigned as Director in February 1979 to be succeeded by Dr John Villiers from 1 October 1979, again an historian and someone with considerable administrative and diplomatic experience who was a leading scholar of the early European (Portuguese and Spanish) mercantile period in Southeast Asia. Under John Villiers the Institute embarked on a broad range of activities. It provided research funds through its own and Leverhulme-funded Fellowships and travel grants; it organized symposia, conferences and seminars, launched its own newsletter and developed a small library. In July 1982 it also appointed an Assistant Director, Dr Gregory Forth, an Oxford-trained anthropologist who had worked in eastern Indonesia and who took up his post in Singapore from January 1983.

In 1982 the Management Committee in London, under William Watson's tutelage, extended its membership to include the then Chair of ASEASUK, David Bassett. Ian Glover, a leading archaeologist of Southeast Asia, was also appointed. In addition, Victor King, then Honorary Secretary of ASEASUK, took up the newly created post of Honorary Secretary of the Management Committee from 1 August 1982. Thus the relationship between the Academy, the Institute and ASEASUK increased immeasurably from this time. Prior to this and with the exception of Jeremy Cowan, a founding member of ASEASUK, the Management Committee had comprised Fellows of the Academy, who, though they possessed Asian experience and expertise, had no direct links to or membership in the Association.

Unfortunately during the first part of the 1980s the Institute then began to suffer from the increasing costs of operating in Singapore (to economise it moved from Orchard Road to cheaper rented premises on Beach Road), the need to continue to support the wider range of activities it had developed and to fund its increased staff base. There was also a more general squeeze on public finances. To that end the decision was taken to close the office in Singapore and move to premises in Bangkok where it was hoped that costs would be considerably reduced. The Institute moved in mid-1984 and was formally registered in Bangkok in October 1984. Yet the financial situation did not improve and the decision was taken to close the Institute officially in December 1985. Its operations were gradually run down and the library sold off, and sadly the Institute, just over a decade after its foundation, ceased operations in Bangkok in June 1986.

THE BRITISH ACADEMY COMMITTEE FOR SOUTH-EAST ASIAN STUDIES: THE ACADEMY RETURNS HOME

Very fortunately for Southeast Asian scholarship in the United Kingdom the Academy sustained its firm commitment to the support of advanced research on the region. It decided to establish a London-based Committee for South-East Asian Studies in 1986, on a very modest budget, whose main responsibilities were to approve and sponsor research projects and activities, and to keep the Academy informed about the needs of British-based researchers in Southeast Asia and the opportunities for research there. The Committee, under the chairmanship of Professor William Beasley, received its first grant in 1987 and began the task of developing a programme of work, which was continued by Professor Jeremy Cowan as chair from 1990 to 1998. Victor King continued as Honorary Secretary and then took over as Chair in 1998. Links between the Academy through its Committee for South-East Asian Studies and ASEASUK became even closer from 1986, particularly because several members of the Association served on the Committee and funds were provided to support various Association activities and the research of many of its members. However, in this ever closer relationship between the Association and the Academy, ASEASUK did not develop into a "Society of Friends" of an Academy-funded Learned Society. Indeed, it was not until 2005 that the Academy's Committee was eventually incorporated (officially and constitutionally) into the Association as its Research Committee. This followed discussions with the Academy conducted on ASEASUK's behalf by the then Chair of the Academy Committee, Professor Robert Taylor and the Secretary, Professor Jonathan Rigg and his successor Dr Tim Harper.

ASEASUK was also successful in securing continuing research funding for a five-year period from 2005–06 from the Academy and is recognized currently as an Academy-funded Learned Society with the responsibility of disbursing grants for field research and for the support of conference panels, publications, and related outreach activities. Unfortunately, recent reductions in the Academy's budget will see this support discontinued in

2012, although the Association has been charged with the evaluation of a Research Fellowship scheme for Southeast Asia, with modest funding from the British Academy, which will be implemented from 2011.

THE PARKER REPORT (1986):
A BRIEF RESPITE

Let us now return to the mid-1980s at a time when the British Institute was in process of winding down and the severe cuts in university staffing had also impacted on area studies provision (Carey 1986, pp. 17–20). The situation had become so difficult for area studies from the second half of the 1970s that even in 1981 the Vice-Chancellor of London, supported by the Vice-Chancellors of Oxford and Cambridge, called for a new enquiry into area studies to review national provision twenty years after Hayter. Eventually Sir James Craig, former British Ambassador to Syria (1976–79) and Saudi Arabia (1979–84) was appointed to undertake the enquiry in 1984. Sadly he retired from it in May 1985 because of the pressure of other commitments and was succeeded by Sir Peter Parker, a businessman and former Chairman of British Rail, who had wide-ranging international experience and a particular interest and expertise in East Asia (Carey 1986, pp. 19–20). The Parker Review was done on a shoestring budget, in a short space of time, with no committee and little administrative support; it also concentrated much more narrowly on national needs in diplomacy and commerce which required expertise in Asian and African languages and area studies (King 1990, p. 4). Parker's conclusions expressed the same disappointments and anxieties as the previous reports. In his letter which accompanied his report delivered to the UGC, he says "We have to face the fact that since at least the early 70s there has existed no national policy for Oriental and African Studies, nor any effective system of coordination between those institutions engaged in them" (1986, p. 2). Again the reference point is primarily the USA and not other European neighbours when Parker emphasizes that this predicament was "in sharp and shaming contrast with the United States" (ibid., p. 1). In his international comparisons he devotes some time to considering the American funding system for area studies (ibid., pp. 79–83), with brief reference to the French Institute in Paris, Oriental Studies at Leiden and Utrecht in the Netherlands (ibid., p. 84), and the fact that in Germany "no government policy on Asian and African Studies has been formulated" (ibid., p. 85).

In his view the UK had seen "an unwitting retreat from the Scarbrough-Hayter principles" (ibid., p. 4) and the national system developed in response to them is "already gradually breaking down" (ibid., p. 11). For Parker this was happening because "there has been no monitoring of the national stock of expertise in studies of Africa and Asia ... Nor has there been any systematic planning of provision" (ibid.). In his observations on national foreign language capability he contrasts Britain's weaker commitment to language training with the approach of its main European partners and competitors (ibid., pp. 1–18). Following the submission of the Parker Report there was a brief respite in that some funds were forthcoming for a limited number of posts, studentships and training fellowships in Asian and African Studies (some funds were provided for Southeast Asian Studies at SOAS and Hull, but not Kent). In some cases they enabled the position to be retrieved somewhat from the 1970s and early 1980s but with no real prospect of expansion.

THE AFTERMATH OF PARKER: "PETERING OUT"

The Gold Report (1989)

Four years after the Parker Report doubts were already being raised about the effectiveness and scale of the measures which had been introduced. In a Report by the National Council for Modern Languages in Higher and Further Education (NCML), Dr Peter Gold, its author, presented a rather pessimistic picture of the provision in those languages which Parker had reviewed (1989). The NCML survey was not comprehensive but it pointed to particular areas of concern and that the ambitions which Parker had set down clearly had not been fulfilled (see King 2001b, pp. vii–viii). Although some language provision had maintained a steady state, including Japanese and Chinese, other languages including those in Southeast Asia had "struggled for survival". Gold also noted that "there remain gaps in some areas which a nation with Britain's wide interests cannot leave indefinitely unfilled without damage to its diplomatic credibility or commercial capacity" (1989, p. 9). This national demise continued to worsen.

The Area Studies Monitoring Group and the Hodder-Williams Report (1993)

Parker had also proposed strongly that national provision in Oriental and African Studies and Languages be monitored and to this end in the early

1990s an Area Studies Monitoring Group was established, chaired by HRH The Prince of Wales (King 2001*b*, p. xi). The Group commissioned a Report and the compilation of a database of Area Studies in the United Kingdom under the auspices of the Coordinating Council of Area Studies Associations (CCASA) and funded by the Economic and Social Science Research Council (ESRC) (Hodder-Williams 1993). The Report noted that the Parker Report's proposal for "on-going monitoring" of national provision had not been implemented. With regard to provision in Southeast Asian languages, the *Executive Summary* concluded that this was "relatively weak" (Taylor 1994, p. 4). Overall the Report concluded that though area studies in the United Kingdom was not in a critical condition, "it is a cause for concern" and that a national approach and monitoring was essential (1993, p. 60).

CONTINUING DECLINE IN THE 1990s

In the event much of what Parker and others proposed has not been implemented and there has been no further national review of provision and future needs, although there have been *ad hoc* national exercises and reviews covering particular areas, such as the HEFCE provision for "minority subjects" (see, for example, 2000) and the British Academy's reviews of its learned societies (see, for example, 1996). More generally the efforts at national monitoring, following Parker, deteriorated dramatically. The Area Studies Monitoring Group ceased to operate after a few years and the Coordinating Council of Area Studies Associations seemed to slip into oblivion, though the Council produced another report on "area studies monitoring" in the late 1990s (Werbner 1999), and an Area Studies Directory was launched in 1998 at the University of Manchester, though now apparently no longer active (CCASA 1998). In his Report Professor Richard Werbner drew attention to the lack of representation of Area Studies and non-Western academic interests on the Boards of the ESRC and the Research Committee and Board of the HEFCE, which, for him, in turn helped explain "the almost complete lack of substantial funds for major fields of research in many disciplines of the Arts, Humanities and Social Sciences throughout whole regions of the world" (1999, pp. 3–4). But following the disappearance of CCASA it was not until 2003 that a new body emerged to replace it: the United Kingdom Council for Area Studies Associations (UKCASA), operating through the Subject Centre for Languages, Linguistics and Area Studies at the University of Southampton and embracing all the major professional area studies associations. But even with the more recent reconstitution of area studies in the UK no new national review has been commissioned and no active monitoring of provision is currently taking place. In this regard the future looks bleak.

INTO THE TWENTY-FIRST CENTURY (WITH TREPIDATION)

It has now been over twenty years since the last major review of area studies and since then Southeast Asian Studies specifically has continued to decline with the closure of the Kent Centre in 1991 and Hull's phasing out of its Southeast Asian programmes from 2002 to 2005. Invariably it is noted in public documents that the state of Southeast Asian Studies has decreased further from the level which was envisaged in the 1960s and 1970s (see, for example Asian Studies Panel 2009). This decline is not the case with some other regional studies in the Asian context with more recent injections of funding of the order of £25 million under the joint HEFCE/ESRC/AHRC Language Based Area Studies initiative from 2006–11 for Chinese and Japanese Studies, along with Arabic and Middle Eastern Studies and Russian and East European Studies. There were also reviews following Parker: the UGC Review of Soviet and East European Studies (Wooding 1989) and the Higher Education Funding Council for England Review of Chinese Studies (1999). These provided some funding in areas considered to be vulnerable and of strategic importance to the UK and this initiative is likely to be carried forward, with more modest funding, from 2011 to 2015.

However, Southeast Asia, which is clearly not considered to be of sufficient strategic importance by government and other agencies in the UK, has failed to secure any substantial additional funding since the 1980s. The study of its languages and cultures has continued to lose ground. But it should be noted that the current national landscape is a mixed one. The decline in the main area centres has pushed provision back to what was available in the 1960s when the UK was beginning to gain momentum from Hayter funding. However, the ASEASUK remains buoyant with some 190 members and a survey undertaken in the year 2000 identified about 220 individuals who had a professional interest in the region (King 2001*b*; 2009, pp. 27–28; Khng and King 2001); currently the register is being updated and over 100 individuals have been listed so far (King 2009, p. 36). ASEASUK is the longest established professional association focusing on Southeast Asia in Europe along with the South-East Asia Library Group (SEALG) which was founded in the UK in 1968 and which then extended its membership to other parts of Europe. The only comparable professional national body in continental Europe is L'Association Française pour la Recherche sur l'Asie du Sud-Est (l'AFRASE), established in 1984. Germany has always emphasized Asian Studies rather than the sub-regions and it set up an Association for Asian Studies in 1967. At the European level the European Association for South East Asian Studies (EUROSEAS) was launched in 1992; the specialist European Association of Southeast Asian Archaeologists (EurASEAA) emerged in the 1980s and held its first conference in London in 1986, and the European Colloquium on Indonesian and Malay Studies came into being in 1977.

Aside from its longevity ASEASUK also continues to produce its biannual newsletter, which is the longest standing national newsletter of its kind on the region in Europe; it maintains a website and continues to hold an annual conference (other than in every third year when the European Association of Southeast Asian Studies [EUROSEAS] holds its conference). An important development in the UK, which began to gather pace from the 1980s was the increasing geographical spread of those professionally involved in Southeast Asian Studies and the decline in concentration in the three main centres (King 2005, pp. 20, 23–24). Now the majority of ASEASUK members are scattered in ones and twos, sometimes threes in some forty institutions when in the 1970s they were heavily concentrated in just three centres. There has also been a movement away from area studies and the traditional disciplinary interests of Southeast Asian Studies into the multi- and inter-disciplinary fields of development, environment, media and communication, business and management, drama and performance, museum and library studies.

Interestingly some twenty years ago Professor Bernhard Dahm perceived an important difference between Asian Studies in Germany which he indicated was a much more dispersed enterprise with over thirty universities involved, including eighteen institutes with some interest in Southeast Asia, and the UK which at that time concentrated its work on Southeast Asia in three centres of study (n.d., p. 2). As he noted this was a product of the "cultural autonomy of the various German states" which has resulted in the absence of any notable national approach or policy for Asian Studies, apart from the coordinating function performed by the Institute of Asian Studies in Hamburg (ibid., p. 3). However, much has changed since then and the UK, with the demise of two of its centres, has become increasingly like Germany in its disparate Southeast Asian Studies constituency, notwithstanding the continued dominance of SOAS. Of course, in contrast Southeast Asian expertise in France is heavily focused in Paris. Nevertheless, in an attempt to decentralize some of this activity, a Southeast Asian programme was established at the University of Provence (Maison Asia Pacifique).

We might see these developments in the UK as a welcome means of spreading risks, but there may be very little synergy between research undertaken by the solitary academic or academics working on Southeast Asia in widely scattered institutions, and with staff turnover expertise can disappear from an institution as suddenly as it appears. Another problem occasioned by the decline in the centres is the difficulty of accessing language training for researchers, and this in spite of the availability of e-based and distance learning. The current financial difficulties experienced by universities in the UK also suggests that we shall go through a similar process of retrenchment as in the 1980s and this at a time when a significant number of scholars in Southeast Asian Studies are within retirement range with probably no prospect of replacement (King 2009, p. 35).

An interesting recent development in the UK is the closer collaboration between researchers on those sub-regions of Asia which, for mainly Western colonial considerations, were separated, particularly between East and Southeast Asia. We have already seen that in the 1960s and 1970s the British Academy's deliberations on the establishment of an overseas institute in Asia wavered between a location in Japan and Singapore and between a focus on either East Asia or Southeast Asia. Recently the Academy has set up several international advisory panels, one of them an East Asian Panel which includes Southeast Asia. Following the closure of the Hull Centre for South-East Asian Studies the remaining staff members were absorbed into the Department of East Asian Studies at Leeds University. For a time SOAS brought its South East Asia department into a coalition with that on South Asia. Oxford with its Faculty of Oriental Studies and Cambridge with its Faculty of Asian and Middle Eastern Studies have long combined the sub-regions of Asia into an all-embracing field of study.

In this respect the character of and developments in the study of Southeast Asia in the UK are now following those in other European countries where the emphasis has generally been on the integrated study of Asia, exemplified particularly in the French EFEO which covers all the major regions of Asia and other programmes of study in the Parisian Écoles, the founding by the Scandinavian countries of the Nordic Institute of Asian Studies (NIAS) in Copenhagen in 1968, the Dutch establishment of the International Institute for Asian Studies (IIAS) (Leiden and Amsterdam) in 1993 and the Institute of Asian Studies within the German Institute of Global and Area Studies (GIGA) in Hamburg established in 1956. These three institutes along with SOAS, the Centre for International Studies and Research (CERI-Sciences Po) in Paris, the Centro de Estudios de Asia Oriental at the Universidad Autonoma de Madrid, the European Institute for Asian Studies in Brussels and the Swedish School of Advanced Asia-Pacific Studies have also come together to form the European Alliance for Asian Studies which was established in 1997. Interestingly even when Southeast Asia is designated as a region in University programmes in other parts of Europe they are often brought together with the study of East Asia as in Lund and Gothenburg. Nevertheless, there are separate centres of research and teaching in Southeast Asian Studies elsewhere in Europe, but as in the UK they are few and far between, though they are in well recognized departments and programmes in such places as Leiden, Passau and Provence.

BRITISH AND OTHER EUROPEAN TRADITIONS: ARE WE ALIKE?

Let us finally consider some of the academic contributions of British-based scholars in creating a region. It was the late Professor Ralph Smith, in what I still consider to be a key paper on British intellectual efforts and perspectives on Southeast Asia, who posed the question back in the mid-1980s of whether or not we are able to discern a "British tradition in Southeast Asian Studies"? (1985). So far as I know it was one of the first, if not the first attempt to pose such a question. It came at a time when Southeast Asian Studies programmes were under threat from the financial stringencies of the early Thatcher years. Smith's proposals need to be considered in relation to Southeast Asian Studies programmes elsewhere in Europe and in the USA.

The German-Austrian Contribution

I have already touched on the advantages which British sojourners and travellers in Southeast Asia enjoyed in the attempts to look beyond a particular colonial territory. However, this did not ensure that Southeast Asia would emerge as a region in much of British scholarship until we reach the 1930s. Indeed, as Reid has argued the term "Southeast Asia" had "a much longer pedigree" in German language scholarship on the Far East. It was to be two German-speaking émigrés to the USA who were to play a very significant role in the development of the concept of Southeast Asia in the period from the late 1930s into the 1940s. Reid suggests that the reason for this wider regional perspective of German and Austrian scholars, who interestingly were all working in the field of prehistory and ethnology, apart from Karl Pelzer who was a geographer, is that

Germany and Austria had no Asian colonies [and] their scholars were free of obligations or restrictions in any one of the colonial traditions which had divided the region. They appear thereby to have perceived its unities (1999, p. 10).

I think it is more than this in that their perspectives were also influenced by their interest in specific areas of preclassical ethnology and the occurrence across the region of certain cultural artefacts whose distribution they wished to explain. It was Robert Baron van Heine-Geldern, the Austrian ethnologist and prehistorian, who came to have an enormous early influence on the popularization of the term "Southeast Asia" (Südostasien) in his work in prehistory and material culture and on the contacts and exchanges between the people who settled the region (see, for example 1923, 1927). He wrote a number of publications in German in the 1920s and 1930s using the term "Southeast Asia" whilst working at the Natural History Museum in Vienna and then at the University of Vienna, where he held a Chair from 1931. But it was not until his later work, which he published in English during his temporary residence in the United States that his influence became much more significant (Heine-Geldern 1942/1956). He had left Austria for the sanctuary of the USA in 1938 where he worked at the American Museum of Natural History in New York. He also took a leading role in establishing the East Indies Institute in New York in July 1941 which was to become the Southeast Asia Institute, the first organization in America to carry the name "Southeast Asia" (see Heine-Geldern 1943). He returned to Vienna in 1950.

Heine-Geldern was predated and had been influenced by the research of Franz Heger, another Austrian ethnologist who also worked at the Natural History Museum in Vienna, and who published an influential paper on Dongson drums, also using the term "Southeast Asia" in the title of the publication (1902). Indeed Reid traces German scholarship back still further, again in work on bronze drums in Southeast Asia by Adolf Bernard Meyer and Wilhelm Foy, who published *Bronze-Pauken aus Sudost-Asien* in the Dresden Ethnographic Museum's series in 1897. Yet another German-speaking scholar, Karl Josef Pelzer, similarly wrote his early work on Southeast Asia in German (1935), but in moving to the USA and becoming a central figure in the development of Southeast Asian Studies at Yale University he, like Heine-Geldern, made several important contributions not just to the popularization of the term "Southeast Asia" in English-speaking scholarly circles but also to the creation of a region (1945).

French Classical Studies and the British Shift to Modern Studies

On the other hand colonial French scholarship primarily confined itself to Indochina, although Denys Lombard makes the important point that, even from the sixteenth century, and especially from the seventeenth century French observers made important contributions to our understanding of other parts of Southeast Asia, particularly the island world (1981, p. 53). However, from the nineteenth century, when territories began to be claimed exclusively by one or another colonial power, French scholarship became increasingly focused on France's Indochinese possessions. Even then there were a few French scholars who realized that there were important cultural and historical links between mainland and island populations. The main contributor to this wider perspective was Georges Coedès, Director of the EFEO in Hanoi before the Second World War, who examined the common experiences and character of the "Hinduized" states of Indochina and Indonesia. The work of Coedès and indeed Lombard and many other French scholars also demonstrates the very significant commitment of the French to the study of what we might term "classical studies" in archaeology, material culture, philology, literature, art history and ethnology rather than in what Hayter and others in the UK came to refer to as "modern studies" (see, for example, Lombard 1981, pp. 55–56; and see Braginsky 2002).

In fact, it was the major shift in emphasis effected by Hayter in 1960–61 that began to move the focus of earlier British scholarship, which at that time was located mainly at SOAS, but also at Oxford and Cambridge, from what Braginsky has called the study of "classical civilizations" (in early history and prehistory, philology, anthropology, archaeology, linguistics, languages, literatures, religion, art and more broadly culture) towards the study of modern history, politics, geography, economics and sociology. However, I think we need to qualify this observation to some degree. British attention to modern Southeast Asian politics and economics and to the problems of late colonialism and the issues posed by the newly emerging nations of the region were certainly not insignificant in the pre-Hayter period. An important source of inspiration in these fields was John Furnivall who produced several important studies from the late 1930s on the political economy of British Burma and the Dutch East Indies and on more general issues of social and economic welfare, education and progress in the region (1931, 1939*a*, 1939*b*, 1941, 1943, 1945, 1948) (see below). Furthermore, if attention is confined to research and teaching within the UK in the immediate years after Scarbrough, as Braginsky does, then again the emphasis on classical studies is understandable. However, if our vision is widened to include British scholarship in Malaya and Singapore in the 1950s and early 1960s, then a rather different picture emerges. It was precisely within the region that the study of current issues by expatriate British and Commonwealth researchers was nurtured. In this respect the often assumed contrast between post-war American studies of development, change and nation-building and the classical traditions of Asian Studies in Europe, conducted mainly by scholar-administrators and colonial servants, does require qualification (see, for example, Braginsky 2002, pp. 11–23).

Asian Studies in Europe: Colonialism, Orientalism, Classical Studies and All That

Before returning to examine British scholarship on the region it is instructive to consider briefly Bernhard Dahm's attempt to identify the distinctive differences between "Asian Studies [including Southeast Asian Studies] in Europe" and other parts of the world as well as those between German and other traditions (n.d., pp. 1–5; and see Stokhof 2003 and Van der Velde, n.d.). He identifies three important features of European Asian Studies. First, there is the long-established European scholarly interest in Asia (n.d., p. 1). As we have seen, if we include studies of the Near and Middle East, within the scope of what was referred to in Europe as "Oriental Studies" this scholarly interest within universities goes back almost 400 years. This longevity is also supported by extensive library, archival, manuscript and museum collections.

Secondly, there is the fact that this field of study was "designed and practised as part and parcel of colonial expansion" (ibid.). This has given a particular edge and anxiety to the contemplation of the history of European scholarship on Asia, in the debates which have been engaged in about the European construction of the Orient, and in the European attempts to rethink that contribution and to reposition themselves in relation to scholarship from within Southeast Asia itself. It was of course also a focus for debates with American scholars about the need to move away from imperialist assumptions about the post-war development of Southeast Asia to one which, from an American perspective, recognized "national" aspirations and priorities and the need to promote social, economic and political development (Smith 1986, p. 16).

Thirdly, Dahm argues for the "high quality" of European philological studies on Asia, "unparalleled up to the end of the colonial period which continued to make deep imprints on Asian Studies in Europe thereafter" and which were also "appreciated" by "the emerging new elite in the various colonies" (n.d., p. 2). In this respect he refers to the work in classical studies by Krom, Stutterheim, Coedès, Luce and Harvey among others. This tradition is also emphasized by Martin Platt who, in comparing Southeast Asian Studies between the United States and Europe, suggests that in European universities "the study of language and literature is taken more seriously", an approach which is in turn based on their long-established "textual and philological tradition" (2006, pp. 91–95).

However, in his rather stern judgement of British classical scholarship, Smith suggests that "the scholarly achievement of the Dutch and the French in South-East Asia was on a far higher level than that of the British" (1986, p. 4). According to Smith the possible reasons for this were two-fold: first, "the more systematic approach of 'continental' scholarship; by the side of which the British approach was often said to be 'amateurish'"; it was above all the "thoroughness of French and Dutch scholars" which impressed Smith, and he states categorically that "no British scholar could compete with the erudition and achievements of Georges Coedès" (ibid., p. 5); second, there was the important fact that "the *principal* territorial possessions of both the Dutch and the French in Asia lay in our region [i.e. Southeast Asia]" (ibid., pp. 4, 15).

In this latter respect Smith's argument turns on the preoccupation which the British had with the Indian subcontinent and the fact that the major centres of British scholarship were located in Bombay, Calcutta and Madras, with Rangoon and Singapore as distant outliers of scholarly activity. Of course the British also had scholarly interests in Hong Kong and the Shanghai Concession and more generally in China which may help explain an important focus of British Sinologists on the Chinese in Southeast Asia (see, for example, Freedman 1957; Purcell 1951, 1956). On the other hand, the French and Dutch founded research centres for the coordination and support of scholarly work in Southeast Asia itself, in their institutes in Hanoi and Batavia and the quantity and quality of their work in prehistory, history, culture and language was undoubtedly enhanced by virtue of this more intense focus on and within the region. Nonetheless, it is my argument that the breadth of British interest, despite the preoccupation with India and China, did provide a view of Southeast Asia which was more expansive than other colonial powers, though it did not compete with the early vision of European scholars, German and Austrian in particular, who were citizens of countries which had no colonial preoccupations in Asia.

In this connection Dahm proposes that the European focus on classical studies and on the past and its understanding, appreciation and construction rather than on new political developments tended to endure longer "in countries with no colonial past in Asia such as Germany or the Scandinavian countries" (ibid.; and see Stokhof 2003). In contrast, he suggests that in France, the Netherlands and the UK, in response to decolonization problems, and following "some initial hesitations here or there" the former colonial institutes came to focus increasingly on modern Asia (and Southeast Asia).

Of course, the study of modern Southeast Asia has advanced considerably in Germany and Scandinavia since Dahm wrote his paper. But even he drew attention to the increasing interest on the part of German scholars in modern developments in the region (ibid., pp. 2–3), through studies undertaken particularly at the Institute of Asian Affairs in Hamburg. There was also the work undertaken, among others, in Dahm's own Southeast Asia programme at Passau University and in Southeast Asian sociology under Professor Hans-Dieter Evers at Bielefeld. In Scandinavia Dahm also referred to the establishment of the Nordic Institute of Asian Studies in Copenhagen whose mission was to focus increasingly on modern issues (ibid., p. 2).

I concur with Dahm that there was clear evidence of increasing post-war interest in modern developments in Southeast Asia among the former colonial powers. Yet I think that this did not go as far in France as it did in the UK in that the French, through such well established institutions as the EFEO, have maintained a strong commitment to classical scholarship. On the other hand the case of the Netherlands seems to me to come closest to that of post-war British scholarship in that, in spite of the continuation of the classical tradition in Southeast Asian Studies at Leiden University and the Koninklijk Instituut voor Taal-, Land- en Volkenkunde (now called the Royal Netherlands Institute of Southeast Asian and Caribbean Studies), there was a strong development of modern studies at the University of Amsterdam. This was particularly so in the field of studies associated with Professor Wim F. Wertheim and usually referred to as "Non-Western Sociology". As for the British there was some wavering for a time because the British Academy and SOAS ensured that pre-war and early post-war traditions would continue for a time (Braginsky 2002, pp. 8–27). But the considerable influence of the American model of area studies, which so impressed the Hayter Sub-committee, resulted in a substantial shift towards modern studies in the UK from the 1960s.

A British Tradition? Yes and No

Although there were certain broadly common features of European scholarship on Asia and Southeast Asia, there were also differences in emphasis, focus and development between various European countries. What then were the distinctive features which Smith identified in his attempt to demonstrate a British tradition? He draws attention to (1) a focus on colonial possessions but with a pronounced regional vision; (2) a commitment to discipline despite the post-war move towards interdisciplinary studies; and (3) the background of early scholars of Southeast Asia in colonial administration (and one might add military service) which helps explain their more pragmatic and empirical approach. Importantly, in his attempt to delineate a British tradition he makes comparisons specifically with Southeast Asian Studies in the United States and not with continental Europe. In my own later work I have been unable, in the same fashion, to resist the temptation to draw out differences between European and American approaches and interests in the fields of Southeast Asian anthropology and sociology (King and Wilder 2006, pp. 68–155, 308–19; King 2000, pp. 24–35, 246–48).

First Smith makes the obvious point that the colonial powers focused on those peoples, cultures and places which fell within their colonial domains. This is true to a point, but in the British case it needs to be qualified not simply because of the spread of territories administered by the British which bridged mainland and island Southeast Asia, but also because of the extensive commercial interests which Britain had along the sea routes between India and China. The British presence in Singapore in particular which became a cosmopolitan, outward-looking entrepôt encouraged some expatriate residents to take a wider view of the region, and the early commercial involvement of the British in the Indonesian archipelago and beyond to Siam and those places along the trade routes to Hong Kong and China gave some observers an appreciation of some of the connections between these far-flung territories. Smith is correct when he points to the nineteenth century and especially from the beginning of the British presence in Singapore in 1819 as "a truly formative period" in British scholarship on the region (1986, p. 1).

Smith is also correct that the geographical extent of British writing on the region, reflected "diplomatic, commercial and colonial interests"; yet he seems to imply that this was in some way limiting. However, even in his own survey, we find that British interests not only focused on Burma, Singapore and what is now Malaysia (including Borneo), but also the western regions of the Indonesian archipelago (especially Sumatra and Java), "with some extension northwards to include Thailand (and more occasionally

Indochina)"; furthermore, as extensions to their presence in Singapore, northern Borneo, Labuan and Brunei we should also include parts of the Philippines (ibid., p. 2). This already embraces much of the region which came to be known as Southeast Asia. Therefore, from a "heavy concentration of detailed research in the Malaysia-Singapore area" as a feature of the "British approach" Smith then proposes that, in spite of this focus, British scholarship demonstrates "the desire … for a broad understanding of the region as a whole" (ibid., p. 18). In demonstrating this Smith concentrates mainly on post-war scholarship, but several other observers, including Reid and Harrison, have drawn attention to long-standing British regional interests which go back some 200 years.

In the late eighteenth and the first half of the nineteenth century British writers began to establish themselves as major contributors to our understanding not only of the Malay-speaking regions of the Indonesian-Malay archipelago including the Philippines but also to the wider Southeast Asian region embracing the mainland areas of Siam and Indo-China; in this connection the work of John Crawfurd, John Leyden, J.R. Logan, William Marsden, J.H. Moor, and Thomas Stamford Raffles come to mind, and the papers contained in the twelve volumes edited by Logan of the *Journal of the Indian Archipelago and Eastern Asia* published in Singapore between 1847 and 1862 (see Braginsky 2002, p. 9; Harrison 1961, pp. 245–54; Reid 1999, p. 12). Although the terms used expressed British preoccupations with India and China, including "Indian Archipelago", "Indian Islands and Adjacent Countries" and "Indo-Chinese Nations" these early studies, primarily by writers based in Singapore, gave evidence of a much wider vision of a distinctive region.

However, as Cowan has indicated these contributions were usually seen "as an obscure and unimportant branch of colonial history" (1963, p. 7), falling outside the mainstream of British academic circles, and certainly outside of what was considered to be more significant and advanced British scholarship on Indian and Chinese civilization. Nevertheless, for the "realists" who consider Southeast Asia to be "a coherent empirical reality" rather than a "constructed artefact" this early British scholarship, prior to the emergence of clearly defined colonial territories and the later nationalist movements which went with them, was "explicitly regional … drawing particular sustenance from the central location of the Straits Settlements in the 19th century and earlier" (Reid 1999, p. 12). Therefore, Ralph Smith's defining feature of British scholarship as geographically constrained should be modified and more boldly replaced by the defining principle, at least in certain periods of history, of a significantly developed regional consciousness.

This regional awareness tended to become dimmed as the colonial powers consolidated their hold on particular territories and focused their attention increasingly upon them. It was not until the 1940s and into the early 1960s that we begin to witness again the development of a strong British stream of regional scholarship, as strong in this period, I would venture to suggest as that which emerged from the United States, and culminating in the publication of Charles Fisher's geography of Southeast Asia in 1964. Along with Fisher, Smith singles out Hall's general history and Victor Purcell's study of the Chinese in Southeast Asia as publications which became "standard works" (1986, p. 12); to these I would add the body of work by Furnivall. In my view there is a cluster of studies which mark British scholarship out for special consideration and for their contribution to the creation of Southeast Asia as a field of study. These comprise: EHG Dobby's *South-East Asia* (1950); Charles A. Fisher's *South-East Asia: A Social, Economic and Political Geography* (1964); J.S. Furnivall's *Progress and Welfare in Southeast Asia: A Comparison of Colonial Policy and Practice* (1941), *Problems of Education in Southeast Asia* (1943), and *Colonial Policy and Practice: A Comparative Study of Burma and Netherlands India* (1948); DGE Hall's *A History of South-East Asia* (1955) and his edited volume *Historians of South-East Asia* (1961); Brian Harrison's *South-East Asia: A Short History* (1954); Reginald S. Le May's *The Culture of South-East Asia: The Heritage of India* (1954), and Victor Purcell's *The Chinese in Southeast Asia* (1951).

Of these scholars there are three who stand out for me in their contribution to a field of study: John Sydenham Furnivall (1878–1960) because he predated post-war modern studies of the political economy and national development of Southeast Asia; Daniel George Edward Hall (1891–1979) because he was instrumental, not only in marking out the field of Southeast Asian history, but also because he was the driving force behind the creation of a multi-disciplinary programme of work on Southeast Asia at SOAS during the 1950s, focused on the classical tradition of British scholarship, and the building of a world class Department of History; and finally Charles A. Fisher (1916–1982) because he was an eloquent exponent of both the unity and diversity of Southeast Asia in geographical terms and a major international force in regional geography from the 1950s through to the 1970s.

Firstly, let me say something about Furnivall. In the English literature on the area it was most certainly Furnivall's work on the political economy of British Burma and Netherlands India and on the comparative study of colonial policy and practice which had a significant impact on the development of our thinking. He revealed and examined common themes uniting different colonial dependencies which hitherto had been thought of as separate and as tied to other parts of colonial empires and not interlinked within an identifiable regional context. Furnivall's work has been celebrated in many publications particularly with regard to his concept of the plural society (Evers 1980), but above all he began to conceptualize Southeast Asia as both incorporated into wider systems of economic and political control which had different consequences for the colonized peoples and territories, but which also resulted in them sharing certain common experiences in the emerging era of globalization (Furnivall 1941, 1943).

By the late 1930s Furnivall had already grasped the importance of studying Southeast Asia as a regional unit, though he preferred to use the term "Tropical Far East" or "Tropical Asia" (1941, 1943, 1945). It may be that his American publishers decided to introduce the term "Southeast Asia" in the titles of his two general books published in 1941 and 1943. Nevertheless, he had already captured what Southeast Asia comprised and, despite the intervention of different Western powers, he argued that there were common experiences in the encounter between West and East which needed to be compared in that the West had based its colonial dominion and the social and economic relations so formed "on reason, impersonal law and individual rights" (1948, p. 3). Furnivall says, in his study of "progress and welfare" that

> Few regions are so fertile in material for the study of colonial policy and practice as the Tropical Far East, the region extending from Burma across Thailand (Siam) and Indo-China to the Philippines, and including Malaya and Indonesia. Within this region many peoples, with much in common in their racial character and cultural history, have come at different times and in different ways under the influence of Western nations — Spain and Portugal, Holland, England, France and the United States — which, for all their diversity of traditions and colonial objectives, yet have in common a fundamental unity of culture (1941, p. 3).

Secondly there was Hall who was appointed to the Chair of History at the University of Rangoon in 1920 and took up his position in 1921. He returned to the UK in 1934 to become Headmaster at Caterham School in Surrey until 1949. During the 1930s he had already expanded his interests in British relations with "Further India" into Dutch trade and commerce and more general European commercial relations with Burma. Not only did he have a reading knowledge of Dutch but also French and German which provided him with the basis for a history of the whole of Southeast Asia (Cowan 1980, pp. 152–53). After the war and the expansion occasioned by the *Scarbrough Report* he was appointed to the Chair of South East Asian History at SOAS in 1949. During the early 1950s he travelled to many parts of Southeast Asia, and following his retirement in 1959 he was appointed to a Visiting Professorship of Southeast Asian History in the American heartland of Southeast Asian Studies, at Cornell, which he held until 1973. The close links between Anglo-American Southeast Asian Studies, particularly after the Hayter Enquiry, was also forged by Hall and others through the London-Cornell Project (1962–72). Not only did Hall bring together an outstanding team of historians including Charles Boxer, Jeremy Cowan, Hugh Tinker, Oliver Wolters and Merle Ricklefs, but he also presided over the development and expansion of the Department of South East Asia and the Islands (Braginsky 2002, p. 16). The staff involved in the study of the languages, literatures and art of Southeast Asia during the 1950s reads like a "Who's Who of British-based Southeast Asian Studies": Anna Allott, Johannes de Casparis, Anthony Christie, Patrick Honey, Christiaan Hooykaas, Judith Jacob, Gordon Luce, Gordon Milner, Harry Shorto, Stuart Simmonds and Cyril Skinner (ibid.).

Hall, in the "Preface to the Fourth Edition" of his *tour de force*, *A History of South-East Asia* (1955/1981) re-emphasizes the point that he made in the 1955 edition, that his objective has been "to present South-East Asia as an area worthy of consideration in its own right" and to understand its history in terms of local rather than external perspectives, and not just as a part of the world which in much previous scholarship has been depicted as being influenced, shaped, understood and given meaning from Indian, Chinese and Euro-American activities and perspectives (1981, p. xvi). As Smith notes, Hall was also "rebelling, above all, against the idea that Burma (of which he had most experience) was merely a part of 'greater India'" (1986, p. 18). Also of great importance in understanding Hall's approach to regional history was the influence which other European scholars had on his work including such Dutch writers as Jacob van Leur, Bernard Schrieke and Wim Wertheim and, from the French academy, Georges Coedès' whose study of the Hinduized states of Indo-China and Indonesia Hall regarded as "a work of rare scholarship", but more than this "for presenting for the first time the early history of South-East Asia as a whole" (1981, p. xxviii). What also interests me in Hall's prefatory statements is the broad experience that he had of the region; located primarily in Burma for much of his

Asian career, his book was also based on university lecture courses delivered in London, Rangoon and Singapore, and papers delivered in Jakarta and Bangkok (1981, p. xxix).

Hall also makes reference to the work of his colleague, Charles Fisher at SOAS to the effect that for both of them Southeast Asia has an integrity, distinctiveness and personality of its own in historical, geographical and cultural terms (1981, pp. xvi–xvii). In his introductory chapter he also refers approvingly to the contributions of Purcell and Dobby to our understanding of the region (ibid., p. 3). Hall, in his *History* sets the grounds for the debate about the integrity of Southeast Asia as a region in uncompromising terms. Here the argument for the newly created post-war Southeast Asian programmes at SOAS was given its scholarly justification. As I have argued elsewhere historians were vitally important in the delimitation of a field of study and Hall was the pioneer (King 2005a, 2006). Hall says

> The use of such terms as "Further India", "Greater India" or "Little China" is to be highly deprecated. Even such well-worn terms as "Indo-China" and "Indonesia" are open to serious objections, since they obscure the fact that the areas involved are not merely cultural appendages of India or China but have their own strongly-marked individuality. The art and architecture which blossomed so gorgeously in Angkor, Pagan, central Java and the old kingdom of Champa are strangely different from that of Hindu and Buddhist India. For the key to its understanding one has to study the indigenous cultures of the peoples who produced it. And all of them, it must be realized, have developed on markedly individualistic lines (ibid., p. 4).

Nevertheless, and as has been pointed out on numerous occasions, in the first edition of his *History* Hall did not include an examination of the Philippines, which was seen to be part of an American-oriented Pacific sphere and not properly part of the Indian-influenced sphere of the largest part of Southeast Asia (Smith 1986, p. 12). In this regard Hall was still conforming to an Indian-centric perspective on the region shared by the French and Dutch. Nor had the Philippines for military-strategic reasons, been included in Lord Louis Mountbatten's South East Asia Command (SEAS) based in Ceylon during the Pacific War. However, Hall remedied this omission in his second edition. Furthermore, given the rather fluid character of British Southeast Asian Studies, when Hall was later to address an audience in British Hong Kong in May 1959 on the subject of "East Asian History", he sometimes had the tendency to bring Southeast Asia under the umbrella of East Asian or Far Eastern Studies (1959). Nevertheless, what he did do in that address, referring admiringly to the work of van Leur (1955) among others, was to return to one of his favourite Southeast Asian themes, and argued decisively for the understanding of Southeast Asian history "from within" and in terms of local categories and perspectives (ibid., pp. 7–9, 14–15).

In this connection Brian Harrison, who had been Senior Lecturer in History in the University of Malaya before taking up the Chair in History in Hong Kong, and who hosted Hall's visit there in 1959, had managed to beat Hall to the finishing line in the publication of a general history of Southeast Asia, though Harrison's book was intended only as "a short history" (1954/1966) and it did not compare with the depth and breadth of Hall's study. Harrison was somewhat equivocal in putting his case on behalf of Southeast Asia, reminiscent of the later "constructivist" position when he tells us that the regional designation "South-east Asia ... is a convenient one". For him "the area to which it refers does not form either a political or a cultural entity" (1966, p. ix). Though, on the other hand, he suggests, that the region comprises "a group of countries whose social structures have much in common", and what is most important for him is that their "past history and present politics show many similarities" (ibid.).

Finally, my third major figure in British Southeast Asian Studies was Charles Alfred Fisher. He joined SOAS in 1964 on the creation of a new Department of Geography there, having held posts in Leicester, Aberystwyth, Oxford and Sheffield, and was appointed as Professor of Geography with reference to Asia in the University of London. In the introduction to his monumental study of Southeast Asian geography he says "I certainly regard South-east Asia as a major part of the world, possessing a sufficient measure of overall unity to justify its being viewed first as a single entity" (1964, p. v). Moreover his military experience in Southeast Asia with the Survey Service of the Royal Engineers and in the Japanese POW camp at Changi in Singapore and then on the Burma-Siam Railway in Thailand where he endured enormous privation and hardship, helped him, he says, learn "in some degree to look at South-east Asia from within rather than, as I had hitherto done, from without" (ibid., p. vii).

Fisher firmly presents the view that it was the encounter with the Japanese that brought the Western colonial powers to the realization of the region as an entity in its own right (ibid., p. 3). Having said this, as others have done before and since, he sets out to demonstrate in a truly eloquent and compelling fashion, that this military-strategic-political dimension merely served to give belated recognition to "a distinctive region" in geographical, demographic, historical, cultural, racial, and mental-psychological terms (ibid., p. 7). Although one might consider Fisher's book to be located firmly in the rather old-fashioned tradition of regional geography, Michael Parnwell has argued for the recognition of Fisher as "one of the greatest Southeast Asian geographers" and particularly that "he engaged with, and informed, the issues of the day". Above all it was his dedication to the study of an area from "a solid disciplinary foundation" which marked him out as a scholar of international standing (1996, pp. 108, 122). In an obituary B.H. Farmer also tells us that "Charles Fisher's work amply demonstrates that he had the pen of a ready writer perhaps more so than any other geographer of his generation. He deplored opacity and jargon" (1984, p. 252).

The second feature which Smith identifies in his examination of the British tradition has been "the tendency ... for individual scholars to remain firmly attached to their own departments and to feel that they are making contributions to a specific 'discipline'" (1986, p. 19). I am not entirely convinced that this is a sufficiently distinctive feature of the British approach to the study of Southeast Asia. In my view it is found in continental Europe as well. Smith was attempting to draw a contrast between the British and American approaches, but I am not sure that it works in this respect either. However, I do accept that, in spite of the Hayter proposals to establish multi- and inter-disciplinary centres, the major thrust of the scholarly study of regions in the UK has been firmly rooted in academic disciplines. Apart from relatively brief periods in which the British contribution to the study of Southeast Asia was organized across disciplines the overwhelming weight of work has been located in departments. This was a feature of the way in which the University of Malaya organized its teaching and research on the region; it was also the principle on which the academic structures of the three centres of study in the UK were built. It is now, with the demise of two of the three centres, and the fact that the centre at SOAS has never been overwhelmingly interdisciplinary, an even more dominant feature of the study of Southeast Asia in the UK.

Finally, Smith refers to the early development of Southeast Asian Studies as primarily dependent on "people whose experience of the region ... has been acquired in an official capacity as members of the colonial or the diplomatic services" (ibid., p. 19). We should also include those who worked in higher education in the period of late colonialism in Burma, Malaya and Singapore and draw attention to the involvement of (mainly) young men in the military campaigns in Asia, some of whom subsequently went on to academic careers (among others Fisher, Honey, Shorto and Simmonds at SOAS). In contrast to the American approach this route to scholarly activity seems to be broadly distinctive, but in comparison with the continental European experience it is unexceptional. It is hardly surprising that many of our post-war British scholars in Southeast Asian Studies had seen military action in the East, and taken together with those who had served in the British dependent territories and colonies, then it does mark out a particular cast of mind in approaching the study of a region in which one has been personally involved. In the post-war period this also applies to those who worked in the University of Malaya and lived in Singapore and Kuala Lumpur.

In this respect Smith's comments about the more comfortable engagement of British scholars with the region — in that they were familiar with it and less prone to culture shock — and that they were generally working and serving there, explains their "highly pragmatic approach" (ibid.). Above all, for Smith the British approach, at least in its immediate post-war manifestations, "begins by accepting the discipline of the available source materials and seeking to reconstruct situations or sequences to which they relate: and only afterwards risks a generalisation or two" (ibid., p. 20). Smith contrasts this with the more "conceptual orientation of American historians and political scientists" (ibid., p. 19). There is a measure of truth in this: British academe has not produced a Clifford Geertz or a James Scott. However, in a special issue of the Singapore journal *Sojourn. Journal of Social Issues in Southeast Asia* (April 2009) which compiled a league table of the most influential books on Southeast Asia, whilst American writers were dominant, the UK at least claimed three authors (Furnivall, Leach and Reid [who was British-trained]), whilst the Netherlands delivered two (van Leur and Wertheim [with two books]).

CONCLUSION

In this wide-ranging excursion into the development of the study of Southeast Asia from a British-based and to some extent a European perspective I have emphasized the important, although sometimes contested contribution which Western scholars have made to our understanding of Southeast Asia. Some of my discussion has turned on whether or not there is a distinctive European approach to the study of the region and within that whether or not there is an identifiable British tradition. I have not reached any definite conclusion on these matters; Ralph Smith's attempt to discover such a British tradition is equivocal as is Bernhard Dahm's excursion into European-based Asian Studies. Nevertheless, I do suggest that there were British scholars and observers in the first half of the nineteenth century and in the interwar years and the immediate post-war period who attempted to conceptualize a Southeast Asian region or at least had a wider regional

vision, though so did early German and Austrian scholars. The British
played a not insignificant role in the making of Southeast Asia, and for a
few senior scholars in the 1950s and 1960s both in the UK and in Malaya
and Singapore put down the foundations and developed the academic
infrastructure for the advanced study of the region.

What is very clear from my excursion into the official and institutional
history of the development of Southeast Asian Studies in the United
Kingdom is that it has not been a startling success overall, and to some
extent the success that has been enjoyed is in spite of rather than because
of government policy. All the official inquiries with their recommendations
have, after an initial injection of funds and energy, lost momentum, and,
at the time of writing, there is still no integrated and coherent national
policy for the study of the major areas of the world including Southeast
Asia and the monitoring of national provision. The blame cannot be placed
at the door of any one government or public agency, but it reflects a
popular indifference, even a public ignorance of the Southeast Asia region,
an ignorance which was highlighted by the Scarbrough Commission some
sixty-five years ago. One cannot but feel a degree of sadness and regret that
the long tradition that British scholarship has established in its engagement
with Southeast Asia is in danger of becoming something of an irrelevance
in terms of British national and educational priorities. There does seem
to be possible salvation in the coming together of British-based scholars
who are working across Asia in that there is strength in numbers; this
trend towards an Asian Studies perspective which has always been much
more pronounced in continental Europe, seems to me to be a positive
development. But returning to the theme of the historical construction of
Southeast Asian Studies (and Southeast Asia) perhaps those of us in the
United Kingdom who do have a commitment to the study of the region
might, as consolation, claim some small credit for the healthy condition
of this field of endeavour in the former British dependencies of Singapore
and Malaysia.

Note

*   I mainly render the name of the region as "Southeast Asia", but in institutional
     and other titles in the United Kingdom and in some quotations and biblio-
     graphical references it appears variously as "South-East Asia", "South East Asia"
     and "South-east Asia". I use these other renderings where appropriate.

     Some of the materials for this essay have been taken, mainly in revised
     form, from my recent history of the Association of Southeast Asian Studies in

the United Kingdom (ASEASUK), published by the Association (King 2009) and from King (1990).

References

Acharya, Amitav and Ananda Rajah, eds. "Reconceptualizing Southeast Asia". Special focus. *Southeast Asian Journal of Social Science* 27, no. 1 (1999).

Anderson, Benedict. "Studies of the Thai State: The State of Thai Studies". In *The State of Thai Studies: Analyses of Knowledge, Approaches, and Prospects in Anthropology, Art History, Economics, History, and Political Science*, edited by E. Ayal. Athens, OH: Ohio University Centre for International Studies, Southeast Asia Program, 1978.

———. "The Changing Ecology of Southeast Asian Studies in the United States". In *Southeast Asian Studies in the Balance: Reflections from America*, edited by Charles Hirschman, Charles F. Keyes, and Karl Hutterer. Ann Arbor, MI: The Association for Asian Studies, 1992.

Asian Studies Panel. *RAE2008, Panel Reports: Panel L, Asian Studies*. Bristol: HEFCE, Chair, Victor T. King, 2009.

Bassett, D.K. "Southeast Asian Studies in the United Kingdom". In *A Colloquium on Southeast Asian Studies*, edited by Tunku Shamsul Bahrin, Chadran Jeshurun, and A. Terry Rambo. Singapore: Institute of Southeast Asian Studies, 1981.

[The] British Academy. *The British Schools and Institutes Overseas and Sponsored Societies: An Enquiry by a British Academy Review Committee 1994–95*. Final Report. London: The British Academy, April 1996.

Braginsky, Vladimir I. "Introduction: Research into Classical Civilisations of South East Asia at SOAS and in *BSOAS*". In *Classical Civilisations of South East Asia: An Anthology of Articles Published in The Bulletin of the School of Oriental and African Studies*, edited by Vladimir Braginsky. London and New York: RoutledgeCurzon, 2002.

Carey, Peter. *Maritime Southeast Asian Studies in the United Kingdom: A Survey of Their Post-war Development and the Current Resources*. JASO Occasional Papers, no. 6 (1986).

Chou, Cynthia and Vincent Houben. "Introduction". In *Southeast Asian Studies: Debates and New Directions*, edited by Cynthia Chou and Vincent Houben. The Netherlands: International Institute for Asian Studies and Singapore: Institute of Southeast Asian Studies, 2006*a*.

———, eds. *Southeast Asian Studies: Debates and New Directions*. The Netherlands: International Institute for Asian Studies and Singapore: Institute of Southeast Asian Studies, 2006*b*.

Coedès, George. *Histoire Ancienne des États Hindouisés d'Extrême Orient*. Hanoi: Imprimerie d'Extrême Orient, 1944.

Coordinating Council of Area Studies Associations (CCASA). *Area Studies Database of Expertise in the UK*. Manchester: University of Manchester, 1998.

Cowan, C.D. "South East Asian History in London". Inaugural lecture, University of London School of Oriental and African Studies, 1963.

————. "Obituary: Daniel George Edward Hall". *Bulletin of the School of Oriental and African Studies* 43 (1980): 149–54.

Cribb, Robert. "Region, Academic Dynamics, and Promise of Comparitivism: Beyond Studying 'Southeast Asia'?". In *Southeast Asian Studies: Debates and New Directions*, edited by Cynthia Chou and Vincent Houben. The Netherlands: International Institute for Asian Studies and Singapore: Institute of Southeast Asian Studies, 2006.

Dahm, Bernard. *Asian Studies in Europe with Emphasis on Germany*. Available at <http://www.iias.nl/iiasn/iiasn2/emphasis.txt>, n.d.

Dobby, E.H.G. *Southeast Asia*. London: University of London Press, 1950.

Dunn, C.W. and J.R. Firth. "Obituary: J.A. Stewart". *Bulletin of the School of Oriental and African Studies* 13 (1949): 259–64.

Evers, Hans-Dieter, ed. *Sociology of South-East Asia: Readings on Social Change and Development*. Oxford in Asia University Readings. Kuala Lumpur: Oxford University Press, 1980.

Farmer, B.H. "Obituary: Charles Alfred Fisher, 1916–1982". *Transactions of the Institute of British Geographers*, n.s., 9 (1984): 252–54.

Fisher, Charles A. *South-East Asia: A Social, Economic and Political Geography*. London: Methuen and Co. Ltd., 1964.

Freedman, Maurice. *Chinese Family and Marriage in Singapore*. London: HMSO, 1957.

————. *Proposed British Institute for and in South-East Asia*. London: The British Academy, typescript, November 1971.

Furnivall, John S. *An Introduction to the Political Economy of Burma*. Rangoon: Burma Book Club, 1931.

————. *Netherlands India: A Study of Plural Economy*. Cambridge: Cambridge University Press. 1939*a*.

————. *The Fashioning of Leviathan*. Rangoon: Zabu Meitswe Pitaka Press, 1939*b*.

————. *Progress and Welfare in Southeast Asia: A Comparison of Colonial Policy and Practice*. New York: International Secretariat, Institute of Pacific Relations, 1941.

————. *Problems of Education in Southeast Asia*. New York: International Secretariat, Institute of Pacific Relations, 1943.

————. *The Tropical Far East*. London: Oxford University Press, 1945.

————. *Colonial Policy and Practice: A Comparative Study of Burma and Netherlands India*. Cambridge: Cambridge University Press, 1948.

Gold, Peter. *Post-Parker: The State of Oriental and African Languages Four Years On (with an Addendum of East European Languages)*. Sheffield: For National Council for Modern Languages in Higher and Further Education, mimeo, November 1989.

Hall, D.G.E. *A History of South-East Asia.* 4th ed. London: Macmillan Press Ltd., 1981. First published 1955.

———. *East Asian History Today.* Hong Kong: Hong Kong University Press and Oxford University Press, 1959.

———, ed. *Historians of South East Asia.* London, New York, Toronto: Oxford University Press, Historical Writing on the People of Asia, 1961*a*.

———. "Introduction". *Historians of South East Asia,* edited by D.G.E. Hall. London, New York, Toronto: Oxford University Press, Historical Writing on the People of Asia, 1961*b*.

Harrison, Brian. *South-East Asia: A Short History.* 3rd ed. London: Macmillan and Co. Ltd., 1966. First published 1954.

———. "English Historians of 'The Indian Archipelago': Crawfurd and St. John". In *Historians of South East Asia,* edited by D.G.E. Hall. London, New York, Toronto: Oxford University Press, Historical Writing on the People of Asia, 1961.

Hartog, P.J. "The Origins of the School of Oriental Studies". *Bulletin of the School of Oriental Studies* 1 (1917): 5–22.

Hayter, Sir William. *Report of the Sub-committee on Oriental, Slavonic, East European and African Studies.* University Grants Committee. London: Her Majesty's Stationery Office, 1961.

HEFCE (Higher Education Funding Council for England). *Review of Chinese Studies: Report of a HEFCE Review Group on Chinese Studies.* Bristol: HEFCE, Report, February 99/09, 1999.

———. *Minority Subjects. Allocation of Funding.* Bristol: HEFCE, Report, April 00/17, 2000.

Heger, Franz. *Alte Metalltrommeln aus Südost-Asien.* Leipzig: K. von Heirsemann, 1902.

Heine-Geldern, Robert von. "Südostasien". In *Illustrierte Völkerkunde,* edited by G. Buschan. Vol. 2. Stuttgart: Strecker und Schroder, 1923.

———. "Die Steinzeit Sudostasiens". *Mitteilungen der Anthropologischen Gesellschaft in Wien* 57 (1927): 47–54.

———. "Conceptions of State and Kingship in South East Asia". *Far Eastern Quarterly* 2 (1942): 15–30. Reprinted in the Cornell Southeast Asia Program, Data Paper 18, Ithaca, New York, 1956.

———. *A Survey of Studies on Southeast Asia at American Universities and Colleges.* New York: East Indies Institute of America, 1943.

Hodder-Williams, Richard. *Area Studies in the United Kingdom: A Report to the Area Studies Monitoring Group.* Bristol: mimeo, December 1993.

Jackson, Peter A. "Space, Theory, and Hegemony: The Dual Crises of Asian Area Studies and Cultural Studies". *Sojourn: Journal of Social Issues in Southeast Asia* 18 (2003*a*): 1–41.

———. "Mapping Poststructuralism's Borders: The Case for Poststructuralist Area Studies". *Sojourn: Journal of Social Issues in Southeast Asia* 18 (2003*b*): 42–88.

Khng, Pauline and Victor T. King, eds. and comps. *Register of South-East Asianists in the United Kingdom*. Hull, UK: University of Hull, Association of South-East Asian Studies, under the auspices of the British Academy Committee for South-East Asian Studies, 2001.

King, Victor T. "Social Anthropology and Sociology". In *Research on South-East Asia in the United Kingdom: A Survey*, edited by V.T. King. Hull, UK: Centre for South-East Asian Studies, University of Hull, for the Association of South-East Asian Studies in the United Kingdom, 1989.

————. *Between West and East: Policy and Practice in South-East Asian Studies in Britain*. Hull, UK: Hull University Press, 1990.

————. "Southeast Asia: An Anthropological Field of Study". *Moussons: Social Science Research on Southeast Asia* 3 (2001*a*): 1–31.

————. "Introduction". In *Register of South-East Asianists in the United Kingdom*, edited and compiled by Pauline Khng and Victor T. King. Hull, UK: University of Hull, Association of South-East Asian Studies, under the auspices of the British Academy Committee for South-East Asian Studies, 2001*b*.

————. *Defining Southeast Asia and the Crisis in Area Studies: Personal Reflections on a Region*. Working Papers in Contemporary Asian Studies, no. 13. Lund, Sweden: Lund University Centre for East and South-East Asian Studies, 2005*a*.

————. "Notes on the Current Situation of Southeast Asian Studies in the United Kingdom". *ASEASUK News* 37 (2005*b*): 18–26.

————. "Southeast Asia: Personal Reflections on a Region". In *Southeast Asian Studies: Debates and New Directions*, edited by Cynthia Chou and Vincent Houben. The Netherlands: International Institute for Asian Studies and Singapore: Institute of Southeast Asian Studies, 2006.

————. *The Sociology of Southeast Asia: Transformations in a Developing Region*. Copenhagen: NIAS Press and Honolulu: University of Hawai'i Press, 2008.

————. *A History of ASEASUK: On Its 40th Anniversary*. School of Oriental and African Studies, London: ASEASUK, 2009.

————. "The Development of Southeast Asian Studies in the United Kingdom (and Europe): The Making of a Region". Paper presented at SIEAS International Conference of Research Clusters, The Historical Construction of Southeast Asia, Sogang University Institute for East Asian Studies (SIEAS), Seoul, 2010.

King, Victor T. and William D. Wilder. *The Modern Anthropology of South-East Asia: An Introduction*. London, RoutledgeCurzon and New York: Routledge, reprint, 2006. Originally published in 2003.

Kratoska, Paul, Remco Raben, and Henk Schulte Nordholt, eds. *Locating Southeast Asia: Geographies of Knowledge and Politics of Space*. Singapore: Singapore University Press and Athens, OH: Ohio University Press, 2005.

Le May, Reginald S. *The Culture of South-East Asia: The Heritage of India*. London: Allen and Unwin, 1954.

Lieberman, Victor. "Local Integration and Eurasian Analogies: Structuring Southeast Asian History, c.1350–c.1830". *Modern Asian Studies* 27 (1993): 475–572.

————. "An Age of Commerce in Southeast Asia? Problems of Regional Coherence — A Review Article". *The Journal of Asian Studies* 54 (1995): 796–807.

————. *Strange Parallels: Southeast Asia in Global Context, c800–1830.* Vol. 1, *Integration on the Mainland,* and Vol. 2, *Mainland Mirrors: Japan, China, South Asia, and the Islands.* Cambridge: Cambridge University Press, 2003/2009.

Lombard, Denys. "Southeast Asian Studies in France". In *A Colloquium on Southeast Asian Studies,* edited by Tunku Shamsul Bahrin, Chadran Jeshurun and A. Terry Rambo. Singapore: Institute of Southeast Asian Studies, 1981.

Macdonald, A.W. "The Application of a South East Asia-centric Conception of History to Mainland South East Asia". In *Historians of South East Asia,* edited by D.G.E. Hall. London, New York, Toronto: Oxford University Press, Historical Writing on the People of Asia, 1961.

McVey, Ruth. "Change and Continuity in Southeast Asian Studies". *Journal of Southeast Asian Studies* 26 (1995): 1–9.

————. "Globalization, Marginalization, and the Study of Southeast Asia". In *Southeast Asian Studies: Reorientations,* edited by Craig J. Reynolds and Ruth McVey. Ithaca, NY: Cornell University, Southeast Asia Program Publications, 1998.

Malleret, L. "The Position of Historical Studies in the Countries of Former French Indo-China in 1956". In *Historians of South East Asia,* edited by D.G.E. Hall. London, New York, Toronto: Oxford University Press, Historical Writing on the People of Asia, 1961.

Meyer, A.B. and W. Foy. *Bronze-Pauken aus Südost-Asien.* Dresden: Königliches Ethnographisches Museum zu Dresden, XI, 1897.

Parker, Sir Peter. *Speaking for the Future. A Review of the Requirements of Diplomacy and Commerce for Asian and African Languages and Area Studies.* London: University Grants Committee, 1986.

Parkinson, C. Northcote. *Trade in the Eastern Seas, 1793–1813.* Cambridge: Cambridge University Press, 1937.

Parnwell, Michael J.G. "Geography". In *An Introduction to Southeast Asian Studies,* edited by Mohammed Halib and Tim Huxley. London and New York: I.B. Tauris Publishers, Tauris Academic Studies, 1996.

Pelzer, Karl. *Die Arbeiterwanderungen in Südost-Asien. Eine Wirtschafts- und Bevölkerungs-geographische Untersuchung.* Hamburg: Friederichsen, de Gruyter and Co., 1935.

————. *Pioneer Settlement in the Asiatic Tropics: Studies in Land Utilization and Agricultural Colonization in Southeastern Asia.* New York: American Geographical Society, 1945.

Phillips, C.H. *The School of Oriental and African Studies, University of London 1917–1967: An Introduction.* Winchester: Gabare Ltd., 1967

————. "A History of SOAS, 1917–67". In *SOAS: Since the Sixties,* edited by David Arnold and Christopher Shackle. London: SOAS, précis of Phillips 1967 by David Arnold, 2003.

Platt, Martin. "The Academic's New Clothes: The Cult of Theory *versus* the Cultivation of Language in Southeast Asian Studies". In *Southeast Asian Studies: Debates and New Directions*, edited by Cynthia Chou and Vincent Houben. The Netherlands: International Institute for Asian Studies and Singapore: Institute of Southeast Asian Studies, 2006.

Purcell, Victor. *The Chinese in Southeast Asia*. London and New York: Oxford University Press, Geoffrey Cumberlege, 1951. New edition 1964.

————. *The Chinese in Modern Malaya*. Singapore: D. Moore, 1956.

Reay, Lord. *Report of the Committee Appointed by the Lords Commissioners of HM Treasury to Consider the Organisation of Oriental Studies in London*. London: HM Treasury, 1909.

Reid, Anthony. *Southeast Asia in the Age of Commerce: 1400–1600*. Vol. 1, *The Land Below the Winds*, and Vol. 2, *Expansion and Crisis*. New Haven: Yale University Press, 1988/1993.

————. "A Saucer Model of Southeast Asian Identity". In "Reconceptualizing Southeast Asia", edited by Amitav Acharya and Ananda Rajah. Special focus, *Southeast Asian Journal of Social Science* 27 (1999): 7–23.

Scarbrough, The Earl of. *Report of the Interdepartmental Commission of Enquiry on Oriental, Slavonic, East European and African Studies*. Foreign Office, London: His Majesty's Stationery Office, 1947.

Selth, Andrew. "Modern Burma Studies: A Survey of the Field". *Modern Asian Studies* 44 (2010): 401–40.

Shackle, Christopher. "Language Studies: A Play in Three Acts". In *SOAS: Since the Sixties*, edited by David Arnold and Christopher Shackle. London: SOAS, 2003.

Smith, Ralph. "The Evolution of British Scholarship on South-East Asia 1820–1970: Is there a 'British Tradition' in South-East Asian Studies?". In *Britain and South-East Asia*, edited by D.K. Bassett and V.T. King. Special Issue, Occasional Paper no. 13. Hull, UK: University of Hull, Centre for South-East Asian Studies, 1986.

Stockwell, A.J. "British Imperial Strategy and Decolonization in South-East Asia 1947–1957". In *Britain and South-East Asia*, edited by D.K. Bassett and V.T. King. Special Issue, Occasional paper no. 13. Hull, UK: University of Hull, Centre for South-East Asian Studies, 1986.

Stokhof, Wim. *Development of Asian Studies in Europe*, 2003. <http://www.ndl. go.jp/jp/publication/proceedings/asia2003/asia_sympo04_e.pdf>.

Taylor, R.H. "Executive Summary" of Richard Hodder-Williams, *Area Studies in the United Kingdom: A Report to the Area Studies Monitoring Group*. Bristol: mimeo, December 1993, March 1994.

Van der Velde, Paul. *Re-orienting Asian Studies*, n.d. <ttp://www.paulvandervelde. nl/publications/re_orientingAsianStudies.pdf>.

Van Leur, J.C. *Indonesian Trade and Society*. The Hague: W. van Hoeve, 1955.

Villiers, John. "Editorial". *South-East Asian Studies Newsletter* (British Institute in South-East Asia, Singapore) 1 (1980): 1.

Vlekke, Bernard. *Nusantara: A History of the East Indian Archipelago.* Cambridge, MA: Harvard University Press, 1943.

Werbner, Richard. *Area Studies Monitoring Report: Public Funding of Research.* Coordinating Council of Area Studies Associations, mimeo, November 1999.

Wolters, O.W. *History, Culture and Region in Southeast Asian Perspectives.* Ithaca, NY: Cornell University, Southeast Asia Program Publications, Studies on Southeast Asia, no. 26, 1999; revised edition in cooperation with the Institute of Southeast Asian Studies. Originally published by the Institute of Southeast Asian Studies, Singapore, 1982.

Wooding, Norman. *Review of Soviet and East European Studies.* London: University Grants Committee, mimeo, 1989.

Other materials

These have been consulted in the archives housed at the British Academy in London of the British Institute in South-East Asia, the Management Committee of the Institute, the British Academy Committee for South-East Asian Studies, the Association of South-East Asian Studies in the United Kingdom. Miscellaneous papers of the ASEASUK are also housed in the Wilberforce Building, University of Hull. Annual Reports and Calendars of SOAS, University of Hull and University of Kent at Canterbury have been consulted as well as the Newsletter of the ASEASUK published continuously since November 1984. These have not been referenced in the main text.

9

IT IS HARD TO TEACH AN OLD DOG NEW TRICKS, BUT THERE IS LIFE IN IT YET
The Decolonization of Indonesian Studies in the Netherlands

Freek Colombijn[1]

INTRODUCTION

How can people shake off the yoke of colonization? The question pertains as much to the colonizers as the colonized and by the time most of the citizens of a country ignore this question as something from an irrelevant, distant past social scientists are still motivated, perhaps they feel compelled, to reflect on the matter. In this chapter I want to consider how Dutch social scientists who currently work on Indonesia have come to terms with the colonial ties, which, whether they like it or not, bind them to their subject.

The importance of these colonial ties weighs very unevenly on different disciplines in the social and natural sciences, and the humanities and technical fields. I do not think Dutch anthropologists concentrating on contemporary issues or culture (vernacular architecture, *batik*, informal sector, urban waste), geographers, economists, linguists, and communication scientists looking at the modern media are very much influenced by the former colonial relationship, and for them Indonesia is just another country from the Global South.[2] For Dutch botanists Indonesia is definitely not just any country, and there is for instance a direct ancestry from *De landbouw in den Indische archipel* (*Agriculture in the Dutch Indies Archipelago*, Van Hall and Van de Koppel 1946–1950) to the *Plant Resources of South-East Asia* project (Westphal and Jansen 1989), but this field is not overly burdened by value judgements. Dutch civil engineers, who are sometimes called upon to rehabilitate drainage systems in Indonesia, are strongly aware of the colonial heritage, but with a positive, unproblematic feeling. A recent work on Dutch civil engineering in Indonesia (Ravesteijn and Kop 2008), for instance, gives an excellent overview of Dutch technical achievements, but uses an unashamedly Eurocentric perspective and by and large ignores indigenous solutions found to technical problems.[3]

The need to come to terms with the colonial past has been most pertinent for historians, and for anthropologists and sociologists with a historical inclination. In the remainder of this chapter I will also call these anthropologists and sociologists "historians" for the sake of brevity. Much, if not most, of their work dealing with issues like, for example, ethnic and class relations, nation-building, the functioning of the state, and violence takes a historical perspective partly as a means to understand better what is happening today.

In a broad sense these "historians" carry a colonial burden in three ways. The first burden is formed by the rich library and archival resources in the Netherlands: the National Archive in The Hague, the KITLV (Koninklijk Instituut voor Taal-, Land- en Volkenkunde, Royal Netherlands Institute of Southeast Asian and Caribbean Studies) in Leiden and other institutes together comprise a unique repository of source material, arguably the richest source on Indonesia in the world. The importance of the KITLV for Indonesian Studies lies not only in its historical collection, but also in its policy to acquire every publication in the social sciences and languages on Indonesia that appears today. It is especially strong in books published in Indonesia itself, which are often hard to find in Indonesia. The presence of this wealth of source material is as much a boon as a burden, but in any case it has definitely shaped the way Dutch scholars approach their subject. The presence of these resources has also resulted in a strong empirical orientation in research.

The second colonial burden is the question of how to position oneself *vis-à-vis* the policies and practices of the colonial state, the balance of failures and accomplishments. The Dutch colonial presence in Indonesia is discussed over and over again in Dutch public forums and the media, and it is difficult to avoid moral judgements. For a long time Dutch colonialism in Indonesia was usually constructed in novels, movies, documentaries, exhibitions and history textbooks as something positive and benign (albeit not heroic). The dominant mood was that: "We were doing a nice job, which was prematurely ended by the Japanese invasion and Indonesian revolutionaries." This view has been backed by formal and informal lobbies by people who have personal experience and recollections of colonial life in Indonesia (people of at least 70 years old nowadays). Also younger generations share this romantic view, for example former Dutch Prime Minister Balkenende once publicly called for a reinvigoration of the good-old VOC mentality.[4] The positive appreciation of Dutch colonialism fuses with a broader, warm self-assessment of historically being a seaborne major power in global politics. Taking a critical stand towards colonialism, or only a detached position — as most contemporary historians probably do — gets quickly loaded with a moral judgement in the Netherlands: "If you are not pro colonialism, you must be against." If the historian is not passing a moral judgement, others will do it. I experienced this myself when I presented a research project on urban housing during decolonization to an unreceptive audience of elderly people. "Why are state funds squandered on such research? If you want to do something useful, sort out which Indonesian or Japanese stole my house and where I can place a financial claim!"

The third colonial burden, an inward orientation, is connected to moral debate in the Netherlands. In a way, of course, the public interest in Indonesia has not only been a burden, but also a boon for Dutch historians, because it provides legitimacy — and funds — to their research subject. The price Dutch historians have paid for this domestic public interest in their work is the difficulty of disentangling themselves from the Dutch audience and the moral quibbles about colonialism. The engagement with discussions relevant to the Dutch public and scholarly audience made the work of Dutch historians less relevant for an international scholarly community working on Indonesia. This inward looking orientation is the third colonial burden. Even if Dutch work does relate to international debates (and is written in English), Dutch scholars still seem to suffer from an image problem.

In this chapter, I wish to analyse how the subject of Indonesian Studies has evolved in the Netherlands, and how Dutch historians have been handling this triple colonial burden in order to decolonize the subject. I will start with a sketch of the historical construction of Indonesia as a subject of studies in the Netherlands, and then continue with an analysis of the ways in which Dutch historians have handled the three burdens just mentioned.

Part of the argument is based on interviews with eight historians based in the Netherlands who have devoted a large part, and usually most of their research time to Indonesia. I talked to three retired professors from three Dutch university centres of Indonesian Studies and in each case, at least one of their respective former doctoral students, who have all made successful academic careers. They are Jan Breman from the University of Amsterdam with his doctoral student Mario Rutten, Cees Fasseur (Leiden University) with Wim van den Doel, and Heather Sutherland (VU University Amsterdam) with Peter Boomgaard and Henk Schulte Nordholt. I have also talked to Elsbeth Locher-Scholten (Ph.D. Leiden University, but with non-Indonesianist Ivo Schöffer as supervisor and a career at the University of Utrecht) as a more independent figure.[5] I have also made a content analysis of a selection of their doctoral theses, inaugural lectures, valedictory lectures, and *Festschriften*. These four types of writing are, more than ordinary articles and monographs, texts in which people express their position *vis-à-vis* their research subject.

Of course, my analysis is coloured by my own history. As an undergraduate student of anthropology my interest in Indonesia was aroused by Clifford Geertz's *Agricultural Involution*, and from there, I gradually specialized in Indonesia, realizing that Dutch anthropologists and historians are uniquely positioned to study Indonesia because of the library resources in the Netherlands. I hold a Ph.D. from Leiden University, supervised by anthropologist Reimar Schefold, sociologist Peter Nas and historian Thomas Lindblad, definitely not representatives of what is sometimes called the Leiden School of Indonesian Studies. All in all, my colonial roots are negligible, but like other Dutch scholars I find it impossible to ignore totally the colonial sentiments (for or against) in Dutch public discourse.

THE CONSTRUCTION OF INDONESIAN STUDIES IN THE NETHERLANDS

Indonesian studies in the Netherlands began as a direct result of their colonial bond. From the first contact onwards, the Dutch produced works about the Indonesian Archipelago. The first Dutch ships arrived in Indonesia in 1596, and one of the sailors, Willem Lodewycksz (1598), produced a fine account of the places they visited along their way. During the second Dutch voyage, the merchant Frederick de Houtman was taken hostage and spent two years at the court of Aceh, from 1599 to 1601. He used his time to compile a grammar and vocabulary of the Malay language, published in 1603. Somewhat earlier Jan Huyghen van Linschoten, sailing on Portuguese ships in the 1580s, had compiled an overview of the Asian waters (Van Linschoten 1596).

In the seventeenth and eighteenth centuries all Dutch dealings with Indonesia (and the whole of Asia) were in the hands of the trading company, the VOC. The VOC controlled tiny parts of the Archipelago, which were of strategic importance to its business interests. The Company promoted three kinds of scholarly work: travelogues, studies of the Malay language (partly in order to develop missionary activity), and works on the flora and fauna. These works had the function to facilitate trade, understand the functioning of Asian polities, discover the potential of agricultural products, and undertake missionary work. Some writings, however, may have been borne out of sheer curiosity. In 1778 the *Bataviaasch Genootschap van Kunsten en Wetenschappen* (Batavian Society of Arts and Sciences) was established in Batavia (today's Jakarta), the VOC's headquarters in Asia. It was the oldest learned society in Asia and it was established in order to stimulate a more systematic study of the Archipelago (Boomgaard 2006, pp. 193–96; Teeuw 1994, pp. 653–54).

The VOC also produced a stream of handwritten letters from its various offices, from Mocha in Arabia to Japan, extensive summary reports (*generale missiven*) sent from Batavia to the Directors of the company in the Netherlands, and local diaries and books of sales and purchases. This material is probably the most valuable European source for the historical study of the early modern period of Southeast Asian maritime history. The sheer amount of VOC archives and the time required to sift through the primary material (written in a now unfamiliar handwriting, spelling and grammar) induce scholars, Dutch and non-Dutch, to focus on a locality as the unit of analysis to reduce the topic to a manageable size (the archives are organized by place) (Andaya and Andaya 1995, pp. 94–95).

The economic fortunes of the VOC declined towards the end of the eighteenth century and the Dutch state liquidated the company on 31 December 1799. The VOC possessions in Indonesia became a colony administered by the Dutch state. During the Napoleonic wars (when the Netherlands became a vassal of France and hence an enemy of England), England seized Dutch colonial territory in Asia, but returned most of it after the Napoleonic wars were over, in order to strengthen a Dutch counterweight to France. The duration of British rule varied from place to place in Indonesia, but on the core island, Java, it lasted from 1811 to 1816.[6] From 1816 onwards, the Dutch began to put together a colonial state, starting with the isolated fragments that had been controlled by the VOC. Building a colonial state included both gradual territorial expansion, which was not completed until the twentieth century, and the development of a state apparatus.

The transfer from VOC rule to colonial rule caused a change in the purpose of the Dutch presence in the Archipelago, but did so only gradually. After all, the VOC had often acted like a state, because its charter allowed the Company to wage war and conclude peace east of the Cape of Good Hope and it had already acquired some territories in parts of Java, the Moluccas and various, separated strongholds on other islands. The colonial state, conversely, behaved in many ways like an enterprise. The colony was meant to make a profit for the mother country, certainly after the Netherlands was drawn into the expensive Java War (1825–1830), and the foremost way to achieve this was by selling colonial products in Europe. The shipment and sale of the products was consigned to a trading company (NHM, *Nederlandsche Handelmaatschappij*), with which the state closely cooperated. It is no big mistake therefore that into the twentieth century many Indonesians referred to the Dutch colonial state as "*kumpeni*" (company). Nevertheless, Dutch attention gradually shifted from making money in the first place, to administering properly the people and the territory. A milestone, in this respect, was the initiation of a new welfare policy, dubbed *Ethische Politiek* (Ethical Policy) in 1901.

As a result of the expansion of the colonial state after 1816, works on Indonesia really began to flow. Civil servants at various local posts compiled an Annual (Administrative) Report (*Algemeen Verslag* or *Algemeen Administratief Verslag*), which more than VOC missives, described the local situation, also in the interior of islands: change in population size, health, trade and market prices, political affairs, and the state of agriculture. In the course of the nineteenth century, some sections of the report were split off and written as a separate series of Political or Cultural Reports (*Politiek Verslag, Cultuurverslag*). It became administrative routine that an outgoing local administrator compiled a summary report about the state of affairs (*Memorie van Overgave*) for his successor. These summary reports included also sections on the physical landscape, settlements, and noteworthy customs and formed a general ethnography *avant-la-lettre*.[7]

The quality of these reports tended to increase as the civil service was professionalized. The high-ranking civil servants received an academic training in the Netherlands, which included three years of study of Sanskrit, Arabic, Islam and Indian classical cultures. Language study was important to the Dutch, A. Teeuw asserts, because of various reasons: the system of indirect rule, the diversity of local languages which aroused curiosity, missionary interest in making Bible translations, and a lack of pride in the Dutch language itself (Teeuw 1994, pp. 656–59).

Civil servants with literary or scientific ambitions recycled their bureaucratic reports into articles for scientific journals, which were published in either the Netherlands Indies or the Netherlands. Compared to the renowned colonial archives, the treasure found in these journals is somewhat underrated by historians today; the articles are especially useful, since many of them are essentially civil servants' reports presented in a more structured form. Despite the close connection between colonial rule and scientific knowledge, it is not clear to what extent most scientific work was written with the conscious aim of dominating the colony. This link was obvious, however, in the case of the explorations to places hitherto unknown to the Dutch in the late nineteenth and early twentieth centuries (Boomgaard 2006, pp. 202–4).

The most important journals are worth noting: *Tijdschrift voor Nederlandsch Indië* (1838–1902), founded in 1838; *Bijdragen tot de Taal-, Land- en Volkenkunde van Neêrlandsch Indië* (*BKI*, 1852–today); *Tijdschrift voor Indische Taal-, Land- en Volkenkunde* (*TBG*, 1853–1955);[8] *De Indische Gids* (1879–1941); *Tijdschrift voor het Binnenlandsch Bestuur* (1887–1917), later incorporated in *Koloniaal Tijdschrift* (1912–41); *Koloniale Studiën* (1916–41). Other journals specialized in specific domains: *Het Regt in Nederlandsch Indië* (1849–1914, on law) incorporated in *Indisch Tijdschrift voor het Recht* (1915–42); *Geneeskundig Tijdschrift van Nederlandsch-Indië* (1852–1942, on health); *Natuurkundig Tijdschrift van Nederlandsch-Indië* (1850–1942, on science); *Locale Belangen* (1913–42, on urban development and local administration); *Indisch Bouwkundig Tijdschrift* (1898–1933, on architecture and civil engineering) later changed into *Locale Techniek* (1932–40); *Tectona* (1908–55, on forestry); *Djawa* (1921–41, on the culture of Java). I present this list, which is not comprehensive, to give an idea of the enormous amount of material available. The production of articles is comparable to today's academic journals on Southeast Asia or Indonesia (*Journal of Southeast Asian Studies, Archipel, Indonesia, Review of Indonesian and Malaysian Affairs, Southeast Asia Research, Sojourn*, etcetera), but then focusing on only Indonesia and sustained over a longer period.

The nature of this astounding work has continued to exert influence on Indonesian Studies in the Netherlands after decolonization, perhaps until today. Most work was based on intimate knowledge of the country, founded on proficiency in Indonesian languages. The corollary was that most work was factual, descriptive, and inward-looking. No comparison with societies outside Indonesia was attempted and there was no effort to link case studies with theoretical issues. A lot of work avoided political issues, especially the articles written by civil servants, who were expected to refrain from political commentary, and published in the journals most closely associated with the state (BKI and TBG). In their descriptions and classifications, the Dutch scholars, as possibly any scholar at the time, maintained a strict separation between themselves and their research subjects, as if they were able to transcend this gap (Philpott 2000, p. 42).

The Japanese occupation of the Netherlands Indies, followed by the Indonesian Revolution ended Dutch colonial rule in Indonesia. The only journal that survived these historical events and has continued to appear until today is *BKI*. The editors were well aware of the changing times. In 1949 *BKI* dropped the words "*van Nederlandsch Indië*" from its name and already in 1947 the Board discussed the desirability to use English. As of the 1970s English language articles have outnumbered Dutch articles. Started as a journal to promote knowledge among those people who had to administer the colony, it has now become a journal produced by academics and for academics (Knaap 1994, pp. 645–47, 651). Although these editorial changes have kept *BKI* in business, on the whole decolonization had a disastrous effect on Indonesia studies in the Netherlands.

Career opportunities for civil servants were closed in Indonesia; some moved to the Netherlands, others became expatriate development experts in what is nowadays called the Global South. After diplomatic relations between Indonesia and the Netherlands deteriorated in the late 1950s, the last Dutch were expelled, including professors working at Indonesian tertiary institutions. The need for knowledge about Indonesia dwindled in the Netherlands, contacts were lost, financial resources dried up, and attention turned to other countries.

While interest in Indonesian Studies declined in the Netherlands, the USA stepped in and became the centre of this field. Well-funded, multi-disciplinary area studies emerged in America in the 1950s in response to the Cold War. Knowledge was needed as part of a broad counter-insurgency strategy to prevent the realization of the domino theory of one state after the other falling to communism in Southeast Asia. Most of the extant knowledge in the Netherlands seemed irrelevant for this American project and few Americans bothered to learn Dutch — why should they? The Americans wished to learn about the two most pertinent processes taking place at the time: nationalism or nation-building and modernization. Dutch colonial studies were not framed in these terms, certainly not in terms of nation-building. The few Dutch works that still drew interest were English translations of pre-war studies of a more explicit sociological

nature, such as the work by B. Schrieke and J.C. van Leur, and the contemporary studies of W.F. Wertheim written along similar lines. No Dutch
expert joined the emerging American centres of expertise. For geopolitical
reasons also Australia set up centres of Southeast Asian Studies after the
Second World War (Chou and Houben 2006, pp. 4–5; Editor's note
2009; McVey 1995; Philpott 2000, p. 104; Sutherland 1994, p. 789;
Wertheim 1995).

Ironically, the fall of the first Indonesian President, Sukarno, and the
establishment of the New Order regime in Indonesia, founded on the killing
of perhaps 500,000 communists, was positive for Indonesian Studies in the
Netherlands. Dutch scholars were allowed to return to Indonesia and did
so, despite some mixed feelings about the nature of the New Order state.
Interest in Indonesia revived and in the 1970s state funds for Indonesian-
Dutch scientific cooperation began to flow. The Indonesian Studies
Programme (started in 1975) brought young Indonesian academics to the
Netherlands for doctoral studies. History writing became less Eurocentric;
sensitive political and social issues were by and large avoided in most studies
in order not to put the delicate relationship at risk. In 1992, however,
diplomatic relations experienced a rather unexpected downturn and formal
scholarly cooperation came to an abrupt end when Dutch Minister of
Development Cooperation, J.P. Pronk, backed by the full Dutch parliament,
offended the Indonesian government by insisting on tying economic aid
to human rights; the Indonesian state unilaterally rejected any further
Dutch funds (Sutherland 1994, p. 790; Teeuw 1994, pp. 661–62). This
diplomatic break coincided with the custom of social scientists in the
Netherlands (and perhaps anywhere else outside Indonesia) reaching easily
the morally heavily loaded conclusion that the state was always doing a
bad job (corrupt, not respecting the rights of the citizens, including land
rights, violence, and so on).

Despite the diplomatic rupture, low-profile cooperation continued and
has now formally been re-established. In the late 1980s Dutch university
policies expanded opportunities for Ph.D. students and established so-
called research schools where Ph.D. students and senior staff could meet.
Two reports produced for the Ministry of Education pleaded successfully
for support for area studies in Asia, not only in Indonesia, but also in
South and East Asia, where the Netherlands have had a long research
tradition. The second report, focusing on Asia, pleaded for extra funding
and apart from that a hands-off policy from the Ministry. The past rapid
succession of new university policies had been disastrous according to this
report; quoting a Chinese proverb: "Ruling a large country is like frying

little fish; when you often turn them over, they fall apart."[9] (*Baby Krishna* 1991; *Krishna in de delta* 1991). As a minor point, the second report pleaded for extra funds to maintain the rich library and archival resources in the Netherlands. The 1990s were a prosperous period for Indonesian Studies in the Netherlands.

In the first decade of the twenty-first century, the situation is no longer so bright. Few people who obtained a Ph.D. degree found tenured positions and consequently many have pursued careers outside academia. The number of Master's and Ph.D. students writing on Indonesian subjects seems to have declined and the membership of the KITLV association (for Indonesia) has fallen off from around 1,600 in 2000 to 1,100 in 2008, and dropped to 750 in 2009 (KITLV 2010, p. 7). The reading room of the KITLV seems to be increasingly used by foreign visitors. University researchers working on Indonesia are mostly found in disciplinary departments (anthropology, history, law) and not in specific departments or programmes for Indonesia. Insofar as undergraduate students learn about Indonesia, they usually do as part of either disciplinary courses or courses on the whole of Southeast Asia and few seize the opportunity to learn the language skills necessary to be able to do fieldwork.[10] In general, the imposition of business models on universities, with efficiency and production targets as important key terms, has gone at the expense of the quality of research (and teaching).

Perhaps, these recent developments do not need to be regretted. It can be argued that the decolonization of Indonesian Studies has finally been completed in the Netherlands. Studying Indonesia has become an ordinary thing, no different from the study of other countries in the Global South. The above historical overview will help to better understand some of the characteristics of Indonesian Studies as perceived by the practitioners themselves. The remaining part of this chapter is predominantly based on interviews with eight Dutch scholars. They were originally interviewed for a study on the transfer of academic values. As the discussion of academic values became a discussion of the general state of affairs and future directions of Indonesian Studies, the material is very appropriate for this chapter too and has been organized around the triple colonial burden, starting with the wealth of sources, which has resulted in a strong empirical orientation.

EMPIRICAL ORIENTATION

Dutch scholars on Indonesia have demonstrated a strong empirical orient-ation. For historians the rich archives and libraries are very tempting to use. Also anthropologists have the ideal of doing fieldwork, although for senior staff it has practically become impossible to spend prolonged periods in the field, due to duties at the university.

More important than the method is the inclination to seek research topics that stem from empirical curiosity and not from a question that is derived from an analytical problem or theoretical debate. "Indonesian history writing in the Netherlands is only beginning to free itself from the restraints created by a strong past", Heather Sutherland wrote in the 1990s, "We remain somewhat parochial and conventional in the questions we ask [...] the notion persists that history consists of getting the facts straight, a sort of superior clerical work" (Sutherland 1994, p. 786).

The exemplary representative of scholars working in the archives is eminent Dutch historian Cees Fasseur. For several years he used his lunch break while at work in the Department of Justice to collect the necessary data for his Ph.D. thesis (on the nineteenth century Cultivation System or *Cultuurstelsel*). This preference for archival work, preferably in the National Archives in The Hague, is also obvious in the work of Fasseur's students. The decision to undertake archival work was, for Fasseur and his students, not a matter of calculation driven by the nature of the topics they chose. Rather, the material available in the archives determined the range of topics available for investigation. Alternative methodologies (literature study, oral history, discourse analysis of photographs) do not seem to be considered very seriously, or at least were not considered so for a long time. The physical proximity of this group of Leiden-based scholars to the treasury of the National Archives in The Hague (ten minutes by train) may have influenced this preference.

As a corollary of the Leiden tradition to equate historical research with empirical study in the archives the most important works from this group are, or at least used to be until recently, published in the form of Dutch books. When one writes in Dutch, it is not necessary to make the difficult, never fully satisfying, translation into English of quotes found in the archives to the delight of the historian. "Why would I write in English?" Fasseur reportedly once said, "everybody who wants to study Indonesian history must be able to read Dutch." It required an outsider, Australian Professor Heather Sutherland (Ph.D. Yale University) appointed at VU University Amsterdam in 1976, to open the windows and to force the Dutch Indonesianists to realize that science is an international activity. Peter Boomgaard, a student of Heather Sutherland, was probably the first to write his Ph.D. thesis in English (Boomgaard 1987) and the language choice definitely helped him to achieve international acclaim. The days that Dutch scholars felt they could claim a self-evident authority to speak about Indonesia are gone. Western but non-Dutch Indonesianists outnumber Dutch scholars by far and Indonesian historians have developed their own narratives about the past. Non-Dutch historians still learn Dutch to have access to colonial archives, but they do so in such large numbers that also in Dutch archives and libraries Dutch researchers sometimes seem a minority (which is not a bad thing, of course).

The absence of theoretical debate and the use of the Dutch language is connected to the widely felt obligation that historians should write for a larger audience than just professional historians, and this view is certainly not only held by Leiden-based scholars (see, e.g., Schulte Nordholt 2008). In the Netherlands, there exists a large potential readership of people with a personal relationship to colonial Indonesia: by ancestry, or place of birth, work, military service, or the place of one's childhood. To reach this readership, books are a more appropriate medium than articles in journals. Texts should be easy to read. (But easy reading is damned hard writing, Ernest Hemingway has reminded us!) In order to achieve this aim, Cees Fasseur and his students are fond of anecdotes and playful (but often incomprehensible) titles of books and chapters. A nice example is formed by the Ph.D. thesis of Wim van den Doel (1994), *De stille macht* (The silent force), a variation on Couperus' famous novel *De stille kracht*, and even better the thesis of Hans van Miert (1995), *Een koel hoofd en een warm hart* (literally: A cool head and a warm heart) with the chapter "Petruk met sportmuts" (Petruk with a sports cap).

As a corollary of the richness of the archives and the desire to serve a large readership, the Dutch historical world values thick books. Fasseur's best known student, Wim van den Doel, told me that when he was writing his Ph.D. thesis on the colonial civil service, Fasseur was writing a monograph on the School for Colonial Administration. They vied for who would write the most voluminous work, so that in hindsight, Van den Doel admits, his thesis (581 pages) carries superfluous ballast. One particular consequence of the empirical orientation, namely the general conviction, emphasized by almost every scholar interviewed by me, is the attempt by scholars to be objective.

MORAL JUDGEMENTS AND OBJECTIVITY

A scientific statement on colonial Indonesia is quickly weighed in moral terms in the Netherlands, and this habit has been extended among Indonesianists to the post-colonial state. Nevertheless, almost all Dutch scholars would agree on the importance of objectivity. The critique of Edward Said on

Orientalism is of course well known, but most scholars take it first and foremost as a methodological recipe and not a fundamental critique of their work.[11] Punching discursive strategies in colonial sources is considered a matter of doing good research, and quite often the contemporary discourse itself has become a subject of study. Having said that, most people believe, or have convinced themselves, that something meaningful can be said about the empirical world (past or present), somewhere out there. Now that postmodern studies seem to be over their peak, the stand of most Dutch scholars in this respect seems far less outdated than they did ten years ago.

In practice, the desire to remain objective is translated into the prescription to show respect for the sources, or more precisely respect for the integrity of the people who produced those sources. People need to be understood in their own historical context. So, for instance, it is easy in hindsight to disparage the Eurocentrism of colonial civil servants, but at the time they considered themselves enlighteners (*opheffers*). By the way, this respect for one's subject seems to apply far less to representatives (military, civil service, judiciary) of the New Order or, to a lesser extent, the contemporary state of Indonesia, than to the colonial state.[12]

Not only is every statement about Indonesia morally loaded, but also the need to remain objective is a strong value. To draw a conclusion that is not supported by empirical fact, or worse contradicted by the facts, is not only bad scholarship, but also morally wrong. Because of these moral overtones, some debates were very heated. The debate among Dutch historians is less about the political, selective nature of the sources, than about the degree that the social production of the historical records needs to be contextualized. Related to this difference of opinion is the question of how much attention needs to be paid to the oppressed people in Indonesia. If we accept the moral primacy of objectivity, immediately the paradoxical question emerges: why then have scholars at the University of Leiden and the University of Amsterdam repeatedly clashed over colonial issues, while basing their positions on more or less the same colonial archival and printed sources?[13] The paradox is solved by the meaning given to the word objectivity.

The most outspoken during the interviews in this respect was Jan Breman. Objectivity — he used the more active form objectifying (*objectivering*) — is important in his view, precisely because scholars are influenced by their personal preferences and social background. Objectifying then is the process of being on guard against one's own presuppositions and constantly trying to falsify them. Coming from, in his own words, a lower class milieu and writing about labour relations in India and Indonesia, Breman had always tried to falsify his own supposition that the labourers were exploited by the landowners. Yet, at the end of the analysis, the labourers are exploited. The closing sentences of his dissertation are: "Like their comrades elsewhere, the Dubla [the lowest caste in his research site in Gujarat, India] daily labourers are paralysed by apathy and suspicion. They lead a life without prospects and demonstrate a lack of interest for the future. It can never become better than what life of today offers. And that is too little."[14] The impressive closing sentence, which Breman must have considered over and over again, is clearly a moral judgement. Life brings too little to the Dubla according to whose standard?

Objectifying, then, seems less a matter of writing, than of doing fieldwork, during which Breman made an effort to hear both sides, also the landowning caste. In an interesting section of his thesis, Breman (1970, pp. 95–98) describes how he tried to speak with both landowners and landless labourers up to a certain point. Faced with the choice that the landowners were not or no longer willing to receive him if he continued to meet the low Dubla caste, Breman unequivocally chose the side of the landless. He defends his choice by pointing at the fact that it took more time to gain the confidence of the labourers. In the field, he never made a secret of his own sympathies for the labourers; "[p]recisely for that reason I have always striven to act as objectively as possible when collecting information" (Breman 1970, p. 98). During my interview with him, Breman readily mentioned the class background of (scientific) friend and foe, but I think the relationship between one's class and work is subtler than that. Critical work has also been written by Dutch scholars from the middle or upper classes. Moreover, depending on the subject under study gender and ethnicity (being "white" in the case of Dutch scholars) can be just as important (e.g., Locher-Scholten 1997, 1998).

Paradoxically, the argument between Leiden and Amsterdam is not about the ideal of objectivity nor about the importance of empirical sources, but an epistemological issue of how to treat the sources. Scholars in Amsterdam search for what is left out of the colonial (or contemporary, for that matter) sources and rejoice when unexpectedly a window opens that allows them to peep behind the front stage (Schulte Nordholt 2000). Respect for the sources in Leiden, conversely, has resulted in a more positive appreciation of the colonial state. When (not if) there were abuses, these were described as excesses (hence exceptions) and not as a structural pattern. However, precisely because of this respect for sources, the best Leiden scholars will not let the colonial state off the hook when facts are clear. Fasseur (in the *Excessennota*), for example, speaks unequivocally of Dutch war crimes during the Indonesian Revolution.

INWARD- OR OUTWARD-LOOKING

Joost Coté, an Australian with intimate knowledge of the Dutch "scene", has addressed the question why the Dutch and Australian-American historiography have kept each other at a distance. His argument is worth addressing in some detail. Whereas Americans and Australians operated from a critical, post-colonial frame since the 1950s, the Dutch accepted only belatedly the fact that the Netherlands Indies was an imperial project at all. For a long time the sense that the colonial mission had been terminated prematurely, and perhaps unfairly, was dominant among Dutch scholars, not a few of them originating from the colonial civil service. The Dutch historical attention for Dutch critical voices in colonial times, and some-times positive state responses to that critique (notably the termination of the nineteenth century Cultivation System, or the launching of the Ethical Policy in the early twentieth century) suggested that Dutch colonialism did comparatively well; the Dutch academic focus on critical debate in the colony pre-empted a readiness to accept the more fundamental critique from American and Australian post-colonial scholarship (Coté 2009).

Accepting Coté's analysis it almost becomes self-evident that Ameri-cans and Australians (and other non-Dutch writers) on the one hand and Dutchmen on the other ignored each other's work. Coté definitely has a point, although his self-imposed, though not consistently honoured, restriction to Dutch language publications clearly limits the scope of his analysis. On a list of the fourteen "most influential" English-language books of Southeast Asia, compiled by the editorial board and advisory members of *Sojourn* (Editor's note 2009), no less than three Dutch-authored books figure, albeit all from the 1950s and 1960s (by J.C. van Leur and W.F. Wertheim). Since then, Dutch scholarship has lost much ground. Coté ends with a positive note on a new generation of scholars, who "by deploying international perspectives [...] have not only opened up the colonial archive to fresh insights for Dutch historians, but notably, provided and encouraged the entry point for Anglophone historians. Their influence has certainly been felt abroad" (Coté 2009, p. 88).

According to Coté, in short, the major obstacle between Dutch and American-Australian scholars was the inability of the Dutch to accept a critical attitude towards colonialism. He definitely has a point, but I believe also the features of Dutch Indonesian Studies sketched so far have had consequences for the third burden, the inward orientation of Dutch scholars. Both Leiden and Amsterdam have, no doubt, profited from their mutual controversies to increase their profile. By taking sides, a person could feel assured to become automatically part of a "circle of esteem" (Cribb 2005) and perhaps it was fun to pull each other's leg as well. Dutch scholars who were bystanders in the Leiden-Amsterdam duels sometimes felt impatient about or annoyed by the parochial quibbles (Raben 1996, *stelling* 14). The fact that a lot of the Dutch work has been published in the form of voluminous, Dutch-language books has formed a barrier to communicate with non-Dutch scholars, a point that Coté strangely has not considered important.[15] Regardless of the degree to which one takes colonial sources at face value or sees through the pages, almost all Dutch Indonesianists have a strong inclination to write empirical studies (and this chapter is no exception).[16]

I believe the presence of the very rich depositories has exerted a very powerful influence on the Dutch scholars. The temptation to use these rich sources looms large. Studies are started with empirical curiosity about particular phenomena as the driving force. Theories are called upon at a second stage to analyse data and frame writings, as is common in all area studies (MacDonald 2004), but research projects very rarely start from a theoretically deduced problem. The strategy of starting with an empirical question (with the ultimate goal to understand empirical matters and not to build theory) extends to studies of today's Indonesia.[17] Usually the outcome is a "thick description" (Geertz) of the phenomena; at best the theoretical consequences of the study concerned are analysed, at worst there is only description.

The flipside of the empirical studies is that many Dutch Indonesianists demonstrate, in the words of Henk Schulte Nordholt, a "shyness" (*bedeesdheid*) to take part in broader discussions. As a result of this shyness, others, basing themselves on the work of Dutch authors (and sometimes not even that), take the limelight. For instance, it is easy to demonstrate that Ann Stoler makes serious empirical flaws (Beaulieu-Boon 2009; Colombijn 2010, pp. 81–82), but she definitely makes her points and is much more widely read than her critics. It is, as Robert Cribb has observed, that although empirical knowledge is a powerful weapon in academic debate, empiricists always run the risk of "being trumped by an assertion of superiority in theory", partly because "theory is remarkably resistant to falsification" (Cribb 2005, pp. 298–99).

The focus on empirical studies, ignoring the broader picture is found not only among Dutch Indonesianists, but is perhaps characteristic of Dutch

social science at large (Kloos 1989, p. 32). To nuance this position somewhat, I can refer to comments made by two interviewees. One said that a
narrow scope is a problem of *all* social science, and the other remarked that
the focus on only Indonesia is also characteristic of Australian historians.[18]
In a similar vein, Ariel Heryanto (2002, p. 23) has observed that *all*
Southeast Asianists tend to emphasize the uniqueness of their respective
areas over universalizing social theories.

To counter this inward-looking attitude, according to my interlocutors,
Dutch Indonesianists should add a comparative dimension to their work.
A lot is to be learnt from work on India, Malaysia, or China, for instance.
This can be done either by reading case studies about those countries, or
by using more theoretical insights or concepts. The need to write compara-
tive studies and use social theory has particularly been promoted by Wim
Wertheim and Heather Sutherland, but the principle is now widely accepted.
A fine example is a large research project comparing Indonesia with three
other Southeast Asian countries and four African countries, directed by
David Henley of the KITLV. Comparative work does not only need to be
between societies, but it is also common to compare contemporary and
historical situations: sociologists and anthropologists historicize their work.

Societal changes push Dutch scholarship in the same direction of a
broader view. At home, the natural readership of those Dutch people who
have known colonial Indonesia from personal experience is dying out.
University courses on Indonesia draw a diminishing number of students in
the Netherlands,[19] and in response have broadened the subject to Southeast
or Southeast and South Asia. Indonesianists have nowadays to explain to
other Dutch area specialists why Indonesia is interesting, instead of — as
used to be the case — the other way around. In this uncertain landscape,
Dutch Indonesianists have to reassess their position.

CONCLUSION

The Netherlands has had a long tradition of scholarly research on Indonesia.
Research has finally become by and large decolonized. If studies take the
colonial past into account, the Dutch are increasingly seen as just one
segment of the wider Netherlands Indies society. The two opposing stand-
points that the Dutch were essentially bringing something positive to the
Archipelago or that they were the source of most inequality, violence and
lack of development — both views are Eurocentric — have been abandoned.

Dutch Indonesianists can no longer afford not to legitimize the choice
of topic and they are gradually losing their natural home audience of people

who lived in the Netherlands Indies; Indonesia is no longer a self-evident area of research and most scholars who kept the Leiden-Amsterdam controversies (and research) alive have retired. New legitimization is sought and found in making connections to wider debates (on ethnicity, nation-building, urban development, and so on). In order to connect to these wider debates, most work is published in English. Has this shift been enough to reconnect to the outside scholarly world?

One almost unavoidable problem for Dutch Indonesianists is the general belief that area studies are "charged with being old-fashioned, [...] parochial [...] and empiricist [...] in an increasingly changing, globalising world" (King 2005, p. 2). This problem can be partly overcome, of course, because processes of globalization always must touch ground somewhere, if they are not to remain *in abstracto*. Globalization always implies localization and scholars must make a convenient choice for a region (King 2005, p. 9; see also Jackson 2003, p. 2). At the very least Dutch Indonesianists share the image problem of area studies with their colleagues in other countries.

It is telling that the strongest international cooperation exists with Australians, the only other country which has a special relationship with Indonesia (because of geography, not history), although the Netherlands is nowadays hopelessly outdone by Australia in terms of the number of Indonesia specialists.[20] In my experience, Americans often seem to overlook Dutch expertise, including a long tradition of knowledge about Islamic activism in the Archipelago. Future scholarly cooperation can better be sought with other European countries and with Asian countries that have the academic resources and economic motive to develop Indonesian Studies: Japan, and Singapore. More recently, the entry of South Korea into the field has been very fortunate, also for the Dutch.

If Dutch scholars are able to ask better questions and connect to broader debates, they will be able to reclaim some ground of a field they once dominated. The available library and archival resources will continue to be a tremendous depository, and Dutch scholars have a competitive edge by the speed and accurateness with which they can read historical sources written in their mother tongue. This advantage is offset, of course, by the requirement to write in English. Non-native writers of English will always remain less productive than native writers, because writing in another language than one's own slows down the writing process, and involves an extra round (hence time) of corrections by a native speaker (repeated when editors of a journal ask for revisions). It will also inevitably consume extra financial resources to pay for corrections, and ultimately, regardless of the quality of the editor, there remains some imprecision of expression and limited vocabulary. Scholars coming from countries that seem doubly cursed (speaking neither English, nor Dutch or an Indonesian language as their mother tongue) can find solace in an academic system that allows prolonged sabbaticals to do fieldwork (as in South Korea).

POSTSCRIPT

Early in 2011 the Royal Netherlands Academy of Arts and Sciences announced unexpectedly that in reaction to cuts in its own budget it intended to stop funding the KITLV and to dismantle the institute. Indonesianists in the Netherlands were at first dazed at this total lack of respect for the quality and wealth of resources of the KITLV. The directors of the KITLV are currently trying to find a solution (for instance, moving to Amsterdam, closer to the Royal Netherlands Academy of Arts and Sciences, looking for closer cooperation with an Indonesian counterpart, or becoming an institute of Leiden University) and the institute will definitely survive in some form. Nevertheless, it is certain the KITLV will not come through this crisis unscathed and, most importantly, it has stopped its independent publishing activities. The KITLV Press and the publication of *Bijdragen tot de Taal-, Land- en Volkenkunde* were handed over to Brill Publishers in 2012. Whatever the ultimate outcome, Indonesian Studies in the Netherlands will certainly experience a serious setback.

Notes

1   Preliminary versions of this chapter were presented at the conference *The Transmission of Academic Values in Asian Studies*, hosted by the Australian National University on 25–26 June 2009, and at the conference *The Historical Construction of Southeast Asia*, Sogang Institute for East Asian Studies, Seoul, 19–20 March 2010. I am grateful for the comments received during those conferences.

2   According to Victor King (2005), referring to John Bowen and Mary Steedly, the focus on an interpretative concept of culture in Indonesian Studies is also dominant in American anthropology.

3   It might be argued that the focus on Dutch achievements in this work is merely a necessary, and therefore justifiable, albeit somewhat arbitrary delimitation of the subject. In my view, however, it should have been acknowledged that, for instance, effective transportation networks existed throughout the Archipelago long before the Europeans had even discovered Indonesia. Notwithstanding the Dutch contribution to irrigation works, wet rice cultivation is of course an Asian, and not a European, invention. Downright irritating is the remark that

in the 1883 Krakatau eruption "37 Europeans and 36,380 native inhabitants" (p. 48) lost their lives; as if 37 Europeans were of equal importance to the thousand-fold number of indigenous casualties. Why do the Europeans need to be singled out here anyway?

⁴   *Vereenigde Oostindische Compagnie*, the Dutch East India Company.

⁵   I realize that by juxtaposing the comments of the interviewees, I may unintentionally criticize them (or rather, make them criticize each other); therefore I would like to emphasize that I appreciate the work of all, each in its own way, and greatly enjoyed interviewing them. The generous help of my interlocutors is gratefully acknowledged.

⁶   The British interregnum gave a boost to scholarly research and resulted in some standard works written by William Marsden, Thomas Raffles and John Crawfurd (Teeuw 1994, p. 655).

⁷   Most *Memories van Overgave* can be found at the Dutch National Archive in The Hague; the *Algemene Verslagen*, *Politieke Verslagen* and *Cultuurverslagen* have been kept at the Indonesian National Archive in Jakarta.

⁸   The abbreviations of the two most scholarly journals refer to the institutes that published them. *Bijdragen tot de Taal-, Land- en Volkenkunde van Neêrlandsch Indië* was published, and still is, by the Koninklijk Instituut voor Taal-, Land- en Volkenkunde and abbreviated as *BKI* (Bijdragen of the Koninklijk Instituut, Contributions by the Royal Institute); *Tijdschrift voor Indische Taal-, Land- en Volkenkunde* was published by the Bataviaasch Genootschap van Kunsten en Wetenschappen hence abbreviated as *TBG*. Because of the relative difficulty of international communication, authors living in the Netherlands preferred to publish in *BKI* and authors in the Netherlands Indies chose *TBG*; some prolific authors in *BKI* never visited Indonesia (Teeuw 1994, pp. 658, 660). *TBG* was continued under an Indonesian name and appeared irregularly until 1958.

⁹   "*Een groot land regeren is net als kleine visjes bakken (Als je ze vaak omdraait gaan ze kapot)*" (*Baby Krishna* 1991, p. 83).

¹⁰   There are some remarkable similarities here with the UK, another former colonial power (King 2005, p. 11).

¹¹   For a textual example of this stand, see Boomgaard (2006, p. 211).

¹²   The New Order is the name of the long dictatorial rule of Soeharto (1965–98), characterized by economic growth, mass corruption, and state violence against its own citizens.

¹³   Jan Breman and Vincent Houben on coolies (indentured labour) in nineteenth-century Sumatra, Henk Schulte Nordholt and Wim van de Doel on the Ciomas Affair (the shooting of unarmed Indonesians yelling at a distance), Cees Fasseur and Jan Breman on the cultivation system.

¹⁴   The original quote (Breman 1970, p. 257) and following quotes from Breman are in Dutch.

¹⁵   Many non-Dutch Indonesianists, and certainly historians, will be able to read Dutch, but I believe it is one thing whether, say, an Australian, reads essential

Dutch sources from colonial times and another thing whether he or she is willing to read a Dutch-language historical or sociological analysis.

[16] This chapter starts with empirical curiosity and a descriptive question and does not take for instance concepts like "Orientalism" or "circles of esteem" (Cribb) as its starting point.

[17] We should not forget in this respect that the KITLV collection on contemporary Indonesia is as outstanding as its historical collection.

[18] The same point can be made about political scientists writing on Indonesia (Philpott 2000, p. 50).

[19] See (King 2005, p. 3) on the similar phenomenon in the UK.

[20] The ANRC (Australian-Netherlands Research Collaboration) is a successful, recent attempt to develop institutional cooperation between Dutch and Australian scholars, expanding their relationship to include Southeast Asians.

References

Andaya, Leonard Y. and Barbara Watson Andaya. "Southeast Asia in the Early Modern Period: Twenty-five Years On". *Journal of Southeast Asian Studies* 26 (1995): 92–98.

Baby Krishna: Rapport van de Adviescommissie Kleine Letteren, 1951.

Beaulieu-Boon, Hendrika H. *So Far Away from Home: Engaging the Silenced Colonial; the Netherlands-Indies Diaspora in North America*. Ph.D. thesis, Leiden University, 2009.

Boomgaard, Peter. *Children of the Colonial State: Population Growth and Economic Development in Java, 1795–1880*. Ph.D. thesis, Vrije Universiteit, Amsterdam, 1987.

———. "The Making and Unmaking of Tropical Science: Dutch Research on Indonesia, 1600–2000". *Bijdragen tot de Taal-, Land- en Volkenkunde* 162 (2006): 191–217.

Breman, Johannes Cornelis. *Meester en knecht: Een onderzoek naar de veranderingen in de betrekkingen tussen landheren en landarbeiders in Zuid-Gujarat, India*. Ph.D. thesis, Universiteit van Amsterdam, 1970.

Breman, J.C., G.A. de Bruijne, O.D. van den Muijzenberg, J.W. Schoorl, and H. Sutherland. *Voorstel voor een postdoctorale opleiding "Comparatieve Studie van Aziatische Samenlevingen"*. Amsterdam: Centre for Asian Studies Amsterdam CASA, 1987.

Chou, Cynthia and Vincent Houben. "Introduction". In *Southeast Asian Studies: Debates and New Directions*, edited by Cynthia Chou and Vincent Houben. Leiden: IIAS and Singapore: Institute of Southeast Asian Studies, 2006.

Colombijn, Freek. "Hoe de Nederlanders op Sumatra aan de weg timmerden: De ontwikkeling van het wegennet op Midden-Sumatra, 1600–1870". In *Macht en majesteit: Opstellen voor Cees Fasseur bij zijn afscheid als hoogleraar in de geschiedenis van Indonesië aan de Universiteit Leiden,* edited by J. Thomas Lindblad and Willem van der Molen. Leiden: Opleiding Talen en Culturen van Zuidoost-Azië en Oceanië, Universiteit Leiden (Semaian 22), 2002.

———. *Under Construction: The Politics of Urban Space and Housing during the Indonesian Decolonization.* Leiden: KITLV Press, 2010.

Coté, Joost. "Strangers in the House: Dutch Historiography and Anglophone Trespassers". *Review of Indonesian and Malaysian Affairs* 43, no. 1 (2009): 75–94.

Cribb, Robert. "Circles of Esteem, Standard Works, and Euphoric Couplets: Dynamics of Academic Life in Indonesian Studies". *Critical Asian Studies* 37 (2005): 289–304.

Doel, Wim van den. *De stille macht: het Europese binnenlands betuur op Java en Madoera, 1808–1942.* Ph.D. thesis. Amsterdam: Bert Bakker (Rijksuniversiteit Leiden), 1994.

Editor's note. "The Most Influential Books of Southeast Asian Studies". *Sojourn* 24, no. 1 (2009): vii–xi.

Hall, C.J.J. van and C. van de Koppel, eds. *De landbouw in den Indische archipel,* 3 vols. 's-Gravenhage: Van Hoeve, 1946–50.

Heryanto, Ariel. "Can There be Southeast Asians in Southeast Asian Studies?" *Moussons* 5 (2002): 3–30.

Jackson, Peter A. "Space, Theory, and Hegemony: The Dual Crises of Asian Area Studies and Cultural Studies". *Sojourn* 18, no. 1 (2003): 1–41.

King, Victor T. *Defining Southeast Asia and the Crisis in Area Studies: Personal Reflections on a Region.* Working paper 13. Lund: Centre for East and South-East Asian Studies, Lund University, 2005.

KITLV. *Financieel jaarverslag 2009.* Leiden: Vereniging van het Koninklijk Instituut voor Taal-, Land- en Volkenkunde, 2010.

Kloos, Peter. "Anthropology in the Netherlands: The 1980s". In *Tropical Research in the Development, Wotro 1964–1989.* The Hague: Stichting Wetenschappelijk Onderzoek in de Tropen, 1989.

Knaap, Gerrit. "One Hundred and Fifty Volumes of Bijdragen". *Bijdragen tot de Taal-, Land- en Volkenkunde* 150 (1994): 637–52.

Krishna in de delta: De Azië-studies op weg naar de 21ste eeuw. Amsterdam: Adviescommissie Maatschappijwetenschappen Azië van de Koninklijke Nederlandse Akademie van Wetenschappen, 1991.

Linschoten, Jan Huyghen van. *Itinerario: Voyage ofte schipvaert van Jan Huyghen van Linschoten naer Oost ofte Portugaels Indien* etc. Amstelredam: Cornelis Claesz, 1596.

Locher-Scholten, Elsbeth. "Summer Dresses and Canned Food: European Women and Western Lifestyles in the Indies, 1900–1942". In *Outward Appearances: Dressing State and Society in Indonesia,* edited by Henk Schulte Nordholt. Leiden: KITLV Press, 1997.

————. "So Close and Yet So Far: The Ambivalence of Dutch Colonial Rhetoric on Javanese Servants in Indonesia, 1900–1942". In *Domesticating the Empire: Race, Gender, and Family Life in French and Dutch Colonialism*, edited by Julia Clancy-Smith and Frances Gouda. Charlottesville/London: University Press of Virginia, 1998.

Lodewycksz, Willem. *De eerste schipvaart naar Oost-Indië onder Cornelis de Houtman, 1595–1597, opgetekend door Willem Lodewycksz*. Reprint Linschoten Vereniging 7, 's-Gravenhage: Nijhoff, [1598] 1915.

MacDonald, Charles J.H. "What is the Use of Area Studies". *IIAS Newsletter* 41 (2004). Available at <via www.iias.nl> (accessed 25 September 2006).

McVey, Ruth. "Change and Continuity in Southeast Asian Studies". *Journal of Southeast Asian Studies* 26 (1995): 1–9.

Miert, Hans van. *Een koel hoofd en een warm hart; nationalisme, javanisme en jeugdbeweging in Nederlands-Indië, 1918–1930*. Ph.D. thesis. Amsterdam: De Bataafsche Leeuw (Rijksuniversiteit Leiden), 1995.

Philpott, Simon. *Rethinking Indonesia: Postcolonial Theory, Authoritarianism and Identity*. Houndsmills, Basingstoke: MacMillan, 2000.

Raben, Remco. *Batavia and Colombo: The Ethnic and Spatial Order of Two Colonial Cities 1600–1800*. Ph.D. thesis, Rijksuniversiteit Leiden, 1996.

Ravesteijn, Wim and Jan Kop. *For Profit and Prosperity: The Contribution Made by Dutch Engineers to Public Works in Indonesia 1800–2000*. Leiden: KITLV Press and Zaltbommel: Aprilis, 2008.

Schulte Nordholt, Henk. *Een staat van geweld*. Oratie Erasmus Universiteit Rotterdam, 2000.

————. *Indonesië na Soeharto: Reformasi en restauratie*. Amsterdam: Bert Bakker, 2008.

Sutherland, Heather. "Writing Indonesian History in the Netherlands: Rethinking the Past". *Bijdragen tot de Taal-, Land- en Volkenkunde* 150 (1994): 785–804.

Teeuw, A. "The Role of the Bijdragen in Dutch Colonial Studies". *Bijdragen tot de Taal-, Land- en Volkenkunde* 150 (1994): 636–64.

Wertheim, Wim F. "The Contribution of Weberian Sociology to Studies of Southeast Asia". *Journal of Southeast Asian Studies* 26 (1995): 17–29.

Westphal, E. and P.C.M. Jansen, eds. *Plant Resources of South-East Asia: A Selection*. Wageningen: Pudoc, 1989.

PART IV
AUSTRALIA AND THE U.S.

10

A GENEALOGY OF SOUTHEAST ASIAN STUDIES IN AUSTRALIA
Scholars and Their Works

James J. Fox

INTRODUCTION: A CRITICAL PROVISO

Southeast Asian studies have developed to become a considerable field of study in Australia. Southeast Asia, as Australia's neighbouring region, has been the focus of national interest and this interest has encouraged considerable research and teaching in Australian universities for several decades. Yet "Southeast Asian Studies" as a whole has never been a unified subject of investigation nor can the study of Southeast Asia be extricated from other specific fields of research. Many of the individuals who have made the greatest contribution to the general field of Southeast Asian Studies have seen themselves primarily as contributors either to a particular discipline such as anthropology, politics, economics or demography or to the study of a particular country within Southeast Asia.

One might go further and argue that Southeast Asia could well be seen as a "transitory" category created in the period after the Second World War. Despite the existence of a political foundation through ASEAN for the present conception of Southeast Asia, views of this grouping of countries could well be reformulated in the future.

Although the category of Southeast Asia may be useful for certain purposes, there are other perspectives from which to view this same collection of countries. At different periods of history, various countries within the region have come under the cultural influence of either India or China and it is still possible to distinguish countries within the region accordingly. It is also possible to view these countries in terms of their predominant language families. Thus most of island Southeast Asia forms part of an Austronesian-speaking world. Similarly it is possible to view these countries in terms of their main constituent religions, in which case, Indonesia and Malaysia in particular form part of a Middle Eastern religious sphere.

This chapter offers a "genealogy" of some of the principal contributors to "Southeast Asian Studies" in Australia, even though many of these individuals would not themselves have identified their contribution as primarily directed to the creation of Southeast Asian Studies as such. In Australia, Southeast Asian Studies began through efforts to build disciplinary expertise on particular countries. In some cases, this involved a clear government-supported effort. This chapter will therefore proceed by looking first at the founding period and the initial founder figures in particular disciplines. These founder figures were responsible both for educating and recruiting the next generation. The chapter will also examine the institutional framework within which particular individuals carried out their research and teaching, focusing on specific disciplines and the intellectual succession that occurred within these disciplines.

I do this in relation to particular countries in Southeast Asia beginning with Indonesia because of its signal importance to Australia. This combination of discipline and area more closely approximates the way in which Southeast Asian Studies has been organized in Australia. In this chapter, I focus on the individual scholars and cite some of their chief scholarly work. For many versatile and prolific scholars, this thumbnail identification can, I admit, be misleading. I have called this examination a genealogy rather than a history because it provides the bare outline of the complex succession of scholars who together contributed to the creation of Southeast Asian Studies in Australia.

The development of Southeast Asian Studies in Australia is a story within a story. That larger story concerns the development of Australian universities in the post-war period, beginning with the establishment of the Australian National University (ANU) and continuing thereafter with the creation of new universities (Monash, University of New South Wales, Flinders, Griffith and Murdoch), all of which in varying degrees were open to the pursuit of studies on Southeast Asia.[1]

THE FOUNDATION PERIOD:
THE FIRST GENERATION FROM 1955

Four universities figured in the initial development of Southeast Asian Studies in Australia. They were the Australian National University, Sydney University, Melbourne University, and Monash University. Sydney and Melbourne were long established centres of learning in Australia. The Australian National University and Monash University were founded after the Second World War. The Australian National University was established in 1946 with a special charter that required a focus on Asia and the Pacific. The ANU's focus on Southeast Asia was given impetus when it was merged with Canberra University College in 1961. It was also in 1961 that Monash was founded in Melbourne and began its initial efforts to create a Southeast Asian focus.

Although the University of Queensland never established a full-blown Southeast Asia studies programme and instead concentrated, from the mid-1950s, on the study of the history of the region, it could also be included among universities that initially contributed to the development of Southeast Asian Studies in Australia.

THE AUSTRALIAN NATIONAL UNIVERSITY

The Australian National University was established in the immediate post-war period as a grouping of Schools within the Institute of Advanced Study. Among these Institutes was the Research School of Pacific Studies. "Pacific", at this time, was conceived of, according to one of the University's founders, as ranging "from the Americas to India". The anthropologist, Raymond Firth, was invited to be a member of the planning council of the University and was offered the position as the first Director of the Research School of Pacific Studies.

Although better known for his initial research on the Pacific, Firth had done research in Malaya and, had he accepted the position as Director, he might have contributed impressively to Southeast Asian Studies in Australia. When he declined the position, the task of shaping the School fell to others with different interests. Initial research focused on Papua New Guinea, the Pacific Islands, Aboriginal Australia and, within Asia, on China and to a lesser extent Japan. It was not until Professor Wang Gungwu was appointed as Director of the Research School in 1975 that research on Southeast Asia began to develop rapidly.

At the time of the founding of the ANU, Canberra already had a "Canberra University College" which was affiliated with Melbourne University. Eventually in 1961, this College was merged with the ANU to become The School of General Studies. Already in 1952, a School of Oriental Languages was established within the Canberra University College and Professor Hans Bielenstein was appointed as its Chair. The initial Oriental languages taught within this School were Chinese, Japanese and Russian.

After the merger with the ANU, Bielenstein's Department became the Faculty of Oriental Studies and continued as such until 1970 when its name was changed to the Faculty of Asian Studies. For a period, Oriental Studies and the Department of Far Eastern History in the Research School of Pacific Studies formed the "Centre of Oriental Studies" at the ANU.

THE ESTABLISHMENT OF INDONESIAN STUDIES IN AUSTRALIA

In 1955, during Prime Minister Menzies' government, the Commonwealth Office of Education wrote to three universities in Australia offering funding for Indonesian and Malayan Studies. The three universities to which this money was offered were: the Australian National University (more specifically, Canberra University College with its already established School of Oriental Languages), Sydney University and Melbourne University. Each of these universities took a different pathway for developing these studies.

In some government circles, expertise on Indonesia, Australia's neighbour to the north, was felt to be vital for future relations, even though in academic circles, there was preference to continue to develop a more traditional Orientalist focus on China, Japan and India.[2] Thus, for example, the Canberra University College submitted an alternative proposal for Indian Studies but the Office of Education insisted on Indonesian Studies. Finding suitable staff to build such a programme was, at the time, a considerable task.

Professor Bielenstein, a China scholar, was given this recruitment task in Canberra and he decided upon a young scholar, Anthony H. Johns, trained at the School of Oriental and African Studies in London who was at the time teaching in Indonesia. It took over two years before Johns could conclude his contract and come to Australia. He arrived in 1958 and in 1960, as the ANU-CUC merger was occurring, began the recruitment of a remarkable group of Indonesians who provided the basis for the teaching of the Indonesian language as the first Southeast Asian language to be taught at the ANU.

In 1956, in the initial phase of the Indonesian teaching programme, lectures in Bahasa Indonesia were given at the College by the Cultural Attaché, Mr Supangkat, of the Indonesian Embassy in Canberra. In 1957, for a period of two years, the Indonesian government provided a member of the Indonesian Ministry of Education, Mr Amir Hamzah to teach Indonesian language.

DEPARTMENT OF INDONESIAN LANGUAGES IN CANBERRA: FROM PHILOLOGY TO LITERATURE

Anthony H. Johns was a key figure in the development of Southeast Asian Studies at the ANU. In 1964, he was appointed as Professor of Indonesian Languages and Literature. He was a seminal figure in the training of successive generations of Indonesianists who did major research on Malay, Indonesian, Javanese and Balinese. He was also a scholar with a deep interest in Arabic and he was critical in directing researchers to the study of Islam in Southeast Asia. Remarkably, as Emeritus Professor, he continues to carry on his research and to advise students at the ANU to the present.

In his inaugural lecture as Professor, Johns noted that "philology for its own sake has dominated Indonesian studies" and that he intended to foster an effort that would lead to a wider purview of Malay and Javanese literary traditions: "…philology is a good servant, but a very bad master". Johns trained students who adopted this view. All of his initial appointees as teaching staff were Indonesians who could provide ANU students with a solid grounding in Indonesian and Javanese and all of them went on to produce major works of their own. S. Soebardi who was appointed in 1961, Soewito Santoso who was appointed in 1964, and Soepomo who was appointed in 1970 all produced nuanced studies of important Javanese texts: Soebardi: *The Book of Cabolèk* (1975), Soewito Santoso: *Sutasoma: A Study in Javanese Wajrajana* (1975), and Soepomo: *Arjunawijaya: A Kakawin of Mpu Tantalar* (1977). The noted writer and author of *Atheis*, Achdiat Miharja was also appointed in 1961 and he was joined in 1975 by Yohanni Johns who went on to produce what became for many years the most popular textbook for learning Indonesian in Australia, *Bahasa Indonesia: Langkah Baru, A New Approach.*[3]

DEPARTMENT OF ECONOMICS IN CANBERRA

Another founder figure at the ANU was Heinz Arndt in Economics. Like Johns, Arndt was originally a member of the Canberra University College and became part of the Australian National University at the time of the merger of the two entities. While Johns was located in the "Faculties" at the ANU, Arndt became the Head of Economics in the Research School of Pacific Studies. In this position, he went on to establish the study of the Indonesian economy in Australia but, as he himself recounts (Arndt 1985), this was initially a formidable task. In fact he was strongly discouraged from undertaking such work because of the state of the Indonesian economy during the chaotic, inflationary phase of the Sukarno government in late 1964. He nonetheless visited Indonesia and made contact with the group of economists, popularly known as the "Berkeley Mafia", who later became ministers in the Soeharto government.

With a grant from the Ford Foundation and the editorial assistance of Ruth Daroesman, he was able to publish the first issue of the *Bulletin of Indonesian Economic Studies* — an eighty-page offset-print produced by the printery of the Research School of Pacific Studies that appeared in June 1965. The *Bulletin* as a journal continues today in more or less the same format and is certainly one of Arndt's notable achievements. The *Bulletin* appears three times a year and each year includes a "Survey of Recent Developments" in the Indonesian economy. Arndt produced seventeen of these surveys in the early days of the journal's existence, which required him to make frequent visits to Indonesia. From 1966, he visited Indonesia four or five times a year, staying for three to four weeks to write his survey.

In building a programme on Indonesia and then more widely on Southeast Asia, Arndt recruited to his department a number of research scholars. Three individuals were particularly important: David Penny who came from Cornell University with a strong rural sociology background to do research on Indonesia, R.M. Sundrum who came from Rangoon University and did research on a range of countries, and E.K. (Fred) Fisk who arrived from the University of Malaya.

Penny's 1964 thesis at Cornell was on the transition from subsistence to commercial farming in North Sumatra. At the ANU, he developed a productive collaboration with Masri Singarimbun in the study of Javanese village poverty in a site known as Sriharjo (Penny and Singarimbun 1973). Sundrum's appointment led to a long and varied career in the Department of Economics and collaboration with different colleagues, including Arndt. A good example of their early collaboration was a short monograph they did together on transmigration in Indonesia (1977). Fisk's work, like Penny's, had a rural focus. In 1964, he published a book on the rural economies of Southeast Asia and in his early years in the department edited two books on Malaya/Malaysia with different colleagues (Fisk and Silcock 1963; Fisk and Osman-Rani 1982). Thomas Silcock, Fisk's first collaborator on Malaya, was a Visiting Fellow in Economics. He was a fluent Thai-speaker and was responsible for an early edited volume on development in Thailand (1967) as well as a study of Thai agriculture (1970). He maintained a productive association with the department and continued to work on Thailand.

ANTHROPOLOGY IN THE RESEARCH SCHOOL OF PACIFIC STUDIES AT THE ANU

Another less prominent but nonetheless important founding figure in a genealogy of Southeast Asian Studies at the ANU was Derek Freeman. Trained in London and at Cambridge University, Freeman wrote one of the finest ethnographies of its kind on the Iban of Sarawak.[4] Until his retirement, his work continued to attract students interested in the Iban in particular and in Borneo in general but not long after his arrival in Canberra in 1955, he turned his attention to Samoa where he had done previous research and then to issues in the intersection of anthropology and biology.

The founding Professor of Anthropology was Siegfried Nadel who died suddenly in 1956 and was replaced by John Barnes who was already a Professor at Sydney University. Barnes took upon himself the task of requiring students to do research on Indonesia and thus Anthropology was among the first departments to produce Indonesianist graduates, all of whom did research on Sumatra. Donald Tugby received his Ph.D. in 1960 for research on the Mandailing Batak; Mervyn Jaspan in 1964 for research on the Rejang; and Masri Singarimbun in 1965 for research among his own people, the Karo Batak.

Masri Singarimbun was a remarkable individual who not only published a "classic" study on the Karo (1975); he also collaborated in early work with the rural economist, David Penny. More significantly, he stayed on in Canberra to train himself as a demographer. When he returned to Indonesia, he was able to establish the Population Studies Centre (*Lembaga Kependudukan*) at Gadjah Mada University which became a significant centre for research, particularly on Java. Toward the end of his career, the ANU awarded him an Honorary Doctorate for his many achievements.

Another early graduate of this period who combined archaeology and anthropology was Campbell Macknight who wrote his thesis (1969) on the Macassan *trepang* industry in Northern Australia. The book based on his thesis was published in 1976; he went on to do substantial research, at the ANU and later in Tasmania, on the Bugis of South Sulawesi.

Gehan Wijeyewardene joined the Anthropology Department in 1964 with a research background in Ceylon. However, he soon shifted his interests to northern Thailand and created the long-standing Thai-Yunnan Research Project.

ARCHAEOLOGY AND PREHISTORY AT THE ANU

Almost from the outset, archaeological research of various kinds was carried out in different parts of the ANU: through a Prehistory Department that separated from Anthropology in the Research School of Pacific Studies, through a Department of Prehistory and Anthropology in the Faculty of Arts and by particular individuals in the Faculty of Asian Studies. This research focused on very different time periods: ranging from the early Pleistocene to the late Pleistocene and Holocene and into the classical period of Southeast Asian kingdoms.

The first ANU archaeological research in Southeast Asia was carried out by English students, J. M. Matthews and Ian Glover. Matthews wrote a thesis in 1964 on "Hoabinian" in Southeast Asia. Glover, on the other hand, carried out extended excavations in what was then Portuguese Timor in 1966–67. Two years later, in 1969, John Mulvaney, in cooperation with the Indonesian archaeologist R.P. Soejono who had been a visitor to Canberra the year before, led a major expedition to South Sulawesi, bringing with him Macknight who had just finished his Macassan thesis and Glover who was still working on his. Much of this initial research set a pattern for the future.

Glover finished his thesis in 1972 and published the major monograph on this work in 1986. On taking up a position at the Institute of Archaeology in London, Glover excavated adjacent sites to the first ANU sites and produced a number of studies establishing a long sequence for the area.

Helmut Loofs-Wissowa who had joined the Faculty of Asian Studies was at this time beginning his ANU career focusing on the classical archaeology of mainland Southeast Asia. In 1970, he published a basic volume on Vietnamese archaeology.

HISTORY IN THE RESEARCH SCHOOL OF PACIFIC STUDIES AT THE ANU

The history of Southeast Asia had its first hesitant beginnings in the study of British colonial history and as a consequence there was to begin with more interest in Malaya than with Indonesia. Much depended on an initial cohort of graduates. Emma (Emily) Sadka who came to the ANU in 1954 from Singapore as a Ph.D. student and wrote her thesis on the residential system in the protected Malay states (1960) was invited by the founding professor in History, Jim Davidson, a specialist on the Pacific, to assist him in developing a focus on Southeast Asia. She was instrumental in training a number of Ph.D. graduates to do this research. Among them were William Roff, Chris Wake and Chris Penders.

Roff did his thesis (1965) on the origins of Malay nationalism, which was published as a book in 1967; he went on to have a distinguished research career which focused on the study of Malaysia. Wake's thesis (1966) looked at nineteenth-century Johore but was never published as a book. Penders wrote his thesis (1968) on Dutch colonial education policy and practice in Indonesia in the first part of the twentieth century and continued to publish regularly on the colonial period and some of Indonesia's key nationalists. He took up an appointment at the University of Queensland where he continued the tradition begun by Bastin and Tarling, focusing on the history of Southeast Asia.

When Sadka died unexpectedly in 1968, Davidson recruited the Oxford-trained Indianist, Christine Dobbin as a research fellow. She turned her attention to Indonesia and published a number of studies, including an excellent examination of the Padri war (1983).

DEMOGRAPHY IN THE RESEARCH SCHOOL OF SOCIAL SCIENCE AT THE ANU

Demography at the ANU established the beginnings of a Southeast Asian interest through the training of its students. Jack Caldwell, who pioneered the development of demographic research in a wide spectrum of directions, wrote a thesis on the population of Malaya in 1962. He was joined in the Department by Gavin Jones who wrote his thesis on labour in Malaya in 1966. Together these two figures became a mainstay of the Department of Demography into the 1990s. Jones' work on an array of issues in the demography of Indonesia and of Southeast Asia (1984, 1994) laid a strong foundation for this field. In the early days of the Department, however, Jones and Caldwell were responsible for recruiting Masri Singarimbun as a research fellow to work on the demography of Indonesia. This led to a close relationship between demography at the ANU and what was to develop as the Population Institute in Yogyakarta.

INDONESIAN STUDIES AT SYDNEY UNIVERSITY

As in the case of the ANU, Indonesian studies at Sydney was begun through initial funding from the Commonwealth. At Sydney, it was decided to use these funds to establish a separate Department of Indonesian and Malayan Studies and to appoint as Head of this Department a notable scholar of Old Javanese, F.H. van Naerssen, who had been trained in Leiden, and later a young expert on Malay texts, Russell Jones who had been trained at the School of Oriental and African Studies. Both were oriented to the philological study of texts and their two most notable students, Peter Worsley and Stuart Robson carried on and extended this tradition. As students both Worsley and Robson did their Honours degrees at Sydney but went on to do their Ph.D.s at Leiden. Robson reworked his Sydney MA on the Classical Malay text, *Hikajat Andaken Penurat*, publishing it in 1969 and thereafter did his major work on Javanese. Worsley did his doctoral work on a Balinese dynastic genealogical text, the *Babad Buleng* which he published in 1972. He returned to Sydney as Professor and was responsible for promoting research on Bali and the Balinese. Robson remained in Leiden after the completion of his degree; he produced critical editions of a number of important Javanese texts, among others a new translation of the *Deśawarnana* (or *Nāgarakrtāgama*) by Mpu Prapañca but also useful materials for teaching colloquial Javanese. He, too, eventually returned to Australia.

In 1967, the Department established a journal, *Review of Indonesian and Malayan* (later to become *Malaysian*) *Studies*, popularly known as *RIMA* which has continued to the present to be published with two issues each year. It is the oldest continuing journal of its kind in Australia. In 2003, an independent association was formed in Canberra to publish the journal and since that time, the journal has been successfully edited by Campbell Macknight.

In the Anthropology Department at Sydney was W.H. Geddes who, like Derek Freeman, had carried out fieldwork in the British Crown Colony of Sarawak under the auspices of the Colonial Social Science Research Council.[5] He, like Freeman, wrote a study which is also a classic of its kind, *Nine Dayak Nights*, a superb account of the recitation of a long Dayak tale. Like Freeman, he also shifted his fieldwork interests to the Pacific but also to Thailand where he did research among the highland Hmong or Blue Miao. He was thus partially responsible for the development of Thai studies at Sydney. One of the first students to take Introductory Indonesian at Sydney was Douglas Miles who went on under Geddes' supervision to do fieldwork among the Dayak of Kalimantan. After the publication of his first ethnography (1976), he followed Geddes' lead in doing further research in northern Thailand and then went on to do research on Bali. Another of Geddes' students was Peter Hinton who continued research on Thailand at Sydney.[6]

Among the first to develop interests in the politics of Southeast Asia at Sydney University was Michael Leigh who did his Ph.D. at Cornell on political leadership in Sarawak in 1967. His first study of Sarawak, *The Rising Moon: Political Change in Sarawak,* was published by Sydney University Press in 1974. In his long career, Leigh held various positions including a Professorship in Sarawak before being appointed as the Director of the Asia Institute in Melbourne. In the 1970s, Leigh was joined by Michael van Langenberg who completed a Ph.D. thesis at Sydney on national revolution in North Sumatra in 1976. Langenberg continued a tradition of critical analysis at Sydney that was focused on political economy. This was a tradition begun by Rex Mortimer who was appointed at Sydney after obtaining his Ph.D. at Monash in 1970. Richard Robison, another student in this tradition, finished his thesis at Sydney on capitalism and the bureaucratic state in Indonesia in 1979 and moved to Murdoch University in Western Australia where he had a distinguished and prolific career. One of Robison's important early studies was *Indonesia: The Rise of Capital* (1986); his work became directed to the study of Southeast Asia as a whole. With one of his students, Garry Rodan, he produced *The Political Economy of South-East Asia: An Introduction* (1997) and followed this with a succession of books on various aspects of the political economy of the region.

INDONESIAN AND MALAYAN STUDIES IN MELBOURNE

The third bequest of funding from the Commonwealth government for the establishment of Indonesian and Malay studies was made to Melbourne University. Melbourne adopted another model for the development of these studies. As in Canberra, the initial teaching of Indonesian at Melbourne in 1956 was provided and supported by the Indonesian government through the secondment of a member of the Indonesian Ministry of Foreign Affairs, Mr Zainu'ddin. Thereafter, for the creation of its Department of Indonesian and Malayan Studies, the University appointed one of its own scholars, a Melbourne graduate, Jamie Mackie, who had studied at Oxford and had spent two years working as a Colombo Plan expert in the Indonesian Planning Bureau. On his appointment in 1958, Mackie set out to establish a programme that would examine Indonesia's political and economic development. The programme included the study of the Indonesian language. Together with J.P. Sarumpaet, Mackie produced an introductory text for the study of Indonesian. Mackie, by his determination to create a broader understanding of Indonesia in Australia, can be considered the first Australian to develop a distinct focus on contemporary Indonesia as a political, social and economic entity.

When, however, Monash University was established in 1961, the historian John Legge was appointed as a foundation professor. He recruited the political scientist Herb Feith to join him in establishing the programme that led to the creation of the Centre of Southeast Asian Studies at this new university. To a certain extent, the Monash Centre was modelled on the Southeast Asia Program at Cornell University. Feith did his Ph.D. at Cornell and Legge had spent time there. They were among the first wave of Australians to make their way to study at Cornell and then return to Australia, thus initiating a long-standing connection between Southeast Asian Studies programmes there and in Australia.

The Centre became a remarkable confluence of scholars of different political persuasions who were nevertheless united in a common interest in Indonesia in particular and the region in general. Besides Legge and Feith, these scholars included Cyril Skinner. Michael Swift from the British Anthropology tradition and Lode Brakel from Leiden's "*Indische*" studies tradition added to this group. In 1968, Jamie Mackie was lured from Melbourne University to Monash to become the Research Director of the Centre making it the leading centre in Australia for the study of Indonesia and Southeast Asia. Another figure to join this group was Barbara Harvey, an American with diplomatic experience in Indonesia and a degree from Cornell (1974) for a thesis on Islam and rebellion in Sulawesi.

Each of these scholars made notable contributions to the study of Southeast Asia. Legge first gained recognition for his Cornell monograph on central authority and local autonomy in Indonesia (1961), then for his general book on Indonesia (1964) and, most significantly for his political biography of Sukarno (1972). Feith also wrote a Cornell monograph on Indonesian politics (1961) and then followed this with his influential study of the decline of constitutional democracy (1962). Mortimer wrote the first of the Monash Southeast Asia Centre papers on the Communist Party's campaign for land reform (1972) and two years later, produced his major study of Communism under Sukarno (1974). Harvey's monograph on the *Permesta* rebellion was published in 1977. Mackie's publications were wide-ranging. As Research Director, he published a monograph on Sukarno's Confrontation (1974) and on the Chinese in Indonesia (1976). Skinner provided a contrast in the group. He was the elder of the Monash group and maintained a scholarly tradition of historical and textual analysis focused as much on Malaya as on Indonesia through such works as his edited translation of a rhymed chronicle of the Macassar war (1963) and his monograph on the civil war in Kelantan in 1839 (1966). Michael Swift wrote about Malay peasant society (1965) and Brakel worked on Malay manuscripts (1975). Rex Mortimer was one of the first students to study with Feith; his thesis on the Indonesian Communist Party, completed in 1970, was published in 1974.

Some years later, David Chandler joined the Monash Centre providing it with greater focus on mainland Southeast Asia, in Chandler's case, Cambodia. His extensive publications (1972, 1983, 1996) covered the land, people and history of Cambodia.

One of the most useful initiatives begun in 1959 at Melbourne University was the formation of an informal discussion group that extended well beyond academia to include anyone with an interest in Indonesia. The group would meet regularly to discuss current developments in Indonesia and became known as the Contemporary Indonesia Study Group. Eventually the organization for this group shifted to Monash University where it still exists and continues to meet to this day.

SOUTHEAST ASIAN HISTORY AT THE UNIVERSITY OF QUEENSLAND

The University of Queensland was not a recipient of the initial Australian government funding provided to the universities in Canberra, Melbourne and Sydney. It did not therefore develop a language programme for Indonesian but instead came to focus attention on the study of the history of the region and its politics. The British historian, John Bastin, was the first to teach on Southeast Asian history during a year's appointment from 1955 to 1956 and he was succeeded by Nicholas Tarling who taught at the university until 1965 when he accepted a position in New Zealand. Over his long career, Tarling has been enormously prolific. During his time at Queensland, he wrote on Anglo-Dutch rivalry (1962) and also on piracy and politics (1963) in the Malay world and published a short history of Southeast Asia (1966). Later he was responsible for editing *The Cambridge History of Southeast Asia* (1992).

THE TRANSITION TO A SECOND GENERATION
AT THE ANU

At the ANU, two figures of the founding generation were notable for the number of students whom they trained and who then continued their careers in Indonesian studies. These two figures are Professor Anthony Johns and Professor Heinz Arndt.

Professor Johns produced a number of distinguished students who, in turn, contributed to the development of Indonesian, Javanese and Balinese studies. Among these students were scholars who stayed on to teach at the Australian National University: Ann Kumar whose dissertation on Surapati published in 1976 combined both historical and textual analysis, and Ian Proudfoot who wrote his thesis on a tale told within the *Mahabharata* (1977). Both Kumar and Proudfoot published extensively across a wide range of subjects: thus, for example, Kumar's *The Diary of Javanese Muslim* (1985) which provides a marvellous glimpse into nineteenth century relations about key figures in Islamic learned society. Proudfoot wrote on early printed Malay books (1993) but also delved deeply into the study of old Muslim calendars (2006).

Other students who did their undergraduate study at the ANU in Indonesian studies went on elsewhere for their further degrees. Heather Sutherland went from the ANU to Yale University where she wrote her thesis on the Javanese *priayi* that was eventually published in 1979; Barbara Hatley also went on to Yale where she did an MA but returned to Australia to complete her Ph.D. at Sydney University on *Kethoprak* theatre in Yogyakarta in 1985. The book based on her long study of Javanese performance was finally published in 2008, by which time she had been appointed as the Foundation Professor in Indonesian at the University of Tasmania. Chris Manning, another of these undergraduate students, went on to do his Ph.D. in Economics at the ANU.

In Economics, Arndt produced a significant number of able students: Peter McCawley, Ross Garnaut, Anne Booth, Howard Dick, Hal Hill and Chris Manning, all of whom went on to have distinguished careers. McCawley wrote his thesis on the Indonesian electricity industry in 1971, Garnaut on Australian trade with Southeast Asia in 1972, Booth on Indonesian land tax in 1974, Dick on the Indonesian interisland shipping industry in 1977, Hill on the Indonesian weaving industry in 1979, and Manning on the labour market in Indonesian manufacturing also in 1979.

For a while, all of these scholars were in Canberra and worked together in various ways. Garnaut and Manning co-authored a monograph on

Irian Jaya (1974) which was valuable for its time. Booth and McCawley edited an important volume, *The Indonesian Economy during the Suharto Era* (1981), which Arndt, in his autobiography, *A Course through Life* (1985, p. 66), considered a coming-of-age for the department in its research on Indonesia.

McCawley eventually left the Department to work first in AusAID and then for the Asian Development Bank. Booth was a productive stalwart of the department for many years writing on agriculture. One of her most important books while she was in the Department was *Agricultural Development in Indonesia* (1988) as a Southeast Asian Studies monograph. Dick moved to the University of Melbourne. He published a revised version of his thesis in 1986 and, in 2002, a socioeconomic history of Surabaya, *Surabaya, A City of Work*, that covers the whole of the twentieth century. Garnaut remained in the Department but turned his attention to China. For several years during the Hawke government, he served as Australian Ambassador to the People's Republic of China. Hill, too, stayed on in the Department. Hill's research looked at Indonesian industry but he also studied the Philippine economy and edited several important volumes on the Philippines and on Indonesian regional economic development. Manning also remained in the Department, continuing to write on labour in Indonesia culminating in his major study in 1998. They were joined by Ross McLeod who had also done a Ph.D. at the ANU. Together the three of them took over, in turn, the running of the "Indonesia Project" at the ANU and in particular, the continuing publication of the *Bulletin of Indonesian Economic Studies (BIES)*, which, in 2012, had reached its 48th volume. The *Bulletin* has provided an extraordinary record, in many ways unique of its kind, in documenting the development of the Indonesian economy.

DEVELOPMENTS IN THE RESEARCH SCHOOL OF PACIFIC STUDIES

The Research School of Pacific Studies [later, the Research School of Pacific and Asian Studies] was part of the Institute of Advanced Study at the ANU and as such, it received its research support in a "block grant" from the Australian government. Its primary task was research and its Ph.D. programme was considered part of its research effort. Those enrolled for a Ph.D. in the Research School were referred to, at the time, as Research Scholars. The School had a relatively small number of tenured faculty with a large number of "Research Fellows" and "Senior Research Fellows" whose appointments could range from two to five years and could, in some instances, be renewed for another five years. This arrangement gave the Research School the capacity to hire outstanding individuals for extended periods of time to concentrate on their research and publications. In addition, the Research School had a strong Visiting Fellows programme that offered scholars support for several months to participate in research programmes within the School.

Several developments in the Research School set the stage for further research on Southeast Asia. One important appointment in 1968 was that of Wang Gungwu, who — though appointed to head East Asian History — was a person with a deep interest and knowledge of Southeast Asia. When he became Director of the Research School in 1975, he actively promoted the development of Southeast Asian Studies.

An important appointment was that of Anthony Reid. He began in Wellington where he had studied with Emma Sadka before moving to Cambridge to do his doctorate on Aceh. Although he was appointed in 1970, he took leave in 1973 for two years to teach at Yale and only returned in 1975. Reid, in particular, maintained a commitment to the study of the whole of Southeast Asia and was intimately involved in promoting interdisciplinary research on the region. While continuing to work on Aceh and Sumatra in general, Reid was an enthusiastic organizer of symposia and maintained a continuing commitment to the history of Southeast Asia. He gained international recognition for his *Southeast Asia in the Age of Commerce, 1450–1680* and after leaving the ANU for the University of California, Los Angeles (UCLA) and, later, to become Director of the Asia Research Institute at the University of Singapore, he continued to be a vital figure in Southeast Asian Studies.

One can date the emergence of another generation from the early 1970s. By this time, a number of students of Johns and Arndt held positions at the ANU and were soon joined by a cohort of graduates from Cornell or Yale along with a few graduates, like Reid, from either Oxford or Cambridge. Thus, for example, in 1972, Lance Castles returned from Yale to a research fellowship in the History Department; Leonard Andaya and Rey Ileto arrived in 1973–74. They were the first Cornell appointees to history, though Herb Feith had himself held a position briefly in the Research School before moving to Monash.

Leonard Andaya was accompanied by his wife, Barbara Watson Andaya. She had been educated at Sydney, did her MA at Hawai'i, submitted her Ph.D. at Cornell in 1975 and took up a position at the ANU in 1977. Leonard's study of the kingdom of Johor (1975) and Barbara's study of Perak (1979) were a beautifully complementary set of early historical studies.

Indicative of this new effort was a symposium held in Canberra in April 1973 and published in 1975 on "Pre-colonial state systems in Southeast Asia". Contributors included a range of young scholars: Reid, Castles, Worsley who returned to Sydney to take over the Department of Indonesian and Malayan Studies, Dobbins who was teaching at Flinders, Leonard and wife Barbara Andaya, Campbell Macknight who was lecturing in history at the ANU and students such as Virginia Matheson Hooker who was doing her Ph.D. at Monash and Alfons van der Kraan who was doing his at the ANU.

Virginia Matheson Hooker, a graduate of Monash University, was later appointed in Anthony John's Department; she cooperated with Barbara Andaya to produce an annotated translation of the *Tuhfat al Nafis*, entitled *The Precious Gift* (1982), which was inspired by Johns' early study, *The Gift Addressed to the Spirit of the Prophet* (1965). She went on to write a perspicacious examination of the development of the Malay novel (2000) and, together with Greg Fealy, to compile a major source book on contemporary Islam in Southeast Asia: *Voices of Islam in Southeast Asia* (2006).

In 1975, when Wang Gungwu was appointed Director of the Research School there was beginning to emerge a critical mass of research scholars across several disciplines that was able to attract students interested in studying Southeast Asia.

In 1975, James J. Fox was appointed to a position in the Department of Anthropology and given the explicit task of developing a strong programme on the anthropology of Indonesia. Fox came from Oxford via Harvard with a primary interest in eastern Indonesia, which, at the time, was a region that was hardly studied, despite its proximity to Australia. His first book, *Harvest of the Palm* (1977), had both an historical and ecological focus on the Timor region and was followed by various comparative volumes on the social structure (1980) and ritual languages (1988) of eastern Indonesia. Soon after his arrival, however, he developed an interest in Java and made this his second area of research. Later, in the 1980s, he initiated the Comparative Austronesian Project at the ANU, thus viewing island Southeast Asia as socially and culturally a distinct part of the Austronesian-speaking world. The Project produced a series of publications that has continued.

David Marr took up a permanent position in History in 1977 adding a focus on modern Southeast Asian history, particularly Vietnam. His work provided a continuing exploration of twentieth century Vietnamese history (1971, 1981, 1995).

Also significantly, in 1978, Jamie Mackie was appointed Foundation Professor in the new Department of Political and Social Change in the

Research School; he was joined by Ron May who did his research both on New Guinea and the Philippines. As his first staff member, he recruited William O'Malley from Cornell University and not long afterwards, two other recent Australian Ph.D. graduates, Colin Brown and Ken Young for his first major project on Java. Thereafter he hired Brian Fegan to do research on the Philippines, specifically Luzon, to provide a comparative perspective on Java. More importantly, he appointed Harold Crouch whose work on the Indonesian military (1978) and on Malaysian politics (1982, 1996) was particularly notable. At about this same time, both Colin Barlow and Peter Warr were appointed in Economics: Barlow to do research on rubber and other export crops from Indonesia and Malaysia (1978) and Warr on the agricultural development of both the Philippines and Thailand (1993).

Elsewhere in the University, there was also a developing interest in Southeast Asia. Although members of the Demography Department cooperated closely with colleagues in the Research School, it always remained within the Research School of Social Sciences. Its Ph.D. programme was particularly productive at an early date. Peter McDonald finished his thesis in 1972 and in 1975, three more distinguished graduates — Terry Hull, Valerie Hull and Graeme Hugo — submitted their Ph.D.s, all written on demographic issues in Indonesia.

Although McDonald's thesis was on the demography of Australia, he published various substantial works on marriage and divorce in West Java and on the Indonesian census (1983). Hugo's thesis was on population mobility in West Java. He published extensively on the demographic dimension of development in Indonesia and in the Asia-Pacific region (1981, 1987). Both of these researchers went on in their careers to concentrate their attention on Australian demographic development. The Hulls, on the other hand, remained focused on Indonesia and the Asian region. They co-operated and collaborated on research on Java through Masri Singarimbun's Population Institute in Yogyakarta (1976). At the ANU, Terry Hull also published with Gavin Jones (1999) as well as publishing a host of reports on fertility, child mortality and family planning.

In 1973, Anthony Forge was appointed Foundation Professor in Anthropology in the Faculties. Although his major work had been in the Sepik, prior to coming to Australia, he had done a year's fieldwork on Bali, studying, in particular, Balinese art. Fox and Forge had met on Bali and had spent time together so that, once in Canberra, they were able to develop strong cooperation between anthropology in the Research School and in the Faculties.

Initially, as a return gesture for Australian Aid under the Colombo Plan, the Thai government supplied a teacher Ajar Wiphut Sophawong (1975–78) to begin the teaching of Thai. In 1978, Anthony Diller took up a position to teach Thai on a permanent basis. Diller had done his Ph.D. at Cornell on the southern Thai dialect. During his time at the ANU, while continuing his linguistic research, he developed a vigorous programme of Thai language studies.

Anthony Milner, a graduate of Monash University who completed his Ph.D. at Cornell in 1978, returned to Australia in 1980 via the University of Kent at Canterbury to teach in the History Department in the Faculties. His early work was on Malay political culture but soon broadened to take in a wider range of issues relating to Southeast Asia.

Peter Bellwood in the Department of Prehistory and Anthropology in the Faculties, whose first research had been on Polynesia, shifted his interests to focus on the archaeology and early history of what he called the Indo-Malaysian archipelago (1985). In the late 1970s, Margo Lyon was appointed in this same Department to provide Indonesian anthropological expertise.

The milestone event at the ANU in the study of Indonesia was a seminar organized over several weeks in late 1979 that drew on all the expertise throughout the university to examine the course of Indonesia's development from its geological beginnings to its most current political and economic policies. The results of this seminar were published as a single massive volume, *Indonesia: Australian Perspectives* (Fox et al. 1980) and as three separate volumes, *Indonesia, The Making of a Culture* (1980); *Indonesia: Dualism, Growth and Poverty* (1980); and, *Indonesia: The Making of a Nation* (1980)

NATIONAL DEVELOPMENTS IN ASIAN STUDIES FROM THE MID-1970s ONWARD

The formation of a second generation of Southeast Asianists in Australia occurred rapidly in the 1970s. Australia widened its focus to other countries in the region and made a considerable effort to develop an appropriate range of scholarly expertise. At the same time, the early efforts to advance the study of Indonesia in Australia led to a veritable explosion of further scholarly research on Indonesia. This was in particular a period of expansion of the teaching of Indonesia in many universities in Australia.

1976 was an important year for Asian Studies in Australia. This was the year that the Asian Studies Association of Australia was founded and immediately set to work to promote Asian Studies, including Southeast Asian Studies, in Australia. At the time, the main Asian languages studied in Australia were Japanese, Chinese and Indonesian. In the early 1970s, Indonesian was taught only at Sydney University, Melbourne University, Monash and the ANU. However in 1975, the School of Modern Asian Studies was established at Griffith University in Brisbane and began teaching Indonesian and a year later in 1976, Flinders University in South Australia established an Asian Studies programme featuring Indonesia. For a period in the 1970s, James Cook University in Townsville also taught Indonesian in its Modern Languages programme. This was also the period when a number of variously named Asian Studies or Southeast Asian Studies centres were established in universities. Some of these centres prospered while others failed to reach the critical mass necessary for a viable programme.

The School of Modern Asian Studies recruited Julia Howell from the United States and Robert Elson, one of Legge's students. Howell had an interest in Javanese religion and from this base developed a particular interest in Sufism in Java. Elson proved to be perhaps the most prolific of Indonesian historians, publishing major studies at regular intervals that began with studies on Java's sugar industry and the cultivation system and went on to include a biography of Soeharto and a history of the idea of Indonesia (1984, 1994, 2001, 2008). These two scholars were joined by John Butcher who began his career doing research on the colonial history of Southeast Asia at Hull University (1979) and then moved on to write an important study on the marine fisheries of the region (2004).

Robert Cribb, who did Asian Studies at the University of Queensland before going on to do his Ph.D. at the School of Oriental and African Studies, also taught for a period at Griffith University as well as the University of Queensland. In 2003, he joined the Department of Asian and Pacific History in the Research School of Pacific and Asian Studies at the ANU. His early historical research focused on the revolution in Indonesia: *Gangsters and Revolutionaries: The Jakarta People's Militia and the Indonesian Revolution, 1945–1949* (1991). While at Griffith he wrote a modern history of Indonesia with Colin Brown (1995) and at the ANU he produced a *Digital Atlas of Indonesian History* (2005a).

Other graduates who did their doctoral research in England before taking up positions in Australia were Clive Kessler whose Ph.D. research at the University of London was on the Malaysian state of Kelantan and then, some years later, Kenneth Young whose research, also at the University of London, was on the Minangkabau anti-tax rebellion of 1908. Kessler became an established researcher and commentator on Malaysia at the University of

New South Wales while Young did his research on Indonesia at a number of universities in Melbourne, Canberra and Wollongong. Another graduate with an overseas Ph.D., Jean G. Taylor whose research was done at the University of Wisconsin, has taught for many years at the University of New South Wales. Her splendid book on the social world of Batavia, first published in 1983, was republished in a 2nd edition in 2009.

Graduates of Monash who trained at the Centre of Southeast Asian Studies dispersed throughout Australia. Besides Elson who went to Griffith and Crouch who went to the ANU, Ulf Sundhaussen moved to the University of Queensland, John Ingleson to the University of New South Wales and Charles Coppel to Melbourne University; James Schiller, with his wife Barbara Martin-Schiller, established themselves at Flinders University. Richard Tanter, after teaching in Japan, took up an appointment at the Royal Melbourne Institute of Technology. The anthropologist, Michael Pinches, took a position at the University of Western Australia after completing his Ph.D. on a shanty town in the Philippines and somewhat later the political scientist David Bourchier who did his thesis on Indonesia also went to the University of Western Australia. Yet another Monash graduate, Damien Kingsbury was appointed at Deakin University. Susan Abeyasekere–Blackburn who wrote her thesis on Indonesian nationalism remained at Monash.

Sundhaussen whose thesis focused on the Indonesian officer corps published his study of Indonesian military politics in 1982; some years later, he and Chris Penders collaborated to write the political biography of Indonesian general, Abdul Haris Nasution (1985). Ingleson published an important study of the Indonesian nationalist movement in 1979 as the first volume in the Southeast Asia publication series of the Asian Studies Association; his study of workers' unions in colonial Java appeared in 1986 as the 12th volume in this series; Coppel's study on Indonesian Chinese published in 1983 was the 8th volume in the series. He continued to publish on the ethnic Chinese of Indonesia (2002) and on the violence affecting them and others in the country (2006). Schiller's work focused on local government; his wife, whose Monash thesis was on an upland village in Java, joined him in a study of the town of Jepara on Java's north coast (1996).

Tanter's Ph.D. was on the intelligence agencies in Indonesia, an interest which he continued to develop to include the wider Asian region. His research has also been on the politics of the middle class in Indonesia. Bourchier's concerns with Indonesian political thought have also drawn him to research on issues of democracy and dissent in the country. Kingsbury has extended his critical research on Indonesia to the Southeast Asian region in general and to East Timor in particular.

Susan Abeyasekere published variously on the Indonesian nationalist movement (1976) and then wrote a history of Jakarta (1987); later as Susan Blackburn, she did research on a range of feminist issues (2004).

FACILITATING ASIAN STUDIES AT THE NATIONAL LEVEL

In 1980, the Asian Studies Association published a comprehensive report on Asian Studies in Australia, officially known as "Asia in Australian Education" but unofficially referred to as the "FitzGerald Report" after the Chairman of the Report's Committee, Stephen FitzGerald. This was the first and perhaps the most important report of its kind. It was in three volumes. The first volume consisted of 99 pages with 75 detailed resolutions/recommendations, many of them made up of several parts; the second, shorter volume provided a survey of Asian Studies in the country; while the third merely summarized the Report's resolutions. The Report called for the development of Asian Studies in schools, leading to more advanced study at university level. In particular, it recommended the teaching of "second-tier" languages — in the case of Southeast Asia, Thai, Vietnamese and Tagalog — at a tertiary institution.

This Report did not attempt to promote an area-studies approach in Australia. It pressed for the teaching of languages as essential to the study of Asia and then remarked on the practice, already developed in several Australian universities, of combining a discipline with knowledge of a country and its language. The Report thus called for "Asian content in discipline-based courses" (Resolution 11, in particular).

A key element in the development of Southeast Asian Studies in Australia was the existence in Canberra of the National Library of Australia. The Library had a long-standing policy acquiring books on and from the Asia-Pacific region and continues to maintain this policy to the present. The Library collects language and other research materials on (1) Indonesia, (2) Thailand, (3) Vietnam, (4) Cambodia and (5) Burma/Myanmar and has a separate "Regional Asia" collection devoted to Malaysia, Singapore and the Philippines. The ANU Menzies Library, located directly opposite the Research School of Pacific and Asian Studies, has the second largest collection of books on Asia, making Canberra a focus for research on Asia.

Another innovation that began in the early 1980s at the ANU had a far-reaching effect on the way that Southeast Asian Studies was publicly perceived. On the 3rd of November 1983, the first Indonesia Update was held. The idea behind this and all subsequent "Updates" was to provide a public presentation of current developments in a particular country along with lectures on a specific topic in relation to that country. Indonesian Updates have been held each year in Canberra (and in recent years in Jakarta as well) since 1983. Other scholars have emulated this practice so that most every year there are Updates on the various countries in Southeast Asia, particularly Thailand, Vietnam, the Philippines and Myanmar.

These Updates are open to the public and are well attended. The annual Indonesia Update is now held over two days and generally attracts 400 or more attendees — many, in Canberra, from government departments. Each year there is a lecture devoted to recent political developments and another devoted to economic developments, plus various presentations on the chosen topic. The goal is to increase public awareness but also to promote a more general understanding of academic research on these countries.

GRADUATES IN SOUTHEAST ASIAN STUDIES IN THE 1980s AND THE 1990s

Whereas a majority of Australians in the 1970s went overseas for their Ph.D. training and only a minority managed to do their Ph.D.s in Australia, things changed dramatically in the 1980s. Southeast Asian Studies in Australia, particularly the study of Indonesia and to a lesser extent, Thailand, expanded in the 1980s as a whole new generation of students did their doctoral work in Australia and then took up positions in various universities throughout the country.

Among Anthony Johns' students was Helen M. Creese whose dissertation in 1981 was on an Old Javanese *kakawin*, the *Subhadrāwiwāha;* she followed this with a study of an eighteenth-century Balinese text, *Parthayana* (1998) and an even more fascinating study of women of the Indic court world of Java and Bali (2004). Peter Riddell was another of Johns' students whose Ph.D. in 1984 on *'Abd Al-Ra'ūf Al- Singili* was eventually published in 1990. This work reflected Johns' ever increasing interest in Islam in Southeast Asia. Creese moved to teach in Queensland and Riddell to Brunel in London. Yet another graduate was Tim E. Behrend who submitted his doctoral dissertation on the various manuscripts of the Javanese poem, the *Serat Jatiswara*, in 1987. This study was published in Indonesian translation in 1995. Behrend was involved with Alan Feinstein in the microfilming of Javanese manuscripts particularly from the Museum Sonobudoyo in Yogyakarta.

As retirements occurred in the Department, George Quinn was recruited to strengthen the programme, particularly in Javanese. His teaching and his research on Java, especially his study of the Javanese novel (1992) added considerably to the programme.

The Department of Political and Social Change produced a number of distinguished graduates: Andrew MacIntyre who wrote his Ph.D. on business-government relations in Indonesia, John Maxwell on the Indonesian political intellectual and activist, Soe Hok-Gie and Ed Aspinall on the political opposition in Indonesia. After teaching elsewhere, both MacIntyre and Aspinall returned to take up positions at the ANU where they continued their research and teaching. Each published books based on their theses — MacIntyre: *Business and Politics in Indonesia* (1991) and Aspinall: *Opposing Suharto: Compromise, Resistance and Regime Change in Indonesia* (2005). The book based on Maxwell's thesis was published in Indonesian translation (2001) and was used as the basis for a widely acclaimed Indonesian film on the life of Soe Hok-Gie.

In History, under the supervision of David Marr, Nola Cooke wrote a Ph.D. thesis on Vietnamese colonial history (1991) and a year later in 1992, Li Ta Na completed her thesis which was published as *Nguyễn Cochinchina: Southern Vietnam in the Seventeenth and Eighteenth Centuries* (1998). Cooke and Li later collaborated in editing a valuable history of Chinese commerce in the Mekong (2004). Another student, jointly supervised by Marr and Wijeyewardene was Philip Taylor who was one of the first Australians to carry out extended fieldwork in southern Vietnam. Taylor published his first book, *Fragments of the Present* (2001), based on his thesis and has subsequently published extensively on Vietnam (2004, 2007). Li and Taylor were eventually appointed to positions at the ANU. Jane Drakard, who completed her Ph.D. on the history of a Sumatran kingdom in 1993, took up a position at Monash University. The book, *A Kingdom of Words*, based on her thesis appeared in 1999.

In Anthropology, there were a significant number of new graduates supervised by Fox. In 1982, Patrick Guinness completed his thesis on an urban kampong in Yogyakarta; in 1983, E. Douglas Lewis submitted his thesis on a community in central east Flores; in 1984, Kathryn Robinson on a mining development in Sulawesi. Thereafter, in 1989, Andrew McWilliam completed his thesis on West Timor, Greg Acciaioli his thesis on a Bugis settlement in central Sulawesi and Lynette Parker her thesis on a Balinese village. Finally in 1990, Christine Helliwell submitted her thesis on a community in Borneo.

Guinness and Helliwell were appointed to teach in the Faculties at the ANU. Robinson, after a time at Newcastle and McWilliam, after a period of Aboriginal research, returned to Anthropology in the Research School. Lewis began in Western Australia but was then appointed to teach anthropology at Melbourne University. Acciaioli moved to teach anthropology at the University of Western Australia where he joined another of Fox's former students, John Gordon who received his Ph.D. from Harvard, while Lyn Parker took up a position in Asian Studies at the University. Penelope Graham who finished her thesis on eastern Flores in 1991 after having completed an MA thesis at the ANU on the Iban of Borneo (1987) moved to Monash to teach anthropology.

All of these graduates produced important publications based on their fieldwork. Guinness published his book, *Harmony and Hierarchy*, as an Asian Studies monograph in 1986; Robinson published her book, *Stepchildren of Progress*, also in 1986; Graham, her book, *Iban Shamanism* in 1987; Lewis his book, *People of the Source*, in 1988. Helliwell's book, *Never Stand Alone* appeared in 2001; McWilliam's, *Paths of Origin, Gates of Life* in 2003.

A later group of Fox's students also went on to teach in Australia: Minako Sakai who began the Indonesian language programme at the Australian Defense Force Academy (ADFA), attached to the University of New South Wales, Thomas Reuter who taught at Monash was awarded a Future Fellowship at Melbourne University while Phil Winn is currently at the ANU. Sakai's research was on Sumatra, Reuter's on Bali and Winn's on Banda Island in the Moluccas. Reuter published two volumes of ethnography on the Bali Aga: *Custodians of the Sacred Mountains* (2002*a*) and *The House of our Ancestors* (2002*b*).

In all, Fox supervised fifty-five doctoral dissertations in Anthropology at the ANU. Twenty of these Ph.D. theses were written by Indonesians. This number of Indonesian students points to another development that gained momentum in the 1980s and increased rapidly in the 1990s. A large number of students, from Indonesia but also from Thailand and Vietnam, began coming to the ANU and other Australian universities for advanced training. On their return, these students contributed to the development of a network of cooperation throughout the region.[7]

Fox was also responsible for the creation of an Ethnographic Film Unit attached to the Research School. With the support, collaboration and impetus provided by two outstanding film-makers, Timothy and Patsy Asch, he and some of his students (Bubandt, Lewis, Suwandi and Vischer) made a series of films on eastern Indonesia and Java.

At the ANU, Bellwood had a seminal influence on Southeast Asian archaeology. He trained a host of Southeast Asian students from Brunei, Malaysia, Thailand, Laos and particularly Indonesia, most of whom did their own important excavations under his guidance. In cooperation with his students and other local colleagues, he also carried out a succession of investigations on regional prehistory: in the 1970s, in North Sulawesi including Talaud and Sangihe, in the 1980s, in Sabah, in the 1990s, in the northern Moluccas and thereafter on the Batanes Islands of northern Philippines. On all of these sites, he published valuable papers and monographs and at the same time, he has written the key volumes that have synthesized current knowledge (1997) and argued for the importance of the spread of farming cultures in the region and into the Pacific. He was a key participant in the *Comparative Austronesian Project* initiated by Fox in the 1990s and served as one of the editors of *The Austronesians* (1995).

Among Bellwood's Australian students, David Bulbeck, who finished his thesis in 1992 and was a participant in the *Comparative Austronesian Project,* carried out research on the historical archaeology of Gowa and Tallok in South Sulawesi. He and Ian Caldwell, an ANU student of Campbell Macknight, and now at Leeds University, have gone to work together on the history and archaeology of Luwu and the Cenrana valley of Sulawesi (2000).

In 1995, another ANU graduate based at the University of New England, Mike Morwood, whose Ph.D. thesis was on the prehistory of central western Queensland, joined a major excavation project in central Flores that continued for almost a decade and resulted in the discovery of a possible new species, *homo floresiensis,* popularly known as the "hobbit". These skeletal remains have been the subject of continuing controversy since their discovery (Morwood and Oosterzee 2007).

In the same year, 1995, two archaeologists from the ANU, Sue O'Connor and Matthew Spriggs together with Peter Veth from James Cook University, began excavations on the Aru Islands, hoping to find evidence of early migration that may have carried via New Guinea into Australia. O'Connor and Veth edited a substantial interdisciplinary volume, *East of Wallace's Line,* in 2000 and all three collaborators published the results of the Aru research in 2005.

With the end of the Indonesian occupation of East Timor, these same archaeologists have turned their attention to Timor following on from the original work of Glover in the 1960s. Their excavations have uncovered evidence of human settlement dating back 35,000 years.

THE BLOSSOMING OF SOUTHEAST ASIAN STUDIES AT UNIVERSITIES AROUND AUSTRALIA

Monash University sought new talent from overseas. The University appointed the anthropologist Joel Kahn and, a few years later, the historian Merle Ricklefs to professorships. Both scholars were highly productive. After some years at Monash, Kahn moved to La Trobe University and Ricklefs to the ANU where he became the Director of the Research School of Pacific and Asian Studies. From the ANU, he moved, for a time, to be Director of the Melbourne Institute of Asian Languages and Societies.

Monash continued to produce significant graduates. Two such graduates, Greg Barton, a student of Herb Feith, and, later, Greg Fealy, a student of Merle Ricklefs both produced important theses on Indonesian Islam. Barton wrote his thesis on several leading Islamic thinkers, including Djohan Effendi who himself came to Monash for a Ph.D. Fealy wrote his thesis on the history of Nahdlatul Ulama, Indonesia's largest Muslim organization. Together the two edited a volume on Nahdlatul Ulama (1996). Barton went on to write a biography of Abdurrahman Wahid (2002) and was eventually appointed Herb Feith Professor for the Study of Indonesia at Monash. Fealy whose thesis has been published in Indonesian (2003) took up a position in Political and Social Change, the Department founded by Jamie Mackie. At the ANU, he has collaborated with various colleagues on a variety of publications on Islam: Bubalo (2005) and Hooker (2006).

Melbourne appointed the well-known Indonesian researcher and commentator, Arief Budiman, to a professorship in its Institute of Asian Languages and Societies. In 1990, Timothy Lindsey who had done his doctorate in Indonesian studies took up a position in the Asian Law Centre, where he became Director and was exceptionally influential in promoting the study of both Islamic and Indonesian law as well as law reform. In addition to a major work, *Indonesia: Law and Society* (1st ed., 1999), he has edited a book with his Melbourne colleague, Howard Dick, on corruption in Asia, particularly Indonesia and Vietnam (2002).

Sydney University where Bali had been a focus of study under Worsley produced two distinguished Bali researchers: Adrian Vickers who completed his thesis on a Balinese Malat text in 1986 and Linda Connor who did extensive fieldwork in Bali for her Ph.D. Vickers published a version of his thesis in 2005 after a variety of other publications on Bali (1989, 1996); Connor worked with Patsy and Tim Asch to produce a monograph on the films that they had made together on Balinese trance. After teaching careers elsewhere (Newcastle and Wollongong and involvement in the joint Newcastle-Wollongong

CAPSTANS initiative) both returned to teach at Sydney University. One of the Sydney Department's earlier graduates, Keith Foulcher who had submitted his thesis on Malay literature in 1974 and then taught at both Monash and Flinders Universities, returned to Sydney to head the Department of Indonesian Studies in 1996.

Sydney produced and was associated with other important researchers on Indonesia. Jennifer Lindsay did notable research in Yogyakarta, studying the Javanese performing arts. She wrote a study of Javanese gamelan (Lindsay 1979; 2nd ed. 1992); she published her thesis in Indonesian translation in 1991 and then translated essays by the distinguished editor of *Tempo* magazine, Goenawan Mohamad (Lindsay 1994, 2002). She was also involved in a project supported by the Ford Foundation to microfilm manuscripts of the Kraton Yogyakarta. These microfilms with a preliminary descriptive catalogue were made available in 1987 (Lindsay et al. 1987); a final catalogue was published in Indonesian translation in 1994 (Lindsay et al. 1994). The anthropologist Jennifer Alexander also carried out valuable research in Indonesia. Her initial research was on Javanese rural trade (1987); her husband, Paul Alexander whose original dissertation research was on Sri Lanka, took up an interest in Indonesia and worked with her. He edited the volume, *Creating Indonesian Cultures* (1989). Jennifer Alexander then went on to do further research in Sarawak, particularly among the Lahanan. The historian, Michael Laffan did seminal research on Islam during the colonial period (Laffan 2003); he taught for a period at the ANU, before taking up a fellowship in Leiden and eventually a professorship at Princeton.

The Asia Centre at Flinders University was only established in 2000. Prior to its establishment, Southeast Asian research at the University was directed primarily to Indonesia through a programme begun by Anton Lucas who graduated in history at the ANU in 1980; his study of revolutionary north coast Java appeared as a Southeast Asia monograph in 1991.

At different stages in its development, the Flinders programme included notable scholars such as Colin Brown, Jim Schiller and his wife Barbara Martin Schiller. Now the Asia Centre is headed by Elizabeth Morrell, a graduate of Flinders who has done research on the Toraja of Sulawesi (2005), and includes Michael Barr who has done research on Singapore (2000) and Malaysia, and Anthony Langlois whose focus is on human rights in Southeast Asia (2001).

The universities in Western Australia began to develop their Southeast Asia expertise a generation or more after universities on the east coast but they were soon able to rival these universities with their array of talented research scholars. James Warren who did his Ph.D. at the ANU and

Richard Robison who did his at Sydney were among the first scholars to take up positions at Murdoch University; they were followed later by Krishna Sen and David Hill whose research examined the role of cinema (Sen 1994), the media and the internet (Hill and Sen 2005) in Indonesia. Together with graduates of Murdoch, Kevin Hewison whose research was on capital formation and state politics in Thailand (1989), Carol Warren whose initial research was on Bali (1993) and Garry Rodan whose research on the political economy of authoritarian regimes in Southeast Asia had a focus on Singapore (1989), they became part of Murdoch's Asia Research Centre that was created in 1991 to cover the whole of the Asia region. Ian Chalmers, an ANU graduate whose research is on government-business relations in Indonesia and who teaches at Curtin University of Technology, is also a member of Murdoch's Asia Research Centre. He has edited a book on the politics of economic development with Vedi Hadiz (1997), a graduate of Murdoch, who has now returned to the university as a Future Fellow and will continue Murdoch's tradition of research on political economy.

As research on Southeast Asia continued to develop at the University of Western Australia, scholars were recruited from a wide number of Australian universities: Greg Acciaioli and Lyn Parker, graduates from the ANU, Michael Pinches and David Bourchier who graduated from Monash, Lenore Lyons from Wollongong, Stephen Dobbs from Murdoch and most recently, Krishna Sen who has become Professor and Dean of the Faculty of Arts, Humanities and Social Sciences.

Charles Darwin University in Darwin, formerly the Northern Territory University (NTU), offers itself as "Australia's Gateway to Asia". During the time that it was still the NTU, Paul Webb established a small but notable Centre for Southeast Asian Studies at the University that had its focus primarily on eastern Indonesia, which he had made his special interest (1986). This Centre did not, however, survive various internal reorganizations of the university and subsequent efforts at teaching Indonesian were intermittent. Despite these setbacks, the University still maintains a small group of scholars working on Southeast Asia: Dennis Shoesmith whose research is on the comparative politics of the region, David Mearns whose research has been on both Malaysia and on Maluku, Natasha Stacey whose research is on the maritime populations of eastern Indonesia and Steven Farram whose research is on Timor, both East and West. In recent years, more efforts have been directed to Timor-Leste than to Indonesia.

James Cook University of Northern Queensland has been more successful in maintaining its Centre for South-East Asian Studies. This has been due in large part to the work of B.B. Hering who has also maintained the biannual journal, *Kabar Seberang Sulating Maphilindo* which is a multidisciplinary journal that publishes on Southeast Asia and adjacent areas of the western Pacific. Hering's Ph.D. research at the University of Queensland focused on a key nationalist figure in Indonesia, Mohammed Thamrin (1996). He, too, collaborated with Chris Penders, in this case, in editing the memoires of an Indonesian diplomat, Ganis Harsono (1977). With the close cooperation of Pramoedya Ananta Toer, Hering devoted a special issue of *Kabar Seberang* to a commemorative volume to honour the writer on his 70th birthday (1995).

A successful programme of Indonesian studies was established in 1999 at the Australian Defence Force Academy in Canberra which forms part of the University of New South Wales. The programme, which has been headed by Minako Sakai with the support of Paul Tickell, provides a full major in Indonesian studies and has become one of the larger Indonesian language programmes in Australia.

Elsewhere at other Australian universities, even where there have been no major programmes in Asian or Southeast Asian Studies, there have been notable research scholars who have contributed to the field: Amarjit Kaur at the University of New England, Carl Trocki at Queensland University of Technology, David Reeve at the University of New South Wales, Barbara Leigh at the University of Technology Sydney, Steven Drakeley at the University of Western Sydney, Alberto Gomes at La Trobe University and Pamela Allen at the University of Tasmania. Margaret Kartomi is another scholar who as Professor at Monash University, has charted her own distinct but highly productive research programme in the ethnomusicology of Southeast Asia, in particular Indonesia.

One of the innovations of the early 1990s was the creation of "The Australian Consortium for 'In-Country' Indonesian Studies (ACICIS)" which was established in 1994 to develop and coordinate a programme for students interested in the study of Indonesian at university level in Indonesia. It was especially useful to draw together students from universities across Australia.

ACICIS has developed to include nineteen Australian universities (plus The School of Oriental and African Studies, University of London and Leiden University) which are now partnered with six different universities and institutes in Indonesia. Over a period of more than fifteen years, the programme has channelled hundreds of students to Indonesia for accredited in-country academic training. Currently ACICIS is coordinated by a secretariat based at Murdoch University.

CONTRIBUTIONS TO SOUTHEAST ASIAN STUDIES
FROM BEYOND THE ACADEMY

Any survey of the development of Southeast Asian studies in Australia cannot ignore the considerable contributions to scholarship by independent researchers who, for the most part, did their work outside the confines of universities. Such contributions would include Bruce Grant's *Indonesia* (1964), Peter Polomka's *Indonesia since Sukarno* (1971), Hamish McDonald's *Suharto's Indonesia* (1980), David Jenkins's *Suharto and His Generals* (1984) and Max Lane's *Unfinished Nation: Indonesia before and after Suharto* (2008). Among this group would also be Graeme Dobell who has consistently reported on Southeast Asia for the Australian Broadcasting Corporation (2000) and Patrick Walters who has done the same in *The Australian*. Those who pursued diplomatic and government careers would include Jeff Forrester and Ken Ward (1974). Also included within this group would be both Max Lane and Harry Aveling whose translations from the Indonesian, particularly of Pramoedya Ananta Toer's work and whose critical commentary have been notable. Milton Osborne needs also to be added to this group. Osborne, whose work includes *Southeast Asia: An Introductory History* (1979*a*), was a member of the wave of Australians to return from Cornell with their Ph.D.s. His thesis was submitted in 1978. Although he has spent time in academia, like the others in this group, he has spent more time in a variety of other occupations but he has published prolifically. Harry Aveling is another scholar who is difficult to categorize. He has held numerous visiting and adjunct positions in Australia, the United States and Southeast Asia. As a wandering scholar, he has been enormously productive in his translations and commentaries on Indonesian literature.

Academic research on Southeast Asia has also been supported through cooperation with various museums in Australia. In the 1980s, the Australian National Gallery under its Director, James Mollison, established a four member committee consisting of Anthony Forge, James J. Fox, Robyn and John Maxwell to advise on the creation of a collection of Southeast Asian textiles. This collection has now grown to be the largest and probably the most distinguished collection of its kind in the world and has opened the way to the study of trade patterns and cultural influences throughout the region. Robyn Maxwell, who for many years held positions at the ANU and the National Gallery, has published two major volumes (1990, 2003) on the collection.

In 1980, Don Hein at the Art Gallery of South Australia formed the Thai Ceramics Dating Project, which became the Thai Ceramics Archaeological

Project when the Gallery began cooperating with the University of Adelaide. In 1984, the two institutions formed the Research Centre for Southeast Asian Ceramics. Initially the Centre investigated fifty or more kilns in central Thailand, collecting and cataloguing thousands of ceramic finds (Hein and Sangkhanukit 1984); eventually the Centre extended its research elsewhere in Thailand and into Laos (Hein et al. 1989).

At about this same time, in 1979–80, the Western Australian Maritime Museum began the development of maritime archaeology in Southeast Asia, forming a joint Thai-Australia team to excavate the Ko Kradat ship wreck in the Gulf of Thailand. The Museum went on to investigate other shipwrecks near Pattaya and Bangkok in the 1980s and since that time has continued research on pre-colonial ships and ship-building in the Indian Ocean and South China Sea, including the Philippine coast (Green and Harper 1983; Green 1990; Clark et al. 1993).

THE DEVELOPMENT OF THE STUDY OF "OTHER" COUNTRIES IN SOUTHEAST ASIA

It is instructive to contrast the concerted efforts that went into establishing Indonesian studies in Australia with the way in which studies on other countries in Southeast Asia — such as Thailand, Vietnam, the Philippines, Cambodia and Myanmar developed. From the beginning, it was deemed essential that Indonesian/Malay language teaching form the basis for further study. In the case of Thailand, research in various disciplines preceded the beginnings of proper language teaching. In the case of Vietnam, there was a lag in the development of language training compared to other research efforts and in the case of the Philippines, despite some short-term efforts, no language programme ever became established. For Myanmar, only an occasional summer course in Burmese has ever been offered.

At the ANU, for example, early on, Silcock in economics provided some research coverage of Thailand. The anthropologist, G. Wijeyewardene turned his interests to Thai from an early interest in Ceylon; the political scientist, Ron May and the geographer, Ted Chapman conducted research in Thailand before the Thai language began to be officially taught. Similarly the anthropologist/historian, Baas Terwiel, whose doctoral fieldwork for a European university involved spending a year in a Thai monastery, began teaching in the Faculties as did the economist, Peter Warr, before the initiation of Thai language study. Peter Jackson did his ANU Ph.D. dissertation on Buddhist philosophy and only afterwards began his study of Thai with Tony Diller. Nicholas Tapp, whose primary interests were on the ethnic minorities of upland Thai region, replaced Wijeyewardene on his retirement to continue the long-running Thai-Yunnan Project. The same could be said for Sydney University where there was no language programme for Thai. Geddes and others at Sydney were able to shift interests to Thailand despite a lack of Thai language training in Sydney and the Cornell-trained historian, Craig Reynolds successfully taught on Thailand at Sydney for many years before moving to the ANU. Only in 1989 was the National Thai Studies Association of Australia established to provide a national forum to promote the development of Thai language and Thai studies teaching in Australia.

At the ANU, the combination of interests provided through the work of Diller, Warr, Reynolds, Jackson and, later, by one of Wijeyewardene's students, Andrew Walker produced a varied but substantial programme of Thai studies.

Much the same can be seen in the development of Vietnam studies: David Marr was doing fundamental research on Vietnam decades before the establishment of Vietnamese at the ANU. Similarly, although Tagalog was never established as a regular language programme, a number of scholars managed to pursue research on the Philippines. At the ANU, this group included at one time Ron May, Peter Warr, Hal Hill, Rey Ileto and later Ben Kerkvliet who was appointed as Professor of Political and Social Change to replace Jamie Mackie. The tradition has continued with the appointment of Paul Hutchcroft after the retirement of Ben Kerkvliet. Hutchcroft who did his Ph.D. at Yale University has published extensively on Philippine politics, most notably on the politics of banking (1998). The Research School also supported a number of research fellows, such as Brian Fegan, who did his research on the Philippines.

Martin Stuart-Fox at the University of Queensland stands out, among Southeast Asian scholars in Australia, in his remarkable commitment to the study of Laos, on which he has published over a dozen books and monographs from the early 1980s to the present (1982, 2010).

CONCLUSION

Robert Cribb has written of "circles of esteem" that define and enhance relationships among groups of scholars (2005*b*). Members of these clusters respect each others' research and often regard themselves as engaging in a similar effort or as Cribb describes it, "working a related part of the same story, manufacturing pieces, perhaps, for the same jigsaw puzzle" (2005*b*, p. 292). Certainly clusters of this sort, often initiated by a particular teacher, are recognizable in the generations of scholars in Australia. Early on in the development of Southeast Asian Studies, Anthony Johns' students were one such group — or perhaps two groups, those interested in philology and those interested in Islam; Heinz Arndt's group of economists formed another clear cluster. There were common features among the many graduates of Monash but they were also a diverse group with separate interests. Peter Worsley at Sydney stimulated a number of students to do research on Bali as did James Fox at the ANU for the ethnography of eastern Indonesia, though a majority of his Indonesian students did research on Java and particularly on Islam in Java. (Seven of these studies have been published by the ANU E Press in a series entitled *Islam in Southeast Asia*.)

Clearly, too, the group of political economists — Hewison, Rodan, Hadiz, all inspired by Robison, along with a number of other similarly oriented colleagues — can be recognized as an important circle of esteem. However, possibly the largest of these circles of esteem is that group of women scholars who have contributed publications to the *Women in Asia* series, created by the Asian Studies Association of Australia. Their work on Southeast Asia comprises over a dozen publications including books by Linda Bennett (2005), Michele Ford and Lyn Parker (2008), Sharyn Graham (2010), Anne-Marie Hilsdon (1995), Elizabeth Martyn (2005), Nina Nurmila (2009), Kathryn Robinson (2009*b*), Kate O'Shaughnessy (2009), Maila Stivens (1996), Norma Sullivan (1994) and Andrea Whittaker (2000, 2004). Were one to add to this, the work of Susan Blackburn (2004), one of the editors of the series, this would represent a formidable circle of esteem within Southeast Asian Studies.

Yet despite the existence of these clusters that extend research throughout Southeast Asia, Australia has never committed itself to the study of Southeast Asia as an "area studies programme". Australia is, however, committed to the study of Asia but it does this by promoting Asian content in recognized disciplines: Anthropology, Demography, Political Science, History, Economics, Law, and the Arts. This is now an accepted aspect of Australian university teaching. A consequence of this is that language programmes for the major languages of Asia have found a place at some Australian universities but less prominent Southeast Asian languages have failed to gain an appropriate position.

In 1964, Anthony Johns entitled his inaugural lecture as Foundation Professor of Indonesian studies at the ANU as "An Open Horizon". He asserted that "orientalism in the old sense" was dead but "phoenix-like, out of its ashes, something new is arising [that] takes on new life as it informs and sustains work in the fields of literature, linguistics, history, anthropology, and the other social sciences" (1964, p. 17). What was envisaged was a new wave of studies whose pursuit was to be based on a deep knowledge and a thorough command of a major language of the region whose understanding informed investigations, within particular disciplines, of the full context of particular research. At the core of these specialized studies was a commitment to specific locations — an area, a country, a region — and a discipline that was grounded in a focused understanding. To a considerable extent, this vision has indeed characterized a succession of several generations of scholarship in Australia since the mid-1960s and has allowed Southeast Asian Studies to flourish.

These studies have indeed opened a wide horizon. By their very success, however, they have lost much of their original specialist appeal. In Australia, general knowledge of Southeast Asia has become more widespread as specific knowledge of particular countries within the region has developed. In the 1960s, Australians visiting Southeast Asia were a small minority; today the number of Australians visiting countries like Indonesia, Malaysia, Singapore or Thailand number in the hundreds of thousands with tens of thousands of Australian residents in the region. Knowledge gained in-country has added immeasurably to the understanding of the region as have the decades of education and training offered by Australian academics to students both in Australia and from Southeast Asia. Knowledge and expertise on Southeast Asia has thus diffused widely.

In attracting new students, Southeast Asian Studies have also had to compete with other studies, particularly the study of China, in the past two decades. This is particularly evident in the language programmes that originally served as the foundation for specialized study. In Australian universities, at present, language programmes for the study of Chinese, Japanese and Korean now attract more students than do any of the programmes for the study of languages of Southeast Asia. All of these programmes show a steady decline.

A report, dated the 10th of April 2008, commissioned by the Asian Studies Association of Australia and prepared by Anne McLaren on Asian language enrolments in Australian Institutes of Higher Education in 2006–07 noted strong growth (31 per cent) in enrolments in Chinese, reasonable growth (15 per cent) in Korean, and limited growth (1.5 per cent) in Japanese but a marked decline (24 per cent) in Indonesian and precipitous declines (77–79 per cent) for the already minor teaching programmes in Thai and Vietnamese.

In 2006–07, there were 32 institutions in Australia teaching Japanese, 26 institutions teaching Chinese and 20 institutions teaching Indonesian but between 2001 and 2004, four universities had dropped their Indonesian programmes. Three universities had dropped their Thai language programmes, leaving only two universities teaching Thai and only two universities teaching Vietnamese. Only the ANU continued to teach all three languages — Indonesian, Thai and Vietnamese.

At the same time, many — possibly a majority — of those whose work is cited in this chapter have retired, are about to retire, or are preparing to retire within the decade. There will be considerable generational change in Southeast Asian Studies in Australia in the near future. A new generation — many of whom have not been cited in this historical review — is taking over, but they do so in the context of a globalized world of internet communication and rapid dissemination of knowledge.

Notes

[1] I should properly indicate my own personal background (and bias) in offering this genealogy. I have spent the whole of my career in Australia at the Australian National University (ANU) and as a consequence, am better acquainted with its development than that of any other university in the country. Since its foundation, the ANU has had a prominent role in the study of the Asia-Pacific region. It is difficult therefore not to give emphasis to its importance.

This chapter has gone through various drafts which I have shown to colleagues to ask for comment and advice. I would like to thank Robert Cribb, Jamie Mackie and Campbell Macknight in particular for their considerable assistance. I have also relied on a number of articles written by others on the development of Southeast Asian Studies in Australia. All of these articles are included in the bibliography.

[2] It is important to appreciate the political climate of this period and the significance given by key government figures to orienting Australia to the Asia-Pacific region. A book that provides a good background to these efforts is Daniel Oakman's *Facing Asia: A History of the Colombo Plan* (2004).

[3] *Bahasa Indonesia, Langkah Baru, A New Approach* was first produced in 1975 within the Faculty of Asian Studies in collaboration with Robyn Stokes. It was subsequently published and republished by the Australian National University Press as it went through successive revisions and expansions.

[4] This was first published as a government report but was later reprinted in the London University Anthropology series.

[5] Like Freeman, the report on his fieldwork among the Land Dayak was published as a government document.

⁶   In the early 1970s, Geddes' association with the Tribal Research Center (TRC) in Chiang Mai in Thailand was the subject of criticism and controversy because of accusations that the TRC was involved in counter-insurgency. See Robinson (2004).

⁷   The establishment of extensive cooperative links between individual scholars in Australia and former students and colleagues in Southeast Asia was perhaps the most important achievement of Australia's decades-long efforts in establishing its Asian studies programmes. Although some of these connections are indicated in this chapter, to discuss these connections in any adequate way would require another long paper.

References

Asia in Australian Education. Asian Studies Association of Australia, 1980.

Bulletin of Indonesian Economic Studies. Basingstoke: Taylor & Francis, 1965–the present.

Kabar Seberang Sulating Maphilindo. Centre for Southeast Asian Studies, James Cook University of North Queensland, Townville.

Abeyasekere, Susan. *One Hand Clapping: Indonesian Nationalists and the Dutch, 1939–1942.* Clayton: Centre for Southeast Asian Studies, 1976.

———. *Jakarta: A History.* Singapore: Oxford University Press, 1987.

Acciaioli, Gregory, C. van Dijk, and Roger Tol, eds. *Authority and Enterprise among the Peoples of South Sulawesi.* Leiden, KITLV Press, 2000.

Alexander, Jennifer. *Trade, Traders and Trading in Rural Java.* Singapore: Oxford University Press, 1987.

Alexander, Paul, ed. *Creating Indonesian Cultures.* Sydney: Oceania Publication, 1989.

Allen, Pamela. *Membaca dan Membaca lagi: Reinterpretasi Fiksi Indonesia, 1980–1995.* Magelang: Indonesia Tera, 2004.

Andaya, Barbara W. *Perak, the Abode of Grace: A Study of an Eighteenth-Century Malay State.* Kuala Lumpur: Oxford University Press, 1979.

Andaya, Leonard Y. *The Kingdom of Johor, 1641–1728.* Kuala Lumpur: Oxford University Press, 1975.

Arndt, Heinz W. *The Indonesian Economy. Collected Papers of H.W. Arndt.* Singapore: Chopmen, 1984.

———. *A Course through Life: Memoirs of an Australian Economist.* Canberra: The Australian National University, 1985.

Arndt, Heinz W. and R. M. Sundrum. *Transmigration: Land Settlement or Regional Development?* Canberra: Research School of Pacific Studies, 1977.

Aspinall, Edward. *Opposing Suharto: Compromise, Resistance and Regime Change in Indonesia.* Stanford, CA: Stanford University Press, 2005.

Aveling, Harry, ed. and trans. *Contemporary Indonesian Poetry: Poems in Bahasa Indonesia and English.* St. Lucia: University of Queensland Press, 1975.

————, ed. *The Development of Indonesian Society: From the Coming of Islam to the Present Day.* St. Lucia: University of Queensland Press, 1979.

————. "Literature and the Australian Study of Indonesia". *RIMA* 43, no. 1 (2009): 35–50.

Barlow, Colin. *The Natural Rubber Industry: Its Development, Technology, and Economy in Malaysia.* Kuala Lumpur: Oxford University Press, 1978.

Barr, Michael D. *Lee Kuan Yew: The Beliefs behind the Man.* Washington, D.C.: Georgetown University Press, 2000.

Barton, Greg. *Abdurrahman Wahid: Muslim Democrat, Indonesian President: A View from Inside.* Honolulu: University of Hawai'i Press, 2002.

Bastin, John. "Indonesian and Malayan Studies in Australia". Korte Mededelingen, *Bijdragen tot de Taal-, Land- en Volkenkunde* 113, no. 2 (1957): 201–4.

Behrend, Timothy E. *Surat Jatiswara: Stuktur dan Perubahan di dalam Puisi Jawa, 1600–1930.* Jakarta: INIS, 1995.

Behrend, Timothy E. and Alan H. Feinstein. *Naskah-Naskah Museum Sonobudoyo Yogyakarta.* [Microform 1–162 reels] n.d.

Bellwood, Peter S. *Prehistory of the Indo-Malaysian Archipelago.* Sydney: Academic Press, 1985; Revised edition, Honolulu: University of Hawai'i, 1997.

————. *First Farmers: The Origins of Agricultural Societies.* Malden: Blackwell Pubs, 2005.

Bellwood, Peter, James J. Fox, and Darrell Tryon, eds. *The Austronesians: Historical & Comparative Perspectives.* Canberra: ANU, 1995. ANU E Press Publication, available at <http://epress.anu.edu.au>.

Bennett, Linda Rae. *Women, Islam and Modernity: Single Women, Sexuality and Reproductive Health in Contemporary Indonesia.* London: Routledge, 2005.

Blackburn, Susan. *Women and the State in Modern Indonesia.* Cambridge: Cambridge University Press, 2004.

Booth, Anne. *Agricultural Development in Indonesia.* Sydney: Allen & Unwin, 1988.

Booth, Anne and Peter McCawley, eds. *The Indonesian Economy during the Suharto Era.* Kuala Lumpur: Oxford University Press, 1981.

Bourchier, David and Vedi Hadiz, eds. *Indonesian Politics and Society: A Reader.* New York: Routledge, 2003.

Brakel, Lode F. *The Hikayat Muhammad Hanafiyyah: A Medieval Muslim-Malay Romance.* The Hague: Nijhoff, 1975.

Bulbeck, David. "A Historical Perspective on the Australian Contribution to the Practice of Archaeology in Southeast Asia". *Australian Archaeology* 50 (2000): 45–53.

Bulbeck, David and Ian Caldwell. *Land of Iron: The Historical Archaeology of Luwu and the Cenrana Valley.* Hull: Centre for South-East Asian Studies, University of Hull, 2000.

Butcher, John. *The British in Malaya, 1880–1941: The Social History of a European Community in Colonial South-East Asia.* Kuala Lumpur: Oxford University Press, 1979.

———. *The Closing of the Frontier: A History of the Marine Fisheries of Southeast Asia, 1850–2000.* Singapore: Institute of Southeast Asian Studies, 2004.

Chalmers, Ian and Vedi R. Hadiz, eds. *The Politics of Economic Development in Indonesia: Contending Perspectives.* London: Routledge, 1997.

Chandler, David. *The Land and People of Cambodia.* Philadelphia: Lippincott, 1972.

———. *A History of Cambodia.* Boulder: Westview Press, 1983.

———. *Facing the Cambodian Past: Selected Essays 1971–1994.* Sydney: Allen & Unwin, 1996.

Clark, P., J. Green, T. Vosmer, and R. Santiago. "The Butuan Two Boat Known as a Balangay in the National Museum, Manila, Philippines". *The International Journal of Nautical Archaeology* 22 (1993): 143–59.

Connor, Linda, Patsy Asch, and Tim Asch. *Jero Tapakan, Balinese Healer: An Ethnographic Film Monograph.* Cambridge: Cambridge University Press, 1986.

Cooke, Nola and Li Ta Na, eds. *Water Frontier: Commerce and the Chinese in the Lower Mekong Region, 1750–1880.* Lanham: Rowman & Littlefield. 2004.

Coppel, Charles. *Indonesian Chinese in Crisis.* Sydney: George Allen & Unwin, 1983.

———. *Studying Ethnic Chinese in Indonesia.* Singapore: Singapore Society of Asian Studies, 2002.

———, ed. *Violent Conflicts in Indonesia: Analysis, Representation and Resolution.* London: Routledge, 2006.

Creese, Helen M. *Parthayana: The Journeying of Partha: An Eighteen Century Balinese Kakawin.* Leiden: KITLV Press, 1998.

———. *Women of the Kakawin World: Marriage and Sexuality in the Indic Courts of Java and Bali.* London: M.E. Sharpe, 2004.

Cribb, Robert. *Gangsters and Revolutionaries: The Jakarta People's Militia and the Indonesian Revolution, 1945–1949.* Honolulu: University of Hawaii Press, 1991.

———. *Digital Atlas of Indonesian History.* Copenhagen: NIAS, 2005a.

———. "Circles of Esteem, Standard Works, and Euphoric Couplets: Dynamics of Academic Work in Indonesian Studies". *Critical Asian Studies* 37, no. 2 (2005b): 289–304.

Cribb, Robert and Colin Brown. *Modern Indonesia: A History since 1945.* London: Longman, 1995.

Crouch, Harold A. *The Army and Politics in Indonesia.* Ithaca: Cornell University Press, 1978.

———. *Malaysia's 1982 General Election.* Singapore: Institute of Southeast Asian Studies, 1982.

————. *Government and Society in Malaysia*. Ithaca: Cornell University Press, 1996.

Dick, Howard W. *The Indonesian Interisland Shipping Industry*. Singapore: Institute of Southeast Asian Studies, 1986.

————. *Surabaya, City of Work: A Socioeconomic History, 1900–2000*. Athens: Ohio University Press, 2002.

Dobbin, Christine. *Islamic Revivalism in a Changing Peasant Economy: Central Sumatra 1784–1847*. London: Curzon Press, 1983.

Dobell, Graeme. *Australia Finds Home: The Choices and Chances of an Asia Pacific Journey*. Sydney: ABC Books, 2000.

Drakard, Jane. *A Kingdom of Words: Language and Power in Sumatra*. New York: Oxford University Press, 1999.

Elson, Robert E. *Javanese Peasants and the Colonial Sugar Industry*. Singapore: University of Oxford Press, 1984.

————. *Village Java under the Cultivation System*. Sydney: Allen & Unwin, 1994.

————. *Suharto: A Political Biography*. Cambridge: Cambridge University Press, 2001.

————. *The Idea of Indonesia: A History*. Cambridge: Cambridge University Press, 2008.

Fealy, Greg. *Ijtihad Politik Ulama: Sejarah Nahdlatul Ulama, 1952–1967*. Yogkakarta: LKiS, 2003.

Fealy, Greg and Greg Barton, eds. *Nahdlatul Ulama, Traditional Islam and Modernity in Indonesia*. Clayton: Monash Asia Institute, Monash University, 1998.

Fealy, Greg and Anthony Bubalo. "Joining the Caravan? The Middle East, Islamism and Indonesia". Lowy Institute Paper no. 5, Lowy Institute for International Policy. Sydney: Longueville Press, 2005.

Fealy, Greg and Virginia Hooker, eds. *Voices of Islam in Southeast Asia: A Contemporary Source Book*. Singapore: Institute of Southeast Asian Studies, 2006.

Feith, Herbert. *Indonesian Politics 1949–1957: The Decline of the Representative Government*. Ithaca: Cornell University, 1961.

————. *The Decline of Constitutional Democracy in Indonesia*. Ithaca: Cornell University Press, 1962.

Fisk, E.K. *Studies in the Rural Economy of South-East Asia*. Singapore: Eastern Universities Press, 1964.

Fisk, E.K. and H. Osman-Rani, eds. *The Political Economy of Malaysia*. Oxford: Oxford University Press, 1982.

Fisk, E.K and Thomas H. Silcock, eds. *The Political Economy of Independent Malaya: A Case Study in Development*. Canberra: ANU Press, 1963.

Ford, Michele and Lyn Parker, eds. *Women and Work in Indonesia*. London: Routledge, 2008.

Foulcher, Keith. *Pujangga Baru: Literature and Nationalism in Indonesia, 1933–1942*. Bedford Park, S.A.: Flinders University Asian Studies Monographs, 1980.

————. *Social Commitment in Literature and the Arts: The Indonesian "Institute of Peoples' Culture" 1950–1965.* Clayton: Centre of Southeast Asian Studies, Monash University, 1986.

Fox, James J. *Harvest of the Palm: Ecological Change in Eastern Indonesia.* Cambridge, MA: Harvard University Press, 1977.

————, ed. *The Flow of Life: Essays on Eastern Indonesia.* Cambridge, MA: Harvard University Press, 1980.

————, ed. *To Speak in Pairs: Essays on the Ritual Languages of Eastern Indonesia.* Cambridge: Cambridge University Press, 1988.

————, ed. *Inside Austronesian Houses: Perspectives on Domestic Designs for Living.* Canberra: Anthropology, Research School of Pacific Studies, 1993. ANU E Press Publication, available at <http://epress.anu.edu.au/>.

Fox, James J., R.G. Garnaut, P.T. McCawley, and J.A.C. Mackie, eds. *Indonesia: Australian Perspectives.* Canberra: Research School of Pacific Studies, The Australian National University, 1980. [includes *Indonesia: The Making of a Culture*; *Indonesia: Dualism, Growth and Poverty*; and, *Indonesia: The Making of a Nation*]

Fox, James, Timothy Asch, and Patsy Asch. *The Water of Words: A Cultural Ecology of an Eastern Indonesian Island.* 16 mm colour film. Watertown, MA: Documentary Educational Resources, 1983.

Freeman, Derek. *Iban Agriculture.* London: Her Majesty's Stationery Office, 1955.

————. *Report on the Iban.* London: University of London, The Athlone Press, 1970.

Garnaut, Ross. "Real Australians in Economics". In *The Coombs: A House of Memories,* edited by Brij V. Lal and Allison Ley. Canberra: Research School of Pacific and Asian Studies, The Australian National University, 2006.

Garnaut, Ross and Chris Manning. *Irian Jaya: The Transformation of a Melanesian Economy.* Canberra: Australian National University Press, 1974.

Geddes, W.H. *Land Dayaks of Sarawak.* London: H.M. Stationery for the Colonial Office, 1954.

————. *Nine Dayak Nights.* Melbourne: Oxford University Press, 1957.

————. *Migrants of the Mountains: The Cultural Ecology of the Blue Miao (Hmong Njua) of Thailand.* Oxford: Clarendon Press. 1976.

Glover, Ian. *Archaeology in Eastern Timor, 1966–67.* Terra Australis No. 11. Canberra: Department of Prehistory, Research School of Pacific Studies, The Australian National University, 1986.

Gomes, Alberto. *Modernity and Malaysia: Settling the Menraq Forest Nomads.* New York: Routledge, 2007.

Graham, Penelope. *Iban Shamanism.* Canberra: Research School of Pacific and Asian Studies, 1987.

Graham, Sharyn Leanne. *Gender Diversity in Indonesia: Sexuality, Islam and Queer Selves.* London: Routledge, 2010.

Grant, Bruce. *Indonesia*. London: Melbourne University Press, 1964.

Green, J. "Maritime Archaeology in Southeast and East Asia". *Antiquity* 64 (1990): 347–63.

Green, J. and R. Harper. *The Excavation of the Pattaya Wreck Site and Survey of Three Other Sites in Thailand*. Fremantle: Australian Institute for Marine Archaeology, 1983.

Guinness, Patrick. *Harmony and Hierarchy in a Javanese Kampung*. Singapore: Oxford University Press, 1986.

Hadiz, Vedi. *Workers and the State in New Order Indonesia*. London: Routledge, 1997.

Harvey, Barbara. *Permesta: Half a Rebellion*. Ithaca: Cornell Modern Indonesia Project, 1977.

Hatley, Barbara. *Javanese Performances on an Indonesian Stage: Contesting Culture, Embracing Change*. Singapore: NUS Press, 2008.

Hein, Don and P. Sangkhanukit. *Report on the Excavation of the Ban Tao Hai Kilns Phitsanulok, Thailand*. Research Centre for Southeast Asian Ceramics Papers No. 1. Adelaide: University of Adelaide and Art Gallery of South Australia, 1984.

Hein, Don, Mike Barbetti, and Thongsa Sayavongkhamdy. *An Excavation at the Sisattanak Kiln Site, Vientiane Lao P.D.R.* Sydney: NWG Macintosh Centre for Quarternary Dating, University of Sydney, 1989.

Helliwell, Christine. *"Never Stand Alone": A Study of Borneo Sociality*. Phillip, ME: Borneo Research Council, Inc., 2001.

Hering, B.B., ed. *Pramoedya Ananta Toer 70 Tahun: Essays to Honour Pramoedya Ananta Toer's 70th Year*. Yayasan Kabar Seberang, 1995.

———. *Mohammed Hoesni Thamrin and His Quest for Indonesian Nationhood, 1917–1941*. Yayasan Kabar Seberang, 1996.

Hewison, Kevin. *Bankers and Bureaucrats: Capital and the Role of the State in Thailand*. New Haven, CT: Yale University Southeast Asian Studies, 1989.

Hill, David and Krishna Sen. *The Internet in Indonesia's New Democracy*. London: Routledge, 2005.

Hill, Hal, ed. *Unity and Diversity: Regional Economic Development in Indonesia since 1970*. Singapore: Oxford University Press, 1989.

———. *Indonesia's Industrial Transformation*. Singapore: Institute of Southeast Asian Studies, 1997.

Hilsdon, Anne-Marie. *Madonnas and Martyrs: Militarism and Violence in the Philippines*. St Leonard's, N.S.W.: Allen & Unwin, 1995.

Hooker, Virginia Matheson. *Writing a New Society: Social Change through the Novel in Malay*. Sydney: Allen & Unwin, 2000.

Hooker, Virginia and Barbara Watson Andaya. *The Precious Gift/Raja Ali Haji ibn Ahmad: An Annotated Translation*. Kuala Lumpur: Oxford University Press, 1982.

Howell, Julia Day and Martin van Bruinessen, eds. *Sufism and the "Modern" in Islam.* London: St Martins Press, 2007.

Hugo, Graeme. *Migration, Urbanization and Development in Indonesia.* New York: United Nations, 1981.

Hugo, Graeme, et al., eds. *The Demographic Development in Indonesian Development.* Singapore: Oxford University Press, 1987.

Hull, Terrence H. and Valerie E.J. Hull. *The Relation of Economic Class and Fertility: An Analysis of Some Indonesian Data.* Yogyakarta: Population Institute, Gadjah Mada University, 1976.

Hull, Terence H., Gavin Jones, and Endang Sulistyaningsih. *Prostitution in Indonesia: Its History and Evolution.* Jakarta: Pustaka Sinar Harapan, 1999.

Hutchcroft, Paul D. *Booty Capitalism: The Politics of Banking in the Philippines.* Ithaca: Cornell University Press, 1998.

Ileto, Reynaldo C. *Pasyon and Revolution: Popular Movements in the Philippines, 1840–1910.* Quezon City: Ateneo de Manila University Press, 1979.

Ingleson, John. *Road to Exile: The Indonesian Nationalist Movement, 1927–1934.* Singapore: Asian Studies Association of Australia, 1979.

———. *In Search of Justice: Workers and Unions in Colonial Java, 1906–1926.* Singapore: Asian Studies Association of Australia, 1986.

Jackson, Peter A. *Buddhadasa: A Buddhist Thinker for the Modern World.* Bangkok: Siam Society, 1988.

———. *Dear Uncle Go: Male Homosexuality in Thailand.* Bangkok: Bua Luang Books, 1995.

Jenkins, David. *Suharto and His Generals.* Ithaca: Cornell Modern Indonesia Project, Cornell University, 1984.

Johns, Anthony H. "Indonesian Studies in Australia: An Open Horizon". Inaugural Lecture, The Australian National University, Canberra, 30 June 1964.

———. *The Gift Addressed to the Spirit of the Prophet.* Canberra: Centre of Oriental Studies, The Australian National University, 1965.

———. *Cultural Options and the Role of Tradition: A Collection of Essays on Modern Indonesian and Malaysian Literature.* Canberra: Faculty of Asian Studies with the ANU Press, 1979.

Johns, Anthony H. and Nelly Lahoud, eds. *Islam in World Politics.* London: Routledge, 2005.

Johns, Yohanni. *Bahasa Indonesia: Langkah Baru, A New Approach.* Canberra: The Australian National University Press, 1976–90.

Jones, Gavin. *The Demographic Transition in Asia.* Singapore: Maruzen Asia, 1984.

———. *Marriage and Divorce in Islamic Southeast Asia.* Melbourne: Oxford University Press, 1994

Kahn, Joel S. *Constituting the Minangkabau: Peasants, Culture and Modernity in Colonial Indonesia.* Providence: Berg, 1993.

———. *Other Malays: Nationalism and Cosmopolitanism in the Modern Malay World.* Singapore: Singapore University Press, 2006.

Kartomi, Margaret J. *Matjapat Songs in Central and West Java*. Canberra: The Australian National University Press, 1973.

Kaur, Amarjit. *Economic Change in East Malaysia: Sabah and Sarawak since 1850*. New York: St. Martin's Press, 1998.

Kessler, Clive S. *Islam and Politics in a Malay State, Kelantan, 1838–1969*. Ithaca: Cornell University Press, 1978.

Kingsbury, Damien. *The Politics of Indonesia*. Melbourne: Oxford University Press, 1st ed. 1998; 2nd ed. 2002.

———. *South-East Asia: A Political Profile*. Melbourne: Oxford University Press, 1st ed. 2001; 2nd ed. 2005.

Kumar, Ann. *Surapati, Man and Legend: A Study of Three Babad Traditions*. Leiden: E.J. Brill, 1976.

———. *The Diary of Javanese Muslim: Religion, Politics and the Pesantren, 1883–1886*. Canberra: Faculty of Asian Studies, The Australian National University, 1985.

Laffan, Michael Francis. *Islamic Nationhood and Colonial Indonesia: The Umma below the Winds*. London: Routledge, 2003.

Lane, Max. *Unfinished Nation: Indonesia before and after Suharto*. London: Verso, 2008.

Langlois, Anthony J. *The Politics of Justice and Human Rights: Southeast Asia and Universalist Theory*. Cambridge: Cambridge University Press, 2001.

Legge, John. *Central Authority and Regional Autonomy in Indonesia: A Study in Local Administration, 1950–1960*. Ithaca: Cornell University, 1961.

———. *Indonesia*. Englewood: Prentice Hall, 1964.

———. *Sukarno: A Political Biography*. London: Allen Lane, 1972.

Legge, John D. and Herbert Feith. "J.A.C. Mackie: Biographical Notes; I. Kandy to Monash". In *Observing Change in Asia: Essays in Honour of J.A.C. Mackie*, edited by Ron J. May and William J. O'Malley. Bathurst: Crawford House Press, 1989.

Leigh, Barbara. *The Changing Face of Malaysian Crafts: Identity, Industry, and Ingenuity*. Kuala Lumpur: Oxford University Press, 2000.

Leigh, Michael. *The Rising Moon: Political Change in Sarawak*. Sydney: Sydney University Press, 1974.

Lewis, E. Douglas. *People of the Source: The Social and Ceremonial Order of Tana Wai Brama on Flores*. Dordrecht: Foris Publications, 1988.

Li, Ta Na. *Nguyễn Cochinchina: Southern Vietnam in the Seventeenth and Eighteenth Centuries*. Ithaca: Cornell University, Southeast Asia Program, 1998.

Lindsay, Jennifer. *Javanese Gamelan*. Kuala Lumpur: Oxford University Press, 1979. 2nd ed., 1992.

———. *Klasik, Kitsch, Kontemporer: Sebuah Studi tentang Seni Petunjukan Jawa*. Yogyakarta: Gadjah Mada University Press, 1991.

———, trans. *Sidelines: Writings from Tempo, Indonesia's Banned Magazine/Goenawan Mohamad*. South Yarra, Vic: Hyland House, 1994.

————, trans. *Conversations with Difference: Essays from Tempo Magazine/Goenawan Mohamad*. Jakarta: PT Tempo Inti Media, 2002.

Lindsay, Jennifer, R.M. Soetanto, Alan H. Feinstein. *A Preliminary Descriptive Catalogue of the Manuscripts of the Kraton Yogyakarta*. Yogyakarta: Proyek Mikrofilm Kraton Yogyakarta, 1987.

Lindsay, Jennifer, R.M. Soetanto, Alan H. Feinstein, and T.E. Behrend. *Kraton Yogyakarta*. Jakarta: Yayasan Obor Indonesia, 1994.

Lindsey, Timothy, ed. *Indonesia: Law and Society*. Annandale: Federation Press, 1st ed. 1999; 2nd ed. 2008.

Lindsey, Timothy and Howard Dick, eds. *Corruption in Asia: Rethinking the Governance Paradigm*. Annandale: Federation Press, 2002.

Loofs-Wissowa, H.H.E. *Vietnamese-English Archaeological Glossary with English Index*. Canberra: Faculty of Asian Studies, The Australian National University, 1970.

Lyon, Margo L. *The Basis of Conflict in Rural Java*. Berkeley: Center for South and Southeast Asian Studies, The University of California, 1970.

Lucas, Anton. *One Soul, One Struggle: Region and Revolution in Indonesia*. Sydney: Allen & Unwin, 1991.

MacIntryre, Andrew J. *Business and Politics in Indonesia*. Allen & Unwin, 1991.

Mackie, J.A.C. *Konfrontasi: The Indonesia-Malaysia dispute, 1963–1966*. Kuala Lumpur: Oxford University Press, 1974.

————. *The Chinese in Indonesia: Five Essays*. Melbourne: Australian Institute of International Affairs. 1976

Macknight, C.C. *The Voyage to Marege': Maccassan Trepangers in Northern Australia*. Melbourne: University of Melbourne Press, 1976.

Manning, Chris. *Indonesian Labour in Transition: An East Asian Success Story?* Cambridge: Cambridge University Press, 1998.

Marr, David G. *Vietnamese Anticolonialism, 1885–1925*. Berkeley: University of California Press, 1971.

————. *Vietnamese Tradition on Trial, 1920–1945*. Berkeley: University of California Press, 1981.

————. *Vietnam 1945: The Quest for Power*. Berkeley: University of California Press, 1995.

Martyn, Elizabeth. *Women's Movement in Postcolonial Indonesia: Gender and Nation in a New Democracy*. London: RoutledgeCurzon, 2005.

Maxwell, John. *Soe Hok-Gie: Pergulatan Intelektual Muda Melawan Tirani*. Jakarta: P.T. Pusaka Grafiti, 2001.

Maxwell, John, Ron J. May, and William J. O'Malley. "J.A.C. Mackie: Biographical Notes; II The Canberra Years". In *Observing Change in Asia: Essays in Honour of J.A.C. Mackie*, edited by Ron J. May and William J. O'Malley. Bathurst: Crawford House Press, 1989.

Maxwell, Robyn. *Textiles of Southeast Asia: Tradition, Trade and Transformation*. Australian National Gallery. Melbourne: Oxford University Press, 1990.

————. *Sari to Sarong: Five Hundred Years of Indian and Indonesian Textile Exchange*. Canberra: The National Gallery of Australia, 2003.

McDonald, Hamish. *Suharto's Indonesia*. Blackburn,Vic.: Fontana/Collins, 1980.

McDonald, Peter, ed. *Pedoman Analisa Data Sensus Indonesia, 1971–1980*. Canberra: Australian Vice-Chancellors' Committee, Universities International Development Program, 1983.

McLaren, Anne. "Report on Asian Languages Enrolments in Australian Higher Education, 2006–07". For the Asian Studies Association of Australia, 10 April 2008, available at <http://www.griffith.edu.au/__data/assets/pdf_file/0008/145790/ASAA-Language-Stats-Summative-Report-April-2008.pdf>.

McWilliam, Andrew. *Paths of Origin, Gates of Life: A Study of Place and Precedence in Southwest Timor*. Leiden: KITLV Press, 2003.

Mearns, David and Christopher J. Healey, eds. *Remaking Maluku: Social Transformation in Eastern Indonesia*. Darwin: Northern Territory University, 1996.

Miharja, Achdiat. *Atheis*. Melaka: A. Bandong, 1966.

Miles, Douglas. *Cutlass and Crescent Moon: A Case Study of Social and Political Change in Outer Indonesia*. Sydney: Centre for Asian Studies, 1976.

Milner, Anthony C. *Kerajaan: Malay Political Culture on the Eve of Colonial Rule*. Tucson: Arizona Press, 1982.

Morrell, Elizabeth. *Securing a Place: Small-Scale Artisans in Modern Indonesia*. Ithaca: Southeast Asia Program Publications, Cornell University, 2005.

Mortimer, Rex. *The Indonesian Communist Party and Land Reform: 1959–1965*. Monash Papers on Southeast Asia, no. 1. Clayton: Monash University, 1972.

————, ed. *Showcase State: the Illusion of Indonesia's Accelerated Modernisation*. Sydney: Angus & Robertson, 1973.

————. *Indonesian Communism under Sukarno, Ideology and Politics, 1959–1965*. Ithaca: Cornell University Press, 1974.

Morwood, M. J. and Penny Oosterzee. *The Discovery of the Hobbit: The Scientific Breakthrough that Changed the Face of Human History*. Milsons Point: Random House, 2007.

Nurmila, Nina. *Women, Islam and Everyday Life: Renegotiating Polygamy in Indonesia*. London: Routledge, 2009.

Oakman, Daniel. *Facing Asia: A History of the Colombo Plan*. Canberra: Pandanus Books, ANU, 2004.

O'Connor, Sue and Peter Veth, eds. *East of Wallace's Line: Studies of the Past and Present Maritime Cultures of the Indo-Pacific Region*. Rotterdam: A.A. Balkema, 2000.

O'Connor, Sue, Matthew Spriggs, and Peter Veth. *The Archaeology of the Aru Islands, Eastern Indonesia*. Canberra: Pandanus Books, The Australian National University, 2005.

Osborne, Milton E. *The French Presence in Cochinchina and Cambodia: Rule and Response, 1859–1905*. Ithaca: Cornell University Press, 1969.

————. *Southeast Asia: An Introductory History*. Sydney: Allen & Unwin, 1979a.

————. *Before Kampuchea: Preludes to Tragedy*. Sydney: Allen & Unwin, 1979*b*.

————. *The Mekong: Turbulent Past, Uncertain Future*. New York: Atlantic Monthly Press, 2000.

O'Shaughnessy, Kate. *Gender, State and Social Power: Divorce in Contemporary Indonesia*. London: Routledge, 2009.

Penders, C.L.M., Ganis Harsono, and B.B. Hering, eds. *Recollections of an Indonesian Diplomat in the Sukarno Era, Ganis Harsono*. St. Lucia: University of Queensland Press, 1977.

Penders, C.L.M. and Ulf Sundhaussen. *Abdul Haris Nasution: A Political Biography*. St. Lucia: University of Queensland Press, 1985.

Penny, David and Masri Singarimbun. *Population and Poverty in Rural Java: Some Economic Arithmetic from Sriharjo*. Ithaca: Cornell International Agriculture Monograph, 1973.

Polomka, Peter. *Indonesia since Sukarno*. Harmondsworth: Penguin Books, 1971.

Proudfoot, Ian. *Early Malay Printed Works*. Kuala Lumpur: University of Malaya, 1993.

————. *Old Muslim Calendars of Southeast Asia*. Leiden: Brill, 2006.

Quinn, George. *The Novel in Javanese: Aspects of Its Social and Literary Character*. Leiden: KITLV Press, 1992.

Reeve, David. *Golkar of Indonesia: An Alternative to the Party System*. Singapore: Oxford University Press, 1985.

Reid, Anthony. *The Contest for North Sumatra: Atjeh, the Netherlands and Britain 1858–1898*. London: Oxford University Press, 1969.

————. *The Blood of the People: Revolution and the End of Traditional Rule in Northern Sumatra*. Kuala Lumpur: Oxford University Press, 1974.

————. *Southeast Asia in the Age of Commerce, 1450–1680*. New Haven: Yale University Press, 1988–93.

————. "Anthony Hearle Johns with 'List of A.H. John's Publications'". In *Islam: Essays on Scripture, Thought & Society: A Festschrift in Honour of Anthony H. Johns*, edited by Peter G. Riddell and Tony Street. Leiden: Brill, 1997.

————. "Indonesian Studies at the Australian National University". *RIMA* 43, no. 1 (2009): 50–74.

Reid, Anthony and Lance Castles, eds. *Pre-Colonial State Systems in Southeast Asia*. Kuala Lumpur: The Malaysian Branch of the Royal Asiatic Society, 1975.

Reuter, Thomas. *Custodians of the Sacred Mountains: Culture and Society in the Highlands of Bali*. Honolulu: University of Hawai'i Press, 2002*a*.

————. *The House of Our Ancestors: Precedence and Dualism in Highland Balinese Society*. Leiden: KITLV Press, 2002*b*.

Reynolds, Craig J. *Thai Radical Discourse: The Real Face of Thai Feudalism Today*. Ithaca: Cornell University Modern Southeast Asia Program, 1987.

Ricklefs, Merle. *A History of Modern Indonesia*. London: Macmillan, various editions, 1981–90.

————. *War, Culture and Economy in Java, 1677–1726*. Sydney: Allen & Unwin, 1993.

————. *The Seen and Unseen Worlds in Java, 1726–1749: History, Literature and Islam in the Court of Pakubuwana II*. Sydney: Allen & Unwin, 1998.

Riddell, Peter. *'Abdul al-Ra'ūf Al-Singilī's Rendering into Malay of the Jalalayn Commentary: Transferring a Tradition*. Berkeley: Centers for South and Southeast Asian Studies, University of California, 1990.

Robinson, Kathryn. *Stepchildren of Progress: The Political Economy of Development in an Indonesian Mining Town*. Albany: State University of New York Press, 1986.

————. "Chandra Jayawardena and the Ethical 'Turn' in Australian Anthropology". *Critique of Anthropology* 24, no. 4 (2004): 379–402.

————. "We the Ethnographers". In *The Coombs: A House of Memories*, edited by Brij V. Lal and Allison Ley. Canberra: Research School of Pacific and Asian Studies, The Australian National University, 2006.

————. "Anthropology of Indonesia in Australia: The Politics of Knowledge". *RIMA* 43, no. 1 (2009*a*): 7–33.

————. *Gender, Islam and Democracy in Indonesia*. London: Routledge, 2009*b*.

Robison, Richard. *Indonesia: The Rise of Capitalism*. London: Allen & Unwin, 1986.

————. *Reorganizing Power in Indonesia: The Politics of Oligarchy in an Age of Markets*. New York: Routledge, 2004.

Robison, Richard and Garry Rodan. *The Political Economy of South-East Asia: An Introduction*. Melbourne: Oxford University Press, 1997.

Robson, Stuart. *Hikajat Andaken Penurat*. The Hague: Nijhoff, 1969.

————. *Patterns of Variation in Colloquial Javanese*. Monash: Centre for Southeast Asian Studies, 1991.

————. *Deśawarnana (Nāgarakrtāgama) by Mpu Prapañca*. Leiden: KITLV Press, 1995.

Rodan, Garry. *The Political Economy of Singapore's Industrialization: National State and International Capital*. Basingstoke: Macmillan, 1989.

Rodan, Garry, Richard Robson, and Kevin Hewison, eds. *The Political Economy of South-East Asia: Markets, Power and Contestation*. 3rd ed. Melbourne: Oxford University Press, 2006.

Roff, William. *The Origins of Malay Nationalism*. New Haven: Yale University Press, 1967.

Sakai, Minako, Glenn Banks, and J.H. Walker, eds. *The Politics of the Periphery in Indonesia: Social and Geographical Perspectives*. Singapore: NUS Press, 2009.

Santoso, Soewito. *Sutasoma: A Study in Javanese Wajrajana*. New Delhi: International Academy of Indian Culture, 1975.

Sarumpaet, J.P and Jamie Mackie. *Introduction to Bahasa Indonesia*. Melbourne: Melbourne University Press. 1967.

Sen, Krishna. *Indonesian Cinema: Framing the New Order*. London: Zed Books, 1994.

Schiller, James. *Developing Jepara: State and Society in New Order Indonesia*. Clayton: Monash Asia Institute, 1996.

Silcock, Thomas H. *Thailand: Social and Economic Studies in Development*. Canberra: Australian National University Press. 1967

———. *Economic Development of Thai Agriculture*. Ithaca: Cornell University Press, 1970.

Singarimbun, Masri. *Kinship, Descent and Alliance among the Karo Batak*. Berkeley: University of California Press, 1975.

Skinner, Cyril. *Sja'ir Perang Mengkasar: The Rhymed Chronicle of the Macassar War by Entji'Amin*. The Hague: M. Nijhoff, 1963.

———. *The Civil War in Kelantan in 1839*. Singapore: Monographs of the Malaysian Branch, Royal Asiatic Society, 1966.

Soebardi, S. *The Book of Cabolèk*. The Hague: Martinus Nijhoff, 1975.

Soepomo. *Arjunawijaya: A Kakawin of Mpu Tantalar*. The Hague: Martinus Nijhoff, 1977.

Stacey, Natasha. *Boats to Burn: Bajo Fishing Activity in the Australian Fishing Zone*. Canberra: ANU E Press, 2007.

Stivens, Maila. *Matriliny and Modernity: Sexual Politics and Social Change in Rural Malaysia*. St Leonard's, N.S.W.: Allen & Unwin, 1996.

Stuart-Fox, Martin, ed. *Contemporary Laos: Studies in the Politics and Society of the Lao People's Democratic Republic*. St Lucia: University of Queensland Press. 1982.

———. *The A to Z of Laos*. Lanham: Scarecrow Press, 2010.

Sullivan, Norma. *Masters and Managers: A Study of Gender Relations in Urban Java*. St Leonard's, N.S.W.: Allen & Unwin, 1994.

Sundhaussen, Ulf. *The Road to Power: Indonesian Military Politics 1945–1967*. Oxford: Oxford University Press, 1982.

Sutherland, Heather. *The Making of a Bureaucratic Elite: The Colonial Transformation of the Javanese Priayi*. Singapore: Asian Studies Association of Australia, 1979.

Swift, Michael G. *Malay Peasant Society in Jelebu*. London: Athlone Press. 1965.

Tanter, Richard and Kenneth Young, eds. *The Politics of Middle Class Indonesia*. Clayton: Monash University, Centre of Southeast Asian Studies, 1990.

Tapp, Nicholas. *Sovereignty and Rebellion: The White Hmong of Northern Thailand*. Singapore: Oxford University Press, 1989.

Tarling, Nicholas. *Anglo-Dutch Rivalry in the Malay World, 1780–1824*. Brisbane: University of Queensland Press, 1962.

———. *Piracy and Politics in the Malay World: A Study of British Imperialism in Nineteenth-Century South-east Asia*. Melbourne: F.W. Cheshire, 1963.

———. *A Concise History of Southeast Asia*. New York: Praeger, 1966. Originally published as *Southeast Asia, Past and Present*.

———, ed. *The Cambridge History of Southeast Asia*. Cambridge: Cambridge University Press, 1992.

Taylor, Jean G. *The Social World of Batavia: European and Eurasian in Dutch Asia*. Madison: University of Wisconsin Press, 1983; 2nd ed. 2009.

Taylor, Philip. *Fragments of the Present: Searching for Modernity in Vietnam's South.* St Leonards, N.S.W.: Allen & Unwin, 2001.

———. *Goddess on the Rise: Pilgrimage and Popular Religion in Vietnam.* Honolulu: University of Hawai'i Press, 2004.

———. *Cham Muslims of the Mekong Delta: Place and Mobility in the Cosmopolitan Periphery.* Singapore: NUS Press, 2007.

Trocki, Carl. *Opium and Empire: Chinese Society in Colonial Singapore, 1800–1910.* Ithaca: Cornell University Press, 1990.

———. *Singapore: Wealth, Power, and the Culture of Control.* New York: Routledge, 2006.

Vickers, Adrian. *Bali: A Paradise Created.* Berkeley: Periplus, 1989.

———. *Being Modern in Bali: Image and Change.* New Haven: Yale University Southeast Asia Studies, 1996.

———. *Journeys of Desire: A Study of the Balinese Malat.* Leiden: KITLV Press, 2005.

Walker, Andrew. *The Legend of the Golden Boat: Regulation, Trade and Traders in the Borderlands of Laos, Thailand, China and Burma.* Richmond: Curzon, 1999.

Ward, Ken. *The 1971 Election in Indonesia: An East Java Case Study.* Clayton: Centre for Southeast Asian Studies, Monash University, 1974.

Warr, Peter G., ed. *The Thai Economy in Transition.* Cambridge: Cambridge University Press, 1993.

Warren, Carol. *Adat and Dinas: Balinese Communities in the Indonesian State.* Kuala Lumpur: Oxford University Press, 1993.

Warren, James F. *The Sulu Zone: 1768–1898: The Dynamics of External Trade, Slavery and Ethnicity in the Transformation of a Southeast Asian Maritime State.* Singapore: Singapore University Press, 1981.

Webb, R.A.F. Paul. *Palms and the Cross: Socio-economic Development in Nusatenggara, 1930–1975.* Townsville: James Cook University of Northern Queensland, Centre for South East Asian Studies, 1986.

Whittaker, Andrea. *Intimate Knowledge: Women and their Health in North-east Thailand.* St Leonard's, N.S.W.: Allen & Unwin, 2000.

———. *Abortion, Sin and the State in Thailand.* London: RoutledgeCurzon, 2004.

Wijeyewardene, Gehan. *Place and Emotion in Northern Thai Ritual Behaviour.* Bangkok: Pandora, 1986.

Worsley, Peter. *Babad Buleng: A Balinese Dynastic Genealogy.* The Hague: Nijhoff, 1972.

11

SOUTHEAST ASIAN STUDIES IN THE U.S.
Construction of Traditions of an Autonomous History, Its Limitations, and Future Tasks

Song Seung-Won

INTRODUCTION

This chapter examines the current state and future objectives of Southeast Asian Studies in the U.S. The U.S. is a leading country in terms of Southeast Asian Studies within the general field of area studies. Area studies began to assume importance in the U.S. in the context of American concerns about the expansion of Third Word Communism during the Cold War period. Amidst this tense international atmosphere, Southeast Asianists in the U.S. set themselves against what they considered to be the limitations of European colonial studies preoccupied with the Western presence and role in Southeast Asia and the reconstruction of the history and cultural traditions of those whom they governed. They instead focused more on the circumstances of modern Southeast Asia, post-colonial nation-building and the prospects and problems for socio-economic and political development. Some scholars also argued for the need to consider and understand the region from local perspectives and to construct an autonomous history of the region, which focused on local genius, views, interests and initiatives. American scholars in the field of Southeast Asian Studies have been dominant in the post-war development of theoretical and conceptual frameworks in order to understand processes of change and modernization in the region and to capture the main characteristics of what it is to be Southeast Asian. The outcomes of these theories have often served as templates for students in the field.

Yet, the "Western-oriented perspectives" that American scholars intrinsically sustain have functioned as epistemological barriers in investigating the "peculiarities of Southeast Asianness" in further depth. Thus, while recognizing the major contributions of American scholars in establishing Southeast Asian Studies as a positive and meaningful field, it should be pointed out that some of the scholarly themes and discourses on Southeast Asia must now to some extent be questioned.

To examine the general state of Southeast Asian Studies in the U.S., this chapter commences with a consideration of its development and the intellectual climate in which it flourished over the last several decades; and, second, it addresses popular scholarly themes in the past and currently emerging themes. Through an examination of these two sets of themes, this chapter will examine how American scholars have perceived Southeast Asia; what scholarly contributions they have made; and what have been pointed out as the limitations of their scholarly work. I recognize that the American contribution has been very substantial indeed, and it is impossible to capture the scale and diversity of this scholarship in a brief chapter. I have therefore selected a few themes which, I think, capture some of the significant issues which emerged and shaped American research in the first few decades after the Second World War.

A BRIEF HISTORY OF THE DEVELOPMENT OF SOUTHEAST ASIAN STUDIES IN THE U.S.

The scholarly roots of Southeast Asian Studies in the U.S. stem from European colonial studies. While European scholarship comprised the first serious efforts to understand the region's history and culture, these studies were primarily characterized by the Orientalist preoccupation with the "great" traditions of the region (Buddhism Hinduism, Islam) which implicitly emphasized Southeast Asian history as a hybrid, or more precisely, and at best, as a region which had come under Indian and/or Chinese influences. Except for the Philippines, a former colonial territory of the U.S. from the turn of the twentieth century, Southeast Asian Studies in the U.S. prior to the Pacific War were seen to be peripheral and part of the histories of Europe.

The end of the colonial period and the advent of the new nation-states in Southeast Asia created the opportunity to develop fresh perspectives on how the region's past might better be studied. Hence, in contrast to pre-Second World War research, post-war work signified a break in the historiography as well as in the history of the region, which was no longer viewed as a "cultural appendage" of India or China or as simply a branch of Indology or Sinology or indeed as the dependent territories of outside powers.

Initially, the study of Southeast Asia benefitted from the rapidly rising political need to understand the region in the context of Cold War politics. During this period, the U.S. government expended huge efforts to contain the expansion of Communism in the region, which emerged as its critical concern after the establishment of a Communist regime in mainland China, and then the partition of Vietnam and the Korean Peninsula. American and more broadly Western concerns for the region resulted in a veritable boom in area studies.

Owing to enormous government support, the first generation of Southeast Asian Studies specialists was trained, appointed and funded, and this field of study, formerly perceived merely as an undeveloped and marginal enterprise, began to develop to a significant degree, peaking in the 1950s and 1960s. During this period, scholarly Centers for Southeast Asian Studies were established at Cornell,[1] Yale,[2] the University of California-Berkeley,[3] the University of Hawaii,[4] the University of Michigan,[5] Northern Illinois University,[6] Ohio University,[7] and the University of Wisconsin,[8] with broad and long-term support from, among others, the Rockefeller Foundation and the Carnegie Corporation.[9]

The initial attention of these academic Centers was concentrated on the exploration of the current conditions of the area. Language, cultural studies, geography and contemporary history as "a background to current affairs" (Bowen 2003, p. 21) gained popularity, while other fields of social science such as political science and international relations, anthropology, and history emerged as the leading fields of study subsequently. In this mode, the humanities and classical studies have remained less important fields in the U.S. even today.

After two decades of growth, Southeast Asian Studies was in a state of decline by the 1970s, in part due to America's failure to contain the Communists in the former French Indochinese countries and more general disillusionment with the capacities of regional specialists to provide information and advice to policy-makers and to capture accurately the mainsprings of political processes. The academic credibility of area studies in terms of its disciplinary rigour, methodologies and preoccupation with bounded regions was also questioned. This caused the loss of official interest in sustaining the huge funding of area studies, resulting in the general decline of student interest as well.

The 1980s marked a revival in Southeast Asian Studies in the U.S. First, Charles Keyes pointed to the influx of several hundred thousand refugees from the former Indochina countries and their resettlement in the U.S. as a boost for interest in the region (Keyes 1992, p. 12). Not only were the students from this refugee background interested in knowing about their original homelands, but Americans also saw this addition of a multi-ethnic population as the chance to get to know and understand the region through immediate contacts with local people. Second, the growing contacts of Americans with the region through travel and their fascination with the local cultures and peoples resulted in the formation of various cultural centres and academic institutes. Third, the internal developments in Southeast Asia itself accelerated scholarly interest in the region. The major boost in this regard was the growth and development of the ASEAN (Association of Southeast Asian Nations) as a unified regional unit in the 1980s and the considerable economic development which the member countries achieved. Fourth, rapprochement between Indochina and the U.S. helped revive regional studies. It was during this period that many Southeast Asian students went to the U.S. to learn about their countries. The U.S. government provided scholarships for many Southeast Asian students, which related to the political agenda to train pro-American intellectuals from the region. For instance, combined with its strategy of supporting liberal Islam in Southeast Asia, the U.S. government offered many students prominent in liberal Islamic circles (i.e., students at The State Institute of Islamic Studies (IAIN) in Indonesia), a chance to pursue Masters or doctoral degrees in American universities.

Subsequently the 1990s came as a time of crisis for American Southeast Asian Studies. As Anderson and many others pointed out, it was seen as a critical moment in the field, which decided its future direction in a more fundamental manner. The reasons which Anderson has given for this overall decline from the 1970s are "the context-dependent, fragile nature of area studies as a product of American post-war and Cold War involvement and intervention in the developing world; area studies' lack of methodological and theoretical sophistication; and its distance from disciplinary specialization" (Anderson 1978, p. 232). It was in this time period that many scholars in the field began to challenge the previously constructed study patterns and seek alternative themes and research methodologies. Detailed discussions in this regard will be examined later in this chapter, but in short, their concerns were to develop and adopt more appropriate scholarly perspectives in their studies.

Finally, the trend in Southeast Asian Studies in the 2000s can be summarized as studies carried out during a time of serious introspection on the problems raised in the 1990s and a time for a new beginning. The focal point in terms of Southeast Asian Studies was the trend toward globalization and the growing importance of cross-boundary relations and also interests in ethnic and religious groups as more appropriate research units than nation-states. As was often pointed out, with growing ethnic tensions and religious conflicts since the 1990s, Southeast Asia has been identified as a strategic place where Christian-Muslim conflicts, perhaps politically overemphasized by the West, symbolically and physically collided. The Islamic terrorist attack on the World Trade Center on September 11, 2001 provided another motive for the U.S. government to enhance its strategic interests in area studies. Although the increased budget for promoting area studies was targeted to Middle Eastern and South Asian studies, Reid (2003, p. 2) suggested that "it was possible to believe that the curious pendulum of strategically motivated government spending on area studies had begun to swing in a direction that might again encourage Southeast Asian studies as well".

In this globalization mode, the academic themes became diversified. Not only have the topics widened or become more sophisticated to understand small-scale communities, units and locations rather than national frames of reference, the study fields have extended to the humanities. "[M]usicology, popular literature, and the visual and performing arts have perhaps had more revealing things to say on the transformation of Southeast Asia society than has sociology itself" (McVey 1995, p. 5). In sum, the current time is a moment of new departure, seeking fresh approaches to Southeast Asian Studies.

CONSTRUCTION OF AN AUTONOMOUS HISTORY AND ITS LIMITATIONS

A Brief Review of Some Major Works

The autonomous history approach which began to emerge more firmly in the 1960s in which scholars have attempted to interpret historical events and figures in a local context and from a Southeast Asian perspective, stemmed from criticisms of colonial perspectives developed by European scholars. Yet, it was not only to correct the flawed paradigm of the colonial scholars, but also to find a balanced historiography by criticizing the equally flawed paradigm of the so-called "Asia-centric" and nationalist versions of historiography. The agenda of writing an autonomous history became an influential scholarly agenda in Southeast Asian historiography since the famous two papers of the American-based scholars Harry Benda (1962) and John Smail (1961) appeared in the early 1960s.

The search for an autonomous history then became the rallying point for scholars onwards. The subsequent generation, who could also speak local languages and thus interpret indigenous sources, has further enhanced the autonomy of Southeast Asian history writing. Michael Aung-Thwin stated that "autonomous history was seen as an 'opening up', a progressive development, towards a more objective and universal history of Southeast Asia" (Aung-Thwin 2009). Balancing the official national histories of the independent Southeast Asian countries, American historians with deep insight into indigenous patterns of political, economic, cultural and social development produced valuable histories of a different kind.

Just a few of the scholars whose concepts and analyses were influential in Southeast Asian studies in the U.S. include: John F. Embree's (1950) "loosely structured social system in Thai society"; William Skinner's (1957) study of Chinese society in Thailand; Clifford Geertz's (1960, 1963, 1980) "agricultural involution and shared poverty", "theatre state", "notions of primordial loyalties", "cultural streams", and "syncretic religion" in Java and Bali; Hildred Geertz's (1961) work on Javanese kinship; David Wyatt's (1969, 1984) study of "Thai politics and autonomous history"; Charles Keyes's work (1977, 1995) on "Thai patron-client relations" and "ethnic relations"; James Scott's (1976) and Michael Adas's (1981) "moral" and "rational" approaches to the understanding of rural protest movements; Michael Aung-Thwin's (1991) "spiral approaches to history" primarily in a Burmese context; Benedict Anderson's (1972, 1990, 2006) "Javanese charisma" and "imagined communities" in Southeast Asia and more widely; Donald Brown's (1976) "principles of social structure of Southeast Asia" developed from his work on the Brunei sultanate; F.K. Lehman's (1963), and A. Thomas Kirsch's (1973) "models of hill tribe social structures" in mainland Southeast Asia; Robbins Burling's (1965) "differentiation between lowland and upland cultures in Southeast Asia"; Lauriston Sharp's and Lucien Hank's (1978) "ethnographies of the social and economic organizations of a Central Thai village and the utility of the notion of 'loose structure' in understanding Thai social forms"; Melford Spiro's (1967, 1971) analysis of the "relationships between Buddhism and folk religion in the Mandalay region of Burma" and "Burmese Buddhism from a psychological perspective"; Barbara Andaya's (1993) "upstream/downstream relationship"; Leonard Andaya's (1993) "centre/periphery conception"; and John Pemberton's (1994) study of "cultural inheritance" in Java. In the discussion below, some characteristics and the limitations of the previously-constructed autonomous history will be explored.

An Autonomous History and Its Limitations

Before entering into thematic reviews of Southeast Asian Studies in the U.S., I think it would be useful to recall what Charles Tilly discussed as a way to understand world history. He suggested that the world can be understood through wide-ranging comparisons of some "big structures" and "large processes" across various regions (Tilly 1984). By and large, what Tilly embraced in these two concepts included nation-states, regional modes of production, capitalist structures, industrialization, proletarianization, urbanization, and bureaucratization, and he set himself the task of finding differences and similarities across cases, according to which indigenous particularities could be generated. While pointing out some previous methods of comparison by Fernand Braudel and William Hardy McNeill, Tilly suggested more effective ways to compare cases across the world and draw some generalizations.

The "big structures" and "large processes" suggested by Tilly, then, bear some similarity to the research themes that were adopted by Southeast Asianists in the U.S. to examine the Southeast Asian region. In order to understand the internal development of and dynamics within Southeast Asia, these scholars paid attention to such phenomena as political centralization processes, the establishment of nation-states, the formation of strong kingship and leadership relations, bureaucratization processes, the development of capitalism, the influx of foreign workers and settlers and their dispersion, and territorial expansion.

However, to trace these large-scale structures and processes poses certain problems. In short, these structures and processes are essentially outcomes of Western perceptions, based on their ideas of the "modes of development" of non-Western societies. In actual fact, there is more potential for objective and detailed examination of the character and trajectory of Southeast Asian societies from the consideration of what we might term "small structures" and "small processes", which were previously hidden behind large-scale forms and processes. For instance, there were certain time periods in Southeast Asia during which agricultural development or decentralization were more necessary for social development. In addition, while large-scale formation is indeed taking place, what has been missing is the point that, perhaps as the consequence of such centralization, some other parts of nation-states, societies and cultures were actually experiencing "decentralization" (i.e., decapitalization, de-industrialization, or ruralization) at the same time. Indeed, in examining the region from a macro-perspective, these decentralized regions have occupied much larger spaces than the centralized regions in Southeast Asia.

In this regard, what has been reconstructed as the autonomous history of the region is in some sense monolithic. While these scholars were successful in illuminating local societies through the comparison of "big structures" and "large processes", what have been missing or neglected are the serious attempts to find different or indigenous ideas of development and the cases beyond the realms of the large-scale.

In my opinion, at the current time we need to expand our research scope precisely to those "invisible" areas, in order to grasp more holistic pictures of the region. This means that, apart from the realms of the autonomous history of Southeast Asia established in American scholarship so far, we need to ask "What has to be continued?" and "Where does the twenty-first century go for the further development of the writing of Southeast Asian history?" These questions are related to what Manning suggested, that is, "new evidence and previously unknown relationships" about which "we should spend much of our time updating the ideas and interpretations bequeathed to us by our forebears" (2003, p. 36). In order to discuss the previous trends in scholarship, the following section of the chapter provides a brief introduction to some of the previous major works, which are evaluated as important in establishing the autonomous history of Southeast Asia, then a discussion of such big frames on which American scholars have focused and on their limitations, and finally it offers some suggestions for alternative answers to those limitations.

The Problem of the Nation-State as the Research Unit

As mentioned earlier, the study of Southeast Asia as a region in the U.S. started as one of the fields within what has been called "area studies". Until roughly the 1990s, an area studies approach was still seen as useful. In addressing the utility of area studies as the basis of understanding world history, Patrick Manning wrote, "The interdisciplinary and transregional approaches of area studies, in sum, brought great new strengths to the historical analysis of large areas of the world, and were absolutely requisite to developing cosmopolitan approaches to world history" (Manning 2003, p. 36). Indeed, the growth of area studies or area specific histories made it possible for historians to make more truly global connections in history, and expand the scope of world histories.

For instance, the Cornell Southeast Asia programme under the direction of George Kahin in the 1950s began to produce country studies focused on recent and current political developments in the region. Certainly these endeavours "kept the exigencies of nation-building and nationalism very much in mind" (Bowen 2003, p. 23). Anderson and Kahin (1982) referred to the "Kahinian" approach as historical in method and pro-nationalist in orientation. Most scholars in the field such as Clifford Geertz produced their famous writings in this straightforward manner to "catch the sense of new and unfamiliar developments in the 'new nations'" (Bowen 2003, p. 24).

Yet, while the usefulness of area studies is still sustained, some criti-cisms have emerged since the 1990s because the nation-state is an artificial creation which emerged from colonial, international and domestic power struggles in the nineteenth and twentieth centuries. In fact, this emphasis on the nation-state as a research unit stems from an earlier period, from colonial scholarship, which more or less established the current territories of the Southeast Asian nation-states as they are now. It is true that scholars in the post-colonial period utilized European colonial sources, deliberately or not, based on which indigenous peoples gained a certain legitimacy to claim their territory as a "unified entity". As Nordholt remarks, "National historiography also emphasised the authority of the colonial state archives as repositories of 'reliable facts' in contrast to local historiographies that were categorised under folklore" (2004, p. 7). Similarly, Ahmad and Tan have also pointed to a "story of anti-colonial struggles laying the foundations for the formation of the nation-state after the departure of a colonial power" (Ahmad and Tan 2003, p. xiii). In this trend, local histories, which were largely ignored by the Dutch in Indonesia, simply could not be established.

Although anthropologists have never been "entirely satisfied with the term [nation-state] because the political borders of the region frequently cut across ties of ethnicity and religion, and largely reflect colonial spheres of influence" (Hill and Hitchcock 1996, p. 11), most American political scientists and historians depended on colonial source materials, resulting in affixing their spectrum of thinking to the nation-state or colonial geographical boundaries. As a result, marginal and minority history have been deemed irrelevant or unimportant for the construction of state narratives and have therefore been poorly explored (Ahmad and Tan 2003, pp. ix–xxv).

Many uncertainties and complex circumstances have been blurred in the nation-state framework. Several scholars have pointed out what has been missing in the previous research frames. For instance, while challenging the perception of seeing a nation-state as a homogeneous entity, Taylor argued that "northern Vietnam polities resemble China, [but] southern ones, the Theravada neighbors, oversimplifies the matter, because kings drew on different features for different purposes, giving locally distinctive forms to Theravada concepts (such as the *sangha*), and incorporating Confucian terms without creating Confucian-style bureaucracies" (Bowen 2003, p. 40). McVey, emphasizing the need to deconstruct this boundary, also argued that "until the end of the last century at least, Southeast Asian people's lives were dominated by religion, trading, and patronage relationships which had little to do with boundaries and hierarchy as defined by the state" (McVey 1998, p. 59).

How, then, can we overcome the scholarly preoccupation with the nation-state as that entity which determines the boundaries and scope of research, and would this even be possible? In "Redefining World History", Ross Dunn has introduced various scholarly debates on the most appropriate way to go about writing or presenting world history (Dunn 2000, pp. 109–60). In the debates, Hodgson, Barraclough, Wolf, Curtin, and McNeill have argued for the need to approach world history thematically through an examination of interregional exchange, comparative development, and global concerns, patterns, and communication. Manning also writes that, although interregional exchanges and comparative development approaches can provide in-depth views of different parts of the world, it is the history of global patterns and exchanges, and the emphasis on connections, which can provide a history unrestricted by nation-states or limited to certain areas. Certainly, Curtin's focus on "comparative and interregional themes" or McNeill's on "communication nets" are practical frameworks for looking at the larger changes affecting most of the globe (Dunn 2000, pp. 111–12).

Similar debates were held among Southeast Asianists in the U.S. as well. While stating that "what we intend to study is not Southeast Asia as a geopolitical space but Southeast Asians as the study subjects", McVey, for instance, argued that "their histories, cultures, and environments may intertwine and come apart over time; depending on what aspect we study, a space far smaller or far wider than regional or national boundaries may be relevant, but what matters are patterns of human conditions, perceptions, and experience" (McVey 1998, p. 53). Bowen also suggested that, "in a less boundary-obsessed way", Southeast Asia may be viewed "as a geographical and cultural openness, toward all the seas, distributing throughout the archipelago and the mainland a panoply of cultural forms, including quite particular *stupa* constructions, images of Siva, Vishnu and Buddha, Perso-Islamic ideas of governance, and modernist Islamic critiques of ritual" (Bowen 2003, p. 2).

What they suggested is the need to study history "at the interstices" (Winichakul 2003); "histories from below" (Yeoh 2003); or boundless history, histories of the flows, networks, or diasporas, rather than "the territories controlled by modern states" (Kratoska 2003). More challengingly, McVey suggested putting aside the nation-state as the research focus and moving to the examination of "virtual states", "whose power is based on control of technology, knowledge, and investment rather than territory" (McVey 1998, p. 59) as an alternative framework. She argued that:

> In Southeast Asia we have been brought to a new awareness of trans-national business and labor networks, ethnic diasporas, the influence of global corporations, and the creation of multinational entities such as ASEAN and "growth triangles".
>
> (McVey 1998, p. 59)

In this regard, many scholars in the field of Southeast Asian Studies suggested focusing on some emerging networks beyond the boundaries of the nation-state, and Lombard, for example, has proposed studying Chinese, Muslim, or Christian networks (Lombard 1995, p. 11), which express trans-boundary relations. On this basis Lombard has criticized studies of Islam in Southeast Asia carried out in the U.S.:

> [Scholars] have a tendency of confining themselves only to the countries where Islam is predominant today. One tends to forget quite easily that in Phnom Penh, King Chan (1942–1959) became a Muslim.... Even in Ayuthia, during the seventeenth century there was a big Muslim community, with in particular some Persians and Makassars.... A study of mystical brotherhoods, or *Tarekat*, could provide a better comprehension of these networks.
>
> (Lombard 1995, p. 15).

Besides, an effort to deconstruct ethnic divisions within a state and to define ethnicity as not a fixed entity but as one which is frequently changing and fluid has been made consistently by anthropologists. For instance, Leach (1954), Eggan (1941, 1967), and Kirsch (1973) have "defined a 'type' society or culture which embraces several communities" in the upland regions of mainland Southeast and which crosses national borders. In a similar vein, the emphasis on the nation-state has resulted in a lack of concern for the people of the margins. Nevertheless, one significant study in this regard is Anna Tsing's work on the Dayaks of the Meratus Mountains of south-eastern Kalimantan and the "cultural and political construction of marginality" (1993). King and Wilder summarized the significance of her work in the following terms: "It is not only about how the Meratus Dayaks are marginalised by the powerful forces of the state and the actions and perceptions of neighbouring lowland majorities such as the Banjar Malays but also how the people themselves respond to their marginal identity through protest, challenge, negotiation, and the reinterpretation and explanation of their status in stories, songs and narratives of people and events" (King and Wilder 2003, p. 217).

Yet in concluding this section I have to draw attention to Winichakul's observations on the difficulties of writing alternative histories. His fundamental criticism is of the question of whether the optimistic views of scholars of Southeast Asian history about the possibility of providing counter-narratives to national histories would be a straightforward enterprise. The intrinsic problem of going beyond the autonomous history approach is related to the question of how to avoid the politicization of history. In historiography, whether Southeast Asian or American, there are all kinds of sensitivities expressed by those in power about what can and cannot be said and investigated. For example, people are not allowed to argue that nationalists in Indonesia had European wives; that the founder of Ayutthaya in Thailand was Chinese; or that the history of ethnic minorities in Burma should be written in their local contexts. Unless present governments and their attitudes toward minorities change dramatically, post- or anti-nationalistic history will never be allowed, but this change is unlikely to happen in the near future.

In this political atmosphere, it is not only local Southeast Asian scholars but also American scholars, who have to pay frequent visits to their research areas, and who will be at the greatest disadvantage in the writing of marginal history because of government pressures. In addition, national unity in Southeast Asian states is still in process. History can be utilized for political purposes; for example, Sukarno used history to mobilize his people for the struggle for independence. Marginal history might stimulate marginal groups to initiate struggle for independence or autonomy. Of course, these histories represent national history for marginal people. Yet, it should be noted that the nation-state is still the most important framework within which marginal history should be constructed because history constitutes the concept of the nation. Do historians have a right to deny nation-building for their own interests? The view mentioned above does not mean that marginal history is not important, but that, perhaps, Southeast Asia is not ready for it. The perspectives generated by the narratives of marginal history in Southeast Asian historiography appear to be difficult to promote in today's Southeast Asian political realities, so it may be necessary to leave the task of writing counter-histories to the next generation.

The Issue of Development

In addition to the nation-state as the framework to understand Southeast Asia, frequently applied themes, which resonate with Tilly's "large processes", would need to engage with the issues of "development" and "underdevelopment", which are concerns "running through the disciplines of economics, geography, sociology, anthropology, and politics" (Halib and Huxley 1996, p. 7). These disciplines are concerned with examining the processes of capital accumulation, urbanization, social differentiation and poverty, rural development, and the development of civil society and political institutions in the region. As indicated here, the term *development* has a broad meaning, encompassing issues of political complexity, economic progress, and the structural completeness of the bureaucratic system, legal codes, and other social norms. Except for the subject of civil society, the themes addressed above were widely applied in constructing the histories of states since the classical period, or even earlier, in Southeast Asia.

Based upon the analysis of these large processes, scholars in the field of Southeast Asian Studies have made significant progress in reconstructing an autonomous history in the region. Their works are prominent in the sense that many of them attempted to move away from what Sutherland has described as the Western-perception of development. Sutherland criticized this concept:

> Western historiography assumes a chronological linear unfolding of progress, and early Western commentators on Asian societies tended to see them as stagnant variants of earlier phases in European history, as feudal despotisms and passive, unchanging village communities. In assessing levels of "development" or "progress" such observers looked for

recognizable specialist institutions in politics and the economy; finding
few such institutions, they saw only "backwardness"....

To most Europeans, trying to make sense of unknown societies and
cultures, the alien could only be made comprehensible by identifying it
with the familiar. It was then all too easy to proceed as if the unknown
was simply a mutant or primitive version of the known. Ideas, social
relationships and values which were literally beyond their ken, were
often simply not seen at all. In their observations of both political and
economic systems, they saw decline, corruption and confusion because
they failed to recognize the patterns which structured society.

(Sutherland 1995, p. 133)

What matters here is that the limits of such "autonomous work" on the
subject of classical economy suppose rather imprudently that such Western
modes of development as the expansion of capitalism and the market,
urbanization, and political centralization, would, without doubt, mean
"development" in Southeast Asia in the classical period.

Contrary to what Sutherland argued, American Southeast Asianists
were eager to find local development models, which were sufficiently
distinct from Western ones. For instance, Geertz argued convincingly that
political centralization in the Western sense does not always translate as
an identifiable strength of a Southeast Asian state. While criticizing the
previously common Western-derived notion of "Oriental Despotism" which
was used to analyse early Southeast Asian political systems, Geertz argued
that *negara* (an example of a Southeast Asian political system which was
based on his analysis of the Balinese state) politics could possibly be called
"fragmentary", but not "weak". Even though political actions in *negaras*
did not necessarily have the sanction of political power, Geertz argues,
their ability to act came from their symbolic power based on the Indic
concept of kingship. Without significant economic or military power, in
the "theatre state", the kings and princes of Bali "were the impresarios,
the priests, the directors, and the peasants the supporting cast, stage crew,
and audience" (Geertz 1980, p. 13) and the kings conveyed their power
to their subjects with "court ceremonies", which identified royalty with
the Hindu gods (ibid.).

In addition, in terms of political development, the well-known work
of Anderson and others was related to this theme. Based on his analysis
of the shadow theatre tradition in Java, Anderson distinguished Weberian
charisma and the Southeast Asian concept of charisma, and argued that in
Java a ruler's charisma came from mystical power. By this, Anderson argued

that Javanese ideas of power were "perfectly rational once its assumptions about the nature of power were properly understood" (Sears 2007, pp. 54–55).

Yet, on the subject of economic history, it seems that scholars in the field held a linear concept of development derived from the Western experience. Their scholarly interests were focused on finding some development processes through larger processes such as urbanization, or capitalization.

For instance, Wheatley (1983), a British scholar, though much of his career was spent in the U.S., explored the question of what gave rise to urbanism in Southeast Asia in the early classical period. While he rejects the concept of Indianization through military expansion as the determining factor for urbanization, Wheatley sought it in Hinduism. He maintains that the rulers of chiefdoms could attain sacred authority through religious practices, which consequently brought the birth of a more centralized political system. Similarly in *Circles of Kings*, Hagesteijn (1989), a Dutch scholar, follows the Wheatley line of evolutionary approach. She begins her book with a criticism of Geertz's interpretation that prehistoric polities were localized and fragile. Hagesteijn argues that prehistoric Southeast Asian regions already had developed a significant level of political centralization. As the necessary force for urbanization, Hagesteijn cites the importance of a rice-agricultural mode of production, long-distance trade, and Indic influence. However, she emphasizes that there were already indigenous initiatives in attaining the status of a chiefdom before the introduction of any other external influence. Unlike Wheatley who does not see trade as a necessary condition for the formation of cities, Hagesteijn argues that interregional maritime trade played an important role in political centralization in some areas. With the influx of foreign products, hierarchies and armies could be formed. Political leaders would then have opportunities to be cultural brokers through trade.

Wheatley's and Hagesteijn's fundamental ideas of "development" were challenged by Michael Aung-Thwin. His criticism is reflected in his differing opinions on the mode of development of the Burmese kingdoms in the classical period from those of Victor Lieberman. Lieberman (1984, 1987) constructed the Burmese history of dynasties based on the Western development model, which emphasizes trade and maritime kingdoms over agriculture or agrarian states, according to which a conclusion was derived that the transfer of the capital of the state from lower Burma to the central dry zone meant retrogression in terms of state development. However, according to Aung-Thwin, the transfer should be understood as the Burmese choice of a better option and the different mode of development for their society.

Aung-Thwin (1991), in his article, "Spirals in Early Southeast Asian and Burmese History", introduced the term the cyclical or the *spiral approach* to history. This directed our attention to the fact that Burmese history has shown several dynastic cycles, which have shared patterns similar to previous dynastic cycles. But the cycles were not the same because each dynasty had different structural transformations. Aung-Thwin stated that there were "usually agrarian-demographic cycles of the inland states and the trade-commercial cycles of the coastal polities" (Aung-Thwin 1991). He argued that the Pagan dynasty, which kept its trade-commercial cycle, experienced social disorder through rebellions and Ava's failure to occupy the coastal areas was a lesson to the Burmese that "to forsake the stability of the heartland for the commercial revenues of the coasts invited disaster, not only physically but psychologically" (ibid., p. 589). The attempt to occupy Lower Burma was attained by the Toungoo dynasty, but it did not last long because of the rulers' anxiety to retreat to the interior of Burma, where most dynastic traditions were alive. It was their bitter lesson that without controlling its heartland, interior Burma could not survive long. Based upon this lesson, the Second Ava Dynasty was relocated inland. In this way, Aung-Thwin suggested a different idea of development in Burmese dynasties.

This pressure to find an indigenous model of development does not come only under the purview of studies of earlier periods, but also should be applied to contemporary studies. For instance, while citing the example of the concept of Islamic modernism, McVey argued that one particular interest to reconceptualize Southeast Asian Studies is the attempt to "re-formulate ideas of modernity, society, and the state" (McVey 1995, p. 8).

On the other hand, whether conducted in Western or Southeast Asian development models, what we have to be careful of is the research that is undertaken in the areas and among the populations which were alienated from these processes. For instance, Tilly argued that industrialization in towns is accompanied by de-industrialization of the countryside. Thus, he argues, "stage theories impose a standardisation on experience which disappears on close observation of real life". This is reminiscent of Tilly's argument that social change does not follow any standard pattern of stages (Tilly 1984).

This discussion of the research focused on the Western development model connects with the issue of subaltern studies. As seen in the scholarly work on "development", we can still see where those scholars' interests were concentrated: on the powerful strata of society, such as kings and the wealthy, traders, and urban people, rather than on the commoners or those in the marginal areas.

The demand to explore the commoners' lives was met by some American scholars. In American scholarship history from below or research on rural resistance movements have appeared since the 1970s. Michael Adas's (1981) idea of "avoidance protest" and James Scott's (1985) notions of "moral economy" and "hidden transcripts" can be included in this category. Nevertheless, studies of a subaltern class or the social history of commoners are still rather sparse, and we are thus waiting for much more research on these subjects in the future.

Beyond the Realm of an Autonomous History? Issues of Ideology, Religion, and Gender

While American scholars generally emphasized local specificity in recon-structing historiography in Southeast Asia, there was still a tendency to apply prevalent perceptions to ideology, religion, or gender issues without more elaborated efforts to refine or rectify them in Southeast Asian contexts. First, as Bowen argued, "most scholars took for granted the idea that states should, and perhaps were, moving toward secular, liberal constitutional orders" (Bowen 2003, p. 24).

This preoccupation with liberalism resulted in the study of Southeast Asian politics lagging behind other fields of study. McCargo and Taylor have argued that:

> [T]he dominant intellectual traditions of American political science have not been comparative in scope; nor have they given a central place to the understanding of societies that do not accord with liberal democratic paradigms (see Crick 1959; Ricci 1984). American political science had its origins in a moral enterprise, an attempt to foster an understanding of American institutions and practices in such a way as would contribute to the continuation and development of democracy.... When this discipline turns its attention to the non-Western world, it often does so with a particular purpose, looking to identify evidence of incipient liberalism and to nurture democratic thoughts. However, these terms of reference are not always appropriate to the central analytical issues at the heart of most polities — European, American, African, or Asian. American-trained political scientists have often been inclined to approach Southeast Asian politics with questions such as "How democratic is this polity?" rather than the more fundamental

question for political analysis of "How is power distributed in this society?" The concepts of liberalism, rationalism and individualism that lie at the heart of American political thought militate against an accurate understanding of Southeast Asian political realities.

(McCargo and Taylor 1996, p. 211)

Based on such presumptions, many scholars tend to analyse political or economic discourses within the boundaries of Western ideologies of liberalism, socialism, Communism, or a mix of these, while failing to see some indigenous values reflected in the discourses. This does not, however, mean that American scholars are ideologically biased as they were in the 1950s or 1960s, when anxieties about Communism and the preference for local Nationalisms provided the foundational direction for most Southeast Asian Studies.

For instance, some scholars began to emphasize the different natures of what had previously been considered merely Communist-influenced movements. Benda and McVey also saw in the Banten revolt against the Dutch in 1926 that these revolts were not part of a nationalist uprising, but were instead a localized expression of anti-Dutch sentiment in which Communist ideology played a small part (McGregor 2003, p. 106). These views departed from Indonesian historiography, which analysed these events not in terms of Communist-led anti-colonial movements but rather as national revolts in which other forces also participated. On the other hand, Anderson (1970–71) "rehabilitated" Tan Malaka's (who was evaluated as the "true socialist" in Indonesia) place in the history of the nation. Anderson's portrayal of the man and his interpretation of the "July 3rd Affair" are in marked contrast to the classic account in Kahin's *Nationalism and Revolution in Indonesia* (1952), wherein Tan Malaka and his colleagues are depicted as masterminding the kidnapping of the Prime Minister Sjahrir. In Anderson's view, Tan Malaka was still under arrest at the time and his colleagues were only informed of the "coup" after it happened. Anderson sees this as the first betrayal in the new republic, in which the republican leaders, though they "were well aware of Tan Malaka's innocence", needed a scapegoat so "Tan Malaka, always an outsider, was expendable" (Anderson 1972, p. 404). Anderson's interpretation departed from how Indonesian national historiography deals with these Communist or socialist actors.

Despite efforts to free themselves from the reins of ideological matters, however, certainly a relatively unquestioned "belief" that societies are evolving into more liberal political modes still exists. While liberalism holds the universal values that are advocated by a majority of people, this belief generated a tendency to think that political systems which differed from liberal ones must be authoritarian in one way or another.

The study of religion can be included in this context of applying Western values without elaboration. For instance, in the case of Indonesia, Islam has often been analysed as a political ideology, together with such other beliefs as nationalism and Communism. Yet, the major preferences of the American scholars were liberalist rather than orthodox Islam; apparently the latter has been described as a malicious or dangerous social ideology. It is the common view which American scholars or students carry into their research on the so-called Neo-Modernist Muslims, who are liberalist Muslims.

In addition, many American universities invite young liberalist Muslim scholars to be educated there, and many from IAIN (The State Institute of Islamic Studies) in Indonesia have been given scholarships. This has emerged from the U.S. strategy developed from the 1970s to train liberalist Muslims, and Nurcholish Madjid or Amien Rais were actually educated in the U.S. While it is true that liberal Islam is a strong pillar of the Islamic forces in Indonesia, the description of orthodox Islam as reactionary or immoral brings up the question of whether it provides an objective observation.

A similar kind of consideration should be given to gender studies in Southeast Asia. As Sears pointed out, it was only after the 1990s that theories of gender and feminism came into sight within Southeast Asian Studies (Sears 2007, p. 38). Accordingly, critical feminist works on Southeast Asia have not been produced in abundance (ibid., p. 54). A few scholars who have addressed these issues include Aihwa Ong and Peletz (1995), Anna Tsing (1993), Suzanne Brenner (1998), and Barbara Watson Andaya (2000).

Southeast Asian gender studies began to develop as a whole due to the application of Western concepts and theories. The gender studies scholars evaluated new gender roles and identities in Southeast Asia, comparing them with those roles and identities that are labelled traditional in Western discourse (housewife and breadwinner) and the contemporary egalitarian gender patterns in the West (wage-earning woman, caring fathers). Indeed, within this Western framework of gender studies, major themes that were discussed included those which were on the agenda of women's movements, such as solutions to social problems. The topics dealt with included the exclusion of women from the public sphere, female unemployment, protective legislation, the reproductive rights of women, and the risky involvement of women in small businesses.

Based on these concerns, feminists criticized the New Order government. They argued that the regime, through the endowment of functions
to every part of society, attempted to institutionalize the female status as
obedient housewives and mother figures. To the feminists, this meant
that the military regime suppressed female rights to participation in social
development. In this regard, *Dharma Wanita*, a social association of wives
of Indonesian civil servants, which the "patriarchal" New Order government
promoted heavily as an exemplary organization for women, was especially
criticized. Many feminists argued that this social organization "inculcates
an ethos of unquestioning obedience and acceptance of hierarchy and
discourages independent thinking on political or social issues" (Mackie
and MacIntyre 1994, p. 27). They also argued that the formation of this
organization was merely a tactic of the New Order regime to confine the
roles of women to the household.

Yet, to my knowledge, women in *Darma Wanita* were never marginalized in their roles in society in any sense, because they sustained their
careers while participating in this social gathering. Furthermore, it seems
that this organization widened their social boundaries, increased their
opportunities to get information, i.e. which was conducive to their husbands'
promotions, by these activities. It seems to me that the women in *Darma
Wanita* enjoyed their participation in this gathering, rather than seeing it as
a suppression of women or as a sign of their status as second-class citizens.
Then why would women agree to be organized into a government-sponsored
organization for the wives of civil servants? In my opinion, perhaps they
agreed with the New Order view of the roles of women, primarily as good
housewives and mothers, and secondly as actors in national development.
In addition, it does not appear that, with the exception of some feminists,
Indonesian women of the New Order era were annoyed by the bestowal
by the government of gender roles in national development. Furthermore,
my empirical observations indicate that this opinion, perhaps they were in
name only, and in practice, the numbers of career women taking advantage
of the New Order promotion of formal education, dramatically increased in
the period. Thus, in gender studies, the Western feminist context that the
role of housewife is viewed as traditional or that the wage-earning woman is
part of the liberation effort for and on behalf of women should be carefully
examined before applying it to indigenous societies in Southeast Asia.

Yet, some American scholars in the field of history and gender studies
also tried to apply the approach of autonomous history in gender studies
in Southeast Asia. For instance, Suzanne Brenner (1998) discussed the
strong position of women in Javanese society, who kept their domestic

sphere becoming a site of cultural production and social reproduction, and thus women are seen to play a central role in defining the status hierarchies of men. The work edited by Barbara Watson Andaya (2000) also provides Southeast Asian concepts on "maleness", "femaleness", and the "third gender".

In sum, beyond the numerous outcomes by American scholars in constructing an autonomous history in Southeast Asia, there are still many themes which require the rethinking of these perspectives, i.e., on the issues of ideology, religion, or gender. Indeed, future scholars should give more serious and careful consideration to the local specificity before applying their "universal values".

CONCLUSION

Southeast Asian Studies in the U.S. started from the strategic needs of America, which resulted in the creation of the multi-disciplinary enterprise of area studies as the main field of study. Since the early period of the development of Southeast Asian Studies, American scholars focused their scholarly efforts on constructing an "autonomous history" of the region. With enormous public and private support and well-established research bases, Southeast Asian Studies in the U.S. achieved substantial success, which then attracted numerous students from all over the world including from within Southeast Asia itself to study Southeast Asian Studies there.

The resultant scholarly work generally presented certain characteristics. First, American scholarship was relatively free from the reins of nationalism or patriotism, which preoccupied local historians to a degree. Being thus free meant they could establish more objective histories. Second, based on the tradition of establishing an autonomous history, their research concentrated on finding "local genius", whereby the roles of indigenous people were emphasized. Third, on the issue of the marking out of the boundaries of area studies which were used to define units for analysis, theirs tended to be confined to the realms of the nation-state, which obscured the social realities of ethnic or religious boundaries or cross-boundary flows and networks. Fourth, particularly on the issue of economic history, they tended to adopt monolithic perspectives in the definitions of development, by which they meant the expansion of capital, and the processes of urbanization, or industrialization. Fifth, on some issues such as ideology, religion, and gender, American scholars tended to apply their Western-contextualized universal values without further elaboration to adapt it to Southeast Asia.

The achievements and limitations presented in this earlier scholarship, then, began to be challenged by some scholars. These scholars argued for the need to go beyond the boundary of the nation-state and to examine smaller, more specific and cross-boundary realities, i.e. issues to do with ethnic or religious groups that cut across national boundaries, trans-Pacific connections based on diaspora, family, tourism, media, migrants, international commercial networks, intensified flows of labour migrants within and beyond the region, new labour markets that cut across Southeast Asia, and the formation of cross-national identities. Besides, as social history calls for further studies, economic histories need to be studied in depth, especially for the colonial era. Most colonial studies placed their focus on political issues. Finally, future scholarship should be carefully designed to understand indigenous values and discourses in relation to the issues of ideology, religion, and gender, among others, in order to avoid overgeneralization or some unfounded conclusions on these issues.

Notes

[1] The Southeast Asia Program at Cornell University was established in 1950.

[2] The Southeast Asian Studies Program at Yale University was established in 1947. It was the first area studies programme in the United States to embark on the study of Southeast Asia in all disciplines.

[3] The Center for Southeast Asian Studies at the University of California at Berkeley was formally established during the Second World War.

[4] The Center for Southeast Asian Studies at the University of Hawaii, Manoa represents the largest concentration of specialists on the region in the U.S. The Center represents the largest concentration established in 1972.

[5] The University of Michigan has produced scholars working on Southeast Asia since the 1870s. The Center for Southeast Asian Studies emerged in 1999 from the former Center for South and Southeast Asian Studies, which was established in 1961.

[6] The Center for Southeast Asian Studies at Northern Illinois University was established in 1963. The Center has been funded as a National Resource Center since 1997.

[7] Southeast Asian Studies at Ohio University was established in 1967.

[8] The Center for Southeast Asian Studies at the University of Wisconsin, Madison was formally established in 1973.

[9] By the early 1980s, there were eight Centers, five of which were receiving federal (NDEA) funds. In the 1990s, three new university Centers — Arizona State University, the University of Oregon, and the University of Washington — were installed (Hirschman 2003, p. 43).

References

Adas, Michael. "From Avoidance to Confrontation: Peasant Protest in Precolonial and Colonial Southeast Asia". *Comparative Studies in Society and History* 23 (1981).

Ahmad, Abu Talib and Tan Liok Ee. Introduction to *New Terrains in Southeast Asian History*, edited by Abu Talib Ahmad and Tan Liok Ee. Athens, OH: Ohio University Press, 2003.

Andaya, Barbara Watson. *To Live as Brothers: Southeast Sumatra in the Seventeenth and Eighteenth Centuries*. Honolulu: University of Hawaii Press, 1993.

————, ed. *Other Pasts: Women, Gender and History in Early Modern Southeast Asia*. Honolulu: Center for Southeast Asian Studies, University of Hawaii at Manoa, 2000.

Andaya, Barbara and Leonard Andaya. *A History of Malaysia*. Houndmills: University of Hawaii Press, 1982.

Andaya, Leonard Y. *The World of Maluku, Eastern Indonesia in the Early Modern Period*. Honolulu: University of Hawaii Press, 1993.

Andaya, Leonard Y. and Barbara Watson Andaya. "Southeast Asia in the Early Modern Period: Twenty-Five Years On". *Journal of Southeast Asian Studies* 26, no. 1 (1995).

Anderson, Benedict R.O'G. "The Cultural Factors in the Indonesian Revolution". *Asia* 20 (1970/1971).

————. *Java in a Time of Revolution*. Ithaca: Cornell University Press, 1972.

————. "Studies of the Thai State: The State of Thai Studies". In *The State of Thai Studies: Analyses of Knowledge, Approaches, and Prospects in Anthropology, Art History, Economics, History, and Political Science*, edited by E. Ayal. Athens, OH: Ohio University Center for International Studies, Southeast Asia Program, 1978.

————. *Language and Power: Exploring Political Cultures in Indonesia*. Ithaca and London: Cornell University Press, 1990.

————. *Imagined Communities: Reflections on the Origin and Spread of Nationalism*. Rev. ed. London and New York: Verso, 2006.

Anderson, Benedict R.O'G and Audrey Kahin. *Interpreting Indonesian Politics: Thirteen Contributions to the Debate, 1964–1981* (Interim Reports Series). Cornell University Modern Indonesia Project, 1982.

Aung-Thwin, Michael. "Spirals in Early Southeast Asian and Burmese History". *Journal of Interdisciplinary History* 31, no. 4 (1991).

————. "'The Classical' in Southeast Asia: The Present in the Past". *Journal of Southeast Asian Studies* 26, no. 1 (1995).

————. *Myth and History in the Historiography of Early Burma: Paradigms, Primary Sources, and Prejudices*. Athens, OH: Ohio University Center for International Studies, 1998.

———. "Continuing, Re-emerging, and Emerging Trends in the Field of Southeast Asian History". Paper delivered at the Sogang Institute for East Asian Studies (SIEAS) International Conference, 2009.

Benda, Harry. "The Structure of Southeast Asian History: Some Preliminary Observations". *Journal of Southeast Asian History* 3 (1962).

Bowen, John. "The Development of Southeast Asian Studies in the United States". In *Location: Global, Area, and International Archive*, 2003. Available at <http://www.escholarshp.org/uc/item/88z8x738>.

Brenner, Suzanne. *The Domestication of Desire: Women, Wealth, and Modernity in Java*. Princeton, NJ: Princeton University Press, 1998.

Brown, D.E. *Principles of Social Structure: Southeast Asia*. Boulder, CO: Westview Press, 1976.

Burling, Robbins. *Hill Farms and Padi Fields: Life in Mainland Southeast Asia*. Englewood Cliffs, NJ: Prentice-Hall, 1965. Reprint, 1992.

Crick, Bernard. *The American Science of Politics: Its Origins and Conditions*. Berkeley: University of California Press, 1959.

Dunn, Ross E. "Redefining World History". *The New World History: A Teacher's Companion*. Boston: Bedford/St. Martin's, 2000.

Eggan, Fred. "Some Aspects of Culture Change in the Northern Philippines". *American Anthropologist* 43 (1941).

———. "Some Aspects of Bilateral Social Systems in the Northern Philippines". In *Studies in Philippine Anthropology: In Honor of H. Otley Beyer*, edited by Mario D. Zamora. Quezon City: Alemar Phoenix, 1967.

Embree, John F. "Thailand, a Loosely Structured Social System". *American Anthropologist* 52 (1950).

Geertz, Clifford. *The Religion of Java*. New York: The Free Press of Glencoe, 1960.

———. *Agricultural Involution*. Berkeley and Los Angeles: University of California Press, 1963.

———. *Negara. The Theatre State in Nineteenth Century Bali*. Princeton: Princeton University Press, 1980.

Geertz, Hildred. *The Javanese Family: A Study of Kinship and Socialization*. New York: The Free Press of Glencoe, 1961.

Hagesteijn, R. Renee. *Circles of Kings*. Dordrecht: Foris, 1989.

Halib, Mohammed and Tim Huxley. Introduction to *An Introduction to Southeast Asian Studies,* edited by Mohammed Halib and Tim Huxley. New York: I.B. Tauris & Co. Ltd., 1996.

Hanks, Lucien M. *Rice and Man: Agricultural Ecology in Southeast Asia*. Chicago: Aldine-Atherton, 1972.

Hill, Lewis and Michael Hitchcock. "Anthropology". In *An Introduction to Southeast Asian Studies,* edited by Mohammed Halib and Tim Huxley. New York: I.B. Tauris & Co. Ltd., 1996.

Hirschman, Charles. "Southeast Asian Studies in American Universities". *Southeast Asian Studies in the Balance*, edited by Charles Hirschman, Charles F. Keyes, and Karl Hutterer. Ann Arbor, MI: The Association for Asian Studies, 1992.

Kahin, George McTurnan. *Nationalism and Revolution in Indonesia*. Ithaca: Cornell University Press, 1952.

Keyes, Charles. "A Conference at Wingspread and Rethinking Southeast Asian Studies". In *Southeast Asian Studies in the Balance,* edited by Charles Hirschman, Charles F. Keyes, and Karl Hutterer. Ann Arbor, MI: The Association for Asian Studies, 1992.

————. *The Golden Peninsular: Culture and Adaptation in Mainland Southeast Asia.* Rev. ed. New York: Macmillan, 1995. First published in 1977 by University of Hawaii Press.

King, Victor T. and William D. Wilder. *The Modern Anthropology of South-East Asia: An Introduction*. London and New York: RoutledgeCurzon, 2003.

Kirsch, A. Thomas. *Feasting and Social Oscillation: A Working Paper on Religion and Society in Upland Southeast Asia*. Ithaca, NY, Cornell University, Southeast Asia Program, Data Paper no. 92 (1973).

Kratoska, Paul H. "Country Histories and the Writing of Southeast Asian History". In *New Terrains in Southeast Asian History*, edited by Abu Talib Ahmad and Tan Liok Ee. Athens, OH: Ohio University Press, 2003.

Leach, E.R. *Political Systems of Highland Burma: A Study of Kachin Social Structure*. LSE Monographs on Social Anthropology no. 44. London: Athlone Press, 1954. Reprint, 1970.

Lehman, F.K. *The Structure of Chin Society: A Tribal People of Burma adapted to a Non-Western Civilization*. Urbana, IL: The University of Illinois Press, 1963.

Lieberman, Victor. *Burmese Administrative Cycles: Anarchy and Conquest, c.1580–1760*. Princeton, NJ: Princeton University Press, 1984.

————. "Reinterpreting Burmese History". *Comparative Studies in Society and History* 29, no. 1 (1987).

Lombard, Denys. "Networks and Synchronisms in Southeast Asian History". *Journal of Southeast Asian Studies* 26, no. 1 (1995).

Mackie, Jamie and Andrew MacIntyre. "Politics". In *Indonesia's New Order: The Dynamics of Socio-economic Transformation*, edited by Hal Hill. Honolulu: University of Hawaii Press, 1994.

Manning, Patrick. *Navigating World History.* New York: Palgrave Macmillan, 2003.

McCargo, Duncan. "Rethinking Southeast Asian Politics". In *Southeast Asian Studies: Debate and New Directions*, edited by Cynthia Chou and Vincent Houben. Singapore: Institute of Southeast Asian Studies, 2006.

McCargo, Duncan and Robert H. Taylor. "Politics". In *An Introduction to Southeast Asian Studies*, edited by Mohammed Halib and Tim Huxley. New York: I.B. Tauris & Co. Ltd., 1996.

McGregor, E. Katharine. "Representing the Indonesia Past: The National Monument History Museum from Guided Democracy to the New Order". *Indonesia* 75 (2003).

McVey, Ruth. "Change and Continuity in Southeast Asian Studies". *Journal of Southeast Asian Studies* 26, no. 1 (1995).

———. "Globalization, Marginalization, and the Study of Southeast Asia". In *Southeast Asian Studies: Reorientations*, edited by Craig J. Reynolds and Ruth McVey. Ithaca: Cornell Southeast Asia Program Publications, 1998.

Nash, Manning. *The Golden Road to Modernity: Village Life in Contemporary Burma.* New York: John Wiley, 1965.

Nordholt, Henk Schulte. "De-colonising Indonesian Historiography". Paper delivered at the Centre for East and South-East Asian Studies public lecture series "Focus Asia", May 2004.

Ong, Aihwa and Michael G. Peletz, eds. *Bewitching Women, Pious Men: Gender and Body Politics in Southeast Asia.* Berkeley and Los Angeles: University of California Press, 1995.

Pemberton, John. *On the Subject of "Java".* Ithaca, NY and London: Cornell University Press, 1994.

Reid, Anthony. Introduction to *Southeast Asian Studies: Pacific Perspectives.* Tempe, AZ: Arizona State University, 2003.

Ricci, David. *The Tragedy of Political Science: Politics, Scholarship and Democracy.* New Haven and London: Yale University Press, 1984.

Scott, James C. *The Moral Economy of the Peasant: Rebellion and Subsistence in Southeast Asia.* New Haven and London: Yale University Press, 1976.

———. *Weapons of the Weak: Everyday Forms of Peasant Resistance.* New Haven: Yale University Press, 1985.

Sears, Laurie J. "Postcolonial Identities, Feminist Criticism, and Southeast Asian Studies". In *Knowing Southeast Asian Subjects,* edited by Laurie Sears. Seattle: University of Washington Press, 2007.

Sharp, Lauriston and Lucien M. Hanks. *Bang Chan: Social History of a Rural Community in Thailand.* Ithaca, NY and London: Cornell University Press, 1978.

Skinner, William G. *Chinese Society in Thailand: An Analytical History.* Ithaca, NY: Cornell University Press, 1957

Smail, John R.W. "On the Possibility of an Autonomous History of Modern Southeast Asian History". *Journal of Southeast Asian Studies* 2 (1961).

Spiro, Melford E. *Burmese Supernaturalism: A Study in the Explanation and Reduction of Suffering.* Englewood Cliffs, NJ: Prentice-Hall, 1967.

———. "Religion: Problems of Definition and Explanation". In *Anthropological Approaches to the Study of Religion,* edited by M. Banton. London: Tavistock Publications, 1971.

Sutherland, Heather. "Believing is Seeing: Perspectives on Political Power and Economic Activity in the Malay World 1700–1940". *Journal of Southeast Asian Studies* 26, no. 1 (1995).

Tilly, Charles. *Big Structures, Large Processes, Huge Comparisons.* New York: Russell Sage Foundation, 1984.

Tsing, Anna Lowenhaupt. *In the Realm of the Diamond Queen: Marginality in an Out-of-the-Way Place.* Princeton, NJ: Princeton University Press, 1993.

Wheatley, Paul. *Nagara and Commandery.* Chicago: University of Chicago Department of Geography, 1983.

Winichakul, Thongchai, eds. "Writing at the Interstices: Southeast Asian Historians and Postnational Histories". In *New Terrains in Southeast Asian History,* edited by Abu Talib Ahmad and Tan Liok Ee. Athens, OH: Ohio University Press, 2003.

Wyatt, David. *The Politics of Reform in Thailand: Education in the Reign of Rama V.* New Haven: Yale University Press, 1969.

———. *Thailand: A Short History.* New Haven and London: Yale University Press, 1984.

Yeoh, Brenda S.A. "Changing Conceptions of Space in History Writing: A Selective Mapping of Writings on Singapore". In *New Terrains in Southeast Asian History*, edited by Abu Talib Ahmad and Tan Liok Ee. Athens, OH: Ohio University Press, 2003.

INDEX

Vietnam's regional research
  capacity in, 198
Institute's Management Committee
  in London, 291
institutional developments, 7,
  131–35, 270, 271
institutional dislocation, 45
institutional infrastructure of
  Southeast Asian Studies in
  China, 49
institutionalization of foreign
  policy-making, 45
institutionalized network, future of,
  252
integrative approach to study of
  Southeast Asia, 136
Inter-Asia Cultural Studies project,
  252
interdisciplinary approaches of area
  studies, 406–7
inter-disciplinary regional studies,
  7, 14
interdisciplinary research, 213
inter-/multi-disciplinary approach,
  136
international audiences, 243
international character of
  scholarship, 22
international communication,
  diverse channels for, 51
International Conference on Thai
  Studies, 274
international economics, field of,
  119
International Institute for Asian
  Studies (IIAS), 300
internationalization of Southeast
  Asian Studies in China, 54–55
international marriages, 128
international order, 50

international relations, 98
international trade
  field of, 123–24
  Southeast Asia, 97
interviewees, list of, 192, 193
intra-regional cultural flows, 237–44
  in Southeast Asia, 247–48
intra-regional popular culture, 227,
  244, 252
Inul Daratista, 250
inward-looking attitude, 340
inward orientation, 326
  of Dutch scholars, 339
ISEAS. *See* Institute of Southeast
  Asian Studies (ISEAS)
Ishii Yoneo, 95, 99
Islam, 99
  cultural politics of, 248
  in Malaysia and Indonesia, 99
  in Southeast Asia, 409
Islamic films in Indonesia, 249
Islamic forces in Indonesia, 417
Islamic identity, 248
Islamic lifestyles, commodification
  of, 248
Islamic popular culture, 248
Islamic terrorist attack, 403
Islamization, 248
Islam-themed Film Festival, 252
Iwanami koza tonan ajiashi, 96
*Iwanami Lectures of Southeast Asian
  History*, 99
Iwao Seiichi, 31, 81

J
James Cook University of Northern
  Queensland, 377–78
Japan
  advancement in *nanyo*, 77
  American policy toward, 78

www.ingramcontent.com/pod-product-compliance
Lightning Source LLC
Chambersburg PA
CBHW072039020426
42334CB00017B/1328